AUSTRALIAN CRIMINAL LAWS

CRITICAL PERSPECTIVES

Bernadette McSherry

Bronwyn Naylor

**Claudiu Ilisei
Solicitor
Auckland**

OXFORD

UNIVERSITY PRESS

OXFORD
UNIVERSITY PRESS

253 Normanby Road, South Melbourne, Victoria 3205, Australia

Oxford University Press is a department of the University of Oxford.
It furthers the University's objective of excellence in research, scholarship,
and education by publishing worldwide in

Oxford New York

Auckland Bangkok Buenos Aires Cape Town Chennai
Dar es Salaam Delhi Hong Kong Istanbul Karachi Kolkata
Kuala Lumpur Madrid Melbourne Mexico City Mumbai Nairobi
São Paulo Shanghai Taipei Tokyo Toronto

OXFORD is a trade mark of Oxford University Press
in the UK and in certain other countries

Copyright © Bernadette McSherry and Bronwyn Naylor 2004
First published 2004

This book is copyright. Apart from any fair dealing for the purposes
of private study, research, criticism or review as permitted under the
Copyright Act, no part may be reproduced, stored in a retrieval system,
or transmitted, in any form or by any means, electronic, mechanical,
photocopying, recording or otherwise without prior written permission.
Enquiries to be made to Oxford University Press.

Copying for educational purposes
Where copies of part or the whole of the book are made under Part VB
of the Copyright Act, the law requires that prescribed procedures be
followed. For information, contact the Copyright Agency Limited.

National Library of Australia
Cataloguing-in-Publication data:

McSherry, Bernadette.
  Australian criminal laws: critical perspectives.

  Bibliography.
  Includes index.
  ISBN 0 19 550790 8.

  1. Criminal law—Australia. I. Naylor, Bronwyn Glynis.

  345.94

Typeset by OUPANZS
Printed through Bookpac Production Services, Singapore

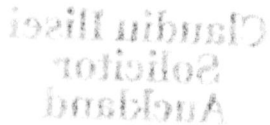

Summary of Contents

Part 1 Introduction
1	Defining criminal laws	3
2	Structuring criminal law	49

Part 2 Offences against the person
3	Homicide	89
4	Assault and related offences	152
5	Sexual assault	203

Part 3 Property offences
6	Property offences involving stealing	251
7	Property offences involving deception	333

Part 4 Extending criminal responsibility
8	Inchoate offences	373
9	Complicity	424

Part 5 Defences
10	Self-defence and provocation	469
11	Mental state defences	502
12	Defences based on external pressures	553

Contents

Preface	xiii
Table of Cases	xv
Table of Statutes	xxxv

Part I Introduction — 1

1 Defining criminal laws — 3

Introduction	3
Defining crime: differing perspectives	4
Realism	6
Critical legal studies and critical criminology	8
Postmodernism	11
Feminist theories	12
Critical race theory	15
Critical perspectives in this book	16
Aims of the criminal law: differing perspectives	17
Punishment	17
Prevention of harm	18
Preservation of morality	19
Social welfare	21
Measuring crime	22
Jurisdiction	24
Territorial theory	25
Terminatory theory	27
The protective approach	28
The territorial nexus/substantial link approach	29
The way ahead: the Model Criminal Code	30
Individual and corporate criminal responsibility	31
Reason and rationality in the criminal law	38
Legal reasoning and rationality	39
The rational actor	40
Mental illness	41
Children	41
The reasonable man	46
Conclusion	48

2 Structuring criminal law — 49

Introduction	49
Offences	50
Defences	51

Justification and excuse	53
The burden of proof and defences	54
The evidential burden	55
The legal burden	56
The main exceptions	56
Elements of 'serious' crimes	58
Strict and absolute liability offences	61
Subjective versus objective fault	63
Physical elements	65
Voluntary conduct	66
Acts and omissions	66
Fault elements	69
Intention	69
General or basic intention	70
Specific intention	71
Oblique intention	72
Intention and motive	74
Knowledge and recklessness	74
The role of wilful blindness	76
Negligence	77
Concurrence of physical and fault elements	79
Causation	81
Conclusion	85

Part 2 Offences against the person   87

3 Homicide   89

Introduction	89
Murder and manslaughter—physical elements	95
Background	95
The current law	97
Death of a human being	98
Causation of death	99
Critique	104
Murder—fault elements	106
Background	106
The current law	107
Intention to kill	108
Intention to cause grievous bodily harm	109
Recklessness as to causing death or grievous bodily harm	109
Transferred malice	110
Critique	112
Constructive murder	115
Background	115
The current law	116
Constructive murder	116
Escape murder	118
Critique	118
Manslaughter	119
Background	119
The current law—gross or criminal negligence manslaughter	121
Critique	122
The current law—negligent omissions	124
Critique	126
The current law—unlawful and dangerous act manslaughter	127
Unlawful	128
Dangerous	129
Critique	129

Euthanasia	131
Background	131
The current law	132
Voluntary euthanasia	132
Non-voluntary euthanasia	133
Critique	134
Offences relating to childbirth	137
Background	137
The current law	138
Abortion	139
Child destruction	140
Infanticide	141
Critique	142
Corporate homicide	144
Background	144
The current law	147
Critique	148
Conclusion	151
4 Assault and related offences	**152**
Introduction	152
Assault	155
Background	155
The current law—physical elements	158
Assault by the threat of force	158
Assault by the use of force	159
Aggravated assaults	160
Assaults with intention to commit another crime	160
Assaults on particular classes of people	160
Assaults resulting in harm	161
Female genital mutilation	163
Critique	163
Assaults by the threat of force	164
Factors of aggravation	166
The current law—fault elements	167
Critique	170
Threats and stalking	171
Background	171
The current law	173
Critique	174
Offences endangering life or personal safety	176
Background	176
The current law	178
Critique	179
Lawful assaults and consent	181
Background	181
Lawful assaults	181
The current law	182
The use of reasonable force	182
Defences to assault	183
Critique	185
The use of reasonable force	185
Defences to assault	188
Consent	188
The current law	190
Personal adornment	191
Surgery	192
Rough horseplay and violent sports	193
Sadomasochism	194

viii Contents

Female genital mutilation	196
Indigenous customary law	197
Critique	198
Sports violence	198
Female genital mutilation	198
Indigenous customary law	199
Sadomasochism	200
Conclusion	202

5 Sexual assault — 203

Introduction	203
Rape and indecent assault	206
Background	206
The current law—physical elements	207
Sexual intercourse/indecent assault	207
Without consent	209
Critique	211
The social context of consent	211
Fraud and consent	220
The current law—fault elements	222
Intention and recklessness	222
A mistaken belief in consent	224
Critique	225
Sexual offences against children and young people	228
Background	228
The current law	230
Critique	233
The age of consent	233
Defences	234
Overlap between offences	236
Sexual offences against individuals with mental impairment	238
Background	238
The current law	240
Critique	242
Conclusion	246

Part 3 Property offences — 249

6 Property offences involving stealing — 251

Introduction	251
Theft	260
Background	260
Physical elements	263
Property	263
Belonging to another	268
Taking or appropriating the property	272
Critique—physical elements	278
Property the subject of theft	278
Property belonging to another	280
The meaning of appropriation	281
The current law—fault elements	283
Intention to permanently deprive	283
Acting dishonestly	288
Critique—fault elements	295
The meaning of dishonesty	295
The requirement of intent to permanently deprive	307
Robbery	308
The current law: physical elements	309
Steals	309
Uses force/violence	310

	Threatens violence/seeks to put any person in fear of immediate force	312
	Immediately before, after or at the time of stealing	313
	The current law—fault elements	314
	Critique—the law of robbery	315
	Degree of force or violence	315
	Timing of the use of force	315
	Nature of the threats	316
	Armed/aggravated robbery	316
	Critique—armed robbery	318
	Burglary	319
	Background	319
	The current law—physical elements	322
	Entry	322
	Entry as a trespasser	323
	Entry to a building or part of a building	325
	The current law—fault elements	326
	With intent to commit another offence	326
	Critique—the law of burglary	328
	Aggravated burglary	329
	Critique—aggravated burglary	330
	Conclusion	331
7	**Property offences involving deception**	**333**
	Introduction	333
	Obtaining property by deception	338
	Background	338
	The current law—physical elements	339
	Deception	339
	Obtains	341
	Property	343
	Belonging to another	344
	Critique—physical elements	344
	Obtaining by deception	344
	Fault elements	346
	Intention to permanently deprive	346
	Dishonesty	346
	Critique—fault elements	348
	Intention to permanently deprive	348
	Dishonesty	348
	Obtaining a financial advantage by deception	349
	Background	349
	The current law—physical elements	351
	Deception	351
	Obtains	351
	Financial advantage	352
	Critique—physical element	353
	The meaning of 'financial advantage'	353
	The current law—fault element	356
	Dishonesty	356
	Critique—fault element	357
	Should fraud and theft be separate offences?	357
	Computer fraud	360
	Background	360
	The current law	361
	Critique	362
	Offences involving corporations	364
	Background	364
	The current law	365
	Critique	365
	Conclusion	367

Part 4 Extending criminal responsibility — 371

8 Inchoate offences — 373
Introduction — 373
Attempts — 376
    Background — 376
    The current law—physical elements — 380
    Critique — 384
    The current law—fault element — 385
    Critique — 387
Conspiracy — 388
    Background — 388
    The current law–physical elements — 391
        The agreement — 393
        Agreement between two or more persons — 396
        The unlawful act — 398
    Critique — 399
    The current law—fault element — 403
    Critique — 406
Incitement — 408
    Background — 408
    The current law—physical element — 409
    Critique — 410
    The current law—fault element — 412
    Critique — 412
Impossibility — 413
    Background — 413
    The current law — 414
        Attempts — 415
        Conspiracy — 416
        Incitement — 418
    Critique — 419
Conclusion — 422

9 Complicity — 424
Introduction — 424
Principal offenders and acting in concert — 428
    Background — 428
    The current law — 428
    Critique — 432
Innocent agency — 434
    Background — 434
    The current law — 434
    Critique — 436
Accessorial liability — 437
    Background — 437
    The current law—definitions and physical elements — 438
    Critique — 441
        Mere presence, omissions and supplying goods and advice — 442
        Withdrawal by an accessory — 445
    The current law—fault elements — 448
        Assisting and encouraging crime — 448
        Accessories after the fact — 450
    Critique — 450
The doctrine of common purpose — 453
    Background — 453
    The current law — 457
    Critique — 460
Conclusion — 462

Part 5 Defences — 467

10 Self-defence and provocation — 469
Introduction — 469
Self-defence — 472
  Background — 472
  The current law — 473
  Critique — 475
    Excessive self-defence — 475
    Women's reactions to violence — 478
    Subjective/objective elements — 482
Provocation — 484
  Background — 484
  The current law — 486
    Provocative conduct — 486
    The accused's loss of self-control — 488
    The ordinary person test — 490
  Critique — 495
    Characteristics of the ordinary person — 495
    Should there be an ordinary person test? — 497
    Should there be a defence of provocation at all? — 499
Conclusion — 501

11 Mental state defences — 502
Introduction — 502
Mental impairment and involuntary conduct — 507
  Background — 507
  The current law — 508
    The internal cause theory of insane automatism — 511
    The continuing danger theory — 512
    The sound/unsound mind theory — 512
  Critique — 514
Mental impairment and unintentional conduct — 517
  Background — 517
  The current law — 518
  Critique — 520
Intoxication — 521
  Background — 521
  The current law — 523
  Critique — 526
The defence of mental impairment — 530
  Background — 530
  The current law — 531
    Internal causes of mental impairment — 531
    The effect of the mental impairment on understanding — 535
    The effect of the mental impairment on volition — 537
  Critique — 538
Diminished responsibility — 540
  Background — 540
  The current law — 541
    Abnormality of mind — 542
    Cause of the abnormality of mind — 542
    Effect of the abnormality of mind — 543
  Critique — 544
Infanticide — 546
  Background — 546
  The current law — 548
  Critique — 548
Conclusion — 551

12	Defences based on external pressures	553
	Introduction	553
	Duress and marital coercion	555
	Background	555
	The current law	559
	Threats of the infliction of death or grievous bodily harm	560
	The objective element	564
	Critique	565
	Elements of the defence	565
	Should duress be available to a charge of murder?	568
	Should marital coercion exist?	569
	Necessity	570
	Background	570
	The current law	573
	The nature of the emergency	574
	The accused's belief	575
	The objective component	576
	Critique	577
	The elements of the defence	577
	Should necessity be available to a charge of murder?	579
	Conclusion	582
Bibliography		**583**
Index		**612**

Preface

The general 'principles of criminal law' have traditionally been viewed as authoritatively set out or 'posited' and therefore understandable without reference to their historical and social context. This book aims to move beyond this approach in order to place the foundations of criminal laws in a broad historical and social context, to offer critical perspectives on the law's development and operation, and to highlight law reform issues.

We decided to use case studies to analyse serious criminal offences and defences in detail, rather than referring only to 'general principles' gleaned from numerous cases with the facts omitted. We hoped that by adopting this method, we would give criminologists and social scientists an understanding of current criminal laws and criminal lawyers an understanding of the law's social context.

Our general approach is that by adopting broader critical perspectives beyond positivist conceptions of the criminal law, we can provide more realistic accounts of current laws and their operation and encourage debate about them.

While one author initially wrote a draft of each chapter, each of us jointly contributed to its ultimate form. Bronwyn wrote the first drafts of the chapters on homicide and property offences, while Bernadette wrote the first drafts of the other nine chapters.

Many colleagues and students have helped and encouraged us to explore critical and contextual perspectives in criminal law scholarship. Bernadette would particularly like to thank Simon Bronitt of the Australian National University, Adjunct Professor Ian Freckelton of Monash University and Professor Alan Norrie of Kings College, London, in this regard. Bronwyn dates her introduction to critical and contextual criminal research to her work at the former Law Reform Commission of Victoria with Professor Louis Waller, and particularly thanks him for his encouragement then and at all times. She thanks Dr David Neal, also formerly of the Law Reform Commission of Victoria, and Dr Loraine Gelsthorpe and Dr Allison Morris of Cambridge University. Bronwyn also thanks Professor Bob Williams of Monash University for helpful comments on two draft chapters.

Thanks to our commissioning editor, Jill Henry, who has since moved on from Oxford University Press, as well as the current commissioning editor, Katie Ridsdale, for their unceasing enthusiasm for this project. Thanks also to Tim Fullerton for his excellent and painstaking editorial work and to Chris Wyness, Senior Editor, for overseeing the production process with such aplomb. We are also exceptionally grateful to our research assistants, Tamara Pallos, Owen Griffiths, Joanna Kyriakakis and Caterina Popa, for their excellent work on successive drafts. The encouraging and constructive comments of our anonymous reviewers are also greatly appreciated. All errors are of course our own and the law is current as at 30 June 2003.

On a personal level, Bernadette thanks her mother, Doris, partner John, and brothers Tony, Paul and Mark, for their love and support. She dedicates this book to her late aunt, Sister Teresa McSherry. Bronwyn thanks Simon for his patience and encouragement, and dedicates this book to Rebecca and Jessica, who give meaning to all her academic endeavours.

We welcome any comments or suggestions. We can be contacted at: Bernadette.McSherry@law.monash.edu.au and Bronwyn.Naylor@law.monash.edu.au

Dr Bernadette McSherry and Dr Bronwyn Naylor, Melbourne

The authors and publishers would like to thank the following copyright holder for permission to reproduce copyright material for Figure 1.1 in Chapter 1:

Figure 13.1 from *The Oxford Handbook of Criminology*, edited by R. Maguire et al. (second edition, 1997). Reprinted by permission of Oxford University Press UK.

Table of Cases

A v The United Kingdom unreported, 23 September 1998, Eur Court HR, No 100/1997/884/1096   186
Abbott v The Queen [1977] AC 755   554
Abbott v The Queen unreported, 25 July 1995, CCA of WA, No 98 of 1995   194
Adams (1812) R & R 225   435
Ahern v The Queen (1988) 165 CLR 87   390
Airedale NHS Trust v Bland [1993] 2 WLR 316   68, 133, 135–6
Airedale NHS Trust v Bland [1993] AC 789   68, 125, 132, 133
Alford v Riley Newman Ltd (1934) 34 SR (NSW) 261   34
Allen v United Carpet Mills Pty Ltd [1989] VR 323   34, 61, 62
Allsop (1976) 64 Cr App R 29   392
Andrews v DPP [1937] AC 576   78
Annakin (1987) 37 A Crim R 131   110
Athanasiadis (1990) 51 A Crim R 292   223
Attorney-General's Reference (No 1 of 1975) [1975] QB 773   438, 439
Attorney-General's Reference (No 6 of 1980) [1981] QB 715   189, 190, 191, 210
Attorney-General's Reference (No 1 of 1983) [1985] QB 182   272
Attorney-General's Reference (No 3 of 1994) [1996] QB 581 (CA)   111, 139
Attorney-General's Reference (No 3 of 1994) [1998] AC 245 (HL)   111
Attorney-General's Reference (No 1 of 1996) [1998] 7 Tas R 293   526
Attorney-General's Reference (No 2 of 1999) [2000] QB 796   145
Attorney-General's Reference (No 3 of 1994) [1997] 3 WLR 421   113
Attorney-General's Reference (No 3 of 1998) [1999] 2 Cr App R 214   520
Attorney-General v Able (1984) QB 795   440, 441
Attorney-General v Whelan [1934] IR 518   556
Attorney-General (Northern Ireland) v Gallagher [1963] AC 349   526
Australian Stevedoring Industry Authority v Overseas & General Stevedoring Co Pty Ltd (1959) 1 FLR 298 (Fed Ct)   34

B unreported, 3 July 1995, SC of Vic, Teague J   179
Baker and Ward (1999) 2 Cr App R 335   558, 563
Bannen (1844) 1 Car & K 295   434
Baragith (1991) 54 A Crim R 240   493
Barker v The Queen (1983) 153 CLR 338   323, 324, 328
Barton v Armstrong [1969] 2 NSWR 451   164
Beal v Kelley [1951] 2 All ER 763   159
Becerra (1975) 62 Cr App R 212   445, 446
Bedi v The Queen (1993) 61 SASR 269   178
Beer v McCann [1993] 1 Qd R 25   190
Bennett (1989) 45 A Crim R 45   168, 524
Betts and Ridley (1930) 22 Cr App R 148   439
Billinghurst [1978] Crim LR 553   193
Bleasdale (1848) 2 Car & K 765   435
Board of Trade v Owen [1957] AC 602   28, 389
Boughey v The Queen (1986) 161 CLR 10   71, 75, 110, 128, 170, 182, 190
Bowker v Premier Drug Co Ltd [1928] 1 KB 217   438
Brady v Schatzel; Ex parte Brady [1911] St R Qd 206   165
Bratty v Attorney General for Northern Ireland [1963] AC 386   55, 505, 512
Brennan v Bass (1984) 35 SASR 311   559
Brisac and Scott (1803) East, *PC* iv 164, 102 ER 792   435
Britten v Alpogut [1987] VR 929   379, 380, 385, 415
Brown (1987) 32 A Crim R 162   110
Bull (1845) 1 Cox 281   434
Burnett v Mental Health Tribunal unreported, 21 November 1997, SC of ACT, Crispin J, [1997] ATSC 94   534
Burns (1984) 79 Cr App R 173   411
Butcher (1858) Bell 6   435
Butt (1884) 15 Cox 564   435
Buttigieg (1993) 69 A Crim R 21   487
Byrne [1960] 2 QB 396   505, 542, 543

C (A Minor) v DPP [1994] 3 WLR 888 (CA)   44
C (A Minor) v DPP [1995] 2 WLR 383 (HL)   45
Callaghan v The Queen (1952) 87 CLR 115   78
Cameron (1990) 47 A Crim R 397   524
Campbell (1995) 80 A Crim R 461   171, 181
Campbell v The Queen [1981] WAR 286   82
Canadian Dredge & Dock Co Ltd v The Queen (1985) 19 CCC (3d) 1   34
Carroll v Lergesner [1991] 1 Qd R 206   190
Carter and Savage; Ex parte Attorney-General (1990) 47 A Crim R 55   440
Case of Prohibitions del Roy (1607) 12 Co Rep 63; 77 ER 1342   39
Catalano (1992) 61 A Crim R 323   402

Censori v The Queen [1983] WAR 89   486
Chayna (1993) 66 A Crim R 178   503, 540, 545
Chhay (1994) 72 A Crim R 1   487
Christie v Foster Brewing Co Ltd (1982) 18 VLR 292   34
Churchill v Walton [1967] 2 AC 224   403, 406
Clark (1980) 2 A Crim R 90   561
Clark (1991) 52 A Crim R 180   302
Clarkson [1987] VR 962   346
Clarkson and Lyon (1986) 24 A Crim R 54   282
Clifford (1845) 2 Car & K 202   434
Codere (1916) 12 Cr App R 21   535
Collins v Wilcock [1984] 1 WLR 1172   160, 182, 190
Comer v Bloomfield (1971) 55 Crim App R 305   382
Commissioner of Police of the Metropolis v Caldwell [1982] AC 341   76
Commissioner of Police v Charles [1977] AC 177   345, 346
Commissioner of Police v Wilson [1984] AC 242   160
Condon (1995) 83 A Crim R 335   302, 356
Considine v Kirkpatrick [1971] SASR 73   317
Coombes (1785) 1 Leach 388   434
Cooper (1846) 8 QB 533   435
Cooper v The Queen (1979) 51 CCC (2d) 129   536
Coulter v The Queen (1988) 164 CLR 350   168
Crabbe v The Queen (1990) 101 FLR 133   107
Croton v The Queen (1967) 117 CLR 326   274
Cundy v Le Cocq (1884) 13 QBD 207   61

D unreported, 1 May 1996, Supreme Court of Victoria, Hampel J; (1997) 21 Crim LJ 40   179
Dawson and James (1976) 64 Cr App R 170   310
Dawson v The Queen (1961) 106 CLR 1   440
Dennis v Plight (1968) 11 FLR 458   444
Department of Health and Community Services (NT) v JWB (Marion's case) (1992) 175 CLR 218   192
Dharmasena v The King [1951] AC 1   402
Dimozantos (1991) 56 A Crim R 345   408, 410
Dimozantos v The Queen (1992) 174 CLR 504   408
Dimozantos v The Queen (No 2) (1993) 178 CLR 122   409
Ditta [1988] Crim LR 42   234, 559
Dixon-Jenkins (1985) 14 A Crim R 372   554
Donaghy and Marshall [1981] Crim LR 644   314
Doodeward v Spence (1908) 6 CLR 406   267
Dowey (1868) 11 Cox 115   435
DPP v Beard [1920] AC 479   117, 523

DPP v Blady [1912] 2 KB 89   396
DPP v Camplin [1978] AC 705   495
DPP v Esso Australia Pty Ltd (2001) 124 A Crim R 200   145
DPP v Esso Australia Pty Ltd [2001] VSC 103 14 February 2001   145
DPP v M and J (1993) 9 WAR 281   208
DPP v Majewski [1977] AC 443   168, 523, 525
DPP v Morgan [1976] AC 182   63, 224, 527
DPP v Newbury and Jones [1977] AC 500   129
DPP v Nock [1978] AC 979   416, 418, 419
DPP v Parmenter [1991] 3 WLR 914   159, 168
DPP v Ray [1974] AC 370   340, 343, 344, 351, 352
DPP v Rogers [1953] 2 All ER 644   159
DPP v Shannon [1975] AC 717   397
DPP v Smith [1961] AC 290   109, 162, 290, 560
DPP v Stonehouse [1978] AC 55   377, 380, 383, 435
DPP v Sutcliffe unreported, 1 March 2001, SC of Vic, Gillard J, [2001] VSC 43   24
DPP v Withers [1975] AC 842   389, 400
DPP (Northern Ireland) v Lynch [1975] AC 653   555, 558, 574
DPP (Northern Ireland) v Maxwell [1978] 3 All ER 1140   452
DPP (UK) v Majewski [1977] AC 443   168, 523, 525
DPP (UK) v Nock and Alsford [1978] AC 979   416, 418
DPP Reference (No 1 of 1991) (1992) 60 A Crim R 43   473
Drago v The Queen (1992) 8 WAR 488   223
Duffy v The Queen [1981] WAR 72   168
Duong (1992) 61 A Crim R 140   459

Egan (1985) 15 A Crim R 20   223
Emery (1978) 18 A Crim R 49   560
Esau v The Queen [1996] NWTR 242   203
Ex parte Parker: Re Brotherson (1957) 57 SR (NSW) 326   444

F (1998) 101 A Crim R 578   228
Fagan v Metropolitan Police Commissioner [1969] 1 QB 439   80, 158, 159, 164, 169
Fairclough v Whipp [1951] 3 Cr App R 138   209
Falconer (1989) 46 A Crim R 83   469, 488, 489, 491, 509
Ferguson v The Queen [1979] 1 WLR 94   56
Ferguson v Weaving [1951] 1 KB 814   438
Fisher v Bennett (1987) 85 FLR 469   352
Fitzgerald (1980) 4 A Crim R 233   302
Fitzgerald (1999) 106 A Crim R 215   168
Fitzgerald v Kennard (1995) 38 NSWLR 184   224
Flatman (1880) 14 Cox 396   435
Foster v The Queen (1967) 118 CLR 117   285, 307

Franklin (2001) 119 A Crim R 223   463
Fraser v Dryden's Carrying & Agency Co Pty Ltd [1941] VLR 103   34
Freundt v Hayes (1992) 59 A Crim R 430   318

Gerakiteys v The Queen (1984) 153 CLR 317   394, 395, 396, 397, 403
Gardner; re BWV unreported 29 May 2003, SC of Vic, Morris J, [2003] VSC 173   136
Gibbins (1918) 13 Cr App R 134   67
Giles (1827) 1 Mood CC 166   434
Giorgianni v The Queen (1985) 156 CLR 473   385, 403, 404, 412, 439, 445, 448, 449, 460
Glennan (1970) 91 WN (NSW) 609   449
Goddard v Osborne (1978) 18 SASR 481   555, 561, 563
Goodes v General Motors Holden's Pty Ltd [1972] VR 386   34
Green v The Queen (1997) 191 CLR 334   493, 500
Green v The Queen unreported, 18 May 1999, CCA of NSW, [1999] NSW CCA 97   493

Haggie v Meredith (1993) 9 WAR 206.   524
Hale (1978) 68 Cr App R 415   313
Hales v Jamilmira unreported, 15 April 2003, CA of NT, [2003] NTCA 9   197, 200, 235
Hall v Fonceca [1983] WAR 309   168
Harkin (1989) 38 A Crim R 296   209
Harley (1830) 4 C & P 369   434
Harvey [1993] 2 Qd R 389   302
Haughton v Smith [1975] AC 476   58, 413, 414, 415
Hawkins (No 2) (1993) 68 A Crim R 1   518
Hawkins v The Queen (1994) 179 CLR 500   518, 519
Hawkins v The Queen (No 3) [1994] 4 Tas R 376   519
Hayes v Fries (1988) 49 SASR 184   268
He Kaw Teh v The Queen (1985) 157 CLR 523   55, 61, 72, 385, 412
Heaney et al (1992) 61 A Crim R 241   457
Heddich v Dike (1981) 3 A Crim R 139   358
Helmhout v R (1980) 49 FLR 1   185
Helmsley (1988) 36 A Crim R 334   223
Hendrickson v The Commonwealth 3 SW 166 (1887)   223
Hewitt (1996) 84 A Crim R 440   434, 435
Hickling v Laneyrie (1991) 21 NSWLR 730   62
Hill (1981) 3 A Crim R 397   496
Hind and Harwood (1995) 80 A Crim R 105   457
HM Advocate v Dingwall (1867) 5 Irvine 446   541
HM Coroner for East Kent, ex parte Spooner and Others (1989) 88 Cr App R 10   144
Hoessinger v The Queen (1992) 107 FLR 99   178
Holmes v DPP [1946] AC 588   487

Hood (2000) 111 A Crim R 556   311
Howe [1987] 1 AC 417   568
Hubert (1993) 67 A Crim R 181   166
Hyam v DPP [1975] AC 55   73, 74, 114

Ilich v The Queen (1987) 162 CLR 110   271, 280
In re London and Globe Finance Corporation Limited [1903] Ch 728   340, 347
Invicta Plastics Ltd v Clare [1976] Crim LR 131   409, 410

Jadurin (1982) 7 A Crim R 182   199
Jayasena v The Queen [1971] AC 618   56
Jerome [1964] Qd R 595   311
Jervis (1991) 56 A Crim R 374   161
Jiminez v The Queen (1992) 173 CLR 572   80, 508
Johns v The Queen (1980) 143 CLR 108   458
Johnson (1805) 29 St Tr 81   435
Johnson v The Queen (1976) 136 CLR 619   491
Jones (1990) 91 Cr App R 351   381
Jordan (1956) 40 Cr App Rep 152   101

Kaitamaki v The Queen [1985] AC 147   208
Kamara v DPP [1974] AC 104   404
Kaporonovski v The Queen (1973) 133 CLR 209   184, 486
Kay (1857) Dears & B 231   435
Kearon v Grant [1991] 1 VR 321   61, 62
Kennison v Daire (1985) 38 SASR 404   361
King v The Queen (1986) 161 CLR 423   429
Knight (1988) 35 A Crim R 314   158, 159, 385
Knight v The Queen (1992) 175 CLR 495   385
Knuller (Publishing & Printing Promotions) Ltd v DPP [1973] AC 435   399
Kowbel v The Queen [1954] 4 DLR 337   396
Kural v The Queen (1987) 162 CLR 502   77

La Fontaine v The Queen (1976) 136 CLR 62   71, 75
Lanciana (1996) 84 A Crim R 268   560
Larner v Dorrington (1993) MVR 75   575, 576
Laskey, Jaggard and Brown v The United Kingdom Eur Court HR, 19 February 1997, *Reports of Judgments and Decisions* 1997-I   190
Lawrence v Commissioner of Police for the Metropolis [1972] AC 626   276, 357
Leaman v The Queen [1986] Tas R 223   450
Lee (1917) 13 Cr App R 39   67
Lee (1994) 76 A Crim R 271   394
Leonard v Morris (1975) 10 SASR 528   168
Lergesner v Carroll (1989) 49 A Crim R 51   191, 193

Libman v The Queen (1985) 21 CCC (3d) 206   29
Limbo v Little (1989) 45 A Crim R 61   575, 576
Lipohar v The Queen (1999) 200 CLR 485   25, 29
Logdon v DPP [1976] Crim LR 121   169
Low v Blease [1975] Crim LR 513   279, 327, 360
Lowery v King (No 2) [1972] VR 560   429

M'Naghten Rules (1843) 10 Cl & Fin 200; 8 ER 718   56, 531
Mabo v Queensland (No 2) (1992) 175 CLR 1   264
Macklin and Murphy's case (1838) 2 Lew CC 225   428
Macleod v The Queen (2003) 197 ALR 333   282
MacPherson v Brown (1975) 12 SASR 184   168, 169
Mahadeo v The King [1936] 2 All ER 813   440
Mamote-Kulang of Tamagot v The Queen (1964) 111 CLR 62   78, 166
Manley (1844) 1 Cox 104   435
Markby v The Queen (1978) 140 CLR 108   459
Marshall (1987) 26 A Crim R 259   118
Martin (1995) 85 A Crim R; 13 WAR 472   112, 139
Martin (No 2) (1996) 86 A Crim R 133   139
Masciantonio v The Queen (1995) 183 CLR 58   490, 491, 497
Matthews v Fountain [1982] VR 1045   349, 352, 354
Matusevich v The Queen (1977) 137 CLR 633   429
Mawji v The Queen [1957] AC 126   396
Mazeau (1840) 9 C & P 676   434
McAuliffe and McAuliffe v The Queen (1995) 183 CLR 108   454
McAvaney v Quigley (1992) 58 A Crim R 457   194
McConville (1989) 44 A Crim R 455   313, 314
McDonough (1962) 47 Cr App R 37   418
McGhee v The Queen (1995) 183 CLR 82   386
McLiney v Minster [1911] VLR 347   182
Meissner v The Queen (1995) 184 CLR 132   404
Meyers v The Queen (1997) 147 ALR 440   109
Meyrick and Ribuffi (1929) 21 Cr App R 94   395
Michael (1840) 9 C & P 356   434
Middap (1992) 63 A Crim R 434   450
Miller v Hrvojevic [1972] VR 305   317
Mills (1963) 47 Cr App R 49   393
Minor (1992) 59 A Crim R 227   199
Moffa v The Queen (1977) 138 CLR 601   46, 485, 487, 498
Mogul Steamship Company v McGregor, Gow & Co [1892] AC 25   390
Mohan v The Queen [1967] 2 AC 187   430
Moore v Hussey (1609) Hob 93; 80 ER 243   572

Moore v Regents of the University of California 271 Cal Rptr 146 (Cal 1990)   268
More v The Queen [1963] 41 DLR (2d) 380   519
Morgan v Babcock and Wilcox Ltd (1929) 43 CLR 163; 30 SR(NSW) 218   34
Moriarty v Brooks (1834) 6 C & P 684   161
Mouse's case (1608) 77 ER 1341   572
Mousell Bros Ltd v London and Northwestern Railway Co [1917] 2 KB 836   34
Mulcahy v The Queen (1868) LR 3 HL 306   391
Murray v McMurchy [1949] 2 DLR 442   192
Murray v The Queen [1962] Tas SR 170   429, 440, 441
Mutemeri v Cheesman [1998] 4 VR 484   179
Mutton (1793) 1 Esp 62   435

National Coal Board v Gamble [1959] 1 QB 11   439
Nationwide News Pty Ltd v Bitter (1985) 38 SASR 390   62
New South Wales Sugar Milling Co-op Ltd v EPA (1992) 59 A Crim R 6   79
Nicholson (1994) 76 A Crim R 187   382
Nirta v The Queen (1983) 10 A Crim R 370   376
Norwich Union Fire Insurance Society Ltd v Williams H Price Ltd [1934] AC 455   272
Nydam v The Queen [1977] VR 430   78, 121, 170

O'Brien (1974) 59 Cr App R 222   394
O'Leary v Daire (1984) 13 A Crim R 404   526
O'Sullivan v Thurmer [1955] SASR 76   429
O'Sullivan v Truth and Sportsman Ltd (1957) 96 CLR 220   439
Ohlson v Hylton [1975] 1 WLR 724   318
Osland v The Queen (1998) 197 CLR 316   425, 429, 430–1, 434, 454, 464, 479, 480
Oxford v Moss (1978) 68 Cr App R 183   267, 269, 362

P (1997) 98 A Crim R 419   237
P & O European Ferries (Dover) Ltd (1991) 93 Cr App R 73   33
Pagawa v Mathew [1986] PNGLR 154   575
Pagett (1983) 76 Cr App R 279   83, 84
Pallante v Stadiums Pty Ltd (No 1) [1976] VR 331   193
Palmer (1804) 2 Leach 978   434
Papadimitropoulos v The Queen (1957) 98 CLR 249   210, 220
Parker v Alder [1899] 1 QB 20   61
Parker v The Queen (1963) 111 CLR 610   489
Parsons v The Queen (1999) 195 CLR 619   265
Paterson [1976] NZLR 394   435
Pemble v The Queen (1971) 124 CLR 107   64, 128, 560
People v MacEoin (1978) 112 ILTR 43   498
Pereira v DPP (1988) 82 ALR 217   77
Perka et al v The Queen (1985) 14 CCC (3d) 385   554, 574

Peters v The Queen (1998) 192 CLR 493   64, 292, 295, 300, 303, 304, 305, 337, 338, 348, 392, 404, 405, 407
Phillips (1987) 86 Cr App R 18   396
Pitman (1826) 2 C & P 423   435
Podinsky v The Queen (1990) 3 WAR 128   229
Police v Kawiti [2000] 1 NZLR 117   554
Polyukovich v Commonwealth (1991) 172 CLR 501   26
Poulterers' Case (1611) 9 Co Rep 55b; 77 ER 813   389
Proudman v Dayman (1941) 67 CLR 536   62

R and Minister for Customs v Australasian Films Ltd (1921) 29 CLR 195   34
R v Abusafiah (1991) 24 NSWLR 531   560, 561, 562–3, 564
   v *AC Hatrick Chemicals Pty Ltd* unreported, 29 November 1995, SC of Vic, Hampel J   35
   v *Aitken* [1992] 1 WLR 1006   193
   v *Allan* [1965] 1 QB 130   442
   v *Alley; Ex parte Mundell* (1886) 12 VLR 13   396
   v *Anderson* [1986] AC 27   407
   v *Anderson and Morris* [1966] 2 QB 110   459
   v *Arden* [1975] VR 449   448
   v *Aspinall* (1876) 2 QBD 48   394
   v *Austin* [1981] All ER 374   429
   v *Baba* [1977] 2 NSWLR 502   392
   v *Bacash* [1981] VR 923   168
   v *Bainbridge* [1960] 1 QB 129   452
   v *Ball* [1911] AC 47   238
   v *Baltzer* [1974] 27 CCC (2d) 118   519
   v *Barbouttis* (1995) 37 NSWLR 256   417
   v *Barbouttis, Dale and Single* unreported, 2 October 1996, SC of NSW, S51/1996   418
   v *Barker* [1924] NZLR 865   381, 384
   v *Barlow* (1962) 79 WN (NSW) 756   441, 450
   v *Barlow* (1997) 188 CLR 1   455, 463
   v *Baruday* [1984] VR 685   277, 358
   v *Battisti and Wilson* unreported, 13 September 1995, NSW CCA, 60284/9   391
   v *Battle* (1993) 8 WAR 449   524
   v *Beattie* (1981) 26 SASR 481   239, 242, 244
   v *Beck* [1985] 1 All ER 571   437, 439
   v *Beckett* (1836) 1 Mood & R 526   161
   v *Beharriell* (1995) 130 DLR (4th) 422   471
   v *Bell* [1972] Tas SR 127   386
   v *Berwick* [1979] Tas R 101   161

v *Bingapore* (1975) 11 SASR 469   102
v *Bingley* (1821) Russ & Ry 446   428
v *Bland* [1988] Crim LR 41   442
v *Blaue* [1975] 1 WLR 1411   102
v *Bonollo* [1981] VR 633   291, 298, 299, 306, 347, 349, 356
v *Bonora* (1994) 35 NSWLR 74   223
v *Bournewood Community and Mental Health NHS Trust, ex parte L* [1998] 3 WLR 107   581
v *Brain* (1834) 6 C & P 349   98
v *Brow* [1981] VR 783   291, 298, 347, 356
v *Brown* (1986) 43 SASR 33   561, 562, 563
v *Brown* [1990] VR 820   402
v *Brown* [1992] 2 WLR 441   189
v *Brown* [1992] 2 WLR 441 (CA)   189
v *Brown* [1993] 2 WLR 556 (HL)   189, 191, 194
v *Browning* [1976] 34 CCC (2d) 200   519
v *Bulmer* [1987] 1 S.C.R. 782   225
v *Burgess* [1991] 2 QB 92   514
v *Burr* [1969] NZLR 736   70
v *Butcher* [1986] VR 43   115, 117, 311
v *Butterfield* (1843) 1 Cox CC 39   440
v *Buttsworth* [1983] 1 NSWLR 658   78
v *Byrne* [1960] 2 QB 396   505, 542, 543
v *Cahill* [1978] 2 NSWLR 453   400
v *Calhaem* [1985] QB 808   439
v *Campbell* [1933] St R Qd 123   391
v *Campbell* [1991] Crim LR 268   382
v *Campbell* [1997] 2 VR 585   169
v *Camplin* (1845) 1 Cox CC 220   211
v *Carr* unreported, 17 October 1990, CCA of NSW   194
v *Carroll* (1835) 7 C & P 145; 173 ER 64   523
v *Carter* [1959] VR 105   512
v *Carter* [1990] 2 Qd R 371   440
v *Cato* [1976] 1 WLR 110   128
v *Chai* unreported, 25 August 2000, CCA of NSW, [2000] NSW CCA 320   463
v *Chai* (2002) 187 ALR 436   463
v *Chan-Fook* [1994] 2 ER 552   162
v *Chapple* (1840) 9 Car and P 355   441
v *Charles Fletcher* (1866) LR 1; CCR 39   243
v *Chaulk* [1990] 3 SCR 1303   57
v *Chellingworth* [1954] QWN 35 (Circuit Court)   380
v *Cheshire* [1991] 1 WLR 844   101

v *Chrastny (No 1)* [1991] 1 WLR 1381   394
v *Chrichton* [1915] SALR 1   410
v *Clarke and Wilton* [1959] VR 645   67, 428
v *Clarkson* [1971] 1 WLR 1402   439, 432
v *Cline* [1956] OR 539   382
v *Cockburn* [1968] 1 WLR 281   288
v *Cogan and Leak* [1976] 1 QB 217   435
v *Coleman* (1990) 19 NSWLR 467   79, 165
v *Collingridge* (1976) 16 SASR 117   383, 415
v *Collins* [1973] 1 QB 100   324
v *Coney* (1882) 8 QBD 534   191, 439, 442
v *Conway* [1989] 1 QB 290   554, 555
v *Costa* unreported, 2 April 1996, CA of SC of Vic   223
v *Court* [1989] AC 28   209, 223
v *Cox* (1992) 12 BMLR 38   132
v *Crabbe* (1985) 156 CLR 464   71, 75, 77, 110, 114, 169, 170
v *CRH* unreported, 18 December 1996, CCA of NSW, BC9606725   45
v *Croft* [1944] 1 KB 295   445, 448
v *Croft* [1981] 1 NSWLR 126   487
v *Cuerrier* [1998] 2 SCR 371   221
v *Cugullere* [1961] 1 WLR 858   317
v *Cunningham* [1982] AC 566   162
v *Damson* [1978] VR 536   554, 562, 563
v *Daniels* [1972] Qd R 323   429
v *Darby* (1982) 148 CLR 668   392, 402, 429
v *Darrington and McGauley* [1980] VR 353   558
v *Darryl Raymond Reid and Wayne Matthew Reid* unreported, 28 August 2001, SC of ACT, Crispin J [2001] ACTSC 88   152
v *Davidson* [1969] VR 667   139, 574, 576, 581
v *Davis* (1823) 168 ER 917   322
v *Dawson* [1961] VR 773   440
v *Day* (1841) 9 Car & P 772   210
v *Day* (1845) 1 Cox 207   160
v *De Stefano* [2003] VSC 68   251
v *Dee* (1884) 15 Cox CC 579   210
v *Demirian* [1989] VR 97   71, 79, 170, 429, 430
v *Denbo Pty Ltd & Timothy Ian Nadenbousch* unreported, 14 June 1994, SC of Vic, Teague J   37, 148
v *Dickie* [1984] 3 All ER 173   536
v *Dincer* [1983] VR 460   500
v *Ditta* [1988] Crim LR 42   559
v *Donnelly* [1970] NZLR 980   414

v *Donovan* [1934] 2 KB 498   190, 191
v *Dudley and Stephens* (1884) 14 QBD 273   52, 572, 575, 582
v *Duguid* (1906) 94 LT 887   397
v *Duru* [1974] 1 WLR 2   286
v *Duvivier* (1982) 29 SASR 217   185
v *Eagleton* (1855) 6 Cox CC 559   380
v *Easom* [1971] 1 QB 315   307
v *Edwards* [1956] QWN 16   380
v *Emmett* unreported, 18 June 1999, Court of Appeal, No 9901191/Z2   194
v *Esau* [1997] 2 SCR 777   203, 226
v *Evans* (1987) 48 SASR 35   386
v *Evans and Gardiner (No 2)* [1976] VR 523   101
v *F, ex parte Attorney-General* [1999] 2 Qd R 157   45
v *Falconer* (1990) 171 CLR 30   47, 58, 472, 507, 508, 509, 513, 532, 533, 534, 566
v *Farrar* [1992] 1 VR 207   185
v *Feely* [1973] 1 QB 530   291, 296
v *Fitzmaurice* [1983] QB 1083   418
v *Flattery* (1877) 1 QBD 410   210
v *Fletcher (Richard)* (1859) 8 Cox CC 131   211, 243
v *Fletcher (Charles)* (1866) LR 1   243
v *Fletcher* [1962] Crim LR 551   448
v *Francis* [1993] 2 Qd R 300   211
v *Fry* (1992) 58 SASR 424   182
v *Gallienne* [1964] NSWR 919   210
v *Ghosh* [1982] 1 QB 1053   291, 296, 303, 347, 405, 407
v *Gilks* [1972] 1 WLR 1341   272
v *Gilmartin* [1983] QB 953   340
v *Giorgi* (1983) 31 SASR 299   439
v *Glenister* [1980] 2 NSWLR 597   290, 292, 302
v *Gomez* [1993] AC 442   276, 281, 358
v *Gotts* [1992] 2 AC 412   557, 558
v *Governor of Brixton Prison; Ex parte Levin* [1997] QB 65   362
v *Graham* [1982] 1 WLR 294   562
v *Greenberg* [1972] Crim LR 331   269
v *Griffith* (1553) 75 ER 152   427
v *Griffiths* [1966] 1 QB 589   394, 395
v *Grimes* [1968] 3 All ER 179   374, 392
v *Grundy* [1977] Crim LR 543   448
v *Gullefer* [1990] 3 All ER 882   380
v *Gunn* (1930) 30 SR (NSW) 336   393
v *Hadfield* (1800) 27 St Tr 1281   520, 537
v *Hall* [1973] QB 126   270

v *Hallett* [1969] SASR 141   83, 100
v *Hansford* (1974) 8 SASR 164   28
v *Harris* [1964] Crim LR 54   444
v *Hartridge* (1966) 57 DLR (2d) 332   508
v *Helene* unreported, 28 July 1999, CCA of NSW, [1999] NSW CCA 203   463
v *Hennessy* [1973] 1 QB 910   514
v *Hersington* [1983] 2 NSWLR 72   391, 404
v *Hickey* (1992) 16 Crim LJ 271   479
v *Higgins* (1801) 2 East 5   409, 410
v *Hill* [1986] 1 SCR 313   495, 498
v *Hinks* [2000] 4 All ER 833   277
v *Hoar* (1981) 148 CLR 32   376
v *Holey* [1963] 1 All ER 106   440
v *Holzer* [1968] VR 481   120, 127, 128
v *Hopley* 2 F & F 202   183
v *Hornbuckle* [1945] VLR 281   72
v *Horsington* [1983] 2 NSWLR 72   391, 404
v *Howard* [1966] 1 WLR 13   211
v *Howe* [1987] AC 417   52, 557, 558, 568, 579
v *Howes* (1971) 2 SASR 293   404
v *Hudson and Taylor* [1971] 2 QB 202   562, 563
v *Hurley and Murray* [1967] VR 526   558, 559, 561, 562, 564
v *Hutty* [1953] VLR 338   98, 138
v *ICR Haulage Ltd* [1944] KB 551   33, 396
v *Instan* [1893] 1 QB 450   67
v *Ireland; R v Burstow* [1998] AC 147   167
v *J* (1982) 45 ALR 331   237
v *Jackson* [1891] 1 QB 671   183
v *Jarvis* (1837) 2 Mood and R 40   441
v *JC* unreported, 18 August 2000, SC of the ACT, Higgins J, [2000] ACTSC 72   208
v *Jensen and Ward* [1980] VR 194   445, 446
v *Johnson* [1964] Qd R 1   486
v *Jones* [1949] 1 KB 194   450
v *Joudrie* unreported, 9 May 1996, Court of Queen's Bench of Alberta, No 9501-1280-C6   514
v *Karounos* (1994) 63 SASR 451   404, 406
v *Kastratovic* (1985) 42 SASR 59   295, 304
v *Kelly* [1998] 3 All ER 741   267
v *Kemp* [1957] 1 QB 399   505, 512
v *Khan* [1990] 2 All ER 783   386
v *Khan* [1998] EWCA Crim 971   126
v *Kimber* [1983] 1 WLR 1118   223

v *Kitchener* (1993) 29 NSWLR 696   76, 223
v *Kolb and Adams* unreported, 14 December 1979, SC of Vic   317
v *Kontinnen* (1992) 16 Crim LJ 360   478
v *Kovacs* [1974] 1 WLR 370   338, 343
v *Krause* (1902) 66 JP 1902   410
v *Kumar* [2002] 5 VR 193   488
v *Kusu* [1981] Qd R 136   524
v *L* (1991) 174 CLR 379   206
v *Lamb* [1967] 2 QB 981   128
v *Lambie* [1982] AC 449   333, 343, 345
v *Langham* (1984) 36 SASR 48   288, 292, 310
v *Lawrence* [1997] 1 VR 459   300, 348
v *Laz* [1998] 1 VR 453   215
v *Lechasseur* [1977] 38 CCC (2d) 319   519
v *Lee* (1990) 1 WAR 411   376, 415
v *Leonboyer* unreported, 7 September 2001, CA of the SC of Vic, [2001] VSCA 149   488, 516
v *Levy* [1912] 1 KB 158   441
v *Lloyd* [1967] 1 QB 175   543
v *Lloyd* [1985] 3 WLR 30   285, 362
v *Lock* (1872) LR 2 CCR 10   210
v *Lopatta* (1983) 35 SASR 101   260, 292
v *Lopuszynski* [1971] QWN 33   429
v *Loughnan* [1981] VR 443   46, 554, 555, 572, 573, 574, 575, 576, 577
v *Love* (1989) 17 NSWLR 608   290, 302, 348, 356
v *Lovett* [1975] VR 488   169
v *Lynsey* [1995] 3 All ER 654   157
v *Macdonald* [1904] QSR 151   428
v *Machirus* [1996] 6 NZLR 404   393
v *Maes* [1975] VR 541   212
v *Mai* (1992) 26 NSWLR 371   415
v *Malcherek*; *R v Steel* [1981] 1 WLR 690   102
v *Maloney* [1985] AC 905   73
v *Mansfield* unreported, acquittal 5 May 1994, SC of Vic, Hampel J   514, 515
v *Marshall* (1987) 49 SASR 133   182
v *Martin* (1881) 8 QBD 54   111
v *Martin* (1983) 32 SASR 419   129
v *Martin* [1989] 1 All ER 652   576
v *Maryanne Jane Cooper* unreported, 31 August 2001, SC of NSW, Simpson J, [2001] NSWSC 769   547
v *Masters* (1992) 26 NSWLR 450   390
v *Matchett* [1980] 2 WWR 122   508

v *Mayers* (1872) 12 Cox CC 311   211
v *McCormack* [1969] 2 QB 442   159
v *McDonnell* [1966] 1 QB 233   396
v *McGrath and Simonidis* [1983] 2 Qd R 54   392
v *McIntosh* unreported, 3 September 1999, SC of Vic, Vincent J, No 1412 of 1999, [1999] VSC 358   196
v *McIver* (1928) 22 QJPR 173   223
v *McKechie* [1926] NZLR 1   396
v *McKenna* [1960] 1 QB 411   440, 441
v *McNamara* [1954] VLR 137   165
v *Meech* [1974] QB 549   270
v *Menniti* [1985] 1 Qd R 520   445
v *Meredith* [1973] Crim LR 253   269
v *Metharam* [1961] 3 All ER 200   162
v *Middleton* (1873) LR 2 CCR 38   270
v *Miers* [1985] 2 Qd R 138   524
v *Miller* [1983] 2 AC 161   67, 79, 80, 125
v *Mitchell* [1983] QB 741   110
v *Mobilio* [1991] 1 VR 339   221
v *Moore* (1908) 10 WALR 64   537
v *Morgan* [1970] VR 337   240
v *Morhall* [1996] AC 90   495
v *Morris* [1984] AC 320   276
v *Most* (1881) 7 QBD 244   410
v *Mowatt* [1968] 1 QB 421   169
v *Murphy* (1985) 158 CLR 596   374, 392
v *Murphy* (1985) 4 NSWLR 42   374
v *Murray Wright Ltd* [1970] NZLR 476   33
v *Nazif* [1987] 2 NZLR 122   209
v *Newman* [1948] VLR 61   185
v *Nguyen* [1997] 1 VR 551   317
v *Nicholson* [1916] VLR 130   167
v *Nielsen* [1990] 2 Qd R 578   505
v *Nuri* [1990] VR 641   178
v *O'Connor* (1980) 146 CLR 64   72, 168, 523, 524, 528
v *O'Connor* unreported, 26 May 1997, SC of Vic, BC9702350   177
v *Oliphant* (1905) 2 KB 67   435
v *Orton* [1922] VLR 469   393
v *Osland* [1998] 2 VR 636   425
v *Osolin* [1993] 4 SCR 595   225
v *Pace* [1965] 3 Can CC 55   295
v *Page* [1933] VLR 351   383

v *Palazoff* (1986) 43 SASR 99   557, 564
v *Palmer* [1985] Tas R 138   524
v *Parks* [1992] 2 SCR 871   511, 512, 514
v *Parsons* [2000] 1 VR 161 487
v *Patterson* unreported, 29 March 1999, County Court of Vic, Mullaly J   242
v *Patton* [1998] 1 VR 7   157
v *Pawlicki and Swindell* [1992] 1 WLR 827   317
v *Percali* (1986) 42 SASR 46   168
v *Perera* [1907] VLR 240   342
v *Perks* (1986) 41 SASR 335   560
v *Petronius-Kuff* [1983] 3 NSWLR 178   336
v *Phillips* (1971) 45 ALJR 467   97
v *Pickard* [1959] Qd R 475   561, 562
v *Pius Piane* [1975] PNGLR 52   576
v *Porter* (1933) 55 CLR 182   536
v *Potisk* (1973) 6 SASR 389   271
v *Powell; R v English* [1997] 3 WLR 959   455, 460
v *Preddy* [1996] 3 WLR 255   265
v *Prior* (1992) 91 NTR 53   415
v *PS Shaw* [1995] 2 Qd R 97   210
v *Quick* [1989] 1 WLR 287   514
v *R* (1981) 28 SASR 321   487, 496
v *Rabey* (1977) 37 CCC (2d) 461   511
v *Radford* (1985) 42 SASR 266   513, 532, 533
v *Radford (No 2)* (1987) 11 Crim LJ 231   513, 515
v *Ransford* (1874) 13 Cox CC 9   410
v *Ready* [1942] VLR 85   441
v *Red Old Man* (1978) 44 CCC (2d) 123   244
v *Reeves* (1892) 13 LR (NSW) 220   450
v *Richard Fletcher* (1859) 8 Cox CC 131   211, 243
v *Richman* [1982] Crim LR 507   563
v *Robinson* [1915] 2 KB 342   381, 382
v *Roffel* [1985] VR 511   277, 281
v *Rogerson* (1992) 174 CLR 268   391, 392, 393, 400, 402, 404
v *Rose* [1962] 3 All ER 298   441
v *Runjanjic and Kontinnen* (1991) 56 SASR 114   563, 564
v *Russell* [1933] VLR 59   67, 125, 442, 443
v *Ruzic* (1998) 128 CCC (3d) 97   566
v *Ryan* (1890) 11 LR(NSW) 171   182
v *Ryan and Walker* [1966] VR 553   116, 118
v *Salisbury* [1976] VR 452   160
v *Salvo* [1980] VR 401   291, 292, 297, 347, 356
v *Saunders* [1985] Crim LR 230   162

v *Saunders and Archer* (1576) 2 Plowd 473; 75 ER 706   110, 448
v *Savage and Parmenter* [1992] 1 AC 699   159, 168, 169
v *Sayers* [1943] SASR 146   397
v *Saylor* [1963] QWN 14   445
v *Scofield* (1784) Cald Mag Rep 397   377
v *Scott* [1975] AC 819   347
v *Secretary* (1996) 5 NTLR 96   159, 164
v *Secretary of State for the Home Department, ex parte Thompson; ex parte Venables* [1997] 3 WLR 23   43
v *Sew Hoy* [1994] 1 NZLR 257   417
v *Sheriff* [1969] Crim LR 260   160
v *Shields* [1981] VR 717   123, 170
v *Simcox* [1964] Crim LR 402   543
v *Single, Barbouttis and Dale* unreported, 15 March 1996, HC, S134/1995   418
v *Smith* [1959] 2 QB 35   100
v *Smith* [1963] 3 All ER 597   459
v *Solomon* [1959] Qd R 123   439, 441, 445
v *Spratt* [1990] 1 WLR 1073   159, 168
v *Stanley* unreported, 7 April 1995, CCA of NSW, No 60554 of 1994   194
v *Steane* [1947] 1 KB 997   557
v *Stevenson* [1990] 58 CCC (2d) 464   519
v *Stone* [1981] VR 737   450
v *Stone* [1999] 2 SCR 290   58, 511, 514
v *Stone and Dobinson* [1977] 1 QB 354   48, 67, 68, 123
v *Taaffe* [1984] AC 539   414
v *Teremoana* (1990) 54 SASR 30   178
v *Terry* [1955] VLR 114   183, 186
v *Tevendale* [1955] VLR 95   440, 441, 450
v *Thurborn* (1849) 169 ER 293   269
v *Tolmie* (1995) 37 NSWLR 660   76, 223
v *Tout* (1987) 11 NSWLR 251   164
v *Turner* [1962] VR 30   182
v *Turner* [1974] AC 357   353, 354
v *Turner (No 2)* [1971] 1 WLR 901   269
v *Valderrama-Vega* [1985] Crim LR 220   561, 564
v *Vallance* [1960] Tas SR 51   223
v *Venna* [1975] 3 WLR 737   158, 159, 168, 169, 223
v *Wald* [1971] 3 NSWDCR 25   139
v *Walker* (1994) 35 NSWLR 384   62
v *Walker* unreported, 1 September 1994, SC of NT, Martin CJ, No 46 of 1993, [1994] NTSC 79   199
v *Walkington* [1979] 1 WLR 1169   326
v *Walsh and Harney* [1984] VR 474   391

v *Wampfler* (1987) 11 NSWLR 541   62
v *Warner* [1980] Qd R 207   575
v *Waterfall* [1970] 1 QB 148   297, 340
v *Webb; Ex parte Attorney-General* [1990] 2 Qd R 275   428
v *Welch* (1996) 101 CCC (3d) 216   194
v *Wells* (1981) 28 SASR 63   185
v *Welsh* (1869) 11 Cox 336   46, 485
v *White* (1987) 9 NSWLR 427   554, 574
v *Whitehouse* [1977] QB 868   410
v *Whitworth* [1989] 1 Qd R 437   505, 534
v *Williams* [1923] 1 KB 340   210
v *Williams* (1932) 32 SR (NSW) 504   440
v *Williams* [1953] 1 QB 660   296
v *Williams* [1965] Qd R 86   380, 382
v *Williams* (1976) 14 SASR 1   197, 200
v *Williamson* [1972] 2 NSWLR 281   558, 561, 562
v *Wilson* [1996] 3 WLR 125   191, 195
v *Wilson Flanders* [1969] SASR 218   326
v *Wood and McMahon* (1830) 1 Mood CC 278   161
v *Woodrow* (1846) 15 M & W 404; 153 ER 907   61
v *Wyles; Ex parte Attorney-General (Qld)* [1977] Qd R 169   428
Race Relations Board v Applin [1973] QB 815   410
Rance v Mid-Downs Health Authority [1991] 1 QB 587   104
Randall (1991) 53 A Crim R 380   208
Re A (Children) (Conjoined Twins: Surgical Separation) [2001] 2 WLR 480   571, 573, 574, 576, 577
Re F (Mental Patient: Sterilisation) [1990] 2 AC 1   133, 575, 578, 581
Re London and Globe Finance Corporation Limited [1903] Ch 728   340, 347
Re T (Adult: Refusal of Treatment) [1993] Fam 95   192
Reid (1975) 62 Cr App R 109   459
Reniger v Feogossa (1551) 75 ER 1   523
Rhodes (1984) 14 A Crim R 124   109
Rice v McDonald (2000) 113 A Crim R 75   561
Roche v The Queen [1988] WAR 278   486
Rodriguez v Attorney-General (British Columbia) [1993] 3 SCR 519   134
Rogers (1996) 86 A Crim R 542   554, 574, 575, 577
Rolfe (1952) 36 Cr App R 4   159, 208
Rowell (1977) 65 Cr App R 174   374
Royall v The Queen (1990) 172 CLR 378   79, 82, 83, 90, 102, 103, 105
Rozsa v Samuels [1969] SASR 205   158
Russell and Russell (1987) 85 Cr App R 388   428
Ryan v Kuhl [1979] VR 315   165

Ryan v The Queen (1967) 121 CLR 205   79, 508

S & Y Investments (No 2) Pty Ltd v Commercial Union Assurance Co of Australia Ltd (1986) 85 FLR 285   33
S v The Queen (1989) 168 CLR 266   229, 232
Salmon v Chute (1994) 94 NTR 1   67
SC Small v Noa Kurimalawai unreported, 22 October 1997, Magistrates' Court of the ACT, No CC97/01904   522
Schloss v Maguire (1897) 8 QLJ 21   190
Scott v Metropolitan Police Commissioner [1975] AC 819   286, 368, 391, 404, 405, 406
Sharah v The Queen (1992) 30 NSWLR 292   459
Sharp v McCormick [1986] VR 869   286
Shaw v DPP [1962] AC 220   399
Shepherd (1987) 86 Cr App R 47   558
Sherras v De Rutzen [1895] 1 QB 918   63
Smith (1982) 7 A Crim R 437   341, 351, 353
Smith v Byrne (1894) QCR 252   183
Smith v Desmond [1965] AC 960   269, 310
Smith v The Queen unreported, 6 March 1979, CCA Tas   558
Snow v The Queen [1962] Tas SR   524
Sodeman v The Queen (1952) 86 CLR 358   537
Sreckovic v The Queen [1973] WAR 85   486
Staines (1975) 60 Cr App R 160   341
State of Queensland v Alyssa Nolan (an infant) unreported, 31 May 2001, SC of Qld, Chesterman J, [2001] QSC 174   581
State v Ford Motor Co, Cause No 11-431 (1980)   147
State v Shackford 127 NH 695, 506 A 2d 315 (1986)   520
Stein v Henshall [1976] VR 612   273
Stephenson v State (1932) 179 NE 633   103
Stewart v The Queen (1988) 41 CCC (3d) 481   279
Stingel v The Queen (1990) 171 CLR 312   490, 491, 495, 566
Stokes and Difford (1990) 51 A Crim R 25   169, 451
Stuart v The Queen (1974) 134 CLR 426   457
Sutherland v United Kingdom (1997) 24 EHRR CD22–CD35   233

T v The United Kingdom and V v The United Kingdom unreported, 16 December 1999, Eur Court HR Strasbourg, Application No 00024724/94   43
Taaffe (1983) 77 Crim App R 82   414
Taktak (1988) 34 A Crim R 334   125
Tesco Supermarkets Ltd v Nattrass [1972] AC 153   35, 148
Thabo Meli v The Queen [1954] 1 WLR 228   79
Thambiah v The Queen [1966] AC 37   438, 439
Thomas (1985) 81 Cr App R 331   160

Thompson v Nixon [1966] 1 QB 103   273
Tietie (1988) 34 A Crim R 438   446
Trade Practices Commission v Tubemakers of Australia Ltd (1983) 47 ALR 719   386
Tyler and Price (1838) 1 Mood CC 428   434

US v Kissel 218 US 601 (1910)   400

Vallance v The Queen (1961) 108 CLR 56   161, 168
Valler (1844) 1 Cox 84   434
Van Den Hoek v The Queen (1986) 161 CLR 158   486, 488
Varley v The Queen (1976) 12 ALR 347   459
Viro v The Queen (1978) 141 CLR 88   475, 476, 477
Vose (1999) 109 A Crim R 489   172

Wai Yu-tsang v The Queen [1992] 1 AC 269   391, 392
Walden v Hensler (1987) 163 CLR 561   291, 292, 294
Walker v Bradley unreported, 15 December 1993, NSW Dist Ct, Kirkham J, 1919 of 1989   192
Walsh (2002) 131 A Crim R 299   348, 388
Ward v The Queen (1980) 142 CLR 308   27
Warner (1970) 55 Cr App R 93   285
Warren, Coombes and Tucker (1996) A Crim R 78   197
Watherston v Woolven (1988) 139 LSJS 366   194
Wau Yu-tsang v The Queen [1992] 1 AC 269   391, 392
Welham (1845) 1 Cox 192   435
Wesley-Smith v Balzary (1977) 14 ALR 681   376
Westaway (1991) 52 A Crim R 336   168, 171
White v Ridley (1978) 140 CLR 342   435, 445, 446
Wilcox v Jeffery [1951] 1 All ER 464   439
Wilkinson (1985) 20 A Crim R 230   223
Willer (1986) 83 Cr App R 224   554
Willgoss v The Queen (1960) 105 CLR 295   535, 536
Williams (1990) 50 A Crim R 213   168, 169
Wilson v Kuhl [1979] VR 315   318
Wilson v The Queen (1992) 174 CLR 313   127, 129
Wooley v Fitzgerald [1969] Tas SR 65   190
Woolmington v DPP [1935] AC 462   55, 56
Wray v The King (1930) 33 WALR 67   537, 538

Yip Chiu-Cheung v R [1995] 1 AC 111   398
Youssef (1990) 50 A Crim R 1   56

Zaharias (2001) 122 A Crim R 586   560
Zanker v Vartzokas (1988) 34 A Crim R 11   159
Zecevic v DPP (Vic) (1987) 162 CLR 645   53, 183, 321, 473, 475, 482

Table of Statutes

Commonwealth

Cheques Act 1986   265, 266
Constitution: s 51 (vi) and (xxiv)   26
Corporations Act 2001   260, 365
Crimes Act 1914   27, 44, 182, 259, 300, 335, 338, 361, 367, 373, 374, 378, 380, 384, 391, 392, 394, 396, 398 401, 407, 409, 415, 416, 418, 421, 427, 438, 440, 450
    s 3ZC(2)(a)   182
    s 4N   44
    s 5   427, 438
    s 6   440, 450
    s 7   378, 379
    s 7(2)   380, 384
    s 7(3)(a)   415, 416, 421
    s 7A(a)   409
    s 29D   367
    s 42   392
    s 43   373, 374
    s 86   338, 391
    s 86(1)(e)   300
    s 86A   300
    s 86(3)(b)   407
    s 86(3)(c)   394, 401
    s 86(4)(a)   416, 421
    s 86(4)(b)   396
    s 86(5)(a)   398
    s 86 (6)   394
    s 86(9)   391

Crimes (Child Sex Tourism) Amendment Act 1994   27
Criminal Code
    s 4.2(4)   123, 126, 131
    s 4.2(3)   511
    s 5.2(3)   109
    s 5.4(1)   175
    s 5.4   114, 462
    s 5.5   36, 122, 123
    s 7.1   42
    s 7.2   44
    s 7.3   531
    s 7.3(1)(c)   537
    s 7.3(1)(b)   536
    s 7.3(8)   533
    s 7.3(9)   533
    s 10.2   557, 565, 566, 567, 582
    s 10.3   573, 578, 580
    s 10.3(1)   577
    s 10.3(2)   582
    s 10.4   474
    s 10.4(2)   483, 576
    s 11.1(2)   384
    s 11.1(4)   421
    s 11.2   427, 438
    s 11.2(3)   461
    s 11.2(3)(a)   453
    s 11.2(4)   447
    s 11.3   436
    s 11.4   409
    s 11.4(3)   421
    s 11.5   259
    s 11.5(2)   401, 412
    s 11.5(2)(b)   407
    s 11.5(3)(a)   421
    s 11.5(5)   464
    s 12.2   148
    s 12.3(1)   149
    s 12.3(2)   149
    s 12.3(6)   36, 149
    s 12.4   36
    s 12.4(3)   36
    ss 76A–76F   361

s 134.1(15), (16)   283, 360
s 130.3   305, 349
s 131.3(1)   282
s 131.7   281
s 132.2   316
s 132.3   318
s 132.4   329
s 132.5   330
s 133.1   361, 362
s 135.1   335, 338, 357, 367
s 135.1(a)   367
s 135.4   259
s 142   367
s 142(1)   367
ss 476.1–478.4   361, 363
Criminal Code Act 1995   30
Criminal Code Amendment (Theft, Fraud, Bribery and Related Offences) Act 2000   259, 305, 338, 362
  ss 143.1–144.1   362
Customs Act 1901
  s 233B   415
  s 233B(1)(b)   77
Cybercrime Act 2001   27, 31
Euthanasia Laws Act 1997   132
  Sch 1   132
Family Law Act 1975   469
Marriage Act 1961
  s 11   231
  s 12   231
Parliamentary Commission of Inquiry Act 1986   374
Social Security (Administration) Act 1999
  Part 6   335
Trade Practices Act 1974   150, 260, 366, 368
  ss 53–53C   365
War Crimes Act 1945
  s 11   26

Australian Capital Territory

Children and Young People Act 1999
  s 71(2)   44
Crimes Act 1900   25

s 2E(2)   230
s 4   162
s 10   138
s 11(1)   97
s 12(1)(a)   107
s 12(1)(b)   107
s 13(2)   486
s 12   96
s 14   540
s 14(1)   542, 543
s 15   96
s 15(1)   120
s 17   131
s 19   168, 327
s 20   168, 327
s 21   161, 327
s 22   160, 327
s 24   162, 327
s 25   42, 170
s 26   44, 157
s 27   327, 533
s 27(4)(c)   160
s 29   123
s 29(4)(b)   123
s 30   173, 174
s 31   174
s 32(1)(b)   160
s 34A   174
s 39   179
s 42   104, 141, 474
s 47   158, 409
s 83   263
s 84   259, 263, 268, 283, 288
s 85   270
s 85(1)   268
s 85(3)   270
s 85(4)   271, 272
s 86   336
s 86(1)   259
s 86(3)   294
s 86(4)   295, 347
s 86(4)(b)   303

s 86(4)(c)   293
s 87   284, 346
s 91(1)   309, 311, 316
s 91(2)   309
s 92   316, 317
s 92(a)   207
s 92(b)   207
s 92(d)   207
s 92(e)   208
s 92D   74, 222
s 92E(1)   234
s 92E(2)   231
s 92E(2)–(3)   231
s 92E(2), (3)   231
s 92EA   232
s 92J   208, 209
s 92K(1)   231
s 92K(2)   231
s 92L   232
s 92L(6)   232
s 92L(7)   232
s 92P(1)(a)–(j)   210
s 92P(1)(e)   211
s 92P(1)(f)   210
s 92P(1)(g)   210, 220
s 92P(1)(i)   210, 240
s 92P(2)   209, 210
s 93   321
s 93(1)   321, 327
s 93(2)   325, 326
s 94   330
s 95   288, 338, 351
s 95(2)   355
s 95(2)(a), (b)   352
s 96   352
s 97(2)   355
s 98   344, 352, 356
s 98(2)   353
s 98(3)(a), (b)   356
s 102   365
s 106   280
s 111   287

s 116   327
s 117   327
s 339   522
s 346   440, 450
s 349ZE   182
s 428B   534, 538
s 428N   534
Pt 111B   163, 191, 197
Crimes (Amendment) Act (No 2) 1986   258
Criminal Code
   s 15(5)   523
   s 25   42
   s 26   44,
   s 27   533
   s 28   531, 534
   s 31   522, 526
   s 40   557
   s 41   573, 577
   s 42   474
   s 44   379
   s 45   427, 438
   s 47   409
   s 47(4)   409
   s 48   391
   Pt 2.7   31
   Pt 4.2   363
Mental Health (Treatment and Care) Act 1930   534
Transplantation and Anatomy Act 1978
   s 45   99

New South Wales

Children (Criminal Proceedings) Act 1985
   s 5   42
Crimes Act 1900
   s 4   109
   s 4(1)   162, 326, 350
   s 17A   97
   s 18(1)   116
   s 18(1)(a)   107, 108, 116
   s 18(1)(b)   120

s 19A 96
s 20 138
s 22A 141, 547
s 22A(1) 141
s 22A(1), (2) 548
s 23(2) 486
s 23A 540
s 23A(8) 542, 543
s 24 96, 162
s 27 160
s 27–30 379
s 31 173, 174
s 31C 131
s 33 161, 169
s 35 161, 169
s 43 179
s 44 67, 161, 179
s 45 163, 191, 197
s 52A 81, 123, 448, 449
s 54 170
s 58 160, 161
s 59 162
s 61 157
s 61D(2) 74, 222
s 61H(1)(a) 207
s 61H(1)(b) 207
s 61H(1)(c) 207
s 61H(1)(d) 208
s 61J 241
s 61J(2)(f) and (g) 241
s 61L 208
s 61M(3)(b) 231
s 61R 209
s 61R(2)(a)(i) 210
s 61R(2)(a)(ii) 221
s 61R(2)(a1) 210, 221
s 61R(2)(d) 210
s 66C 230
s 66EA 232
s 66F(2) 241
s 66F(3) 241

s 73   230
s 77   231
s 78A   232
s 78Q   231
ss 82–84   139
s 94   330
s 94(1)   309
s 95   317
s 96   317
s 97   317
s 98   317
s 109   321, 322, 327
ss 109–113   320, 326
s 110   322
s 111   322
s 112   322
s 114(1)(c)   321
s 116   261
s 117   261
s 118   285, 294
s 124   272
ss 124–162   262
s 125   258, 274
s 139   264
s 140   264
s 154A   287
s 154AA   287
154B   287
s 157   258
s 160   258
s 173   302
s 176   365
s 178A   258, 336
s 178B   340
s 178BA   258, 302, 336, 340, 351, 355, 356, 362
s 178BA(1)   339, 350
s 178BB   336, 339, 350
s 178C   336, 350
s 179   258, 274, 336, 339, 340, 346, 347, 350
s 183   359
s 249F   427
s 308–308I   361

s 319   392
s 326   161
s 341   392
s 342   392
s 344A   378, 379
s 346   427, 438
s 347   440
s 407A   559
s 421   476
ss 428A–428I   526
s 428C   526
s 428G   524
s 521A   264
s 562AB   174

Crimes Amendment (Diminished Responsibility) Act 1997   544
Crimes Amendment (Self-defence) Act 2001   476
    s 4   321
Crimes Amendment (Sexual Offences) Act 2003
    Sch 1   221, 230
Crimes (Application of Criminal Law) Amendment Act 1992
    s 3A   29
Crimes Legislation Amendment Act 1996   526
Crimes (Public Justice) Amendment Act 1990   392
Education and Public Instruction Act 1987
    s 14   183
Home Invasion (Occupants Protection) Act 1998
    s 5   321
    s 11   321
Human Tissue Act 1983
    s 33   99
Liquor Act 1982
    s 114   62
Mental Health (Criminal Procedure) Act 1990
    s 22(1)(b)   533
Motor Traffic Act 1909
    s 4E(7)   62

Northern Territory

Criminal Code
    s 1   109, 162, 163, 207–8, 542, 560
    s 4   380, 381, 385

s 4(2)   383
s 4(3)   415, 416
s 7(1)   132, 525
s 7(1)(b)   525
s 8(1)   457
s 11   183
s 12   427, 438, 558
s 13   440, 450
s 15   28
s 16   98
s 27   182
s 27(g)   182
s 28   182
s 28(f)   182
s 30(2)   289, 29, 303
s 31   168, 526
s 32   576
s 33   573
s 34   184, 484, 486
s 37   540, 543
s 38(1)   42
s 38(2)   44
s 40   561, 562, 563
s 40(1)(b)   562, 563
s 40(1)(c)   564
s 40(1)(d)   563
s 40(2)   558
s 41   554, 568, 577
s 43A   533, 534
s 43C   531
s 43C(b)   536
s 126   231
s 128(1)(a)   230
s 128(1)(b)   230
s 129   231
s 129(1)(b)   231
s 129(3)   231
s 130(1)   241
s 131A   232
s 132(2)   231
s 133   230
s 134   232

s 135   232
ss 149–155   124
s 150   179
s 154   178
s 155   67
s 156   138
s 157   100
s 158   99
s 159   102
s 160   101
s 162(1)   104
s 162(1)(a)   107
s 162(1)(b), (2)   117
s 162(1)(c), (d)   116, 118
s 162   108, 116
s 163   120, 121
s 164   96
s 165   160, 379
s 166   173, 174
s 167   96
s 168   131
s 170   104, 141
s 172   139
s 173   139
s 177   168
s 181   168
s 183   67, 179
s 184   179
s 186   162
s 187   158, 159, 190
s 187(a)   159, 160
s 187(b)   158, 164, 165
s 187(e)   182
s 188   157
s 188(2)(b)   161
s 188(2)(d)   161
s 188(2)(e)   161
s 188(2)(f)   161
s 188(2)(h)   161
s 188(2)(k)   208
s 189   174
s 190   161

s 192   210
s 192(2)(c)   211
s 192(2)(d)   210, 240
s 192(2)(f)   210, 221
s 192A   210
s 193   160
s 200   174
s 209   268, 274, 283
s 209(1)   272, 284, 289, 303
s 209(2)   264
s 209(3)–(5)   270
s 209(4)   270
s 209(5)   271
s 210(1)   262
s 211   313, 316
s 211(1)   315
s 213   321, 327
s 213(6)   322, 330
s 216   287
s 217   287
s 218   287
s 221   280, 360
s 222   279
s 226(1)   283
s 226A(2)   322
s 226B   321
s 227   338, 347
s 227(1)   339
s 227(2)   342
s 227(3)   338
s 227(4)   338
s 276   362
s 277(1)   379
s 278   378
s 279   378
s 279(1)   383
s 280   409
ss 282–289   391
s 284   392
s 286   392
s 287   399
s 291   396

s 292   397
s 292(d)   398
s 292(e)   397
s 315   158
Pt VI Div 4A   163, 191, 197
Criminal Law and Procedure Ordinance 1933
    s 55(2)   559
Emergency Operations Act 1973
    s 3(1)   192
Human Tissue Transplant Act 1979
    s 23   99
Rights of the Terminally Ill Act 1995
    s 3   132
    s 7(1)(c)   132
    s 7(1)(c)(iv)   132

Queensland

Criminal Code
    s 1   109, 162, 264, 560
    s 4   380, 381, 385
    s 4(2)   383
    s 4(3)   416
    s 6   207
    s 7   427, 438, 558
    s 8   457
    s 10   440, 450
    s 12(2)   28
    s 12(3)   27
    s 22(2)   291
    s 23   168, 508
    s 23(1A)   102
    s 24   576
    s 25   573
    s 27   531
    s 28   72, 526
    s 29(1)   42
    s 29(2)   44
    s 31(1)(d)   561, 562, 563, 564
    s 31(2)   558
    s 32   559
    s 33   396

s 132   392
s 208   232, 234
s 208(1)   230
s 210   231
s 215   234
s 215(1)   230
s 215(5)   232
s 216   241
s 218   221
s 222   232
s 224   139
s 225   139
s 229B   232
s 245   158, 159, 160, 164, 165, 190, 209
s 245(1)   158
s 256   182
s 257   182
s 268   185
s 269   184, 484
s 271   182
s 280   183
s 282   139, 140
s 283   184
s 285   67, 179
ss 285–290   124
s 288   179
s 291   127
s 292   98, 138
s 293   100
s 294   99
s 295   102
s 297   102
s 298   101
s 302   116
s 302(1)   107
s 302(1)(a)   107
s 302(1)(b)   116
s 302(1)(c)–(e)   108, 116, 118
s 303   120, 121
s 304   486
s 304A   540, 542, 543
s 305   96

s 306   160, 379
s 308   173
s 309   399
s 310   96
s 311   131
s 313   104, 141
s 317   162
s 319   177
s 319A   177
s 320   162, 168
s 323(1)   161
s 323A   163, 191
s 323A(2)   197
s 326   179
s 328   162, 170, 177
s 328A   123
s 335   157
s 340(a)   160
s 340(b), (e)   161
s 348   209
s 348(1)   210, 240
s 348(2)   210
s 348(2)(a)–(d)   210
s 348(2)(e)   210
s 348(2)(f)   210
349(2)(a), (b)   207
s 349(2)(c)   207
s 352(1)(a)   208
s 359   174
s 359A   174
s 359B(b)   176
s 359B(d)(i)   174
s 364   179
s 390   264, 272
s 391   258, 264
s 391(1)   274, 275, 284
s 391(2)   283, 289
s 391(2)(a)   284
s 391(2)(c)   284, 286
s 391(2)(d)   284, 286
s 391(2)(e)   284, 286
s 391(2)(f)   284, 290

s 391(2A), (2B)   288
s 391(7)   272
ss 393–396   272
s 398   362
s 405   338
s 407   338
s 408   280, 338, 360
s 408A   287
s 408C   258, 275, 336, 337
s 408C(c)   347
s 408C(1)   347
s 408C(1)(a)   337, 344
s 408C(1)(b)   344
s 408C(1)(c)   341
s 408C(1)(d)   337, 350, 351
s 408C(1)(h)   344, 350
s 408C(3)(a)   343, 337
s 408C(3)(b)   347
s 408C(3)(c)   347
s 408C(3)(d)   344
s 408C(3)(e)   342
s 408C(3)(f)   275, 337
s 408D   362
s 409   309, 310, 312, 313, 315, 316
s 411   316
s 411(2)   317
s 413   309
s 418(1)   323
s 418(2)   322
s 418(4)   326
s 419   322
s 419(1)   322, 325, 327
s 419(2)   325
s 419(3)   330
s 421   321, 322
s 425(1)(e)   321
s 425   322
s 430   392
s 438   365
s 467A   177
s 535   379
ss 536–578   378

s 538   383
s 539   409
ss 541–543   391
s 541(2)   391
s 543(2)   391
s 575   158

District Courts Act 1967
  s 129   161
Fauna Conservation Act 1974   290
Penalties and Sentences Act 1992
  s 207   97
Transplantation and Anatomy Act 1979
  s 45   99
Voluntary Aid in Emergency Act 1973
  s 3   192

South Australia

Consent to Medical Treatment and Palliative Care Act 1995
  s 13(1)   192
Criminal Law Consolidation Act 1935
  s 5(1)(a)   207
  s 5(1)(b)   182, 207
  s 5(1)(c)   207
  s 5C   29
  s 5G   29
  s 11   96
  s 12A   108, 116, 117
  s 13   96
  s 13A(3)   132
  s 13A(5), (7)   131
  s 15(1)   184, 474
  s 15(1)(b)   182
  s 15(2)   476, 477
  s 18   97
  s 19   173, 174
  s 19(3)   173
  s 19A   123
  s 19AA   174
  s 19AA(1)(a)   176
  s 21   161, 162
  s 21(b)   168

s 23   161, 162
s 29   178
s 29(2)(b)   168
s 30   67, 179
s 33A   163, 191
s 33A(2)   197
s 39   157
s 40   162
s 42   161
s 43(b)   161
s 48   74, 209, 210, 222
s 49(3)   230
s 49(4)   231, 232
s 49(5)   230
s 49(6)   240, 241
s 49(8)   231
s 56   208
s 58   231
s 64(b)   221
s 72   232
s 73(6)   210
s 73(5)   207, 210, 221
s 74   232
s 82A   140
s 81   139
s 82   139
s 86A   287
s 130   263, 280, 340
s 131   347
s 131(1)   289, 292, 305
s 131(3)   294
s 131(4)   289
s 131(5), (6)   289, 292, 293, 294
s 132(2)   293
s 132(3)   282, 358
s 134   278, 351
s 134(1)   263, 282
s 134(1)(c)   283, 284
s 134(1)(b)   268, 272, 273
s 134(2)   284
s 134(2)(b)   284

s 134(2)(b)(ii)   286
s 134(3)   270
s 134(3)(b)   272
s 134(5)   259
s 135   263
s 135(1)   264
s 137   316
s 137(1)(a)   311, 312, 316
s 137(1)(b)   313
s 137(2)(a)   317
s 137(2)(b)   316
s 139   279, 337, 342, 343, 346, 350, 351
s 140   362
s 141   362
s 142   277, 367
s 144   344
s 168   320, 321, 327
s 168(3)   329
s 169   320, 321, 326
s 169(1)   322
s 169(2)   330
s 169(3)   326
s 170   321
s 170(1)   322
ss 170(s)(a)(b)   320
s 170(2)(c)   322, 330
s 170(3)   326
s 170A   320, 322
s 179(3)   326
s 241   440
s 241(1)   450
s 241(2)   450
s 267   427, 438
s 269A(1)   533
s 269C   531
s 270A(3)   378
s 270B   160, 309
s 279A(1)   379
s 328A   554, 555, 559
s 330   359
Pt 3, Div 9   327

liv Table of Statutes

Criminal Law Consolidation (Intoxication) Amendment Act 1999   525
Criminal Law Consolidation (Offences of Dishonesty) Amendment Act 2002   260
Criminal Law Consolidation (Self-defence) Amendment Act 1997   184
Death (Definition) Act 1983
    s 2   99
Evidence Act 1929
    s 69   62
    s 71   62
Young Offenders Act 1993
    s 5   42

Tasmania

Criminal Code
    s 1   109, 207, 208, 264, 561
    s 2   380
    s 2(1)   385
    s 2(2)   383, 415
    s 2A   190
    s 2A(2)   210
    s 2A(2)(a)   210
    s 2A(2)(c)   211, 240
    s 3   427, 438
    s 4   29, 97, 457
    s 6   440
    s 8   185
    s 13(1)   508
    s 16   531
    s 16(1)(a)(i)   536
    s 16(1)(b)   537
    s 17(2)   72
    s 18(1)   41
    s 18(2)   44
    s 20   561, 562, 563, 564
    s 20(1)   558, 561, 562, 563
    s 20(2)   559, 569
    s 26   182
    s 27   182
    s 30   183
    s 31   182
    s 46   483
    s 50   183

s 51(1)   192
s 51(3)   192
s 124   230
s 124(3)   231
s 125A   232
s 125B   231
s 126(1)   241
s 127(1)   208
s 127A   207, 208
s 129(b)   221
s 133(1)   232
s 133(2)   232
s 133(4)   232
s 134   139
s 135   139
s 144   67, 179
ss 144–152   124
s 153(2)   100
s 153(4)   98, 138
s 153(5)   99
s 154(a)   101
s 154(b)   102
s 154(c)   103
s 156(2)   124
s 156(2)(b)   121
s 156(2)(c)   127
s 157(1)(a)   107
s 157(1)(c)   107, 110
s 157(1)(d)   108, 116
s 157(1)(d)–(f)   116, 118
s 157(2)   118
s 158   96
s 159   120
s 160(2)   486
s 161   440
s 162   173
s 163   131
s 165   104, 141
s 165A   141, 547, 548
s 167A   123
s 170   168
s 172   161

s 178   179
ss 178A–178C   163, 191, 197
s 182   158, 159, 168, 174, 190
s 182(1)   158, 159, 160, 165
s 182(2)   164
s 182 (3)   182
s 183   161
s 183(a)   160
s 184   157
s 185   209
s 192   174
s 226   258
s 226(1)   274, 283, 337, 339
s 226(2)   275
s 228   284
s 233   280, 338, 360
s 240(1)   310, 311, 312, 313, 315
s 240(2)   317
s 240(3)   317
s 240(4)   317
s 243(3), (4)   325
s 243(6)   325
s 243(7)   326
s 243(8)   322
s 244   321, 325, 327
s 245   330
s 245(a)(iii)   322
s 248(c)   321
s 249   339
s 250   337, 339, 346, 347
s 252   337
s 252A   337
s 257A–F   362
s 282   365
s 297   391
s 297(1)(d)   392
s 297(1), (2)   392
s 297(2)   396
s 298   409
s 299   379
s 300   440
s 334A   158

s 342(3)   376
Criminal Code Amendment (Year and Day Rule Repeal) Act 1993
    s 4   97
Criminal Law (Territorial Application) Act 1995
    s 4   29
    s 4(1)   29
Police Offences Act 1935
    s 34B(1)   161
    s 35(2)   161
    s 55   182

Victoria

Children and Young Persons Act 1989
    s 127   42
Crimes Act 1958
    s 2A(1)   409
    s 3   96
    s 3A   108, 116
    s 3A(1)   117
    s 5   96
    s 6   141
    s 6(1)   547, 548
    s 6(2)   548
    s 6B(1)   132
    s 6B(2)   131
    s 9AA   97
    s 10   104, 141
    s 10(1)   141
    s 10(2)   104, 141
    s 15   162
    s 16   162, 168, 327
    s 17   162, 327
    s 18   170, 327
    s 20   173, 174, 531
    s 21   174
    s 21A   24, 28, 172
    s 21A(3)   174, 175
    s 22   178, 179
    s 23   178
    s 24   162, 170
    s 31   158

s 31(1)(a)   160
s 31(1)(b)   161
ss 32–34A   163, 191
s 34   197
s 35   207, 208
s 36   210
s 36(a)   210
s 36(b)   210
s 36(c)   210
s 36(d)   211
s 36(e)   210, 240
s 36(f)   210
s 36(g)   210, 221
s 37   209, 210
s 37(a)   214, 215, 216, 217, 218, 219, 220, 246
s 37(c)   224
s 38   74, 222
s 38(2)   209
s 38(2)(b)   208
s 38(3)   208
s 39   208
s 44   232
s 44(1)   232
s 44(2)   232
s 44(4)   232
s 44(7)(a)   232
s 45   234
s 46   231
s 46(1)   230
s 47   231
s 47A   232
s 49   231
s 51   241, 242
s 52   241
s 57   221
s 58   231
s 60(1)   231
s 63A   117
s 65   139
s 66   139
s 71(1)   263, 265, 267, 343

s 71(2)   268, 270, 344
s 72   327
s 72(1)   263, 268, 283, 287
s 72(2)   262
s 73(2)   295, 300, 346
s 73(2)(a), (b), (c)   289, 292, 293, 294, 295, 297, 298, 303
s 73(2)(b)   289, 293, 295
s 73(2)(b), (c)   297
s 73(3)   294
s 73(4)   272, 274, 358
s 73(6), (7)   263, 264
s 73(8)   270
s 73(8)–(10)   270
s 73(9)   270
s 73(10)   271, 272
s 73(12)   284, 285, 286, 287, 307, 346
s 73(13)   346
s 73(14)(a)   287
s 75   117, 312, 316
s 75(1)   311
s 75(2)   309
s 75A(1)   317
s 76   321, 326
s 76(1)   321
s 76(1)(a)   327
s 76(2)   325
s 77   316
s 77(1)(a)   317
s 77(1)(b)   330
s 77(1A)   330
s 80A   364
s 80A(2)   364
s 81   288
s 81(1)   339
s 81(2)   341
s 81(3)   346
s 81(4)   340, 351
s 81(4)(a)   340
s 81(4)(b)   351, 361, 362
s 82   288
s 82(1)   351

s 83A   361
s 85   365
s 197   327
ss 247A-1   361, 363
s 318   123
s 318(2)   123
s 318(2)(b)   123
s 318(2)(c), (d)   123
s 321   391
s 321(1)   399
s 321(2)   407
s 321(3)   416
s 321(4)   391
s 321B   398
s 321F(1)   392, 400
s 321F(2)   392
s 321F(3)   411
ss 321G–321I   409
s 321G(1)   409, 410
s 321G(2)   412
s 321G(3)   418
s 321M   379
s 321N(1)   380, 384
s 321N(2)   385
s 321N(3)   415
s 321P   378
s 323   427, 438
s 324   438
s 325   440
s 325(1)   450
s 336   554, 559
s 336(1)   559
s 336(2)   559
s 336(3)   563, 564
s 336(4)   564
s 339(1)   396
s 421(2)   315
Crimes (Computers) Act 1988
    s 80A   361
    s 81(4)(b)   361
Crimes (Married Person's Liability) Act 1977   570

Table of Statutes **lxi**

Crimes (Mental Impairment and Unfitness to be Tried) Act 1997
    s 20   531
    s 20(1)(b)   536
Education Act 1958
    reg XVI   183
Environment Protection Act 1970
    s 39(1)   62
Magistrates' Court (Koori Court) Act 2002   200
Medical Treatment Act 1988   136
Occupational Health and Safety Act 1985   45, 146
Road Safety (Traffic) Regulations 1988
    s 1001(1)(c)   62
Sentencing Act 1991
    s 5(1)   18
Summary Offences Act 1966
    s 9A   361

Western Australia

Criminal Code
    s 1   109, 162, 264, 275, 409, 533, 561
    s 1(4)   109, 162
    s 4   380, 381, 383, 384, 385, 415, 416
    s 7   427, 438, 558
    s 8   457
    s 10   440, 450
    s 12(1)   28
    s 22   291
    s 23   168, 508
    s 24   576
    s 25   573
    s 27   531
    s 28   72, 526
    s 29   42, 44
    s 31(4)   558, 561, 562, 563, 564
    s 32   554, 559, 561
    s 135   392
    s 192   221
    s 199   139
    s 222   158, 159, 160, 164, 165, 190, 210
    s 237   182

s 245   185
s 246   184, 484
s 248   182
s 257   183
s 259   139, 140
s 260   184
s 262   67, 179
s 262–267   124
s 265   138, 179
s 268   127
s 269   98, 138
s 270   100
s 271   99
s 272   102
s 274   102
s 275   101
s 277   120
s 278   472
s 279   108
s 279(1)(a)   107
s 279(2)   116
s 279(3)–(5)   116, 118
s 280   120, 121
s 281   486
s 281A(1)   141, 458
s 281A(2)   548
s 282   96
s 283   160, 379
s 287   96
s 287A   547
s 288   131
s 290   104, 141
s 294   162
s 296   177
s 296A   177
s 297   162, 168
s 301   161
s 304   179
s 306   162, 177
s 313   157
s 317A   160
s 318(1)(d)–(f)   161

s 318A   161
s 319(1)   207, 208
s 319(2)   210
s 319(2)(a)   210
s 319(2)(b)   210
s 320(4)   231
s 321   230
s 321(4)   231
s 321(9)   232
s 321(10)   231
s 321A   232
s 322A   230
s 323   208
s 325   210
s 329   232
s 329(11)(a)   232
s 330(1)   241
s 338   174
s 338B   173, 174
s 338D   174
s 344   179
s 370   264, 272
s 371   258, 264, 271
s 371(1)   274, 275, 287, 337
s 371(2)   283, 284, 289
ss 371(2)(c)-(e)   286
s 371(2)(f)   290
s 378   262
s 385   338
s 390   272, 280, 338, 360
s 391   309, 313, 317
s 392   309, 310, 312, 315, 317
s 393   316
s 394   309
s 400(1)   326, 330
s 401   322, 327
s 401(1)(b)   322
s 407   322
s 409   258, 275, 344, 368
s 409(1)   337
s 409(1)(b)   342
s 409(1)(c)   337, 350

s 420   365
s 440A   362
s 552   379
s 553   409
s 554   378, 409
s 555A   378, 379, 409
s 556   409
s 558   391
s 560   391
s 594   158
Criminal Code Amendment Act (No 2) 1987
    s 6   396
Criminal Law Amendment Act 1991
    s 6   97
Health Act 1911
    s 334   140
Human Tissue and Transplant Act 1982
    s 24(2)   99
Road Traffic Act 1974
    s 59   123

Canada

Charter of Rights and Freedoms
    s 1   57
Constitution Act 1982
    Sch B   57
Criminal Code
    s 202A(2)(a)   519
    s 231   519
    s 273.2   227
    s 322   307
    s 380   367
Criminal Law Amendment Act (No 2) 1976   519
Sexual Sterilization Act RSA 1970   245
Sexual Sterilization Act RSBC 1960   245

International

Convention on the Rights of the Child
    Art 19(1)   187

Declaration on Violence Against Women (1993)   198
European Convention on Human Rights
    Art 3   186–7
    Art 6   43
International Covenant on Civil and Political Rights 1966
    Art 7   200
    Art 27   200

United Kingdom

An Act to Prevent the Destroying and Murthering of Bastard Children 1624   547
Accessories and Abettors Act 1861
    s 8   427
Crime and Disorder Act 1998   45
Criminal Attempts Act 1981
    s 1(1)   384
    s 1(2)   415, 421
Criminal Lunatics Act 1800   504
Criminal Law Act 1977   399, 400, 407
    s 5(8)   402
Homicide Act 1957
    s 2   541
Infanticide Act 1938   548
Larceny Act 1916
    s 1(1)   261
Lord Ellenborough's Act 1803   547
Misuse of Drugs Act 1971   416
Offences Against the Person Act 1828
    s XIV   547
Offences Against the Person Act 1861   154
    s 47   195
Prohibition of Female Circumcision Act 1985
    s 1   163
Sexual Offences Act 1956
    s 1(1)   410
Sexual Offences (Amendment) Act 2000   233–4
Theft Act 1968   285, 291, 343
    s 2   296
    s 15(2)   377
    s 15A   278
    s 16   352

s 16(2)(a), (b), (c)   353
s 24(3)   413
Theft Act 1978
ss 1–3   352

USA

Model Penal Code
    s 211.2   178
Montana Code Ann., Stat. 46-14-102 (1979)   520
Idaho Code, Stat. 18-207 (1982)   520
Utah Code Ann., 76-2-305 (1990)   520
Kansas Stat. Ann., 22-3220 (1995)   520

Part 1
INTRODUCTION

CHAPTER 1

Defining criminal laws

Introduction

There are numerous perspectives of what the law is or what it should be. The way in which Australian criminal laws are generally outlined in textbooks reflects a 'positivist' approach to the law.

Positivism has formed the basis of scientific, economic, legal and philosophical scholarship since the period during the eighteenth century known as the Enlightenment, where reason was seen as the source of progress in knowledge. Positivist theorists rely on the presumption that we can use objective methods to establish a verifiable knowledge or truth about events and human behaviour. The positivist tradition in criminology, defined as the study of the causes of crime and human behaviour, entails a commitment to scientific methods of empirical enquiry and it originally had a close connection with the biological sciences. For example, Cesare Lombroso, often referred to as the founder of criminology, tried to relate particular physical characteristics to the innate predisposition of certain individuals towards sociopathy and criminal behaviour: *L'uomo Delinquente* (Turin: Fratelli Bosca, 1876). In such writings, the criminologist is viewed as a separate, uninvolved, emotionally detached observer of the criminal population.

In relation to criminal laws, the positivist approach presumes that whatever is a crime can be objectively verified and is institutionally certain. For those often referred to as 'black letter lawyers', the criminal law is seen as something that has been authoritatively set out or 'posited' and therefore is understandable without reference to politics, economics, history, social values and the like. Generations of law students have been taught how to identify laws by recourse to statute or case law. The role of criminal justice institutions such as the police and prosecution and their discretionary powers in law enforcement have been usually ignored. There may have been a discussion of criminal law and morality as exemplified by the debate during the late 1950s and early 1960s between Lord Patrick Devlin and Professor Herbert Hart on the aims of the criminal law, which we will explore later in this chapter. However, the causes of crime and its cultural underpinnings have been left to courses in criminology or the administration of criminal justice.

In the past decade, there has been a substantial increase in critical writing on the criminal law in both Britain and Australia. This book is very much situated among these recent attempts to move beyond a positivist approach to the criminal law by providing a critical understanding of current Australian criminal laws. Margaret Davies has described the term 'critique' as 'the process of attaining an understanding of the foundations of any approach, theory or system of thought': *Asking the Law Question: The Dissolution of Legal Theory* (2nd edn, Sydney: Lawbook Co, 2002) p 1. We are concerned to understand the foundations of current criminal laws through placing them in a broad social and historical context. By doing this, we aim to identify current problems with criminal laws and work towards reforming them.

It is important at the outset to state that while our focus is on critiquing certain laws, we do not wish to abandon or ignore them. We accept that criminal laws are necessary to the proper functioning of society, but we do not have to unquestioningly accept the laws that do exist. Our aim is to write a book that can be as easily accessible to criminal lawyers as to criminologists and those working in disciplines other than law.

This chapter will examine different perspectives on defining crime and the role of the law in relation to crime, the problems associated with measuring crime and the presumptions behind notions of the rational actor and individual criminal responsibility. It is divided into six main sections: Defining crime: differing perspectives; Aims of the criminal law: differing perspectives; Measuring crime; Jurisdiction; Individual and corporate criminal responsibility; and Reason and rationality in the criminal law. The next chapter will take a critical look at how the study of criminal laws has been traditionally structured. It will also examine the traditional elements of a crime such as the division between physical and fault elements and causation. Discussion of these traditional elements underpins the analysis in the remaining chapters on specific offences. From there we move on to examining individual offences and defences within the framework of setting out the current law, providing a critique of it, then suggesting ways towards law reform.

Defining crime: differing perspectives

The frequent everyday use of the terms 'crime' and 'criminal' may lead to the false impression that the meaning of these terms is self-explanatory. A positivist approach may define crime as an act or omission prohibited and punishable by the criminal law and the criminal as the agent who carries out such an act or omission. For example, Glanville Williams defined a crime as 'a legal wrong that can be followed by criminal proceedings which may result in punishment': *Textbook of Criminal Law* (2nd edn, London: Stevens & Sons, 1983) p 27. Such an approach raises a number of problems.

- There are a wide variety of behaviours punishable by law, from intentional killing (other than in wartime) to parking a car at an expired parking meter. Such a definition fails to take into account differences in the gravity of offences. A substantial number of motorists violate the speed limit every day, yet they are not seen as criminals in the same way that murderers are.
- If crime is an act or omission prohibited and punishable by the criminal law, then it is possible for a government to decree that any form of conduct is a crime. If a law is passed making it an offence to eat sandwiches at lunchtime, that will be a crime, despite its nonsensical nature.
- On the other hand, Jerome Michael and Mortimer Adler have pointed out that if one accepts this definition of crime, then to get rid of crime, all that needs to be done is to abolish the relevant Criminal Code or Criminal Law Act: *Crime, Law and Science* (Montclaire, NJ: Paterson Smith, 1933).
- If an act is prohibited, but the consequence is not punishment, but is some form of restitution or community service order, or a civil or administrative penalty, is it still a crime? Perhaps not, although Glanville Williams hedges his bets by using the word 'may' in his definition of crime.
- Most importantly, this definition of crime fails to explain why certain types of behaviour are considered criminal and others not. The positivist approach fixes clear boundaries to the criminal law and does not extend its analysis beyond case law and legislation.

It is more realistic to think of crime as relative in both time and space and as being culturally defined. What is deemed criminal in one society may not be deemed criminal in another. New crimes may develop, such as pollution offences or stalking, while others are taken out of legislation such as homosexual practices between consenting adults. In Australia, the existence of nine different criminal law jurisdictions (six states, two territories and the Commonwealth) shows how the definition of crime is relative. As we will set out throughout this book, certain crimes and defences to them exist in some jurisdictions and not others. More broadly, there are the well-publicised differences in criminal laws across different countries such as the retention of adultery as a crime under Islamic law: HR Kusha, *The Sacred Law of Islam* (Aldershot: Ashgate, 2002); N Khouri, *Honor Lost: Love and Death in Modern Day Jordan* (New York: Atria Books, 2003).

From around the 1980s onwards, a number of theorists have sought to challenge the positivist approach to criminal law and pointed out problems with the positivist definition of crime. We turn now to considering alternative approaches to the definition of crime.

Realism

Realist theories can be viewed as marking the start of the modern critical approaches to Anglo-American law. One school originated in America during the late 1920s and concentrated on debunking the belief that law was 'simply a set of doctrines which are the sole determinants of legal issues': Margaret Davies, *Asking the Law Question: The Dissolution of Legal Theory* (2nd edn, Sydney: Lawbook Co, 2002) p 143. Karl Llewelyn was one of the main proponents of this approach: 'Some Realism about Realism—Responding to Dean Pound' (1931) 44 *Harvard Law Review* 1222–64. For the realist, the nature of law could only be understood by reference to its historical, social and empirical context.

Legal realism formed part of a broader movement away from metaphysical methods to practical experiential ways of exploring notions of 'truth'. Law was seen as a social instrument that should be used towards the achievement of certain social goals. The previous emphasis on principles and rules of law and methods of formal reasoning was criticised as being too abstract and removed from the everyday life of lawyers and the courts. A distinction was thus made between 'law in books' and 'law in action'.

The criminological movement known as 'left realism' grew out of earlier realist theories. Since the late 1970s, a group of British and Canadian criminologists have reacted to what they termed 'left idealism' in much the same way as earlier realists reacted to the abstract ideal of law as a set of doctrines. A group of criminologists including Jock Young, John Lea and Roger Matthews in Britain and John Lowman and Brian MacLean in Canada have examined the impact of crime and the social context in which it occurred: J Young, 'Left Realist Criminology: Radical in its Analysis, Realist in its Policy' in M Maguire, R Morgan and R Reiner (eds), *The Oxford Handbook of Criminology* (2nd edn, Oxford: Oxford University Press, 1997) pp 473–98; J Lowman and BD MacLean (eds), *Realist Criminology: Crime Control and Policing in the 1990s* (Toronto: University of Toronto Press, 1992); J Lea and J Young, *What is to Be Done About Law and Order? Crisis in the Nineties* (London: Pluto Press, 1993); R Matthews and J Young (eds), *Issues in Realist Criminology* (London: Sage Publications, 1992).

These theorists have focused on working class victims of crime and working class offenders and concerns about specific neighbourhoods as a way of exploring methods of dealing with crime arising from working-class communities themselves. While still concerned with the consequences of the crimes of the powerful, left realists have begun focusing on intra-class and intra-racial crime. From an empirical perspective, left realists concentrate on localised rather than national crime surveys in order to gain an understanding of the effects of crime on certain groups.

For realists, a definition of crime must focus on the social context. Jock Young poses a model of crime that looks at crime in terms of victim–offender relations as well as the social control of crime, as shown in Figure 1.1.

```
Police,                              Offender
multi-agencies  ┌─────────────────┐
                │                 │
                │                 │
Social control  │                 │  The criminal act
                │                 │
                │                 │
                │                 │
                └─────────────────┘
   The public                         Victim
```

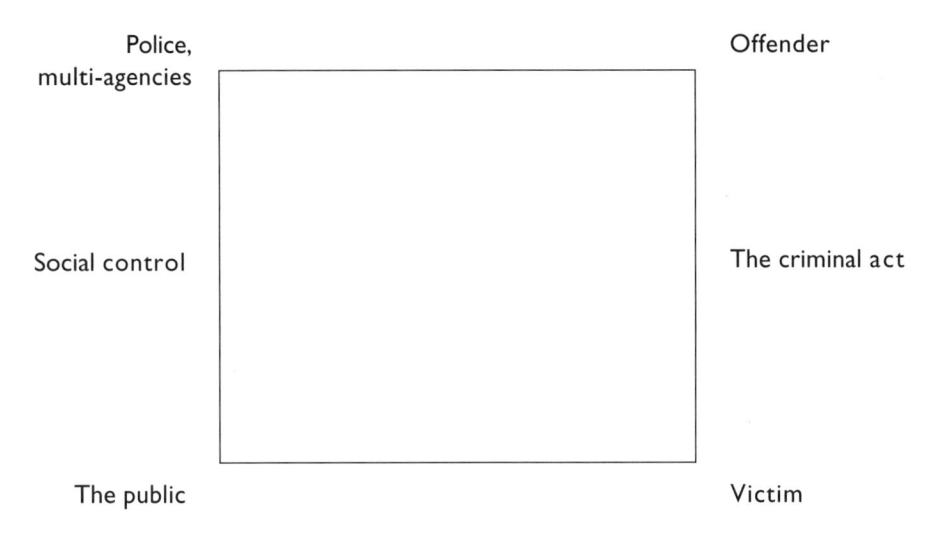

Figure 1.1 The Square of Crime

Source: J Young in R Maguire, R Morgan and R Reiner (eds), *The Oxford Handbook of Criminology* (2nd edn, Oxford: Oxford University Press, 1997) p 486.

On the left-hand side are situated the agencies of social control including the police and public institutions such as the family and schools. On the right-hand side are individuals associated with the criminal act, namely the offender and victim. The nature and form of crime are influenced by relationships between not only individuals such as victims, offenders and members of the public, but also the agencies of social control. Both left and right realists would agree on the existence of this complex interrelationship. For example, James Q Wilson, the American political scientist, who can be classified as writing from a right-wing perspective, views crime as being influenced by a multitude of relationships between individuals and institutions: JQ Wilson (ed), *Crime and Public Policy* (San Francisco: ICS Press, 1983); JQ Wilson and RJ Herrnstein, *Crime and Human Nature* (New York: Simon and Schuster, 1985). Where left and right realists differ is in their analysis of the relationships surrounding crime.

Jock Young gives the following definition of crime in 'Incessant Chatter: Recent Paradigms in Criminology' in M Maguire, R Morgan and R Reiner (eds), *The Oxford Handbook of Criminology* (Oxford: Oxford University Press, 1994) pp 69–124 at 106–7:

> Crime as an activity involves a moral choice at a certain moment in changing determinant circumstances. It has neither the totally determined quality beloved of positivism, nor the wilful display of rationality enshrined in classicist legal doctrine. It is a moral act, but one which must be constantly assessed within a determined social context. It is neither an act of determined pathology, nor an obvious response to desperate situations. It involves both social organization and disorganization.

According to realists, defining crime is thus more complex than a positivist conception would allow. The problem, of course, is that this 'definition' of crime seems overly broad. What is meant by a moral choice and a moral act in the above quotation is left unanswered.

One of the main criticisms of left realism by critical criminologists is that it accepts the status quo, rather than working to overturn or at least challenge it. We will now turn to these radical approaches to the analysis of crime.

Critical legal studies and critical criminology

The terms 'critical legal studies' and 'critical criminology' may encompass a wide range of theories such as feminist theories, postmodern theories, race theories and so on. Here, we concentrate on foundational or narrower versions of the terms.

'Critical legal studies' was a movement originating in the USA in the late 1970s mainly among white male academics at Yale and Harvard Law schools in response to what was seen as an increasingly conservative political and legal agenda. The movement assembled a number of left-wing scholars who 'came together for political education, sustenance, and activity': M Tushnet, 'Critical Legal Studies: A Political History' (1991) 100 *Yale Law Journal* 1515–44 at 1515, n 2. Along with left realism, it can be seen as a successor to earlier realist theory and it shares a concern with exposing pervasive inequality and oppression.

A major part of the movement concentrated on situating the law within its historical and social context in order to demystify it. Another strand was more concerned with showing the contradictions, incoherence and relativism of the existing law, such that it should be rejected or abandoned: A Hutchinson and P Monahan, 'Law, Politics and the Critical Legal Scholars: The Unfolding Drama of American Legal Thought' (1984) 36 *Stanford Law Review* 199–245 at 206.

There are a number of themes that can be drawn from the critical legal studies movement. The first is the inseparability of law and politics. Legal reasoning was seen as a technique for rationalising political decisions. A major criticism of previous realist authors was that while they had influenced mainstream legal thinking, they had failed to challenge its doctrinal emphasis.

A second theme or goal was to point out the contradictions in liberal legalism. One of the most pervasive traditional theories concerning the scope of the criminal law is that originally outlined by John Stuart Mill in his work *On Liberty* (Harmondsworth: Penguin, 1974, first published 1859). He stated (p 68):

> [T]he only purpose for which power can be rightfully exercised over any member of a civilised community, against his [or her] will, is to prevent harm to others. His [or her] own good, either physical or moral, is not a sufficient warrant. He [or she] cannot rightfully be compelled to do or forbear because it will be better for him [or her] to do so, because it will make him [or her] happier, because, in the opinion of others, to do so would be wise, or even right.

This translates in the criminal law to the idea that for the state to intervene against the individual, there must be a clear public interest or benefit in doing so. The criminal law is the ultimate prohibitory norm that should only be used as a 'last resort': A Ashworth, *Principles of Criminal Law* (3rd edn, Oxford: Oxford University Press, 1999) pp 32–7. This position has led, for example, to the identification and criticism of 'overcriminalisation' in areas such as public order and drug offences. It also leads to the rejection of 'paternalist' laws aimed at protecting people from harming themselves.

While critical legal scholars did not concentrate on the criminal law, they were concerned that liberal ideology works by concealing oppressive and alienating societal structures. John Stuart Mill's statement leaves open what is meant by 'harm' (are economic/psychological/indirect harms included?) and 'others' (are foetuses/animals included?).

Mark Kelman is one author in the critical legal studies movement who has focused on the criminal law: 'Interpretive Construction in the Substantive Criminal Law' (1981) 33 *Stanford Law Review* 591–673. His view was that the 'general principles' of criminal law were in fact indeterminate and contradictory rather than based on any grand theory of legal reasoning. He concentrated on how the subjectivist approach to criminal responsibility was in fact a muddle of free will and determinist accounts of human action and behaviour. This approach will be explored further in Chapter 2.

A third theme in the critical legal studies movement has been the inadequacy of applications of traditional rights theory. The concept of liberty has been translated in positivist theory into specific legally protected rights such as privacy rights. For critical legal scholars, such rights discourse should be abandoned because it has nothing to do with the reality of pervasive inequality and oppression. Formal rights do not produce substantive justice.

To some extent, the ideas of critical legal scholars have now been accepted by the Australian legal academy through a 'law in context' approach. The notion that law is linked to or is in reality a part of politics has become a mainstream one. This could explain why there has been a decline in critical legal studies scholarship in favour of more specific critical approaches such as those from feminist or postmodern perspectives.

Critical criminology (or 'left idealism' as its left-realist opponents would have it) also began in the late 1970s and views crime as being associated with broad political processes. It is probably best to think of this as a movement rather than any one theory and it is sometimes referred to as radical or conflict criminology. Roger Hopkins Burke writes in *An Introduction to Criminological Theory* (Cullompton, Devon: Willan Publishing, 2001) p 173:

> For the powerful, there are pressures associated with the securing and maintaining of state and corporate interests in the context of global capitalism. In the case of

the less powerful, criminal behaviour is seen to be the outcome of the interaction between the marginalisation or exclusion from access to mainstream institutions and that of criminalisation by the state authorities. Particular attention is paid to the increasing racialisation of crime, in which the media and police in the 'war against crime' and public disorder target certain communities.

Critical criminology was initially influenced by the emergence of Marxism as a field of study during the 1960s and 1970s. Though Karl Marx wrote little about crime, critical criminologists extended his theories to an analysis of the criminal law system. Capitalism was seen as leading to certain harmful acts committed by those in the working class being defined and treated as crimes, whereas harmful acts committed by those in positions of power were either not treated as crimes or treated as minor regulatory offences. Similarly, criminalised 'harms' were defined in terms of powerful interests. For example, the creation of notions of private property leads to the creation of criminal laws to punish actions that challenge property ownership: D Hay, 'Property, Authority and the Criminal Law' in D Hay, P Linebaugh, JG Rule, EP Thompson and C Winslow (eds), *Albion's Fatal Tree: Crime and Society in Eighteenth Century England* (London: Allen Lane, 1975) pp 17–63. For critical criminologists, social empowerment and the redistribution of resources should be the methods of combating crime.

A number of critical theorists have pointed out that the criminal law often reflects the values of powerful interest groups. Howard Becker, for example, refers to groups of elites or 'moral entrepreneurs', who use their own value systems and social and economic interests to define what is and what is not criminal behaviour: *The Outsiders* (New York: The Free Press, 1963).

One of the most prominent theorists in the Marxist/critical criminology tradition is Richard Quinney. He defines crime as 'a definition of human conduct that is created by authorized agents in a politically organized society': *The Social Reality of Crime* (Boston: Little Brown and Co, 1970) p 15. These authorised agents have the power to enforce and apply their definition of crime against those considered deviant. Various means of communication construct and diffuse the definition of crime throughout segments of society.

For Quinney, the main failure of the positivist method of analysis was that it failed to consider how to transcend the established order. The same criticism has been made of left realism. Too much attention has been given to changing the criminal rather than the system. For Quinney and others, only a new society based on socialist principles can provide a solution to crime control and this cannot occur without the collapse of capitalist society. He writes in *Critique of Legal Order* (Boston: Little Brown and Co, 1974) p 170: 'Capitalism itself is the problem. Liberal reforms, therefore, can do little more than support the capitalist system, which is also to say that the capitalist problem (and its associated forms of exploitation) cannot be solved within the liberal reformist framework.'

Critical criminology has undergone a number of changes in response to criticisms by left realists and others. It has moved away from treating social class as the predominant explanation for crime. It now includes explanations that focus on gender, race, ethnicity and cultural processes such as language and mass media: ML Lynch, R Michalowski and W Byron Groves, *The New Primer in Radical Criminology: Critical Perspectives on Crime, Power and Identity* (3rd edn, Monsey, NY: Criminal Justice Press, 2000). This change reflects the development of postmodern and feminist intellectual movements and it is to these approaches that we now turn.

Postmodernism

Michel Foucault has identified the modern age as beginning at the start of the nineteenth century: *The Order of Things* (New York: Vintage Books, 1973). Modernity is viewed as an age characterised by certainty and confidence in the explanatory power of grand theories to set out how individuals should live.

'Postmodernism' is a term with a range of meanings deriving initially from the fields of architecture and art. It refers to a mode of thinking aimed at overturning the basic premises of modernism. Postmodern societies are viewed as having lost certainty, with no expectation of its return. Some of the central themes of postmodernism include:
- an aversion to 'metadiscourses' or grand theories that are self-legitimising;
- an awareness of the indeterminacy of knowledge and the impossibility of discovering 'truth'; and
- a recognition of eclecticism and variety of perspectives such that a range of different discourses can be legitimate for different people.

For example, Foucault has attempted to explain power in terms of local relationships, seeing it as dynamic and complex: *Power/Knowledge* (Brighton: Harvester Press, 1980). Power is not something that is located in a sovereign or elite, but is something that circulates or functions by way of a chain process. People are powerful because of their place in a system of relationships. Power in the legal system cannot simply be described in terms of a hierarchy of those who have authority to make decisions. It is necessary to examine the particular, rather than the general, in order to see how the networks of power and control work. These networks are governed by the concepts and knowledge that define them as well as by the intentions of individuals: A Hunt and G Wickham, *Foucault and Law* (London: Pluto, 1994). In the legal arena, the increasing use of instruments such as speed cameras and video surveillance to regulate behaviour can be seen as an expanding mechanism of social control.

Deconstruction is a key method of postmodernism, premised on the notion that all language is value-laden, carrying particular political, historical and cultural meanings. An important focus of deconstruction is the attempt to analyse the language of various disciplines so as to understand the values embedded in that discipline. Language is seen as the means by which power, authority and status are conferred. The deconstructive method of analysis suggests that no form of empirical knowledge can be divorced from the prior world view of the subject. This challenges the meanings associated with binary oppositions such as man/woman, mind/body, speaking/writing and so on. This is particularly salient for the law, which uses many binary terms such as public/private, objective/subjective, individual/state and law/policy. Because people inhabit multiple worlds simultaneously, foundational theories of law must be seen as reflecting dominant social practices and conventions rather than speaking for all members of society. Jacques Derrida has pointed out that binary oppositions are interdependent: *Positions* (Chicago: University of Chicago Press, 1981). This, however, is rarely acknowledged and thus it is assumed that one term is primary and has a separate meaning. The positioning of the primary term is dependent on the historical use of power. Thus, for example, 'man' is seen as gaining a dominant position by the negation or oppression of 'woman', who is viewed as the other.

Ngaire Naffine points out the limits of deconstruction in effecting change: *Feminism and Criminology* (St Leonards: Allen & Unwin, 1997) p 89:

> There are powerful institutional reasons why many continue to think that 'man' is quite naturally the dominant and more important term, even when deconstruction reveals the dependence of that term on 'woman'...Deconstruction may do some of the job of effecting change, but alone it is insufficient to undo the institutional systems that have been built upon, and that help to sustain, the economic and political power of men over women.

Postmodernist theories in relation to the law are still developing and only recently have there been attempts to show how legal theory is being transformed: HM Stacy, *Postmodernism and Law: Jurisprudence in a Fragmenting World* (Aldershot: Ashgate/Dartmouth, 2001). What is important is that the postmodernist movement allows for a multitude of perspectives to develop such as those dealing with gender, race and ethnicity. It is to these perspectives that we now turn.

Feminist theories

Feminist theories cover a range of different approaches to explaining the oppression and inequality of women in particular cultures by the analysis of gender relations and of the different power locations of women and men in that culture. There is no single feminist theory that explains crime and criminal behaviour, but there are a number of approaches that have their roots in broader theories such as liberalism, Marxism, socialism and cultural studies.

Two main feminist approaches to the study of crime and criminal behaviour can be clearly identified, with a third continuing to develop and merging in some respects with theories of race and class: S Harding, *Feminism and Methodology* (Milton

Keynes: Open University Press, 1987); C Smart, 'Feminist Approaches to Criminology or Postmodern Woman Meets Atavistic Man' in A Morris and L Gelsthorpe (eds), *Feminist Perspectives in Criminology* (Milton Keynes: Open University Press, 1990) pp 71–84; L Gelsthorpe, 'Feminism and Criminology' in M Maguire, R Morgan and R Reiner (eds), *The Oxford Handbook of Criminology* (3rd edn, Oxford: Oxford University Press, 2002) pp 112–43. These approaches will be discussed in turn. It is interesting to note that the developing third approach is occurring in tandem with the rise of 'masculinist' theories of social control: I Breines, R Connell and I Eide (eds), *Male Roles, Masculinities and Violence* (Paris: UNESCO Publishing, 2000); SP Schacht and DW Ewing, *Feminism and Men: Reconstructing Gender Relations* (New York: New York University Press, 1998).

Feminist empiricism provides a critique of the presumed objectivity of the criminal law, while still accepting that it is possible to be objective and neutral. It has focused on incorporating a gender dimension into criminal law and on the need for equality and fairness in the concept of justice and its delivery. Feminist empiricism can be seen as not particularly threatening to the established legal order, as it broadly aims to 'add women and stir' to dominant notions of positivist, liberal theory. In relation to criminology, it endeavours to develop a scientific understanding of female offenders and victims. A major criticism that has been made of this stance is that it still accepts men as the 'norm' and women as 'the other'.

Standpoint feminism is based on the premise that laws are constructed and experienced differently by different groups of people. Law, legal studies and criminology have traditionally been constructed and analysed from a male standpoint. The approach of standpoint feminism challenges this by focusing on the experience of women towards existing criminal laws. It has been particularly prominent in the analysis of criminal offences such as rape, indecent assault and domestic violence. Larissa Behrendt, for example, has emphasised the importance of oral histories in explaining the standpoints of Aboriginal women: 'Women's Work: The Inclusion of the Voice of Aboriginal Women' (1995) 6(2) *Legal Education Review* 169–74. The motivating drive has been to let women's experiences be told in order to reveal the real levels of female victimisation. The problem with such an approach is that it can assume that there is only one female (and one male) standpoint or experience, ignoring race and class differences.

Postmodern feminism is a developing approach that attempts to explore the criminal law through pluralities of standpoints. It rejects the possibility of one universal reality of criminal law in favour of a gender-based analysis of a multiplicity of women's (and men's) experiences.

Postmodern feminism embraces the notion of 'intersectionality', which highlights the intermeshed operations of inequalities of class, race and gender. For example, Kathy Daly refers to Lisa Maher's 1997 study of the street drug scene as an example of how 'sex-gender interacts with race/ethnicity, and both in turn interact with economic disadvantage to produce different outcomes and opportunities for different groups': 'Inequalities of Crime' in A Goldsmith, M Israel and K Daly (eds), *Crime and Justice: An Australian Textbook in Criminology* (2nd edn, Sydney: Lawbook Company, 2003) pp 116–17; L Behrendt, 'Meeting at the Crossroads: Intersectionality, Affirmative Action and the Legacies of the Aborigines Protection Board' (1997) 4(1) *Australian Journal of Human Rights* 98–119.

Authors such as Carol Smart, Ngaire Naffine and Nicola Lacey have been influenced by postmodern thought in their criticisms of the criminal law. Carol Smart has questioned whether a feminist criminology is in fact theoretically possible or desirable. She poses the question, what does criminology have to offer feminism (rather than what does feminism have to offer criminology), and concludes that it offers very little: 'Feminist Approaches to Criminology or Postmodern Woman Meets Atavistic Man' in A Morris and L Gelsthorpe (eds), *Feminist Perspectives in Criminology* (Milton Keynes: Open University Press, 1990) pp 71–84. She argues that there is a danger that feminist criminology is being marginalised both by feminist and criminological theories because it continues to engage with modernist thought. That is, theories of the causes of crime and criminal behaviour have yet to break out of the presumption that 'truth' can be sought through 'objective' scientific enquiries.

Naffine and Lacey appear to be more optimistic as to what feminist theories may bring to the study of the criminal law. Naffine argues that, in line with postmodern theories, it is necessary to reject the intransigence of categories of meaning of words such as 'crime' or 'rape' in favour of exploring the 'referential, "relational" and metaphorical nature of meaning' more fully: *Feminism and Criminology* (Cambridge: Polity Press, 1997) p 98. This can be done by using insights of deconstruction and standpoint feminism (at 98–119). For Naffine, meaning and interpretation *can* change. She illustrates this with an account of how images in crime fiction have changed from the hardboiled male detective current during the 1950s and 1960s to the independent, physically active female investigator as the protagonist.

For Lacey, the challenge is to reconstruct notions of neutrality, rights, equality and justice through the inclusion of different standpoints. She argues that the process of criminal justice should be seen as a 'social ordering practice' rather than a method of crime control in order to allow for the investigation of its symbolic and instrumental aspects. Lacey refers to 'criminalisation' as a dynamic, conceptual framework for analysing the connections between criminal law and criminology: 'Legal Constructions of Crime' in M Maguire, R Morgan and R Reiner (eds), *The Oxford Handbook of Criminology* (3rd edn, Oxford: Oxford University Press, 2002) pp 264–85. She states at 282:

> [T]he idea of criminalization captures the dynamic nature of the field as a set of interlocking practices in which the moments of 'defining' and 'responding to' crime can rarely be completely distinguished and in which legal and social (extra-legal) constructions of crime constantly interact. It accommodates the full range of rele-

vant institutions within which those practices take shape and the disciplines which might be brought to bear upon their analysis; it allows the instrumental and symbolic aspects of the field to be addressed, as well as encompassing empirical, interpretive and normative projects.

Lacey poses the challenge for those influenced by postmodernism and feminism as how best to approach the criminal law through the wider lenses of criminology and criminal justice studies. This challenge will be referred to again after we examine critical race theory.

Critical race theory

The origins of 'critical race theory' can be traced back to the mid-1970s in the USA when writers such as Derek Bell and Alan Freeman wanted to hasten the slow pace of racial reform.

As outlined above, critical legal studies theorists focused, among other things, on critiquing the importance of rights in liberal political theory. From the perspective of race theorists, rights are only insignificant to those who already have them, such as the white male academics in the critical legal studies movement. While critical race theorists are discontented with liberalism, safeguarding the rights of minorities is still seen as a priority. For example, Girardeau Spann has criticised the United States Supreme Court in its failure to recognise legal claims asserted by racial minorities and urged the latter to turn away from reliance on judicial review in favour of advancing minority interests via the political branches of government: 'Pure Politics' in R Delgado and J Stefancic (eds), *Critical Race Theory* (2nd edn, Philadelphia: Temple University Press, 2000) pp 21–34.

Similarly, early feminist theories were criticised for assuming that the female norm was white, middle-class and heterosexual: A Moreton-Robinson, *Talkin' Up the White Woman: Indigenous Women and Feminism* (St Lucia: University of Queensland Press, 2000); 'Troubling Business: Difference and Whiteness Within Feminism' (2000) 15 *Australian Feminist Studies* 343–52. The criticism was that whiteness remained invisible because it was the norm and that white middle-class academics simply assumed that race was something that could be added to their theories. For example, Marilyn Lake writes in 'Between Old World "Barbarism" and Stone Age "Primitivism": The Double Difference of the White Australian Feminist' in N Grieve and A Burns (eds), *Australian Women: Contemporary Feminist Thought* (Melbourne: Oxford University Press, 1994) p 80: 'Feminism's great animating insight lies in the recognition of the systematic nature of men's power over women; its concomitant blindspot is the frequent failure to see that the sisterhood of women also involves systematic relations of domination between women.'

Those writing from a critical race perspective may take differing focal points. Some argue that the primary concern should be the struggle against racism: P O'Shane, 'Is There Any Relevance in the Women's Movement for Aboriginal Women?' (1976) 12 *Refractory Girl* 31–4. Others have been concerned with mapping out distinct identities for non-white individuals.

Many critical race theorists have been influenced by postmodernism in using techniques such as autobiography, stories and parables to expose the presumptions of white critical theory. Race itself is seen as a social construct: L Jayasuriya, 'Understanding Australian Racism' (2002) 45(1) *Australian Universities Review* 40–4. Drawing on deconstruction methodology, cultural racism has been described as focusing on the exploitation and negation of the Other: M Wieviorka, *The Arena of Racism* (London: Sage, 1995); A Markus, *Race: John Howard and the Re-Making of Australia* (Sydney: Allen & Unwin, 2001).

The challenge for critical legal perspectives is to recognise issues of race without assuming that like the older version of 'add women and stir' feminist empiricism, one can 'add race and stir' to existing theories. Chris Cunneen's book *Conflict, Politics and Crime* (Crows Nest, NSW: Allen & Unwin, 2001) provides a useful starting point in this regard in relation to Aboriginal perspectives on crime.

Critical perspectives in this book

We are writing from the standpoint of being white, middle-class, female academics. Our own perspectives have been influenced by our experiences as white middle-class women learning and teaching criminal law, the administration of criminal justice and criminology. We acknowledge that it is difficult, if not impossible, for us to fully appreciate critical race perspectives, but we will nevertheless refer to approaches based on race and culture in the analyses of criminal laws that follow.

This book will draw on the newer critical perspectives that incorporate postmodern and feminist approaches to the criminal law. As stated above, Nicola Lacey has recommended approaching the criminal law through the wider lenses of criminology and criminal justice studies. She sees the task for current legal scholars as 'developing an integrated yet non-reductive critical approach to criminal legal and criminal justice practices': 'In(de)terminable Intentions' (1995) 58 *Modern Law Review* 692–5 at 695. We hope that by framing our analysis within interdisciplinary perspectives, the critical perspectives explored here will pave the way for such an integrated critical approach.

We are also concerned with bringing the impact of criminal laws to the fore through the use of case studies. We thus focus on one main case or a handful of cases in the chapters on the main offences and analyse them in detail rather than referring to 'general principles' gleaned from numerous cases with the facts omitted. This is quite a different method of approaching the criminal law and we hope it will bring the current laws to life in ways that have not been achieved in other books on the criminal law.

Because this book is aimed at readers from different disciplines, we provide a section setting out the current laws before engaging in a critique of them. Criminologists have been accused in the past of researching areas where a necessary knowledge of the law was lacking. Setting out the chapters on the main offences in this way will address this. Similarly, those practising or learning criminal law will gain an understanding of the social context of this area through the critique sections.

Aims of the criminal law: differing perspectives

As with defining crime, there are numerous perspectives on the aims of the criminal law or what those aims should be. In this section we will outline some of the main theories that suggest that the aims of the criminal law include punishment of the offender, protection of individuals from harm, preservation of morality and promotion of social welfare.

Punishment

We stated in the previous section that Glanville Williams describes a crime as 'a legal wrong that can be followed by criminal proceedings which may result in punishment': *Textbook of Criminal Law* (2nd edn, London: Stevens & Sons, 1983) p 27. This connection between crime and punishment indicates that a positivist approach to the criminal law often focuses on the main aim of the criminal law as being to punish offenders. However, within that general aim are subcategories dealing with the purpose of punishment. These subcategories of aims include retribution, deterrence, incapacitation and rehabilitation. There are further approaches that can be identified within these subcategories. For example, Mirko Bagaric identifies three approaches to punishment as retribution: punishment only for the guilty; the principle of proportionality; and punishment as good in itself: *Punishment and Sentencing: A Rational Approach* (London: Cavendish Publishing Limited, 2001) pp 38 ff.

HLA Hart has stated that theories of punishment constitute 'moral *claims* as to what justifies the practice of punishment—claims as to why, morally, it *should* or *may* be used': *Punishment and Responsibility* (Oxford: Oxford University Press, 1968) p 72. There is therefore a strong normative component in theories of punishment in that they deal with what the punishment *should* be.

Retribution is often seen as the main purpose of punishment. In order for it to be distinguished from revenge, a common law principle has developed that is generally referred to as the principle of proportionality. This means that the type and extent of punishment should be proportionate to the seriousness of the harm and the degree of responsibility of the offender: R Fox, 'The Meaning of Proportionality in Sentencing' (1994) 19 *Melbourne University Law Review* 489–511.

Deterrence as an aim of punishment is concerned with preventing crime. It is generally seen as having two arms: specific deterrence and general deterrence. The former is aimed at preventing the offender from committing a crime in the future and general deterrence is aimed at preventing others from committing crimes. Rehabilitation is similarly concerned with the prevention of crime, but through the treatment of the offender. This aim was particularly popular during the 1970s, but has since been somewhat played down with governments being more attracted to retributive and deterrent theories. It still has influence, however, with the development of specialised drug courts that aim to provide supervision of treatment for drug abuse and with the provision of therapeutic and educational programs in prisons.

Incapacitation as an aim is tied in with the protection of the community at large. For example, an offender found not guilty because of mental impairment can nevertheless be detained in a mental health facility on the basis of the protection of the public. Incapacitation as an aim of punishment is now also used to justify the detention of those considered 'dangerous' on the basis that past criminal behaviour can be predictive of certain offenders being at risk of offending in the future.

Sentencing legislation tends to take a mixed bag approach to these sub-categories of punishment aims. For example, s 5(1) of the *Sentencing Act* 1991 (Vic) sets out that the only purposes for which sentences may be imposed are just punishment, deterrence, rehabilitation, denunciation and community protection. How these sometimes competing aims can be balanced is not mentioned in the legislation, but is left to the judge's discretion.

David Garland has suggested that it is illusory to try to explain punishment according to a sole aim: *Punishment and Moral Society* (Oxford: Clarendon Press, 1990). Instead, he writes (at 281) that there is a need to see punishment as possessing multiple causality, multiple effects and multiple meanings. He states (at 287): 'Punishment is, on the face of things, an apparatus for dealing with criminals—a circumscribed, discrete, legal-administrative entity. But it is also…an expression of state power, a statement of collective morality, a vehicle for emotional expression, an economically conditioned social policy, an embodiment of current sensibilities, and a set of symbols which display a cultural ethos and help create a social identity.'

Viewing punishment as having a multitude of aims seems appropriate, but of course theorists will continue to debate just exactly what those aims are and should be.

Prevention of harm

We have already mentioned that one of the most pervasive traditional theories concerning the scope of the criminal law is that originally outlined by John Stuart

Mill in his work *On Liberty* (Harmondsworth: Penguin, 1974, first published 1859). His view (at 68) was that the power of the state should only be exercised to prevent harm to others. The main aim of the criminal law should therefore be the prevention of harm and the criminal law should only be used as a 'last resort': A Ashworth, *Principles of Criminal Law* (3rd edn, Oxford: Oxford University Press, 1999) pp 32–7.

The primary problem with this approach is to define what is meant by harm to others. Does it include psychological and economic harm as well as physical harm? Does it encompass indirect or potential harm? Would environmental damage be considered harm to others? Is the word 'others' limited to humans or does it encompass animals? Joel Feinberg in *The Moral Limits of the Criminal Law: Harm to Others* (New York: Oxford University Press, 1984) has (at 215) defined harm as meaning 'a setback to a person's interest'. However, this fails to take into account wider social or indirect harms. It also fails to take into account what Regina Graycar and Jenny Morgan refer to as gendered harms; that is, those harms caused by injuries that happen to women as women: *The Hidden Gender of Law* (2nd edn, Annandale: The Federation Press, 2002) p 300.

The prevention of harm approach to the criminal law may help explain why certain activities should *not* be criminalised, but runs into difficulties in explaining why certain conduct *should* be criminalised. At the same time, this approach has the potential to considerably expand the reach of the criminal law because there is no clear delineation between state-enforced sanctions and civil or quasi-criminal sanctions in punishing harmful behaviour.

In addition, the broader the definition of harm, the weaker the harm principle becomes for maximising individual freedom. For example, on a very broad definition of harm to others, it could be argued that drug-taking in private leads to over-reliance on publicly funded health and social welfare programs, which is a form of indirect economic harm to others. Yet, how does this explain public acceptance of the use of alcohol and tobacco, yet not drugs such as marijuana and heroin? Neil MacCormick has pointed out that the concept of harm itself is 'morally loaded': *Legal Right and Social Democracy* (Oxford: Oxford University Press, 1982) p 29.

Despite these problems, the harm principle is pervasive in law and order debates. Nicola Lacey and Celia Wells state that the prevention of harm is best seen 'neither as ideal nor as explanation but rather as an ideological framework in terms of which policy debate about criminal law is expressed': *Reconstructing Criminal Law: Critical Perspectives on Crime and the Criminal Process* (2nd edn, London: Butterworths, 1998) pp 7–8.

Preservation of morality

There is undoubtedly a fundamental connection between the criminal law and morality. In medieval England, the Church's doctrine that serious wrongs were sins influenced notions of blameworthiness in the development of the theory of criminal responsibility: F McAuley and JP McCutcheon, *Criminal Liability* (Dublin: Round Hall Sweet & Maxwell, 2000) pp 4–10. Even now, the *Criminal Codes* of the Northern Territory, Queensland, Tasmania and Western Australia group certain crimes under the heading 'Offences Against Morality'. But stating that the development of the law has been influenced by morals is different from saying that the aim of the criminal law is or should be to preserve morality. The usefulness of this latter approach was hotly debated in England during the late 1950s and early 1960s.

In the late 1950s, a movement developed in England to decriminalise homosexual acts that were conducted in private between consenting male adults. The Wolfenden Committee enquired into the matter and recommended decriminalisation: *Report of the Committee on Homosexual Offences and Prostitution* (London: HMSO, 1957) Cmnd 257. The eminent English judge Lord Patrick Devlin took issue with this recommendation. He argued that certain kinds of conduct should be prohibited by the criminal law because they are immoral according to the prevailing norms of a given society: *The Enforcement of Morals* (London: Oxford University Press, 1965). He stated that certain types of consensual conduct such as homosexual acts should be criminalised in order to preserve society, its essential institutions and what he termed its 'positive morality' from disintegration. Devlin stated (at 15) that morality could be determined by enquiring into what 'every right-minded person' considered immoral.

For Devlin, John Stuart Mill's harm principle could not explain why certain conduct was criminal. He referred to the criminalisation of voluntary euthanasia, suicide pacts, duelling, abortion and sibling incest. He stated (at 7) that these acts 'can be done in private and without offence to others and need not involve the corruption or exploitation of others...[t]hey can be brought within [the criminal law] only as a matter of moral principle'.

The legal philosopher HLA Hart criticised Devlin's position and argued that what people did with consent in private was their own business and not that of the criminal law: *Law, Liberty and Morality* (London: Oxford University Press, 1963). Hart took John Stuart Mill's harm principle as his starting point, but qualified it by arguing that the state is permitted to pass laws to protect the vulnerable from exploitation. He wrote (at 47): 'Recognition of individual liberty as a value involves, as a minimum, acceptance of the principle that the individual may do what he [or she] wants, even if others are distressed when they learn what it is he [or she] does—unless of course there are other good grounds for forbidding it.'

Hart raised a number of criticisms of Devlin's theory. First, he was sceptical about whether or not a shared common morality could in fact be identified. Second, he argued that even if there is a 'positive' morality in a given society, it could be used to discriminate against minority groups. He pointed to the example of Nazi Germany in this regard.

Third, Hart questioned Devlin's notion of preserving society from disintegration through criminalising immoral acts. He argued that Devlin produced no evidence to support his contention that any deviation from positive morality such as homosexuality threatens the existence of society.

Finally, Hart argued (at 51) that the proposition that 'a society is identical with its morality...so that a change in its morality is tantamount to the destruction of society' was again unsupportable and unacceptable.

Hart's approach to the aims of the criminal law became the prevailing one during the 1960s. It appears a useful approach given that most criminal offences such as motor traffic offences are regulatory in nature and do not have a moral component. However, there is a link between some of the serious criminal offences and morality. Paul McCutcheon re-frames this in terms of the tolerance or intolerance societies show towards certain conduct: 'Morality and the Criminal Law: Reflections on Hart–Devlin' (2002) 47 *The Criminal Law Quarterly* 15–38 at 34 ff. We will explore in Chapter 4 how Devlin's approach can be seen to have influenced the majority decision of the House of Lords in *R v Brown* [1993] 2 WLR 556 in holding that consent was irrelevant to sadomasochistic acts causing actual bodily harm. Moral considerations are therefore still relevant to certain areas of the criminal law.

Social welfare

Spurred on by the criticisms that can be made of the aims of the preservation of morality and the prevention of harm, some theorists have explored social welfare as an aim that should be highlighted by the criminal law. For example, the Swedish theorist and politician, Anders Vilhelm Lundstedt has stated that lawmakers must always keep in mind what is socially useful: *Legal Thinking Revisited* (Stockholm: Almqvist & Wiksell, 1956). He stressed that social welfare should be viewed as a real outcome that could be measured empirically and that it should not be seen as some sort of metaphysical concept. His view was that individuals strive for adequate food, clothing and property as well as spiritual interests and that the law should at the very least protect these material benefits. Similarly, Nicola Lacey refers to social welfare as including 'the fulfilment of certain basic interests such as maintaining one's personal safety, health and capacity to pursue one's chosen life plan': *State Punishment* (London: Routledge, 1986) p 104.

But, how should the law deal with competing or opposed social welfare interests? Lundstedt refers to the protection of the 'greatest possible' freedom of each individual. This seems to hark back to the importance of freedom and autonomy central to John Stuart Mill's theory. Andrew Ashworth, in *Principles of Criminal Law*

(3rd edn, Oxford: Oxford University Press, 1999) p 30, suggests there may be a way of combining the two approaches:

> Clearly there are conflicts between the two principles [of welfare and autonomy], but that may not always be the case. If the principle of autonomy is taken to require a positive form of liberty rather than negative liberty, then the principle of welfare may work towards the same end by ensuring the citizens benefit from the existence of facilities and structures which are protected, albeit in the last resort, by the criminal law.

As with approaches to the definition of crime, this brief overview of theories on the scope of the criminal law shows that it is impossible to state that there is only one aim that should underlie the criminal law. As Paul McCutcheon writes in 'Morality and the Criminal Law: Reflections on Hart–Devlin' (2002) 47 *The Criminal Law Quarterly* 15–38 at 37–8: '[T]he limits of the criminal law cannot be set by reference to a "simple principle", be it harm, individual liberty or whatever. Instead the boundaries of the law are shaped by a variety of forces that operate as broad guidelines rather than as clear-cut criteria.'

Measuring crime

In the previous sections, we have made the point that there is no single definition of crime or criminal law or the aims of the criminal law. There is a further problem associated with measuring crime and crime trends. Various forms of media are adept at referring to what are deemed to be 'facts' about crime trends. However, since the meaning of crime is relative, it pays to be sceptical about how crime is measured. 'Official' statistics relating to crime can be obtained through such organisations as the Australian Bureau of Statistics, the New South Wales Bureau of Crime Statistics and Research, the Australian Institute of Criminology or through police, court and correctional records. These statistics, however, while accurate in their own terms, suffer from a number of limitations.

Only a small proportion of crime comes to the attention of the police. The failure to report crime gives rise to what has been termed the 'dark figure' in measuring crime. People may fail to report crime for many reasons. It may be because they believe the offence is trivial or that nothing can be done about it or because they have a relationship with the offender or because they fear that they will be further victimised by the criminal justice system. Even if a crime is reported to police, it may go unrecorded. The police exercise a great deal of discretion in the recording and processing of offences: M McConville, A Sanders and R Leng, *The Case for the Prosecution: Police Suspects and the Construction of Criminality* (London: Routledge, 1991).

Official crime statistics are often used for the policy purposes of budget and resource allocation and may therefore be open to misinterpretation. Ezzat Fattah writes in *Criminology: Past, Present and Future* (Basingstoke: Macmillan Press Ltd, 1997) p 98:

> Scepticism regarding statistics in general, and criminal statistics in particular, is reinforced by frequent misuse of these statistics. For instance, when they are used in support of demands for money and manpower for the police, higher *figures* may be cited regardless of whether the *rate* itself has increased or declined and without mentioning that the upward figures may be the result of increased police activity or improved reporting and recording practices. [Emphasis in original.]

The levels of detection, reporting or recording of offences may influence fluctuations in crime statistics. For example, it may be difficult to identify when there is a rise in the general crime rate rather than a rise caused by improvements in data gathering and processing. Because of different police practices and different legal definitions of offences, it is often difficult to compare levels of crime across Australian jurisdictions and nationally.

Criminologists often look beyond official criminal statistics to victimisation surveys and self-report studies to give a more realistic version of the 'dark figure' of criminal statistics. Again, there are limitations with these methods of measuring crime.

Victimisation surveys often reveal high levels of unreported and unrecorded crimes. Often these surveys are conducted by telephone or mail using a national sample of households. The British Crime Survey, for example, has become a major source of data about crime. Usually over 10,000 people aged 16 and over are interviewed for the purposes of this survey. The problem with such a method is that it can be difficult to get a truly representative sample. For example, if interviews are conducted during the day, household workers and the elderly may be over-represented. If the survey is conducted by mail, response rates can be very low. If it is conducted by telephone, the homeless and those in lower income brackets may be under-represented. A sample constructed on the basis of telephone listings immediately cuts out those who have unlisted numbers.

Self-report studies ask individuals whether they have committed criminal acts. Problems of sampling and low response rates are common. Many individuals may be reluctant to reveal illegal activities while others may feel tempted to exaggerate the frequency and seriousness of offences. Nevertheless, these studies add another facet to the picture provided by official statistics and have been used with varying degrees of success in measuring levels of crime.

It is important to recognise that there are many difficulties associated with the measurement of crime. Yet, this does not mean that the collection and use of statistical measures of levels of crime should be abandoned. As Mike Maguire states in 'Crime Statistics, Patterns, and Trends: Changing Perceptions and their Implications' in M Maguire, R Morgan and R Reiner (eds), *The Oxford Handbook of*

Criminology (2nd edn, Oxford: Oxford University Press, 1997) pp 135–88 at 142: '*[S]o long as their limitations are fully recognized,* crime-related statistics undoubtedly offer a valuable aid to understanding and explanation, as well as to the very necessary task of description. The key point to take...is that no conclusions should ever be drawn from any such data without a clear understanding of how they were compiled and what they represent.' [Emphasis in original.]

Throughout this book, we will refer to various surveys and official statistics to give an overview of the levels of the type of crime being analysed. However, we are careful to point out wherever possible that the 'true' picture may be somewhat different given the 'dark figure' of crime and the problems associated with compiling criminal statistics.

Jurisdiction

One area that will be of increasing importance to the criminal law is that of jurisdiction. In most criminal law cases, the crime occurs within a particular state or territory and is tried within that jurisdiction. The traditional approach has been that all crime is local and a country or state should only exercise its powers to try and punish offenders where the offence was committed within its territorial boundaries. That is, crimes should be tried where they were committed. This is known as the 'territorial theory' of jurisdiction.

This local territorial focus has, however, been challenged in recent years with the advent of crimes that may begin in one area, but have consequences in another. Take, for example, the facts of *DPP v Sutcliffe* unreported, 1 March 2001, SC of Vic, Gillard J, [2001] VSC 43.

Brian Sutcliffe was charged with stalking Sara Ballingall, who was an actor in the television series *Degrassi High* between 1985 and 1990 and who lived and worked in Canada. Sutcliffe had visited Canada in 1993 and there he obtained Sara Ballingall's address. After his return to Australia he proceeded to mail her numerous letters, some of which mentioned his interest in guns. The final letters contained sentences such as 'this is your final warning' and 'If this isn't resolved there is going to be trouble'.

The magistrate dismissed the charge on the basis that there was no jurisdiction to try Sutcliffe in Victoria. One of the elements of the crime of stalking set out in s 21A of the *Crimes Act* 1958 (Vic) is that the course of conduct caused apprehension or fear in the victim for his or her own safety. The magistrate was of the view that this element of the crime could only have occurred in Canada and therefore the charge should have been brought there and could not proceed in Victoria. The case went on appeal to the Supreme Court of Victoria. Before analysing how the Court saw the matter, it is worthwhile taking a step back and examining how the concept of 'jurisdiction' has evolved in the criminal law.

Territorial theory

The term 'jurisdiction' is used widely in both domestic and international law, but it is also a generic term that may relate to geography, control over persons and procedures as well as to constitutional and judicial structures and powers: *Lipohar v The Queen* (1999) 200 CLR 485 at 516 per Gaudron, Gummow and Hayne JJ. In this section, we are referring to jurisdiction in the sense of a geographic political unit that has power to prosecute an accused person.

An individual may be made subject to the laws of a number of different political units that can regulate behaviour such as local government, state or territory government, the Commonwealth government and supranational organisations such as the United Nations. The territorial theory of jurisdiction holds that a criminal court has jurisdiction only over crimes committed within its geographical boundaries. Once a criminal court has such jurisdiction, it applies its own laws in relation to the offence. Territorial jurisdiction in this limited sense refers to the power of the state to exercise control over events occurring domestically or within its boundaries.

In Australia, there are nine different sets of criminal laws operating. Each of the six states, the two territories and the federal jurisdiction has its own criminal laws. Each state or territory has control over crimes occurring within its borders and a corresponding duty not to interfere with the affairs of other jurisdictions. The Northern Territory, Queensland, Tasmania and Western Australia have Criminal Codes based on a draft produced by Sir Samuel Griffith in 1897. He saw codification as leading to an explicit statement of the criminal law in a form that could be ascertained by an intelligent person: 'Explanatory Letter to the Attorney-General Queensland with Draft Code' in E Edwards, R Harding and I Campbell, *The Criminal Codes* (4th edn, Sydney: The Law Book Company Ltd, 1992) p 5. However, Codes do not supersede the system of precedent as the provisions are not free of all ambiguity and need to be interpreted. The differences between the Code and common law jurisdictions have probably been overstated in the past as the common law jurisdictions of the Australian Capital Territory, New South Wales, South Australia and Victoria all rely for the most part on legislation which, while it does not seek to codify the common law, is also open to interpretation by the courts. The Australian Capital Territory is in the process of reforming its criminal legislation and has enacted the *Criminal Code* 2002 (ACT). Some of its provisions have immediate application, but others will not be in force until 1 January 2006, or earlier if prescribed under regulations. Further chapters are to be added to the Code over the next few years. We will mention the Code provisions throughout this book in tandem with appropriate provisions of the *Crimes Act* 1900 (ACT) that are still in force.

Jurisdiction is viewed more broadly in international law than the territorial theory allows. In international law, jurisdiction has been used to denote the exercise of powers by a nation state over events, persons and property: IA Shearer, *Starke's International Law* (Sydney: Butterworths, 1994) p 183. Matthew Goode has identified four principles of criminal jurisdiction in addition to the territorial theory: 'The Tortured Tale of Criminal Jurisdiction' (1997) 21 *Melbourne University Law Review* 411–59. These are:

- the **protective principle** whereby a state has jurisdiction in relation to any conduct engaged in by a person anywhere that threatens the state's peace, security or good government;
- the **nationality principle** whereby a state has jurisdiction in relation to any conduct contrary to local law engaged in anywhere by a national of the state;
- the **passive personality principle** whereby a state has jurisdiction in relation to any conduct committed anywhere that victimises a national of the state;
- the **universality principle** whereby a state has jurisdiction simply because the offender is within the state.

Until recently, the conceptions of jurisdiction under international and domestic law were viewed as differing and potentially conflicting. For example, Toohey J noted in *Polyukovich v Commonwealth* (1991) 172 CLR 501 at 658 that the 'term "jurisdiction" has different meanings in international and municipal law'. However, while the territorial theory of jurisdiction applied domestically is still current at common law, it has been particularly influenced by the protective principle of international jurisdiction. We shall explore a little later how the *Criminal Code* (Cth) has moved towards incorporating principles of international jurisdiction into domestic criminal law. In the next section we will explore how the territoriality theory has been adapted to take into account where the elements of a crime occurs, whether the conduct threatens peace, order or good government and whether there is a substantial link or 'nexus' to the state.

The territorial theory has also been challenged by the rise of extraterritorial offences. There are many offences where federal, state and territory legislatures have exercised their sovereign power to apply the criminal law beyond their territorial borders. For example, s 11 of the *War Crimes Act* 1945 (Cth), as amended by the *War Crimes Amendment Act* 1988 (Cth), provides that Australian nationals or residents may be prosecuted for war crimes that have occurred outside Australia, whether or not the offender was an Australian national at the time. In *Polyukovich v Commonwealth* (1991) 172 CLR 501 the High Court upheld the validity of the *War Crimes Act* 1945 (Cth) as a proper exercise of the Commonwealth's external affairs power pursuant to ss 51 (vi) and (xxiv) of the Constitution. The majority concluded that the legislation was a valid exercise of these powers and applied to past conduct of persons who at the relevant time had no connection with Australia: G Triggs, 'Australia's War Crimes Trials' in TLH McCormack and GJ Simpson, *The Law of War Crimes: National and International Approaches* (The Hague: Kluwer Law International, 1997).

There is a growing global interest in expanding the ambit of what are known as extraterritorial offences to include crimes against human rights such as torture, terrorism and sexual trafficking in women and children. For example, there are provisions in the *Crimes Act* 1914 (Cth) criminalising sexual intercourse with children committed overseas: Part IIIA inserted by *Crimes (Child Sex Tourism) Amendment Act* 1994 (Cth). Similarly, the *Cybercrime Act* 2001 (Cth) inserted new computer offences into the *Criminal Code* (Cth), which apply to Australian citizens anywhere in the world.

We now turn to examining how the territorial theory of jurisdiction has been challenged by crimes that have elements or consequences occurring across states.

Terminatory theory

The early common law in England adopted a highly localised view of jurisdiction, limiting trials to the county in which the crime occurred. This approach related to the need to ensure that the jury empanelled to hear the matter had 'local knowledge' of the offender and offence: A Leaver, *Investigating Crime* (Sydney: LBC Information Services, 1997) pp 33–50.

In *Ward v The Queen* (1980) 142 CLR 308 the High Court had to consider the problem of how to apply the territorial theory where the crime began in one jurisdiction, but had consequences in another. The accused, standing on the Victorian bank of the Murray River, shot and killed his victim who was standing on the opposite bank in New South Wales. Jurisdiction was particularly important in this matter because the defence of diminished responsibility was available to the accused in New South Wales, but not in Victoria. The accused was tried and convicted of murder in Victoria. He appealed on the basis that because the conduct causing death terminated or had its consequences in New South Wales, he should have been tried there. The High Court was therefore faced with a decision as to whether jurisdiction should be determined by where the conduct occurred (the initiatory theory) or by the place where the *consequences* of that conduct occurred (the terminatory theory). The High Court held that the terminatory theory applied to these facts and that the accused should have been tried in New South Wales.

The terminatory theory works best with those crimes that have 'one core element which dictates where it may be tried': D Lanham, *Cross-Border Criminal Law* (Melbourne: FT Law & Tax Asia Pacific, 1997) p 3. It is problematic when applied to crimes that have multiple elements that may be committed at different times and from different locations such as stalking or complex fraudulent financial dealings.

Since jurisdictional disputes are resolved on a case-by-case basis, there is some uncertainty whether the principle, theory or test of territoriality endorsed by the court applies to all offences or rather is crime specific. The terminatory test in *Ward v The Queen* forms the basis for criminal jurisdiction under the common law. It has also been incorporated into the tests of territorial jurisdiction in the Codes adopted in Queensland and Western Australia: *Criminal Code* (Qld) s 12(3); *Criminal Code*

(WA) s 12(1). These Codes do, however, also include reference to the initiatory theory: *Criminal Code* (Qld) s 12(2); *Criminal Code* (WA) s 12(1).

While some judges apply *Ward v The Queen* as a general principle for determining jurisdiction, others have acknowledged the limitations of the terminatory theory and have adopted more flexible tests or conceptions of territoriality. Certain cases explored in the following sections seem to be moving away from the terminatory theory towards other approaches such as looking at whether or not the crime affects the peace, order and security of the state or whether or not the crime committed elsewhere has a substantial link to the jurisdiction in which it is sought to be tried.

The protective approach

In international law, a state may exercise jurisdiction over those who are not nationals of the state who commit acts abroad that interfere with the state's security. This is seen as a form of protection of state interests. This approach has been adapted to trying those within a jurisdiction who are planning to commit offences abroad. For example, in *Board of Trade v Owen* [1957] AC 602 at 624, Tucker LJ set out the test as considering whether or not the contemplated crime would be recognised 'to aid in the preservation of the Queen's peace and the maintenance of law and order within the realm'. Wells J in *R v Hansford* (1974) 8 SASR 164 at 195 translated this as considering whether or not the accused's conduct affects 'the peace, welfare and good government of the State'. This test means that the offence or intended offence need not have any physical connection to a territory. It is therefore very broad and potentially open to abuse.

A version of this test is set out in s 15 of the *Criminal Code* (NT). This section states that if 'a person is guilty of the conduct proscribed by any offence it is immaterial that that conduct or some part of it did not occur in the Territory if that conduct affected or was intended to affect the peace, order or good government of the Territory'.

Returning to the facts of *DPP v Sutcliffe*, the *effects* of Sutcliffe's conduct were felt in Canada. On the terminatory approach, the magistrate was correct in holding that the Canadian authorities should have tried Brian Sutcliffe rather than the Victorian authorities. However, Gillard J in the appeal to the Supreme Court did not discuss this theory, but applied the protective approach instead.

Gillard J viewed the matter as one of statutory construction. He examined whether or not Parliament intended that the offence of stalking have extraterritorial effect. It was a matter of territorial ambit rather than jurisdiction as the Magistrates' Court had jurisdiction to hear a charge under s 21A of the *Crimes Act* 1958 (Vic). He went on to find that the Victorian Parliament had power to pass a law that has extraterritorial operation providing it was 'for the peace, order and good government' of the state of Victoria. He found that when the provision was enacted in 1994, Parliament was well aware that with the advent of new technologies, stalking could take place via the Internet or email and therefore could occur partly within Victoria and partly outside it. Gillard J therefore found that the Magistrate had been wrong in dismissing the charge of stalking and remitted the matter back to the Magistrates' Court for determination.

The territorial nexus/substantial link approach

New South Wales, South Australia and Tasmania have enacted provisions that set out a 'territorial nexus' test: *Crimes (Application of Criminal Law) Amendment Act* 1992 (NSW) s 3A; *Criminal Law Consolidation Act* 1935 (SA) ss 5C, 5G; *Criminal Law (Territorial Application) Act* 1995 (Tas) s 4.

For example, s 4(1) of the *Criminal Law (Territorial Application) Act* 1995 (Tas) sets out that a crime against the law of Tasmania is committed if all elements of the crime exist and a 'territorial nexus' exists between the state and at least one element of the crime. These provisions, however, have been construed very narrowly and Matthew Goode has argued that they will 'be so interpreted as to achieve nothing that was not already achieved by common law': 'The Tortured Tale of Criminal Jurisdiction' (1997) 21 *Melbourne University Law Review* 411–59 at 459.

A common law test of a real and substantial link seems to have the potential to fare better than these statutory provisions. This test was established by the Supreme Court of Canada in *Libman v The Queen* (1985) 21 CCC (3d) 206 at 232 and now seems to be finding favour in Australia. This examines whether or not there is a 'real and substantial link' between the offence and the country or state seeking to try it. In *Libman*'s case, the accused was charged in Canada with fraud and with conspiracy to defraud in relation to a telemarketing scheme. The accused rang residents of the USA from Canada asking them to invest in bogus South American companies. The money was then sent to South America and the accused collected it there before returning with it to Canada.

The Supreme Court of Canada held that the accused could be tried in Canada because a significant portion of the activities constituting the offence took place in that country and this meant that a real and substantial link between the offence and Canada had been established.

The majority of the High Court in *Lipohar v The Queen* (1999) 200 CLR 485 recently endorsed formulations similar or identical to the Canadian formulation, which ranged from a 'sufficient connection' (at 501 per Gleeson CJ; at 535 per Gaudron, Gummow and Hayne JJ) to a 'real link' (at 588 per Callinan J) between the offence and the state.

If this approach were applied to the facts in *Sutcliffe*'s case, Brian Sutcliffe could have been tried in Victoria because, as most elements of the crime of stalking had occurred there, a real and substantial link existed with the state of Victoria.

Matthew Goode has criticised the concept of domestic jurisdiction as being a muddle of approaches. He writes in 'Contemporary Comment—Two New Decisions on Criminal "Jurisdiction": The Appalling Durability of Common Law' (1996) 20 Crim LJ 267–82 at 269: 'Any reader seeking a common thread of reason, rationale or plain legal reasoning in these and other decisions will be bitterly disappointed.'

Notwithstanding the diversity of tests and theories, jurisdiction rarely forms the basis for objection by the defence. This is probably because a sufficient territorial connection can usually be found through whichever test is applied.

The way ahead: the Model Criminal Code

Because of the discrepancies that occur between jurisdictions in relation to criminal law and procedure, in 1990, the Standing Committee of Attorneys-General placed the question of the development of a national Model Criminal Code for Australian jurisdictions on its agenda. The Model Criminal Code Officers Committee (MCCOC) was subsequently established to provide discussion papers and draft the Model Criminal Code.

As part of this process, the *Criminal Code* (Cth) came into force on 1 January 1997. The Commonwealth Criminal Code is appended as a schedule to the *Criminal Code Act* 1995 (Cth). Amendments to it came into force on 5 December 2001. The Code only applies to Commonwealth offences, but it was hoped that it would serve as a model to be adopted in due course by the other eight Australian jurisdictions. The Australian Capital Territory is in the process of reforming its criminal legislation and has enacted the *Criminal Code* (ACT), which is largely based on the Commonwealth model. Part of the *Criminal Code* (Cth) relates to jurisdictional issues. The Code does not refer to any of the tests mentioned above. Rather, it retains the common law as the 'standard geographical jurisdiction', supplemented by four categories of 'extended geographical jurisdiction'. It thus attempts to incorporate international law approaches to jurisdiction within Australia.

Section 14.1 sets out that standard geographic jurisdiction applies where the conduct or a result required by the offence occurred wholly or partly in Australia. Sections 15.1 to 15.4 set out the four categories of extended geographic jurisdiction as follows:

- Category A—covers Australian citizens or bodies corporate anywhere in the world, subject to a foreign law defence (that is, there is no corresponding crime in the foreign jurisdiction).
- Category B—covers Australian citizens, bodies corporate as well as Australian residents anywhere in the world, subject to a foreign law defence.
- Category C—covers anyone anywhere regardless of citizenship or residence, subject to a foreign law defence.
- Category D—covers anyone anywhere regardless of citizenship or residence and there is no foreign law defence.

Under this model the 'default setting' for jurisdiction is based on the terminatory theory. The four categories of extended geographic jurisdiction are intended to attach to specific offences such as those dealing with computer crimes. For example, the *Cybercrime Act* 2001 (Cth) inserted s 476.3 into the *Criminal Code* (Cth). This states that the extended geographical jurisdiction—Category A—now applies to the computer offences specified in the Code. These categories do not require the offence to be geographically connected to Australia and are similar to approaches to jurisdiction at international law. The danger is that they may be over-inclusive although there are some safeguards such as the necessity for permission from the Attorney-General to institute proceedings against a person who is not a citizen or resident of Australia in relation to conduct that occurs wholly in a foreign country.

It would seem that given recent terrorist actions in New York and Bali, the concept of extended geographical jurisdiction will be fostered and legitimated. Drug laws, more than any other area of domestic law, have already been shaped by international efforts to combat the trafficking of drugs.

The new federal approach to jurisdiction represents a radical departure from the territorial theory of jurisdiction. This model might be considered acceptable for federal criminal law since 'Commonwealth legislation does not deal with the general law (except where it needs to be applied for specific situations) but with particular interests and concerns that, being of a national character, fall within the Commonwealth sphere': Model Criminal Code Officers Committee, *Chapter 4, Damage and Computer Offences*, Discussion Paper (January 2000) p 177. The Australian Capital Territory has enacted similar provisions dealing with geographical application: *Criminal Code* (ACT), Part 2.7. It remains to be seen whether or not this model will be adopted by the other Australian jurisdictions.

Having provided an overview of different approaches to crime, its measurement and jurisdictional issues, we now turn to an application of critical perspectives to what are usually viewed as the underlying principles of criminal law.

Individual and corporate criminal responsibility

Much of the writing about criminal laws assumes individual responsibility. The notions of voluntary action, intention, recklessness, causation and even the infliction of punishment very much depend upon the notion of an individual offender capable of choosing between committing a criminal act or not. Ian Dennis describes the criminal law as being based on Immanuel Kant's idea of the person as a rational, free and autonomous being: 'The Critical Condition of Criminal Law' (1997) 50 *Current Legal Problems* 213–49. He writes (at 237) that this model 'accords individuals the status of autonomous moral agents who, because they have axiomatic freedom of choice, can fairly be accountable and punishable for the rational choices...they make...[I]nformed voluntary choices of action are both necessary and sufficient to justify blame and punishment'.

In the next section, we will examine further the idea of the 'rational' individual. In this section, we will concentrate on problems that have arisen with this notion of *individual* criminal responsibility.

The attribution of criminal responsibility to individuals is so well accepted now that it seems difficult to imagine any other form of attribution. Yet, until the eighteenth century, the law also attributed criminal responsibility to animals: EP Evans, *The Criminal Prosecution and Capital Punishment of Animals* (London: Faber and Faber, 1987, first published 1906). If an individual domestic animal such as a pig, cow, horse or dog had killed a human being, it could be tried in a secular tribunal, with capital punishment the usual result. Evans writes (p 2) that in addition, the Ecclesiastical courts could institute judicial proceedings against 'rats, mice, locusts, weevils, and other vermin in order to prevent them from devouring crops, and to expel them from orchards, vineyards, and cultivated fields by means of exorcism and excommunication'. Even today the rationale of eliminating a social danger can be found in the removal and destruction of, for example, dogs that attack children.

Possibly the biggest challenge to the centrality of individual criminal responsibility, however, has been the development and acceptance of corporate criminal responsibility. For many years, corporate misbehaviour was not seen as criminal at all or was considered a lesser form of criminality that could be regulated by a range of minor offences. Alan Norrie traces this back to the social context of the development of criminal law in the nineteenth century when categories of crime were developed in order to control primarily working-class deviance: *Crime, Reason and History: A Critical Introduction to Criminal Law* (2nd edn, London: Butterworths, 2001) p 81.

The need for rules as to corporate criminal responsibility developed in tandem with the growth of corporations and the occurrence of recent major disasters such as the Air New Zealand Mount Erebus crash, the Bhopal disaster in India, the Chernobyl nuclear explosion and the Exxon Valdez oil spill. There are, however, problems with assigning criminal responsibility to corporations.

The first is that because the criminal law developed to deal with individuals, its categories are ill defined to cope with the type of crimes corporations commit. Some crimes are peculiar to the corporate form, whereas others are simply variations on offences aimed at individuals such as conspiracy to defraud. We will explore this further below. Second, the criminal law has traditionally not been seen as a proper mechanism for dealing with corporate deviance. From a criminological perspective, Edwin H Sutherland noted that the vast majority of criminal data compiled dealt with working-class offenders, but that business people committed a high level of crime: 'White-collar Criminality' (1940) 5 *American Sociological Review* 1–12. He considered traditional explanations of criminality to be misleading and concentrated on developing a theory of 'differential association' to explain why business people committed crimes. He saw different normative cultures existing within corporations as producing deviance through exposure to unethical and illegal behaviour.

The crimes that corporations commit can have more far-reaching consequences than those committed by individuals. The loss of lives and the damage to the environment caused by the above-mentioned disasters was enormous. In addition, in Australia, there are a significant number of work-related deaths occurring every year. In a study of occupational health and safety offences, Santina Perrone found that between January 1987 and December 1990, 353 work-related deaths had occurred in Victoria alone: 'Workplace Fatalities and the Adequacy of Prosecutions' (1995) 13(1) *Law in Context* 81–105 at 87. Of those deaths, 203 occurred in a corporate context and twenty-five of those were related to an 'extreme level of company negligence'.

Celia Wells writes that the 'history of the development of corporate criminal liability has a number of intervening strands and the resulting cloth is uneven': *Corporations and Criminal Responsibility* (Oxford: Oxford University Press, 1993) p 94. The criminal responsibility of corporations was virtually unrecognised until the latter half of the nineteenth century and then, it was on the basis of vicarious liability. As we shall outline, liability has now developed to be 'direct' as well as vicarious.

A corporation is considered a 'legal person' and may therefore in theory be criminally liable to the same extent as a natural person. The main restriction to this principle is that a corporation cannot be tried for an offence that can only be punished by imprisonment and therefore it is arguable that a corporation cannot be held criminally responsible for the crime of murder: *R v ICR Haulage Ltd* [1944] KB 551 at 556; *R v Murray Wright Ltd* [1970] NZLR 476 at 484 per McCarthy J. There is, however, nothing to stop the legislature providing an alternative punishment for murder such as a substantial fine. There is also no reason for a corporation to be exempted from prosecution for manslaughter: *P & O European Ferries (Dover) Ltd* (1991) 93 Cr App R 73; *R v ICR Haulage Ltd* [1944] KB 551; *S & Y Investments (No 2) Pty Ltd v Commercial Union Assurance Co of Australia Ltd* (1986) 85 FLR 285 at 306–7 per Asche J. A corporation cannot be held criminally responsible for certain crimes that only an individual can commit such as perjury or bigamy. It may, however, be held criminally liable for the offences of complicity, conspiracy, attempt and incitement.

The main problem with ascribing criminal responsibility to a corporation is that the concept of individual responsibility does not fit with what is in reality a set of social processes for labour and profit-making. Richard Quinney has argued that corporate crime is not seen as truly criminal because corporate practices are essential to developing a capitalist political economy: 'Class, State and Crime' in J Jacoby (ed), *Classics of Criminology* (New York: Waveland Press Inc, 1994, first published 1980) pp 106–15 at 110. Quinney's approach points out that corporations are largely protected from scrutiny because they are central to the functioning of capitalist society. This issue is examined further in Chapter 7.

Because a corporation does not have a physical existence, it is only perceived as being able to form an intention through its directors or employees. There are two ways in which corporate criminal liability has been established:
- by holding a corporation vicariously liable for the conduct of its employees where those employees were acting within the scope of their employment; or
- by holding a corporation directly liable for the acts of certain persons such as the corporation's board of directors, its managing director or person to whom the functions of the board have been delegated, who are considered to be the embodiment of the company.

Borrowing from civil law principles, it is now well established that a corporation may be held vicariously liable for the acts of its employees providing that they acted within the scope of their employment: *Christie v Foster Brewing Co Ltd* (1982) 18 VLR 292; *R and Minister for Customs v Australasian Films Ltd* (1921) 29 CLR 195; *Morgan v Babcock and Wilcox Ltd* (1929) 43 CLR 163; 30 SR (NSW) 218; *Alford v Riley Newman Ltd* (1934) 34 SR (NSW) 261; 51 WN (NSW) 82; *Fraser v Dryden's Carrying & Agency Co Pty Ltd* [1941] VLR 103; *Australian Stevedoring Industry Authority v Overseas and General Stevedoring Co Pty Ltd* (1959) 1 FLR 298. The status of the employee is irrelevant for this purpose. However, a corporation will not be vicariously responsible for the conduct of an independent contractor except where so provided by statute: *Allen v United Carpet Mills Pty Ltd* [1989] VR 323; *Goodes v General Motors Holden's Pty Ltd* [1972] VR 386. It is usually in respect of strict liability offences (explained in Chapter 2) that corporations will be found vicariously liable for the acts of their employees.

In general, the prosecution needs to prove three elements for vicarious criminal liability to be established. First, the relevant legislation must intend that legal liability be applied vicariously. In *Mousell Bros Ltd v London and Northwestern Railway Co* [1917] 2 KB 836 at 845 Lord Atkin stated: '[R]egard must be had to the object of the statute, the words used, the nature of the duty laid down, the person upon whom it is imposed, the person by whom it would in ordinary circumstances be performed, and the person upon whom the penalty is imposed.'

Secondly, the employee must have committed the relevant act within the course of employment or within the scope of his or her authority. In this regard, there is no requirement that the corporation explicitly authorise the employee to commit the offence: *Fraser v Dryden's Carrying & Agency Co Pty Ltd* [1941] VLR 103; *Australian Stevedoring Industry Authority v Overseas & General Stevedoring Co Pty Ltd* (1959) 1 FLR 298 (Fed Ct); *Canadian Dredge & Dock Co Ltd v The Queen* (1985) 19 CCC (3d) 1.

Thirdly, the employee must have possessed the state of mind required for the offence in question, unless the offence is one of strict or absolute liability: *Moussell Bros Ltd v London and Northwestern Railway Co* [1917] 2 KB 836.

By contrast, corporate criminal liability for serious offences such as manslaughter is based on direct liability. Rather than holding the corporation criminally responsible *for* the acts of its employees, direct liability views the employee's acts as those *of* the corporation. The mere fact that an employee performed an act will not be sufficient to establish liability for a serious offence. It must be shown that an act or omission was performed by someone with authority to act *as the corporation*. That person must be said to embody the corporation and this is sometimes referred to as 'the identity rule' or 'the attribution rule'. The leading case in this area is that of *Tesco Supermarkets Ltd v Nattrass* [1972] AC 153, which has been widely followed in Australia.

In *Tesco*, the company operated more than eight hundred supermarkets throughout the UK. It was charged under the Trade Descriptions Act with offering goods to consumers at a price for which they could not be bought. An assistant had placed normally priced soap powder on the shelf despite it having been advertised at a reduced price. The assistant had failed to notify the manager of the store and he had failed to check that the soap powder was displayed at the advertised price. It was held at first instance and by the Court of Appeal that the company was vicariously liable for the manager's lack of care. The House of Lords held, however, that the company was not liable as the manager was not of sufficient status in the company's organisation for his lack of care to be attributable to the company. He did not, as it were, 'embody' the company. The company's conviction was therefore quashed.

The *Tesco* principle limits the criminal liability of a company to the conduct and fault of those who may be said to embody the company such as the company's board of directors, its managing director or person to whom the function of the board has been fully delegated. This can lead to problems of proof. Proving that a top-level manager was at fault will be easier to prove if the corporation is small. If the fault comes from middle-level management, it will be more difficult to prove. For example, in *R v AC Hatrick Chemicals Pty Ltd* unreported, 29 November 1995, SC of Vic, Hampel J, the corporation, a plant engineer and a plant manager were charged with manslaughter in relation to a tank that had exploded during a welding operation, causing the death of one worker and seriously injuring another. The manslaughter charges against the individuals were withdrawn prior to committal and Hampel J directed a verdict of acquittal against the corporation on the basis of legal argument prior to the trial. One of the main arguments forming the basis of the direction was that the plant engineer and the plant manager were not 'the guiding mind' of the company: D Neal, 'Corporate Manslaughter' (1996) *Law Institute Journal* 39–41. Corporate responsibility for homicide is discussed further in Chapter 3.

Harry Glasbeek writes in *Wealth By Stealth: Corporate Crime, Corporate Law, and the Perversion of Democracy* (Toronto: Between the Lines, 2002) p 147:

> Often, distinct legal entities operate under the same general corporate umbrella, so that, in the end, a multitude of people—not always legally linked—play a role in the thinking and doing that, together, make up the corporate conduct that is the object of investigation. The authorities find it difficult to identify any one person,

let alone the requisite senior person, as having had the legally required intention and hands-on participation.

Other, alternative approaches to corporate responsibility have been tried, but bring with them their own difficulties. One alternative approach, which has been taken up in the *Criminal Code* (Cth), is to look to 'corporate culture' as a way of proving the authorisation of an offence. This approach draws on the work of Professor Brent Fisse on corporate liability: 'Corporate Criminal Responsibility' (1991) 15 Crim LJ 166 at 173; B Fisse, 'Criminal Law: The Attribution of Criminal Liability to Corporations: A Statutory Model' (1991) 13 *Sydney Law Review* 277 at 281 ff, 286; B Fisse and J Braithwaite, *Corporations, Crime and Accountability* (Cambridge: Cambridge University Press, 1993).

'Corporate culture' is defined as 'an attitude, policy, rule, course of conduct or practice existing within the body corporate generally or in the part of the body corporate in which the relevant activities take place': *Criminal Code* (Cth) s 12.3(6). In its Final Report on *General Principles of Criminal Liability* (Canberra: AGPS, December 1992) pp 112–13, the MCCOC explained that this idea would allow 'the prosecution to lead evidence that the company's unwritten rules tacitly authorised non-compliance or failed to create a culture of compliance. It would catch situations where, despite formal documents appearing to require compliance, the reality was that non-compliance was expected. For example, employees who know that if they do not break the law to meet production schedules (eg by removing safety guards on equipment) they will be dismissed'.

The *Criminal Code* (Cth) also contains provisions dealing with negligent actions by a corporation: ss 5.5, 12.4. Negligence may be evidenced by inadequate corporate management, control or supervision of the conduct of one or more of the corporation's employees, agents or officers or by the failure to provide adequate systems for conveying relevant information to relevant persons in the body corporate: s 12.4(3).

The provisions in the *Criminal Code* (Cth) may go some way towards securing a greater measure of corporate accountability, but the problem with the 'corporate culture' approach is that some critical theorists would argue that rule breaking is expected and condoned within corporations due to ideals such as market efficiency. Alan Norrie writes in *Crime, Reason and History: A Critical Introduction to the Criminal Law* (2nd edn, London: Butterworths, 2001) p 105:

> If a company's grossly inadequate safety standards lead to death and injury, is that a matter for liability, or simply a regrettable fact of life in a world of profit-driven motivation? The answer to that question can only be political, but it is precisely the connection between crime and politics that the criminal law has sought to obscure in relation to 'ordinary' crime for a hundred and fifty years. Once again, the crimes of the powerful and the way they are treated cast a powerful, critical light on the crimes of the powerless and how they are treated.

Another approach to corporate liability is to follow the model of environmental protection legislation that exists in some jurisdictions whereby senior company officials are nominated as those personally liable for breaches of legislation by the company. Andrew Hopkins suggests that nominated accountability has caused directors of large companies to take their organisation's environmental responsibilities very seriously: *Making Safety Work: Getting Management Commitment to Occupational Health and Safety* (St Leonard's: Allen & Unwin, 1995) pp 105–7. However, the idea of nominating an individual to bear responsibility does not sit well with traditional notions of holding only blameworthy individuals criminally responsible for their actions.

A further problem associated with corporate criminal responsibility lies in the sanctions that may be enforced against a corporation. In *R v Denbo Pty Ltd & Timothy Ian Nadenbousch* unreported, 14 June 1994, SC of Vic, Teague J, the accused corporation pleaded guilty to manslaughter resulting from a workplace death. One of the corporation's truck drivers died in a truck accident after attempting to drive down a steep incline of which he had not been warned. The truck itself had faulty brakes and the manslaughter charge was based on the argument that the corporation had failed to set up an adequate maintenance system for its plant and vehicles, had failed to train its employees properly, and had allowed the truck to be used without proper maintenance. Teague J fined the corporation $120,000. However, by that stage, the company was in liquidation so the punishment was ineffectual.

There is some reason to believe that such a fine only has a limited deterrent effect, particularly if the company is large: S Perrone, 'Workplace Fatalities and the Adequacy of Prosecutions' (1995) 13(1) *Law in Context* 81–105 at 100. A law and economics approach to the matter of fines is that unless the penalty is hurting the corporation financially, it is of little benefit. One of the basic concepts of economic theories is that of cost–benefit analysis. That is, the true cost of choosing to do something is measured in terms of the opportunities that are sacrificed to do it. If members of a corporation know that the costs of failing to set up an adequate maintenance system will be higher than the initial outlay on maintenance, they will take steps to put it in place: R Johnstone, 'Economic and Sociological Approaches to Law' in R Hunter, R Ingleby and R Johnstone (eds), *Thinking About Law* (St Leonards: Allen & Unwin, 1995) pp 61–85. One example, explored further in Chapter 3, concerns a small car called the Pinto, which was sold by Ford USA throughout the 1970s. Crash tests during design of the vehicle showed that in rear-end crashes over 25 miles per hour, the petrol tank always ruptured. There was evidence from an internal company memorandum that a cost–benefit analysis had been carried out that led to the decision not to correct the faulty design. However, the cost–benefit analysis failed to take into account the substantial civil damages that were subsequently awarded to the families of those who died or were seriously injured when the petrol tank burst into flames in rear-end collisions.

Brent Fisse has suggested that other forms of sanctions apart from fines should be used in sentencing companies such as adverse publicity orders, punitive injunctions and liquidation orders: 'Sentencing Options Against Corporations' (1990) 1(2) *Criminal Law Forum* 211. See also J Braithwaite and B Fisse, *The Impact of Publicity on Corporate Offenders* (Albany: State University of New York Press, 1983). There may be different motivations and attitudes expressed by company directors towards compliance: P Grabosky and J Braithwaite, *Of Matters Gentle: Enforcement Strategies of Australian Business Regulatory Agencies* (Melbourne: Oxford University Press and the Australian Institute of Criminology, 1986). It remains to be seen whether or not such sanctions would have an effect on a structure that is built around economic motivation.

Overall then, the concept of individual criminal responsibility does not fit easily with the creation of the corporation as a legal entity. The failure to define many actions by corporations as criminal has its roots in political and social history. The failure to see some corporate activities as criminal and the failure to gain convictions in the rare cases where corporations are prosecuted can partly be explained by the limits of individual responsibility as a method of social control.

Reason and rationality in the criminal law

The Enlightenment, the intellectual movement that was predominant in the Western world during the eighteenth century, saw the development of the idea of reason as the source of progress in knowledge. From René Descartes' theories onwards, reason was seen as the means of constructing theoretical ideals upon which systems of thought and practice could be structured. For example, the French and American revolutions sought to replace the feudal notions of privilege with egalitarian societies embodying the notions of reason and progress.

The idea of the rational individual also has its roots in the Enlightenment. For example, the normative works on punishment of Cesare Beccaria in Italy and Jeremy Bentham in England rely on the notion of rational individuals who possess free will and whose primary motivation is to maximise pleasure and minimise pain: C Beccaria, *On Crimes and Punishment*, H Paolucci (trans) (Indianapolis: Bobbs-Merrill Educational, 1963, first English edn 1767); J Bowring (ed), *The Works of Jeremy Bentham* (New York: Russell and Russell, 1962). They reasoned that if a rational person knows that a particular, painful punishment will almost certainly follow the commission of a particular crime, he or she would not commit the crime. Margaret Davies explains in *Asking the Law Question* (2nd edn, Sydney: Lawbook Co, 2002) p 300:

> [The] idea of a unified actor who is independent and rational forms the basis not only of many areas of substantive law, but also of the idea of law itself, as it has been traditionally presented. In substantive law, it is clearly a notion of the autonomous thinking and acting subject which underlies the criminal law, contract,

torts, and so on. The system is constructed as a coming together of lots of these independent rational units, who simply act and react on each other.

In the criminal law, the focus on reason as an ideal together with the rational individual came together in the objective standard of the 'reasonable man'. Although this has developed into the 'ordinary person' in some areas of the criminal law, feminist authors have suggested the ideal largely remains that of the reasonable man.

The influence of reason and rationality in the criminal law will be examined by focusing on three areas, that of legal reasoning, the rational actor and the reasonable man test.

Legal reasoning and rationality

The common law has traditionally been seen as something that cannot be understood through 'natural' reasoning, but only by legal reasoning that has accumulated over a period of time and is articulated through the doctrine of precedent. Legal reasoning is seen as a method of reaching correct decisions that only those who have been educated in the law can understand. Thus, individual judges do not determine the law through personal opinions, but through applying legal reason. Legal education is therefore all about teaching students to 'think like a lawyer'. For example, Sir Edward Coke proclaimed in the *Case of Prohibitions del Roy* (1607) 12 Co Rep 63; 77 ER 1342 at 1343 that common law cases 'were not to be decided by natural reason but by the artificial reason and judgment of law, which law is an act [sic] which requires long study and experience'.

Jeremy Bentham described this view of the common law as 'dog law': J Bowring (ed), *The Works of Jeremy Bentham* (New York: Russell and Russell, 1962) Vol 5 at 235:

> When your dog does anything you want to break him of, you wait till he does it, and then beat him for it. This is the way you make laws for your dog: and this is the way the judges make law for you and me. They won't tell a man beforehand what it is he *should not* do...they lie by till he has done something which they say he should not *have done*, and then they hang him for it. [Emphasis in original.]

Bentham saw the common law as an incoherent 'mass of rubbish' and lacking in rationality. His criticisms have been echoed in realist and critical legal studies perspectives of the law. Bentham's aim, however, was to replace the common law with a comprehensive legal code similar to the Codes of continental Europe. The aims of realist and critical legal studies scholars have been much more diverse and more responsive to the social context in which laws have developed and operated.

In relation to the criminal law, a commitment to the rationality of the law is seen as a central legal principle. In many criminal law texts, general principles are seen as natural and ahistorical and legal reasoning the method of discovering them. This has been criticised by a number of scholars. For example, Nicola Lacey has viewed the attempt to find universal principles in areas such as the search for meaning of intention as not only elusive, but also illusory: 'A Clear Concept of Intention: Elusive or Illusory?' (1993) 56 *Modern Law Review* 621–42. She writes (at 637) that the contradictions that exist within the criminal law are 'symptomatic of deeper substantive political questions that cannot be submerged by doctrinal rationalization or by formal conceptual analysis'.

Alan Norrie has shown that many areas of the criminal law are neither rational nor principled: *Crime, Reason and History: A Critical Introduction to the Criminal Law* (2nd edn, London: Butterworths, 2001). He writes that the origins of modern criminal law must be seen against a background of social and political conflict such that any principles are historic and relative.

From Norrie's perspective, it is necessary to understand that while the criminal law can be seen as irrational, this does not mean that 'anything goes'. Rather, there is a tension between the normative principle of rationality and the historical limits of such a principle. It is through being aware of this tension, that theoretical progress can be made.

Historical analysis can lead to a complex and more comprehensive understanding of the criminal law than positivist conceptions allow. Lindsay Farmer suggests that melding historical and procedural perspectives can give a fuller overview of the process of criminalisation. He refers to this as 'critical positivism': *Criminal Law, Tradition and Legal Order* (Cambridge: Cambridge University Press, 1997).

In this book, we wish to move away from legal reasoning as an attempt to find universal principles of responsibility that are applicable to *all* crimes. Through drawing on broad critical perspectives we aim to move towards an appreciation of the complex social context of criminal laws.

The rational actor

As stated above, the rational individual legal subject was a powerful ideal that developed during the Enlightenment. For postmodern theorists, the presence of such a being presupposes the possibility of the opposite. For Foucault, madness can be seen as the 'other' against which reason is defined: *Madness and Civilisation: A History of Insanity in the Age of Reason* (London: Tavistock, 1967). In the criminal law, the notion that those with some form of mental illness lack the ability to reason has long been found in laws excusing them from responsibility for criminal acts. The other antithetical category to that of the rational actor is that of the child.

These categories of the insane and children as the 'other' may be found in Roman law through Justinian's codification in the sixth century that '[a]n infant or a madman who kills a man is not liable under the *lex cornelia*, the one being protected by the innocence of his intent, the other excused by the misfortune of his condition': *The Digest of Justinian*, T Mommsen (trans), P Krueger and A Watson (eds) (Pennsylvania: University of Pennsylvania Press, 1985) Book Forty-Eight, 8.12. The same conclusion was reached in Henrici de Bracton's first systematic treatise on the laws and customs of England when he stated that the 'lack of reason in committing the act' excused the madman and 'the innocence of design' protected the infant from the boundaries of the criminal law: Henrici de Bracton, *De Legibus et Consuetudinibus Angliae* 135b, quoted in FB Sayre, 'Mens Rea' (1932) *Harvard Law Review* 974–1026 at 985–6.

Mental illness

Foucault has analysed the way in which certain marginalised individuals, particularly the mentally ill, have been treated by society: *Madness and Civilisation: A History of Insanity in the Age of Reason* (London: Tavistock, 1967). He argues that the process of confinement of the mentally ill developed in conjunction with the notion of reason. Reason and madness did not naturally exist, but were formulated as dominant and mutually exclusive discourses in the context of forms of social control.

Modern conceptions of the insanity defence generally serve to exculpate an accused from criminal responsibility because of the accused's inability to know the nature and quality of the conduct or that the conduct was wrong. In some jurisdictions, there is an added component that the mental disorder caused an inability to control the accused's conduct. The law completely disregards the social circumstances in which the person's mental illness may have occurred. The law relating to defences dealing with mental disorder will be explored in Chapter 11.

The law's view of mental illness as 'unreason' contrasts with the aims of the psychiatric profession to find the physiological causes of mental illness in order to treat the illness. A person's inability to reason is only one potential symptom of mental illness. The tension between law and psychiatry was seen historically in murder cases when punishment was the execution of the offender. Psychiatrists were forced to use classificatory systems as a way of saving a person from execution. The legal concept of assigning blame to those considered rational was viewed with disdain by psychiatrists while lawyers viewed psychiatrists as letting sane people who deserved to be executed get away with murder. The abolition of capital punishment in the UK and Australia has somewhat alleviated the differing aims of law and psychiatry in assigning criminal responsibility as against classification and treatment. However, in the jurisdictions of the USA where capital punishment is still allowed, the tensions between the law and psychiatry are still very much present: A Stone, 'The Ethical Boundaries of Forensic Psychiatry: A View from the Ivory Tower' (1984) 12(3) *Bulletin of the American Academy of Psychiatry and Law* 209–19.

Children

Like those with some form of mental impairment, children have traditionally been viewed as lacking the ability to reason. For example, Aristotle associated children with animals because of their lack of reason and rational desire: Aristotle, *The Nichomachean Ethics*, T Irwin (trans) (Indianapolis: Hackett Publishing Co, 1985) i 9 1100a1. In the criminal law, children under a certain age have been exempted from criminal responsibility because of their incapacity to understand the consequences of their acts and because they have not fully developed an appreciation of the difference between right and wrong. The minimum age for criminal responsibility varies from jurisdiction to jurisdiction. At common law, there is an irrebuttable presumption that a child aged seven or under cannot be guilty of a crime: Sir William Holdsworth, *A History of English Law* (London: Sweet & Maxwell, 1966) Vol 3, at 372; Sir James Stephen, *A History of the Criminal Law of England* (3rd edn, London: Richard Clay & Sons, 1883) Vol 2, p 98. In Tasmania, the phrase used is 'under seven years of age': *Criminal Code* (Tas) s 18(1).

In the Australian Capital Territory, Victoria, New South Wales, the Northern Territory, South Australia, Queensland and Western Australia, the minimum age of criminal responsibility has been raised to 10 years, so that a person under that age cannot be found guilty of a crime: *Criminal Code* (ACT) s 25; *Children and Young Persons Act* 1989 (Vic) s 127; *Children (Criminal Proceedings) Act* 1985 (NSW) s 5; *Young Offenders Act* 1993 (SA) s 5; *Criminal Code* (WA) s 29; *Criminal Code* (Qld) s 29(1); *Criminal Code* (NT) s 38(1). This is the position taken also in s 7.1 of the *Criminal Code* (Cth). This general minimum age of 10 is very much a construct as to a child's capacity to distinguish between right and wrong. Much higher minimum ages apply in certain European countries: T Crofts, *The Criminal Responsibility of Children and Young Persons: A Comparison of English and German Law* (Aldershot: Ashgate, 2002).

Having a minimum age of criminal responsibility is occasionally questioned, particularly when a serious crime is committed by a child. For example, in New South Wales, the 1999 manslaughter trial of an eleven-year-old boy for throwing his six-year-old companion, Corey Davis, into a river attracted widespread comment from judges, politicians and the public. The Director of Public Prosecutions, Nicholas Cowdrey brought an ex-officio indictment against the boy after Magistrate Stephen Scarlett dismissed the charge at the committal hearing. The boy was subsequently acquitted by the jury: R Phillips, 'Young Boy Acquitted of Manslaughter', 9 December 1999, *World Socialist Web Site*, <http://www.wsws.org/articles/1999/dec1999/tria-d09_prn.shtml>, accessed 11 June 2003. The murder of two-year-old James Bulger in Liverpool, England, by Robert Thompson and Jon Venables, both of whom were aged 10 at the time, also gave rise to much public concern and outrage. The trial was held in the Preston Crown Court before Morland J in November 1993. Alan Norrie analyses the responses in the context of law's hegemony over such events: 'Legal and Moral Judgment in the "General" Part' in P Rush, S McVeigh and A Young (eds), *Criminal Legal Doctrine* (Aldershot: Ashgate/Dartmouth Publishing Company Limited, 1997) 1 at 4–8. Norrie argues that the law's division between guilt and innocence and good and bad sets the agenda for other responses. These simplistic dichotomies fail to take into account the broader environment and social conditions in which the boys were raised.

In *R v Secretary of State for the Home Department, ex parte Venables; R v Secretary of State for the Home Department, ex parte Thompson* [1997] 3 WLR 23 at 76, Lord Hope of Craighead pointed out that had the two boys been born a few months earlier, they could not have been held responsible for the killing because they would have been deemed not criminally responsible. The accused boys subsequently complained to the European Court of Human Rights that they had been denied a fair trial: *T v The United Kingdom and V v The United Kingdom* unreported, 16 December 1999, Eur Court HR Strasbourg; Application No 00024724/94. There was evidence that the accused had found the trial distressing and frightening and had not been able to concentrate during it. The Court held by sixteen votes to one that there had been a violation of the right to a fair trial under Article 6 of the *European Convention on Human Rights*. This was on the basis that given the accused boys' immaturity and emotional state and the tense courtroom and public scrutiny, they would not have been capable of consulting with their lawyers and giving them information for the purposes of their defence.

The main rationale behind treating children as not criminally responsible is that they are viewed as somehow morally different to adults. This has been questioned by social science researchers who argue that children and adolescents' moral reasoning, in the sense of knowing the difference between right and wrong, may be very similar to that of adults. See, for example: T Grisso, 'Society's Retributive Response to Juvenile Violence: A Developmental Perspective' (1996) 20 *Law and Human Behavior* 229–47; JL Woolard, ND Repucci and RE Redding, 'Theoretical and Methodological Issues in Studying Children's Capacities in Legal Contexts' (1996) 20 *Law and Human Behavior* 219–28; L Steinberg and E Cauffman, 'Maturity of Judgement in Adolescence: Psychosocial Factors in Adolescent Decision Making' (1996) 20 *Law and Human Behavior* 249–72; ES Scott, ND Reppucci and JL Woolard, 'Evaluating Adolescent Decision Making in Legal Contexts' (1995) 19 *Law and Human Behavior* 221–44. The main difference between children and adolescents as compared to adults is that children differ in relation to judgment and self-control. Stephen Morse writes in 'Immaturity and Irresponsibility' (1998) 88(1) *The Journal of Criminal Law and Criminology* 15–67 at 53 that adolescents '(1) have a stronger preference for risk and novelty; (2) subjectively assess the potentially negative consequences of risky conduct less unfavorably; (3) tend to be impulsive and more concerned with short-term than long-term consequences; (4) subjectively experience and assess the passage of time and time periods as longer; and (5) are more susceptible to peer pressure'. Morse argues that differential treatment of children because of these findings is a normative judgment that only society can make.

The way in which children have been treated by the criminal law has differed markedly according to societal concepts of childhood. In the seventeenth and eighteenth centuries, children were treated as miniature adults and were subject to fierce punishments such as whipping, branding and even hanging: I Pinchbeck and M Hewitt, *Children in English Society* (London: Routledge and Kegan Paul, 1973) Vol 1. It was only during the nineteenth century that children began to be treated differently and only at the turn of the twentieth century that separate courts for children's crime were established in common law countries: JN Turner, 'The James Bulger Case: A Challenge to Juvenile Justice Theories' (1994) 68(8) *Law Institute Journal* 734–7 at 735; F Gale, N Naffine and J Wundersitz (eds), *Juvenile Justice: Debating the Issues* (St Leonards: Allen & Unwin, 1993); A Borowski and I O'Connor (eds), *Juvenile Crime, Justice and Corrections* (South Melbourne: Addison Wesley Longman, 1997).

When a child reaches the age of 14 he or she is regarded as an adult in terms of criminal responsibility. A problem arises as to how to treat those children of and over the minimum age of criminal responsibility but below the age of 14. A legal presumption developed that once a child reaches the age of minimum criminal responsibility but is under the age of 14 he or she does not know the difference between right and wrong. This is sometimes referred to by the Latin term *doli incapax* (incapable of wrongdoing). The presumption can be rebutted by evidence that the child did in fact know the difference between right and wrong. The common law presumption has been replaced by legislation in certain jurisdictions: *Criminal Code* 1995 (Cth) s 7.2; *Crimes Act* 1914 (Cth) s 4N; *Criminal Code* (ACT) s 26; *Children and Young People Act* (ACT) s 71(2); *Criminal Code* (NT) s 38(2); *Criminal Code* (Qld) s 29(2); *Criminal Code* (Tas) s 18(2); *Criminal Code* (WA) s 29. A rationale for the presumption is that it protects children from the 'full rigour of criminal law enforcement': B Fisse, *Howard's Criminal Law* (5th edn, Sydney: Law Book Co, 1990) pp 479–80.

The presumption that a child between the minimum age of criminal responsibility and 14 is incapable of committing a crime was severely criticised by Laws J sitting in the Divisional Court of Queen's Bench Division in *C (A Minor) v DPP* [1994] 3 WLR 888 (CA). In that case, two twelve-year-old boys were caught tampering with a motorcycle. One boy held the handlebars while the other used a crowbar in an attempt to force open the padlock and chain around the motorcycle. The police approached on foot and one chased C, who climbed a wall, but who was then caught by another officer. C was convicted of interfering with a motorcycle with the intention to commit theft. The magistrate considered a submission that C was *doli incapax*, but held that the presumption had been rebutted on the basis that it could be inferred from C's running away and the criminal damage that C knew that what he was doing was wrong. The Divisional Court dismissed C's appeal on the basis that the presumption of *doli incapax* was outdated and should be treated as being no longer good law.

In the course of his judgment, Laws J criticised (at 895–6) the presumption on a number of grounds. One criticism was that the presumption operated in favour of children with impoverished backgrounds and antisocial tendencies:

It must surely nowadays be regarded as obvious that, where a morally impoverished upbringing may have led a teenager into crime, the facts of his [or her] background should not go to his [or her] guilt, but to his [or her] mitigation; the very emphasis placed in modern penal policy upon the desirability of non-custodial disposal designed to be remedial rather than retributive...offers powerful support for the view that delinquents...who may know no better than to commit anti-social and sometimes dangerous crimes, should not be held immune from the criminal justice system, but sensibly managed within it.

The judgment of the Divisional Court was overturned by the House of Lords, which held that abolition of the presumption was a matter for Parliament: *C (A Minor) v DPP* [1995] 2 WLR 383 (HL). Lord Lowry stated (at 38) that the prosecution must prove beyond reasonable doubt that the child knew that his or her act was wrong as distinct from an act of 'mere naughtiness or childish mischief'. Secondly, the prosecution must prove this from the evidence and not presume it from the mere commission of the act. In *R v CRH* unreported, 18 December 1996, CCA of NSW, BC9606725, the New South Wales Court of Criminal Appeal reviewed the English and Australian cases on *doli incapax* and held that the law as expressed by Lord Lowry in *C*'s case is the law in Australia. In *R v F, ex parte Attorney-General* [1999] 2 Qd R 157, Davies JA, with whom McPherson JJA and Shepherdson J agreed, clarified that while the mere commission of the act will not be enough to rebut the presumption, the surrounding circumstances of the commission of the act may go to prove the relevant capacity to know that the act was wrong. The presumption was subsequently abolished by the *Crime and Disorder Act* 1998 (UK), but it remains firmly in place in Australia.

This outline of how those considered insane and those under a certain age are considered in the law as unable to reason very much reflects the social context of how such individuals are perceived. The ideal of the rational individual legal subject means that the social issues underlying the problems of those with mental illness and children who commit crimes can be obscured. In reality, many people may have difficulty with moral reasoning and certainly many have trouble following the legalities of a criminal trial. Questions have been raised in particular concerning the language and cultural barriers faced by Indigenous people in criminal trials: D Mildren, 'Redressing the Imbalance Against Aboriginals in the Criminal Justice System' (1997) 21 Crim LJ 7–22. Such individuals are still held criminally responsible for their behaviour.

Alan Norrie, concentrating on the competing legal and psychiatric conceptions of madness is of the view that it is necessary to integrate analyses of social and individual conduct rather than purely relying on the artificial construct of the rational individual: *Crime, Reason and History: A Critical Introduction to Criminal Law* (2nd edn, London: Butterworths, 2001). He writes (at 196): '[T]he underlying social conditions, which generate madness and reproduce mad crime, remain all the while untouched and untreated. Despite the evidence of the dramatic causes célèbres, the legal-psychiatric complex combines to process the individual symptoms of a desperate social problem without ever getting to its roots.'

The first step is to recognise that the rational individual is an ideal that is a product of historical processes. This reinforces Mark Kelman's idea that notwithstanding the rhetorical commitment to rationalism in the criminal law, determinism plays a significant, yet suppressed role: 'Interpretive Construction in the Substantive Criminal Law' (1981) 33 *Stanford Law Review* 591–673. The challenge of course is to move beyond the notion of rationalism in an attempt to fully address the problems that occur in assigning criminal responsibility to some and not others without appreciating the social context of their behaviour.

The reasonable man

In the previous section, we outlined how the idea of the rational individual that arose during the Enlightenment was an ideal one. Alan Norrie writes in *Crime, Reason and History: A Critical Introduction* (2nd edn, London: Butterworths, 2001) p 29:

> It was the image of 'man' as either a metaphysical or a calculating self-interested being, conceived of in an asocial way…Here is one key to understanding the nature of modern criminal law. At its heart there exists a 'responsible individual', or rather a universe of equally responsible individuals, regarded in isolation from the real world, the social and moral contexts in which crime occurs of which they are part. The legal categories rarely take the realities of crime and conflict on board.

Seeing the rational actor as an ideal helps explain how the concept of 'the reasonable man' became enshrined in the criminal law as an objective standard against which certain behaviour could be measured. In relation to the law of provocation, the 'reasonable man' test developed as a way of controlling the scope of the defence. In *R v Welsh* (1869) 11 Cox 336, Keating J stated (at 338): 'The law contemplates the case of the reasonable man, and requires that the provocation shall be such as that such a man might naturally be induced, in the anger of the moment, to commit the act.'

The 'reasonable man' still crops up in the defence of necessity. In *R v Loughnan* [1981] VR 443 at 448, the test was stated as 'would a reasonable man in the position of the accused have considered that he had any alternative to doing what he did to avoid the peril?' With provocation, however, the reasonable man has developed into the ordinary person. As will be explored further in Chapter 10, Barwick CJ in *Moffa v The Queen* (1977) 138 CLR 601 at 606 noted that it is preferable to characterise the objective standard in terms of an ordinary rather than a reasonable person because the use of the term 'reasonable' might be taken as excluding severe emotional reactions from consideration. The reasonable, rather than the ordinary, person still appears in tests for criminal negligence.

The notion of the ordinary person also ties in with the ideal of the rational individual already discussed. In the defence of duress, in Australian jurisdictions other than Queensland, Tasmania and Western Australia, there is a requirement that the circumstances must have been such that a person of 'ordinary firmness of mind' would have yielded to the threat in the way the accused did. Similarly, the ordinary person crops up when courts attempt to distinguish between sane and insane automatism. In *R v Falconer* (1990) 171 CLR 30 Toohey J, Mason CJ, Brennan and McHugh JJ proposed an objective standard gloss to the sound/unsound mind distinction. They stated (at 55):

> [T]he law must postulate a standard of mental strength which, in the face of a given level of psychological trauma, is capable of protecting the mind from malfunction to the extent prescribed in the respective definitions of insanity. That standard must be the standard of the ordinary person: if the mind's strength is below that standard, the mind is infirm; if it is of or above that standard, the mind is sound or sane. This is an objective standard which corresponds with the objective standard imported for the purpose of provocation.

Objective standards of behaviour posed by reasonable or ordinary person tests are predicated on the existence of a 'community consensus' about what constitutes reasonable and ordinary behaviour. They also reflect a community of white males. Carol Gilligan has pointed out that women and men may subscribe to different standards of risk and to different expectations of levels of care and levels of self-serving or self-sacrificing behaviour within a society: *In a Different Voice: Psychological Theory and Women's Development* (Cambridge, MA: Harvard University Press, 1982). There may also be widely different standards and values between the currently dominant white community and groups with different racial or ethnic backgrounds.

Gender and race are also significant in particular areas of criminal law. For example, in relation to the defence of provocation, replacing the reasonable man with the genderless ordinary person may give lip service to the reaction of women who kill. It does not, however, address the historical origin of the defence that was based on a man killing his wife and/or lover after finding them together. This was seen as the ultimate insult: J Horder, *Provocation and Responsibility* (Oxford: Clarendon Press, 1992). It also fails to recognise the gendered nature of a sudden violent response to an insult. While some feminist scholars see the defence as fatally flawed, others have endeavoured to recast concepts of the reasonable or ordinary person into more inclusive terms. This will be explored further in Chapter 10.

Similarly, there is an ongoing debate as to whether the ordinary person should be imbued with an accused's race in relation to provocation. Denying racial characteristics reinforces the ordinary person as being white. On the other hand, imbuing the person with specific racial or ethnic characteristics may lead to stereotyping of racial groups: S Bronitt and K Amirthalingam, 'Cultural Blindness and the Criminal Law' (1996) 20(2) *Alternative Law Journal* 58–64.

Even if the reasonable or ordinary person can be identified, the objective standard poses severe problems for those people who may have a physical or intellectual disability. For example, in *R v Stone and Dobinson* [1977] 1 QB 354 the two accused, a 67-year-old man and a 43-year-old woman, both of whom had physical and intellectual disabilities, were convicted of manslaughter by negligent omission after the male accused's sister died from toxaemia and prolonged immobilisation. There was evidence that the sister suffered from anorexia nervosa and when she died she weighed only five stone and five pounds. The victim was found dead in bed in 'a scene of dreadful degradation' (at 359). She was soaked in urine and excreta and had ulcers on her legs that contained maggots. Both accused had made some ineffectual attempts to obtain medical attention for the sister and the female accused had given her food. On appeal, the Court of Appeal held that both accused had undertaken a duty of care for the woman and that they had been criminally negligent in failing to give her proper care.

The facts of this case show that the objective standard can operate harshly against those who have a physical or intellectual disability. The Victorian Law Reform Commission was critical of the Court of Appeal's decision in *Stone and Dobinson* and recommended that special circumstances exist where an accused is incapable of meeting a reasonableness standard: Law Reform Commission of Victoria, *Homicide*, Report No 40 (Melbourne: LRCV, 1991) p 116. The Commission proposed that any person charged with manslaughter by criminal negligence should be afforded a defence if by reason of some physical or intellectual disability he or she could not reach the standard expected from non-disabled persons. This issue is further discussed in Chapter 3.

The problems associated with the 'reasonable person' will be taken up in Part 5 of this book when we consider criminal defences. Suffice to say that replacing the reasonable man with the reasonable or ordinary person does little to change the underlying historical context of objective standards of behaviour.

Conclusion

This introductory chapter has sought to show that there is no single definition or concept of crime and criminal laws. Rather, there is a range of very different and often conflicting perspectives on the nature and function of criminal laws. Many textbooks are constrained to presenting a positivist account of crime. In contrast, we want to open up the criminal law to analyses from a number of critical perspectives.

Many of the underlying assumptions of positivist accounts of the criminal law, such as individual criminal responsibility, rationality and legal reasoning, the rational actor and the reasonable man, must be viewed in their historical context. Adopting broader critical perspectives beyond positivist conceptions of the criminal law allows more realistic accounts of current laws and encourages debate about law reform endeavours.

CHAPTER 2

Structuring criminal law

Introduction

On 1 April 1992, the Consultative Committee of State and Territorial Law Admitting Authorities, chaired by Mr Justice Priestley, prescribed eleven 'areas of knowledge' that law students must successfully study before admission to practice. This prescribed set of law subjects, which became known as the 'Priestley Eleven', has become embodied in rules and regulations of each state and territory in Australia. In relation to the criminal law, the prescribed course requires the teaching of offences of homicide, non-fatal offences against the person, offences against property and relevant defences. It also requires the teaching of a selection of topics dealing with the elements of criminal procedure and other topics such as attempts and participation in crime. While the Priestley criminal law syllabus provides some flexibility in topics covered, it makes no mention of any required understanding of the context of criminal offences and defences. It also emphasises offences against the person and property offences to the exclusion of other crimes such as drug and public order offences: S Bronitt and B McSherry, *Principles of Criminal Law* (Sydney: LBC Information Services, 2001) p vi.

The Priestley Eleven also refers to an approach to teaching topics to provide 'knowledge of the general doctrines of criminal law'. This presumes that there are clearly identifiable general doctrines. Andrew Ashworth writes in 'Is the Criminal Law a Lost Cause?' (2000) 116 *The Law Quarterly Review* 225–56 at 225:

> The number of offences in English criminal law continues to grow year by year. Politicians, pressure groups, journalists and others often express themselves as if the creation of a new criminal offence is the natural, or the only appropriate, response to a particular event or series of events giving rise to social concern. At

the same time, criminal offences are tacked on to diverse statutes by various governement departments, and then enacted (or, often, re-enacted) by Parliament without demur. There is little sense that the decision to introduce a new offence should only be made after certain conditions have been satisfied, little sense that making conduct criminal is a step of considerable social significance. It is this unprincipled and chaotic construction of the criminal law that prompts the question whether it is a lost cause.

This quotation highlights that, in reality, statutory crimes are usually enacted without any recourse to general doctrines or principles of criminal law. This book will follow the Priestley approach of structuring criminal law into specific offences and defences, but will examine them from a range of critical perspectives. As set out in Chapter 1, our view is that the context of criminal laws should not be seen as an optional extra, but as a necessity for understanding the way in which criminal laws have developed and continue to develop. The current book differs from previous works by introducing the specific offences and defences through the facts of individual cases. Peter Brooks writes in P Brooks and P Gewirtz (eds), *Law's Stories: Narrative and Rhetoric in the Law* (New Haven: Yale University Press, 1996) pp 16–17 that '[narrative] is indeed omnipresent in the law, something that has no doubt always been recognised but has rarely been attended to in an analytic manner'. We have chosen narratives from particular cases to highlight current problems with the law. Jenny Morgan has made the point that factual tales, particularly those concerning alleged provocation by women, are filtered as they move through the court and appeal processes: 'Provocation Law and Facts: Dead Women Tell No Tales, Tales are Told About Them' (1997) 21 *Melbourne University Law Review* 237–76. We highlight the facts of certain key cases in order to emphasise that the development of criminal laws is very much grounded in human stories and often tragic circumstances. The structure of the chapters on specific offences and defences is therefore different to the norm because it explores individual cases, sets out the current law, then provides a critique of the law through the use of those cases.

This chapter provides an introduction to the offences and defences that will be examined in the remainder of the book and the elements of 'serious' offences—physical and fault elements, the requirement of concurrence and the issue of causation—that are usually covered in texts on criminal laws.

Offences

Offences were traditionally divided into felonies and misdemeanours in order to distinguish between the types of punishment that applied. Felonies resulted in the death penalty and the forfeiture of the felon's property to the Crown.

Misdemeanours were less serious offences punishable by imprisonment or fine. The division between the two types of offences lost its significance in relation to punishment when capital punishment and forfeiture were abolished. However, the division still lingers in relation to the manner in which the offences are tried.

While terminology differs among the Australian jurisdictions, serious offences (referred to as 'indictable' in the common law states and 'crimes' in the Code jurisdictions) are tried before a judge and jury whereas less serious offences (referred to as 'summary' in the common law states and 'simple' or 'regulatory' in the Code jurisdictions) are tried before a magistrate. There are also 'hybrid' offences that enable an accused to elect to be tried before a single judge sitting without a jury.

The overwhelming majority of offences (96 per cent) are processed in Magistrates' Courts: Australian Institute of Criminology, *Australian Crime: Facts and Figures 2002* p 55. In 2001, of those accused of serious offences, 69 per cent pleaded guilty: Australian Institute of Criminology, *Australian Crime: Facts and Figures 2001* p 76. Serious offences determined by a judge and jury can therefore be viewed as exceptional. What law students study in the Priestley criminal law syllabus is thus skewed, given that the focus is on appeal cases that usually deal with serious offences that have gone to trial.

In Part 2 of this book, we examine offences against the person—homicide, assault and sexual assault—and in Part 3, offences against property. These are usually seen as the key offences that law students must study and that reflect key societal values. Of course, other offences such as drug and public order offences may be seen as equally socially significant.

In Part 4, we look at ways in which criminal responsibility can be extended through 'inchoate' offences and the doctrine of complicity. The term 'inchoate' is not one in general use. It stems from the Latin *inchoare*, which means to start work on; inchoate offences are therefore offences or behaviour that are only partly formed or just begun. There are three 'inchoate' offences: namely, attempts, conspiracy and incitement. In general, the common thread among these crimes is that they are committed even though the substantive offence that was intended is not completed and no harm is caused.

In Parts 2, 3 and 4, we structure each chapter by analysing a particular case, then describing the current state of the law and providing a critique of it.

Defences

In Part 5, we critically examine defences to homicide and to serious criminal offences such as assault. While the doctrine of mistake could merit a chapter in its own right, we confine looking at mistake and physical impossibility to the chapter on inchoate offences. Defences operate in different ways and with different limitations. Some defences such as provocation and infanticide are considered partial defences in that they operate to reduce intentional killing from murder to manslaughter. Others, such as self-defence and automatism, are complete defences to all serious crimes and operate to give an acquittal to the accused.

It is important to note that because of the prevalence of summary proceedings and pleas of guilty, the raising of defences in a jury trial occurs rarely. Obviously, whether or not there is evidence leading to a defence or defences will affect the decision to plead guilty.

Defence counsel has discretion as to which defences, if any, will be raised at trial. For example, there is some data suggesting that the defences of self-defence and provocation are raised in about a quarter of homicide cases. In a study of all prosecutions for murder and manslaughter in Victoria between 1981 and 1987, the Law Reform Commission of Victoria found that duress was raised in only four cases (1.3 per cent) and necessity was not raised at all. This is not surprising given that duress and necessity at common law are not available as defences to murder, although they may be available on a manslaughter charge: *R v Howe* [1987] AC 417; *R v Dudley and Stephens* (1884) 14 QBD 273. In comparison, self-defence was an issue in 66 cases (20.7 per cent) and provocation in 75 cases (23.5 per cent): Law Reform Commission of Victoria, *Homicide Prosecutions Study*, Report No 40 (Melbourne: LRCV, 1991) Appendix 6, pp 75 ff.

Similarly, in a New South Wales study of 256 homicide prosecutions in New South Wales between January 1990 and September 1993, diminished responsibility was raised in forty-two cases (16.1 per cent) and provocation in twenty-six cases (10.1 per cent): H Donnelly and S Cumines, 'From Murder to Manslaughter: Partial Defences in New South Wales—1990 to 1993', *Sentencing Trends No 8* (Sydney: NSW Judicial Commission, 1994). More recently, in a study conducted by the Victorian Law Reform Commission of one hundred and eighty-two homicide cases, ninety-four accused chose to proceed to trial and of those, twenty-seven (28.7 per cent) raised provocation as a defence and nineteen (20.2 per cent) raised self-defence: *Defences to Homicide*, Options Paper (Melbourne, VLRC, 2003) p 43, table 12.

To our knowledge, no empirical evidence is available as to how often automatism is raised in homicide cases. Automatism was successful in a few Victorian homicide trials in the early 1990s, but it appears that it is rarely raised in practice: B McSherry, 'Automatism in Australia Since Falconer's Case' (1996) December *International Bulletin of Law and Mental Health* 3–8.

Because self-defence and provocation are the most commonly used defences, we deal with them together in Chapter 10. We group together mental state defences in Chapter 11, and then examine the least often raised defences—necessity, duress and marital coercion—in Chapter 12. We now turn to analysing the theoretical basis for these defences.

Justification and excuse

Criminal defences are traditionally used to deny that the act was wrong (justification) or to deny responsibility (excuse). That is, defences 'justifying' a crime focus on the accused's act whereas those 'excusing' a person from criminal responsibility are generally viewed as concentrating on the accused's personal characteristics: P Alldridge, 'The Coherence of Defences' [1983] Crim LR 665–72; S Yeo, 'Proportionality in Criminal Defences' (1988) 12 Crim LJ 211–27 at 212–13. This traditional division arose out of the eighteenth-century common law of homicide whereby justifiable homicide was seen as commendable rather than blameworthy and led to a total acquittal, entailing no forfeiture of goods and requiring no pardon. Excusable homicide in comparison contained an element of blameworthiness, requiring a pardon, and it led to the forfeiture of goods.

In 1828, forfeiture was abolished by statute and therefore the division between justifiable and excusable homicide became obsolete. However, the development of various defences owes much to how they are conceptualised as justifying or excusing behaviour: GP Fletcher, *Rethinking Criminal Law* (Boston: Little Brown and Co, 1978) pp 759 ff; R Schopp, *Justification Defenses and Just Convictions* (Cambridge: Cambridge University Press, 1998).

The division between justification and excuse has also become muddied as defences have developed. Take self-defence as an example. Finbarr McAuley and Paul McCutcheon in *Criminal Liability* (Dublin: Round Hall Sweet & Maxwell, 2000) p 737 trace the classical conception of self-defence to Michael Foster's work in 1762: Fost. 273. He wrote:

> In case of justifiable self-defence the injured party may repel force in defence of his [sic] person, habitation, or property, against one who manifestly intendeth and endeavoreth by violence or surprise to commit a felony upon either. In these cases he is not obliged to retreat, but may pursue his adversary till he findeth himself out of danger, and if in a conflict between them he happeneth to kill, such killing is *justifiable*. [Emphasis added.]

Certainly, self-defence has traditionally been seen in this way. However, this categorisation has been questioned as the defence has developed. In *Zecevic v DPP (Vic)* (1987) 162 CLR 645 at 658, Wilson, Dawson and Toohey JJ stated concerning self-defence: '[I]n scope and in practice nowadays the plea has a greater connection with excusable homicide being in most cases related to the preservation of life and limb rather than the execution of justice.'

As we shall explore in Chapter 10, the emphasis on what the accused believed in relation to self-defence may indeed place it in the category of an excuse. Provocation too can be viewed as containing elements of both excuse and justification. It began as a justification offence with the emphasis on the provocative conduct of the victim and the acceptability of the accused's actions. However, during the twentieth century its focus broadened to an analysis of the accused's lack of self-control as it turned from its rationale as a way of avoiding mandatory capital punishment to a concession to human frailty. Perhaps partly because of this combination of elements of excuse and justification, the conceptual basis for the defence of provocation is often confused and has led to complexity in this defence. That complexity is critiqued in Chapter 10.

Chapter 12 deals with cases in which the physical and fault elements of a crime have been made out, but in which the accused acted in response to threats from another person (duress/marital coercion) or in order to avert dire consequences (necessity). These defences have traditionally fallen within the category of 'justification' defences in that the focus was initially on the justifiability or not of the accused's conduct. However, duress and necessity have developed in such a way as to involve a focus on what the accused believed at the time of the threat or emergency. This means that both defences have taken on characteristics of what have been traditionally labelled 'excuse' defences. For example, in the defence of necessity, the accused's act may be said to be justified because it is recognised that the law can on occasion be broken to avoid a greater harm than would occur by obeying it. The accused's characteristics stemming from human weakness in the face of an emergency may also be seen as excusing his or her behaviour.

The defences thus far mentioned attempted to deny the wrongfulness of the act or responsibility. To this may be added the denial of the voluntariness or willed nature of the act. In a sense the accused is saying, 'I am not the person who performed the act': P Alldridge, *Relocating Criminal Law* (Aldershot: Ashgate, 2000) p 71. The main 'defence' that would fall under this head is that of automatism, which rests upon the claim that the act was involuntary or 'not willed' by the accused. Automatism is very closely allied to other mental state defences such as mental impairment and diminished responsibility, although the latter defences could be said to be excusatory by focusing on the accused's personal characteristics. These mental state defences are examined in Chapter 11.

The burden of proof and defences

In summing up the defence at a trial in Nova Lombaro, the capital of the fictional African country of Neranga, John Mortimer's well-known character, barrister Horace Rumpole, in *Rumpole and the Golden Thread* (Harmondsworth: Penguin Books Ltd, 1983) states at 90: '[W]hen London is but a memory and the Old Bailey has sunk back into the primeval mud, my country will be remembered for three things: the British Breakfast, *The Oxford Book of English Verse* and the Presumption of Innocence! That presumption is the Golden Thread which runs through the whole history of the Criminal Law.'

This Golden Thread presumes that a person is innocent until the prosecution has proven all elements of the offence charged to a high standard of proof. However, Mr Rumpole is somewhat incorrect in his summing up to the jury as it has only been relatively recently that 'the presumption of innocence' has come to the forefront in the trial process. CK Allen wrote in *Legal Duties and Other Essays in Jurisprudence* (Oxford: Oxford University Press, 1931) pp 257–8 that '[W]e may conclude that four hundred years ago in all criminal trials of which we have any record, the dice were loaded heavily against the accused. The presumption of innocence was not only absent from, but antagonistic to, the whole system of penal procedure.'

The presumption of innocence developed importance in the early nineteenth century. It led to the general rule that the prosecution must prove all the elements of the criminal offence beyond reasonable doubt and must also disprove any defences or mitigating circumstances raised by the defence beyond reasonable doubt: *Woolmington v DPP* [1935] AC 462. However, this general rule has been eroded in recent years, not only through the legal burden being placed on the accused with regard to certain defences such as mental impairment and diminished responsibility, but also through statutory provisions, particularly those dealing with drug offences.

In an empirical study conducted in England by Andrew Ashworth and Meredith Blake, it was found that 40 per cent of indictable offences studied violated the presumption of innocence through the legal burden of proof not being on the prosecution in all respects: 'Presumption of Innocence in English Criminal Law' [1996] Crim LR 306–17. The figure would undoubtedly be much higher if summary offences were taken into account given the magnitude of strict and absolute liability offences.

The evidential burden

There is a general rule that the accused has an evidential burden in relation to defences: *He Kaw Teh v The Queen* (1985) 157 CLR 523 at 534–5 per Gibbs CJ, at 593 per Dawson J. This relates to the duty to produce some evidence to support a claim. It is for the judge to decide whether the defence has the support of enough evidence to enable it to be considered by the jury. If there is sufficient evidence for a defence to be considered by the jury, the judge directs it as to the elements of the defence and what needs to be proved or disproved. The jury then makes the ultimate decision as to whether or not the accused should be found guilty or whether, on the facts, a defence reduces the charge to a lesser offence, or leads to a complete acquittal.

The standard of proof in relation to this evidential burden is unclear. In *Bratty v Attorney-General for Northern Ireland* [1963] AC 386 at 413, Lord Denning referred to the requirement that the evidential burden could be fulfilled if the evidence amounted to a 'proper foundation'. In *Hill v Baxter* [1958] 1 QB 277 at 285, Lord Devlin referred to the requirement of 'prima facie evidence'. More recently, the

New South Wales Court of Criminal Appeal stated in *Youssef* (1990) 50 A Crim R 1 at 3 that: '[T]he accused bears an *evidentiary* onus to point to or to produce evidence (or material in an unsworn statement) from which it could be inferred that...there is at least a reasonable possibility that, for example, the act of the accused was accidental, or that it was provoked or done in self-defence.'

Just what amounts to a 'proper foundation' or 'prima facie evidence' or a 'reasonable possibility' will be a matter for a judge to determine.

The legal burden
The standard of proof in relation to the legal burden of proof placed on the prosecution is 'beyond reasonable doubt': *Woolmington v DPP* [1935] AC 462. There is judicial reluctance to define this phrase. The Privy Council stated in *Ferguson v The Queen* [1979] 1 WLR 94 at 99: 'The time-honoured formula is that the jury must be satisfied beyond reasonable doubt...attempts to substitute other expressions have never prospered. It is generally sufficient and safe to direct a jury that they must be satisfied beyond reasonable doubt so that they feel sure of the defendant's guilt. Nevertheless, other words will suffice, so long as the message is clear.'

The main exceptions
The burden of proof differs in relation to mental impairment and diminished responsibility as it rests on the defence. The traditional explanation for this is that it developed as an historical anomaly. Glanville Williams has pointed out in 'Offences and Defences' (1982) 2 *Legal Studies* 233–56 at 235: 'The [burden of proof in relation to mental impairment is] explicable only as a survival from a time before the present rules of burden of proof were established.'

Rule 2 of the *M'Naghten Rules* (1843) 10 Cl & Fin 200 at 210, which sets out the traditional common law defence of insanity, also refers to a presumption that all individuals are presumed to be sane 'until the contrary is proved'. However, it is highly unlikely that this was intended to lay down a special rule for the defence of mental impairment. Prior to *Woolmington v DPP* [1935] AC 462, it was generally accepted that the burden of proof in relation to *all defences* in fact rested upon the accused: *Jayasena v The Queen* [1971] AC 618 at 623 per Lord Diplock. This model of liability followed that of the civil courts, which placed the burden of proving defences upon the defendant: GP Fletcher, *Rethinking Criminal Law* (Boston: Little Brown and Co, 1978) pp 519 ff; GP Fletcher, 'Two Kinds of Legal Rules: a Comparative Study of Burden-of-Persuasion Practices in Criminal Cases' (1968) 77 *Yale Law Journal* 880–935 at 899–901.

In *Woolmington*'s case, however, Viscount Stankey (at 475) referred to *M'Naghten* as standing by itself and laying down the rule that the burden of proof is 'definitely and exceptionally' placed upon the accused.

Since that time, the burden of proof being placed on the accused in relation to the defence of mental impairment and diminished responsibility has rarely been questioned. In *R v Chaulk* [1990] 3 SCR 1303, the majority of the Supreme Court of Canada concluded (at 1330, per Lamer CJC) that 'the presumption of sanity...violates the presumption of innocence'. However, three of the four judges who concluded that there was a conflict with the presumption of innocence went on to hold that the burden of proof being placed on the accused was a reasonable and demonstrably justifiable limitation under s 1 of the Canadian *Charter of Rights and Freedoms*, enacted as Sch B to the *Constitution Act* 1982 (Can). That section states that the rights and freedoms contained in the *Charter* are 'subject only to such reasonable limits prescribed by law as can be demonstrably justified in a free and democratic society'. Lamer CJ (at 1344) pointed to the practical impossibility of the prosecution proving or disproving the insanity of the accused beyond reasonable doubt: 'The presumption of sanity and the reversal of onus...exist in order to avoid placing a virtually impossible burden on the Crown...If an accused were able to rebut the presumption merely by raising a reasonable doubt as to his or her insanity, the very purpose of the presumption of sanity would be defeated and the objective would not be achieved.'

The rationale behind this approach is the fear that if an accused only has to bear an evidential burden in relation to mental disorder, more individuals would be found not criminally responsible than should be the case. SE Sundby has described this as the fear of 'swinging the jail door open to any individual who can stand up in court and claim insanity': 'The Reasonable Doubt Rule and the Meeting of Innocence' (1988) 40 *Hastings Law Journal* 457–510 at 500.

There are a number of questions that arise here. Why should it be easier to fake mental impairment or a condition raising diminished responsibility as opposed to other defences such as necessity or provocation? Why should an accused not have the benefit of reasonable doubt in relation to mental impairment? Where is the evidence that an evidential burden is inadequate? The prosecution may face problems of proof in relation to many other criminal offences, so why should difficulties in proving a person was not mentally impaired justify lessening the standard from the traditional criminal standard of beyond reasonable doubt to a civil standard of more probable than not? TH Jones writes in his article 'Insanity, Automatism and the Burden of Proof on the Accused' (1995) 111 *The Law Quarterly Review* 475–516 at 477: 'One would also have thought that the special dispositional arrangements [that is, the prospect of indefinite detention] for those found not guilty by reason of insanity...made false claims of insanity rather less likely than those of more conventional defences.'

Problems may occur when the defences of mental impairment or diminished responsibility are raised in conjunction with another defence such as provocation. It has been pointed out that juries may become confused by the distinctions in the burden and standard of proof when this occurs: Criminal Law Revision Committee, *Offences Against the Person*, Report No 14 (London: HMSO, Cmnd 7844, 1980) para 94; Law Reform Commission of Victoria, *Provocation and Diminished Responsibility as*

Defences to Murder, Report No 12 (Melbourne: LRCV, 1982) para 2.67. The situation becomes even more complex if the defence relies on evidence of involuntary behaviour arising from automatism and the prosecution wishes to raise mental impairment to rebut sane automatism. The majority in *R v Falconer* (1990) 171 CLR 30 at 62–3 per Deane and Dawson JJ, at 77–8 per Toohey J and at 80 per Gaudron J set out a complicated five-step procedure for use in such a situation.

In *R v Stone* [1999] 2 SCR 290, a majority of five judges to four in the Supreme Court of Canada held that the burden of proof in relation to automatism is on the accused to prove on the balance of probabilities. While this simplifies the procedure when automatism and the defence of mental impairment are raised, it has been criticised as judicial activism gone astray: R Delisle, '*Stone*: Judicial Activism Gone Awry to Presume Guilt' (1999) 25 CR (5th) 91–6; D Paciocco, 'Death by *Stone*-ing: The Demise of the Defence of Simple Automatism' (1999) 26 CR (5th) 273–85. It can also be criticised from the basis that there is no empirical evidence cited as to why automatism is easily feigned whereas other defences such as provocation or duress are not.

If the presumption of innocence is to have any meaning, one would expect the legal burden to be placed on the prosecution in relation to proving all offences and disproving all defences. Otherwise, it appears that the law may be slipping back to the principle that a person who makes a claim under either civil or criminal law must positively prove it.

Elements of 'serious' crimes

In the seventeenth century, Sir Edward Coke referred to the maxim 'actus non facit reum nisi mens sit rea': Coke 3 Co Inst 6; 1 Inst 247b. This maxim, however, seems to have existed prior to Coke's exposition: J Hall, *General Principles of Criminal Law* (2nd edn, Indianapolis: The Bobbs-Merrill Co Inc, 1960) pp 79–83. It can be loosely translated as 'an act does not make a person guilty of a crime unless that person's mind be also guilty': *Haughton v Smith* [1975] AC 476 at 491–2 per Lord Hailsham.

Thus, the traditional view is that a serious offence consists of two elements: a physical (or external) element—the 'actus reus'—plus a subjective fault element—the 'mens rea'. For example, in most jurisdictions, murder is seen as consisting of a voluntary act causing death plus an intention to kill. Different jurisdictions may vary the fault element for murder (an intention to cause grievous bodily harm and/or some form of recklessness may also suffice), but this traditional notion of a physical element plus a fault element is well ingrained in the criminal law. If the prosecution fails to prove that the criminal act or omission occurred and was voluntary, the result is that the accused is acquitted. If the prosecution fails to prove the requisite fault element, the accused will be acquitted of the serious offence, but may still be held liable for a lesser offence. This traditional division can be visualised as shown in Figure 2.1.

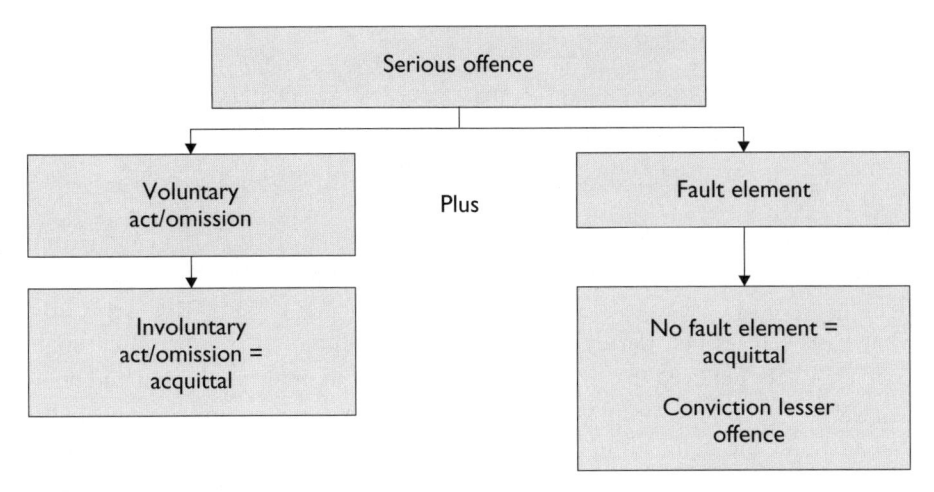

```
                    ┌─────────────────┐
                    │ Serious offence │
                    └─────────────────┘
                     │               │
         ┌───────────┘               └───────────┐
         ▼                                       ▼
┌─────────────────┐                      ┌─────────────────┐
│    Voluntary    │       Plus           │  Fault element  │
│   act/omission  │                      │                 │
└─────────────────┘                      └─────────────────┘
         │                                       │
         ▼                                       ▼
┌─────────────────┐                      ┌─────────────────┐
│   Involuntary   │                      │ No fault element =│
│  act/omission = │                      │    acquittal    │
│    acquittal    │                      │                 │
│                 │                      │Conviction lesser│
│                 │                      │     offence     │
└─────────────────┘                      └─────────────────┘
```

Figure 2.1 Traditional division of serious offences

David Lanham has suggested that it is preferable to think of a serious offence as consisting of a physical element plus a fault element minus a defence: D Lanham, 'Larsonneur Revisited' [1976] Crim LR 276–81. This can be visualised as shown in Figure 2.2.

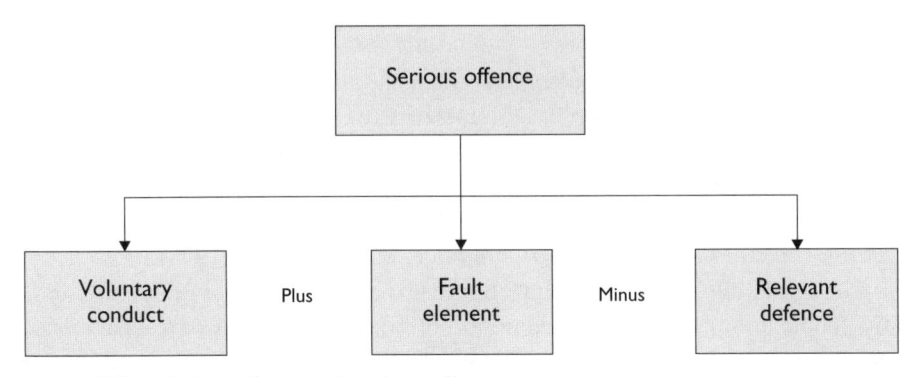

```
                         ┌─────────────────┐
                         │ Serious offence │
                         └─────────────────┘
                                  │
        ┌─────────────────────────┼─────────────────────────┐
        ▼                         ▼                         ▼
┌──────────────┐         ┌──────────────┐         ┌──────────────┐
│  Voluntary   │  Plus   │    Fault     │  Minus  │   Relevant   │
│   conduct    │         │   element    │         │   defence    │
└──────────────┘         └──────────────┘         └──────────────┘
```

Figure 2.2 Modern division of serious offences

The attraction of this approach is that defences can be seen as separate from the physical and fault elements—there is no need to provide a rationale for defences as negating voluntary conduct or intention or other fault element because they exist in a separate realm of their own. As Finbarr McAuley and Paul McCutcheon write, '[t]hus viewed, the somewhat unnatural tension involved in explaining each operative defence in terms of negativing a defined element of the offence is eliminated and, coincidentally, the formulation of a general framework of criminal liability is facilitated': *Criminal Liability* (Dublin: Round Hall Sweet & Maxwell, 2000) pp 114–15.

The notion of a 'guilty mind' is embedded in what has been termed the subjectivist account of the criminal law. That is, one is expected to look inside the accused's head to work out what he or she knew or intended. Central to this is the notion of blameworthiness. We have already outlined how children and those with mental illness have traditionally been excused from criminal responsibility because of their presumed lack of rationality. They are viewed as not to blame for their behaviour because they do not understand the difference between right and wrong.

Basing the concept of criminal responsibility on physical element plus fault element separates an accused's thoughts from his or her actions. This stems from what has been termed Cartesian dualism. The seventeenth-century philosopher René Descartes believed that there was a separation or dualism of mind and body. He viewed the brain as being the major locus for the mind or consciousness of the soul and that the point of interaction between the mind and the soul lay in the pineal gland: TS Hall (trans), *Treatise of Man* (Cambridge: Harvard University Press, 1972, first published 1637). This approach led to action in the sense of a bodily movement being seen as separate from the will or mind's intention. Bodily movement that was directed by the mind was seen as purposeful conduct, while bodily movement not directed by the mind was viewed as reflexive or automatic.

Arguments against the separation of mind and body have been made both on the basis of empirical evidence and on philosophical grounds. Those who have criticised this approach include Antonio Damasio and Paul and Patricia Churchland: A Damasio, *Descartes' Error: Emotion, Reason and the Human Brain* (New York: GP Putnam, 1994); *The Feeling of What Happens: Body and Emotion in the Making of Consciousness* (New York: Harcourt Brace, 1999); Paul Churchland, *A Neurocomputational Perspective: The Nature of Mind and the Structure of Science* (Cambridge, MA: MIT Press, 1989); *The Engine of Reason, The Seat of the Soul: A Philosophical Journey into the Brain* (Cambridge, MA: MIT Press, 1995); P Churchland and P Churchland, *On the Contrary: Critical Essays, 1987–1997* (Cambridge, MA: MIT Press, 1998).

The legal philosopher Antony Duff has also pointed out that in practice, ordinary people do not adopt a refined notion of human behaviour that separates act from will: *Intention, Agency and Criminal Liability* (Oxford: Basil Blackwell, 1990). Rather, people make a global judgment of behaviour that encompasses both act and attitude. As we shall explore below, the Cartesian dualist approach to criminal behaviour also causes problems with separating voluntariness from the fault element of a crime.

In the next sections, we will outline a number of problems with the physical and fault elements, the requirement that they be concurrent and the requirement that an accused's conduct must have caused a certain consequence. Before analysing these issues in detail, it is illuminating to consider how the traditional division between physical and fault elements is challenged by the rise of what are known as strict and absolute liability offences. A further division that is made between subjective and objective fault elements will also be examined.

Strict and absolute liability offences

In terms of numbers of offences, the majority of crimes in fact do not require proof of a fault element. Crimes of strict and absolute liability are creatures of statute and require the prosecution to prove only that the accused committed the physical element of the crime without having to prove that the accused intended to do so. Strict liability offences allow an accused to claim an honest and reasonable mistake of fact in order to be excused from responsibility, but this is not possible in relation to absolute liability offences. In many criminal law textbooks, these types of offences are marginalised to the periphery of the criminal law and described as exceptional and regulatory in nature. Criticisms of this view will be made a little later.

At common law, there is a presumption of subjective fault that may be displaced upon analysis of the particular offence. This does not apply in the Code jurisdictions, where the type of offence is constructed solely by looking at the statutory provision creating it. In the common law jurisdictions, if the section creating the offence uses words such as 'knowingly' or 'dishonestly' or 'wilfully', it will be difficult to show that the presumption of subjective fault has been displaced: *He Kaw Teh v The Queen* (1985) 157 CLR 523 at 594 per Dawson J. The absence of such words, however, does not immediately imply that an offence will be one of strict or absolute liability. Brennan J stated in *He Kaw Teh v The Queen* (1985) 157 CLR 523 at 576 that the 'purpose of the statute is the surest guide of the legislature's intention as to the mental state to be implied'. If the subject matter of the statute is merely to regulate behaviour in some way, then it is likely that the presumption of subjective fault will be displaced. One of the factors behind the rise of strict liability offences is that of administrative efficiency. The presumption of subjective fault has been held to have been displaced in offences dealing with adulterated food and serving liquor to intoxicated people, perhaps partly because it would lead to delays in the court system if subjective fault had to be proved for such offences on each occasion: *Parker v Alder* [1899] 1 QB 20; *R v Woodrow* (1846) 15 M & W 404; 153 ER 907; *Cundy v Le Cocq* (1884) 13 QBD 207.

The consequences to the community have also been taken into account in assessing whether or not the presumption of subjective fault has been displaced. This requirement is generally weighed directly against the potential consequences for the accused if convicted. Consequences to the community have outweighed the latter in the case of environmental damage and speeding offences and the presumption of subjective fault will generally be displaced: *Allen v United Carpet Mills Pty Ltd* [1989] VR 323; *Kearon v Grant* [1991] 1 VR 321.

In general, the more serious the potential consequences for the accused on conviction, the less likely it is that the presumption of subjective fault will be displaced. In *He Kaw Teh v The Queen* (1985) 157 CLR 523 a majority of the High Court held that the severe penal provisions relating to the importation and possession of heroin enforced the presumption that subjective fault was required and should not be displaced. If, on the other hand, the potential consequences to the accused merely involve a financial penalty, it is likely that the presumption of subjective fault will be displaced.

The courts have been reluctant to categorise offences as those of absolute liability in the absence of a clear legislative intention that this be the case. Street CJ stated in *R v Wampfler* (1987) 11 NSWLR 541 at 547 that '[t]here is a discernible trend in modern authorities away from construing statutes as creating absolute liability and towards recognising statutes as falling within the middle or second category [strict liability]'. This appears to be because the courts are uneasy about punishing an accused on the basis of the physical element alone.

With strict liability offences, the courts have allowed the accused's state of mind to be raised by way of the defence of honest and reasonable mistake of fact. That is, while the prosecution need not prove a fault element in relation to strict liability offences, an accused may raise an honest and reasonable belief in a state of facts which, if they existed, would render the act innocent: *Proudman v Dayman* (1941) 67 CLR 536. Provided the accused satisfies the evidential burden in this regard, the prosecution must prove beyond reasonable doubt that the accused did not have an honest and reasonable belief as to the facts asserted.

The courts have interpreted certain offences dealing with the regulation of social or industrial conditions or protecting revenue as imposing absolute liability. For example, the offence of exceeding 60 kilometres per hour in a 60 kilometre zone contrary to cl 1001(1)(c) of the *Road Safety (Traffic) Regulations* 1988 (Vic) has been held to be an absolute liability offence: *Kearon v Grant* [1991] 1 VR 321. Speeding offences are often handled out of court via on-the-spot fines or speeding notices. Similarly, causing pollution to waters under s 39(1) of the *Environment Protection Act* 1970 (Vic) has been interpreted as an absolute liability offence: *Allen v United Carpet Mills Pty Ltd* [1989] VR 323. In these two cases, the courts were persuaded that the consequences for the community overrode any potential consequences to the accused. Other 'regulatory' offences that have been interpreted as absolute liability offences include selling alcohol to underage persons in breach of s 114 of the *Liquor Act* 1982 (NSW), refusing or failing to submit to breath testing pursuant to s 4E(7) of the *Motor Traffic Act* 1909 (NSW) and publishing a name in breach of a suppression order under ss 69 and 71 of the *Evidence Act* 1929 (SA): *Hickling v Laneyrie* (1991) 21 NSWLR 730; *R v Walker* (1994) 35 NSWLR 384; *Nationwide News Pty Ltd v Bitter* (1985) 38 SASR 390 respectively.

In Chapter 1, we explored how imposing criminal responsibility on corporations has proved difficult given the model of individual criminal responsibility that underlies the law. It was pointed out that—as Richard Quinney argues—corporate crime is not seen as truly criminal because corporate practices are essential to developing a capitalist political economy: 'Class, State and Crime' in J Jacoby (ed), *Classics of Criminology* (New York: Waveland Press Inc, 1994, first published 1980) pp 106–15 at 110. The same argument can be made about strict and absolute liability offences. They emerged at a time when the industrial revolution in England led to attempts to regulate employers of those working in factories. The prosecution of factory owners for breaching labour regulations was seen as not part of the 'real' criminal law, for these factory owners were respected members of the community: A Norrie, *Crime, Reason and History: A Critical Introduction to the Criminal Law* (London: Butterworths, 2001) pp 85 ff. Instead of using the criminal law, a regime of civil penalties developed. This approach underlies the argument that strict and liability offences are 'quasi-criminal' or 'regulatory' in nature.

On the other hand, strict and absolute liability offences do provide a way of imposing sanctions on corporations which are most likely to 'unintentionally' harm others through their business practices. They may also be used where intention is difficult to prove or allocate. From a critical criminology perspective, the fact that strict and absolute liability offences are seen as on the periphery of the 'real' criminal law can be viewed as part of a general acceptance of capitalism as requiring different forms of regulation according to social class.

Alan Norrie writes that '[i]t is difficult to imagine a *general* system of law enforcement of the lower social classes based upon advice, consultation and warning as it is to imagine an orthodox label of guilt being imposed on factory owners by a system of vigorous policing': *Crime, Reason and History: A Critical Introduction to the Criminal Law* (London: Butterworths, 2001) p 86. For a Marxist/critical criminologist such as Richard Quinney, only a new society based on socialist principles can alter this division between 'real' and 'regulatory' crimes.

At the other end of the spectrum, a liberal approach may view the expanding categories of strict and absolute liability offences as widening too broadly the scope for state intervention and control in individuals' lives.

Some legal philosophers have argued that strict and absolute liability offences should be discouraged because they offend against the central notion of 'a guilty mind'. Herbert Hart, for example, has described strict liability offences as 'odious' because they sacrifice the valued principle of blameworthiness: *Punishment and Responsibility* (Oxford: Oxford University Press, 1968) p 152. To understand this approach, it is necessary to examine the differences between criminal law 'subjectivists' and 'objectivists'. This will be explored in the next section.

Subjective versus objective fault

The courts have generally shown a preference for subjective fault elements in relation to serious crimes: *DPP v Morgan* [1976] AC 182; *He Kaw Teh v The Queen* (1985) 157 CLR 523. For example, during the nineteenth century, in the face of a growing number of statutory crimes that did not require proof of a subjective fault element, the courts developed a common law presumption that all crimes involve some form of subjective fault element: *Sherras v De Rutzen* [1895] 1 QB 918. This presumption, however, may be displaced at common law.

This preference is related to the liberal philosophical dependence on free will. In *Punishment and Responsibility* (Oxford: Oxford University Press, 1968), Herbert Hart posited that criminal punishment should be restricted to those who have voluntarily broken the law. This approach suggests that a person should be punished only when he or she had recognised the harmful aspect of his or her conduct or its consequences. In other words, the accused must intend, know or at least be aware of the risk of a particular harm occurring.

The subjectivist approach has been criticised by those who prefer an objective approach based on, for example, standards of reasonableness. A major problem with the subjectivist approach is that it necessitates the attribution of intention, knowledge or foresight to another person. Philosophers have spilled much ink debating the problem of 'other minds'. Because we can never know what another person is thinking, we attribute mental states to them that they 'ought to have, in light of [their] environment, perceptual capacities, interests, and past experiences. Moreover, we expect that [they] will act as…rational agent[s]': R Dresser, 'Culpability and Other Minds' (1992) 2(1) *Southern California Interdisciplinary Law Journal* 41–88 at 78. This is sometimes referred to as folk psychology.

The difficulty of determining subjective mental states was recognised by Kirby J in *Peters v The Queen* (1998) 192 CLR 493 at 551:

> Absent a comprehensive and reliable confession, it is usually impossible for the prosecution actually to get into the mind of the accused and to demonstrate exactly what it finds was there at the time of the criminal act. Necessarily, therefore, intention must ordinarily be inferred from all of the evidence admitted at the trial. In practice this is not usually a problem. But the search is not for an intention which the law objectively imputes to the accused. It is a search, by the process of inference from the evidence, to discover the intention which, subjectively, the accused actually had.

Despite the emphasis on 'subjective' intention, it has been accepted that in the process of attributing a mental state to an accused, jurors will often resort to a consideration of what a reasonable person might have intended or known or believed in the circumstances. This practice has been accepted by the courts as being unavoidable: *Pemble v The Queen* (1971) 124 CLR 107 at 120 per Barwick CJ. The idea of intention or knowledge or recklessness being purely 'subjective' is therefore questionable. What the notion of subjectivity in this context really means is that the trier of fact must make an assessment of fault in relation to the particular accused, taking into account his or her behaviour, experiences and characteristics such as age, social and cultural background.

The difficulty in proving intention, knowledge or recklessness beyond reasonable doubt is one factor in the rise of offences where the fault element is expressed as an objective one. Some crimes incorporate an element of negligence as the basis upon which criminal responsibility is assigned. Negligent behaviour is usually assessed by reference to an external standard such as the behaviour of the reasonable person. This, of course, brings its own dangers as previously explored in Chapter 1.

According to the 'subjectivist' approach to criminal responsibility, blame should be ascribed on the basis of an individual's intention or knowledge, not the consequences of an action or omission. Blame should depend on individual choices made and not merely on luck or chance. This underlies many areas of the criminal law such as inchoate offences where the possibility or impossibility of carrying out an offence is viewed as irrelevant.

Objectivists, on the other hand, argue that 'outcome-luck' ought to play a role in ascribing moral and criminal responsibility. For example, Antony Duff argues that consequences have a role to play in determining questions of moral and legal blame even where the actor has no control over them: *Intention, Agency and Criminal Liability* (Oxford: Basil Blackwell, 1990) pp 184–92. Take, for example, the scenario of an act of careless driving that results in a 'near miss' as opposed to an identical act of careless driving that results in the death of a child. Duff suggests the consequences of the same act should serve to differentiate them. Imposing strict equivalence of blame also disregards the fact that the person who caused a 'near miss' is provided with an opportunity to avoid these consequences in the future. Most importantly, not taking account of consequences undermines the censuring function of the criminal law. It would convey the message that from a moral perspective, causing actual harm is unimportant.

These differing approaches will be mentioned throughout the book as we critique various offences. The key is to recognise that both subjectivist and objectivist approaches to the criminal law may be important in different contexts. At certain times, for some crimes, intentions not consequences, are all-important, and vice versa. In Chapter 1, we mentioned that one of the themes in postmodernism is an aversion to 'metadiscourses' or grand theories that are self-legitimising. From that perspective, any quest for the 'grand universal theory', be it subjectivist or objectivist, to account for all forms of culpability is doomed to failure.

Physical elements

We have already pointed out problems with dividing fault elements up into subjective and objective fault. The division between physical and fault elements is also not as neat as it may seem at first glance. The courts have, for example, referred to physical elements as having to be voluntary while leaving considerations of intention to the construction of fault. What is the difference between voluntary and intentional conduct? We will take up that question in the section on intention below. In the next section, we will introduce the concept of voluntary conduct in relation to the physical elements before considering what types of physical elements may be criminalised.

Voluntary conduct

In a criminal trial, the prosecution must prove beyond reasonable doubt that the accused's conduct was voluntary. This requirement is generally treated as quite separate from any consideration of subjective fault and the defence of mental impairment: that is, the defence can raise evidence that the accused's conduct was involuntary in the absence of raising a defence of mental impairment.

There is no legal definition as to what amounts to voluntary conduct. Rather, the case law has developed categories of involuntary conduct such as when the act was involuntary, caused by a reflex action or performed in a state of impaired consciousness. The most problematic category is the latter. This will be explored further in Chapter 11 in the context of mental state defences.

The assumption that individuals freely will their actions is one that has been hotly contested in philosophical literature. Many legal writers acknowledge the debate about determinism and free will, but, as Mark Kelman has pointed out, act as if jurisprudence based on free will is 'ultimately complete, coherent, and convincing': 'Interpretative Construction in the Substantive Criminal Law' (1981) 33 *Stanford Law Review* 591–673 at 598. For example, Herbert Packer has argued that 'the law treats man's [sic] conduct as autonomous and willed, not because it is, but because it is desirable to proceed as though it were': *The Limits of the Criminal Sanction* (London: Oxford University Press, 1969) pp 74–5.

The blurring of the division between voluntary and intentional conduct will be explored further in the section on intention below.

Acts and omissions

The physical element of most offences will consist of the commission of an act or series of acts by the accused. There are also certain offences that criminalise a state of 'being' rather than conduct. An example is that of being drunk or disorderly in a public place or offences relating to vagrancy. These are usually summary offences.

A specified form of conduct may not be a crime *unless* it is performed in certain specified circumstances. For example, in general, the crime of rape is defined by intentional sexual penetration (conduct) that occurs without the other person's consent (the specified circumstance).

In addition, the physical element of an offence may sometimes refer to the results or consequences of conduct rather than the conduct itself. For example, what is prohibited in the crime of murder is the death of the victim rather than the conduct that caused the death. It is irrelevant what conduct was undertaken that caused the death; providing the conduct of the accused *results* in the death of the victim, the physical element of murder will be established. Offences that refer to the consequences of conduct are often referred to as 'result crimes'. In these crimes, it is necessary for the prosecution to prove that the conduct *caused* the requisite consequences. Causation issues will be explored a little later in this chapter.

The most controversial area in relation to physical elements lies in the distinction between acts and omissions. There has been a traditional reluctance to use the criminal law to punish those who omit to act, in the absence of a legal duty to act. It has been thought that the criminal law should not be used to compel or encourage the doing of good and that it is too harsh a method of punishing the ignorant or neglectful: JP McCutcheon, 'Omissions and Criminal Liability' (1993–1995) 28–30 *Irish Jurist* (ns) 56–78 at 57 ff; G Williams, 'Criminal Omissions—the Conventional View' (1991) 107 *Law Quarterly Review* 86–98. A general duty to intervene might also mean that a large number of people who fail to act in certain circumstances would be held responsible. For example, imagine how many people could be held criminally responsible if a beggar dies of starvation or neglect. If a child is substituted in place of the beggar in this scenario, efforts to allocate responsibility, legally and socially, may differ in scope.

In general, there is no legal obligation for persons to act so as to prevent harm or wrongdoing, although there may arguably be a moral duty. There is no duty to prevent a crime, nor does an individual commit a crime or become a party to it simply because he or she could reasonably have prevented it. An omission to act may give rise to criminal liability, however, where a duty arises at common law or is imposed by statute.

At common law, a duty to act may arise as a result of a family relationship between the parties: *R v Russell* [1933] VLR 59; *R v Clarke and Wilton* [1959] VR 645. A duty may also arise as a result of a person undertaking to care for another who is unable to care for him or herself: *R v Instan* [1893] 1 QB 450; (1893) 17 602; *Lee v The Queen* (1917) 13 Cr App R 39 at 41 per Darling J; *Gibbins* (1918) 13 Cr App R 134; *R v Stone and Dobinson* [1977] 1 QB 354. In *R v Miller* [1983] 2 AC 161 at 176 Lord Diplock also referred to there being 'no rational ground for excluding from conduct capable of giving rise to criminal liability conduct which consists of failing to take measures that lie within one's power to counteract a danger that one has oneself created'. This will be explored further in Chapter 3 when we examine negligent manslaughter.

Statutory examples of the imposition of a duty to act include a duty to provide necessities in certain jurisdictions: *Criminal Code* (NT) s 183; *Crimes Act* 1900 (NSW) s 44; *Criminal Code* (Qld) s 285; *Criminal Law Consolidation Act* 1935 (SA) s 30; *Criminal Code* (Tas) s 144; *Criminal Code* (WA) s 262. In the Northern Territory, there is also a duty to rescue or provide help to a person urgently in need of it and whose life may be endangered if it is not provided: *Criminal Code* (NT) s 155; considered in *Salmon v Chute* (1994) 94 NTR 1.

The act/omission distinction has troubled philosophers particularly in relation to euthanasia. In 1975, James Rachels set out two hypothetical cases to argue that there was no moral difference between passive and active euthanasia: 'Active and Passive Euthanasia' in TL Beauchamp and L Walters (eds), *Contemporary Issues in Bioethics* (4th edn, Belmont, CA: Wadsworth Publishing Company, 1994) pp 439–42. In the first case, Smith stands to gain a large inheritance if his six-year-old cousin dies. One evening, as the six-year-old is taking his bath, Smith slips into the bathroom and drowns his cousin, making it look like an accident.

In the second case, Jones also stands to benefit if his six-year-old cousin dies. Like Smith, Jones slips into the bathroom intending to drown his cousin. However, as he enters he sees the child slip, hit his head and fall face down in the bath. Jones watches and does nothing as the child drowns. According to Rachels, Jones' conduct is no less reprehensible than Smith's. From these cases, Rachels argues that there is no moral difference between killing and letting die.

Tom Beauchamp, however, argues that Rachels' cases are not analogous to killing and letting die as they relate to euthanasia: TL Beauchamp, 'A Reply to Rachels on Active and Passive Euthanasia' in TL Beauchamp and L Walters (eds), *Contemporary Issues in Bioethics* (4th edn, Belmont, CA: Wadsworth Publishing Company, 1994) pp 442–9. This was echoed by the members of the House of Lords in *Airedale NHS Trust v Bland* [1993] 2 WLR 316 where it was held that an omission to provide the invasive medical care involved in artificial feeding did not amount to murder, but a lethal injection would have.

There is also a group of cases grappling with omitting to act in relation to negligent manslaughter. In Chapter 1, we outlined the facts in *R v Stone and Dobinson* [1977] 1 QB 354 in which the Court of Appeal held that the two accused, who had a number of physical and intellectual disabilities, had undertaken a duty of care for the male accused's sister and that they had been negligent in failing to give her proper care. We pointed out how an objective standard of fault can operate harshly against those who have a physical or intellectual disability.

Hazel Biggs has highlighted the differing approach of the law in the contexts of euthanasia and negligent manslaughter by omission in 'Euthanasia and Death with Dignity: Still Poised on the Fulcrum of Homicide' [1996] Crim LR 878–88. She compares *R v Stone and Dobinson* [1977] 1 QB 354 with the later decision of *Airedale NHS Trust v Bland* [1993] AC 789. She states (at 883):

> The duty of care...appears to adopt a different criminal significance depending on whether the potential defendant is a member of the public or a medical profession... Why is it that a professionally imposed duty extended only as far as determining the best interests of a patient who could not consent, while the scope of the voluntarily assumed duty in [*R v*] *Stone and Dobinson* included the obligation to overrule the autonomous wishes of the 'patient' [Stone's sister, Fanny]? *Smith* [1979] Crim LR 251 suggests that a person who is capable of *rational* decision-making could relieve a relative of a common law duty of care, but this fails to reconcile conflicting dicta. Bland was incapable of making any decisions and his

carers were absolved of responsibility, while Stone's sister purposefully declined the provision of food and medical aid by her carers and they were culpable.

The law relating to euthanasia and negligent manslaughter will be further explored in Chapter 3.

Fault elements

Fault elements are generally divided between the subjective and objective. Intention, knowledge and recklessness are generally taken to fall under the subjective category whereas negligence falls under the objective category. These are concepts that will be analysed in more detail in relation to individual offences in the following chapters. However, it should be noted that there is a large amount of overlap between these terms. Indeed, in England, recklessness bridges both the subjective and objective categories. The courts have spent much time grappling with what is meant by the various fault elements and the existing state of the law is confusing, particularly in the light of philosophical and psychological conceptions of behaviour. The following sections outline some of the problems associated with the varying definitions of fault elements.

Intention

Legal philosophers usually refer to intention as the central focus of 'mens rea' or fault. Herbert Hart and Antony Duff have very different views on criminal law issues, but both view intention as the cornerstone of the fault elements: HLA Hart, *Punishment and Responsibility* (Oxford: Oxford University Press, 1968); RA Duff, *Intention, Agency and Criminal Liability* (Oxford: Basil Blackwell, 1990). Intentional action is seen as the paradigm of individual choice and control leading to criminal responsibility. It very much reflects the liberal philosophical dependence on free will. Yet, in terms of numbers of offences, intention rarely needs to be proved. As explored above, there has been a rise in strict and absolute liability offences and of those requiring proof of fault, the majority refer to recklessness or negligence as alternatives to intention. Perhaps the central importance of intention in the analysis of fault is that it is philosophically integral to the framework of the subjectivist approach to the criminal law.

The term 'intention' has evaded precise legal definition. Andrew Ashworth has pointed out that appellate courts 'in most cases...insist that intention is an ordinary word that needs no explanation, but on other occasions they adopt broader and narrower definitions and they have never offered a concrete definition of the term': *Principles of Criminal Law* (3rd edn, Oxford: Oxford University Press, 1999) p 182.

Alan Norrie has suggested that the law has recognised three different and potentially conflicting meanings of intention: 'Criminal Law to Legal Theory: The Mysterious Case of the Reasonable Glue Sniffer' (2002) 65(4) *Modern Law Review* 538–55 at 539. These are:

- intention as purpose in the sense of meaning to perform the conduct (sometimes referred to as general or basic intention);
- intention as purpose plus foresight of virtually certain side-effect (sometimes referred to as specific intention);
- intention as purpose plus foresight of probable consequence (sometimes referred to as oblique intention).

These categories of intention will be discussed in turn.

General or basic intention

The definition of intention as purpose is closely connected with the requirement that conduct be voluntary in the sense of it being willed or consciously performed. What is signified by meaning to perform conduct? Here, there is a tension between intention as a form of subjective fault and voluntariness in relation to physical elements.

Legal philosophers have struggled to explain what is meant by voluntary and intentional conduct, sometimes blurring the two. Generally, voluntary conduct is linked to the notion of control, rather than intention, but some theorists have talked about voluntary conduct as being purposeful or goal-oriented. John Austin defined a voluntary act as one resulting from a willed muscular movement: J Austin, *Lectures on Jurisprudence* (5th edn, London: John Murray, 1885) pp 411–15. Similarly, North P stated in *R v Burr* [1969] NZLR 736 at 742 that 'one cannot move a muscle without a direction given by the mind'. Glanville Williams has criticised this approach as presupposing an element of deliberation that does not readily fit in with the ordinary experiences of life where most actions such as walking, eating, gesturing are done in a quasi-automatic fashion: *Textbook of Criminal Law* (2nd edn, London: Stevens & Sons, 1983) p 148.

Herbert Hart posited that an act is voluntary if the individual believes he or she is doing the action: *Punishment and Responsibility* (Oxford: Oxford University Press, 1968) p 105. For example, walking is something that is usually done in a quasi-automatic fashion, but an individual, if asked, would say that he or she believed that he or she was walking. What Hart was concerned to place beyond the realm of voluntary action were acts occurring in a state of impaired consciousness such as during an epileptic seizure or while sleepwalking. Hart's theory, however, does not account for a reflex action in that it is 'unwilled' but the actor is aware that it is occurring.

Another view is that an act is voluntary if it can be described as goal directed or purposeful and it is here that the overlap with intention as meaning to do an act is almost complete. During the early 1930s, Hans Welzel developed in Germany the concept of action as intrinsically purposive rather than simply being an external manifestation of 'the will': GP Fletcher, *Rethinking Criminal Law* (Boston: Little

Brown and Co, 1978) pp 433–9. A voluntary act is one that the actor sought to bring about. The Victorian Law Reform Commission took this approach when stating '[n]o practical distinction can be drawn between voluntary conduct and intentional conduct': *Mental Malfunction and Criminal Responsibility*, Report No 34 (Melbourne: LRCV, 1990) p 67.

This is also the most common approach taken by psychologists in the social cognitive field. Midway through the twentieth century, the Russian psychologists Lev Semenovich Vygotsky and Aleksandr Romanovich Luria posited a view of behaviour as being adapted to the current environment, but determined by an act of conscious choice: LS Vygotsky, *Selected Psychological Investigations* (Moscow: Izd Akad Pedagog Nauk RSFR, 1956); LS Vygotsky, *Development of the Higher Mental Functions* (Moscow: Izd Akad Pedagog Nauk RSFR, 1960); AR Luria, *The Working Brain* (London: The Penguin Press, 1973). This view remains dominant among theories of self-motivation. For example, Albert Bandura writes that '[m]ost human behaviour, being purposive, is regulated by forethought': 'Human Agency in Social Cognitive Theory' (1989) 44(9) *American Psychologist* 1175–84 at 1179. He defines intention as 'the determination to perform certain activities or to bring about a future state of affairs': *Social Foundations of Thought and Action* (Englewood Cliffs, NJ: Prentice Hall, 1986) p 467. Intentional regulation of behaviour is seen as being caused by the exercise of forethought as well as goal setting.

Another approach posited by Finbarr McAulay and Paul McCutcheon, is that the central issue in relation to voluntary and involuntary acts is whether or not the actor can be said to have controlled his or her act: *Criminal Liability* (Dublin: Round Hall Sweet & Maxwell, 2000) p 127. Control does not have to be total, but substantial. Thus, conversely, an involuntary act is one where there is a substantial lack of control.

Perhaps the real crux of the problem of defining voluntary and intentional behaviour from a legal perspective is the assumption that behaviour is *either* voluntary or involuntary and *either* intentional or unintentional. This does not accord with recent work in the behavioural sciences, particularly in the field of psychology. This will be taken up in the section on automatism in Chapter 11 on mental state defences.

Specific intention

Intention as purpose plus foresight of virtually certain side-effect relates to the physical element as the results or consequences of conduct. Here, the prosecution must prove that the accused's purpose was to bring about the results or consequences of the conduct: *La Fontaine v The Queen* (1976) 136 CLR 62; *R v Crabbe* (1985) 156 CLR 464; *Boughey v The Queen* (1986) 161 CLR 10; *R v Demirian* [1989] VR 97. For example, with the crime of murder, it must be proved that the accused intended the death of the victim through his or her conduct.

The difference in intention as it relates to conduct and as it relates to consequences is sometimes referred to as a distinction between basic and specific intention.

In *He Kaw Teh v The Queen* (1985) 157 CLR 523 Brennan J drew a number of distinctions in the use of the term 'intention' in criminal offences. He stated (at 569–70):

> General intent and specific intent are...distinct mental states. General intent or basic intent relates to the doing of the act involved in an offence; special or specific intent relates to the results caused by the act done. In statutory offences, general or basic intent is an intent to do an act of the character prescribed by the statute creating the offence; special or specific intent is an intent to cause the results to which the intent is expressed to relate.

This distinction has become very unclear in relation to the law of intoxication. The distinction is important in this area of law because, as we shall explore in Chapter 11, in Queensland, Tasmania and Western Australia, intoxication may be considered in relation to crimes requiring specific intent, but not basic intent: *Criminal Code* (Qld) s 28; *Criminal Code* (Tas) s 17(2); *Criminal Code* (WA) s 28.

Stephen J pointed out in *R v O'Connor* (1980) 146 CLR 64 at 105 that while murder is generally characterised as a crime of specific intent (that is, the accused intends to cause the result, in this case death), other serious crimes such as assault and manslaughter are characterised as crimes of basic intent. He stated that such a distinction is 'neither clearly defined not easily recognisable [and]...does not reflect or give effect to any coherent attitude either as the relative wrongfulness of particular conduct or the degree of social mischief which that conduct is thought to involve'.

The offence of rape has been viewed as requiring specific intent: *R v Hornbuckle* [1945] VLR 281. However, rape is not a result crime on Brennan J's categorisation. Rather, it is a crime where the physical element is of conduct occurring in specific circumstances. Why should it require a specific rather than a basic intent? The significance in this context is that the accused may be able to obtain an acquittal on the basis of intoxication if it is a crime of specific intent, but not if it is characterised as a crime of basic intent. The division is often arbitrary and inconsistent. This will be taken up further in Chapter 11 in the section on intoxication.

Oblique intention

The third definition of intention is an English invention, sometimes referred to as 'oblique intention'. This refers to intention as purpose plus foresight of probable consequences. This developed partly because the fault element for murder in England is limited to an intention to kill or cause grievous bodily harm and does not include a separate category for recklessness: JC Smith, *Smith and Hogan Criminal Law* (10th edn, London: Butterworths, 2002) pp 359–61. As will be explored in Chapter 3, recklessness as to causing death is an element of murder in the Australian Capital Territory, New South Wales, South Australia, Tasmania and Victoria. The English concept of oblique intention can be seen as overlapping with the concept of recklessness in these jurisdictions.

The facts of *Hyam v DPP* [1975] AC 55 provide a good example of the problems associated with developing a broader approach to intention. The accused poured petrol through a letter box and lit it in order, she claimed, to frighten a woman in the house. In the ensuing fire, two of the woman's daughters died. Hyam claimed that she did not intend to kill them. The House of Lords defined intention broadly to include not only direct intention but also foresight of a probable consequence. Lord Hailsham (at 78) took the view that intentionally and deliberately doing an act that exposes a victim to the risk of probable grievous bodily harm or death are 'morally indistinguishable'. That is, if the accused foresaw that death was a probable consequence of her actions, then she had the relevant intent to kill.

The effect of *Hyam's* case was to introduce into the English criminal law a broad definition of intention, which overlaps with recklessness as it is understood in Australian jurisdictions. Subsequent decisions have attempted to restrict the level of foresight required for oblique intention. In 1985, the House of Lords reconsidered the *Hyam* decision in *R v Maloney* [1985] AC 905. The accused shot his stepfather with a shotgun at close range, but claimed that he had not possessed any intention to kill or hurt his victim. The accused (and the victim) had been drinking alcohol, but this was not raised in defence. The accused gave evidence that he had argued with his stepfather about the former wanting to leave the army. They then started talking about guns and his stepfather claimed that he was faster that the accused at loading, drawing and shooting a gun. The accused went upstairs and brought down two shotguns, presumably so that they could compete with one another. The accused loaded his shotgun faster than the stepfather, who said, 'I didn't think you got the guts, but if you have, pull the trigger'.

Without expressly departing from the decision in *Hyam*, the House of Lords held that the degree of foresight has to be 'little short of overwhelming before it will suffice to establish the necessary intent' (at 925 per Lord Bridge). According to Lord Bridge (at 926), the meaning of intention is best left to the jury to decide:

> The golden rule should be that, when directing the jury on the mental element necessary in a crime of specific intent, the judge should avoid any elaboration or paraphrase of what is meant by intent, and leave it to the jury's good sense to decide whether the accused acted with the necessary intent, unless the judge is convinced that, on the facts and having regard to the way that the case has been presented to the jury in evidence and argument, some further explanation or elaboration is strictly necessary to avoid misunderstanding.

It would seem that as a result of this case, oblique intention has been restricted quite substantially. In practice, fact situations giving rise to an analysis of oblique intention can very well fall within the concept of recklessness, at least for the purpose of the law of homicide, which will be discussed in Chapter 3.

Intention and motive

Intention is not the same as motive, which is generally referred to as an emotion prompting an act. In *Hyam v DPP* [1975] AC 55 Lord Hailsham stated (at 73): 'The motive for murder...may be jealousy, fear, hatred, desire for money, perverted lust, or even, as in so-called "mercy killings", compassion or love. In this sense, motive is entirely distinct from intention or purpose. It is the emotion which gives rise to the intention and it is the latter and not the former which converts an actus reus into a criminal act.'

Motive has traditionally been seen as irrelevant to the question of criminal responsibility. Alan Norrie has criticised the emphasis on intention to the detriment of motive: *Crime Reason and History: A Critical Introduction to Criminal Law* (2nd edn, London: Butterworths, 2001) ch 3. He explains (at 38–9) the origin of this rule: 'Desperate social need and indignant claim of right were the motives of the poor in the seventeenth, eighteenth and early nineteenth centuries. These were hardly motives calculated to win favour or compassion from a social class determined to impose a property order on all regardless of the consequences. Small wonder then that motive's relevance to guilt was very firmly squashed...'.

Yet, despite this general rule, the legal system does allow questions of motive to creep in. It may be relevant in attributing intention to an accused. It may form part of the circumstantial evidence that may establish that the accused did have the requisite state of mind. It may be relevant to decisions as to whether or not to prosecute as well as at the sentencing stage of a trial.

Norrie believes that the criminal law has focused on individual justice to the detriment of social justice: 'From Criminal Law to Legal Theory: The Mysterious Case of the Reasonable Glue Sniffer' (2002) 65 *Modern Law Review* 538–55. Ignoring the relevance of motive underpins the denial of social conditions in which individuals live.

Knowledge and recklessness

An accused may be held criminally responsible if he or she acts with knowledge that a particular circumstance exists or awareness that a particular consequence will result from the performance of the conduct. For example, in New South Wales, Victoria, South Australia and the Australian Capital Territory, the crime of rape occurs where the accused intended to have sexual intercourse with the victim knowing or believing that it was without the other person's consent or being reckless as to the issue of consent: *Crimes Act* 1900 (ACT) s 92D; *Criminal Law Consolidation Act* 1935 (SA) s 48; *Crimes Act* 1900 (NSW) s 61D(2); *Crimes Act* 1958 (Vic) s 38. In these jurisdictions, an accused may claim that although the victim was not in fact consenting, the accused honestly *believed* the victim was. This mistaken belief has the effect of negating the requirement that the accused be aware that the victim was not consenting. This will be taken up in more detail when we explore the law relating to sexual assault in Chapter 5.

Recklessness is a form of the fault element of a crime, which, like knowledge, relates to the physical elements of conduct occurring in specified circumstances or the consequences of conduct. The term 'recklessness' describes the state of mind of a person who, while performing an act, is aware of a risk that a particular consequence is *likely* to result. Awareness of a risk is thus the essence of recklessness. However, this fault element is also expressed as knowledge, foresight or realisation that a consequence is likely to result. The usual shorthand for recklessness is 'foresight' in the sense of foresight of the likelihood of a consequence or of a circumstance occurring.

An accused is said to be reckless where he or she acts in the knowledge that a consequence is a probable or possible result of his or her conduct. For example, a person who foresees death or grievous bodily harm as a probable consequence of his or her conduct is said to be reckless as to those consequences and may be convicted of murder if death results: *La Fontaine v The Queen* (1976) 136 CLR 62; *R v Crabbe* (1985) 156 CLR 464.

For offences other than murder, the courts have not applied the fault element of the high level of recklessness based on foresight of probable consequence. An accused may also be said to be reckless where he or she is aware of the possible existence of certain circumstances but acts regardless of their existence. In *R v Coleman* (1990) 19 NSWLR 467 the New South Wales Court of Appeal considered the definition of recklessness with regard to the offence of maliciously inflicting actual bodily harm with intent to have sexual intercourse. The term 'maliciously' has been interpreted as meaning that intention or recklessness is required for this offence. The New South Wales Court of Appeal held that for all statutory offences other than murder, recklessness is defined as foresight of possibility not probability.

In the jurisdictions where recklessness is an element of crimes such as murder or rape, it is treated as equivalent to intention because of the notion of blameworthiness. This was explained in *R v Crabbe* (1985) 156 CLR 464 as follows (at 469): 'The conduct of a person who does an act, knowing that death or grievous bodily harm is a probable consequence, can naturally be regarded for the purposes of the criminal law as just as blameworthy as the conduct of one who does an act intended to kill or do grievous bodily harm.'

Overall, recklessness relates to a subjective awareness of risks that are substantial and of the 'real and not remote' chance that the consequences will occur: *Boughey v The Queen* (1986) 161 CLR 10. As stated previously, there is a similarity or overlap between recklessness and oblique intention, the latter referring to foresight of a particular consequence as a virtual certainty.

The ordinary common sense use of the term recklessness is much broader than its legal use. The definition of recklessness in *The Macquarie Dictionary* is 'utterly careless of the consequences of action; without caution': *The Macquarie Dictionary* (3rd edn, NSW: Macquarie University, 1997) p 1779. This definition seems to encompass the notion of carelessness that legally falls more squarely within the objective fault element of negligence rather than the subjective fault element of recklessness.

The English courts have adopted a broader interpretation of recklessness than Australian courts. In *Commissioner of Police of the Metropolis v Caldwell* [1982] AC 341 the House of Lords interpreted recklessness as including an objective standard. It held that recklessness has two meanings. It embraces a *subjective* awareness of a risk: the person who is aware of a risk but goes ahead in any case. But it also embraces an *objective* aspect: the person who fails to appreciate the risk when the risk would be obvious to the reasonable person. The House of Lords concluded that inadvertence to an obvious risk was as morally culpable as subjective risk-taking.

Many academics have been extremely critical of this departure from subjectivism in the fault element of serious crimes: JC Smith, 'Case Comment: *R v Caldwell*' [1981] Crim LR 393–6; G Syrota, 'A Radical Change in the Law of Recklessness' [1982] Crim LR 97–106; Glanville Williams, 'Recklessness Redefined' (1981) 40(2) *Cambridge Law Journal* 252–83. See also S Gardiner, 'Recklessness Refined' (1993) 109 *Law Quarterly Review* 21–7. Having such a broad definition blurs the distinction between recklessness and criminal negligence.

Caldwell recklessness has not been applied in Australia. The English position does show the blurring of boundaries between subjective and objective fault that remains the bugbear of those in either camp.

The role of wilful blindness

What if the accused deliberately refrained from making enquiries or was 'wilfully blind' to a particular circumstance or consequence for fear that he or she may learn the truth? The courts have differed in their approach to this question.

In relation to the law of rape, in *R v Kitchener* (1993) 29 NSWLR 696 and *R v Tolmie* (1995) 37 NSWLR 660, the New South Wales Court of Criminal Appeal held that a complete failure to advert to whether or not a person is consenting to sexual intercourse amounted to recklessness. The fault element was thus imputed to the accused. Kirby P (as he then was) stated in *Kitchener* (at 697): 'To criminalise conscious advertence to the possibility of non-consent, but to excuse the reckless failure of the accused to give a moment's thought to that possibility, is self-evidently unacceptable. In the hierarchy of wrongdoing, such total indifference to the consent of a person to have sexual intercourse is plainly reckless, at least in our society today.'

However, Glanville Williams, in his *Textbook of Criminal Law* (2nd edn, London: Stevens & Sons, 1983) p 125, states that judges should not equate wilful blindness with recklessness: 'If knowledge is judicially made to include wilful blindness, and if wilful blindness is judicially deemed to equal recklessness, the result is that a person who has no knowledge is judicially deemed to have knowledge if he [or she] is found to have been reckless…'

The High Court has shown a reluctance to equate wilful blindness with recklessness or actual knowledge. In *R v Crabbe* (1985) 156 CLR 464 at 470–1, the High Court was critical of the trial judge's direction on a charge of murder that equated wilful blindness with foresight of a particular consequence being likely to result. Other decisions by the High Court in this area relegate wilful blindness to an evidential role.

In *Kural v The Queen* (1987) 162 CLR 502 the High Court had to determine the meaning of 'intention to import a prohibited import' in s 233B(1)(b) of the *Customs Act* 1901 (Cth). The majority held that this intention did not require actual knowledge of what was being imported. A belief, falling short of actual knowledge, could sustain an inference of intention. However, the majority pointed out that wilful blindness was not an alternative fault element for this offence, it was simply evidence that a jury could use to infer intention.

In *Pereira v DPP* (1988) 82 ALR 217, the High Court considered the offence of possession of a prohibited import in contravention of the *Customs Act* 1901 (Cth). The accused was delivered a package from Bombay containing cricket balls and a jewellery case that had inside them a quantity of cannabis resin. The accused had taken delivery of the package but had not opened it when the police raided her premises. The trial judge directed the jury as to the importance of proving knowledge and that wilful blindness is the equivalent of knowledge. The jury was directed that the accused could be considered wilfully blind if her suspicions about receiving a parcel from overseas were aroused and she refrained from making any enquiries for fear that she would learn the truth.

The majority of the High Court made some observations about the role of knowledge and wilful blindness. They referred to the previous High Court decision in *Kural* and held that in contrast to the offence of importing a prohibited import, the offence of the possession of a prohibited import *did* require actual knowledge. The majority then went on to state that knowledge means *actual knowledge* and not *imputed knowledge*. A state of mind *less than* actual knowledge is not sufficient. However, the accused's suspicion coupled with a failure to enquire, may be evidence from which a jury can infer knowledge. This reflects Kirby J's comments in *Peters v The Queen* (1998) 192 CLR 493 at 551 that intention must be inferred from the evidence, the focus being on discovering the intention that subjectively the accused had rather than searching for an intention that the law objectively imputes to the accused. This matter will be revisited in Chapter 5 when dealing with the fault element for the crime of rape.

Negligence

Negligence is measured on an objective standard and therefore does not sit well with the concept of the fault element of a crime as referring to a guilty mind. It is sometimes placed in a separate category to that of intention, knowledge or recklessness.

Negligence may apply to any form of the physical element. The objective standard in negligence is generally that of *reasonableness*, often expressed in terms of the standard of a 'reasonable person'. Generally, the accused's behaviour is assessed by reference to what a hypothetical reasonable person would have done in the circumstances. Often it will be difficult to distinguish recklessness from negligent conduct, purely on an external basis. The distinction lies in the accused's awareness of the danger that he or she is creating: *Andrews v DPP* [1937] AC 576 at 583; *Mamote-Kulang of Tamagot v The Queen* (1964) 111 CLR 62 at 79.

Because of the general reluctance to use objective standards in the criminal context, the courts have developed a narrow meaning for negligence and have been concerned to draw a distinction between criminal and civil concepts of negligence. Simple lack of care that may constitute civil liability is normally not enough for a crime to be committed negligently: *Andrews v DPP* [1937] AC 576; *Callaghan v The Queen* (1952) 87 CLR 115; *Nydam v The Queen* [1977] VR 430; *R v Buttsworth* [1983] 1 NSWLR 658.

The leading case on criminal negligence is that of *Nydam v The Queen* [1977] VR 430. In that case, the accused threw petrol over two women and ignited it. He claimed that he only intended to take his own life. The trial judge directed the jury as to murder and also manslaughter by criminal negligence. The accused was convicted of murder. On appeal, the Supreme Court of Victoria considered the trial judge's direction on the meaning of criminal negligence for manslaughter. The Court found that the weight of authority favoured an objective rather than a subjective test. It stated (at 445) that for manslaughter by negligence to be made out, it must be proved that the accused's behaviour involved 'such a great falling short of the standard of care which a reasonable [person] would have exercised and which involved such a high degree of risk that death or grievous bodily harm would follow that the doing of the act merit[s] criminal punishment'. Sometimes the term 'gross negligence' is used in this regard.

For manslaughter by criminal negligence, there are thus three components:
- the accused's conduct must involve a great falling short of the standard of care required of a reasonable person;
- the reasonable person, in the position of the accused, would have foreseen the risk of the particular consequence occurring; and
- the doing of the act must merit criminal punishment.

This last component is inherently circular. It is like defining a crime by saying 'X is criminal when X is sufficient to justify punishment'. This aspect of manslaughter by criminal negligence should be treated with some scepticism. It is perhaps best explained by the court's concern to distinguish criminal negligence from the standard of negligence applied in tort law.

The standard of criminal negligence may differ according to the nature of the offence. If the offence is a serious one, it would seem that the departure from the standard of reasonableness must be greater than if the offence is minor: *New South*

Wales Sugar Milling Co-op Ltd v EPA (1992) 59 A Crim R 6. This area of the law will be explored in Chapter 3 when dealing with further cases on negligent manslaughter.

Concurrence of physical and fault elements

In order for an accused to be convicted of an offence, it must be proved that the fault element coincided with, or existed at the same time as, the physical element: *Ryan v The Queen* (1967) 121 CLR 205; *R v Miller* [1983] 2 AC 161; *R v Demirian* [1989] VR 97; *Royall v The Queen* (1990) 172 CLR 378 at 458 per McHugh J. Mark Kelman has described this as blameworthiness not being 'a hovering wickedness; it is supposed to attach to particular harmful acts': 'Interpretive Construction in the Substantive Criminal Law' (1981) 33 *Stanford Law Review* 591–673 at 633.

The requirement of concurrence has tested the ingenuity of the courts. The courts have occasionally taken a look at a wider timeframe in order to fit particular facts into this requirement. Usually this has been done by imposing the fault element upon a series of acts or a 'continuing act'.

For example, the facts in *Thabo Meli v The Queen* [1954] 1 WLR 228 were that, in accordance with a preconceived plan, the accused men took the victim to a hut, gave him beer so that he was partially intoxicated, then hit him on the back of the head. They then took the victim out of the hut and, believing him to be dead, rolled him over a cliff to create the appearance of an accident. The victim was in fact still alive at that stage and later died of exposure.

The defence took a 'frame by frame' approach to concurrence and argued that there were two acts: the first act was the attack in the hut and while the fault element coincided with this act, it was not the cause of death. The second act was the rolling of the victim off the cliff and while this could be said to be the cause of death, it was not accompanied by the fault element. On appeal against conviction, the Privy Council held that it was impossible to divide up what was really a series of acts in this way. Their Lordships preferred to regard the whole of the conduct as one indivisible transaction causing death. On this reading, the fault element and physical element coincided because the accused possessed the requisite fault element at the time they started the series of acts. Lord Reid stated (at 374):

> There is no doubt that the accused set out to do all these acts in order to achieve their plan, and as parts of their plan: and it is much too refined a ground of judgment to say that, because they were under a misapprehension at one stage and thought that their guilty purpose had been achieved before, in fact, it was achieved, therefore they are to escape the penalties of the law.

Thabo Meli does not contain a clear statement as to *how* the law overcomes the problem of concurrence, except that the criminal law will not be frustrated by a refined application of its general principles. Two later decisions do, however, attempt to provide a conceptual basis for dealing with the concurrence problem, by viewing the physical element as a continuing act. In *Fagan v Metropolitan Police Commissioner* [1969] 1 QB 439 the accused drove his car (accidentally, the accused maintained) onto the foot of a police constable after being told to park his car in a particular space. The police officer stated: 'Get off, you are on my foot!' The accused replied: 'Fuck you, you can wait' and stopped the engine. The accused eventually moved the car off the victim's foot.

On appeal against a conviction for assault, the accused argued that the act of the wheel moving onto the police constable's foot occurred without the fault element. A majority of the Court of Queen's Bench rejected this argument. James J, with whom Lord Parker LJ agreed, held that the relevant act was a continuing one, which started when the wheel was driven onto the victim's foot and ended when it was removed. Viewed this way, the fault element could be superimposed upon the physical element. James J states (at 445): 'It is not necessary that mens rea [the fault element] should be present at the inception of the actus reus [the physical element]; it can be superimposed upon an existing act. On the other hand the subsequent inception of mens rea cannot convert an act which has been completed without mens rea into an assault.'

The issue of concurrence also arose in *R v Miller* (1983) 2 AC 161. In that case, the accused fell asleep while smoking. While he was asleep, his bed caught fire. He awoke to find the mattress smouldering, but instead of extinguishing the fire, he arose and moved into another room of the house and went back to sleep. The house then caught fire and damage was caused.

The accused was charged with and convicted of arson, an offence that requires a fault element of intention or recklessness as to damage to property. The problem of concurrence arose because at the time that the initial act of damage occurred, the accused lacked intention or recklessness as to damage. The prosecution relied on the accused's recklessness *after* he had become aware that the bed was on fire.

The Court of Appeal took a 'continuing act' approach to the problem of concurrence, but justified it on the basis of a duty arising from the creation of a dangerous situation. Lord Diplock stated (at 181): 'I see no rational reason from excluding from conduct capable of giving rise to criminal liability conduct which consists of failing to take measures that lie within one's power to counteract a danger that one has oneself created, if at the time of such conduct one's state of mind is such as constitutes a necessary ingredient of the offence.' Once the accused became aware of the danger he created, a duty arose to take reasonable steps to counteract that danger.

The High Court also took a relaxed approach to concurrence in *Jiminez v The Queen* (1992) 173 CLR 572. This is an important decision because it demonstrates that concurrence problems are not restricted to crimes that contain fault elements. *Jiminez* also raises concerns about voluntariness. The facts were that the accused was driving from the Gold Coast to Sydney with three companions. He took over the driving at 3.30 in the morning and two and a half hours later he fell asleep at the wheel of the car. The car went off the road and crashed into some trees, killing the front-seat passenger. The accused claimed that he had not felt tired before the accident and that he had no warning of the onset of sleep.

The accused was charged and convicted of causing death by culpable driving contrary to s 52A of the *Crimes Act* 1900 (NSW). The physical element of the offence is driving and causing death. There is no fault element required, although the prosecution must prove that the accused was driving the car in a manner dangerous to the public 'at the time of the impact'.

The principle of concurrence here requires the accused's driving both to be dangerous and to cause death. The facts of *Jiminez* posed a problem because *at the time of the impact* that caused death the accused had momentarily fallen asleep and he therefore argued that he was not driving. The High Court affirmed that a person who is asleep is not acting voluntarily and therefore a person cannot be regarded as driving while asleep. However, the majority solved this problem of concurrence by focusing on the earlier conduct of the accused. The Court examined whether the accused was driving in a manner dangerous to the public *before* he fell asleep. This occasioned examining whether he was so tired that his driving was dangerous. On the facts, the Court concluded that there was no real evidence that Jiminez had any warning of the onset of sleep and his appeal against conviction was successful.

This approach is an inversion of the *continuing* act approach: the court is looking at *earlier* conduct that is sufficiently culpable to ground criminal responsibility rather than conduct occurring *after* a dangerous event, which was the situation in *Miller*'s case. In *Jiminez* the High Court was prepared to relax the strict requirement of concurrence, to bridge the gap where the accused's lapse of consciousness was momentary.

In all, the courts have shown a willingness to construct concurrence by either imposing the fault element over a series of acts, or upon a continuing act. In *Miller* the failure to act after awareness of a dangerous situation was enough to make out criminal responsibility. In *Jiminez*, the High Court was prepared to look at antecedent conduct in order to impose criminal responsibility. In Mark Kelman's terms, all these cases show that the courts are prepared to take a broad rather than a narrow time-frame approach to concurrence: 'Interpretative Construction in the Substantive Criminal Law' (1981) 33 *Stanford Law Review* 591–673.

Causation

When the physical element of a crime requires the occurrence of specified results or consequences, the prosecution must prove that the conduct *caused* those results or consequences. Causation is of particular relevance to the crimes of murder and manslaughter in which it must be proved that the accused's conduct caused the death of the victim. It is in the context of these crimes that the tests of causation have been developed and they will be discussed further in Chapter 3. It is also of growing importance in the context of strict and absolute liability offences: N Padfield, 'Clean Water and Muddy Causation: Is Causation a Question of Law or Fact, or Just a Way of Allocating Blame?' [1995] Crim LR 683–94.

In ordinary speech and common usage, the notion of causation is used loosely. In the criminal law, the courts have moved towards a 'substantial cause' test of causation, but other tests have been applied such as 'the natural consequences' test and the 'reasonable foreseeability' test. A word of warning in relation to this area was sounded by McHugh J in *Royall v The Queen* (1990) 172 CLR 378 when he stated (at 448): 'Judicial and academic efforts to achieve a coherent theory of common law causation have not met with significant success. Perhaps the nature of the subject matter when combined with the lawyer's need to couple issues of factual causation with culpability make achievement of a coherent theory virtually impossible.'

Translated into postmodern terms, it may be futile to look for any grand theory of causation. The best that the courts can do is to come up with different legal tests to give juries who must find as a matter of fact whether the accused caused the particular criminal consequences. Burt CJ stated in *Campbell v The Queen* [1981] WAR 286 at 290 that juries are expected to apply their 'common sense' in determining whether an accused's conduct caused the death of a victim. This is particularly salient given that in *Royall v The Queen*, the members of the High Court could not agree as to which test *should* be used. In that case, a majority (Mason CJ, Deane and Dawson JJ) favoured applying the natural consequences test. Toohey and Gaudron JJ showed the greatest fidelity to the substantial cause test and Brennan and McHugh JJ in separate judgments, favoured a reasonable foreseeability test. *Royall*'s case will be explored in detail in Chapter 3.

All of the tests used by the courts are intended to be 'objective' in the sense that they are not based on what the accused subjectively intended or foresaw. This objective requirement may be difficult to apply, particularly in relation to the reasonable foreseeability test: D Lanham, 'Principles of Causation in Criminal Law' in I Freckelton and D Mendelson (eds), *Causation in Law and Medicine* (Hampshire: Ashgate Publishing Ltd, 2002) pp 211–27 at 225–6. That test involves examining whether or not the consequences of the accused's conduct were reasonably foreseeable. In obiter statements in *Royall*'s case, Mason CJ, Brennan and McHugh JJ blurred the distinction between causation and the fault element of a crime. Mason CJ stated (at 390): '[I]n some situations, the accused's state of mind will be relevant to that issue [causation] as, for example, where there is evidence that the accused intended that injury should result in the same way in which it did and where, in the absence of evidence of intention, the facts would raise a doubt about causation.'

The majority in *Royall*'s case stated that juries should not be directed in terms of forseeability because of this very risk of confusion as an objective standard and as a subjective state of mind: at 390 per Mason CJ, at 412 per Deane and Dawson JJ and at 425 per Toohey and Gaudron JJ.

The substantial cause test was developed in the earlier cases on causation and, in particular, by the Supreme Court of South Australia in *R v Hallett* [1969] SASR 141. In that case, the accused had attacked the victim on a beach, rendering the latter unconscious. The forensic evidence suggested that the victim died from drowning in shallow water. The accused claimed that he had not drowned the victim, but had simply left him in what he thought was a position of apparent safety with the victim's ankles in a few inches of water. The accused was convicted of murder and appealed to the Supreme Court of South Australian, which (at 149) posed the test as follows:

> The question to be asked is whether an act or series of acts (in exceptional cases an omission or series of omissions) consciously performed by the accused is or are so connected with the event that it or they must be regarded as having a sufficiently substantial causal effect which subsisted up to the happening of the event, without being spent or without being in the eyes of the law sufficiently interrupted by some other act or event.

The Supreme Court held in *Hallett* that the accused's original blow, which rendered the victim unconscious, started the events that led to the victim drowning. It could not be said that the tide coming in broke the chain of causation. It has subsequently been held that the accused's conduct need not be the sole cause of death in relation to the crimes of murder and manslaughter: *Pagett* (1983) 76 Cr App R 279. Death may result from several causes, but all that must be proved is that the accused's conduct was a substantial cause.

The natural consequence test may apply to situations where the victim has contributed to his or her death by seeking to escape or attempting to avoid being attacked by the accused. The facts of *Royall v The Queen* (1990) 172 CLR 378 were that the victim died after falling from the bathroom window of a sixth floor flat. The victim had previously been assaulted by the accused and the prosecution argued that the victim had either been forced from the window or had fallen from the window in retreating from an attack or had jumped in order to escape from an attack. Mason CJ (at 389) set out the test as follows '…where the conduct of the accused induces in the victim a well-founded apprehension of physical harm such as to make it a natural consequence (or reasonable) that the victim would seek to escape and the victim is injured in the course of escaping, the injury is caused by the accused's conduct'.

Mason CJ, Deane and Dawson JJ in *Royall* applied this 'commonsense' natural consequences test of causation. However, as stated above, the other members of the Court differed in the test of causation to be applied. This case is discussed further in Chapter 3.

As well as developing varying legal tests of causation, the courts have also been concerned with identifying events or actions that might break the 'chain of causation'. Like so many areas of the criminal law, the differing legal tests of causation depend upon imputing criminal responsibility to an individual assumed to have free will and therefore the capacity to control his or her conduct. This may partly explain why it has been rare for the courts to hold that once an accused intentionally sets a series of events in motion, an intervening event or *novus actus interveniens* will break the chain of causation. Types of intervening events that have been considered by the courts include the independent conduct of a third party, particularly in the area of medical treatment and of the victim him or herself. This will be explored more fully in Chapter 3 on homicide. However, it is worthwhile considering one case here that exemplifies the tortured logic that has sometimes been used to maintain the chain of causation.

In *Pagett* (1983) 76 Cr App R 279, the accused shot at armed police while using his ex-girlfriend, Gail Kinchen, as a shield. The police returned his fire and, in the course of doing so, a police officer shot and killed the ex-girlfriend. A subsequent civil action found that the police had been negligent in their handling of the siege: *Guardian*, 4, 5 December 1990.

The accused was convicted of manslaughter. On appeal, he argued that the victim's death was caused by her being shot by the police officer and this was an act of a third party that was a *novus actus interveniens*. The Court of Appeal rejected this argument.

The Court reviewed the relevant principles of causation and in particular those external factors that may operate to break the chain of causation. The Court made reference to the treatise on causation by Herbert Hart and Tony Honoré, *Causation in the Law* (Oxford: Clarendon Press, 1959). After a comprehensive review of the authorities, Hart and Honoré had concluded that the intervention of a third party will have the effect of breaking the chain of causation only where the intervention was 'voluntary' in the sense that it was 'free, deliberate and informed': *Causation in the Law* (2nd edn, Oxford: Clarendon Press, 1985) p 326.

The Court concluded (at 289) that the police officer's actions were not free and deliberate. The shooting was an act performed for the purpose of self-preservation and in performance of a legal duty: '[A] reasonable act of self-preservation, being of course itself an act caused by the accused's own act, does not operate as a novus actus interveniens.'

The Court held that the chain of causation was not broken between the victim's death and the accused's unlawful and dangerous act of firing at the police and holding the victim as a shield in front of him. On this approach, the accused was said to have caused the death of the victim through the unintended actions of another. This is a very broad approach to the issue of causation. Herbert Hart and Tony Honoré have conceded that this analysis can lead to the odd description of an armed offender who is killed by a police officer as having committed suicide: *Causation in the Law* (2nd edn, Oxford: Clarendon Press, 1985) pp 332, 334.

The Court's decision in *Pagett* can be explained by the Court's disapproval of the accused's conduct in placing the victim in a position of danger and the desire to protect police officers acting in self-preservation and in pursuit of a legal duty. The finding of police negligence in the subsequent civil action casts a doubt over the legal duty argument, but the policy behind the Court's finding is understandable. Perhaps all that can be concluded about this particular area of the law is that the notion of causation has considerable flexibility.

Conclusion

In this chapter we have examined how conceptualisations of criminal law in textbooks and the requisite syllabus for law students structure the study of criminal law into certain key offences and defences with uniform components and principles. This structure is philosophically justifiable but should be recognised as being a long way from the practice of criminal law, given that the majority of offences are heard in the Magistrates' Courts and the vast majority of statutory offences are ones of strict or absolute liability. We have also examined how a number of ideas that are meant to be central to the criminal law can be challenged. First, the presumption of innocence has been challenged by the legal burden of proof not being placed on the prosecution in many statutory offences and through the accused having to bear the burden of proving mental impairment or diminished responsibility. Secondly, the idea that serious crimes consist of a physical and fault element and the presumption of subjective fault have been confronted by the proliferation of strict and absolute liability offences. Thirdly, the notion that the physical and fault elements must be concurrent at one moment has been challenged by the courts taking a broad time-frame approach to certain cases. Finally, the issue of causation has, albeit on rare occasions, forced the courts to use a broad-brush approach to differing legal tests.

These challenges to the traditional underpinnings of the criminal law will be raised again throughout this book. We now turn to a critical examination of specific offences, starting with offences against the person.

Part 2
OFFENCES AGAINST THE PERSON

CHAPTER 3

Homicide

Introduction

In the days leading to her death, Kelly Healey's relationship with Kym Royall was 'far from serene'. Following a serious quarrel, Kelly had left their flat, planning to move in permanently with a friend. When she returned to the flat on the evening of 15 November 1986, a violent argument took place. Royall admitted punching Kelly in the face, shaking her and pulling her hair. There was evidence that Kelly had bruising to her neck, a dislocated nose and cuts to her eye and lips. Blood was found splashed in various parts of the flat. The bathroom door had been forced open and there were signs of a struggle within. There was a chipped glass ashtray in the basin and gouge marks in the bathroom wall consistent with someone swinging it. Kelly Healey's body was found on the street, under the bathroom window of their sixth-floor flat. Her body was naked and her hair was wet.

The prosecution case was that Royall had either pushed the victim out of the window, or attacked her such that in retreating from the attack she fell from the window, or that she had jumped out of the window to escape Royall's life-threatening violence. Royall claimed that when he broke into the bathroom, out of concern for Kelly's health, she jumped out the window. At trial Royall gave an unsworn statement that he knew Kelly had used amphetamines for a long time and suffered from epilepsy that caused her to become unconscious. When he heard a noise on the wall after Kelly had gone to take a shower he said he became concerned. He stated that he forced the lock with a knife and banged open the door. When interviewed he said, 'I just saw the back of Kelly going out the window. She just jumped out'.

Royall was convicted of murder. He was granted special leave to appeal to the High Court, but a majority of four judges to two dismissed his appeal: *Royall v The*

Queen (1990) 172 CLR 378. The main issue under consideration was whether Royall 'caused' Kelly's death.

The circumstances of this case not only raise the issue of causation, but also exemplify the fact that homicide, as with most crime, is a largely masculine offence, and that homicide most frequently arises in the context of a relationship between the accused and the victim. In a study conducted by Jenny Mouzos of all homicides reported to police in Australia, drawing on the Australian Institute of Criminology's National Homicide Monitoring Program, it was found that most offenders were male: only 12.8 per cent of offenders (where the gender was known) were female: *Homicidal Encounters—A Study of Homicide in Australia 1989–1999* (Canberra: AIC, 2000) p 51. However, almost two-thirds of victims (63 per cent) in the period 1989–99 were male and 37 per cent were female (at 30).

Killings of males by males was the single largest category: about half of all homicides (at 103). Men were therefore most likely to be the victim of another man. Women and girls were also more likely to be killed by a man (see 33–34).

'Homicide' is a general term used to refer to the unlawful killing of a human being. It includes offences such as murder, manslaughter, infanticide and culpable driving causing death. It is also closely allied to offences relating to childbirth such as abortion and child destruction, as well as offences of assisting and encouraging suicide. All of these offences are discussed in this chapter. We also include a discussion of euthanasia and corporate homicide in order to show the importance of social and historical factors in determining what is considered to be unlawful killing.

Murder and manslaughter most commonly occur within a relationship of some sort. Random or stranger killings are relatively rare (contrary to Hollywood and other media representations). Mouzos found that most homicides occurred between people known to each other; 20.9 per cent involved intimate partners, 14.3 per cent involved family members, 27.6 per cent involved friends/acquaintances, and 9.8 per cent other relationships. Only 19.3 per cent of homicides involved strangers, while in 8.1 per cent of cases the relationship was unknown: Jenny Mouzos, *Homicidal Encounters—A Study of Homicide in Australia 1989–1999* (Canberra: AIC, 2000) p 68.

The relationships within which homicides occur are very different for male and female victims. As illustrated by the facts in *Royall*, Jenny Mouzos' study (at 66) showed that female victims were most likely to be killed in an intimate relationship (15.3 per cent); male victims were most likely to be killed by a friend or acquaintance (23 per cent).

While the relationship between victim and offender is clearly important, it is also necessary to try to define the context in which the incident arose: why this particular offender killed this particular victim. What was the nature of their relationship or of the incident within which the killing occurred? Both the characterisation of the primary incident and the applicability of possible defences turn on understanding how the homicide arose.

Mouzos' study (at 115) found that across Australia if an adult woman was a victim of homicide she was most likely to be killed by a male intimate partner as a result of a domestic altercation. An earlier study by Alison Wallace of all homicides reported to the police in New South Wales from 1968 to 1981 found that 47 per cent of women victims were killed by their partner or spouse, compared with 10 per cent of male victims who were killed by their female partner/spouse: *Homicide: The Social Reality* (Sydney: NSW Bureau of Crime Statistics and Research, 1986) p 83.

These deaths often occurred in the context of a history of physical abuse by the male partner, who had used violence as a form of control for some time prior to the killing: J Mouzos and C Rushforth, 'Family Homicide in Australia', *Trends and Issues* No 255 (Canberra: AIC, 2003) p 3. Where women have killed a man in an intimate relationship, a history of physical abuse by the male victim has been found to have existed in a significant percentage of cases. The link between male violence and homicide raises important issues for the understanding of the broader occurrence of domestic violence, which is discussed in Chapter 4. It is also relevant to the discussion of defences such as provocation and self-defence, which are examined in Chapter 10.

A study of prosecuted homicide cases in Victoria found that women and men killed in response to different circumstances and in different relationships: Law Reform Commission of Victoria, *Homicide*, Report No 40 (Melbourne: LRCV, 1991) p 16. Men were accused of killing a stranger in 32 per cent of male homicide cases, an acquaintance/friend in 28 per cent of male cases, and their spouse or sexual partner in 16 per cent of male cases. The main circumstances in which women were accused was of killing their child (36 per cent of female cases) and a spouse or partner (34 per cent).

The context of men's and women's killings is also different. The Victorian study found that the majority of women's killings, 70 per cent of cases, took place in a 'domestic' context. Men's killings, on the other hand, showed different patterns, with the largest category, 34 per cent of cases, arising out of an argument, followed by 25 per cent domestic, and 12 per cent in the context of a robbery (at 51): see further B Naylor, 'The Law Reform Commission of Victoria Homicide Prosecution Study: The Importance of Context' in H Strang and S Gerull (eds) *Homicide: Patterns, Prevention and Control* (Canberra: Australian Institute of Criminology, 1993) pp 93–119. The importance of gender has also been identified by Ken Polk, for example, who has observed that a significant category of male killings of males arises from 'confrontations which begin as a contest over honour or reputation': 'Masculinity, Honour, and Confrontational Homicide' in K Daly and L Maher (eds), *Criminology at the Crossroads: Feminist Readings in Crime and Justice* (New York: Oxford University Press, 1998) pp 188–205 at 190. See also on these issues Jenny Mouzos, *Homicidal Encounters: A Study of Homicide in Australia 1989–1999* (Canberra: AIC, 2000) pp 101–65.

It is likely that domestic violence is much more prevalent than official reports indicate, but it does not receive significant press coverage. The media's focus on stranger killings deflects attention from the fact that women, and children, are most at risk of homicide in their own homes and among their intimates. The growth in public awareness of domestic violence generally has made this a more widely known phenomenon, but the impact of continuing media focus on stranger violence, particularly stranger violence against women, may be significant. First, it does not reflect the reported occurrence of crimes against women. The criminal statistics previously outlined suggest that most *reported* violence is between men, and that violence by men against women usually occurs in intimate relationships. Secondly, the predominance of such stories raises issues about the perceived demand for them, and the effect on readers and viewers of the high volume of these stories. They suggest to women that the public sphere is unsafe but the private sphere is safe, and confirm men's fears about women's safety in public places. Thirdly, the repetition of such stories can influence public policy making about the allocation of funding, towards for example street lighting and increased policing and away from refuges or indeed any broader structural analysis of violence: See B Naylor, 'Reporting Violence in the British Print Media: Gendered Stories' (2001) 40 *Howard Journal* 180–94.

In Australia, Indigenous people are significantly over-represented both as homicide victims and as offenders, as is the case in the criminal justice system generally. In cases where race or racial appearance was recorded by the police, 12.9/100,000 Indigenous people were victims of homicide compared to 1.6/100,000 non-Indigenous people. Whereas Indigenous people constitute 2 per cent of the total Australian population, they represent 13 per cent of homicide victims and 16.6 per cent of offenders: Jenny Mouzos, *Homicidal Encounters: A Study of Homicide in Australia 1989–1999* (Canberra: AIC, 2000) p 34. Judy Atkinson points out that 'Aboriginal men are four times more likely to die a violent death than are non-Aboriginal men, and women are 6.5 times more likely to die a violent death than are non-Aboriginal women': 'Voices in the Wilderness—Restoring Justice to Traumatised Peoples' (2002) 25(1) *UNSW Law Journal* 223–41 at 224–5 citing Fitzgerald, *Cape York Justice Study Report No 1: Summary, Conclusions and Recommendations* (2001) 19, Queensland Government Department of the Premier and Cabinet.

There are important differences in the patterns of Indigenous and non-Indigenous homicides. For example, whereas women offenders are involved in around one-tenth of non-Indigenous homicides, they constitute around one-fifth of offenders in Indigenous homicides. Further, three-quarters of Indigenous women's homicides are directed against their partner. By comparison, as noted earlier, non-Indigenous women are equally likely to kill their child or their partner: Jenny Mouzos, 'Indigenous and Non-Indigenous Homicides in Australia—A Comparative Analysis', *Trends and Issues* No 210 (Canberra: AIC 2000) p 4.

The over-representation of Indigenous offenders in the criminal justice system reflects a range of factors including the long-term effects of colonisation and dispossession, the operation of criminal justice processes and Indigenous offending behaviour, examined most comprehensively in the 1991 Report of the Royal Commission into Aboriginal Deaths in Custody: see also Chris Cunneen and David McDonald, *Keeping Aboriginal and Torres Strait Islander People out of Custody: An Evaluation of the Implementation of the Recommendations of the Royal Commission into Aboriginal Deaths in Custody* (Canberra: ATSIC, 1997).

There has also been a rapid growth in recent years in research on the extremely high levels of violence within Indigenous communities, particularly violence by Indigenous men against their family members: see Judy Atkinson, 'Voices in the Wilderness—Restoring Justice to Traumatised Peoples' (2002) 25(1) *UNSW Law Journal* 233–41 at 235; Judy Atkinson, 'Violence against Aboriginal Women: Reconstitution of Community Law: The Way Forward' (1990) 46 (2) *Aboriginal Law Bulletin* 6–9; Jenny Mouzos, 'Indigenous and Non-indigenous Homicides in Australia: A Comparative Analysis', *Trends and Issues* No 210 (Canberra: AIC, 2000).

The Queensland Aboriginal and Torres Strait Islander Women's Task Force on Violence (2000) found evidence of 'physical, psychological, cultural and structural violence in Indigenous communities': <http://www.qldwoman.qld.gov.au/publications/atsiviolence.doc>, accessed 24 October 2003, p xii. The Report states:

> Appalling acts of physical brutality and sexual violence are being perpetrated within some families and across Communities to a degree previously unknown in Indigenous life. Sadly, many of the victims are women and children, young and older people who now in many cases are living in a constant state of desperation and despair.
>
> Throughout the consultations, there was a strong message from Indigenous women that they recognise that their men are hurting too, and if there is to be a break in the cycle of violence, they must work collectively to reunite their families and to address the effects of alcohol and drug misuse and to eradicate these illnesses from their lives.

The problems associated with prosecuting domestic violence and violence in Indigenous communities will be explored further in Chapter 4 when we examine the law relating to assault.

Most writers, and most societies, accept that not all killings are in fact morally wrong. The criminal law, similarly, deals with only some forms of homicide. How a particular society classifies different sorts of killing is an important reflection of its values and how it perceives human relationships and human motivations. This is not to say that the law represents a coherent set of values. Especially in such an emotive and powerful area as taking life, the law as it stands at any particular time represents a balance between a range of conflicting interests and moral positions. Tom Sorell writes in *Moral Theory and Capital Punishment* (Oxford: Blackwell, 1987) p 2: 'But if killing people is permissible in some cases but not in others, which cases are which? Is it possible to qualify the principle that killing people is always wrong and still be left with a principle that tells us when it is wrong?'

The law may fail to distinguish between certain killings where it is arguable that a distinction should be made. For example, the law treats as murder both intentionally killing a loved parent in the terminal stages of illness and intentionally killing a drug dealer competing for the accused's illegal market. The law may also make distinctions that may seem to some to be inappropriate or problematic such as, for instance, distinguishing between murder and causing death by failing to observe occupational health and safety standards, and between manslaughter and culpable driving causing death.

While 306 deaths (1.6 per 100,000) were recorded as murders in Australia in 2001 and 246 (1.3 per 100,000) as driving causing death (Australian Bureau of Statistics), 319 were recorded as compensated workplace fatalities (4 per 100,000 employees): National Occupational Health and Safety Commission, *Compendium of Workers' Compensation Statistics Australia 2000–2001* (Canberra, 2002). Further, in 2001, deaths recorded as being 'drug-induced' amounted to 1038: Australian Bureau of Statistics, *Drug-induced Deaths 1997–2001* (Canberra: ABS, 2002). These figures raise questions as to which harms society labels as criminal, and when it is appropriate to employ the criminal justice system, and when civil or medical frameworks are apposite.

Enforcement and prosecution also reflect social values (although perhaps less in homicide than in other areas of criminal law). There may be differences in the enforcement or prosecution of the law, for example in the context of euthanasia, the non-treatment of defective neonates, abortion, and unsafe work practices that breach statutory requirements. These issues will be discussed in more detail below.

Currently, lawful homicides are considered:

- those that do not fall within any criminal category (for instance, an accidental killing); and
- those that are 'authorised' in some way, such as killings in wars, or those that are excused, for example because the accused acted in self-defence.

What is an 'acceptable' or authorised killing can vary over time. For example, killings in war may later be seen as criminal, as may the use of force by police in particular situations. The USA has resisted ratifying the International Criminal Court for fear that the actions of its soldiers fighting wars around the world might subsequently be characterised as criminal: M Leigh, 'The United States and the Statute of Rome' (2001) 95(1) *American Journal of International Law* 124–31.

Unlawful homicide is generally regarded as the most serious of criminal offences because it is aimed at human beings (as distinct from serious offences against the state such as treason) and because it produces the worst harm, that is, the irremediable harm of loss of life. However, the significance of homicide, both philosophically and as a focus for development of legal principle, is not related to its frequency.

The occurrence of homicide in Australia is fortunately relatively infrequent. The homicide rate is also essentially stable. Unlike some other offences, the homicide rate does not change significantly from year to year. In the ten-year period 1989–99 there were 3150 homicide incidents (which include a number of types of criminal killings) recorded by the police: an average of 315 homicide incidents each year across Australia. In this period the number of homicide incidents varied from a low of 297 in 1998 to highs of 331 in 1993, and 327 in 1995 and 1999: Jenny Mouzos, *Homicidal Encounters—A Study of Homicide in Australia 1989–1999* (Canberra: AIC, 2000) p 16.

In 2001, the Australian Bureau of Statistics recorded 340 homicides in Australia. Other personal offences were more frequent, but these in turn were much less frequent than offences against property. In 2001, 16,744 sexual assaults and 151,753 assaults were recorded: Australian Institute of Criminology, *Australian Crime Facts and Figures 2002* (Canberra: AIC, 2002) p 5. In the same year the police recorded 435,524 burglaries (unlawful entry with intent to steal or damage) and 699,262 thefts (excluding motor vehicle thefts): Australian Institute of Criminology, *Australian Crime Facts and Figures 2002* (Canberra: AIC, 2002) p 6.

The Australian Institute of Criminology's National Homicide Monitoring Program is an ongoing study of 'homicides' in Australia, based on police data. It examines all deaths where a person has been charged with murder or manslaughter; murder-suicides; and all other deaths classed as homicides although no suspect has been arrested. Many of the killings recorded by police may not in the event lead to prosecution, an obvious example being the murder-suicides, but this and other similar studies give valuable insights into the occurrence of killings, and their social and cultural context. Other studies may focus on cases tried, or convicted, as murder or manslaughter (for example, Law Reform Commission of Victoria, *Homicide*, Report No 40 (Melbourne: LRCV, 1991); Victorian Law Reform Commission, *Defences to Homicide*, Options Paper (Melbourne: VLRC, 2003) or, at the earlier end of the time scale, at coronial inquiries into deaths (for example, K Polk and D Ranson, 'Patterns of Homicide in Victoria' in D Chappell, P Grabosky and H Strang (eds), *Australian Violence: Contemporary Perspectives* (Canberra: AIC, 1991)). See also Jenny Morgan, *Who Kills Whom and Why: Looking Beyond Legal Categories*, Occasional Paper (Melbourne: VLRC, 2002).

In the next section, we will analyse the physical elements for both murder and manslaughter before examining the difference in the fault elements required for both.

Murder and manslaughter—physical elements

Background

Criminal homicides are categorised as 'result crimes', in which the physical element is *causing the death* of the victim, as distinct from engaging in particular prohibited *conduct*: S Bronitt and B McSherry, *Principles of Criminal Law* (Sydney: LBC,

2001) pp 161, 478. All Australian states and territories differentiate unlawful killings into categories based on seriousness. Criminal homicides fall into one of three broad classes: murder, manslaughter, or one of the special statutory categories of homicide. All jurisdictions employ the murder/manslaughter dichotomy except Western Australia, which has in addition the more serious offence of 'wilful murder': *Criminal Code* (WA) ss 277–280. Murder covers the killings regarded as most serious, and manslaughter those regarded as less blameworthy but still requiring punishment.

Seriousness is reflected in the social connotations of the offences and their naming, and also in the severity of penalty. Murder is punishable by life imprisonment (either maximum or mandatory sentence) in all jurisdictions, while the maximum penalty for manslaughter varies from twenty years to life: Murder— *Crimes Act* 1900 (ACT) s 12; *Crimes Act* 1900 (NSW) s 19A; *Criminal Code* (NT) s 164; *Criminal Code* (Qld) s 305; *Criminal Law Consolidation Act* 1935 (SA) s 11; *Criminal Code* (Tas) s 158; *Crimes Act* 1958 (Vic) s 3; *Criminal Code* (WA) s 282. Manslaughter— *Crimes Act* 1900 (ACT) s 15 (twenty years); *Crimes Act* 1900 (NSW) s 24 (twenty-five years); *Criminal Code* (NT) s 167 (life); *Criminal Code* (Qld) s 310 (life); *Criminal Law Consolidation Act* 1935 (SA) s 13 (life); *Criminal Code* (Tas) s 389 (twenty-one years); *Crimes Act* 1958 (Vic) s 5 (twenty years); *Criminal Code* (WA) s 287 (twenty years).

Life imprisonment is mandatory for murder in the Northern Territory (*Criminal Code* (NT) s 164), Queensland (*Criminal Code* (Qld) s 305—life or indefinite sentence), South Australia (*Criminal Law Consolidation Act* 1935 (SA) s 11) and Western Australia (*Criminal Code* (WA) s 282), and discretionary in the Australian Capital Territory (*Crimes Act* 1900 (ACT) s 12), New South Wales (*Crimes Act* 1900 (NSW) s 19A), Tasmania (*Criminal Code* (Tas) s 158) and Victoria (*Crimes Act* 1958 (Vic) s 3). A life sentence generally means that the offender is under the state's control for life. In practice (unless stated otherwise) he or she will be released on parole at some point following review of progress and of the appropriateness of the time served in custody, but will always be subject to possible re-incarceration following serious misbehaviour.

Sir Edward Coke, an eminent seventeenth-century lawyer, described murder as: 'when a man of sound memory, and of the age of discretion, unlawfully killeth any reasonable creature [in being] under the King's peace, with malice aforethought, either expressed ... or implied by law, so as the [death occurs] within a year and a day': *Institutes of the Laws of England: Third Part* (London, 1680) 3 Inst 47. Murder and manslaughter are now defined by statute in most Australian jurisdictions. Only South Australia and Victoria still rely on the common law definition.

The physical elements are the same for murder and manslaughter. The central element in both is causing the death of a human being. The difference between the offences lies in the fault element—the element of blameworthiness. This will be discussed following examination of the physical elements of both offences.

The current law

The two main physical elements that must be proved for murder and manslaughter are:
- that the victim was a living human being; and
- that the accused caused the victim's death.

There are also other matters that must be proved beyond reasonable doubt by the prosecution, which have been referred to in Chapters 1 and 2. For example, the reference by Sir Edward Coke to a person 'of sound memory and of the age of discretion' is really referring to a person who is not mentally impaired or under the age of criminal responsibility. Coke's reference to 'under the King's peace' simply means that the homicide must have taken place within the jurisdiction of the prosecuting authority. The reference to a death taking place 'within a year and a day' was aimed, pragmatically, at excluding criminal liability for long-term effects at a time when medical knowledge made it difficult clearly to ascribe causes to disease. The rule has now been abolished in all jurisdictions: *Crimes Act* 1900 (ACT) s 11(1); *Crimes Act* 1990 (NSW) s 17A; *Penalties and Sentences Act* 1992 (Qld) s 207 (now superseded); *Criminal Law Consolidation Act* 1935 (SA) s 18; *Criminal Code Amendment (Year and Day Rule Repeal) Act* 1993 (Tas) s 4; *Crimes Act* 1958 (Vic) s 59AA; *Criminal Law Amendment Act* 1991 (WA) s 6.

Sir Edward Coke's definition of murder refers to the responsibility of an individual. As explored in Chapter 1, it has been conventionally assumed that only a human being can be charged with homicide. However, there have been attempts recently to prosecute corporations for homicide, and this appears to be technically possible although to date there have been few successful prosecutions. The categorising and prosecution of a significant proportion of deaths each year as 'occupational health and safety' matters is another illustration of the 'constructed' nature of the criminal law. This issue will be considered further in a separate section below on corporate homicide.

Generally, the physical elements for homicide relate to an accused's conduct. This will usually refer to an action by the accused, but there may be circumstances in which a person may be guilty where they caused death by an omission to act (with the relevant intention) where they were under a legal duty to act. It may be noted that the distinction between an act and an omission is not always easy to draw, making this sub-category less significant. As Windeyer J observed in *R v Phillips*, 'If a man intentionally moves when he ought to stand still, or stands still when he ought to move, his conduct can be regarded either as an act or as an omission or as both': (1971) 45 ALJR 467 at 477. This issue primarily arises in the context of manslaughter and is discussed in detail below under that heading. However, there is no reason in principle why a person should not be found guilty of murder, as well as manslaughter, when their inaction, under an obligation to act, coupled with the necessary fault element, causes death.

We turn now to outlining the two main physical elements for both murder and manslaughter.

Death of a human being

A central requirement for criminal responsibility for an unlawful homicide has been that the victim is a *human being*, or, in Sir Edward Coke's words, a 'reasonable creature in being'. In *R v Hutty* [1953] VLR 338 at 339, Barry J held that murder could only be committed on a person who is 'in being' and 'legally a person is not in being until he or she is fully born in a living state'.

This begs the question as to when a child can be considered 'fully born'. Barry J at 339 then set out the test at common law as follows:

> A baby is fully and completely born when it is completely delivered from the body of its mother and it has a separate and independent existence in the sense that it does not derive its power of living from its mother. It is not material that the child may still be attached to its mother by the umbilical cord; that does not prevent it from having a separate existence. But it is required, before the child can be the victim of murder or of manslaughter or of infanticide, that the child should have an existence separate from and independent of its mother, and that occurs when the child is fully extruded from the mother's body and is living by virtue of the functioning of its own organs.

This test is followed in the common law states of South Australia and Victoria and the *Criminal Codes* are very similar in setting out the requirement that the child be 'completely extruded' from the body of its mother and in a 'living' state: *Criminal Code* (NT) s 156; *Criminal Code* (Qld) s 292; *Criminal Code* (Tas) s 153(4); *Criminal Code* (WA) s 269. For example, under *Criminal Code* (Qld) s 292 and *Criminal Code* (WA) s 269: 'A child becomes a person capable of being killed when it has completely proceeded in a living state from the body of its mother, whether it has breathed or not, and whether it has an independent circulation or not, and whether the navel-string is severed or not.' There is no requirement that the child should have breathed, perhaps because a child may be born alive, but not breathe for some time after birth: *R v Brain* (1834) 6 C & P 349 at 350 per Park J.

The tests in the Australian Capital Territory and New South Wales are a little different in specifically requiring that the child has breathed. Section 20 of the *Crimes Act* 1900 (NSW) states: 'On the trial of a person for the murder of a child, such child shall be held to have been born alive if it has breathed, and has been wholly born into the world whether it has had an independent circulation or not.' Additional offences related to pregnancy and childbirth have been developed in all jurisdictions, which will be discussed later in this chapter.

The main exception to the general rule that killing a foetus cannot amount to murder or manslaughter relates to circumstances where a baby was injured in the womb, born alive, but subsequently died as a result of the injuries. In such a case, the accused may be charged with a homicide offence. This is specifically provided for in the Code jurisdictions: *Criminal Code* (NT) s 158; *Criminal Code* (Qld) s 294; *Criminal Code* (Tas) s 153(5); *Criminal Code* (WA) s 271. In *Martin (No 2)* (1996) 86 A Crim R 133, the Western Australian Court of Criminal Appeal held that once there is a live person, who then dies, even from injuries suffered before birth, the unlawful killing offences are applicable. The Court held that s 271 of the *Criminal Code* (WA) applied to an injury to a foetus suffered at any stage of pregnancy, and was not limited to the period shortly before or at birth.

The other issue raised by the requirement that the victim be a living human being relates to when a person may be considered brain dead, for example for the purposes of switching off life support systems. Most jurisdictions now have legislation deeming a person to be dead where there has occurred either irreversible cessation of all functions of the brain or irreversible cessation of the circulation of blood: *Transplantation and Anatomy Act* 1978 (ACT) s 45; *Human Tissue Act* 1983 (NSW) s 33; *Human Tissue Transplant Act* 1979 (NT) s 23; *Death (Definition) Act* 1983 (SA) s 2; *Transplantation and Anatomy Act* 1979 (Qld) s 45 (for the purposes of that Act). There is no statutory definition of death in Western Australia, but s 24(2) of the *Human Tissue and Transplant Act* 1982 states that tissue shall not be removed unless two medical practitioners have declared that 'irreversible cessation of all function of the brain of the person has occurred'.

The requirement for the irreversible cessation of all functions of the brain is significant. The brain stem regulates reflex activities such as heart rate and respiration, whereas the forebrain mediates the complex functions of voluntary movement, sensory input and cognitive processes. A patient may have severe damage to the forebrain causing a lack of awareness, but if the brain stem is still functioning, then the patient is still legally alive. Thus, because those in what is usually termed a 'persistent vegetative state' have some function in the brain stem, they are not considered dead for the purposes of organ transplantation. However, a decision not to keep such patients alive through artificial nutrition and hydration will not necessarily lead to criminal responsibility for causing their death. This will be further explored in the Critique section.

Causation of death

Another central component of the physical elements of homicide is that of causation: the jury must be satisfied that the offender's actions *caused* the victim's death. In most cases, of course, causation is not in dispute. It is clear enough, for instance, where an accused puts a gun to the victim's head and pulls the trigger that he or she has caused the death of the victim. But what about the situation where the shot did not kill the victim, but the victim died from infection caught in the hospital, or from blood loss through having refused a blood transfusion? Or, while the victim was lying in the house immobilised by the shot, the house caught fire and burned down? Or indeed if the accused lured the victim to an unfamiliar part of town, intending to kill, and on the way the victim was hit by a bus and killed?

In a sense there is a connection between each of these actions and the victim's death. But the law requires a relatively specific causal link to be shown, if the accused is to be found criminally liable for causing death. While the accused may be liable in the first and second scenarios above, the third is less clear, and liability would not be imposed in the fourth.

As previously noted in Chapter 2, there is in practice no 'grand theory' of causation, and no single test that will be universally applicable. Several tests have been developed through the case law, depending on the factual issues facing the particular jury. It is important to recall that the focus is on identifying a *legal* test of causation that judge can give jury, so the jury can decide *as fact* whether the accused here caused the death.

In the Northern Territory, Queensland and Western Australia the test simply requires proof of a factual connection: whether the death was caused 'directly or indirectly' by the accused: *Criminal Code* (NT) s 157; *Criminal Code* (Qld) s 293; *Criminal Code* (WA) s 270. In Tasmania the test is stricter. The prosecution has to show that the victim's death was 'directly and immediately connected' with the accused's act or omission: *Criminal Code* (Tas) s 153(2).

The remaining states rely on the following common law principles, which are also applicable in the interpretation of the Code provisions: E Colvin, S Linden and L Bunney, *Criminal Law in Queensland and Western Australia* (3rd edn, Sydney: Butterworths, 2001) p 30.

As set out in Chapter 2, in *R v Hallett* [1969] SASR 141, the Supreme Court of South Australia held that the accused's conduct need not be the *sole* cause of death, but must be a *substantial* cause of it. The Court stated at 149: 'The question to be asked is whether an act...consciously performed by the accused is...so connected with the event that it...must be regarded as having a sufficiently substantial causal effect which subsisted up to the [death], without being spent or without being in the eyes of the law sufficiently interrupted by some other act or event.'

A number of cases have dealt with the issue as to what intervening act or acts may break the nexus or 'chain of causation' between the conduct of the accused and the victim's death. As discussed in *Hallett*'s case, the intervening act may be a natural event such as a tidal wave or earthquake, or the independent actions of a third party or indeed of the victim. This is sometimes referred to as a *novus actus interveniens*. Most simply, if one assailant stabs the victim, who might well have died, but another then comes along and shoots the victim dead, the first assailant will not have 'caused' the death. (The first assailant may however be guilty of *attempted* homicide.)

Some cases have considered the effect of medical treatment, or medical complications, on liability for wounding someone where the victim dies. While the specific facts are crucial when considering causation, the general view now seems to be that treatment, and complications arising from medical treatment, would have to be extremely bad or entirely unpredictable to break the chain of causation.

Take for example the case of *R v Smith* [1959] 2 QB 35, which concerned two soldiers, Thomas Smith and Private Creed. In the course of a fight, Smith stabbed Creed in the arm and back with a bayonet. The victim was carried to a medical station. On the way he was dropped twice. No one recognised that the bayonet had pierced the victim's lung and caused a haemorrhage. He was given oxygen and artificial respiration—treatment that was later described as being 'thoroughly bad' in the circumstances—and died shortly after. There was evidence that if the victim had received a blood transfusion he would probably not have died.

Despite the evidence of highly inappropriate medical treatment, the accused was found to have caused the death. The Court stated at 42–3:

> [I]f at the time of death the original wound [or event] is still *an operating cause and a substantial cause*, then the death can properly be said to be the result of the wound, albeit that some other cause of death is also operating. Only if it can be said that the original wounding is *merely the setting* in which another cause operates can it be said that the death does not result from the wound. [Emphasis added.]

More recent cases have confirmed the courts' unwillingness to find that medical treatment, even inappropriate treatment, absolved the original attacker of responsibility.

The Victorian Supreme Court upheld convictions for murder where the victim was stabbed by the two accused, all being fellow prisoners sharing a cell: *R v Evans and Gardiner (No 2)* [1976] VR 523. The victim had successful surgery, but died eleven months later when he developed obstructive scarring at the site of the operation. This was not an uncommon sequel and could have been diagnosed and corrected. The Full Court affirmed the approach in *Smith*'s case. It distinguished the earlier UK decision in *Jordan* (1956) 40 Cr App Rep 152 at 531 where the Court had held that the attacker was no longer liable where the original wound was healing and the treatment included medication to which the victim had been allergic, and had been 'palpably wrong'.

Similar views have been taken in recent English decisions. The facts of *R v Cheshire* [1991] 1 WLR 844 were that David Cheshire shot and wounded his victim Trevor Jeffrey in the leg and stomach. The victim was improving with treatment, but developed respiratory problems in hospital. A tracheotomy tube was inserted in his windpipe to address the problem. More than two months after the shooting, the victim died of a heart attack, because his windpipe had been obstructed at the site of the tracheotomy. This was a 'rare but not unknown' complication of a tracheotomy, which had not been diagnosed by the hospital. Beldam J in delivering the judgment of the Court of Appeal stated at 852: 'Even though negligence in the treatment of the victim was the immediate cause of his death, the jury should not regard it as excluding the responsibility of the defendant unless the negligent treatment was so independent of his acts, and in itself so potent in causing death, that they regard the contribution made by his acts as insignificant.' Cheshire's appeal against his murder conviction was dismissed.

The Code jurisdictions provide explicitly that if the victim suffers serious harm and dies as a result of proper surgery or medical treatment, applied in good faith, the accused is still deemed to have killed the victim: *Criminal Code* (NT) s 160; *Criminal Code* (Qld) s 298; *Criminal Code* (Tas) s 154(a); *Criminal Code* (WA) s 275.

Where a patient is on a life support system as a result of the accused's attack, and the medical practitioner forms the view that the victim is medically dead and that the machine should be disconnected, turning off the life support system does not break the chain of causation, as the original injury is still 'a continuing or operating cause of death': *R v Malcherek; R v Steel* [1981] 1 WLR 690.

The chain of causation has been held to extend to the killing of another person as a result of the accused's actions. As discussed in Chapter 2, in *Pagett* (1983) 76 Cr App R 279 a police officer, shooting in self-defence, killed the accused's ex-girlfriend, who was being used as a shield by the accused. The accused was held to have caused the victim's death. Rather than being a *novus actus interveniens*, breaking the chain of causation (which, at 279, 280, was a possible reading of the situation), the Court concluded that the police officer's actions were not free and deliberate, but were performed in self-defence, in response to the accused's shots.

What of the situation where, for instance, an elderly victim with a weak heart dies of a heart attack as a result of the accused's assault? The accused's actions will probably be held to have *caused* the death: the accused is required to 'take the victim as they find them'. It will not break the chain of causation if the victim had a special characteristic making him or her more likely to die from the injury or because he or she refused a blood transfusion due to religious beliefs; *R v Blaue* [1975] 1 WLR 1411. This common law rule is embodied in *Criminal Code* (Qld) s 23(1A). Failure by the victim to take proper care will similarly not break the chain of causation: *R v Bingapore* (1975) 11 SASR 469; *Criminal Code* (Qld) s 297; *Criminal Code* (Tas) s 154(b); *Criminal Code* (WA) s 274.

An accused may also be held to have caused death where his or her action made the victim act in a way that led to their death, for example in an attempt at self-preservation. In some cases the courts have said that the accused will only be liable if the victim's response was a natural consequence or 'reasonably foreseeable'. A tendency has been noted in English courts of taking a tough stance on causation where the victim has taken evasive action and died—where a 'daft' or 'unforeseeable' response may break the chain of causation—while upholding the accused's responsibility once the injury has been inflicted, no matter how 'irrational' the victim's action thereafter (such as failure to take proper care of the injury): N Lacey and C Wells, *Reconstructing Criminal Law* (2nd edn, London: Butterworths, 1998) p 241.

A requirement of foreseeability of the victim's response has not, however, been universally accepted, and members of the High Court took different views of this aspect of causation in *Royall v The Queen* (1990) 172 CLR 378 as will be discussed below in the Critique section.

The Code jurisdictions provide that when an accused causes the victim, by threats or deceit, to carry out an act or omission that results in the victim's death, the accused is deemed to have killed the victim: *Criminal Code* (NT) s 159; *Criminal Code* (Qld) s 295; *Criminal Code* (WA) s 272. The Tasmanian provision incorporates a foreseeability test of whether the victim's action/omission, which caused the victim's death, was 'likely to cause death and which he [the accused] knows or ought to have known the other would be likely to do': *Criminal Code* (Tas) s 154(c).

Several cases over the years have dealt with the issue of causation where a female victim has died trying to escape or avoid the violence of her male partner/assailant. The approach taken in some nineteenth-century cases underlines the social and historical context within which issues such as family violence are understood. An example is the Kentucky case of *Hendrickson v The Commonwealth* 3 Southwestern Reporter 166 (1887). The accused's pregnant wife ran out of the house after the accused threatened to kill her, and froze to death. The Kentucky Court of Appeal ordered a retrial on the basis that the jury should have been directed to decide whether the wife's fear was 'well grounded or reasonable'. Such cases raise obvious questions about whose standard of reasonableness was being applied.

While victims seeking escape have sometimes been subjected to a test of the reasonableness of their actions, where victims' reactions to the violence, once perpetrated, resulted in their death, the courts have been satisfied that causation has been shown. This is consistent with the principle noted earlier that an assailant may be required to 'take their victim as they find them'.

An example is the Indiana case of *Stephenson v State* 179 NE 633 (1932). This was an appeal from a conviction for murder where the victim had taken poison after a violent rape by the accused, while still detained by the accused. The accused refused to obtain medical assistance and the victim was then left at her home. She died a month later from the poisoning and possibly from an abscess caused by the accused's bites. The jury had found that the victim had taken the poison while 'distracted with the pain and shame' and that the accused was therefore still responsible for her death. The conviction for murder was affirmed. The case may be limited to the time during which the victim was overwhelmed by the accused's actions. It is not clear whether the finding would have been upheld if the victim had taken poison some time later while depressed.

The contradictions in these approaches were most recently clearly illustrated in the High Court decision in *Royall v The Queen* (1990) 172 CLR 378, the facts of which were outlined at the beginning of this chapter. If Royall had pushed Kelly, or she had fallen out of the window during his attack, it would seem clear that his actions had caused her death. But what of the other two scenarios—that she either jumped to escape him, or simply jumped voluntarily from the window? The accused argued that Kelly acted voluntarily (perhaps as a result of drugs, or depression, or epilepsy) and thereby broke any chain of causation or connection with any actions by him.

The High Court considered the question of the correct test of causation to apply, if the victim *had* jumped out of fear of further assault rather than having been pushed. As previously explored in Chapter 2, Mason CJ held at 389 that the assailant would have caused the victim's injury/death 'where the conduct of the accused induces in the victim a well-founded apprehension of physical harm such as to make it a natural consequence (or reasonable) that the victim would seek to escape'. Similar terminology—a 'well-founded fear or apprehension' making it a 'natural consequence' that the victim should try to escape—was approved by Deane and Dawson JJ (at 410) and this may be regarded as the majority view of the High Court on this point. The 'natural consequences' test endorsed by Mason CJ and Deane and Dawson JJ can therefore be viewed as the Court's authoritative statement of the law on causation for use in the context of self-preservation cases.

Critique

A number of issues are raised by the current state of the law setting out the physical elements of murder and manslaughter. There is a lack of clarity on the law relating to when a human being will be considered alive for the purposes of the law of homicide and, as pointed out in Chapter 2, the concept of causation is a malleable one.

The line between murder and manslaughter and those crimes dealing with pregnancy and childbirth is very much a matter of timing. In jurisdictions other than New South Wales and South Australia, an offence of child destruction has been created to overcome the difficulty that may arise where a child is killed in the process of being born: *Crimes Act* 1900 (ACT) s 42; *Criminal Code* (NT) s 170; *Criminal Code* (Qld) s 313; *Criminal Code* (Tas) s 165; *Crimes Act* 1958 (Vic) s 10; *Criminal Code* (WA) s 290. This offence will be dealt with more fully later in the chapter, but it is worthwhile noting here that one of the elements of the offence is that the child must be 'capable of being born alive'. Section 10(2) of the *Crimes Act* 1958 (Vic) sets out a statutory presumption that a foetus is capable of being born alive after a gestation period of 28 weeks. There is considerable difficulty, however, in establishing whether a foetus of less than 28 weeks is capable of being born alive. In *Rance v Mid-Downs Health Authority* [1991] 1 QB 587 at 621, Brooke J held that a 27-week-old foetus was 'capable of being born alive' if it was capable of 'breathing and living by reason of its breathing through its own lungs alone'.

There is a need for greater clarity in this area as to when a foetus should be considered capable of being born alive and when a child is considered a human being for the purposes of the law of homicide. Robyn Sweet points out that 'the law needs to be clarified in order to take into account the new types of knowledge with which pregnant women can be armed when making decisions about their pregnancies': 'Legal Issues in Reproductive Rights' (2002) 9 *Journal of Law and Medicine* 266–70 at 267. Offences relating to pregnancy and childbirth will be further explored later in this chapter.

At the other end of the life continuum, some have argued that the pressing need for organs for transplantation should lead to the concept of death being redefined to the cessation of functioning of the forebrain or 'higher brain', which would enable those in a persistent vegetative state to be considered legally dead: see discussion in I Kerridge, M Lowe and J McPhee, *Ethics and Law for the Health Professions* (Katoomba, NSW: Social Science Press, 1998) pp 420–36 at 425, and A Asai, 'Should a Patient in a Persistent Vegetative State Live?' (1999) 18(2) *Monash Bioethics Review* 25–39.

The Model Criminal Code Officers Committee (MCCOC) has recommended that there be no change to the legal definition of death because the ramifications of such a change would 'extend beyond the criminal law': *Chapter 5, Fatal Offences Against the Person*, Discussion Paper (June 1998) p 21. Those considered brain-dead do not easily fit within our concept of a dead person in that they are 'pink and warm, their hearts beat and they continue to breathe with the aid of a ventilator': I Kerridge, M Lowe and J McPhee, *Ethics and Law for the Health Professions* (Katoomba, NSW: Social Science Press, 1998) pp 420–36 at 425. The MCCOC recommendation is therefore reasonable in advocating the retention of the status quo, in relation to an issue that requires determination in a broader social and moral context.

In relation to the issue of causation, the MCCOC has proposed that conduct be regarded as causing death or harm if it 'substantially contributed to' the death or harm: *Chapter 5, Fatal Offences Against the Person*, Discussion Paper (June 1998) p 24. The Committee's view was that a substantial contribution (as opposed to cause) test can be applied uniformly even in relation to self-preservation cases: at 29–30.

The question arises as to whether or not the concept of foreseeability should have a role in developing a legal test of causation. As explored in Chapter 2, a majority in *Royall v The Queen* (1990) 172 CLR 378 stated that juries should not be directed in terms of foreseeability because of the risk of confusion between an objective standard and a subjective state of mind: at 390 per Mason CJ, at 412 per Deane and Dawson JJ and at 425 per Toohey and Gaudron JJ.

McHugh and Brennan JJ in separate judgments favoured a reasonable foreseeability test, that is, could a reasonable person have foreseen that the victim would seek to escape. Mason CJ at 390, on the other hand, observed that the reasonableness of the escape act of the victim might be relevant in some situations, but that a victim acting in fear of their life should not be expected to act in an entirely rational fashion, viewed after the event.

There is no logical connection between causation and the foreseeability of the victim's (or another person's) response. Questions of 'causation' should be addressed separately from questions of the accused person's 'intent' or 'foresight'. Incorporating notions of foreseeability as a means of limiting liability to behaviour by a victim, which is in some sense proportionate to the threat posed by the accused, confuses these factors. It should be found that the accused 'caused' the death if in fact his/her acts led the victim to act as they did, reasonably or not. The accused cannot argue that the victim brought on their own death simply because they had a peculiarity or personality or belief that led them to act in the way they did.

The question of causation—did the accused's action cause/contribute to the victim's death—should be assessed objectively without reference to notions of blame. This would seem to be a more realistic approach to the question, and one more manageable by juries. If the accused does not have the necessary mental state or fault element, he or she will not ultimately be held criminally responsible.

Murder—fault elements

Background

Douglas Crabbe was a long-distance truck driver. On 17 August 1983, he drove a road train to Ayers Rock, in the heart of the Northern Territory. He unloaded the vehicle and detached all but one of the trailers. In the evening, he went to the Inland Motel and drank in the crowded public bar. He became louder and more annoying as the evening went on and eventually was physically ejected from the pub. Crabbe said that he went to sleep in the cabin of his prime mover. However in the early hours of the next morning he started it up and drove it through the wall of the bar. Five people died and many were injured. Crabbe stepped out of the cabin and left the motel without assisting the injured.

Crabbe was charged with murder, and the case was heard in the Supreme Court of the Northern Territory. The question for the jury was whether his state of mind amounted to the necessary fault element for him to be guilty of murder: *R v Crabbe* (1985) 156 CLR 464. The Chief Justice of the Northern Territory at 467 directed the jury as follows:

> There appears...to be no dispute that Crabbe killed these people, in the sense that he drove the prime mover and semi-trailer into the bar of this motel at Ayers Rock, and that thereby he caused the deaths of these five people, so that, when you're considering whether or not he is guilty of murder, you have to consider the state of his mind at the time that he did it. If you're satisfied beyond reasonable doubt that when he drove the truck into the motel he intended to cause death or really serious bodily harm to whoever might be in there, then he's guilty of murder. If you're satisfied beyond reasonable doubt that his state of mind was that he knew that it was likely that if he drove the truck into the motel bar, that he would cause death or really serious bodily injury, then he is guilty of murder.

Homicide **107**

This part of the direction was approved by the High Court on appeal, although it regarded at 469 the term 'probable' as equivalent to 'likely'. The case stands as authority for the principle that at common law, a person can be guilty of murder who *intends* to kill or to cause really serious (or 'grievous') bodily harm, or who is *reckless* as to causing death or really serious bodily harm, that is, where the accused knows that death or really serious bodily harm are probable or likely. We will discuss below some differences between jurisdictions in the application of these general principles.

One additional aspect of the Chief Justice's direction in *Crabbe*'s case was, however, rejected by the High Court, and this was the category of 'wilful blindness'. The Chief Justice at 467 directed the jury that Crabbe could also be guilty of murder if he 'foresaw the possibility that there might be some people in the bar, but didn't take any step ... to find out'. The High Court held that this was not a separate category of fault. Instead, the question was whether or not the offender intended to cause death or really serious harm or foresaw the probability of causing such harm. The High Court accepted at 471 that in some cases if the accused deliberately abstained from enquiry this might, at most, be *evidence* of his/her actual knowledge or foresight of the probability of causing the consequences.

Crabbe was granted a new trial. Upon retrial, Crabbe was again convicted on five counts of murder and sentenced to life imprisonment on each count. A further appeal on the basis of new evidence, claimed to support a defence based on automatism, was unsuccessful: *Crabbe v The Queen* (1990) 101 FLR 133.

The facts of *Crabbe*'s case raise the question as to how broad the fault element for murder should be. The English courts take a much stricter approach to the fault element and this will be discussed in the Critique section. First, however, we will outline some of the differences in the current law in the Australian jurisdictions.

The current law

The fault element for murder differs across Australian jurisdictions, and only Victoria and South Australia include all of the four alternative components that were set out in *Crabbe*'s case. Currently the fault elements for murder include some or all of the following:

- intention to kill: *Crimes Act* 1900 (ACT) s 12(1)(a); *Crimes Act* 1900 (NSW) s 18(1)(a); *Criminal Code* (NT) s 162(1)(a); *Criminal Code* (Qld) s 302(1)(a); *Criminal Code* (Tas) s 157(1)(a); *Criminal Code* (WA) s 278. Victoria and South Australia follow the common law;
- intention to inflict grievous (really serious) bodily harm: *Crimes Act* 1900 (NSW) s 18(1)(a); *Criminal Code* (NT) s 162(1)(a); *Criminal Code* (Qld) s 302(1)(a); *Criminal Code* (Tas) s 157(1)(b); *Criminal Code* (WA) s 279(1)(a). Victoria and South Australia follow the common law. The Australian Capital Territory does not include this part of the fault element in its definition of murder;

- recklessness as to death: *Crimes Act* 1900 (ACT) s 12(1)(b); *Crimes Act* 1900 (NSW) s 18(1)(a); *Criminal Code* (Tas) s 157(1)(c). Victoria and South Australia follow the common law; and
- recklessness as to inflicting grievous bodily harm: this is included only in Victoria and South Australia.

These components are all intended to reflect an appropriate level of moral culpability for causing death, and incorporate a test of criminal responsibility based on the harm the offender intended or saw as probable. As discussed in Chapter 2, the focus is on the subjective state of mind of the offender. It can be seen that even within Australia there are different assessments of the level of intentionality that constitute the meaning of 'murder'.

The meaning of each of these terms will be discussed further below. It must, however, be noted that all Australian jurisdictions except the Australian Capital Territory also include in the category of murder the notion of 'constructive murder'. This is a killing (with no intention or recklessness as to causing death or grievous bodily harm) by an act of violence, either in the course of another serious violent crime, or in the course of resisting arrest or escaping from custody: *Crimes Act* 1900 (NSW) s 18(1)(a); *Criminal Code* (NT) s 162; *Criminal Code* (Qld) s 302(1)(c); *Criminal Law Consolidation Act* 1935 (SA) s 12A; *Criminal Code* (Tas) s 157(1)(d); *Crimes Act* 1958 (Vic) s 3A; *Criminal Code* (WA) s 279. This is the exception to the requirement of a subjective fault element. It will be discussed further below in a separate section.

Intention to kill

This is the central, fundamental form of the fault element for murder. The meaning of 'intention' is discussed in general terms in Chapter 2. An intention to kill as presently understood means having the purpose of bringing about the death of another, or knowing that death is certain to result from one's action, even if it is not specifically desired.

The concept of 'intention' is itself a complicated one. As explored in Chapter 2, Alan Norrie has suggested that the law has recognised three different and conflicting meanings of intention: 'Criminal Law to Legal Theory: The Mysterious Case of the Reasonable Glue Sniffer' (2002) 65(4) *Modern Law Review* 538–55 at 539. These are:
- intention as purpose in the sense of meaning to perform the conduct;
- intention as purpose plus foresight of virtually certain side-effect; and
- intention as purpose plus foresight of probable consequence.

In relation to murder, the first two meanings have been used. The third meaning, usually referred to as oblique intention, has been used in England, but falls within the category of recklessness in Australia. It is clear that intention is not the same as 'desire': a person can *want* to kill, but be a bad shot and miss entirely, and not be guilty of murder. On the other hand, a person can firebomb a factory for the insurance money, not wanting to kill the security guard stationed on the premises, but knowing the guard will inevitably be killed. In this case the accused will be guilty of murder. 'Intention' here refers to the intentional achievement of, or knowledge of certainty of, particular *consequences or results*.

Intention is defined in the *Criminal Code* (Cth) as being addressed to either conduct, circumstances or results, and occurring with respect to a result (such as causing death) where the person 'means to bring it about or is aware that it will occur in the ordinary course of events': s 5.2(3).

Intention to cause grievous bodily harm

All jurisdictions except the Australian Capital Territory include as a fault element an intention to inflict grievous or really serious injury less than death. The accused must be shown to have had the purpose of inflicting grievous bodily harm, or to have known that such harm was certain to result. Section 157(1)(b) of the Tasmanian *Criminal Code* defines this aspect of intention more strictly. It refers to intention to cause 'bodily harm which the offender knew to be likely to cause death'.

The level of intended harm is defined in Queensland, Tasmania and Western Australia in terms of bodily injury of such a nature as to endanger life, or to cause permanent injury to health: *Criminal Code* (Qld) s 1; *Criminal Code* (Tas) s 1; *Criminal Code* (WA) s 1. Section 1(4) of the *Criminal Code* (WA) extends this definition to include a 'serious disease'.

The definition in the Northern Territory is in terms of 'physical or mental injury' endangering life or health: *Criminal Code* (NT) s 1. In New South Wales it includes 'any permanent or serious disfiguring of the person': *Crimes Act* 1900 (NSW) s 4. In Victoria and South Australia the common law definition set out in *DPP v Smith* [1961] AC 290 applies; that is, grievous bodily harm means 'really serious injury'. The High Court of Australia confirmed the use of 'really serious injury' in place of 'grievous bodily harm' in *Meyers v The Queen* (1997) 147 ALR 440 at 441. It includes stabbing, punching, and also intentionally making the victim unconscious, as occurred in *Rhodes* (1984) 14 A Crim R 124 where the accused held a pillow over the struggling victim's face to stop her screaming.

The question whether such 'grievous' or 'serious' harm was intended is a matter for the jury to decide. In all jurisdictions that have this element of murder (with the exception of Tasmania) the accused can therefore be guilty of murder without having turned his or her mind in any way to the risk of causing death. This will be discussed in the Critique section.

Recklessness as to causing death or grievous bodily harm

Recklessness as to causing death is one form of the fault element in the Australian Capital Territory, New South Wales, South Australia, Tasmania and Victoria. Recklessness as to causing grievous bodily harm is also included under the common law in South Australia and Victoria.

'Recklessness' has a wide range of meanings in general usage, from foolishness or carelessness to malicious disregard of others. However, it has a very specific meaning in the law of homicide. First, it is subjective; it refers to *knowing* that there is a risk of a particular consequence: in this context, that of death or grievous bodily harm. As explored in Chapter 2, recklessness may also be formulated as foresight or realisation that a consequence is likely to result. It does not include the case of a person who did not know or realise that there was any risk. An exception to this is in Tasmania, where liability for murder includes committing an 'unlawful act or omission which the offender knew, or ought to have known, to be likely to cause death': *Criminal Code* (Tas) s 157(1)(c). Recklessness refers to a high *degree of risk* of causing death or grievous bodily harm that an accused must have foreseen, to be guilty of murder.

The courts in England and Australia have disagreed on the question of the foresight of risk for some time, but the common law test for Australia has been stated conclusively by the High Court in *R v Crabbe* (1985) 156 CLR 464 at 469, as being whether the person did the act *knowing that it was probable that death or grievous bodily harm would result*.

The level of foreseeable risk was elaborated slightly by the High Court in *Boughey v The Queen* (1986) 161 CLR 10. The Court held that the Tasmanian statutory reference to 'likely to cause death' in s 157(1)(c) of the *Criminal Code* was to be distinguished from terms such as 'possibility' and 'more likely than not', which set the standard of foresight too low. But the majority of the High Court accepted (at 22) terms such as 'a substantial or real chance, as distinct from what is a mere possibility' and 'a good chance that it will happen' as equivalent to 'likely'. Similar decisions have been made relating respectively to the Australian Capital Territory and New South Wales provisions: *Brown* (1987) 32 A Crim R 162; *Annakin* (1987) 37 A Crim R 131.

Transferred malice

The doctrine of 'transferred malice' applies where an accused intends to cause death or grievous bodily harm and commits the conduct resulting in death, but the victim who dies is not the person envisaged by the accused. The following two cases exemplify these circumstances.

The sixteenth-century case of *R v Saunders and Archer* (1576) 75 ER 706 concerned a father, John Saunders, who poisoned a roasted apple meant for his wife. The wife gave some to their three-year-old daughter Eleanor, and the father, although he had 'great affection' for his daughter, 'saw her eat it, and did not offer to take it from her lest he should be suspected'. The wife recovered, but the child died. The father was held to be guilty of the child's murder, and hanged.

A more recent case concerned Ronald Mitchell, who was waiting at a busy post office. When Mitchell tried to 'jump the queue' he became involved in an argument with another man. Mitchell hit the other man, who fell against an elderly woman, Mrs Anne Crafts, in the queue. Mrs Crafts fell and broke her leg. She was recovering from the broken leg when, a few days after the incident, she suffered a pulmonary embolism related to the leg fracture, from which she died. Mitchell was found guilty of the manslaughter of Mrs Crafts, on the basis that he had caused her death, and that it was unnecessary to show that he aimed his unlawful and dangerous act at the specific person who died: *R v Mitchell* [1983] QB 741.

The doctrine of applied or transferred malice applies where the accused, with the relevant state of mind, either aims his or her act at one person and kills another, or kills a person by an act that was not specifically aimed at any particular person. Both *Saunders and Archer* and *Mitchell*'s cases illustrate the first category of transferred malice. *Crabbe*'s case illustrates the second. Crabbe was apparently feeling no particular ill-will towards any specific victim when he drove his prime mover into the bar. This did not make any difference to his criminal liability.

The second form of the principle is also illustrated by the nineteenth-century case of *R v Martin* (1881) 8 QBD 54. Edwin Martin blocked the exit from a theatre and turned out the lights on the way to the exit. The audience panicked and rushed to leave. Many people were seriously hurt. His conviction for inflicting grievous bodily harm was affirmed on appeal, the Court finding (at 58) that he intended to cause injury despite having no 'personal malice against the particular individuals injured'. Similarly, a terrorist randomly firing a machine-gun into a crowd is likely to be found to have the fault element for murder.

The offence of criminal homicide exists to protect the community, rather than any particular person. The most serious fault element—the intention to cause the harm—need not be directed against the actual victim. What is required is that the jury find that a relevant intention existed, directed at the victim or someone else, or at people in general.

A recent case that illustrates the doctrine and also raises a number of important related questions is that of *Attorney-General's Reference (No 3 of 1994)* [1996] QB 581 (CA); [1998] AC 245 (HL).

A young woman, 'M', was about 23 weeks pregnant with the child of her boyfriend 'B'. B, who was aware of the pregnancy, stabbed M several times, including in the lower abdomen. M recovered after surgery, but their baby 'S' was born two weeks later, extremely premature, and died four months after the birth from respiratory complications related to her prematurity, despite intensive neonatal care and a number of surgical operations. The trial judge concluded that the causal connection had been shown, but that on these facts (involving an unborn child) it was not possible in law for B to be convicted of murder or manslaughter. The judge directed an acquittal. The legal question was sent for consideration to the higher courts. The English Court of Appeal held that, under the doctrine of transferred malice, B could be held responsible for the murder of the baby girl if he intended to kill or cause grievous bodily harm to M. This was because the foetus was 'an integral part of the mother': [1996] QB 581 at 598. In this case he had in fact pleaded guilty to wounding with intent to cause M grievous bodily harm.

The House of Lords on appeal, however, rejected this approach as an unacceptable extension of the doctrine of transferred malice. The intent to cause grievous bodily harm to the woman could not be 'transferred' into the necessary fault element for murder of the foetus: *Attorney-General's Reference (No 3 of 1994)* [1998] AC 245. Lord Mustill (at 261) was critical of the whole doctrine of transferred malice, which he said lacked 'any sound intellectual basis'. The House of Lords concluded, however, that in such circumstances an accused could be found guilty of unlawful and dangerous act manslaughter.

A case involving similar circumstances arose recently in Western Australia: *Martin* (1995) 85 A Crim R s 87. Sections 278 and 279 of the *Criminal Code* (WA) specifically provide that the fault element for unlawful killing must be directed towards the victim 'or some other person'. Martin had stabbed his pregnant de facto partner and the loss of blood caused severe damage to the foetus. When born, the baby was found to have suffered major brain damage. The death of the baby seven months later was held to be causally related to the damage caused by the accused, and the accused was then convicted given the express statement of the doctrine of transferred malice in the code. Argument in that case was, however, directed to the question as to whether the killing had indeed been directed towards a 'person'. This raised the issue as to whether the physical element of the death of a human being had been proved. In this case the Court stated that the question arose as at the time of the *death*, at which time in this case the victim clearly was a person. An appeal against conviction was dismissed in *Martin (No 2)* (1996) 86 A Crim R 133.

Because the Supreme Court of Western Australia did not view the situation in *Martin*'s case as giving rise to an issue about the doctrine of transferred intention, it is unclear what status the doctrine has in Australia in such fact situations.

Critique

The main criticisms that have been made about the fault elements for murder concern their scope. Before considering this, however, it is worthwhile making a few comments about the doctrine of transferred malice in the context of the death of babies injured in the womb.

Lord Mustill in the House of Lords decision in *Attorney-General's Reference (No 3 of 1994)* [1998] AC 245 particularly objected to the Court of Appeal's decision regarding the foetus as simply part of the mother. Lord Mustill concluded (at 255) that, at least in this context, the foetus is neither a separate person nor part of the mother. He used the rather strange analogy that while the mother's leg was 'part of' her, the foetus was not. It is difficult to see how his Lordship then agreed that the accused could nonetheless be guilty of manslaughter on the basis of unlawful and dangerous act. Nicola Lacey and Celia Wells comment in *Reconstructing Criminal Law* (London: Butterworths, 1998) p 547: 'As a result of Lord Mustill's preoccupation with the house of murder, the opportunity to consider the criminal law's response to a pregnant woman's interest in her foetus has been lost.'

As we will see later, the criminal law has tried to make sense of the complex and sometimes apparently competing interests of the pregnant woman and the foetus she carries, through offences such as abortion, child destruction and infanticide and in the context of euthanasia of neonates. In the course of these attempts, the law sometimes seems to prioritise the interest of the woman and sometimes that of the foetus. However, as Celia Wells and Derek Morgan have pointed out in 'Whose Foetus Is it?' (1991) 18 *Journal of Law and Society* 431–47 at 431, there may be more and overlapping interests to consider: 'The maternal/foetal rights debate seems confounded by the notion that a woman may, in addition to her interest in determining whether her pregnancy is terminated, have an equally compelling interest in ensuring the preservation of her foetus'.

What is clear is that the use of the doctrine of transferred malice is not the best way of dealing with such fact situations. Lord Mustill stated in *Attorney-General's Reference (No 3 of 1994)* [1997] 3 WLR 421 at 435 that the facts in that case required a double transfer of intent, 'first from the mother to the foetus and then from the foetus to the child as yet unborn'. It appears better to address such circumstances through the approach set out in *Martin*'s case.

Turning then to the scope of the fault elements for murder, there has been some criticism of including an intention to cause grievous bodily harm as a fault element. The Law Reform Commission of Victoria was critical of this category of murder, arguing that 'there is a significant difference between someone who intends to cause death and someone who intends to do serious injury but neither intends nor foresees death': *Homicide*, Report No 40 (Melbourne: LRCV, 1991) p 54. The Commission was also critical of the uncertainty of the concept, which may be applied inconsistently by different juries. It recommended the abolition of the category. This was also the view of the MCCOC, which similarly recommended 'that any offence of murder require the prosecution to prove intention or recklessness as to death': *Chapter 5, Fatal Offences Against the Person*, Discussion Paper (June 1998) p 53. It stated: 'The serious harm category of murder diminishes [the] intent-based approach by allowing something less than an intention to kill to constitute murder. The Committee's view is that murder should in some way be linked to death as the contemplated harm rather than merely serious harm.'

The MCCOC has suggested that killing in such circumstances should be viewed as manslaughter rather than murder. Several other law reform bodies have also suggested the abolition of an intention to cause grievous bodily harm as a separate fault element for murder: Mitchell Committee, *Criminal Law and Penal Methods Reform Committee of South Australia* (Adelaide: Government Printer, 1973); House of Lords Select Committee, *Report of the Select Committee on Murder and Life Imprisonment* (London: HMSO, 1989); Law Reform Commission of Canada, *Homicide*, Working Paper No 33 (1984) pp 85–6.

The only jurisdictions in which the fault element extends to recklessness as to grievous bodily harm are Victoria and South Australia. This is clearly a very low standard of fault to be included in the same category of blameworthiness as intention to kill. The MCCOC has recommended that this particular fault element be abolished and that a person who kills in such circumstances be convicted of manslaughter: *Chapter 5, Fatal Offences Against the Person*, Discussion Paper (June 1998) p 59.

The MCCOC has proposed that the fault elements for murder should be an intention to cause death, or recklessness as to the risk of death. Section 5.4 of the *Criminal Code* (Cth) defines recklessness as involving awareness of a 'substantial risk' that a circumstance exists or that a result will occur, where in the circumstances known to the accused 'it is unjustifiable to take the risk'. This is seen as essentially reflecting the common law: MCCOC, *Chapter 5, Fatal Offences Against the Person*, Discussion Paper (June 1998) p 55. It clearly rejects the notion of 'wilful blindness' as being a subset of recklessness. The MCCOC affirmed (at 59) the common law position that the person who kills foreseeing the probability of causing death is 'just as blameworthy' as the intentional killer.

The inclusion of a component of lack of justification in the *Criminal Code* (Cth) formulation was intended to exclude from criminal liability socially justifiable risk taking, such as the doctor performing a heroic operation: at 55. Such a situation was similarly assumed to fall outside the operation of criminal liability by the High Court in *Crabbe* (1985) 156 CLR 464 at 471. As there was no question of justification in that case it was not discussed further and is not generally regarded as forming part of the common law formulation of recklessness. It is likely that justification would have most relevance at the point of deciding whether to prosecute and/or in sentencing. It may also be relevant to the application of the formal defences of necessity and duress, discussed further in Chapter 11.

The English approach has been to limit the fault elements for murder to an intention to kill or cause grievous bodily harm: JC Smith, *Smith and Hogan Criminal Law* (10th edn, London: Butterworths, 2002) p 359. Because recklessness has not formed a separate category of fault, the English courts have taken a broad view of intention as including 'oblique' intention based on the notion of foresight of death as a probable consequence. As explored in Chapter 2, this approach has been somewhat restricted since the influential case of *Hyam v DPP* [1975] AC 55. However, because oblique intention overlaps with Australian versions of recklessness, it seems more appropriate simply to have a category of recklessness as a fault element rather than artificially to stretch the definition of intention.

Overall, it is our view that the MCCOC's recommendation that the fault elements for murder should be an intention to cause death or recklessness as to the risk of death is preferable to having a broad range of fault elements. Given that murder is punishable by life imprisonment (either maximum or mandatory sentence) in all jurisdictions, it seems reasonable to link the fault element to causing death in the contemplation of, or the probable risk of, death.

Constructive murder

Background

Imagine the following scenario. A bank robber enters a bank, points a gun at the waiting customers and shouts, 'Everyone on the floor!'. He swings the gun towards the tellers and orders them to hand over all their money. As he steps towards the counter he trips and the gun goes off, killing one of the tellers. Is the robber responsible for the death? Is it murder? Is it manslaughter? Is it some other offence?

'Constructive murder', or 'felony murder', is a historical category of murder based on the idea that an *accidental* killing, which took place when the accused was carrying out some other serious crime (or escaping arrest), is *as culpable as* an intentional killing, and can therefore be included in the category of murder. The killer is effectively regarded as having accepted responsibility for causing death by deliberately going about the other offence, if death in fact accidentally results.

For example, as in the above scenario, an armed bank robbery can go wrong. The gun may fire accidentally, or a bullet ricochet, and someone may be killed. In such a case, the doctrine of constructive murder means the robber is also a murderer. If the robber had *intentionally* fired the gun at someone, or fired it *recklessly* around the enclosed space of the banking chamber, the robber could of course be guilty of murder under the headings we have already discussed.

One real-life scenario concerning the operation of constructive murder occurred in the case of *R v Butcher* [1986] VR 43. Glen Butcher borrowed a knife, entered a milkbar and demanded money from the proprietor. He held out the knife 'to frighten' the proprietor. The proprietor, however, 'rushed at' Butcher as he held the knife out, and died from a deep knife wound in the stomach. Butcher denied any intention to stab the victim. The charge was put to the jury as either intentional killing or constructive murder. Butcher was convicted of murder in the Victorian Supreme Court on 22 March 1985. On appeal the Victorian Supreme Court confirmed the application of the constructive murder doctrine in such circumstances.

As mentioned above, constructive murder is also known as felony murder. The common law 'felony murder rule' was based on the view that it is murder to cause death by an act of violence in the course of or furtherance of a felony involving violence. The offender was seen to have accepted the risk, when using violent means to commit a serious crime, that death could result.

As we shall explore in the Critique section, there has been considerable criticism of this rule over many years, on the grounds that it disregards the focus on moral culpability embodied (in terms of intentionality) in the alternative components of murder. It therefore wrongly labels as murder, acts that are essentially accidental. The felony-murder rule was abolished in the UK in 1957. However, it remains in all Australian jurisdictions other than the Australian Capital Territory: *Crimes Act* 1900 (NSW) s 18(1); *Criminal Code* (NT) s 162; *Criminal Code* (Qld) s 302; *Criminal Law Con-*

solidation Act 1935 (SA) s 12A; *Criminal Code* (Tas) s 157(1)(d); *Crimes Act* 1958 (Vic) s 3A; *Criminal Code* (WA) s 279. In South Australia and Victoria, a related category of murder exists for death caused while resisting lawful arrest: *R v Ryan and Walker* [1966] VR 553. The Code jurisdictions have an equivalent offence of causing death while intending to cause grievous bodily harm, or administering a stupefying substance, or stopping the victim's breath, to facilitate the flight of the offender: *Criminal Code* (NT) s 162(1)(c) & (d); *Criminal Code* (Qld) s 302(1)(c)–(e); *Criminal Code* (Tas) s 157(1)(d)–(f) and see s 157(2); *Criminal Code* (WA) s 279(3)–(5).

The current law

Constructive murder

Constructive murder has the following components:
- the accused's act must have caused death;
- there must have been a connection between the base offence ('felony') and the act causing death. For example, s 3A of the *Crimes Act* 1958 (Vic) uses the expression 'in the course or furtherance' while s 18(1)(a) of the *Crimes Act* 1900 (NSW) refers to 'during or immediately after the commission' of the relevant offence; and
- the base offence must have been a serious one.

Seriousness may be reflected in the type of base offence required, or in the length of sentence of the base offence. The Victorian legislation incorporates both criteria: the base offence must be 'a crime the necessary elements of which include violence for which a person upon first conviction may...be sentenced to life imprisonment or to imprisonment for a term of 10 years or more': *Crimes Act* 1958 (Vic) s 3A. Section 157(2) of the Tasmanian *Criminal Code* includes in the base offences piracy, murder, escape, resisting lawful apprehension, rape, robbery, burglary and arson.

In Queensland and Western Australia, the operation of constructive murder has been narrowed by including the requirement that the accused's act be 'of such a nature as to be likely to endanger human life': *Criminal Code* (Qld) s 302(1)(b); *Criminal Code* (WA) s 279(2). It is, however, broadened by the inclusion of intending to cause grievous bodily harm 'for the purpose of facilitating the commission of a crime' as defined in the section: *Criminal Code* (Qld) s 302(1)(c)–(e): *Criminal Code* (WA) s 279(3)–(5).

In New South Wales, South Australia and Victoria the common law rule was repealed and replaced with a narrower statutory offence, defined in terms of the seriousness of the base offence. In New South Wales, the base offence must be one punishable by 25 years or life imprisonment: *Crimes Act* 1900 (NSW) s 18(1)(a). In South Australia, the base offence is a major indictable offence punishable by imprisonment for 10 years or more: *Criminal Law Consolidation Act* 1935 (SA) s 12A. The Northern Territory provision limits the offence both by reference to the base offence and the dangerous act: *Criminal Code* (NT) s 162(1)(b) and (2). In Victoria, with the abolition of the felony/misdemeanour distinction in 1981, the felony-murder rule was replaced by s 3A(1) of the *Crimes Act* 1958. It states:

> A person who unintentionally causes the death of another person by an act of violence done in the course or furtherance of a crime the necessary elements of which include violence for which a person upon first conviction may...be sentenced to [life] imprisonment or imprisonment for a term of 10 years or more shall be liable to be convicted of murder as though he had killed that person intentionally.

This was apparently intended to restate the common law position, but its effect has been to give the rule a narrower application through its definition of the requisite base offence. By way of contrast, s 12A of the *Criminal Law Consolidation Act* 1935 (SA) retains the common law position, referring to 'an intentional act of violence while acting in the course or furtherance of a major indictable offence'. The Victorian bill originally referred to 'crimes of violence'. This phrase was replaced with the phrase 'a crime the necessary elements of which include violence' during its passage through Parliament, although with no indication that a change in application was intended: see *R v Butcher* [1986] VR 43 at 51 and House of Assembly, *Hansard*, Vol 358, 6 June 1981 at 8688 per Mr Maclellan, Minister for Transport. In *Butcher*'s case, the Supreme Court of Victoria interpreted this amendment as showing an intention to limit the rule to cases of offences having 'violence as one of its ingredients' and not to extend to an offence simply because it was in fact committed violently.

Few serious crimes are by their definition *necessarily* violent. For instance, a kidnapping can be carried out by enticing the victim away: *Crimes Act* 1958 (Vic) s 63A. The Victorian section has, however, been held to include robbery and armed robbery: *R v Butcher* [1986] VR 43. Robbery is defined as the use of force, or creating fear of use of force, in order to steal: *Crimes Act* 1958 (Vic) s 75. In *Butcher* it was held that both force *and* the threat of force (whether or not the victim is actually put in fear) constitute 'violence': *R v Butcher* [1986] VR 43 at 50, 53.

It is not clear that any other base offences are applicable under s 3A. Aggravated burglary, for example, involves entry to a building as a trespasser with intent to commit particular offences (s 76 *Crimes Act* 1958 (Vic)), while the offender has a firearm or offensive weapon with him or her, or while another person is in the building (s 77 *Crimes Act* 1958 (Vic)). None of these components necessarily involve either violence or 'force': see Chapter 6. A major base offence at common law had been rape. For example, the case of *DPP v Beard* [1920] AC 479 involved a conviction for murder when the young victim died of suffocation as the accused tried to stifle her screams while raping her. Rape is specifically included as a base offence in some jurisdictions such as Tasmania (*Criminal Code* (Tas) s 157(2)) and would continue to apply in, for example, South Australia and the Northern Territory. It is, however, unlikely to fall within s 3A of the *Crimes Act* 1958 (Vic) as it can be committed by fraud, or when the victim was asleep or unconscious: see Chapter 5.

Escape murder

In Victoria, South Australia and the Code states there is an additional form of constructive murder, an unintended killing in the context of an escape from custody. In Victoria and South Australia the 'escape-murder' or 'resisting-arrest murder' rule is separate from the statutory constructive murder provisions, existing at common law only. The rule states that 'the killing of a person by the intentional use of force, knowingly to prevent such a person from making an arrest which he [or she] is authorized by common law to make, is murder even if the person using the force did not intend to kill or do grievous bodily harm': *R v Ryan and Walker* [1966] VR 553 at 564.

The Code jurisdictions have equivalent offences of causing death as a result of causing any of several forms of bodily harm in order to facilitate the flight of an offender, as noted earlier in this section.

The main common law authority for this category of murder is the Victorian case of *R v Ryan and Walker* [1966] VR 553. Ronald Ryan was alleged to have shot at and killed a warder while escaping with a fellow inmate from prison. He was convicted of murder, either on the basis of intent or of constructive murder, although he argued he did not fire the shot at all. On 3 February 1967 he was the last man to be hanged in Victoria, a hanging which has continued to be controversial: B Jones (ed), *The Penalty is Death: Capital Punishment in the Twentieth Century* (Melbourne: Sun Books, 1968); M Richards, *The Hanged Man—The Life and Death of Ronald Ryan* (Melbourne: Scribe Publications, 2002).

The common law rule applies both to escaping from prison and to resisting arrest. It has been suggested in South Australia that the rule may be limited to the situation where the force used involved at least serious violence or serious danger, such as shooting at a police officer, rather than merely tripping the officer: *Marshall v R* (1987) 26 A Crim R 259 at 272 per Johnson J. In such a case, the accused is of course very likely to be found to have intended to commit grievous bodily harm, or been reckless, and to be guilty of murder anyway.

Critique

The categories of constructive murder and escape murder are readily criticised. As noted earlier, felony murder was abolished in the UK in 1957, with no reported detriment. There have been proposals for abolition in various Australian jurisdictions, most recently by the MCCOC, *Chapter 5: Fatal Offences Against the Person*, Discussion Paper (June 1998) p 64. See also Victorian Law Reform Commissioner, *Criminal Procedure: Miscellaneous Reforms* (Melbourne: LRCV, 1974); Law Reform Commissioner of Victoria, *Murder: Mental Element and Punishment* (Melbourne: LRCV, 1984) p 13; Victorian Law Reform Commission, *Homicide*, Report No 40 (Melbourne:

LRCV, 1991) p 64; Criminal Law and Penal Methods Reform Committee of South Australia, *The Substantive Criminal Law*, Fourth Report (The Mitchell Committee) 1977 p 19. These recommendations have not to date been adopted.

National police statistics indicate that around 13 per cent of all homicides occur in the course of another crime, a rate that has remained stable over many years, and that the antecedent crime is most likely to be a robbery. In the period 1989–99, 66 per cent of the homicides occurring in the context of another crime occurred in the context of a robbery: Jenny Mouzos, *Homicidal Encounters—A Study of Homicide in Australia 1989–1999* (Canberra: AIC, 2000) p 71. The homicide may represent an escalation of the violence used in the robbery, for example where a victim resists, or it may be an accident, or it may be an intentional component of the violence.

If the criminal law is to focus on the actual state of mind of the accused in finding criminal responsibility for murder, as discussed earlier, it is clearly wrong to extend responsibility by a concept of constructive murder. We would argue that, if the bank robber or escapee intended to kill or was reckless as to causing death, he or she should be convicted of murder. If the accused committed an unlawful and dangerous act, or was criminally negligent, he or she should be convicted of manslaughter. Otherwise an accused should only be convicted of the offences he or she set out to do, such as armed robbery, or escaping from custody. Further, it is difficult to claim any deterrent effect. The offender cannot prevent the death occurring as, by definition, it was accidental.

Constructive murder may have been retained for reasons of political expediency or to avoid the risk of being seen to abolish it in a community climate of (increasingly punitive) 'law and order' anxiety. However, constructive murder is in fact rarely used: VLRC, *Homicide*, Report No 40 (1990) p 63. It is thus not even realistic to argue that it provides a deterrent, for instance, to the most organised of bank robbers, who might hypothetically factor in such a risk. It is clear that abolition of constructive murder would make no noticeable difference to homicide prosecutions.

Manslaughter

Background

Manslaughter is a form of homicide that carries a lesser penalty and less moral opprobrium than a conviction for murder. Manslaughter has traditionally been divided into two categories: involuntary and voluntary manslaughter. These terms are rather misleading as voluntary manslaughter has nothing to do with willed actions, and involuntary manslaughter has nothing to do with unwilled actions.

Involuntary manslaughter involves killings for which there is not the high degree of intentionality required for murder, but where the accused had a level of responsibility that still warrants punishment. It is 'involuntary' in the sense that the accused did not intend or foresee death (or grievous bodily harm) but intentionally committed some dangerous act, or (without intentionally taking a risk) where he or she grossly failed to fulfil the community standard for responsible behaviour. This is the subject of the following discussion.

Voluntary manslaughter is a killing that would have been murder, in that the accused had the fault element for murder, but where the accused has been able to rely on one of the 'partial defences' to murder. It is 'voluntary' in the sense that the accused did intend to kill or cause grievous bodily harm, but had a legal excuse. This category of manslaughter will be discussed in Chapters 10 and 11 in relation to provocation and diminished responsibility.

The category of involuntary manslaughter covers the situation where the accused causes death, and can be regarded as morally responsible, but where it seems excessive to categorise him or her as a murderer. Take, for example, the following fact situation.

A fight takes place in the street among a group of men outside a café. One man steps in to protect his friend and punches another man standing at the edge of the pavement. The victim staggers back and trips on a gutter. He falls onto the road, hits his head, and dies from the head injury. The person who threw the punch certainly *caused* the death; should he be held *responsible* for the death? As a murderer? As we will set out, this scenario has been viewed as falling within the category of 'unlawful and dangerous act' manslaughter.

The category of involuntary manslaughter is an attempt to define the types of killing that are not as culpable as murder but where the killer should not be allowed to escape without any punishment. The courts have found this a difficult task.

Where the law of homicide is expressed in statute or code in Australia, murder is usually fully defined, and manslaughter is stated to be any other unlawful killing falling short of murder: *Crimes Act* 1900 (ACT) s 15(1); *Crimes Act* 1900 (NSW) s 18(1)(b); *Criminal Code* (NT) s 163; *Criminal Code* (Qld) s 303; *Criminal Code* (Tas) s 159; *Criminal Code* (WA) s 280. The common law exists in South Australia and Victoria. There is no statutory formulation of the meaning of manslaughter in any Australian jurisdiction. The common law approach to manslaughter broadly applies to the Code jurisdictions. The only exception is the Northern Territory, which does not have a category of unlawful and dangerous act manslaughter and where manslaughter is confined to situations where death was foreseen by the accused as possible: see *Criminal Code* (NT) s 31.

While the current common law can be stated reasonably clearly, the categories are neither necessarily exhaustive nor logical. An accused who comes into either of the following categories will be guilty of manslaughter:
- if the accused caused the victim's death by a grossly negligent act or omission; or
- if the accused caused the victim's death by an unlawful and dangerous act.

These categories will be dealt with in turn, with a critique of each category before setting out a critique of the overlap between categories.

The current law—gross or criminal negligence manslaughter

Negligence is a concept used in the civil law to refer to failure to act with the care that a reasonable person would have taken. It requires the application of an objective standard. The criminal law rarely makes a person criminally liable for negligence for *serious* offences, because of the pervasive subjectivist approach requiring that the offender must have actually had a 'guilty mind'. This subjectivist approach was explored in Chapter 2. Where negligence *is* punishable, the level of negligence required must be much higher than in the civil field. This is often referred to as 'gross negligence'. This category of manslaughter is found in some form in all Australian jurisdictions. The Code jurisdictions establish statutory duties of care, breach of which can form the basis of a manslaughter charge: *Criminal Code* (NT) ss 149–155; *Criminal Code* (Qld) ss 285–290; *Criminal Code* (Tas) s 156(2)(b); *Criminal Code* (WA) ss 262–267.

As outlined in Chapter 2, the common law test of negligent manslaughter was stated in 1977 in the Victorian case of *Nydam v The Queen* [1977] VR 430. In that case, the accused had tried to prevent his girlfriend Kathleen from leaving him, but she was determined to end the relationship and return to England. Nydam went to the hairdressing salon where Kathleen was sitting, and threw a bucket of petrol into the salon. He lit the petrol, causing the deaths of Kathleen and a young apprentice working in the shop. Nydam claimed he had only drawn the match lightly over the box, intending to show the strength of his feelings. Nydam was ultimately convicted of murder, but the Supreme Court of Victoria at 445 formulated the test for gross negligence manslaughter on appeal as follows:

> In order to establish manslaughter by criminal negligence, it is sufficient if the prosecution shows that the act which caused the death was done by the accused consciously and voluntarily, without any intention of causing death or grievous bodily harm but in circumstances which involved such a great falling short of the standard of care which a reasonable man [or woman] would have exercised and which involved such a high risk that death or grievous bodily harm would follow that the doing of the act merited criminal punishment.

The test is therefore objective; the fault element for the offence is simply the intention to do the act, in circumstances of negligence as set out. The accused person's negligence could have been failing to see the dangerousness of the situation, or failing to take adequate steps to avoid a recognised danger. In either case, the jury has the ultimate responsibility of deciding whether the accused's failure was such as to merit criminal punishment.

This concept obviously has much in common with recklessness. The crucial difference is that to have been *reckless* the accused must have been aware of the risk, whereas the *negligent* accused will not have been aware of any risk, although a reasonable person would have been.

Critique

The rationale for imposing criminal liability for failing to live up to a particular standard of care is discussed by the legal philosopher HLA Hart in *Punishment and Responsibility* (Oxford: Oxford University Press, 1968) pp 151–2: '[A] hundred times a day persons are blamed outside the law courts for not being more careful, for being inattentive and not stopping to think...*if* anyone is *ever* responsible for *anything*, there is no general reason why [individuals] should not be responsible for such omissions to think, or to consider the situation and its dangers before acting.'

Andrew Ashworth develops this justification for imposing criminal liability for negligence by addressing a number of possible criticisms of the doctrine: *Principles of Criminal Law* (3rd edn, Oxford: Oxford University Press, 1999) p 199. Ashworth argues that it need not be a simple 'objective' standard, as it can include exceptions for people who do not have the capacity for foresight and control of the reasonable citizen. In addition, negligence can be at least as culpable as recklessness, for example where one compares the culpability of a person who knowingly takes a slight risk of harm, with a person who fails to recognise a high risk of harm. Ashworth argues then (at 199) that negligence is an appropriate standard for criminal liability where '(i) the harm is great; (ii) the risk is obvious; and (iii) the defendant has the capacity to take the required precautions'.

If the rationale for negligent manslaughter is accepted, the question then becomes one of how best to draft it. Section 5.5 of the *Criminal Code* (Cth) adopts the *Nydam* definition of criminal negligence. That section states:

> A person is negligent with respect to a physical element of an offence if his or her conduct involves:
> (a) such a great falling short of the standard of care that a reasonable person would exercise in the circumstances; and
> (b) such a high risk that the physical element exists or will exist;
> that the conduct merits criminal punishment for the offence.

The Code does not directly address the question of capacity to comply with the standards of the reasonable citizen. This was an important issue in relation to the facts of *R v Stone and Dobinson* [1977] 1 QB 354, which were discussed in Chapters

1 and 2 and which will be examined again in the next section. Instead, capacity is taken into account in the *Criminal Code* (Cth) in relation to liability for omissions: s 4.2(4). It is also taken into account in relation to liability for producing a particular state of affairs: s 4.2(5).

The definition of criminal negligence in s 5.5 of the *Criminal Code* (Cth) appears adequate, but it may be worthwhile including the question of capacity in relation to negligent acts as well as omissions. It may be unfair to hold a person who suffers from an intellectual disability liable for a criminal act and not an omission in circumstances where his or her behaviour did not comply with the standards of the reasonable person.

Another issue is whether culpable driving causing death should fall within negligent manslaughter or whether a separate category is needed. While some drivers who cause death by their dangerous driving are prosecuted for negligent manslaughter, in most jurisdictions a separate offence specifically covering 'motor manslaughter' is used: *Crimes Act* 1900 (ACT) s 29; *Crimes Act* 1900 (NSW) s 52A; *Criminal Code* (Qld) s 328A; *Criminal Law Consolidation Act* 1935 (SA) s 19A; *Criminal Code* (Tas) s 167A; *Crimes Act* 1958 (Vic) s 318; *Road Traffic Act* (WA) s 59. Section 154 of the *Criminal Code* (NT) creates a general offence criminalising an act or omission that causes serious danger to the life, health or safety of any person. These offences were directed to the perceived reluctance of juries to convict motorists of an offence termed 'manslaughter'.

Such offences clearly overlap with manslaughter. In fact, s 318(2) of the *Crimes Act* 1958 (Vic) includes reckless driving causing death, which overlaps with the offence of reckless murder; s 318(2)(a) refers to 'consciously and unjustifiably disregarding a substantial risk' of causing death or grievous bodily harm, including the element of justification which, as discussed earlier, may also be a part of the common law of murder. Justification may be a particularly relevant concept in fact situations involving driving, for example where a person may claim that they were acting in an emergency. The Victorian Supreme Court confirmed in *R v Shields* [1981] VR 717 that negligent culpable driving under s 318(2)(b) is equivalent to common law negligent manslaughter as defined in *Nydam*'s case and that the statutory test can properly be applied by the jury for both offences. However, some provisions include liability for driving under the influence of alcohol or drugs and causing death, which may extend the offence beyond that of the traditional scope of homicide: *Crimes Act* 1900 (ACT) s 29(4)(b); *Crimes Act* 1900 (NSW) s 52A(a); *Crimes Act* 1958 (Vic) s 318(2)(c) and (d).

The existence of a separate culpable driving offence has been criticised. The Law Reform Commission of Victoria has argued that having a separate offence erroneously suggests that killing while in control of a motor vehicle is a less serious offence than other forms of homicide: *Death Caused by Dangerous Driving*, Discussion Paper (Melbourne: LRCV, 1991). It recommended the abolition of the separate offence and proposed that, where appropriate, offenders be charged with reckless murder or manslaughter. It further proposed (at 15) that an offence of dangerous driving causing death be introduced to cover those cases that did not amount to murder or manslaughter but where the driver's behaviour fell 'substantially below the level of care that a competent and careful driver would take in the circumstances'.

The MCCOC has also been highly critical of having a separate category of culpable driving causing death: *Chapter 5, Fatal Offences Against the Person*, Discussion Paper (June 1998) p 161 ff. It referred to such provisions as 'purely cosmetic' and as arising out of 'unprincipled expediency'. It recommended a separate general offence of 'dangerous conduct causing death' to replace manslaughter by gross negligence. The introduction of such an offence would also make unnecessary the various specific homicide offences such as the vehicular homicides.

There certainly seems to be no valid justification for having a separate offence of culpable driving causing death given the scope of negligent manslaughter and the need to address any existing tolerance for dangerous driving.

The current law—negligent omissions

It will be recalled that an act is usually required for criminal liability to arise. The criminal law does not generally impose *criminal* liability for omissions. For example, a person would not usually be found guilty of manslaughter who stands on a beach and watches a stranger drown, although many may feel the person is *morally* culpable.

However, culpability under the head of negligent manslaughter has been held to arise in certain circumstances from *failing to do* something that a reasonable person would have done in the circumstances.

There are three elements to this imposition of liability:
- the accused was under a duty of care to the victim;
- the accused person's behaviour constituted a gross breach of that duty; and
- the breach of duty caused the death.

Several categories of duties of care have been identified at common law, which will be discussed below. The standard of care required will also be considered, together with what has been held to constitute a breach of the duty.

The Code jurisdictions impose duties to act in some circumstances such as to preserve human life and in the care of children, similar to those at common law, breach of which duty may give rise to criminal liability: *Criminal Code* (NT) ss 149–155; *Criminal Code* (Qld) ss 285–290; *Criminal Code* (Tas) ss 144–152, 156(2); *Criminal Code* (WA) ss 262–267. Section 155 of the *Criminal Code* (NT) specifically includes an offence of 'callously' failing to rescue another whose life is endangered, where the offender was able to have provided rescue or some other aid.

The common law has imposed a duty to act to prevent harm in several situations such as where there is a statutory obligation to prevent harm or where there is a medical duty of care: *Airedale NHS Trust v Bland* [1993] AC 789. A parent also has an obligation to prevent harm to a child and probably also to a spouse: *R v Russell* [1933] VLR 59. An accused may also attract criminal liability for 'failing to take measures that lie within one's power to counteract a danger that one has oneself created': *R v Miller* [1983] 2 AC 161 at 176.

In *R v Instan* (1893) 17 Cox CC 602, Kate Instan was convicted of manslaughter for leaving her elderly aunt unattended when the aunt developed gangrene in her leg, from which she died, death being accelerated by lack of food and medical care. The aunt maintained the house financially and paid for the supply of food to the house. The Court concluded that the niece had a legal obligation at least to give the aunt the food she had paid for. It is not clear whether the Court would have gone further and found a general obligation to take care of the aunt.

A broader obligation to take care was developed in *R v Stone and Dobinson* [1977] 1 QB 334. We outlined the facts of this case in Chapter 1. The Court of Appeal held that the two accused, who suffered from physical and intellectual disabilities, had taken on a duty of care, which, being unfulfilled, gave rise to criminal responsibility for the victim's death.

Recent cases suggest that if the accused voluntarily took on the victim's care and/or left the victim in danger, particularly in circumstances where others were prevented from assisting them, they may be held to have had a duty of care at least to obtain assistance.

In *Taktak* (1988) 34 A Crim R 334, the accused was a heroin addict who arranged for a young woman, also a heroin user, to attend a party to work as a prostitute, for a friend. The friend called Taktak at 3 a.m. to collect the young woman, whom he found unconscious as a result of drug use. Taktak took the young woman back to where he was staying and tried to resuscitate her. He said he slapped her face and splashed her with water, and attempted mouth to mouth resuscitation from time to time. He did not seek medical treatment until later the next morning. The young woman died some time before the doctor arrived. It was found that she had died of a heroin overdose.

The accused was initially convicted of manslaughter by gross negligence. His conviction was quashed on appeal. The NSW Court of Appeal clearly stated that a duty of care had arisen here. It was not, however, satisfied either that the omission to obtain medical treatment had caused the death, or that the accused's delay was a *gross* breach of his duty of care, and on this basis allowed the appeal.

On the question of when a duty of care can arise, the Court said that it was no longer proper to limit the duty of care to legal relationships such as parent and child; it should extend to anyone who has taken on themselves the care of a helpless person. It outlined (at 358) situations where a legal duty to obtain medical care may arise, including 'where one person has voluntarily assumed the care of another who is helpless...and so secluded such person as to prevent others from rendering aid'.

The Court observed that if the accused had simply left her at the party no legal duty would have been found—he would not have 'assumed' a duty and theoretically she would still have had the chance of being found and treated properly.

Critique

In Chapter 1, we outlined how an objective standard of criminal responsibility can pose severe problems for those people who may have a physical or intellectual disability. The case of *Stone and Dobinson* shows that it may be unjust to impose a universal standard of care on those whose decision-making capabilities are significantly impaired. More generally, the case sends the message that it is better to offer no assistance at all in such a situation, to avoid giving rise to the duty to continue to care.

Section 4.2(4) of the *Criminal Code* (Cth) sets out that 'an omission to perform an act is only voluntary if the act omitted is one which the person is capable of performing'. This certainly goes some way towards addressing the harsh operation of an objective standard for manslaughter by omission.

Taktak's case confirms the view that for someone who is primarily interested in possible legal liability, it is better to offer no assistance than to offer unsuccessful assistance. P Williams and G Urbas, in a recent discussion of heroin overdoses, came to the same conclusion. They emphasised, however, that in practice criminal liability would rarely be imposed (noting the decision in *Taktak* on what constitutes a 'gross' breach) and that where someone is found to have taken a drug overdose the most useful intervention—with almost one hundred per cent success rate—is simply the early call for medical assistance: P Williams and G Urbas, 'Heroin Overdoses and Duty of Care', *Trends and Issues* No 188 (Canberra: AIC, 2001). The authors highlighted the importance of community education on the value of the early call for medical assistance.

The issue was raised recently in the UK, in somewhat similar circumstances, in *R v Khan* [1998] EWCA Crim 971. The two accused supplied the victim (a 15-year-old prostitute) with her first heroin in their flat. She overdosed, and collapsed in a coma. The accused men left her alone in the flat without medical attention, where she died. They later returned to dispose of the body. The accused were convicted of manslaughter (and various drug offences). The Court of Appeal found (at 10) the accuseds' behaviour 'about as callous and repugnant as it is possible to imagine' but observed that to extend a duty to summon medical assistance to a drug dealer supplying heroin to a person who then dies would be to enlarge the class of people to whom a duty has been said to have been owed. The question whether such a duty existed had not in fact been addressed by the judge in his direction on negligent manslaughter. The Court of Appeal therefore quashed the conviction, leaving open (at 9), however, the possibility that a duty might be found to exist if the question were put to a jury. *Taktak* does not appear to have been cited to the court. JC Smith, in his commentary on the case, observed that a jury surely would find a duty in those circumstances: JC Smith, 'R v Khan: Commentary' [1998] Crim LR 830–3 at 833.

It is not clear whether the requirement in *Taktak* that the volunteer not only offer care but also 'seclude' the victim 'so as to prevent others from rendering aid' is a necessary part of manslaughter by omission. It was not specifically referred to in the earlier cases of *Instan* and *Stone and Dobinson*, although the victim was in fact 'secluded' in the family home in each case in any event. It may be suggested that the inclusion of this requirement in *Taktak* was intended to limit the obligations of the 'mere' volunteer, as distinct from the person with pre-existing familial or other obligations.

The questions will always be: was there a duty of care? Has there been a gross breach of that duty? And if so, did the breach cause the death? *Taktak* illustrates the high level of breach that must be shown to render the accused liable for criminal punishment. Mere inadvertence or inadequacy of response will not be enough. It also illustrates the undoubted necessity to show the causal connection between the breach and the death.

The current law—unlawful and dangerous act manslaughter

In all jurisdictions except the Northern Territory, a person will be guilty of manslaughter who caused death by intentionally committing a dangerous act. In the common law states the offence is causing death by an 'unlawful and dangerous act'. Section 156(2)(c) of the *Criminal Code* (Tas) refers to causing death by 'any unlawful act'; if it does not amount to murder under s 157 it will be punishable as manslaughter. In Queensland and Western Australia, causing death by the intentional infliction of violence, not amounting to murder, constitutes manslaughter in the absence of any excuse: *Criminal Code* (Qld) s 291; *Criminal Code* (WA) s 268; and see S Bronitt and B McSherry, *Principles of Criminal Law* (Sydney: LBC, 2001) p 502.

At common law, there existed a third category of involuntary manslaughter, 'battery manslaughter', which was committed when a person caused death while intentionally committing bodily harm less than grievous bodily harm. This category was formulated in *R v Holzer* [1968] VR 481. In that case, Holzer punched the victim, Harvey, in the mouth in the course of a fight outside a café. The victim fell backwards onto the road and hit his head. He died from the head injury. Holzer was found guilty of manslaughter on this basis. However, in 1992 the High Court rejected this idea of a separate category of 'battery manslaughter', favouring the higher test of 'dangerousness' as indicating a more serious level of intended harm: *Wilson v The Queen* (1992) 174 CLR 313.

This category of manslaughter can be seen as a parallel of constructive murder. That is, it does not take any account of the actual intention of the accused, but looks at what the accused was doing. The fault element is simply the intention to commit the unlawful and dangerous act.

Unlawful

To be 'unlawful', the act must have been a breach of the criminal law: *R v Holzer* [1968] VR 481; *R v Lamb* [1967] 2 QB 981. How minor a breach will suffice is not clear, but the courts generally have no difficulty in identifying an 'unlawful act'. Any assault will satisfy this requirement; the deciding factor appears in practice to be whether the act was also 'dangerous', which is discussed below.

The common law concept of assault requires that the victim apprehend physical harm: see Chapter 4. Where the victim was unaware of the potential harm—for instance where she or he was approached from behind, or did not believe any harm would arise—the behaviour should not logically constitute in itself the requisite 'unlawful act' to render any killing a manslaughter. In the English case of *R v Lamb* [1967] 2 QB 981, for example, a jocular, and unexpectedly fatal, game of Russian roulette was held not to include an assault bringing it within the doctrine of manslaughter by unlawful and dangerous act, as the victim (who assumed no danger existed) had not been put in fear. However, in *Pemble v The Queen* (1971) 124 CLR 107 the High Court found the offence proven where a man, carrying a loaded gun and walking towards his former girlfriend who had her back to him, claimed to have stumbled, so that the gun discharged and the young woman was killed. (The facts were disputed: the prosecution argument was that Pemble had walked up to the victim, pointed the gun and shot her.) Two judges found 'unlawfulness' to exist on the basis that the accused man's action, on his own agreed statement, amounted to an attempted assault (Barwick CJ at 123; Windeyer J at 137) while McTiernan J (at 127) went so far as to find the unlawful act to be the discharging of a firearm in a public place. The dissenting judges, Menzies and Owen JJ, concluded that there had been no unlawful act as there had been no assault, the victim having been unaware of the threat.

In *R v Cato* [1976] 1 WLR 110, the accused was charged over the death of a friend after he and the friend had consensually taken it in turns to inject each other with heroin. The friend had subsequently died. The accused was convicted of unlawful and dangerous act manslaughter, a conviction upheld on appeal. The Court (at 118) strained to categorise the behaviour as unlawful, given that it had been consensual, and that there was no offence of taking or administering heroin.

Would an 'unlawful act' include driving without a licence? Or does it require something that is itself dangerous as well as unlawful? It has been said in a number of cases that it is only criminal offences that are themselves dangerous that can be considered to be relevant 'unlawful acts': see *Boughey v The Queen* (1986) 161 CLR

10 at 35–6; *R v Martin* (1983) 32 SASR 419 at 451. Cases such as *Cato* and *Pemble* suggest that the courts may conclude that an act was 'unlawful' simply because it was dangerous. This, however, means that the test effectively reads 'dangerous and dangerous act'. This has been the basis for an argument by the Law Reform Commission of Victoria that the separate factor of unlawfulness is not really needed and could be eliminated: *Homicide*, Report No 40 (Melbourne: LRCV, 1991) p 113. As will be discussed further below, others have argued that this category of manslaughter is redundant, and that a single category of negligent manslaughter would be adequate.

Dangerous

At common law the question whether the act done by the accused was 'dangerous' is tested by asking the jury to decide whether the act was such that 'a reasonable person would realise that it was exposing others to an appreciable risk of serious injury': *Wilson v The Queen* (1992) 174 CLR 313 at 335. At trial, the Court had applied the 'battery manslaughter' test from *Holzer*'s case of whether the act involved a risk of 'some harm'. The majority of the High Court (at 333) preferred a stricter test of 'serious injury', meaning an injury that is more than trivial or negligible. The majority (at 334) was concerned to make a closer 'correlation between moral culpability and legal responsibility'. As these categories of manslaughter constitute constructive crime, the Court was keen to limit liability for constructive crime to 'what is truly unavoidable'.

The test is therefore an objective one, based on what a reasonable person would have appreciated, and not a subjective one (based on what the accused actually appreciated).

In England the test for dangerousness is more readily satisfied as it is sufficient if the act was one that reasonable people would realise involved the risk of 'some harm', not necessarily serious harm: *DPP v Newbury and Jones* [1977] AC 500. The minority of the High Court in *Wilson*'s case (at 342) preferred this approach.

Critique

The categories making up involuntary manslaughter have been widely criticised. Some have called for wholesale abolition: Criminal Law and Penal Methods Reform Committee of South Australia, *Fourth Report: The Substantive Criminal Law* (1977). Some have suggested a single category of manslaughter, with the unlawful and dangerous act category merging with negligent manslaughter. The requirement for an 'unlawful' act is said to be inappropriate, 'dangerousness' is effectively an issue of negligence, and attempts by the judiciary to stretch legal principles to bring particular facts within the definition, such as occurred in *Pemble*, also indicate problems with the concepts: see L Waller and CR Williams, *Criminal Law: Text and*

Cases (9th edn, Sydney: Butterworths, 2001) pp 260, 271; J Willis, 'Manslaughter by the Intentional Infliction of Some Harm: A Category that Should be Closed' (1985) 9 Crim LJ 109–24.

What is the difference between an 'appreciable risk of really serious injury', for unlawful and dangerous act manslaughter, and a 'high risk of death or grievous bodily harm' for criminal negligence? *Are* they different? What is the relevance of requiring that the dangerous act also be unlawful? There is no requirement of unlawfulness under the 'negligent manslaughter' category.

The Law Reform Commission of Victoria, *Homicide*, Report No 40 (Melbourne: LRCV, 1991) recommended a single category combining these concepts, 'dangerous act or omission manslaughter', the test for which would be 'whether the defendant did an act in gross breach of duty—or omitted to do an act where there was a duty to act—which a reasonable person in the circumstances would have realised exposed another to a substantial and unjustifiable risk of life-endangering injury': pp 116–17. The High Court in *Wilson* noted the LRCV proposal for reducing involuntary manslaughter to one single category but said it would not take this further step.

The MCCOC (1998) and the Law Commission for England and Wales, *Legislating the Criminal Code: Unintentional Manslaughter*, Report No 237 (London: HMSO, 1996) recommended the abolition of unlawful and dangerous act manslaughter. The MCCOC had earlier proposed a formulation of murder limited to conduct causing death where the offender 'intends to cause, or is reckless about causing, the death of that person or any other person' (cl 5.1.9). Having excluded liability for murder where the offender only intended or foresaw the causing of serious injury, the MCCOC proposal for manslaughter focused on that basis of liability. It proposed that manslaughter be defined as conduct causing death where the offender 'intends to cause, or is reckless about causing, serious harm' (cl 5.1.10). In addition, a separate offence (but subject to the same penalty as manslaughter) of 'dangerous conduct causing death' is proposed, embodying the category of negligent manslaughter. This offence would be defined as conduct causing death where the offender 'is negligent about causing the death of that or any other person' (cl 5.1.11). The offence was also intended to replace the 'motor manslaughter' offences.

We return to *Stone and Dobinson*. On what basis should people apparently not able to comply with their duty of care due to their limited intellectual capacity be held criminally liable? As already noted, Andrew Ashworth proposes that liability for negligence, on the basis of failure to attain a reasonable standard of care—whether by action or omission—should be dependent on the answer to the additional question, 'Could D, given his mental and physical capacities, have taken the necessary precautions?': Andrew Ashworth, *Principles of Criminal Law* (3rd edn, Oxford: Oxford University Press, 1999) p 198. The Law Reform Commission of Victoria recommended that it should be a defence if the accused was unable to meet reasonable standards because of physical or mental deficiency: LRCV, *Homi-*

cide, Report No 40 (1991) p 117. The *Criminal Code* (Cth) addresses this issue by specifying that a person will not be responsible for an omission unless the act omitted is 'one which the person is capable of performing' (s 4.2(4)).

Euthanasia

Background

Imagine that Mary has terminal cancer. She is in great pain and asks the doctor on many occasions what she might take to end her life. Several scenarios may arise:
- the doctor gives her a prescription and tells her the amount of the drug that would be fatal;
- the doctor gives increasing doses of drugs for pain relief, which hasten death; or
- the doctor gives Mary a lethal injection.

In Chapter 2, we outlined how intention is not the same as motive, which is generally referred to as an emotion prompting an act. Motive has traditionally been viewed as irrelevant to the question of fault. Thus, in the first situation, the doctor could be viewed as having assisted Mary's suicide if she takes the drug herself and subsequently dies. This is where a medical practitioner assists a patient to kill him or herself by providing the means to allow the patient to take his or her own life, but does not actually administer any fatal treatment. This is a separate statutory crime in Australian jurisdictions: *Crimes Act* 1900 (ACT) s 17; *Crimes Act* 1900 (NSW) s 31C; *Criminal Code* (NT) s 168; *Criminal Code* (Qld) s 311; *Criminal Law Consolidation Act* 1935 (SA) s 13A(5), (7); *Criminal Code* (Tas) s 163; *Crimes Act* 1958 (Vic) s 6B(2); *Criminal Code* (WA) s 288.

The second scenario is viewed by the law as permissible providing that the giving of drugs is aimed at pain relief. There is some debate about whether such palliative care in fact hastens death: M Ashby, 'Hard Cases, Causation and Care of the Dying' (1995) 3(2) *Journal of Law and Medicine* 152–60.

The final scenario is sometimes termed 'voluntary' euthanasia because there is an intentional taking of life to relieve suffering in response to the sufferer's request. Because motive is irrelevant, it is viewed as murder.

To these scenarios, two more may be added. 'Non-voluntary' euthanasia refers to the intentional taking of life and occurs where the patient is incapable of communicating or forming an opinion as to euthanasia. The most common situation where the question of non-voluntary euthanasia may arise is where a patient is in a persistent vegetative state. 'Involuntary' euthanasia occurs where intentional killing is carried out against the known wishes of the patient.

Euthanasia has been the subject of intense debate in Australia and elsewhere in recent years. In this section, we will concentrate on the existing law relating to voluntary and non-voluntary euthanasia and then look at some of the arguments for and against changing the law in this area.

The current law

As stated above, physician-assisted suicide falls within the separate crime of assisting suicide. In Victoria and South Australia, the survivor of a suicide pact is deemed guilty of manslaughter: *Criminal Law Consolidation Act* 1935 (SA) s 13A(3); *Crimes Act* 1959 (Vic) s 6B(1). Voluntary and involuntary euthanasia generally fall within the category of murder as there is an intention to kill: H Palmer, 'Dr Adams' Trial for Murder' [1957] Crim LR 365–77 at 375; *R v Cox* (1992) 12 BMLR 38; *Airedale NHS Trust v Bland* [1993] AC 789. Non-voluntary euthanasia may be permitted in narrow circumstances through the withdrawal of hydration and nutrition from patients in a persistent vegetative state: *Airedale NHS Trust v Bland* [1993] AC 789. This case is discussed further below.

Voluntary euthanasia

The debate concerning voluntary euthanasia and assisted suicide became prominent in Australia with the passage of the *Rights of the Terminally Ill Act* 1995 (NT). That Act enabled an individual over the age of 18 and suffering from a 'terminal illness' to request a physician to assist him or her to die. Terminal illness was defined in s 3 of the *Rights of the Terminally Ill Act* 1995 (NT) as 'an illness which, in reasonable medical judgment will, in the normal course, without the application of extraordinary measures or of treatment unacceptable to the patient, result in the death of the patient'.

A number of safeguards were built into the Act, including being assessed by a specialist in the illness and a psychiatrist: s 7(1)(c). The latter had to be satisfied that the individual was not suffering from a 'treatable clinical depression in respect of the illness': s 7(1)(c)(iv). A physician who acted in accordance with the Act could not be held guilty of any crime or professional misconduct, nor could he or she be liable in a civil action to any claim for damages: s 20(1).

The *Rights of the Terminally Ill Act* 1995 (NT) was repealed by the *Euthanasia Laws Act* 1997 (Cth). This denied the Northern Territory, the Australian Capital Territory and Norfolk Island the power to make laws 'which permit or have the effect of permitting (whether subject to conditions or not) the form of intentional killing of another called euthanasia (which includes mercy killing) or the assisting of a person to terminate his or her life': Sch 1.

The existence of the NT Act marked the only time in Australian history that voluntary euthanasia was considered lawful. While the Act was in force, Dr Phillip Nitschke used a computerised system that allowed patients to give themselves a lethal dose of medication to end their life. His actions could therefore be more properly described as physician-assisted suicide rather than voluntary euthanasia.

Non-voluntary euthanasia

Anthony Bland was a victim of the 1989 Hillsborough Football Ground disaster in England. At that time he was aged 17 and he suffered a severe crushed chest injury that gave rise to hypoxic brain damage. His condition deteriorated such that he was considered to be in a persistent vegetative state with no hope whatsoever of improvement. His doctors, supported by his parents, formed the view that there was no useful purpose in prolonging his medical care and that it was appropriate to stop artificial feeding and other measures that kept him alive. Because of doubts about the legality of such conduct, the responsible hospital authority sought declarations from the High Court that the doctors could lawfully discontinue all life-sustaining treatment and medical supportive measures including artificial hydration and nutrition. This was granted by the President of the Family Division and, later on appeal, by the Court of Appeal and ultimately the House of Lords: *Airedale NHS Trust v Bland* [1993] AC 789.

In assessing whether the withdrawal of nutrition and hydration could amount to a criminal offence, the House of Lords considered the extent of the duty owed by the hospital and the doctors to their patient. Where a legal duty exists to do a certain act that an accused failed to do, that *omission* may amount to the physical element for unlawful killing, as discussed earlier in this chapter. The House of Lords concluded there was no duty of care to provide Anthony Bland with medical care and food for an indefinite period.

The Court relied upon a previous House of Lords decision *In re F* [1990] 2 AC 1. That case laid down the principle that, based on concepts of necessity, a doctor can lawfully treat a patient who cannot consent to treatment if it is determined to be 'in the best interests' of the patient to receive such treatment. Following on from that principle, the House of Lords held in *Airedale NHS Trust v Bland* [1993] AC 789 that the right to administer invasive medical care is wholly dependent upon such care being in the best interests of the patient.

The critical issue therefore became whether or not it was in the best interests of the patient to continue the invasive medical care involved in artificial feeding. The medical evidence was such that continuation of medical treatment would confer no benefit on Anthony Bland and, accordingly, the House of Lords held that existence in a persistent vegetative state was not in the best interests of the patient. Thus, there was no duty to provide Anthony Bland with medical care and food for an indefinite period of time and the withdrawal of artificial nutrition and hydration would not amount to an unlawful killing.

Critique

International and Australian studies suggest there is strong support for the idea of voluntary euthanasia: for example, H Kuhse and P Singer, 'Voluntary Euthanasia and the Nurse: An Australian Study' (1993) 30(4) Int J Nurs Stud 311–22; H Kuhse,

P Singer, P Baume, M Clarke and M Rickard, 'End-of-Life Decisions in Australian Medical Practice' (1997) 166(4) Med J Aust 191–6; P Baume and E O'Malley, 'Euthanasia: Attitudes and Practices of Medical Practitioners' (1994) 161(2) Med J Aust 137–44. There can, however, be methodological problems associated with opinion surveys, not the least of which is the phrasing of the questions posed. It is also problematic relying on polls and questionnaires to determine what should be legally permissible. As Ian Kerridge, Michael Lowe and John McPhee point out, there are plenty of instances in recent history of both popular approval and legal approval of major violations of human rights: I Kerridge, M Lowe and J McPhee, *Ethics and Law for the Health Professions* (Katoomba, NSW: Social Science Press, 1998) p 468.

A number of arguments have been made as to whether or not voluntary euthanasia should remain criminal. Proponents of voluntary euthanasia argue that if an individual chooses to end his or her own life, the state has no business interfering with that choice or invoking criminal penalties to stop the individual acting on it. Further, 'if the person who has made this decision needs the assistance of another to help him or her carry it out, and that other person is also an adult of sound mind, who after careful reflection is willing to assist the first person in carrying the decision out, the state also ought not to invoke criminal penalties against the person who assists': H Kuhse and P Singer, 'Active Voluntary Euthanasia, Morality and the Law' (1995) 3(2) *Journal of Law and Medicine* 129–35 at 130.

Some have also argued for the existence of a right to die. In his dissenting judgment in *Rodriguez v Attorney-General (British Columbia)* [1993] 3 SCR 519 (at 630) Cory J saw the right to die as an extension of a right to life, which finds expression in the Canadian *Charter of Rights and Freedoms*:

> If, as I believe, dying is an integral part of living, then as a part of life it is entitled to the constitutional protection provided by s 7. It follows that the right to die with dignity should be as well protected as is any other aspect of the right to life. State prohibitions that would force a dreadful painful death on a rational, but incapacitated terminally ill patient are an affront to human dignity.

The eminent philosophers Max Charlesworth and Ronald Dworkin have written about voluntary euthanasia in the context of an expression of autonomy, integrity and dignity: M Charlesworth, *Bioethics in a Liberal Society* (Cambridge: Cambridge University Press, 1993); R Dworkin, *Life's Dominion. An Argument about Abortion and Euthanasia* (London: Harper Collins, 1993).

Voluntary euthanasia has also been advocated where it is in 'the best interests' of the individual concerned. This stems from the ethical principle of beneficence, which holds that there is a moral obligation to promote the welfare of individuals: TL Beauchamp and JF Childress, *Principles of Biomedical Ethics* (4th edn, Oxford: Oxford University Press, 1994) p 249.

In this sense, it has been argued that if there is a choice between a long, drawn out and painful death or a quick death by lethal injection, a person acts with beneficence by giving the appropriate injection. It is this argument that gives rise to voluntary euthanasia sometimes being referred to as 'mercy killing': A Flew, 'The Principle of Euthanasia' in AB Downing and B Smoker (eds), *Voluntary Euthanasia: Experts Debate the Right to Die* (London: Peter Owen, 1986), pp 40–57 at 43.

Those opposed to voluntary euthanasia often refer to the idea that human life has an inherent value such that it is always ethically impermissible to intentionally end human life. Often, but not always, this argument is based on religious principles: see K Amarasekara and M Bagaric, *Euthanasia, Morality, and the Law* (New York: P Lang, 2003).

There is also what has been referred to as the 'slippery slope' argument that the legalisation of voluntary euthanasia will lead to active non-voluntary and involuntary euthanasia in that it will open the way for killing individuals who are not competent to make end-of-life decisions: J Rachels, *The End of Life* (Oxford: Oxford University Press, 1986) pp 170 ff.

Finally, the Australian Medical Association has stated that medical practitioners have an 'ethical obligation to preserve health': *Care of Severely and Terminally Ill Patients*, Position Statement (Canberra: AMA, November 2002), <http://www.ama.com.au/web.nsf/doc/SHED-5FK3DB>, accessed November 2003, p 1. Some doctors have argued that if they are allowed to end their patients' lives, then 'the profession...will never again be worthy of trust and respect as healer and comforter and protector of life in all its frailty': W Gaylin, LR Kass, ED Pellegrino and M Siegler, 'Doctors Must Not Kill' in RM Baird and SE Rosenbaum, *Euthanasia: The Moral Issues* (New York: Prometheus Books, 1989) pp 25–8 at 27. See also, P Mullen, 'Euthanasia: An Impoverished Construction of Life and Death' (1995) 3 *Journal of Law and Medicine* 121–8 at 124; K Healey (ed), *Euthanasia* (Sydney: The Spinney Press, 1997) p 13.

In relation to non-voluntary euthanasia, many commentators have queried the distinction in *Airedale NHS Trust v Bland* [1993] AC 789 between an *omission* to treat and active forms of non-voluntary euthanasia: for example, M Bagaric, 'Active and Passive Euthanasia: Is There a Moral Distinction and Should There Be a Legal Difference?' (1997) 5(2) *Journal of Law and Medicine* 143–54; JM Finnis, 'Bland: Crossing the Rubicon?' (1993) 109 LQR 329–37; G Gillett, 'Euthanasia, Letting Die and the Pause' (1988) 14 J Med Ethics 61–8; J Rachels, 'Active and Passive Euthanasia' (1975) 292(2) *New England Journal of Medicine* 78–80. Lord Goff of Chieveley was careful to point out in *Airedale NHS Trust v Bland* [1993] AC 789 at 865 that an omission is not the same as the taking of some positive step to bring life to an end, because 'the law does not feel able to authorise [active] euthanasia, even in circumstances such as these; for once euthanasia is recognised as lawful in these circumstances, it is difficult to see any logical basis for excluding it in others'.

Lord Browne-Wilkinson (at 879) posed the ethical question arising from *Airedale NHS Trust v Bland* [1993] AC 789 as follows: '[S]hould society draw a distinction (which some would see as artificial) between adopting a course of action designed to produce certain death, on the one hand through the lack of food, and on the other from a fatal injection, the former being permissible and the latter (euthanasia) prohibited?'

The answer to this question is still debated and will continue to have practical significance. For example, in late 2002, a husband sought guardianship of his wife in order to stop artificial feeding and hydration for his wife, who had advanced-stage dementia: J Szego, 'Wife Did Not Want to "Linger On"', *Age*, 25 December 2002; J Davies, 'Guardian to Decide if Woman Dies', *Age*, 12 March 2003. The Victorian Civil and Administrative Tribunal approved the appointment of the Public Advocate as the woman's guardian. The Victorian Supreme Court confirmed the view of the Tribunal that artificial feeding and hydration constituted 'medical treatment' and did not amount to palliative care under the *Medical Treatment Act* 1988 (Vic): *Gardner; re BWV* unreported 29 May 2003, SC of Vic, Morris J, [2003] VSC 173. Under that Act, a person or his or her guardian can refuse any medical treatment other than palliative care: M Ashby and D Mendelson, 'Natural Death in 2003: Are We Slipping Backwards?' (2003) 3 *Journal of Law and Medicine* 260–4. The Public Advocate could therefore refuse the continuation of the artificial feeding and hydration and, with the support of her family, proceeded to do so. Two weeks after removal of her feeding tube 'BWV' died: D Rood, '2 Weeks After Food Stops, "BWV" Dies', *Age*, 8 July 2003.

The MCCOC, in its Discussion Paper on *Fatal Offences Against the Person* (June 1998), has stated (at 187) that the Model Criminal Code should not permit voluntary euthanasia or assisted suicide. It concluded: 'Any such change would be radical, controversial and beyond the Committee's brief to propose a uniform code which reflects a consensus on matters of legal principle.'

Roger Magnusson's thought-provoking book, *Angels of Death: Exploring the Euthanasia Underground* (Melbourne: Melbourne University Press, 2002) shows how the demand for euthanasia services, particularly by those suffering from AIDS, is occurring in an unregulated environment. While Magnusson points out that the realities of the euthanasia underground can be used by both advocates and opponents of legalising voluntary euthanasia, he puts the case for legalising it with legislative safeguards.

As pointed out in Chapter 2, Alan Norrie has stated that ignoring the relevance of motive underpins the denial of social conditions in which individuals live: 'From Criminal Law to Legal Theory: The Mysterious Case of the Reasonable Glue Sniffer' (2002) 65 *Modern Law Review* 538–55. Perhaps it is time to reassess the role of motive in relation to the complex issues raised by euthanasia. David Lanham has suggested a midway point in the debate, arguing that there is a case for treating voluntary euthanasia as manslaughter rather than murder: 'Euthansia, Painkilling,

Murder and Manslaughter' (1994) 3 *Journal of Law and Medicine* 146–55. He argues that one way of approaching voluntary euthanasia is to hold that intention is not established where the primary motive is to relieve pain. Instead, he argues that there should be a partial defence available to reduce murder to manslaughter.

While these approaches give some room for legal change, what is clear is that there are no easy answers to whether or not the law of homicide should encompass voluntary and non-voluntary euthanasia.

Offences relating to childbirth

Background

In January 2000, senior medical staff at the Royal Women's Hospital in Melbourne performed an abortion on a 40-year-old woman who was 32 weeks' pregnant. She had arrived at the hospital in a distressed state requesting an abortion because her doctor had just told her that the foetus had an abnormality consistent with dwarfism: M Toy, 'Doctors Endorse Dwarf Abortion', *Sydney Morning Herald*, 4 July 2000. In July, the hospital suspended three of the senior doctors and the matter was referred to the State Coroner by hospital management.

In January 2002, the coroner ruled that she did not have the jurisdiction to investigate the abortion of a 32-week-old foetus: T Noble, 'Hospital Welcomes Abortion Decision', *Age*, 24 January 2002. This was on the basis that because the foetus was considered stillborn, it was not a 'reportable death' that could be investigated by the coroner.

The facts of this case raise the question as to whether the doctors could and should have been prosecuted under the criminal law. While offences relating to pregnancy and childbirth certainly exist, it is rare for prosecutions to be brought, perhaps because of the complex social issues involved.

In the past, partly due to the lack of safe contraception and the illegality of abortion, the death of new-born babies was not unusual. Judith Allen writes in 'Octavius Beale Re-considered: Infanticide, Babyfarming and Abortion in NSW 1880–1939' in Sydney Labour History Group, *What Rough Beast? The State and Social Order in Australian History* (Sydney: Allen & Unwin, 1982) pp 111–29 at 113–15:

> The Inspector General of Police, Edmund Fosbery, claimed in 1903 that for every one infanticide exposed perhaps seven others remained buried in backyards, vacant lots and rubbish dumps. ...In 1936, a New Zealand Royal Commission into Abortion concluded that the practice of one doctor hushing up the fatal abortion cases of another...by means of 'accidents of pregnancy' certificates was rife...
>
> The tiny handful of deaths which resulted in infanticide or abortion prosecutions were only a fraction of those exposed by coroners [in the early days of the

twentieth century]. Every year in the Sydney metropolitan area, dead babies were found in public places, often wrapped in newspapers. In most cases coroners found that they had been strangled or in some other way deliberately asphyxiated. A majority of these were unidentified and remained so after autopsy. Police energy does not seem to have been expended in locating recently confined women in the neighbourhood where the babies were found. The Eastern Suburbs were over-represented, with a large number of dead babies found there. It seems likely that these were mostly the illegitimate offspring of domestic servants, women too much under surveillance to dispose of the body at work. [footnotes omitted]

A range of offences has developed around causing the death of a baby, before or after birth. Historically, women were heavily penalised for falling pregnant outside marriage. Given the importance of virginity for reasons of religion and marriageability, they were likely to be cast out of the family and/or socially ostracised. Many were in domestic service and, once pregnant, were dismissed. This was potentially devastating, particularly where there were no social services, supporting parents' benefits or other welfare provision. The possibility of an additional child to an already exhausted mother, expected to welcome her husband's sexual requirements regardless of their consequences, could also appear to be the last straw.

For many therefore, strong pressures existed to dispose of the baby. While many of these pressures were external to the offending women, criminal laws were then developed to punish the woman for responding to those pressures.

Judith Allen in the extract above, writing of the period 1880–1939 in New South Wales, highlights both the relatively frequent occurrence of neonaticides and social acceptance of this, and the establishment of a harsh criminal regime, selectively enforced.

Offences in relation to childbirth cover the periods during pregnancy, around the birth, and after the birth: these can be classified as procuring abortion, child destruction, and infanticide.

The current law

As noted in the section on the physical elements of homicide, an unborn child cannot be a victim of homicide as it is not regarded as a 'human being'. The common law in Victoria and South Australia is represented by *R v Hutty* [1953] VLR 338 at 339 per Barry J, in which it was held that a child is only 'in being' when it is 'completely delivered from the body of its mother and has a separate and independent existence' and 'fully extruded from its mother's body and...living by virtue of the functioning of its own organs': see *Crimes Act* 1900 (ACT) s 10; *Crimes Act* 1900 (NSW) s 20; *Criminal Code* (NT) s 156; *Criminal Code* (Qld) s 292; *Criminal Code* (Tas) s 153(4); *Criminal Code* (WA) s 269.

This definition is also of significance for the question of liability of doctors (and others) for the euthanasia of a newly born child with serious abnormalities. This would, on the face of it, constitute murder. Similarly, if a child is injured in the womb, and is born alive but dies of the injuries, this will be treated as a homicide, subject to the attacker having the necessary state of mind as discussed earlier: *Attorney-General's Reference (No 3 of 1994)* [1996] QB 581 (CA); *Martin* (1995) 13 WAR 472; *Martin (No 2)* (1996) 86 A Crim R 133.

Three separate crimes have emerged to supplement the law relating to homicide: abortion, child destruction and infanticide. The latter is also a partial defence to murder in certain jurisdictions and will be discussed in that context in Chapter 10.

Abortion

It is an offence to unlawfully administer poison or use instruments with intent to procure a miscarriage: *Crimes Act* 1900 (NSW) ss 82–84; *Criminal Code* (NT) ss 172–173; *Criminal Code* (Qld) ss 224–225, 282; *Criminal Law Consolidation Act* 1935 (SA) ss 81–82; *Criminal Code* (Tas) ss 134–135; *Crimes Act* 1958 (Vic) ss 65–66; *Criminal Code* (WA) ss 199, 259. Notably, there is no requirement to prove that the miscarriage actually occurred, and in most jurisdictions it is only an offence for a woman to commit the offence in relation to her own miscarriage if she is in fact pregnant. Any other person can be convicted in relation to acting to procure a miscarriage whether or not the woman is pregnant. These provisions therefore indicate a primary aim of protecting women from the consequences of unskilled abortion, rather than of separately protecting the unborn foetus: C Wells and D Morgan, 'Whose Foetus is it?' (1991) 18 *Journal of Law and Society* 431–47 at 434.

The offence is only committed if the abortion was procured 'unlawfully'. The meaning of this term was defined conclusively for Victoria by Menhennit J in *R v Davidson* [1969] VR 667 as importing the elements of necessity and proportion. His Honour stated (at 672) that for an abortion to be lawful, therefore, the person carrying out the abortion 'must have honestly believed on reasonable grounds that the act done by him [or her] was (a) necessary to preserve the woman from a serious danger to her life or her physical or mental health (not being merely the normal dangers of pregnancy and childbirth) which the continuance of the pregnancy would entail; and (b) in the circumstances not out of proportion to the danger to be averted'.

This ruling was followed in New South Wales in *R v Wald* [1971] 3 NSWDCR 25. In that case the Court stated that the matters that might result in serious danger to the woman's physical or mental health included economic, social and medical factors.

In reality, there have been virtually no prosecutions where an abortion was carried out by a doctor who has honestly weighed up the risks to the mother's health. Prosecutions are generally only likely to be considered where the abortion was carried out by an unqualified person, where these requirements would be difficult to prove.

Legislation clarifying the law of abortion was passed in South Australia in the same year as Menhennit J made his liberal ruling in *Davidson*. Section 82A of the *Criminal Law Consolidation Act* 1935 (SA) prohibits abortion after the foetus has become a 'child capable of being born alive' (prima facie at 28 weeks) unless required to preserve the life of the woman. Before this time, however, an abortion can be performed by a qualified medical practitioner satisfied that either there was more risk to the woman's physical or mental health from continuing the pregnancy than if it were terminated, or that there was a substantial risk that the child would be born seriously physically or mentally handicapped. The legislation requires the medical opinion to be held by two doctors, and that the abortion be performed in a prescribed hospital.

Abortion is still politically controversial, although not to the degree encountered on occasions in the USA, where doctors offering abortions have been killed by 'right to life' groups. From time to time, protestors in Australia picket clinics and occasionally attempt to have prosecutions launched. For example, in 1998, two doctors in Perth were prosecuted in relation to an allegedly unlawful abortion. The prosecution was ultimately withdrawn, but the media reports and community reaction led to the Western Australian parliament passing 'Australia's most liberal abortion law to date': N Cica, 'Abortion Law in Australia', Parliamentary Research Paper 1 (1998) p 28. Under s 334 of the *Health Act* (WA), abortion up to 20 weeks of pregnancy may be provided if the woman has given informed consent after receiving legislatively mandated counselling, or (with no requirement of counselling) if the pregnant woman would suffer 'serious personal, family or social consequences' or if her physical or mental health would be seriously endangered if the abortion was not performed: see also *Criminal Code* (WA) s 259 and *Criminal Code* (Qld) s 282. Abortions after 20 weeks are available in more limited, and more supervised, circumstances.

At present the practice is largely settled in Australia. There is currently little political desire to revisit the issues, especially since the events in Western Australia. It is fair to say that abortion is available without, in practice, threat of criminal prosecution upon satisfaction of a form of the 'Menhennit' criteria.

Child destruction

In the case outlined at the beginning of this section, the coroner's conclusion meant that the abortion of the 32-week-old foetus was not to be treated as murder or manslaughter. The facts might, however, have amounted to the offence of child destruction.

This offence deals with the destruction of an unborn child, where the baby was capable of living independently of the mother, but not yet alive and separate from its mother. The offence is closely linked to abortion, the difference being that the foetus must be 'capable of being born alive'. An equivalent offence exists in all jurisdictions except South Australia and New South Wales: *Crimes Act* 1990 (ACT) s 42; *Criminal Code* (NT) s 170; *Criminal Code* (Qld) s 313; *Criminal Code* (Tas) s 165; *Crimes Act* 1958 (Vic) s 10; *Criminal Code* (WA) s 290. Section 21 of the *Crimes Act* 1900 (NSW) is the related narrower offence of contributing to the death of a child during delivery.

In Victoria the offence is defined explicitly by reference to whether the child was capable of being born alive: *Crimes Act* 1958 (Vic) s 10(1). Section 10(2) of the *Crimes Act* 1958 (Vic) states that evidence of pregnancy for 28 weeks or more is prima facie proof that the child was capable of being born alive. In Western Australia, Queensland, the Australian Capital Territory and the Northern Territory, the offence is limited to acts causing death during or in relation to childbirth. In New South Wales and South Australia all unlawful terminations of pregnancy are dealt with under the abortion laws. Differences in the application of the criminal law in different states are discussed by Stephen Gabriel in 'Child Destruction: A Prosecution Anomaly Under Both the Common Law and the Criminal Codes' (1997) 21 Crim LJ 32–9.

It is likely that the offence is not frequently charged. However, issues surrounding the appropriateness and application of such an offence are similar to those surrounding abortion offences.

Infanticide

There is also a separate statutory offence of infanticide dealing with the killing by a mother of her child in the first year of life. This offence exists in New South Wales, Tasmania, Victoria and Western Australia: *Crimes Act* 1900 (NSW) s 22A(1); *Criminal Code* (Tas) s 165A; *Crimes Act* 1958 (Vic) s 6; *Criminal Code* (WA) s 281A(1). It must be proved that at the time of the killing, the mother's state of mind was disturbed by reason of the birth or, in all the relevant jurisdictions apart from Tasmania, the effect of lactation. Interestingly, there is no requirement that there be a connection between the imbalance of mind and the act causing death.

In Victoria and New South Wales, infanticide can either be charged as an offence or raised as a defence: *Crimes Act* 1900 (NSW) s 22A; *Crimes Act* 1958 (Vic) s 6. Infanticide as a defence is discussed in Chapter 11. It appears to be more commonly used as an offence, to which the accused woman will have pleaded guilty, following an initial charge of murder. In Victoria between 1981 and 1987 there were six infanticide presentments (2 per cent) amounting to approximately one per year: LRCV, *Homicide*, Report No 40 (1991) p 65. It is likely to be the final disposition in most cases where a mother kills her child under 12 months, and it usually results in a non-custodial sentence: R Lansdowne, 'Infanticide: Psychiatrists in the Plea Bargaining Process' (1990)16 (1) *Monash University Law Review* 41–63.

A critique of the law relating to infanticide can be found in Chapter 11 where it is examined as a partial defence to murder.

Critique

The facts of the case mentioned at the beginning of this section take us back to our earlier discussion about how the criminal law decides who can be a 'victim' of homicide. Offences relating to pregnancy and childbirth raise issues about the status of the foetus in the criminal law. Because the foetus is not seen as a human being for the purposes of the law of homicide, the offences of abortion and child destruction are viewed as independent but related offences. It is worth considering why this distinction is drawn. Why does the criminal law deal differently with the unborn child?

One answer focuses on the difficulty of knowing at what point to draw a line and say this is a human being and therefore this killing constitutes murder or manslaughter. Should it be homicide if a foetus is killed at 28 weeks or when the foetus is capable of an independent existence or only after the foetus is born? Any answer depends very much on how the foetus is viewed: J Seymour, *Childbirth and the Law* (New York: Oxford University Press, 2000).

The answer also depends on the extent to which the law is seen as protecting the foetus *from* the woman, or as reflecting a pregnant woman's interest in the protection of the foetus (as for example in the case of *Attorney-General's Reference (No 3)* and in *Martin*). At what point does the protected interest of the pregnant woman (in lawful abortion) shift to the protection of the foetus from the woman and/or the protection of the woman from the activities of an assailant?

A social/historical perspective in relation to abortion, child destruction and infanticide would take account of the fact of women's precarious social and economic position. As Judith Allen has pointed out, concern for women and for the practical pressures on them has existed alongside punitive criminalising responses: 'Octavius Beale Re-considered: Infanticide, Babyfarming and Abortion in NSW 1880–1939' in Sydney Labour History Group, *What Rough Beast? The State and Social Order in Australian History* (Sydney: Allen & Unwin, 1982) pp 111–29; for further discussion see Regina Graycar and Jenny Morgan, *The Hidden Gender of Law* (2nd edn, Sydney: The Federation Press, 2002) ch 8.

There is the practical issue of proving the cause of death of a foetus, and the reality that about one in five pregnancies naturally miscarry. There is also the philosophical question of how to conceptualise the status of the foetus, its value as 'potential' or 'future' rather than 'separate' human being, and the (changing) relationship it has with the woman within whom the foetus is developing.

The legal solution—ad hoc and illustrating these conflicting values—has been that while causing the death of a foetus does not fall within the most serious homicide offences, the offences of child destruction and abortion are technically 'fall-back offences' intended to cover the situation where a homicide is suspected but difficult or impossible to prosecute.

It is significant that the criminal law relating to pregnancy and childbirth has in practice required the involvement of the medical profession. For example, Lorraine Hepburn points to the expanding control exercised by the medical profession over women and their reproductive choices: *Ova-Dose? Australian Women and the New Reproductive Technology* (Sydney: Allen & Unwin, 1992). On the other hand, the current state of the law in practice facilitates women's choices and protects women from the dangers of unqualified abortionists. The one certainty was, and is, that women will in some situations feel they have no alternative but to seek a termination of an unwanted pregnancy. Historically the rich paid large amounts for private medical treatment; the poor went to unskilled 'backyard' operators and many died or were seriously injured as a result. Judith Allen writes at 118 (footnote omitted):

> Some Australian and American obstetric research in the late 1920s and 1930s estimated that at least half of the ostensibly non-criminal maternal deaths were likely to have been the result of induced abortion, since there was every medical reason for other forms of maternal mortality to be declining, due to technical advances. Moreover, the ever increasing rates of maternal mortality in NSW (at a time when fewer women were having fewer children), inflated by a higher than acknowledged abortion rate, would still have been a serious under-estimation of abortion deaths, owing to fraudulent certification.

One of the rationales for abortion laws can therefore be viewed as protecting women from dangerous procedures: J Seymour, 'The Legal Status of the Fetus: An International Review' (2002) 1 *Journal of Law and Medicine* 28–40 at 33.

The rarity of prosecutions for abortion and child destruction indicate that there is a difference between what the law criminalises and what the state will prosecute. The MCCOC concluded in 1996 that '[w]ith the exception of South Australia and the Northern Territory, the political process in Australia has been unable to deal with the issue [of abortion] for a century, and that position is unlikely to change': *Chapter 5, Non-Fatal Offences Against the Person*, Discussion Paper (June 1996) p 81. The significant reforms to the Western Australian law that occurred subsequently, and their political provenance, have been discussed earlier. The Committee further concluded that the connection between child destruction and abortion is such that any reform agenda regarding either offence would be driven by political imperatives: *Chapter 5, Fatal Offences Against the Person*, Discussion Paper (June 1998) pp 189–91. The Committee therefore declined to make any recommendation as to legislation about either abortion or child destruction. It seems that, in this area of the criminal law, the practice will continue to receive minimal attention from the criminal justice system.

Corporate homicide

Background

In Chapter 1, we explored how, because the criminal law is predominantly based on a model of individual criminal responsibility, it has been exceptionally difficult to assign criminal responsibility to corporations. The following three cases highlight this problem.

The vehicle ferry *Herald of Free Enterprise* left the port of Zeebrugge, Holland, on 6 March 1987 and capsized shortly thereafter, resulting in the deaths of at least 188 people. A public inquiry found that the immediate cause of the ship's capsizing was that she had sailed from the port with her bow doors open, allowing a rush of water into the vehicle deck. The inquiry was critical of a number of individuals, particularly those responsible for seeing that the bow doors were closed. It was also extremely critical of the operating company, concluding that all concerned in the management were at fault. Key deficiencies were the failure to consider having lights fitted that would inform the Master whether the doors were closed, the failure to report information on previous similar incidents, and the lack of any proper system for ensuring that high safety standards were maintained. The inquiry's finding was cited in *R v HM Coroner for East Kent, ex parte Spooner and Others* (1989) 88 Cr App R 10 at 12 as follows: 'From top to bottom the body corporate was infected with the disease of sloppiness.'

At the subsequent inquest held to determine responsibility for the deaths, the coroner concluded that, as a matter of law, a corporation cannot of itself be guilty of manslaughter. Further, while a corporation can be guilty of manslaughter through vicarious liability for the acts and omissions of its employees, the acts and omissions of individual employees and managers in this case did not together 'add up' to the gross negligence required. Relatives of a number of victims applied to the courts for review of this decision but were unsuccessful. The Divisional Court in *R v HM Coroner for East Kent, ex parte Spooner and Others* (1989) 88 Cr App R 10 was prepared to leave open the possibility that a corporation could be found guilty of manslaughter. However, the Court agreed (at 16) with the coroner's ultimate conclusions:

> A company may be vicariously liable for the negligent acts and omissions of its servants and agents, but for a company to be criminally liable for manslaughter—on the assumption I am making that such a crime exists—it is required that the *mens rea* and the *actus reus* of manslaughter should be established not against those who acted for or in the name of the company but against those who were to be identified as the embodiment of the company itself. The coroner formed the view that there was no such case fit to be left to the jury. ... I see no reason to disagree.

Some ten years after the *Herald of Free Enterprise* disaster, on Friday 19 September 1997, the 10.32 a.m. Swansea to London Paddington high-speed passenger train was travelling at 116 miles per hour when it collided with a freight train as it approached Southall. The driver had been packing his bag in preparation for leaving the train in London and failed to notice two warning signals indicating the presence of the freight train. When he saw the third warning signal he was too late to avert the inevitable collision. Seven passengers were killed and 151 people injured. Two automatic warning systems with which the train was fitted, which would have alerted the driver to the missed signals, had been turned off under the operating company's instructions. The company's safety rules did not prevent a driver operating a high-speed train alone and with the warning systems switched off.

The company was charged with seven counts of manslaughter by gross negligence together with an offence under the English occupational health and safety legislation. At first instance the Court directed verdicts of not guilty on the manslaughter charges, on the basis that corporate liability depended on showing the liability of an individual and this could not be shown here. The company pleaded guilty to the occupational health and safety offence and was fined £1.5 million.

The Attorney-General referred to the Court of Appeal questions on the application of the law of manslaughter to corporate behaviour. The Court of Appeal confirmed that a corporation's liability for manslaughter was based on the principle of identification, which requires that an identified individual's conduct amounting to gross criminal negligence must be attributable to the corporation: *Attorney-General's Reference (No 2 of 1999)* [2000] QB 796.

One further case of corporate wrongdoing to be considered occurred recently in Victoria. On the morning of 25 September 1998, employees of Esso Australia Pty Ltd were attending a problem with leaking equipment at Gas Plant One at Esso's Longford gas plant, on the east coast of Victoria. It was school holiday time and several senior staff were away. As a series of plant components failed, heated oils flowed into an abnormally cold heat exchanger, which 'failed catastrophically...[and] released a vast volume of flammable hydrocarbons, in turn ignited by gas fired heaters...in turn causing a series of explosions': *DPP v Esso Australia Pty Ltd* [2001] VSC 103 14 February 2001, para 12. Two Esso employees, Peter Wilson and John Lowery, were killed in the explosion, and eight other employees were injured.

A Royal Commission into the incident found the disaster to have been due to Esso's withdrawal of experienced engineers from the site and failure to provide adequate training to remaining staff: Longford Royal Commission, Victoria, *The Esso Longford Gas Plant Accident: Report of the Longford Royal Commission* (1999).

Esso was prosecuted for breaches of the *Occupational Health and Safety Act* 1985 (Vic). During the course of the trial, Esso made formal admissions of failure to train staff adequately, and failure to develop procedures for dealing with such predictable hazards and dangers. As Cummins J observed in *DPP v Esso Australia Pty Ltd* (2001) 124 A Crim R 200 at 202 when sentencing the corporation for the breaches: 'It was evident from the evidence given by witness after witness before me that the loyal employees, including supervisors, of Esso were entirely unaware of the deadly danger lurking at GP905 on the Friday morning, 25 September 1998.'

His Honour emphasised (at 202) that this had not been a 'mere accident', as '[t]o use the term "accident" denotes a lack of understanding of responsibility and a lack of understanding of cause'. He went on to comment (at 203): 'As presently the *Crimes (Industrial Manslaughter) Bill 2001* (Vic) is to be considered by Parliament, I consider it is inappropriate for me to say anything here about the limited penalties under the *Occupational Health and Safety Act* [1985] and the limited scope of the Act, other than this: this tragic case once again demonstrates, if it needs further demonstration, the vital importance of workplace safety.'

Esso was convicted on eleven counts, and sentenced to the maximum penalty for two of them. The total penalty was a fine of $2,000,000. Cummins J commented on the corporation's lack of genuine remorse, while accepting the remorse of individual senior officers. In concluding that the corporation itself demonstrated no remorse, Cummins J pointed to its litigious and abusive treatment of key employees during the course of the trial, its obstructive strategies during the trial, and its failure to accept responsibility for the disaster. This was highly relevant to sentencing. Cummins J stated (at 208) that 'Esso's failure still to accept responsibility for these tragic events is a serious deficiency'.

Corporations' activities can lead to death in a range of situations. Many will fall within and overlap with the field of occupational health and safety, in the sense that the cause of death will be defective or dangerous work systems. As noted at the start of this chapter, there were 319 workplace fatalities compensated under civil schemes across Australia in 2000–01, representing four for every 100,000 employees: National Occupational Health and Safety Commission, *Compendium of Workers' Compensation Statistics Australia 2000–2001* (Canberra, 2002). This figure does not include fatalities where no compensation claim was made; nor does it include non-employee fatalities. Indeed, a much higher figure was reported by the Industry Commission, which in 1995 estimated that there were over 500 traumatic deaths from work and up to 2200 deaths from occupational disease each year in Australia: *Work, Health and Safety*, Commonwealth of Australia (1995) Vol 1.

The victim of a 'corporate homicide' is likely to be an employee or contractor, as occurred in the Esso Longford gas disaster, or the user of a service or product, as were most of the victims in the Zeebrugge ferry disaster and the Southall rail crash. A key question then will be which area of law will be given primacy—the quasi-civil occupational health and safety laws or the criminal laws. As we will see, civil regimes, including occupational health and safety laws, have generally been more widely used. Regulatory regimes, focused on encouraging compliance, with enforcement only a last-resort consideration, have been growing in sophistication: see J Braithwaite and P Drahos, *Global Business Regulation* (Melbourne: Cambridge University Press, 2002) pp 500–62. Social scientists such as John Braithwaite have argued convincingly that in many areas it is more useful, and more protective of society, to 'speak softly and carry a big stick'—to identify ways of facilitating compliance with as little as possible resort to sanctions, civil or criminal: John Braithwaite, 'On Speaking Softly and Carrying Big

Sticks: Neglected Dimensions of a Republican Separation of Powers' (1997) 47 *University of Toronto Law Journal* 305–61. There are nonetheless some corporate behaviours that warrant the public censure that only criminal prosecution can provide. Causing avoidable deaths will at times be such a case. The use of criminal homicide laws against corporations is, however, still in the developmental stages.

The current law

In general the relevant criminal law will be the law of manslaughter, but some cases do arise where corporations' actions appear close to the reckless behaviour that might constitute murder. An example is the Ford Pinto case. Throughout the 1970s, Ford USA sold a popular, small, budget-priced car, the Pinto. Crash tests during design of the vehicle showed that in rear-end crashes over 25 miles per hour, the petrol tank ruptured. This was due to the positioning of the fuel tank close to the rear bumper, and could have been corrected by changing and strengthening the design. One woman was killed and her young passenger severely injured in such an incident in 1972. The families were awarded substantial civil damages. Some years later, three young women died in a similar collision when the car exploded in flames upon a relatively minor rear-end collision: *State v Ford Motor Co*, Cause No 11-431 (1980). There was evidence from an internal company memorandum that a cost–benefit analysis had been carried out, on the basis of which the decision had been made not to correct the faulty design. The memorandum, entitled 'Fatalities Associated with Crash-Induced Fuel Leakage and Fires', indicated that the unsafe tanks were likely to result in '180 burn deaths, 180 serious burn injuries, 2100 burned vehicles', which would cost the company $49.5 million in compensation. On the other hand, it would cost $137 million to carry out an adjustment costing $11 per vehicle to 11 million cars and 1.5 million light trucks. In the interests of maintaining market share, the adjustments were not to be made: see, for a summary of the background to the Pinto case, Mark Dowie, 'Pinto Madness' (1977), <http://www.motherjones.com/mother_jones/SO77/dowie.html>, accessed 17 February 2003, also reproduced in D Birsch and JH Fielder (eds), *The Ford Pinto Case: A Study in Applied Ethics, Business and Technology* (Albany, NY: State University of New York Press, 1994) pp 15–36. Public revelation of the company's approach to the safety of its vehicles caused considerable outrage. Mark Dowie observed: 'One wonders how long the Ford Motor Company would continue to market lethal cars were Henry Ford II and Lee Iacocca serving 20-year terms in Leavenworth [federal prison] for consumer homicide.' In *State v Ford Motor Co* the Ford Motor Company was found not guilty of three counts of reckless homicide, on the basis that the car had stopped when it was hit, and that the deaths were therefore not the result of a low-speed collision. Later, in 1980, Ford reached an out-of-court settlement with the family: D Birsch and JH Fielder (eds), *The Ford Pinto Case: A Study in Applied Ethics, Business and Technology* (Albany, NY: State University of New York Press, 1994) 6, 305.

Usually, however, the relevant criminal offence will be manslaughter, primarily by negligent actions or omissions. While there has been an argument that corporations cannot be charged with offences that only carry custodial penalties (such as murder), there are no such technical constraints on the use of manslaughter charges against corporations: J Clough and C Mulhern, *The Prosecution of Corporations* (Melbourne: Oxford University Press, 2002) pp 171 ff.

Critique

A key obstacle to allocating criminal responsibility, as discussed in Chapter 1, has been the problem of proving that the corporation held the requisite fault element for homicide. At common law through the nineteenth century, corporations could only be liable for strict liability offences—offences that were committed irrespective of the intention of the offender. During the twentieth century, with the growth and increasing importance of corporations, criminal responsibility was extended to offences with fault elements. A corporation could be held responsible for the conduct of very senior officers, or someone who could be regarded as acting as the company, where the person's mind could be equated to the mind of the company: *Tesco Supermarkets Ltd v Nattrass* [1972] AC 153; J Clough and C Mulhern, *The Prosecution of Corporations* (Melbourne: Oxford University Press, 2002) ch 3.

For a prosecution to be successful, therefore, there must have been a person in the company who could be found to have had the necessary fault element for manslaughter—that is, who acted with gross negligence or who carried out an unlawful and dangerous act as discussed above. Such prosecutions have to date largely been unsuccessful. It has often been difficult to identify the person with the necessary fault element: Law Reform Commission of Victoria, *Homicide*, Report No 40 (Melbourne: LRCV, 1991) pp 7–14.

In Victoria one corporation recently pleaded guilty to manslaughter; however, the company was in liquidation and the conviction and penalty were thus ineffective: *R v Denbo Pty Ltd & Timothy Ian Nadenbousch* unreported, 14 June 1994, SC of Vic, Teague J. Another corporation charged with manslaughter obtained a directed acquittal on the basis that the two managers responsible for the fatal welding operation did not embody 'the guiding mind' of the company and further that they had not been grossly negligent: *R v AC Hatrick Chemicals Pty Ltd* unreported, 29 November 1995, SC of Vic, Hampel J; D Neal, 'Corporate Manslaughter' (1996) 70 *Law Institute Journal* 39–41.

As explored in Chapter 1, the MCCOC considered the focus on identifying a culpable employee as too narrow in the light of the greater delegation to junior officers in modern corporations, and changing corporate structures: *General Principles of Criminal Liability*, Final Report (December 1992) p 112 ff. It proposed new provisions to make it easier to prove the mental state, or intention, of a corporation.

Under s 12.2 of the *Criminal Code* (Cth), the acts of an employee or officer acting within the scope of his or her employment must be attributed to the corporation.

A fault element—intention, knowledge, recklessness—must be attributed to the corporation if it expressly or impliedly authorised or permitted the commission of the offence: s 12.3(1). Section 12.3(2) sets out that authorisation is established by proving that:

(a) the corporation's board of directors 'intentionally, knowingly or recklessly carried out the relevant conduct' or authorised it;
(b) a 'high managerial agent' (senior person) of the corporation 'intentionally, knowingly or recklessly engaged in the relevant conduct' or authorised it;
(c) a 'corporate culture existed within the body corporate that directed, encouraged, tolerated or led to non-compliance'; or
(d) that the body corporate 'failed to create and maintain a corporate culture that required compliance'.

The concept of 'corporate culture' is an interesting and unusual one in criminal law. It is defined in s 12.3(6) as an 'attitude, policy, rule, course of conduct or practice' within the body corporate. For example, a company's official documents may show commitment to compliance with occupational safety legislation, but there may be in practice pressure to meet production schedules, which requires, for example, removal of safety guards.

In England there have been several high-profile attempts to prosecute senior executives and companies for manslaughter, all of which have been unsuccessful to date. Well-known cases include the prosecution of P&O Ferries after the sinking of the *Herald of Free Enterprise* and the prosecution of Great Western Railways after the 1997 Southall train crash, discussed earlier.

The English Law Commission in *Legislating the Criminal Code: Involuntary Manslaughter*, Report No 237 (London: HMSO, 1996) p 128 recommended an offence of 'corporate killing', focusing on management failure rather than individual fault. The Commission recommended:

(1) that there should be a special offence of corporate killing...
(2) ...the corporate offence should be committed only where the defendant's conduct in causing the death falls far below what could reasonably be expected [of a corporation];
(3) ...the corporate offence should not require that the risk be obvious, or that the accused be capable of appreciating the risk; and
(4) that, for the purposes of the corporate offence, a death should be regarded as having been caused by the conduct of a corporation if it is caused by a failure, in the way in which the corporation's activities are managed or organised, to ensure the health and safety of persons employed in or affected by those activities.

Somewhat ironically, the Court of Appeal in *Attorney-General's Reference (No 2 of 1999)* (the Southall rail disaster case) relied on the Law Commission's proposal as confirming the defence argument that the only basis in common law for corporate criminal liability was the *Tesco* identification principle—as to do otherwise would be to suggest that the Law Commission had 'missed the point'.

The British government also promised a new 'corporate manslaughter' offence in the wake of a second horrific train crash in October 1999, at Ladbroke Grove. Further fatal train crashes have occurred since then, at Hatfield in October 2000 (four deaths) and Potters Bar in May 2002 (seven deaths). Criminal prosecutions against both individual managers and two corporations have been launched in relation to the Hatfield crash: R Verkaik, 'Six Railway Managers Charged with Manslaughter', *Independent*, 10 July 2003. A draft Bill dealing with corporate manslaughter was announced in May 2003. The proposal was, however, immediately criticised for dealing only with corporate liability and excluding the issue of the criminal liability of individual directors: M Becket, 'Change of Heart on Corporate Killing: Legislation Will Target Companies Rather than Individuals', *Daily Telegraph*, 26 May 2003.

The Victorian government introduced the Crimes (Workplace Deaths and Serious Injuries) Bill in 2001, which was intended to utilise the approach developed in the Commonwealth Criminal Code in establishing a new offence of 'corporate manslaughter'. The offence was to apply to corporate practices that were negligent and that resulted in death, using the common law *Nydam* definition discussed earlier in this chapter. The proposed amendment to the Victorian *Crimes Act* would have required the evaluation of negligence by looking at the conduct of the corporation as a whole: Second Reading Speech, Attorney-General Mr Hulls, Crimes (Workplace Deaths and Serious Injuries) Bill, 22 November 2001, *Hansard* at 1921. A concept of failure of management was used that drew on the Commonwealth Criminal Code formulation: J Clough and C Mulhern, *The Prosecution of Corporations* (Melbourne: Oxford University Press, 2002) pp 178–80. The bill was, however, defeated in the Upper House in June 2002. There has also been a proposal in Queensland for an offence of 'dangerous industrial conduct' causing death or grievous bodily harm for which both individuals and corporations could be liable: Department of Justice and Attorney-General, *Dangerous Industrial Conduct*, Discussion Paper, 2000.

There are still difficulties and cultural barriers to characterising the actions of corporations, resulting in serious injury and death, as 'truly' criminal: J Clough and C Mulhern, *The Prosecution of Corporations* (Melbourne: Oxford University Press, 2002) pp 10 ff; Karen Wheelwright, 'Corporate Liability for Workplace Deaths and Injuries—Reflecting on Victoria's Laws in the Light of the Esso Longford Explosion' (2002) 7(1) *Deakin Law Review* 323–47. However, there is increasing support for the extension of criminal liability to corporations for a range of social harms in the wake of recent major corporate collapses and the evidence of serious corporate misbehaviour, and high-profile cases of somewhat euphemistically termed 'failures of corporate governance', in Australia and elsewhere. A recent inquiry into the operation of the *Trade Practices Act* 1974 (Cth) recommended criminal penalties for serious anti-competitive behaviour, including fines for offending corporations and imprisonment and fines for offending individuals: *Review of the Competition Provisions of the Trade Practices Act* (the Dawson Review)

(Canberra: Commonwealth of Australia, 2003) p 164. Jonathan Clough and Carmel Mulhern confirm in *The Prosecution of Corporations* (Melbourne: Oxford University Press, 2002) pp 3–4 that: 'Over relatively recent times, the public has become increasingly aware, sophisticated and often cynical in its attitude towards corporations and corporate conduct'. These issues are examined further in Chapter 7 in the context of corporate frauds.

As broad issues of corporate regulation grow in significance in this early part of the twenty-first century it is inevitable that the question of the criminal responsibility of corporations for deaths caused by their activities will require more adequate solutions than have been considered to date.

Conclusion

In this chapter we have identified a number of problematic areas. The continued advances in medical technology raise issues concerning definitions of a human being in relation to homicide and offences such as abortion and child destruction. The scope of the fault element for murder needs reassessment as intending or being reckless as to causing grievous bodily harm can be viewed as broadening the concept of fault far too much. Constructive murder has also been criticised as going beyond the subjectivist approach to fault for serious crimes.

The different categories of manslaughter are also difficult to support given that they overlap. It may be worthwhile amalgamating existing categories into one single category of dangerous act or omission manslaughter as recommended by the MCCOC.

We then outlined three specific areas related to homicide: euthanasia, offences dealing with pregnancy and childbirth and, finally, corporate crime. All three of these areas raise a central underlying question about the extent to which killing in specific situations should be criminalised. In the corporate arena, it can be argued that the criminal law should spread a wider net in relation to unlawful killing to reflect moral responsibility as well as encouraging, for example, safe working conditions. On the other hand, some would argue that the criminal law should be curtailed in relation to voluntary euthanasia, abortion and child destruction.

Andrew Ashworth has pointed out that 'the culpable causing of another person's death may fairly be regarded as the most serious offence in the criminal calendar': (3rd edn, Oxford: Oxford University Press, 1999) p 263. However, the context in which the killing occurs has traditionally affected how seriously it is taken by police and prosecutors. An exploration of homicide and related offences shows just how important social and historical factors are in determining what is seen as 'truly' criminal.

CHAPTER 4

Assault and related offences

Introduction

Darryl Reid was about to be married and decided to celebrate his 'bucks' night' by going to a private room at Football Park in Canberra. There he became very drunk and later ended up wearing a silver dress and red wig at a local nightclub. Darryl's brother, Wayne Reid, had also been drinking heavily, having consumed at least ten schooners of beer. The proprietor of the nightclub, Ismael Mahommed Salem, had spoken to the group a number of times about their rowdy behaviour. He eventually asked Darryl to leave and escorted him outside. Wayne and several other members of the group followed them.

Darryl began to swear at the proprietor, who pushed him towards the door. Wayne then punched the proprietor and a general mêlée followed involving security staff and other patrons of the nightclub. The proprietor fell to the ground and was kicked in the head a number of times. He lost consciousness and was later found to have suffered a broken jaw, the loss of three teeth, swelling of the face and an injury to his shoulder.

Darryl and Wayne were charged with more serious offences, but the prosecution accepted their pleas of guilty to assault occasioning actual bodily harm. Crispin J of the Supreme Court of the Australian Capital Territory gave both Darryl and Wayne a good behaviour bond for a period of three years: *R v Darryl Raymond Reid and Wayne Matthew Reid* unreported, 28 August 2001, SC of ACT, Crispin J [2001] ACTSC 88.

The facts of this case illustrate some common themes in the law relating to assault, which is the most common of violent crimes. Offenders and victims are most often young and more likely to be male than female: Australian Bureau of Statistics, *Crime and Safety Australia* (April 2002), <http://www.abs.gov.au/websitedbs/

D331O114.NSF/home/statistics>, accessed October 2003; Australian Institute of Criminology, *Australian Crime: Facts and Figures 2002*, pp 16–20.

Many assaults are not reported to the police and due to different definitions in different jurisdictions, statistics need to be treated carefully. The Australian Institute of Criminology found that in 2001, 38 per cent of reported assaults occurred in community locations, with 23 per cent occurring on streets or footpaths.

The pattern of assaults is different for male and female victims. A majority of male victims (58 per cent) were assaulted in non-residential locations, whereas a majority of female victims (71 per cent) were assaulted in residential premises. Thirty-eight per cent of male victims knew the offender compared with 68 per cent of females: Australian Institute of Criminology, *Australian Crime: Facts and Figures 2002*, pp 16–20.

Social attitudes towards particular types of violence can be highly persuasive in defining what constitutes offences against the person. Historically, for example, there has been a reluctance to prosecute assaults that occur in the context of the home: A Cretney and G Davis, 'Prosecuting "Domestic" Assault' [1996] Crim LR 162–74 at 163. This reflects deep-seated beliefs about the privacy of the family. There may also be cultural and social reasons why violence against homosexuals has been under-reported: G Mason, *The Spectacle of Violence: Homophobia, Gender and Knowledge (Writing Corporealities)* (London: Routledge, 2002).

In 1996, the British Crime Survey conducted by the Home Office used a computer-assisted self-interviewing questionnaire on domestic violence: C Mirrlees-Black, Home Office Research Study 191, *Domestic Violence: Findings from a New British Crime Survey Self-Completion Questionnaire* (London: Home Office, 1999). Analysis of the data found that 23 per cent of women and 15 per cent of men aged 16 to 59 said they had been physically assaulted by a current or former partner at some time. Twenty-eight per cent of women aged 20 to 24 said they had been assaulted by a partner at some time and 34 per cent had been threatened or assaulted. Women were more likely to be injured (47 per cent) than men (31 per cent). The majority of female victims said they had been very frightened, compared to a minority of men. Although the questions asked about incidents that would legally be considered assaults, only 17 per cent of incidents counted by the survey were considered by their victims to be crimes.

In Chapter 1, we outlined how 'standpoint feminism' helped turn scholarly and political attention to women's experiences, and revealed high levels of female victimisation. Feminist theory helped put domestic violence against women onto the political agenda in Western countries. In the past few decades, there has been a growing awareness of the personal and social costs caused by domestic violence. This has elicited a range of legislative and policy responses. In September 1996, the Federal Government convened the National Domestic Violence Forum in Canberra. This resulted in a Discussion Paper released in November 1997 and a Report published in April 1999: Domestic Violence Legislation Working Group, *Model*

Domestic Violence Laws, Discussion Paper (Canberra: AGPS, November, 1997) and Domestic Violence Legislation Working Group, *Model Domestic Violence Laws*, Report (Canberra: AGPS, April, 1999). Both papers focus on protection orders and the need for a uniform approach across Australian jurisdictions. However, Rosemary Hunter and Julie Stubbs have criticised the Discussion Paper as being too technical and failing to consider issues of criminal law relevant to domestic violence: 'Model Laws or Missed Opportunity' (1999) 24(1) *Alternative Law Journal* 12–16. The use of the criminal law in relation to domestic violence will be explored further in the following section, which deals specifically with assault.

The criminal law relating to offences against the person is primarily statutory and encompasses a wide range of offences such as assault, unlawful wounding, endangering the safety of others, stalking, and female genital mutilation. In most Australian jurisdictions, offences against the person are based on modifications of the *Offences Against the Person Act* 1861 (UK): 24&25 Vict c 100. This Act largely consolidated the common law together with a variety of statutory provisions.

The structure of the offences in the English Act leaves much to be desired. Sir James Stephen wrote in a letter to Sir John Holker on 20 January 1877, cited by R Cross, 'The Reports of the Criminal Law Commissioners (1833–1849) and the Abortive Bills of 1853' in PR Glazebrook (ed), *Reshaping the Criminal Law* (London: Stevens & Sons, 1978) p 10: 'Their arrangement is so obscure, their language so lengthy and cumbrous, and they are based upon and assume the existence of so many singular common law principles that no-one who was not already well acquainted with the law would derive any information from reading them.'

In 1985, the Victorian Parliament enacted a scheme of offences that departed quite dramatically from the 1861 statutory provisions. This scheme was based on a proposal originally put forward by the English Criminal Law Revision Committee in 1980: *Fourteenth Report, Offences Against the Person* Cmnd 7844. The proposal was again recommended in a modified form by the Law Commission for England and Wales in *Criminal Law: A Criminal Code for England and Wales*, Report No 177 (London: HMSO,1989) and also in *Legislating the Criminal Code: Offences Against the Person and General Principles*, Report No 218 (London: HMSO, 1993). It sets out offences based on causing injury, thereby focusing on the degree of harm caused. The Model Criminal Code Officers Committee (MCCOC) has suggested that a similar scheme based on degrees of fault and seriousness of harm should provide the basis for the Model Criminal Code: *Chapter 5, Non Fatal Offences Against the Person*, Discussion Paper (August 1996); *Chapter 5, Non Fatal Offences Against the Person*, Report (September 1998).

At present, there is much overlap between offences and accordingly a great deal of discretion has been given to the police, prosecuting authorities, magistrates and judges in the trial process. This explains why, in our case study, Darryl and Wayne Reid were allowed to plead guilty to the less serious offence of assault occasioning actual bodily harm rather than being tried for more serious offences.

In this chapter, we will outline the current law relating to the offences of assault, aggravated assault and the related offences of threats and offences endangering life or personal safety. We will also examine the range of circumstances where the law deems an assault to be 'lawful'. It will be argued that the current law is untenable and the approach suggested by the MCCOC has much to recommend it.

Assault

Background

The case study at the beginning of this chapter sets out the archetypal assault: that between young males occurring in a public place after alcohol has been drunk. The data on assault suggests that there is more than a little truth in this archetype. For example, the 1996 British Crime Survey found that victims of assault said the offender was under the influence of drink or drugs in 48 per cent of cases: Home Office, *The 1996 British Crime Survey* (London: Research and Statistics Directorate, 1996). As stated above, it is also young males who are more likely to be both victims and perpetrators of physical violence. This may explain to a certain extent why assaults that occur within families have traditionally been treated differently.

There is considerable debate concerning what constitutes assault in the domestic context, and the statistics mentioned at the beginning of this chapter, as with all statistics, need to be treated carefully. Domestic violence may be defined to include only physical violence, or physical and emotional abuse existing either in a current relationship and/or in a past one. Problems of definition also occur in relation to grading the seriousness of conduct in assault offences because physical force can range from a mere push to a brutal battering and emotional abuse may range from verbal put-downs to threats of serious harm or death.

While the 1996 British Crime Survey, mentioned earlier, suggests that men and women are violent towards one another in the context of relationships, there is overwhelming evidence that women form the majority of domestic assault victims and the majority of victims killed by partners in Australia: A Ferrante, F Morgan, D Indermaur and R Harding, *Measuring the Extent of Domestic Violence* (Sydney: Hawkins Press, 1996) p 121; J Mouzos, *Femicide: The Killing of Women in Australia 1989–1998* (Canberra: Australian Institute of Criminology, 1999) p 45. Some commentators have argued that male-to-female aggression in relationships is built upon a power differential reflecting male domination in most societies: A Taft, K Hegarty and M Flood, 'Are Men and Women Equally Violent to Intimate Partners?' (2001) 25(8) *Australian and New Zealand Journal of Public Health* 498–500. The United Nations Economic and Social Council's Special Rapporteur on violence against women has documented a number of cultural practices that constitute a form of domestic violence such as honour killings and the pledging of girls for economic and cultural appeasement: R Coomaraswamy, *Integration of the Human Rights of Women and the Gender Perspective: Violence Against Women* E/CN.4/2002/83, 31 January 2002. The patterns of victimisation in homicide were explored in Chapter 3 where we examined the law relating to fatal violence. These patterns are also explored in Chapter 10 where we examine defences to homicide.

The view of domestic violence from a perspective based on gender relations has been criticised as being too generalist. In a report on domestic violence by researchers at the University of South Australia, it was noted that women in abusive relations are addressing a diversity of needs: D Bagshaw, D Chung, M Couch, S Lilburn and B Wadham, *Reshaping Responses to Domestic Violence*, Final Report (April 2000) p 20. This report highlighted a range of reasons why women may not seek help, including women's values and beliefs about family and relationships (such as the shame attached to a 'failed' marriage), the need to protect children, the level of restraint exercised by perpetrators, geographical location and limited access to resources to enable them to leave (at 30).

In recent years, there has also been a growing awareness of domestic violence in Australian Indigenous communities. Judy Atkinson has estimated that in some areas, the rate of domestic violence involving Aboriginal women is forty-five times higher than for non-Aboriginal women: 'A Nation is not Conquered' (1996) 3(80) *Law Bulletin* 4–9. A report by the Queensland Domestic Violence Taskforce (1988) stated that in some Aboriginal communities, violence is so high that it is said to affect up to 90 per cent of families (at 256). There are many reasons why women from Indigenous communities may not seek help for domestic violence, ranging from fear of police and government employees to pressure from the community to 'put up with' the violence so as to avoid shame. Aboriginal writers such as Carlie Atkinson state that violence in Indigenous communities must be placed against a history of social and cultural violence against Indigenous people: Domestic Violence Legislation Working Group, *Submission in Response to the Model Domestic Violence Laws Discussion Paper* (Canberra: Attorney-General's Department, 1998). Thus, control of domestic violence in Indigenous communities must reflect cultural understandings. Some have argued it should be based on restorative justice principles rather than traditional punitive sanctions, which predominate in non-Aboriginal society. There is a belief that generic responses to domestic violence are not appropriate to Indigenous communities, but that culturally specific programs are needed. However, there has been criticism of responses to intra-community violence that downgrade its criminal character and the harm suffered by its victims, in the interests of some misplaced 'cultural sensitivity': H Goodall and J Huggins, 'Aboriginal Women are Everywhere: Contemporary Struggles' in K Saunders and R Evans (eds), *Gender Relations in Australia: Domination and Negotiation* (Sydney: Harcourt Brace Jovanovich, 1992) pp 415–21.

Using criminal laws to combat domestic violence has been problematic. While perceptions have changed towards recognising the criminal character of domestic violence, it is still often difficult to prosecute domestic violence successfully. This may be because the victim does not want to give evidence out of fear of her partner's reaction or because of a lack of sufficient evidence to satisfy the burden of proof. Even if there is a successful prosecution, it may be that magistrates or judges are reluctant to impose serious penalties because of the impact this would have on the offender's family: R Alexander, *Domestic Violence in Australia: The Legal Response* (3rd edn, Sydney: The Federation Press, 2002) p 33.

Despite the pressure in recent years by policy makers to treat domestic violence as criminal conduct, some researchers have raised questions about the primacy of the criminal law over other forms of intervention and prevention: R Holder, 'Playing on the Football Field: Domestic Violence, Help-Seeking and Community Development', *Domestic Violence: Current Responses, Future Directions* (Sydney: Relationships Australia, 1998); D Bagshaw, D Chung, M Couch, S Lilburn and B Wadham, *Reshaping Responses to Domestic Violence: Final Report* (Adelaide: University of South Australia, 2000); R Holder, 'Domestic and Family Violence: Criminal Justice Interventions' *Australian Domestic and Family Violence Clearinghouse*, Issues Paper 3 (2001). It may be that hostile criminal proceedings may not help many victims who want an immediate response to a call for help. Obviously the criminal law should not be used as *the* generic solution to domestic violence, but the criminalisation of domestic violence at least serves to clearly stigmatise it as unacceptable.

The term 'assault' encompasses a broad range of unlawful interference with the person of another. It covers putting a person in fear as well as physical violation through the use of force. In the first instance, an assault is any act committed intentionally or recklessly that puts another person in fear of immediate and unlawful personal violence. In addition, the term 'assault' may be used to encompass the situation where a person causes force to be applied to the body or clothing of another. The latter type of assault was formerly referred to at common law as 'battery', but this distinction no longer applies as both statute and case law use the term 'assault' to cover both putting another in fear and the use of force: *R v Lynsey* [1995] 3 All ER 654.

The various statutory provisions also draw a distinction between 'common' assault and a number of more serious offences, generally termed aggravated assaults, which are built upon the proof of the commission of an assault. 'Common' assault exists in statutory form in all jurisdictions apart from Victoria: *Crimes Act* 1900 (ACT) s 26; *Criminal Code* (NT) s 188; *Crimes Act* 1900 (NSW) s 61; *Criminal Code* (Qld) s 335; *Criminal Law Consolidation Act* 1935 (SA) s 39; *Criminal Code* (Tas) s 184; *Criminal Code* (WA) s 313. Despite the new statutory scheme in Victoria, common assault at common law was not abolished and it continues to carry a penalty at the judge's discretion. In *R v Patton* [1998] 1 VR 7, the Supreme Court of Victoria established that although s 31 of the *Crimes Act* 1958 (Vic) is entitled 'assault', it is limited to assaults with intent to commit an indictable offence, assaults on police or those aiding police and assaults permitted in order to resist or prevent lawful detention.

158 Offences against the person

The structure of the more serious assaults divides them into assaults aggravated either by the nature of the intent of the accused, the status of the victim or by the consequential harm. Because these offences share the fact that they are built upon the occurrence of a common assault, an alternative verdict of common assault is generally available where the circumstances of aggravation or its accompanying mental state are not proven. For example, in the Australian Capital Territory, the Northern Territory, Queensland, Tasmania and Western Australia, common assault is an alternative verdict to wounding: *Crimes Act* 1900 (ACT) s 47; *Criminal Code* (NT) s 315; *Criminal Code* (Qld) s 575; *Criminal Code* (Tas) s 334A; *Criminal Code* (WA) s 594.

The following section sets out a brief overview of the current law relating to the physical elements of assault. We then discuss problematic areas in more detail in the Critique section. Following this we turn to outlining the fault element for assaults and criticisms relating to the vagueness of definitions of intention and recklessness in this regard.

The current law—physical elements

As stated above, common assault may occur either by the threat of force or through the use of force. The common law definition of assault applies in the Australian Capital Territory, New South Wales, South Australia and Victoria. The main case setting out this definition is that of *Fagan v Metropolitan Police Commissioner* [1969] 1 QB 439. James LJ stated in that case (at 444): '[An assault is] any act which intentionally…[or recklessly] causes another person to apprehend immediate and unlawful personal violence…and the actual intended use of unlawful force to another person without his [or her] consent.'

The Code jurisdictions offer statutory definitions of assault that are of similar effect: *Criminal Code* (NT) s 187; *Criminal Code* (Qld) s 245(1); *Criminal Code* (Tas) s 182; *Criminal Code* (WA) s 222.

Assault by the threat of force

An assault by the threat of force is any act committed intentionally or recklessly that causes another person to apprehend immediate and unlawful personal violence or, in the Code jurisdictions, indicates an actual or apparent present ability to apply force: *Criminal Code* (NT) s 187(b); *Criminal Code* (Qld) s 245; *Criminal Code* (Tas) s 182(1); *Criminal Code* (WA) s 222; *Fagan v Metropolitan Police Commissioner* [1969] 1 QB 439; *R v Venna* [1975] 3 WLR 737; *Rozsa v Samuels* [1969] SASR 205; *Knight* (1988) 35 A Crim R 314.

'Apprehension' has not been judicially defined, but, at common law, implies awareness or perception of immediate harm. Whether it includes fear is another matter and this will be explored in the Critique section.

At common law there is a requirement of immediacy. The general rule is that where a threat is made, even in the most menacing fashion, of future violence, an assault will not be made out. For example, in *Knight* (1988) 35 A Crim R 314, the accused had made a series of threatening phone calls. The New South Wales Court of Appeal held that since the calls were made from an appreciable distance and the recipients of the calls were not in any danger of immediate violence there was no conduct that could constitute an assault. There is some indication that this requirement may have been relaxed somewhat. For example, in *Zanker v Vartzokas* (1988) 34 A Crim R 11, the victim accepted a lift from the accused. Once in the car, the accused offered the victim money for sex. The victim refused and demanded that she be let out of the car. The accused kept accelerating the car and stated: 'I am going to take you to my mate's house. He will really fix you up.' The victim then jumped out of the car. The Supreme Court of South Australia held (at 14 per White J) that: 'A present fear of relatively immediate imminent violence was instilled in her mind from the moment the words were uttered and that fear was kept alive in her mind, in the continuing present, by continuing progress with her as prisoner, towards the house where she feared sexual violence was to occur.'

The House of Lords in *R v Ireland; R v Burstow* [1997] 3 WLR 534 held that, depending on the circumstances, there may be an apprehension of immediate violence present when a silent telephone call is made. Lord Steyn stated (at 547): '[The silent caller] intends by his silence to cause fear and he is so understood. The victim is assailed by uncertainty about his intentions. Fear may dominate her emotions and it may be the fear that the caller's arrival at her door may be imminent. She may fear the *possibility* of immediate personal violence.'

There is no requirement of immediacy in the Code jurisdictions. Rather, the emphasis is on the 'present ability' of the accused to carry out the threat: *Criminal Code* (NT) s 187; *Criminal Code* (Qld) s 245; *Criminal Code* (Tas) s 182; *Criminal Code* (WA) s 222. This term is said to bear its ordinary meaning: *R v Secretary* (1996) 5 NTLR 96 at 104–5.

There is a discrepancy in the jurisdictions concerning whether or not the victim has to actually be put in fear. This will be taken up in the Critique section.

Assault by the use of force

An assault by the use of force occurs where a person, intentionally or recklessly, causes force to be applied to the body or clothing of another: *Beal v Kelley* [1951] 2 All ER 763; *Fairclough v Whipp* [1951] 2 All ER 834; *DPP v Rogers* [1953] 2 All ER 644; *Rolfe* (1952) 36 Cr App R 4; *R v McCormack* [1969] 2 QB 442; *Fagan v Metropolitan Police Commissioner* [1969] 1 QB 439; *R v Venna* [1975] 3 WLR 737; *R v Spratt* [1990] 1 WLR 1073; *R v Savage and Parmenter* [1992] 1 AC 699; *Criminal Code* (NT) s 187(a); *Criminal Code* (Qld) s 245; *Criminal Code* (Tas) s 182(1); *Criminal Code* (WA) s 222. An assault may occur not only where force is applied to the body of the victim, but also where clothing is slashed or rubbed: *R v Day* (1845) 1 Cox 207; *Thomas* (1985) 81 Cr App R 331. The force used need not be violent, but can be as slight as a mere touch: *Collins v Wilcock* [1984] 1 WLR 1172. Thus, kissing or touching another who does not invite such conduct, expressly or by their behaviour may constitute an assault. If an injury results from the application of force and it is more than minor, then the accused may be charged with an aggravated assault.

Usually an assault is committed by delivering a blow with a limb or using a weapon of some kind. However, the Queensland and Western Australian provisions specifically define the use of force so as to include the application of heat, light, electrical force, gas or odour so as to cause injury or personal discomfort: *Criminal Code* (Qld) s 245; *Criminal Code* (WA) s 222.

At common law, it appears that the application of force must be direct in that it must be aimed at the victim or an object on which the victim is supported: *R v Salisbury* [1976] VR 452; *Commissioner of Police v Wilson* [1984] AC 242; *R v Sheriff* [1969] Crim LR 260. In comparison, in the Code jurisdictions, indirect application of force is sufficient provided that there is adequate evidence of causation: *Criminal Code* (NT) s 187(a); *Criminal Code* (Qld) s 245; *Criminal Code* (Tas) s 182(1); *Criminal Code* (WA) s 222.

Aggravated assaults

A wide variety of statutory offences generally termed 'aggravated assaults' authorise the imposition of greater penalties than for common assault. These statutory offences can be divided into three classes:
- assaults accompanied by an intention of a particular kind;
- assaults committed on particular classes of people; and
- assaults resulting in harm of a particular kind.

Assaults with intention to commit another crime

The most serious form of aggravated assault involving a particular intention is assault with intent to commit murder: *Crimes Act* 1900 (NSW) s 27; *Criminal Code* (NT) s 165; *Criminal Code* (Qld) s 306; *Criminal Code* (WA) s 283. In the other jurisdictions, the crime of attempted murder falls under the general law of attempt. There are also statutory provisions dealing with assaults with intent to commit another crime: *Crimes Act* 1900 (ACT) s 22; *Crimes Act* 1900 (NSW) s 58; *Criminal Code* (NT) s 193; *Criminal Code* (Qld) s 340(a); *Criminal Law Consolidation Act* 1935 (SA) s 270B; *Criminal Code* (Tas) s 183(a); *Crimes Act* 1958 (Vic) s 31(1)(a); *Criminal Code* (WA) s 317A.

Assaults on particular classes of people

Assaults on particular classes of people are viewed as aggravated because of the special status of the people concerned. For example, it is an offence to assault a police officer in the execution of his or her duty: *Crimes Act* 1900 (ACT) s 27(4)(c),

32(1)(b); *Crimes Act* 1900 (NSW) s 58; *Criminal Code* (NT) s 188(2)(h); *Criminal Code* (Qld) s 340(b), (e); *Criminal Law Consolidation Act* 1935 (SA) s 43(b); *Police Offences Act* 1935 (Tas) s 34B(1); *Crimes Act* 1958 (Vic) s 31(1)(b); *Criminal Code* (WA) s 318(1)(d)–(f). However, the range of persons covered in legislation is rather arbitrary and often reflects paternalistic notions of individuals in need of protection. For example, an assault will be considered aggravated if it is carried out on a woman (*Criminal Code* (NT) s 188(2)(b); s 35(2) of the *Police Offences Act* 1935 (Tas) enables the imposition of a heavier penalty if the assault is on a female or a child and is of an aggravated nature) or those unable to defend themselves by reason of infirmity, age, physique, situation or other disability: *Crimes Act* 1900 (NSW) s 44; *Criminal Code* (NT) s 188(2)(d).

Other classes to receive special protection in certain jurisdictions appear to do so because of their status in society. These include members of Parliament where the assault is committed because of such membership (*Criminal Code* (NT) s 188(2)(e); *Criminal Code* (WA) s 318(1)(d)–(f)) and members of the public service or the judiciary: *Crimes Act* (NSW) ss 58, 326; *Criminal Code* (NT) ss 188(2)(f), 190; *District Courts Act* 1967 (Qld) s 129; *Criminal Law Consolidation Act* 1935 (SA) s 42; *Criminal Code* (WA) s 318A.

Assaults resulting in harm

In all jurisdictions, except Tasmania, there also exists a division between assaults causing actual bodily harm or injury and grievous bodily harm or serious injury. There is also a related offence that exists in all jurisdictions apart from Victoria and the Northern Territory of unlawful wounding. In Tasmania, s 183 of the *Criminal Code* creates a separate crime of aggravated assault and describes it as assault with intent to commit a crime or to resist lawful apprehension and the assault of a person in the lawful execution of process against land and goods. However, s 172 provides that any person who 'causes grievous bodily harm to any person by any means whatever is guilty of a crime'.

The main difference between assaults resulting in harm of a particular type and unlawful wounding lies in the definition of the relevant types of harm.

In relation to the offence of unlawful wounding (*Crimes Act* 1900 (ACT) s 21; *Crimes Act* 1900 (NSW) ss 33, 35; *Criminal Code* (Qld) s 323(1); *Criminal Law Consolidation Act* 1935 (SA) ss 21, 23; *Criminal Code* (Tas) s 172; *Criminal Code* (WA) s 301), a wound at common law consists of an injury involving breaking through both the inner and outer skin: *R v Wood and McMahon* (1830) 1 Mood CC 278; *Moriarty v Brooks* (1834) 6 C & P 684; *R v Beckett* (1836) 1 Mood & R 526; *Vallance v The Queen* (1961) 108 CLR 56 at 77; *R v Berwick* [1979] Tas R 101. The term is not defined in the Criminal Codes, but the common law definition has been applied by the Queensland Court of Criminal Appeal in *Jervis* (1991) 56 A Crim R 374. The word 'unlawfully' in relation to this offence appears to be largely redundant in that it does no more than express the principle that certain uses of force may be lawful or justifiable if used in self-defence and arrest situations.

In the Australian Capital Territory, New South Wales and South Australia, the relevant provisions refer to 'actual bodily harm': *Crimes Act* 1900 (ACT) s 24; *Crimes Act* 1900 (NSW) s 59; *Criminal Law Consolidation Act* 1935 (SA) s 40. The Code jurisdictions, apart from Tasmania, use the term 'bodily harm': *Criminal Code* (NT) s 186; *Criminal Code* (Qld) s 328; *Criminal Code* (WA) s 306. In Victoria, the word used is 'injury': *Crimes Act* 1958 (Vic) s 18. At common law, it has been held that the words 'actual bodily harm' should be given their ordinary and natural meaning: *R v Metharam* [1961] 3 All ER 200. In Victoria, injury is defined in s 15 of the *Crimes Act* 1958 as including 'unconsciousness, hysteria, pain and any substantial impairment of bodily function'. In *R v Chan-Fook* [1994] 2 ER 552 the Court held (at 559) that actual bodily harm includes 'psychiatric injury', but it does not include mere emotions such as fear or distress or panic.

The Code jurisdictions' definitions of 'bodily harm' are similar. In the Northern Territory, 'bodily injury' includes any hurt or injury that interferes with health, and in Queensland and Western Australia, this is extended to an interference with health or comfort: *Criminal Code* (NT) s 1; *Criminal Code* (Qld) s 1; *Criminal Code* (WA) s 1.

In all jurisdictions, there exists an offence of assault resulting in some form of serious harm. The term 'grievous bodily harm' is used in most jurisdictions: *Crimes Act* 1900 (ACT) ss 19, 20, 25; *Crimes Act* 1900 (NSW) ss 35, 54; *Criminal Code* (Qld) ss 317, 320; *Criminal Law Consolidation Act* 1935 (SA) ss 21, 23; *Criminal Code* (Tas) ss 170, 172; *Criminal Code* (WA) ss 294, 297. 'Grievous harm' is used in the Northern Territory and 'serious injury' in Victoria: *Criminal Code* (NT) ss 177, 181; *Crimes Act* 1958 (Vic) ss 16, 17, 24.

'Grievous bodily harm' has been interpreted at common law as meaning bodily harm of a serious character: *DPP v Smith* [1961] AC 290 at 334 per Viscount Kilmuir LC; *R v Metharam* [1961] 3 All ER 200; *R v Cunningham* [1982] AC 566; *R v Saunders* [1985] Crim LR 230. In the Australian Capital Territory and New South Wales, grievous bodily harm is defined as including 'any permanent or serious disfiguring of the person': *Crimes Act* 1900 (ACT) s 4; *Crimes Act* 1900 (NSW) s 4(1). In Victoria, 'serious injury' is defined in s 15 of the *Crimes Act* 1958 as including 'a combination of injuries'.

The Code jurisdictions provide statutory definitions of the relevant terms. In Queensland, 'grievous bodily harm' is defined as the loss of a distinct part or an organ of the body, serious disfigurement or 'any bodily injury of such a nature that, if left untreated, would endanger or be likely to endanger life, or to cause or be likely to cause permanent injury to health': *Criminal Code* (Qld) s 1. The Western Australian definition is the same as the latter quoted part. However, s 1(4) of the *Criminal Code* extends it to include a 'serious disease'. The Tasmanian definition is also the same as the quoted part of the Queensland definition, but the words 'serious injury' are used instead of 'permanent injury'. In the Northern Territory, 'grievous harm' is similarly defined as 'any physical or mental injury of such a nature as to endanger or be likely to endanger or to cause or be likely to cause permanent injury to health': *Criminal Code* (NT) s 1.

Female genital mutilation

This overview of the physical element shows that the law of assault and aggravated assault is quite comprehensive. However, during the past twenty years, some legislatures have enacted specific provisions dealing with female genital mutilation. This term describes a variety of ritual practices ranging from scraping or cutting the clitoris to the excision of the clitoris, labia minora and parts of the labia majora: see Queensland Law Reform Commission, *Female Genital Mutilation*, Report No 47 (September 1994), pp 7–8. It was previously referred to as 'female circumcision'. In recent years, however, the language of human rights abuse has displaced the 'traditional' language: see, for example, Australian Medical Association, *Female Genital Mutilation*, Position Statement (Canberra: AMA, November 2002), <http://www.ama.com.au/web.nsf/doc/SHED-5FLUNB>, accessed November 2003, Appendix.

Existing provisions such as those dealing with grievous bodily harm or serious injury could be used to prosecute such conduct. The issue of consent will be considered later. However, it has now been separately criminalised in certain jurisdictions: *Crimes Act* 1900 (ACT), Pt 111B; *Crimes Act* 1900 (NSW) s 45; *Criminal Code* (NT) Pt VI Division 4A; *Criminal Code* (Tas) ss 178A–178C; *Crimes Act* 1958 (Vic) ss 32–34A; *Criminal Code* (Qld) s 323A; *Criminal Law Consolidation Act* 1935 (SA) s 33A. In the UK, s 1 of the *Prohibition of Female Circumcision Act* 1985 (UK) makes it an offence to 'excise, infibulate or otherwise mutilate the labia', but allows a defence if it is performed by a doctor and is intended to benefit the person in a therapeutic context. Other jurisdictions rely on the ordinary law of assault. The Australian Law Reform Commission rejected calls for special female genital mutilation offences, favouring the view that the practice constitutes an offence under the general law: *Multiculturalism: Criminal Law*, Discussion Paper No 48 (1991) p 23.

Critique

A number of criticisms may be made of the existing structure of assaults and aggravated assaults. Most criticisms revolve around the dilemma of how broad should assault offences be. For example, should words alone constitute an assault by the threat of force? Should the focus be on the accused's conduct or on the victim's reaction to it? Should there be an element of immediacy involved? In relation to assault by force, should indirect as well as direct force be involved? How should factors of aggravation be taken into account?

Assaults, whether by the threat of force or use of it, interfere with a person's physical integrity and autonomy. Ian Kerridge, Michael Lowe and John McPhee write that the ethical principle of autonomy is 'often referred to as the principle of respect for persons because it promotes the view that the individual is the rightful determiner of his or her own life. Observance of this principle incurs an obligation upon individuals to not constrain the autonomous actions of others unnecessarily and to treat persons in such a way as to enable them to act autonomously': *Ethics and Law for the Health Professions* (Katoomba, NSW: Social Science Press, 1998) p 72.

Starting from the premise that individual autonomy needs to be respected, a broad view of what should constitute assault can be justified. Many assaults and related offences have psychological effects such as anxiety and depression, which can severely affect a person's ability to function in social and work activities. This has become a central focus point for researchers examining the consequences of domestic violence.

The real problem with defining assaults very broadly is that a great discretion is given to prosecuting authorities as to what charges should be laid against an accused. We will explore this further in the later section dealing with consent issues and assault. In the next sections, we take up a few of the problems associated with defining the physical elements of assault.

Assaults by the threat of force

The first problematic area in relation to assaults by the threat of force relates to whether or not words alone may constitute a threat of force. James LJ in *Fagan v Metropolitan Police Commissioner* [1969] 1 QB 439 at 444 set out a general principle that an omission to act cannot constitute an assault. Some form of positive act is necessary such as a threatening gesture. However, threatening words on their own have amounted to an assault at common law: *Barton v Armstrong* [1969] 2 NSWR 451 at 455 per Taylor J; *R v Tout* (1987) 11 NSWLR 251 at 256–7 per Lee J; *R v Ireland; R v Burstow* [1997] 3 WLR 534 at 546 per Lord Steyn. This is also the case in the Northern Territory: *Criminal Code* (NT) s 187(b); *R v Secretary* (1996) 5 NTLR 96 per Mildren J.

In contrast, in Tasmania, and, by implication, Queensland and Western Australia (where the statutory provisions use wording that is only appropriate to physical gestures), the use of words alone cannot constitute an assault: *Criminal Code* (Tas) s 182(2); *Criminal Code* (Qld) s 245; *Criminal Code* (WA) s 222.

Recent developments in the common law suggest that a very broad approach will be taken to what constitutes a threat. In the case of *R v Ireland; R v Burstow* [1997] 3 WLR 534 the House of Lords held that the making of a series of silent telephone calls that caused fear of immediate and unlawful bodily harm amounted to assault. Lord Steyn stated (at 546–7):

> [T]he critical question [is] whether a silent caller may be guilty of an assault. The answer to this question seems to me to be 'Yes, depending on the facts'....Take now the case of the silent caller. He intends by his silence to cause fear and he is

so understood...As a matter of law the caller may be guilty of an assault: whether he is or not will depend on the circumstance and in particular on the impact of the caller's potentially menacing call or calls to the victim.

Words alone or silence should be enough to amount to threatening conduct, particularly if it forms part of a pattern of conduct. As will be explored later, the crime of stalking may also be relevant in such circumstances.

The second problematic area relating to assaults by the threat of force concerns the victim's mental state. At common law, the act constituting assault must be such as to raise in the mind of the person threatened an apprehension of immediate bodily harm: *R v McNamara* [1954] VLR 137 at 138; *Brady v Schatzel; Ex parte Brady* [1911] St R Qd 206. This requires the accused's knowledge or perception of the threat so that pointing a gun at the back of a person's head or holding a knife over a sleeping person would not amount to an assault. There is some debate, however, as to whether 'apprehension' means that the victim must also be put in fear by the accused's words or actions. In *Ryan v Kuhl* [1979] VR 315, the victim was in a cubicle in a public toilet at a railway station. The accused pushed a knife through a hole in the partition between the cubicles in order, he claimed, to stop the victim from annoying him. McGarvie J of the Supreme Court of Victoria held (at 327) that there was no assault in these circumstances because the victim had not been put in fear:

> [O]n the evidence it could not be inferred that the defendant's conduct created in Matthews [the 'victim'] a fear of violence. Mathews said he realised at the time that the person in the next cubicle could not harm him with the knife while he remained in his cubicle. He also said that the sight of the knife had not scared him and said that he had not gone to the station master because he was frightened. On the other hand, he also gave evidence that the sight of the knife had shocked him, that he said out aloud, 'Are you mad or something?', then opened the door and walked quickly out of the toilet.

This is a decision of a single judge and it could be argued that the question is still open. In contrast, in the Code jurisdictions, it appears possible for an assault to occur where a person has an actual ability to apply force to another regardless of whether or not the victim has knowledge of that ability or is put in fear: *Criminal Code* (NT) s 187(b); *Criminal Code* (Qld) s 245; *Criminal Code* (Tas) s 182(1); *Criminal Code* (WA) s 222. Emphasis in these jurisdictions is placed on an actual or apparent present ability to apply force. Where there is an actual ability, it is irrelevant whether or not the victim has knowledge of that ability: *Criminal Code* (NT) s 187(b); *Criminal Code* (Qld) s 245; *Criminal Code* (Tas) s 182(1); *Criminal Code* (WA) s 222.

It is also irrelevant that the victim actually be put in fear. In *Brady v Schatzel; Ex parte Brady* [1911] St R Qd 206 the victim gave evidence that when the accused pointed a gun at him, he did not believe the accused would fire it. It was argued that because the victim was not afraid, there was no assault. This argument was rejected and it was held that there could be an assault even where the victim was not put in fear. Chubb J of the Queensland Supreme Court stated (at 208): '[I]t is not material that the person assaulted should be put in fear...If that were so, it would make an assault not dependent upon the intention of the assailant, but upon the question whether the party assaulted was a courageous or timid person...All that is needed on this view, is the anticipation of the application of unlawful personal violence.'

Should the common law or Code jurisdictions' approach to the mental state of the victim prevail? Performing an act with the intention of causing fear should be enough to attract criminal liability because it is in itself harmful and because it complies with the general principle of taking one's victim as one finds him or her. This principle has certainly been at the forefront of the law relating to unlawful killing: see, for example, *Mamote-Kulang of Tamagot v The Queen* (1964) 111 CLR 62; *R v Blaue* [1975] 1 WLR 1411; *Hubert* (1993) 67 A Crim R 181. Otherwise the same act may be an assault where the victim is timid, yet not where the victim is heroic.

We shall return to the issue of conduct amounting to threats a little later in this chapter when other specific statutory crimes are explored.

Factors of aggravation

At present, some jurisdictions take rather a paternalistic approach to factors of aggravation when it comes to classes of people. The MCCOC has agreed that there should be increased penalties for assaults where factors of aggravation exist: *Chapter 5, Non Fatal Offences Against the Person*, Discussion Paper (August 1996) p 92; *Chapter 5, Non Fatal Offences Against the Person*, Report (September 1998) p 111 ff. A modified version of these classes of people has been outlined. The MCCOC suggests the following categories:

- public officials defined as including members of Parliament, a Minister of the Crown, a judicial officer, a police officer, a person appointed by or employed by the government or a government agency;
- a person who was involved in any capacity in judicial proceedings;
- a child under the age of 10 years; and
- those to whom the accused is in a position of trust.

The MCCOC approach is to place circumstances of aggravation into the sentencing stage of procedure, rather than set out statutory crimes including harm to certain classes of person. It may, however, be better to retain the existence of different statutory offences and have a jury decide whether the elements of the offence are made out than have a judge take over the fact-finding role during sentencing. Otherwise, the policy behind viewing classes of people as an aggravating factor ties in with having a hierarchy of assaults. Another practical reason for having such offences is to enable convictions for lesser offences should the prosecution fail to make out the aggravating circumstances.

The current law in all jurisdictions differentiates between serious and non-serious harms. The terminology used, however, can be problematic. The House of Lords in *R v Ireland; R v Burstow* [1997] 3 WLR 534 established that bodily harm includes 'recognisable psychiatric illness': see L Dunford and V Pickford, 'Is There a Qualitative Difference Between Physical and Psychiatric Harm in English Law?' (1999) 7 *Journal of Law and Medicine* 36–46 at 42 ff. However, the use of the adjective 'bodily' is misleading as it appears to ignore psychological harm.

The MCCOC has recommended that 'harm' and 'serious harm' are more appropriate terms than actual bodily harm or grievous bodily harm: *Chapter 5, Non Fatal Offences Against the Person*, Report (September 1998) p 21 ff. The MCCOC rejected the Victorian approach of using the terms 'injury' and 'serious injury' on the basis that if the injury is trivial such as trivial touching, there is no harm done. However, as explored in Chapter 1, the scope of the liberal notion of 'harm' is problematic. If broadly interpreted, it could encompass social or economic harm. The terms, if they are to be used, should be clearly defined.

The MCCOC has also recommended that the verb used in the appropriate provisions should be 'causing' rather than 'inflicting'. This covers a broader range of actions. For example, in *R v Nicholson* [1916] VLR 130, the accused entered a house in order to remove two gas meters. He incorrectly reconnected one gas pipe. The occupants came home, lit a lamp, which made the gas explode, injuring them. The accused was charged with negligently causing serious injury. He argued that the offence was limited to 'direct' injury. The Court held that it was not and that the accused had caused the injury as charged. It could not be said, in comparison, that he had 'inflicted' the injury.

Using the word 'causing' does not appear to widen the law too much. The common law has certainly developed such a broad interpretation of 'inflicting' that it is very close to 'causing' in any case. For example, the word 'inflict' has been interpreted broadly in recent years to include causing psychiatric illness: *R v Ireland; R v Burstow* [1998] AC 147.

The MCCOC approach to the hierarchy of assault offences has much to recommend it. It has based its scheme on that proposed by the English Law Reform Committee in its *Fourteenth Report, Offences Against the Person* Cmnd 7844 (1980) upon which the Victorian provisions are based: *Chapter 5, Non Fatal Offences Against the Person*, Report (September 1998); Discussion Paper (August 1996). Having a hierarchy of harms goes a long way towards rationalising what conduct should be considered criminal and enables a broad approach to develop.

The current law—fault elements

In Chapter 2, we outlined the different interpretations of the fault elements of intention and recklessness. The current law of assault displays a degree of confusion as to which interpretations of these terms should prevail. There is also a question as to whether to include negligence as an objective fault element in the hierarchy of assault offences. This section outlines the current laws in relation to the fault element and then we examine some of the criticisms that have been made of them.

In all jurisdictions, a common assault may be committed intentionally or recklessly: *R v Spratt* [1990] 1 WLR 1073; *Vallance v The Queen* (1961) 108 CLR 56; *Leonard v Morris* (1975) 10 SASR 528; *MacPherson v Brown* (1975) 12 SASR 184; *R v Bacash* [1981] VR 923; *Criminal Code* (NT) s 31; *Criminal Code* (Qld) s 23; *Criminal Code* (Tas) s 182; *Criminal Code* (WA) s 23. Although the Queensland and Western Australian Criminal Codes do not specify the fault requirement for an assault, in *Hall v Fonceca* [1983] WAR 309 at 314 it was accepted that the fault element was the same as for common law. Assault has been referred to as a crime of basic intent in that it is a crime involving a specified form of conduct, and intention therefore refers to the accused meaning to perform the conduct: *R v O'Connor* (1980) 146 CLR 64; *DPP (UK) v Majewski* [1977] AC 443; *Duffy v The Queen* [1981] WAR 72. Thus for assault by the threat of force, the accused must mean to commit the act creating an apprehension of immediate and unlawful personal violence. Similarly, for assault using force, the accused must mean to use force on the victim.

The fault element required for assaults resulting in actual bodily harm is the same as for common assault in that intention or recklessness will suffice. The intention or recklessness appears to relate to the use of force, rather than the actual bodily harm, rendering this a conduct rather than a result crime: *R v Venna* [1975] 3 WLR 737 at 742 per James LJ; *R v Percali* (1986) 42 SASR 46; *Coulter v The Queen* (1988) 164 CLR 350; *R v Savage and Parmenter* [1992] 1 AC 699; *Williams* (1990) 50 A Crim R 213. However, in Victoria, s 18 of the *Crimes Act* 1958 (Vic) may require an intention to cause injury rather than simply engage in the conduct that had that result: *Westaway* (1991) 52 A Crim R 336.

The fault element in relation to assaults resulting in grievous bodily harm varies between jurisdictions. Intention (*Crimes Act* 1900 (ACT) s 19; *Criminal Code* (NT) s 177; *Criminal Law Consolidation Act* 1935 (SA) s 21(b); *Criminal Code* (Tas) s 170; *Crimes Act* 1958 (Vic) s 16) and recklessness (*Crimes Act* 1900 (ACT) s 20; *Criminal Code* (NT) s 181; *Criminal Law Consolidation Act* 1935 (SA) s 29(2)(b); *Crimes Act* 1958 (Vic) s 17) are mentioned in most jurisdictions. However, the relevant Queensland, Northern Territory and Western Australian provisions contain no mention of intention or recklessness: *Criminal Code* (Qld) s 320; *Criminal Code* (NT) s 181; *Criminal Code* (WA) s 297. These fault elements will nevertheless be relevant to show that the act did not occur involuntarily or by accident: *Criminal Code* (Qld) s 23; *Criminal Code* (WA) s 23; *Fitzgerald* (1999) 106 A Crim R 215.

It is unclear whether or not the intention required is the same as for the offences of assault and assault resulting in bodily harm. In *Bennett* (1989) 45 A Crim R 45, the Tasmanian provision was viewed as a crime of basic or general rather than specific intent, indicating that this was a conduct rather than a result crime. However, in *Westaway* (1991) 52 A Crim R 336, the Victorian Court of Criminal Appeal held that intention in the offence of intentionally causing serious injury under s 16 of the *Crimes Act* 1958 (Vic) relates to an intention to cause serious injury rather than simply an intention to engage in the conduct that had that result.

The test for recklessness varies between jurisdictions. At common law, an assault will be made out if the accused foresaw unlawful force or the act causing an apprehension of immediate and unlawful personal violence: *Fagan v Metropolitan Police Commissioner* [1969] 1 QB 439 at 444 per James LJ. However, the *degree* of foresight required is uncertain.

Some authorities simply refer to the need for recklessness to be proven without further explanation: *Fagan v Metropolitan Police Commissioner* [1969] 1 QB 439 at 444; *Logdon v DPP* [1976] Crim LR 121 at 122; *R v Venna* [1975] 3 WLR 737. However, in *MacPherson v Brown* (1975) 12 SASR 184, Bray CJ stated (at 187) that it will be enough that the accused foresaw the *possibility* that force might be inflicted: see also *Williams* (1990) 50 A Crim R 213; *R v Coleman* (1990) 19 NSWLR 467 at 475–8 per Hunt J; *R v Lovett* [1975] VR 488 at 493–4 per Harris J: *R v Savage and Parmenter* [1992] 1 AC 699 at 752 per Lord Ackner. The alternative is that the accused must have foreseen that force would *probably* be inflicted. In *R v Campbell* [1997] 2 VR 585 Hayne and Crockett JJ spoke with approval of the High Court test of recklessness in relation to murder as set out in *R v Crabbe* (1985) 156 CLR 464. Hayne and Crockett JJ concluded (at 592–3) in relation to the offence of recklessly causing serious injury: 'We have no doubt that the appropriate test to apply is that it is possession of foresight that injury probably will result that must be proved.'

Campbell's case, however, applies to the statutory offence of recklessly causing injury and not to common assault. At common law, Diplock LJ stated in *R v Mowatt* [1968] 1 QB 421 (at 426) that the offence of inflicting grievous bodily harm required foresight that 'some physical harm in some person, albeit of a minor character, might result', a proposition that was relied upon in *R v Savage and Parmenter* [1992] 1 AC 699 at 716. This seems to imply a lesser standard of foresight.

The weight of common law authority does seem to be in favour of foresight in terms of possibility rather than probability. This requirement is also clearly set out in the Northern Territory. Section 31 of the *Criminal Code* (NT) specifies that an assault is committed whether the harm was 'intended or foreseen…as a possible consequence of [the accused's] conduct'.

The New South Wales provisions refer to 'maliciously inflicting grievous bodily harm with intent to inflict grievous bodily harm' and 'maliciously inflicting grievous bodily harm': *Crimes Act* 1900 ss 33, 35. Section 5 of the *Crimes Act* 1900 (NSW) defines malice as acting with indifference to human life or suffering, or with intent to injure some person or persons, and in any such case without lawful cause or excuse, or acting recklessly or wantonly. If the offence is sought to be established by proof of recklessness, it is sufficient that the accused foresaw the possibility as opposed to probability of some harm resulting from the accused's act: *R v Coleman* (1990) 19 NSWLR 467 at 475; *Stokes and Difford* (1990) 51 A Crim R 25 at 40. Some jurisdictions also have statutory provisions relating to causing grievous bodily harm through a negligent act or omission: *Crimes Act* 1900 (ACT) s 25; *Crimes Act* 1900 (NSW) s 54; *Criminal Code* (Qld) s 328; *Crimes Act* 1958 (Vic) s 24. In *R v Shields* [1981] VR 717, the Full Court of the Supreme Court of Victoria held that the standard of negligence required was the same as for negligent manslaughter. The latter test is set out at common law in *Nydam v The Queen* [1977] VR 430 at 455.

Critique

In Chapter 2, we stated that the term 'intention' has evaded precise legal definition. Andrew Ashworth has pointed out that appellate courts 'in most cases…insist that intention is an ordinary word that needs no explanation, but on other occasions they adopt broader and narrower definitions and they have never offered a concrete definition of the term': *Principles of Criminal Law* (3rd edn, Oxford: Oxford University Press, 1999) p 182.

As stated above, assault and aggravated assaults are generally seen as crimes of basic or general intent in that they involve a specified form of conduct. The current law in relation to assaults resulting in actual bodily harm, for example, views intention as relating to the use of force rather than the bodily harm. Intention is therefore used to refer to the accused meaning to perform the conduct, rather than to achieve the outcome or result.

The MCCOC, however, has recommended that assaults be tiered in terms of the harm caused: *Chapter 5, Non Fatal Offences Against the Person*, Discussion Paper (August 1996) p 26; *Chapter 5, Non Fatal Offences Against the Person*, Report (September 1998) p 13. This implies that another form of intention must be proved, that of intention as purpose plus foresight of the results or consequences of conduct. In regard to this form of intention, the prosecution must prove that the accused's purpose was to bring about the results or consequences of the conduct: *La Fontaine v The Queen* (1976) 136 CLR 62; *R v Crabbe* (1985) 156 CLR 464; *Boughey v The Queen* (1986) 161 CLR 10; *R v Demirian* [1989] VR 97. However, the MCCOC did not clarify whether its scheme contains conduct rather than result crimes: *Chapter 5, Non Fatal Offences Against the Person*, Report (September 1998) pp 41–2. In Chapter 2, we explored how objectivists argue that 'outcome-luck' ought to play a role in ascribing moral and criminal responsibility. For example, Antony Duff argues that consequences have a role to play in determining questions of moral and legal blame even where the actor has no control over them: *Intention, Agency and Criminal Liability* (Oxford: Basil Blackwell, 1990) pp 184–92. Reflecting this approach, it seems logical to use intention in its specific purpose or consequentialist sense in relation to crimes resulting in specific harm.

Thus, taking Antony Duff's approach, there should be a difference in criminal responsibility between two people who punch another, depending on the consequences of the punch. This is the approach taken in the Victorian schema. The definition of intention in relation to intentionally causing injury (s 18 *Crimes Act* 1958

(Vic)) and intentionally causing serious injury (s 16) relates to the consequences of the accused's actions rather than the use of force or threat: *Westaway* (1991) 52 A Crim R 336.

However, even on a 'subjectivist' approach to criminal responsibility, which ascribes blame on the basis of an individual's intention or knowledge rather than on the consequences of conduct, it can be argued that intention should relate to the injury caused rather than the use of force or threat. On this approach, blame should depend on individual choices made and not merely on luck or chance. The focus should therefore be on whether or not the accused intended to cause an injury or a more serious injury.

Recklessness in relation to assaults and related crimes also needs to be clarified. As stated above, the weight of authority appears to be positing a standard of foresight of the possibility of harm apart from the crime of recklessly causing serious injury set out in s 17 of the *Crimes Act* 1958 (Vic) where the test is that of knowledge that serious injury would *probably* result: *Campbell* (1995) 80 A Crim R 461. A low standard of recklessness raises the question as to whether or not the range of assault crimes becomes too broad. Andrew Ashworth writes in *Principles of Criminal Law* (Oxford: Oxford University Press, 1999) p 324: '[O]ne might ask whether the distinction between intention...and recklessness...is so wide in crimes of violence, which are often impulsive reactions to events, as to warrant the difference in maximum penalties between life imprisonment and five years' imprisonment.'

The MCCOC has also recommended that an offence of negligently causing serious harm should form part of the Model Criminal Code partly because it 'is necessary in order to criminalise those instances of gross negligence that cause serious harm, such as the removal of safety equipment in the workplace': *Chapter 5, Non Fatal Offences Against the Person*, Discussion Paper (August 1996) p 33.

A broad hierarchy of assault offences assists in identifying standards of behaviour that should be seen as criminal, such as those arising in the domestic context. A broad hierarchy is also better than having catch-all offences aimed at prosecutorial convenience such as found in public order offences: S Bronitt and B McSherry, *Principles of Criminal Law* (Sydney: LBC, 2001) ch 14. We would therefore recommend setting the standard of recklessness as a possibility rather than probability of harm and introducing a negligence-based offence.

Threats and stalking

Background

In 1995, Paul Vose developed an obsession with an 11-year-old boy, referred to as MA who had featured in a number of advertising campaigns. It was not until 1997, that MA became aware of Vose's obsession. MA and his sister were walking home from a railway station when Vose approached him and asked him whether he was the boy from various advertisements. MA said yes and tried to walk away, but Vose kept asking him questions and followed the children until they turned into their own street. Several weeks later, Vose again approached MA and attempted to engage him in conversation. MA and his sister took an alternative route home and told their mother what had happened.

Over the next year, MA saw Vose near his home, at church where MA sang in the choir and at soccer training where Vose appeared to be taking photos of him. In December 1997, Vose started delivering material to MA's home, which MA's mother and stepfather opened. This material described how to access an Internet site entitled 'Lovable Lads'. When MA's stepfather eventually looked at the website, he saw galleries of photos of MA. MA's parents went to the police and after Vose was arrested and charged with stalking, the police seized electronic listening devices, photographs of MA, various articles of disguise and *Melways* maps indicating MA's school.

Vose eventually pleaded guilty to three counts of stalking contrary to s 21A of the *Crimes Act* 1958 (Vic). He admitted previous convictions for aggravated burglary, one count of causing injury intentionally or recklessly and three counts of possession of unlicensed firearms. He was sentenced to four years' imprisonment for stalking, with a non-parole period of three years. His appeal against sentence was dismissed: *Vose* (1999) 109 A Crim R 489.

Paul Mullen, Michelle Pathé and Rosemary Purcell have identified five primary types of stalkers: intimacy seekers, the resentful, the rejected, the predatory and the incompetents: *Stalkers and Their Victims* (Cambridge: Cambridge University Press, 2000). Paul Vose could be said to fit into the predatory category as these stalkers tend to pursue sexual gratification and control both in and through their stalking. They usually concentrate on furtively following and maintaining surveillance of their victims and their stalking behaviour is usually intended as preparatory to an assault. It is interesting in this regard to note Vose's prior convictions for causing injury and possession of unlicensed firearms. He had also written the following on his website (*Vose* (1999) 109 A Crim R 489 at 493):

> I'm unapologetically dangerous to virtually anyone who threatens me. No one should ever threaten anyone they don't know very well, and since no one knows me very well no one should ever threaten me. Revenge is righteous. I first fell in love with the boy when I was also a boy at the age of 13 years, and he was about 7 years.
>
> I believe that romantic or sexual activity between any two people should be acceptable to the community. It is not appropriate for the Government or society to tell me who I can or cannot love, or the most fitting way in which I can love. I don't understand why people think that children are unable to give consent to

romantic or sexual behaviour. The kid either enjoys the sexual behaviour or they don't. Special laws to protect children are not necessary.

The rejected stalker is one who responds to an unwelcome end to a close relationship. For example, in New South Wales, there was an outcry concerning the murder of Andrea Patrick by an ex-lover after severe harassment that occurred in violation of a protection order and after he had been admitted to bail two days previously. This was one of the catalysts for the enactment of stalking legislation in New South Wales.

While certain stalking behaviours could possibly have been prosecuted under existing laws such as assault through the threat of force or general threat provisions, there is a constellation of behaviours associated with stalking that frequently involves legitimate and otherwise innocuous activities, such as telephone calls and sending 'gifts' and letters. It was thought that specific stalking provisions would help protect victims and prevent unwanted patterns of behaviour. We shall explore in this section the difficulties associated with drafting stalking provisions so that they only encompass the target group rather than, for example, protesters or investigative journalists.

We have outlined previously how assault by the threat of force at common law involves any act committed intentionally or recklessly that causes another person to apprehend immediate and unlawful personal violence. Threats independently of assault may also give rise to a criminal offence. These are usually defined by statute and include threats to kill or cause injury.

The next section sets out the current law relating to threats and stalking and the Critique section looks at the problems associated with distinguishing between behaviours that should be deemed criminal and those that should not.

The current law

The most serious of the threat offences that exist in all jurisdictions are threats to kill and threats to cause harm or injury. In New South Wales, Queensland and Tasmania, a threat to kill must be put in writing: *Crimes Act* 1900 (NSW) s 31; *Criminal Code* (Qld) s 308; *Criminal Code* (Tas) s 162. In the other jurisdictions, the threat can be by words or conduct: *Crimes Act* 1900 (ACT) s 30; *Criminal Code* (NT) s 166; *Criminal Law Consolidation Act* 1935 (SA) s 19; *Crimes Act* 1958 (Vic) s 20; *Criminal Code* (WA) s 338B. For example, in South Australia, a threat may be 'directly or indirectly communicated by words (written or spoken) or by conduct, or partially by words and partially by conduct': *Criminal Law Consolidation Act* 1935 (SA) s 19(3).

All jurisdictions apart from Queensland require an intention to cause the victim to fear that the threat will be carried out. In Queensland, it is enough that there is proof that the accused knew of the contents of any writing threatening to kill another: *Criminal Code Act* 1899 (Qld) s 308. Some jurisdictions also contain recklessness as a fault element: *Crimes Act* 1900 (ACT) s 30; *Criminal Law Consolidation Act* 1935 (SA) s 19; *Crimes Act* 1958 (Vic) s 20.

The Australian Capital Territory and the Northern Territory impose an additional reasonable person test. In the Australian Capital Territory, the circumstances must be such that a reasonable person would fear that the threat would be carried out: *Crimes Act* 1900 (ACT) s 30. Similarly, in the Northern Territory, the threat must be of such a nature as to cause fear to any person of reasonable firmness and courage: *Criminal Code* (NT) s 166. It is a defence in the Northern Territory that the making of the threat was reasonable by the standards of an ordinary person in similar circumstances to the accused: *Criminal Code* (NT) s 166.

It is also an offence in all jurisdictions to threaten harm or injury to another: *Crimes Act* 1900 (ACT) s 31; *Crimes Act* 1900 (NSW) s 31; *Criminal Code* (NT) s 200; *Criminal Code* (Qld) s 359; *Criminal Law Consolidation Act* 1935 (SA) s 19; *Criminal Code* (Tas) s 182; *Crimes Act* 1958 (Vic) s 21; *Criminal Code* (WA) ss 338, 338B. How that harm or injury is constituted varies between jurisdictions. In the Australian Capital Territory, the term is 'grievous bodily harm' and in New South Wales, 'bodily harm'. In the Northern Territory and Queensland, it is 'any injury' or 'any detriment' and in Victoria, 'serious injury'. In Western Australia, the offence covers threats to 'injure, endanger or harm'. In Tasmania, it covers threats to 'apply force' to another.

Stalking is now an offence in all jurisdictions: *Crimes Act* 1900 (ACT) s 34A; *Crimes Act* 1900 (NSW) s 562AB; *Criminal Code* (NT) s 189; *Criminal Code* (Qld) s 359A; *Criminal Law Consolidation Act* 1935 (SA) s 19AA; *Criminal Code* (Tas) s 192; *Crimes Act* 1958 (Vic); *Criminal Code* (WA) s 338D. From the legal viewpoint, stalking refers to a pattern of unsolicited behaviour aimed at causing the fear of harm. Matthew Goode writes in 'Stalking: Crime of the Nineties?' (1995) 19 Crim LJ 21–31 at 21: 'The essence of this behaviour is intentionally harassing, threatening, and/or intimidating a person by following them about, sending them articles, telephoning them, waiting outside their house and the like.'

Each jurisdiction varies in how stalking is defined. Generally a pattern of predatory behaviour is criminalised providing that the accused intended the victim to fear personal injury. The Victorian legislation has the broadest fault element in that it defines intention as including the situation where the accused 'knows, or in all the particular circumstances ought to have understood that engaging in a course of conduct of that kind would be likely to cause such harm or arouse such apprehension or fear': *Crimes Act* 1958 (Vic) s 21A(3). In Queensland, there is a requirement that the conduct be such as to cause the stalked person apprehension or fear, reasonably arising in all the circumstances, of violence: *Criminal Code* (Qld) s 359B(d)(i).

Critique

Many of the issues raised in the Critique section dealing with assaults by threats of force apply to statutory threat provisions. For example, should the focus be on the accused's conduct, or the victims' reaction or a combination of both? Should words alone be enough or should they be reduced to writing? Should there be some requirement of immediacy?

The MCCOC has recommended that threats to kill and to cause serious harm remain offences: *Chapter 5, Non Fatal Offences Against the Person*, Report (September 1998) p 48. The Committee was not certain as to whether to criminalise threats to cause non-serious harm as 'threats to cause minor harms are part of everyday life': at 49. It concluded that such an offence, if it is to be enacted, should be triable summarily: at 51.

The MCCOC has set out the fault element as an intention to instil fear or recklessness in this regard: at 48. Recklessness, however, is not defined. Section 5.4(1) of the *Criminal Code* (Cth) does refer to recklessness in the context of awareness of a 'substantial risk', but this is not further explained.

If a broad approach is to be taken to assaults and related offences, then positing a standard of foresight of the possibility of the fear of harm is justified. The real problem lies in distinguishing between threats that may be blurted out in frustration or momentary anger from those calculated to put another in fear of violence. This could be taken into account at the sentencing stage, but, more realistically, it would seem unlikely for the police to charge a person with threats to kill or cause serious harm in circumstances where they were made through frustration or momentary anger.

The MCCOC was concerned to place the focus on the accused's conduct in relation to threats rather than the victim's reactions. As argued previously, this complies with the general principle of taking one's victim as one finds him or her. Otherwise the same act may be considered a threat where the victim is timid, yet not where the victim is heroic.

Legislative provisions dealing with stalking have been criticised for being too broad in their scope. Paul Mullen, Michelle Pathé and Rosemary Purcell write in *Stalkers and Their Victims* (Cambridge: Cambridge University Press, 2000) pp 277–8:

> [I]n the absence of sufficient safeguards, these laws increase the likelihood that inadvertent and legitimate behaviours will be regarded, and prosecuted, as 'stalking'...[T]here are natural limits to what the law can do to help to protect victims and prevent unwanted forms of conduct. It remains to be seen whether anti-stalking laws in their current form will prove an effective remedy to the problem of stalking, and, in many jurisdictions, in what form these contentious laws will eventually survive.

Certainly, the Victorian provisions seem overly broad: D Weiner, 'Stalking—Does the Law Work?' (2001) 75(8) *Law Institute Journal* 67–71. The definition of intention set out in s 21A(3) goes far beyond the usual interpretations of the term by including knowledge of likelihood as well as a form of objective liability. Deeming intention where the accused 'ought to have understood' that the conduct was likely to cause harm or fear is really confusing negligence with intention. There is also no definition in the Victorian provisions as to what is meant by a course of conduct. The *Crimes (Stalking) Bill* 2003 (Vic) proposes to add 'cyberstalking' to the conduct listed and to remove the requirement that the victim actually be put in fear. In comparison, the South Australian legislation provides for the conduct to take place on at least two occasions: *Criminal Law Consolidation Act* 1935 (SA) s 19AA(1)(a), and in Queensland, one occasion is sufficient providing it is 'protracted': *Criminal Code* (Qld) s 359B(b).

Another matter that needs clarification is how stalking fits into the hierarchy of assault and related offences in terms of sentencing: I Freckelton, 'Stalker Sentencing and Protection of the Public' (2001) 8(3) *Journal of Law and Medicine* 233–9. The penalties differ substantially from up to three years' imprisonment in South Australia with a five-year maximum for aggravating circumstances to up to 10 years' imprisonment in Victoria.

The MCCOC offence provides for a maximum term of five years' imprisonment: *Chapter 5, Non Fatal Offences Against the Person* (September 1998) p 50. The model provision also restricts the fault element to an intention to cause serious harm or to cause the other person to apprehend or fear serious harm. Stalking is then defined to include conduct such as following the other person, loitering outside the other person's residence or place frequented by them, telephoning them, sending them offensive material or keeping them under surveillance. This conduct must occur on at least two separate occasions. The prosecution need not prove that the person stalked actually feared harm.

The MCCOC provision presents an acceptable offence of stalking. It is always going to be difficult to define an acceptable ambit to behaviours that may range from the irritating to the insidious. There is, however, a need to criminalise behaviour such as where a person does not utter threats, but silently follows another around or sits outside their residence for hours on end. While the civil remedy of a restraining order may be one option, they may be inadequate to stop the obsessed stalker.

Offences endangering life or personal safety

Background

On 30 May 1996, Daniel O'Connor and his partner, Cindi McKewen went to the Western Hotel in Warrnambool where they had dinner and a substantial amount of alcohol. They ended up at O'Connor's mother's house at about a quarter to one the next morning. Once there, O'Connor started abusing his mother for past wrongs and claimed that she had caused his father to commit suicide some years before. He found a carving knife in the kitchen and told his mother that he was going to kill her. She ran into a neighbour's house where she called the police.

O'Connor and McKewen barricaded themselves in the house and waited for the police to come. Eventually, McKewen climbed out of a back window and told the police that O'Connor was going to stab them if they came in. She said he wanted the police to shoot him. Sergeant Vick tried to talk to O'Connor, but the latter told him that he had a gas bottle and fifteen aerosol cans in the microwave and that the police had fifteen minutes to leave or he'd blow the place up.

This led to a siege that lasted several hours. Sergeant Vick eventually managed to enter the house through the front door. The kitchen floor was covered with broken glass and debris and there were empty beer bottles piled up on the bench. There was no sign of aerosol cans or gas bottles.

O'Connor was sitting in the doorway of the bedroom and when Vick approached, O'Connor swung at him with a large knife. Vick was able to jump out of the way and then lock O'Connor inside the bedroom. While inside, O'Connor continued to make threats and stabbed at the door a number of times so that the blade of the knife protruded. O'Connor also started slashing his own arm, telling the police it was their fault. He finally surrendered at 7.15 a.m. O'Connor was taken to hospital for his injuries and a blood test showed he had a blood-alcohol level of 0.12.

O'Connor pleaded guilty to making a threat to kill, wilfully damaging property, and reckless endangerment in relation to his conduct towards Sergeant Vick. He had previously been convicted of reckless endangerment and assaulting a member of the police force in 1994.

The overall sentence was imprisonment for three years and four months with a non-parole period of two years and four months. An appeal against sentence was dismissed by the Supreme Court of Victoria: *R v O'Connor* unreported, 26 May 1997, SC of Vic, BC9702350, Winneke P, Brooking JA and Ashley AJA.

This case displays how reckless endangerment is often a charge that is used in combination with others and may sometimes be used to cover situations of threatening conduct towards police officers. In recent years, there have been attempts to use it as a stand-alone offence to prosecute those with HIV who have had unprotected sex. As we shall outline in the Critique section, this has had mixed results.

There are numerous miscellaneous statutory offences dealing with the concept of endangering life or personal safety. There are, for example, provisions against administering drugs or poisons with intent to commit an offence, setting traps and offences relating to explosives. There are also more general offences such as conduct endangering life or personal safety and engaging in dangerous conduct. The Code jurisdictions have endangerment provisions aimed at particular situations such as dangerous conduct on aircraft and railways: *Criminal Code* (Qld) ss 319, 319A, 467A; *Criminal Code* (WA) s 296, s 296A, and which also criminalise negligent endangerment: *Criminal Code* (Qld) s 328; *Criminal Code* (WA) s 306.

The general rationales for penalising conduct that may endanger others are usually the same as for those given in relation to inchoate offences, which are explored in Chapter 8. The 'harm' of inchoate and endangerment offences can be viewed broadly as the *potential* to cause harm. Certain conduct is therefore criminalised in order to prevent the occurrence of substantive harm.

In the 1962 draft of the American Model Penal Code, an attempt was made to construct a single provision that would criminalise all such behaviour. Section 211.2 makes it an offence where a person 'recklessly engages in conduct which places another person in danger of death or serious bodily injury'. This provision has been criticised as being not specific enough as to whether actual danger is required and what level of risk is to be associated with recklessness: KJM Smith, 'Liability for Endangerment: English *Ad Hoc* Pragmatism and American Innovation' [1983] Crim LR 127–36. The MCCOC has also drafted model provisions of endangerment, taking into account previous criticisms. This will be examined after setting out the current law. We will also look at the problems associated with using a general offence such as reckless endangerment to prosecute those with diseases such as HIV/AIDS.

The current law

In the Northern Territory, South Australia and Victoria, there are provisions dealing with endangerment of life or personal safety. In the Northern Territory, any person who causes serious danger to the lives, health or safety of the public is guilty of an offence: *Criminal Code* (NT) s 154. This is assessed on the basis of whether an ordinary person would have foreseen the danger and not done the act or omission. In *Hoessinger v The Queen* (1992) 107 FLR 99 Gallop J held that the accused need not have clearly foreseen the danger, it was enough if an ordinary person 'similarly circumstanced' would have foreseen the danger.

The South Australian provision, in contrast, contains a subjective element. It is an offence in South Australia where a person does an act or makes an omission knowing that it is likely to endanger the life of another or intending to endanger the life of another or being recklessly indifferent as to whether the life of another is endangered: *Criminal Law Consolidation Act* 1935 (SA) s 29; *Bedi v The Queen* (1993) 61 SASR 269; *R v Teremoana* (1990) 54 SASR 30.

Section 22 of the *Crimes Act* 1958 (Vic) sets out the offence of recklessly engaging in conduct that places, or may place, another person in danger of death. Section 23 is similar, but deals with serious injury rather than death. The victim need not have suffered harm. It is enough that he or she was placed in danger of death or serious injury.

In *R v Nuri* [1990] VR 641 the Supreme Court of Victoria held that s 22 involves proof of both subjective *and* objective elements. The prosecution must prove that a reasonable person in the accused's position, engaging in the conduct of the accused, would have realised that his or her conduct had placed, or might place, another person in danger of death. The subjective element requires proof that the accused intended to engage in the relevant conduct, realising that the probable consequence of that conduct would be to place another in danger of death.

Some of the other jurisdictions impose duties on those engaging in conduct that may be dangerous to health such as surgical or medical treatment: *Criminal Code* (NT) s 150; *Criminal Code* (Qld) s 288; *Criminal Code* (WA) s 265. In all jurisdictions apart from the Australian Capital Territory and Victoria, it is a criminal offence to fail to provide the necessaries of life where there is a duty to do so: *Crimes Act* 1900 (NSW) s 44; *Criminal Code* (NT) s 183; *Criminal Code* (Qld) s 285; *Criminal Law Consolidation Act* 1935 (SA) s 30; *Criminal Code* (Tas) s 144; *Criminal Code* (WA) s 262. There is also a range of offences in jurisdictions other than South Australia and Victoria dealing with endangering the life of a child by abandonment or exposure: *Crimes Act* 1900 (ACT) s 39; *Crimes Act* 1900 (NSW) s 43; *Criminal Code* (NT) s 184; *Criminal Code* (Qld) ss 326, 364; *Criminal Code* (Tas) s 178; *Criminal Code* (WA) ss 304, 344.

Critique

It is very difficult to find a satisfactory definition of reckless endangerment that can be used in a variety of circumstances. The MCCOC has recommended the enactment of a general endangerment provision divided into recklessness as to the danger of death and recklessness as to the danger of serious harm: *Chapter 5, Non Fatal Offences Against the Person*, Report (September 1998) p 64. The wording is similar to the Victorian provisions, but the MCCOC did not discuss the objective/subjective test and dismissed the criticism that a comprehensible test for recklessness is difficult to establish (at 71).

The Victorian offence of recklessly engaging in conduct that places, or may place, another person in danger of death has caused problems in prosecuting HIV-positive persons who have engaged in unsafe sexual activity. The objective and subjective test has proved particularly problematic. In *B* unreported, 3 July 1995, SC of Vic, Teague J held that the probability requirement in s 22 required proof of a 'level of dangerousness' in the sense of an appreciable rather than a merely remote risk. In that case, the uncontradicted expert evidence set out that the risk of transmission of HIV arising from unprotected intercourse was around one in 200. The jury was accordingly directed to return a verdict of not guilty: see also the case of *D* unreported, 1 May 1996, Supreme Court of Victoria, Hampel J; (1997) 21 Crim LJ 40.

In *Mutemeri v Cheesman* [1998] 4 VR 484, the accused, who was HIV positive, had been convicted by a magistrate of recklessly engaging in conduct that may place another in danger of death after he had unprotected intercourse on several occasions with the same woman. No evidence was led as to the statistical risk of HIV transmission. On appeal, Mandie J set aside the convictions, sentences and orders of the Magistrates' Court. Mandie J was of the opinion that s 22 was concerned with

foresight of the probability of the other person's exposure to risk of death. Following *Nuri*'s case, he held that the test is whether:
- the accused intended to do an act having realised that the probable consequence of that act would be to place another in danger of death; and
- a reasonable person in the accused's position would realise that that act had placed or may place another in danger of death.

Mandie J held that it was not open for the magistrate to find that the accused's conduct placed his partner in danger of death without expert evidence directed to the risk associated with the particular conduct in issue. Matthew Groves writes in 'Commentary' (1998) 22 Crim LJ 357–61 at 359:

> [T]he essential issue for the magistrate concerned the level of risk of [the victim] contracting HIV by her contact with Mutemeri, *and then* dying as a result. It followed that the expert should have provided evidence on the chances of the survival of [the victim] if she had contracted HIV from Mutemeri, including the possible length of survival, during which a cure or further life prolonging treatments might be developed, and also her chance of outright survival.

This subjective/objective test and the need for expert evidence seems unduly complicated and it may be that having either a subjective or an objective test would provide greater clarity: see further D Lanham, 'Danger Down Under' [1999] Crim LR 960–969. This was not explored by the MCCOC. The model provisions also do not define recklessness. Instead, the MCCOC quoted with approval Hampel J's way of explaining the idea to the jury. In *D* unreported, 1 May 1996, Supreme Court of Victoria; (1997) 21 Crim LJ 40, Hampel J considered the test of recklessness in relation to the transmission of HIV (at 43):

> [T]he question of whether the risk of danger involved is an appreciable risk is one for the jury. The jury is entitled to go beyond the population figure and consider the nature of the infection...the manner in which it is transmitted, and the various epidemiological studies...in order to determine, without relying on statistical or arithmetical calculations of probabilities, whether the risk of infection in respect of each act charged was an appreciable risk of danger or a mere remote possibility.

This seems to relate to an objective measurement. The MCCOC, however, did not make any mention of a reasonable person test or what is meant by an appreciable risk of danger.

Having general endangerment provisions certainly gets around the problems associated with ad hoc statutory provisions. Leaving it up to the jury to decide what is meant by recklessness, however, may lead to inconsistent outcomes. As explored in Chapter 2, awareness of a risk is the essence of recklessness. An accused is said to be reckless where he or she acts in the knowledge that a consequence is a probable or possible result of his or her conduct.

For offences other than murder, the courts have generally applied a level of recklessness based on foresight of possible consequences. In *R v Coleman* (1990) 19 NSWLR 467, as noted earlier, the New South Wales Court of Appeal held that for all statutory offences other than murder, recklessness is defined as foresight of possibility not probability. It is really only the Supreme Court of Victoria that has posed a higher standard of recklessness in relation to the crime of recklessly causing serious injury set out in s 17 of the *Crimes Act* 1958 (Vic): *Campbell* (1995) 80 A Crim R 461.

If a lower standard of recklessness applies in the context of assault and related offences, then it would seem that a lower standard should also apply in relation to reckless endangerment.

We turn now to a consideration of situations that may serve to excuse or justify what would otherwise be considered assaults.

Lawful assaults and consent

Background

As the law of assault and related offences has developed, a number of ways of avoiding criminal responsibility have also arisen. The use of force may be considered lawful if it forms part of ordinary social activity, is used reasonably and moderately to chastise children, forms the basis for an arrest, is used in self-defence or, in some jurisdictions, is used in response to provocation. Consent to a common assault renders the act lawful, but there is considerable debate about the role of consent in relation to aggravated assaults.

We outlined earlier how assaults can be viewed as interfering with a person's physical integrity and autonomy. The ethical principle of autonomy emphasises that each individual has the right to determine his or her own life. One problematic area of individual autonomy is how much liberty each person should have to decide the level of pain to which his or her body should be subjected in relation to, for example, sporting activities, personal adornment, cultural traditions or sexual practices.

The following section outlines the situations in which the law deems an assault to be lawful and offers a critique of the use of reasonable force in relation to children as well as defences that may be used. We then turn to the problematic area of consent to aggravated assaults.

Lawful assaults

There is an eclectic range of activities that the law deems to be lawful assaults. Since the scope of assaults and related offences ranges from an apprehension of fear to a mere touch to a severe battering, reliance is placed upon the prosecutorial process to keep minor matters out of court. The law has also made an exception for physical conduct that is generally acceptable in the ordinary course of everyday life such as the jostling that may occur on public transport or in a busy street: *Collins v Wilcock* [1984] 1 WLR 1172; *Boughey v The Queen* (1986) 161 CLR 10; *Criminal Code* (NT) s 187(e); *Criminal Code* (Tas) s 182(3). This could be justified on the basis that individuals impliedly consent to a certain amount of incidental touching that is part of everyday life. However, the cases generally refer to this as an exception to the general law of assault rather than seeing it as a consent issue: A Ashworth, *Principles of Criminal Law* (3rd edn, Oxford: Oxford University Press, 1999) p 328.

There are other exceptions that make assaults by the use of force lawful. These are outlined in the following section.

The current law

The use of reasonable force

Reasonable force may be used in two very different circumstances. The first is in order to arrest a suspect and the second is in order to chastise children.

A person exercising a lawful power of arrest is entitled to use reasonable force where it is necessary in order to effect that arrest: *R v Turner* [1962] VR 30; *Crimes Act* 1900 (ACT) s 349ZE; *Crimes Act* 1914 (Cth) s 3ZC(2)(a); *Criminal Code* (NT) ss 27, 28; *Criminal Law Consolidation Act* 1935 (SA) s 15(1)(b); *Criminal Code* (Qld) ss 256–257; *Criminal Code* (Tas) ss 26–27, 30–31; *Police Offences Act* 1935 (Tas) s 55; *Criminal Code* (WA) s 237. The old common law drew a distinction between the use of force in relation to resisting arrest and in relation to fleeing from arrest. The provisions in the Queensland and Western Australian Criminal Codes still retain this distinction with more limitations being placed on the force used in relation to fleeing from arrest.

What amounts to reasonable force is a question of fact that depends upon the circumstances of the particular case including the nature of the resistance put up by the accused: *R v Turner* [1962] VR 30. There is also a corresponding right to use reasonable force to resist unlawful arrest: *R v Ryan* (1890) 11 LR(NSW) 171; *McLiney v Minster* [1911] VLR 347; *R v Marshall* (1987) 49 SASR 133; *R v Fry* (1992) 58 SASR 424; *Criminal Code* (NT) ss 27(g), 28(f); *Criminal Code* (Qld) s 271; *Criminal Code* (WA) s 248.

The common law enabled the lawful correction of certain classes or persons such as children, servants, the crew of ships, apprentices and, though subject to debate, wives. It has been claimed that the popular expression 'rule of thumb' originated from English common law, which allowed a husband to beat his wife with a whip or stick no bigger in diameter than his thumb. However, there are doubts as to whether this law really existed: HA Kelly, 'Rule of Thumb and the Folklaw of the

Husband's Stick' (1994) 44(3) *Journal of Legal Education* 341–65. The lawful chastisement of wives, if it ever existed, was ruled out in *R v Jackson* [1891] 1 QB 671.

It appears that currently, parents are entitled to use reasonable and moderate force to chastise their children: *Criminal Code* (Qld) s 280; *Criminal Code* (Tas) s 50; *Criminal Code* (WA) s 257; *Criminal Code* (NT) s 11 (delegation of power); *R v Hopley* 2 F & F 202; *Smith v Byrne* (1894) QCR 252 at 253; *R v Terry* [1955] VLR 114 at 116–17 SC. There is also some authority to the effect that teachers or those *in loco parentis* to the child may use some degree of force to correct a child. For example, s 257 of the *Criminal Code* (WA) states:

> It is lawful for a parent or a person in the place of a parent, or for a school master or master, to use, by way of correction, towards a child, pupil, or apprentice, under his [sic] care, such force as is reasonable under the circumstances: see also *Criminal Code* (Qld) s 280.

In Victoria, corporal punishment in state schools was prohibited by Regulation XVI of the *Education Act* 1958. In New South Wales, s 14 of the *Education and Public Instruction Act* 1987 enabled Discipline Codes to be formulated for state schools after consultation with parents. In 1990, the National Committee on Violence recommended that corporal punishment in all schools be illegal: *Violence: Directions for Australia* (Canberra: Australian Institute of Criminology, 1990).

Defences to assault

The defence of self-defence is available to crimes involving the use of or threat of force to the person such as assault and it results in a complete acquittal. As explored in Chapter 10, the test for self-defence varies across jurisdictions.

In New South Wales and Victoria, the common law holds sway. Wilson, Dawson and Toohey JJ set out the requirements for the defence in *Zecevic v DPP* (1987) 162 CLR 645 (at 661) as follows:

> The question to be asked in the end is quite simple. It is whether the accused believed upon reasonable grounds that it was necessary in self-defence to do what he [or she] did. If he [or she] had that belief and there were reasonable grounds for it, or if the jury is left in reasonable doubt about the matter, then he [or she] is entitled to an acquittal. Stated in this form, the question is one of general application and is not limited to cases of homicide.

This approach was approved by Mason CJ (at 654) and by Brennan J (at 666). It also seems that the dissenting judges approved of this statement of the law: Deane J at 681; Gaudron J at 685.

Section 46 of the Tasmanian *Criminal Code* states that:

184 *Offences against the person*

> A person is justified in using, in defence of himself or another person, such force as, in the circumstances as he [or she] believes them to be, it is reasonable to use.

This Tasmanian test is partly subjective and partly objective. It requires two questions to be answered: First, what were the circumstances as the accused believed them to be? Second, was the use of force reasonable in those circumstances?

Similarly, the South Australian provision allows an accused to use force if that person believes that the force is necessary and reasonable for self-defence and the conduct was reasonably proportionate to the threat that the accused genuinely believed to exist: *Criminal Law Consolidation Act* 1935 (SA) s 15(1) as amended by the *Criminal Law Consolidation (Self-Defence) Amendment Act* 1997 (SA). Section 42 of the *Criminal Code* (ACT) sets out the elements of self-defence as including where the person believes the conduct is necessary to defend him or herself and the conduct is a reasonable response in the circumstances as the person perceives them to be.

The provisions in the Queensland, Northern Territory and Western Australian *Criminal Codes* are more complex and supplement the core element of 'reasonable necessity' with additional rules that limit the use of permissible force. The Queensland and Western Australian provisions distinguish between self-defence as it relates to provoked and unprovoked attacks. In relation to an unprovoked attack:

> [I]t is lawful for [the accused] to use such force to the assailant as is reasonably necessary to make effectual defence against the assault, provided that the force used is not intended and is not such as is likely, to cause death or grievous bodily harm: *Criminal Code* (Qld) s 283; *Criminal Code* (WA) s 260.

Here, the test is objective in determining whether or not the force used by the accused was reasonably necessary. Section 27(g) of the *Criminal Code* (NT) states that the application of force is justified in self-defence provided it is not unnecessary force and it is not intended and is not such as is likely to cause death or grievous harm.

Provocation in some jurisdictions is not only a defence to murder, but may also apply as a defence to assault. In the Northern Territory, Queensland and Western Australia, provocation is also a complete defence to offences that have assault as a defined element: *Criminal Code* (NT) s 34; *Criminal Code* (Qld) s 269; *Criminal Code* (WA) s 246. It is, however, not applicable to offences such as doing bodily harm, grievous bodily harm or wounding where assault is not a defined element: *Kaporonovski v The Queen* (1973) 133 CLR 209.

In the Australian Capital Territory, New South Wales and Victoria, provocation is a qualified defence to an assault that is defined to include the word 'murder' such as wounding with intent to murder: *R v Newman* [1948] VLR 61; *Helmhout v R*

(1980) 49 FLR 1. In South Australia, provocation does not appear to apply as there are no offences of assault defined to include the word 'murder'. Provocation is, however, a defence to an attempted murder in South Australia, but not, it appears, in Victoria: *R v Duvivier* (1982) 29 SASR 217, overruling *R v Wells* (1981) 28 SASR 63; *R v Farrar* [1992] 1 VR 207 at 208–9 per Hampel J.

There is no specific provision relating to provocation in relation to assaults in Tasmania and it has been specifically abolished as a defence to murder. However s 8 of the *Criminal Code* (Tas) states:

> All rules and principles of the common law which render any circumstances a justification or excuse for any act or omission, or a defence to a charge upon indictment, shall remain in force and apply to any defence to a charge upon indictment, except insofar as they are altered by, or are inconsistent with, the Code.

This implies that in theory, the common law definition of provocation can apply to Code offences defining assault as including the word murder. However, in practice, it appears that because there are no Code offences in these terms, provocation no longer exists as a defence.

In the Australian Capital Territory, New South Wales and Victoria, the test for provocation is that for murder (see Chapter 10). It appears that in relation to assaults with an intention to murder, provocation acts as a complete rather than a partial defence: *R v Duvivier* (1982) 29 SASR 217.

In Queensland and Western Australia, the definition of provocation as it applies to assault differs from that of the common law: *Criminal Code* (Qld) s 268; *Criminal Code* (WA) s 245. For example, s 268 of the *Criminal Code* (Qld) provides:

> The term 'provocation', used with reference to an offence of which an assault is an element means and includes...any wrongful act or insult of such a nature as to be likely, when done to an ordinary person, or in the presence of an ordinary person, to another who is under his [sic] immediate care, or to whom he [sic] stands in a conjugal, parental, filial, or fraternal relation, or in the relation of master or servant, to deprive him of the power of self-control, and to induce him [sic] to assault the person by whom the act or insult is done or offered...

Critique

The use of reasonable force

Just what constitutes reasonable force for the purposes of arrest and the chastisement of children is difficult to define. Jude McCullough has argued in her book

Blue Army (Melbourne: Melbourne University Press, 2001) that specialist counter-terrorist units within state police forces have led to increasingly militarised forms of policing. She posits, for example, that Victoria's Special Operations Group has influenced police tactics in arresting suspects and conducting raids such that excessive force is used more frequently. She points to the use of pressure-point neck holds, the use of batons on peaceful protesters and even a series of fatal shootings as being the consequences of militarised forms of policing.

There is scant authority defining the scope and degree of force implied by the words 'reasonable correction' as it relates to parents and children. In *R v Terry* [1955] VLR 114 Sholl J stated (at 116): 'There are exceedingly strict limits to the right [to use reasonable force on a child]. In the first place, the punishment must be moderate and reasonable. In the second place, it must have a proper relation to the age, physique and mentality of the child, and in the third place, it must be carried out with a reasonable means or instrument.'

In a Discussion Paper commissioned by the Commonwealth Department of Human Services and Health, Judy Cashmore and Nicola de Haas undertook an extensive examination of the existing law. They concluded that 'the law relating to the lawful use of physical punishment by parents, teachers and carers does not provide a clear and consistent guide as to what behaviour is and is not acceptable and does not provide children with the protection available to other members of society': *Legal and Social Aspects of the Physical Punishment of Children* (ACT: Commonwealth of Australia, May 1995).

Recently, there have been arguments in favour of holding the use of force against children to be assault. Rochelle Urlich, for example, has argued that physical discipline is ineffective, is linked to child abuse, teaches children that violence is a legitimate means of problem solving and erodes children's rights: 'Physical Discipline in the Home' [1994] *Auckland University Law Review* 851–60.

The common law governing lawful correction was recently challenged before the European Court of Human Rights as violating Article 3 of the *European Convention on Human Rights*. This states that:

> No one shall be subjected to torture or to inhuman or degrading treatment or punishment.

The European Court in *A v The United Kingdom* unreported, 23 September 1998, Eur Court HR, No 100/1997/884/1096 held that Article 3 imposes an obligation to take measures designed to ensure that individuals within their jurisdiction are not subjected to torture or inhuman or degrading treatment or punishment, including ill-treatment administered by private individuals. In *A*'s case, a nine-year-old boy was beaten repeatedly by his stepfather with 'considerable force' resulting in severe bruising. The Court held, and the United Kingdom Government conceded, that the notion of reasonable correction embodied in the common law exception to assault did not offer adequate protection against treatment or punishment contrary to Article 3.

Article 19(1) of the *Convention on the Rights of the Child* (opened for signature 20 November 1989, ATS 1991 No 4, entered into force in Australia 19 January 1991) is similar to Article 3 in that it states:

> [P]arties shall take all appropriate legislative, administrative, social and educational measures to protect the child from all forms of physical or mental violence, injury or abuse, neglect or negligent treatment, maltreatment or exploitation, including sexual abuse, while in the care of parent(s), legal guardian(s) or any other person who has the care of the child.

The MCCOC rejected the argument that this Article requires the prohibition of reasonable correction: *Chapter 5, Non Fatal Offences Against the Person*, Report (September 1998) p 137. It has recommended that reasonable correction be lawful when conducted by a parent or another person who has care of the child where the parent has so consented. In relation to what constitutes reasonable correction, the MCCOC has drafted the following provision:

> Conduct can amount to reasonable correction of a child only if it is reasonable in the circumstances for the purposes of the discipline, management or control of the child. The following conduct does not amount to reasonable correction of a child:
> causing or threatening to cause harm to a child that lasts for more than a short period; or
> causing harm to a child by use of a stick, belt or other object (other than an open hand).

The MCCOC was of the opinion that it would be going too far to criminalise a corrective smack by a parent or guardian. Perhaps the experience of Sweden provides an example of a step-by-step approach to education and law reform in this area. In 1958, Sweden banned all forms of corporal punishment in schools and in 1960 this was extended to social institutions. In 1979 the physical punishment of children was outlawed. However, there was no link to any penalty for violations of this law. The aim was to educate parents into realising that the use of physical discipline was not an acceptable way to raise children. An extensive publicity campaign followed and between 1965 and 1981, the proportion of the population believing that children should be raised without physical punishment rose from 35 per cent to 70 per cent: R Urlich, 'Physical Discipline in the Home' [1994] *Auckland*

University Law Review 851–60 at 858. This shows that criminalisation may have an educative rather than a punitive function and this is one approach that should be followed in order to help change attitudes to physical discipline.

Defences to assault

In Chapter 10 we explore how the defence of self-defence arose out of the regulation of duels and other forms of combat. It developed in the context of fights between two men, the traditional scenario being a bar-room brawl or a one-off duel: I Leader-Elliott, 'Battered But Not Beaten: Women Who Kill in Self-Defence' (1993) 15 *Sydney Law Review* 403–60 at 405. Given this background, it is not difficult to see how a case akin to that of Darryl and Wayne Reid outlined at the beginning of the chapter may bring into play elements of self-defence. How the defence should be constituted is explored in Chapter 10.

Provocation, however, is a different matter. It developed as a partial defence to murder during the seventeenth century at a time when drunken brawls and fights arising from 'breaches of honour' were commonplace. During this time, the law began to distinguish between the most serious types of killing, which required proof of malice aforethought, and killings that were unpremeditated and occurred on the spur of the moment in response to an act of provocation. It was never traditionally considered a defence to assault and the provisions in the Queensland and Western Australian Criminal Codes were inserted without there being such a defence to assault at common law.

The MCCOC has recommended that there be no defence of provocation to assault and related offences: *Chapter 5, Non Fatal Offences Against the Person*, Discussion Paper (August 1996) p 115; *Chapter 5, Non Fatal Offences Against the Person*, Report (September 1998) p 141. There are numerous problems with provocation as a partial defence, which will be explored in Chapter 10. However, if provocation is available to charges of assault, in the domestic violence context, it may raise stereotypes of nagging wives deserving a violent response. For offences that have no mandatory sentence, there is no justification for allowing a defence of provocation. Factors precipitating the offence can always be taken into account at the sentencing stage. For these reasons, provocation should not be available as a defence to assault.

Consent

One of the most intractable problems in the area of assault law is delineating when a person can consent to injury. The following section will show that the law has very much developed on an ad hoc basis so that consent may be relevant to surgery, certain contact sports, 'rough horseplay', body piercing and tattooing, yet not to actual bodily harm that occurs in the context of sexual activity or for cultural practices such as female genital mutilation. Ian Freckelton writes in 'Masochism,

Self-Mutilation and the Limits of Consent' (1994) 2(1) *Journal of Law and Medicine* 48–76 at 55:

> The problem is that the line between what at any particular time is culturally sanctioned and what is sufficiently socially taboo to be regarded as indicative of mental illness is not easy to draw. Homosexuality, after all, was only recently depathologised by orthodox psychiatry. In the more general context, recent debate about practices of female circumcision in the Eritrean and other North African communities residing in Australia has posed poignantly the conflict that can occur between different cultures' views on when violence can legitimately be inflicted on the body.

The issue of consent to actual bodily harm was considered in the controversial case of *R v Brown* [1992] 2 WLR 441 (CA) [1993] 2 WLR 556 (HL). The facts were that in the course of an investigation into child pornography in England, the police discovered a number of videotapes that were originally thought to be 'snuff' movies: S Edwards, 'No Defence for a Sado-Masochistic Libido' (1993) 143 *New Law Journal* 406–7 at 406. The videotapes in fact showed a group of homosexual men engaging in sadomasochistic sex with one another. Some of the acts that were portrayed involved whipping, branding and the infliction of wounds to the genitals, including the insertion of safety pins and fish hooks into the penis, the dripping of hot wax into the urethra and the nailing of a penis into a bench.

These activities had taken place over a period of 10 years at a number of different locations, including rooms equipped as torture chambers. The activities were videotaped and the tapes then copied and distributed among members of the group.

The men involved were charged with a number of offences including charges of assault occasioning actual bodily harm. The men argued that they had committed no crimes as all the activities were consensual. They said there was no permanent injury, and that there was no infection of the wounds, and they used a code word to halt the infliction of pain if necessary.

After a ruling by the trial judge that they could not rely on consent as an answer to the prosecution case, the men changed their pleas of not guilty to guilty. On 19 December 1990, the men were sentenced. Some of the men were given terms of imprisonment, one receiving a prison sentence of four and a half years. Six of the men appealed to the Court of Appeal. That Court reduced the sentences but upheld the convictions: *R v Brown* [1992] 2 WLR 441.

In a joint judgment delivered by Lord Lane CJ, the judges followed *Attorney-General's Reference (No 6 of 1980)*[1981] QB 715 in which the Court stated (at 719): 'It is not in the public interest that people should try to cause, or should cause, each other actual bodily harm for no good reason.'

The Court of Appeal stated in *Brown*'s case (at 449): 'We agree with the trial judge that the satisfying of sado-masochistic libido does not come within the category of good reason nor can the injuries be described as merely transient or trifling.'

Five of the men then appealed to the House of Lords. A majority of three judges to two dismissed their appeal: *R v Brown* [1993] 2 WLR 556. The judges in the majority stressed that consent could not be a defence to a charge of assault occasioning actual bodily harm unless the circumstances fell within pre-existing categories of exceptions such as sporting contests or reasonable surgery. The words used by the majority judges displayed a degree of moral censure. For example, Lord Templeman stated (at 556): 'Society is entitled and bound to protect itself against a cult of violence. Pleasure derived from the infliction of pain is an evil thing. Cruelty is uncivilised.' Similarly, Lord Lowry (at 583) referred to the men suffering injury in order to '…satisfy a perverted and depraved sexual desire. Sado-masochistic homosexual activity cannot be regarded as conducive to the enhancement or enjoyment of family life or conducive to the welfare of society.'

Three of the men then took the matter to the European Court of Human Rights, arguing that the British justice system had violated their human rights, in particular, their right to privacy: *Laskey, Jaggard and Brown v The United Kingdom* Eur Court HR, 19 February 1997, *Reports of Judgments and Decisions* 1997-I, 120. A unanimous nine-judge decision of the European Court held that it found no basis for allegations that the British courts were biased against homosexual men and that it had been necessary to delve into the men's private lives 'for the protection of health'.

In the next section we will outline the pre-existing categories where consent is relevant to aggravated assaults. We will then return to *Brown*'s case in the Critique section.

The current law

Consent to a common assault renders the act lawful: *R v Donovan* [1934] 2 KB 498; *Attorney-General's Reference (No 6 of 1980)* [1981] QB 715; *R v Brown* [1993] 2 WLR 556 (HL); *Criminal Code* (NT) s 187; *Criminal Code* (Qld) s 245; *Criminal Code* (Tas) s 182; *Criminal Code* (WA) s 222. In *Schloss v Maguire* (1897) 8 QLJ 21 the Supreme Court of Queensland commented (at 22): '[T]he term assault of itself involves the notion of want of consent. An assault with consent is not an assault at all.'

Consent may be express or implied: *Beer v McCann* [1993] 1 Qd R 25 at 28–9 per Derrington J; *Collins v Wilcock* [1984] 1 WLR 1172 at 1177–8 per Goff LJ; *Carroll v Lergesner* [1991] 1 Qd R 206. The rule that an act that is part of ordinary social activity is not an assault is sometimes justified on the basis of implied consent: *Boughey v The Queen* (1986) 161 CLR 10 at 24 per Mason, Wilson and Deane JJ. Consent must be freely given and not induced by fraud, force or threats: *Criminal Code* (Tas) s 2A; *Wooley v Fitzgerald* [1969] Tas SR 65.

The situation in relation to aggravated assaults differs quite markedly from consent as it relates to common assault. There are a number of English cases setting out the general rule that a victim cannot consent to an act that has the purpose of, or will, probably cause him or her actual bodily harm: *R v Coney* (1882) 8 QBD 534 (prize fighting); *R v Donovan* [1934] 2 KB 498 (caning a 17-year-old girl for sexual gratification); *Attorney General's Reference (No 6 of 1980)* [1981] QB 715; *R v Brown* [1993] 2 WLR 556 (HL). There are no decisions in Australian common law jurisdictions that directly address this point. In *Lergesner v Carroll* (1989) 49 A Crim R 51 the Queensland Court of Criminal Appeal held that consent may in some cases be a 'defence' to an assault occasioning actual bodily harm. However, consent does not appear to be relevant where the force applied causes grievous bodily harm or wounds.

The rationale for the English rule that consent is irrelevant where actual bodily harm occurs, lies in the notion that it is not in the public interest that a person should cause bodily harm to another for no good reason: *Attorney General's Reference (No 6 of 1980)* [1981] QB 715 at 719.

What constitutes a 'good reason' for causing consensual bodily harm includes:
- for personal adornment such as tattooing, body piercing and branding;
- surgery; and
- rough 'horseplay' and violent sports.

Consensual sadomasochistic sexual activities and the cultural practice of female genital mutilation have been viewed as not providing a 'good reason' for the infliction of bodily harm: *R v Brown* [1993] 2 WLR 556 (HL); *Crimes Act* 1900 (ACT) Pt 111B; *Crimes Act* 1900 (NSW) s 45; *Criminal Code* (NT) Pt VI Division 4A; *Criminal Code* (Tas) ss 178A–178C; *Criminal Law Consolidation Act* 1935 (SA) s 33A; *Crimes Act* 1958 (Vic) ss 32–34A; *Criminal Code* (Qld) s 323A. This also seems to carry over into the non-recognition of certain Indigenous customary practices such as the concept of 'payback'. The law relating to these categories will be examined in turn.

Personal adornment

Various cultures have sanctioned the infliction of harm upon the body in the form of such conduct as tattooing, piercing, footbinding, headmoulding or genital rearrangement: see, in general, AR Favazza, *Bodies Under Siege* (Baltimore: John Hopkins University Press, 1992). In Western society, body piercing has increased in popularity in recent years: see I Freckelton, 'Masochism, Self-mutilation and the Limits of Consent' (1994) 2(1) *Journal of Law and Medicine* 48–76 at 50.

The leading case dealing with bodily harm for 'personal adornment' is that of *R v Wilson* [1996] 3 WLR 125. In that case, the accused branded his initials on his wife's buttocks with a hot knife. He was charged and convicted of assault occasioning actual bodily harm. He argued that the act was consensual. On appeal, the Court of Appeal quashed the conviction on the basis that what the accused did was on a par with tattooing, which did not involve an offence. Russell LJ in delivering the judgment of the court, stated (at 128):

For our part, we cannot detect any logical difference between what the appellant did and what he might have done by way of tattooing. The latter activity apparently requires no state authorisation, and the appellant was as free to engage in it as anyone else. We do not think that we are entitled to assume that the method adopted by the appellant and his wife was any more dangerous or painful than tattooing.

Just where the line is to be drawn between allowing consent to personal adornment by way of tattooing, body piercing and branding and criminalising other conduct that causes bodily harm is very difficult. This issue is taken up further in the Critique section.

Surgery

Surgery is viewed as lawful when performed with the patient's consent despite it involving serious bodily harm: *Department of Health and Community Services (NT) v JWB* (*Marion's* case) (1992) 175 CLR 218 at 232; *Criminal Code* (Tas) s 51(1). Consent may be oral, written or implied: *Re T (Adult: Refusal of Treatment)* [1993] Fam 95 at 102 per Lord Donaldson MR. Valid consent requires that the patient has the capacity to consent and is capable of understanding the treatment: *Department of Health and Community Services (NT) v JWB* (*Marion's* case) (1992) 175 CLR 218. Consent must also be voluntary: *Re T (Adult: Refusal of Treatment)* [1993] Fam 95. It must also pertain to the act performed: *Walker v Bradley* unreported, 15 December 1993, NSW Dist Ct, Kirkham J, 1919 of 1989; *Murray v McMurchy* [1949] 2 DLR 442.

If a patient is unable to give consent, another person may be authorised to give consent on that person's behalf: see B Bennett, *Law and Medicine* (Sydney: LBC Information Services, 1997) pp 21–9; L Skene, *Law and Medical Practice: Rights, Duties, Claims and Defences* (Sydney: Butterworths, 1998), chs 4 and 5. In Tasmania, surgical operations performed in good faith and with reasonable care and skill upon a person incapable of giving consent are lawful: *Criminal Code* (Tas) s 51(3). In the Northern Territory, Queensland and South Australia, doctors have statutory powers to give treatment without consent in an emergency: *Emergency Operations Act* 1973 (NT) s 3(1); *Voluntary Aid in Emergency Act* 1973 (Qld) s 3; *Consent to Medical Treatment and Palliative Care Act* 1995 (SA) s 13(1). It appears that there is a common law doctrine of emergency that is applicable in other Australian jurisdictions: L Skene, *Law and Medical Practice: Rights, Duties, Claims and Defences* (Sydney: Butterworths, 1998) pp 82–3. An emergency situation is one where the treatment is essential to preserve the patient's life or to prevent serious permanent injury: *Walker v Bradley* unreported, 15 December 1993, NSW Dist Ct, Kirkham J, 1919 of 1989; *Murray v McMurchy* [1949] 2 DLR 442. It does not extend to treatment that is convenient. For example, in *Murray v McMurchy* [1949] 2 DLR 442 the patient was undergoing a Caesarean delivery when the doctor discovered fibroids in the patient's uterus. The doctor performed a sterilisation on the basis that the patient should not undergo another pregnancy and it was more convenient to carry out the procedure at that time. The doctor was found liable for damages (at 445) as there was 'no evidence that these tumours were presently at the time of the operation dangerous to her life or health'.

Treatment may also be justified in the absence of consent on the basis of a common law doctrine of necessity. This will be explored in Chapter 12.

Rough horseplay and violent sports

The courts have permitted consent to operate as a defence to bodily harm in the course of certain activities such as 'rough horseplay' and violent sports.

In *R v Aitken* [1992] 1 WLR 1006 the three accused and the 'victim' were members of the Royal Air Force. They went to a party at the completion of their formal flying training and there consumed a 'considerable quantity' of alcohol. Later that night when two officers who were wearing fire-resistant flying suits fell asleep, some of the men set fire to their suits. The suits burned enough to wake the officers and they both treated this as a joke. After the party broke up, the three accused men followed Flying Officer Gibson, caught him, poured spirit over his suit and set fire to it. This time, the flames engulfed Gibson and he suffered extremely severe burning. The three accused were convicted at a general court-martial of inflicting grievous bodily harm. They appealed to the Courts-Martial Appeal Court, which quashed the convictions.

Cazalet J, who delivered the judgment of the Court, stated (at 1020) that the judge advocate had failed to give any direction in relation to Gibson's consent to 'rough and undisciplined horseplay'. Cazalet J went on to set out the direction that should have been given: 'It is common ground that there was no intention to cause any injury to Gibson. In those circumstances, if Gibson consented to take part in rough and undisciplined mess games involving the use of force towards those involved, no assault is proved in respect of any defendant whose participation extended only to taking part in such an activity.'

It is uncertain what status this case has in Australia, given the decision in *Lergesner v Carroll* (1989) 49 A Crim R 51, which implies that consent will be irrelevant to a situation where grievous bodily harm is caused. The injuries suffered by Gibson would seem to fall within this category.

There is slightly more authority on the role of consent in relation to sports violence. Sports such as boxing, wrestling, football and hockey involve body contact that may lead to serious harm. The general rule is by engaging in sport, the participant accepts the inherent risks involved in that sport: *Billinghurst* [1978] Crim LR 553. The status of professional boxing matches was considered in *Pallante v Stadiums Pty Ltd (No 1)* [1976] VR 331. McInerney stated (at 343):

> [B]oxing is not an unlawful and criminal activity so long as, whether for reward or not, it is engaged in by a contestant as a boxing sport or contest, not from motive or personal animosity, or at all events not predominantly from that motive, but

predominantly as an exercise of boxing skill and physical condition in accordance with rules and in conditions the object of which is to ensure that the infliction of bodily injury is kept within reasonable bounds, so as to preclude or reduce, so far as is practicable, the risk of either contestant incurring serious bodily injury, and to ensure that victory shall be achieved in accordance with the rules by the person demonstrating the greater skill as a boxer.

In some sports such as Australian Rules Football, however, it is recognised that the rules will be breached on a regular basis and participants accept this within reasonable limits. Legoe J pointed out in *McAvaney v Quigley* (1992) 58 A Crim R 457 at 459–60 that 'opposing players will not always abide by the rules and it cannot be said that every infringement of the rules resulting in physical contact that directly results in injury can amount to a criminal act'.

Similarly, in *R v Carr* unreported, 17 October 1990, CCA of NSW, the Court upheld the accused's conviction for assault occasioning actual bodily harm. In a particularly violent rugby league match, the accused had executed a head high swinging arm tackle that broke the victim's jaw. The Court upheld the conviction on the basis that the tackle was in breach of the rules of the game and players did not consent to major breaches of the rules that led to injuries of the type sustained on the facts: see also *Watherston v Woolven* (1988) 139 LSJS 366; *R v Stanley* unreported, 7 April 1995, New South Wales Court of Criminal Appeal, No 60554 of 1994; D Garnsey, 'Rugby League Player Jailed for On-Field Assault' (1995) 5(2) *ANZSLA Newsletter* 7; *Abbott v The Queen* unreported, 25 July 1995, CCA of WA, No 98 of 1995; H Opie, 'Aussie Rules Player Jailed for Behind-Play Assault' (1996) 6(2) *ANZSLA Newsletter* 3.

Sadomasochism

The majority opinion in *R v Brown* [1993] 2 WLR 556 (HL) set out the principle that consent is irrelevant to a charge of assault occasioning actual bodily harm where the harm was caused in the course of sadomasochistic sexual activities. A similar approach to the majority view in *Brown*'s case was expressed by the Ontario Court of Appeal in *R v Welch* (1996) 101 CCC (3d) 216. In the course of consensual sadomasochistic activity, the 'victim' suffered 'obvious and extensive bruising' and (possible) injury to the rectum. The Court affirmed (at 239) that the trial judge had been correct in withdrawing the issue of consent from the jury on the following basis: 'Although the law must recognise individual freedom and autonomy, when the activity in question involves pursuing sexual gratification by deliberately inflicting pain upon another that gives rise to bodily harm, then the personal interest of the individuals involved must yield to the more compelling societal interests which are challenged by such behaviour.'

A subsequent decision of the Court of Appeal, *R v Emmett* unreported, 18 June 1999, No 9901191/Z2, Rose LJ, Wright and Kay JJ confirmed the principle arising from *Brown*'s case and refused to draw a distinction between sadomasochistic activity conducted in a heterosexual context and that which is conducted in a homosexual context. In *Emmett*'s case, the accused was living with the 'victim' at the time of the alleged assaults and they afterwards married. The evidence of injuries came from a doctor whom the victim had consulted. The victim herself did not give evidence at the trial. The accused was charged with five offences of assault occasioning actual bodily harm, but this was dropped to two offences at the trial.

Emmett was convicted of assault occasioning actual bodily harm on one count and in the light of the judge's direction, the accused pleaded guilty to a further count of assault occasioning actual bodily harm. He was sentenced to nine months' imprisonment on each count, the sentence being suspended for two years.

The first incident that gave rise to the conviction concerned a process of partial asphyxiation through a plastic bag being placed over the victim's head and tightly tied around her neck during the course of the accused engaging in oral sex with her. The victim lost consciousness due to loss of oxygen. The following day her eyes became progressively bloodshot and when she went to her doctor, he found subconjunctival haemorrhages in both eyes due to the lack of oxygen and bruising around the neck due to the tight ligature holding the plastic bag in place. No treatment was given and after about a week, the bloodshot eyes returned to normal.

The second incident occurred a few weeks later when during sexual activity, the accused poured lighter fuel on the victim's breasts and set light to it. The accused said the victim had panicked and would not keep still, so he could not extinguish the flames immediately. She suffered a 6 cm x 4 cm third degree burn that became infected. The doctor initially thought it might need a skin graft but the burn eventually healed over without scarring.

The accused appealed against conviction upon a certificate granted by the trial judge setting out the following question for the court's determination: 'Where two adult persons consent to participate in sexual activity in private not intended to cause any physical injury but which does in fact cause or risk actual bodily harm, the potential for such harm being foreseen by both parties, does consent to such activity constitute a defence to an allegation of assault occasioning actual bodily harm contrary to section 47 of the Offences Against the Person Act 1861?'

The Court of Appeal held that consent was irrelevant in such circumstances. The accused relied upon *R v Wilson* [1996] 3 WLR 125 in which Russell LJ observed that consensual activity between husband and wife, in the privacy of the matrimonial home, is not a proper matter for criminal investigation or prosecution. However, the Court of Appeal in *Emmett*'s case (at 4) drew a distinction between the type of harm in *Wilson* (branding for personal adornment) and the actual or potential damage suffered by the victim during the course of sexual activity on the facts:

> The lady suffered a serious, and what must have been, an excruciating painful burn which became infected, and the appellant himself recognised that it required medical attention. As to the process of partial asphyxiation, to which she was sub-

jected on the earlier occasion, while it may...now be fairly known that the restriction of oxygen to the brain is capable of heightening sexual sensation, it is also, or should be, equally well-known that such a practice contains within itself a grave danger of brain damage or even death.

The Court of Appeal found that the facts of *Emmett* were similar to that in *Brown*, observing that there was 'no reason in principle...to draw any distinction between sadomasochistic activity on a heterosexual basis and that which is conducted in a homosexual context'. The Court concluded by agreeing with the trial judge's comments (at 4):

> In this case, the degree of actual and potential harm was such and also the degree of unpredictability as to injury was such as to make it a proper cause for the criminal law to intervene. This was not tattooing, it was not something which absented pain or dangerousness and the agreed medical evidence is in each case, certainly on the first occasion, there was a very considerable degree of danger to life; on the second, there was a degree of injury to the body.

It is unclear whether these English decisions will be followed in Australia, although there is some slight indication that they may be. In *R v McIntosh* the accused pleaded guilty to manslaughter: unreported, 3 September 1999, SC of Vic, Vincent J, No 1412 of 1999; [1999] VSC 358. His sexual partner died during bondage sex after the accused deliberately pulled on the rope around the deceased's neck on the theory that near asphyxia can heighten sexual pleasure. There was no evidence that the deceased had not consented to the rope being placed around his neck and there was evidence that the accused and the deceased had periodically engaged in bondage-type sex. In the course of sentencing the accused to five years' imprisonment, Vincent J remarked in relation to whether the activity was unlawful for the purpose of unlawful and dangerous act manslaughter (at 4–5):

> [I]t is not, of itself, and I repeat that expression, of itself, in the case of consenting adult persons, contrary to the law of this jurisdiction to engage in activities that could be described as bondage or sexual sadomasochism...In my opinion, if the sadomasochistic activity or bondage activity to which a victim consents involves the infliction of any such injury or the reckless acceptance of the risk that it will occur, then the consent of the victim will not be recognised.

Here, Vincent J appears, as with the Court of Appeal in *Emmett*'s case, to be focusing on the degree of harm involved in order to provide a cut-off line for consent to sadomasochistic activities.

Female genital mutilation
As outlined in the section on assault, existing provisions such as those dealing with grievous bodily harm or serious injury could be used to prosecute female genital

mutilation. However, it has now been separately criminalised in certain jurisdictions: *Crimes Act* 1900 (ACT), Pt 111B; *Crimes Act* 1900 (NSW) s 45; *Criminal Code* (NT) Pt VI Division 4A; *Criminal Code* (Tas) ss 178A–178C; *Crimes Act* 1985 (Vic) s 34; *Criminal Code* (Qld) s 323A(2); *Criminal Law Consolidation Act* 1935 (SA) s 33A(2).

Indigenous customary law

One question that remains unanswered by the law relating to assault is how to take into account forms of physical punishment such as 'payback' spearing in Indigenous customary law. Should such practices be deemed lawful because of consent to them? At present, there is no indication that the current law will deem such assaults lawful, although customary law has been taken into account in mitigation of sentence in, for example, *R v Williams* (1976) 14 SASR 1.

In *Warren, Coombes and Tucker* (1996) A Crim R 78, the Court of Criminal Appeal of South Australia refused to take into account customary law in an appeal against convictions for causing grievous bodily harm. The three accused men were members of the Dieri tribe, living in Marree. There had been tension concerning members of the Arabanna people claiming Marree as their traditional land. The three accused severely assaulted Dean Ah Chee who had been sent by members of the Arabanna people to warn the Dieri people not to conduct an initiation ceremony. The accused men claimed that the victim had breached their customary law by entering the town without their permission. They argued that customary law applied to them of its own force and that they themselves would be beaten if they did not punish the victim. Interestingly, this case did not revolve around the issue of consent to practices of customary law, but rather the accused claimed that they acted under duress for the purpose of the general criminal law.

The trial judge rejected the claim that the accused were inflicting traditional punishment on the victim, finding that they had acted for other reasons. The Court of Appeal dismissed the accused men's appeals, accepting that there was not sufficient evidence that the accused had been acting under Aboriginal customary law and the trial judge had been correct in rejecting this claim. Justice Debelle and Doyle CJ were careful to point out that they were not stating that duress would never be available as a matter of law when reliance was placed on customary law.

In *Hales v Jamilmira* unreported, 15 April 2003, CA of NT, [2003] NTCA 9 (discussed further in Chapter 5), Martine CJ commented (at para [28]) that '[t]here is a distinction between taking into account the offender being punished in accordance with both the law of the Territory and by the Aboriginal community, and circumstances...where the custom gives rise to the commission of the offence. In my view the latter circumstance does not permit mitigation to the same degree as may be available in the former'.

This statement, together with the dearth of case law directly on point, indicates that at present, consent to Indigenous customary practices such as payback will not constitute a defence to assaults and related offences. The Critique section will explore how certain Indigenous practices have been indirectly accepted as relevant to sentencing.

Critique

Why should the law allow consent to be relevant in relation to rough horseplay and in certain sports and yet not in relation to cultural practices or in the course of sadomasochistic sexual activity? One theme that runs through this area of the law is the degree to which a dominant culture can impinge on another culture or subculture.

Sports violence

In Western culture, there is a general acceptance of sports violence. There has certainly been a marked reluctance to invoke the law of assault in relation to sports violence. Most disciplinary action is brought by the relevant governing bodies. In Canada, where ice hockey involves a great deal of bodily contact, more than one hundred criminal convictions were imposed for offences involving violence between players in the 1970–85 period: DV White, 'Sports Violence as Criminal Assault: Development of the Doctrine by Canadian Courts' (1986) 6 *Duke Law Journal* 1030–54 at 1034. In Australia, however, there have only been a handful of prosecutions and of those cases reported, Paul Farrugia writes that the courts 'have apparently not been concerned with applying, or formulating any form of workable test for the scope of consent on the sports field': PJ Farrugia, 'The Consent Defence: Sports Violence, Sadomasochism, and the Criminal Law' (1997) 8(2) *Auckland University Review* 472–502 at 485.

Female genital mutilation

In Western culture, female genital mutilation is viewed with abhorrence even where an adult woman consents to it, yet while the preponderance of medical opinion is opposed to male circumcision, the law does not criminalise this conduct, even where it is based on ritual rather than therapeutic reasons: D Richards, 'Male Circumcision: Medical or Ritual?' (1996) 3(4) *Journal of Law and Medicine* 371–6. Female genital mutilation and male circumcision can of course be differentiated because the latter has no or only limited impact on sexual or reproductive functioning. However, the example of male circumcision shows that what is acceptable by the dominant culture may vary markedly.

The *Declaration on Violence Against Women* (1993) adopted by the United Nations defined 'violence' as including 'female genital mutilation and other traditional practices to women'. Anticipating the clash between cultural and liberal feminist claims to equality, the Declaration states that 'custom, tradition or religion cannot be invoked by States to avoid their obligations with respect to the elimination of violence against women. The rationale for this is that there are fundamental human rights which can and should be universally upheld. The empirical evidence of the widespread practice of violence against women warrants a unified statement condemning such practices irrespective of any claim to cultural justification'.

This is a powerful statement of principle that there are fundamental human rights that override cultural differences. The practical problem that occurs here is that imposing Western human rights standards on individuals of other cultures may lead to female genital mutilation being driven 'underground'. The Family Law Council points out in its Report, *Female Genital Mutilation* (June 1994), para 5.10, p 31: 'Many people who practise female genital mutilation see western societies as sexually promiscuous, decadent and in the process of disintegration. They cite female genital mutilation as a defence against such corrupting influences. They see the attack on female genital mutilation as an attempt to disintegrate their social order and thereby speed up their Europeanisation.'

Dismissing the freely given consent of adult women who wish to undergo female genital mutilation may only serve to increase feelings of alienation. A different approach to female genital mutilation could be regulation rather than prohibition. As with the case of physical punishment of children, regulation coupled with education programs, such as those run by the Ecumenical Migration Centre in Victoria, may provide a better alternative than criminalisation of consensual female genital mutilation: M Ierodiaconou, '"Listen to Us!" Female Genital Mutilation, Feminism and the Law in Australia' (1995) 20 *Melbourne University Law Review* 562–87. Of course we are referring here to practices consented to by adults rather than the practice on children where consent is not an issue due to their presumed lack of capacity to consent.

Indigenous customary law

The degree to which a dominant culture can impinge on another culture or subculture is also relevant to whether Indigenous customary law should be recognised as a valid and independent source of law alongside Australian criminal laws. The concept of 'payback' covers a wide range of methods used to punish breaches of customary law and may include restitution to the victim in the form of a gift as well as education, shaming, spearing or duelling: Australian Law Reform Commission, *Recognition of Aboriginal Customary Laws*, Report No 31 (1986) para 500. It is not a form of revenge, but is seen as a method of cleansing or atonement and a way of restoring relationships that have been disturbed. The Australian Law Reform Commission recommended that some forms of payback should be incorporated into sentencing orders, but refused to sanction sentencing orders that would involve a breach of, for example, the law of assault.

Some judges have also commented that the deliberate infliction of serious harm in the form of spearing cannot be judicially approved: *Jadurin* (1982) 7 A Crim R 182 at 187 per St John, Toohey and Fisher JJ; *Minor* (1992) 59 A Crim R 227 at 240 per Mildren J; *R v Walker* unreported, 1 September 1994, SC of NT, Martin CJ, No 46 of 1993, [1994] NTSC 79; *Hales v Jamilmira* unreported, 15 April

2003, CA of NT, [2003] NTCA 9 per Martin CJ at para [28]. Justice Mildren, however, went on to state in *Minor*'s case that because spearing into the thigh muscle may not cause any permanent injury to health and the person inflicting the punishment does not intend to kill or cause grievous bodily harm, it could potentially be permitted as part of a sentencing order. In the earlier case of *R v Williams* (1976) 14 SASR 1, Wells J decided not to sentence Williams to imprisonment for the manslaughter of his female drinking companion. Instead, he ordered a two-year suspended custodial sentence on the proviso that Williams submit himself to the customary penalties meted out by Aboriginal elders. Williams was then speared through the legs as required by the elders. This case formed part of the impetus for the Australian Law Reform Commission's brief to determine whether or not Aboriginal customary law should be recognised.

There is a question as to whether forms of payback that involve physical injury offend against Article 7 of the *International Covenant on Civil and Political Rights*, which prohibits 'cruel, inhuman or degrading treatment or punishment'. The Australian Law Reform Commission decided that this article qualified Article 27, which recognises the right of ethnic and religious minorities to enjoy their own culture: *Aboriginal Customary Law—Recognition*, Discussion Paper No 17 (1980) p 53. The Commission was satisfied that prohibiting cruel punishment would not have a significant effect on preserving Indigenous cultures.

This continues to be a problematic area. There have been moves in recent years to set up specialist courts to ensure greater participation of the Indigenous community in the sentencing process of Magistrates' Courts: for example, *Magistrates' Court (Koori Court) Act* 2002 (Vic). There are also major inquiries currently under way by the Law Reform Committees of the Northern Territory and Western Australia as to the recognition of Aboriginal customary law, which may lead to reform in this area: Northern Territory Government, Department of Justice, Law Reform Committee, <http://www.nt.gov.au/justice/graphpages/lawmake/lawref.shtml>, accessed June 2003; H Blagg, N Morgan and C Yavu Kama Harathunian, 'Aboriginal Customary Law in Western Australia' (2002) 80 *Reform* 11–14.

Sadomasochism

Whether sadomasochistic acts should be criminalised also brings into play a balancing act between paternalism and liberalism. As explored in Chapter 1, during the 1950s and 1960s, Lord Patrick Devlin argued that certain kinds of conduct ought to be prohibited and punished by the law simply because they were immoral according to the norms of a given society: *The Enforcement of Morals* (London: Oxford University Press, 1965). He argued that certain types of consensual conduct such as homosexual acts should be criminalised in order to preserve society, its essential institutions and what he termed its 'positive morality' from disintegration.

The opposing view was taken up by Professor Herbert Hart who, following the tradition of John Stuart Mill, argued that conduct should only be criminalised if it caused harm to others: HLA Hart, *Law, Liberty and Morality* (London: Oxford University Press, 1963); JS Mill, *On Liberty* (Harmondsworth: Penguin, 1974, first published 1859). What people did with consent in private was their business and not that of the criminal law.

This latter view was followed by the dissenting judges in *Brown*'s case. Lord Mustill, in particular, stated (at 599) that questions dealing with morally acceptable behaviour 'are questions of private morality: the standards upon which they fall to be judged are not those of the criminal law'. As with Herbert Hart, Lord Mustill sees the main aim of the criminal law as the prevention of harm rather than the preservation of morality.

Should the acts done by the men in *Brown*'s case be punishable by the criminal law? A positive answer could be justified by recourse to Lord Devlin's moralistic approach. A negative answer could be based on Herbert Hart's liberal approach. Interestingly, the European Court of Human Rights' approach seems to fall somewhere in between, in that it could be argued that such conduct should be criminalised because, even though consensual, it is likely to cause harm to health.

Whether consent should be relevant to sadomasochistic activities is a particularly difficult question to answer because such activities combine sex with violence and therefore raise issues for the law relating to sexual offences as well as assault. Susan Edwards, for example, has stated in 'No Defence for a Sado-masochistic Libido' (1993) 143 *New Law Journal* 406–7 at 406:

> In our desire to preserve privacy, individual liberty, and freedom from state intervention we are in danger of missing what lies at the heart of sado-masochism—its potential for violence. Why is it that for some the prefix 'sex' functions as a protective shield? We need to recognise, as we move increasingly into a world of sexual violence, the dangers of placing this so-called 'sex' beyond the rule of law.

The physical expression of sexuality takes many different forms, and this may include sadomasochistic violence: Law Commission, Consultation Paper No 139, *Consent in the Criminal Law* (London: HMSO, 1995) pp 133 ff. The present law may offer some degree of protection by setting limits on the *degree of harm* to which a person can validly consent. An alternative framework for developing safeguards for those engaging in sadomasochistic activities may lie in the concept of consent rather than the degree of harm. The law relating to consent to common assault at present offers little (if any) protection to those individuals who are especially vulnerable because of youth, inexperience or dependency. The general position is that provided the person is sufficiently mature to understand the nature of the relevant act or risk, consent operates as a complete defence. By contrast, recent reforms to the law governing consent to sexual intercourse offer greater protection to vulnerable parties. In Chapter 5, we explore how free agreement to sexual intercourse may be negated by, for example, intoxication, the abuse of authority, threats or mental incapacity.

In the context of offences against the person, similar rules should be developed to ensure that the consent of the parties is given freely, without constraint. This could involve the adoption of a positive consent standard for sadomasochistic activities that involve the risk of bodily harm to the participants. It is in these problematic areas of assault law that education rather than criminalisation could play a very important role in the regulation of behaviour. There is always a danger that heavy-handed criminalisation of certain activities will simply drive them underground and only serve to increase the risk of harm.

Conclusion

A common theme throughout this chapter is the extent to which certain conduct should be criminalised. We have suggested that a broad conception of what constitutes assault and threatening behaviour is warranted, providing that there is a rational hierarchy of offences developed. At present, there is much left to be desired in terms of the existing structure because of the considerable overlap between offences. There is also a lack of clarity as to where the law stands in Australia as to consent to aggravated assaults. As the MCCOC has pointed out in *Chapter 5, Non Fatal Offences Against the Person*, Report (September 1998) p 123: '[A]t common law, there is a general rule, with a host of exceptions, based on ad hoc decisions of courts on the public acceptability of violence in specific situations, which decisions are rationalized as being based on "public policy". In addition, it is quite clear that there is in law no fixed definition of what is "bodily harm".'

The MCCOC scheme replaces assault provisions with those focusing on different types of injury accompanied by different fault elements. Similarly, the Home Office in England circulated a draft Bill for comment in 1998: *Violence: Reforming the Offences Against the Person Act* 1861 (1998), <http://www.homeoffice.gov.uk/docs/vroapa.html>, accessed October 2003. This Bill again proposed a scheme based on the seriousness of the harm caused and the degree of the fault element involved.

The MCCOC scheme is to have four divisions based on the following: causing harm; threats and stalking; endangerment; and kidnapping, child abduction and unlawful detention. The MCCOC scheme has much to recommend it. We have pointed out some minor details that could lead to improvement, but having a hierarchy of offences appears to be fundamentally sound. The traditional separation between 'public' offences against the person and 'private' domestic offences also needs continued review in order to ensure that offences are reported and charged in terms of the harm caused rather than because of where they occur.

An ongoing problem lies in how far a dominant culture can go in imposing its view of acceptable violence on other cultures or subcultures. That is an issue with no easy answer and will no doubt continue to cause much debate as cases dealing with consent to aggravated assault continue to emerge.

CHAPTER 5

Sexual assault

Introduction

'Jane' (the complainant's name was omitted in the law reports) and Abel, who were second cousins, were at a party at Jane's place. Both were drinking alcohol and Jane became so drunk that the next day she could not remember much of what had happened at the party. Her last recollection before going to sleep was climbing the stairs to her bedroom. When she awoke the next day she realised that she must have had sexual intercourse. Charges were laid against Abel.

Abel said that Jane had not been drunk, had participated actively in the sexual activity and had consented. He said she was 'able to control what she was doing' and that after kissing him, had invited him into her bedroom. Jane said she would never have knowingly consented to intercourse with Abel because they were second cousins and in any case she had been too drunk to consent.

At his trial in Canada, the jury convicted Abel of sexual assault (rape in most Australian jurisdictions), evidently concluding beyond a reasonable doubt that Jane had not consented. However, on appeal, Abel raised another scenario. He claimed that Jane in fact did *not* consent to sex, but he honestly, but mistakenly believed that she did. He argued that the trial judge should have put this possibility to the jury despite it not being an issue at the trial. The Court of Appeal for the Northwest Territories in Canada agreed and directed a new trial: *Esau v The Queen* [1996] NWTR 242.

The prosecution then appealed against this decision to the Supreme Court of Canada. A majority of five judges to two dismissed the appeal and ordered a new trial: *R v Esau* [1997] 2 SCR 777. The majority held that the issue of honest but mistaken belief in consent should go to a jury to decide. Interestingly, after the Supreme Court decision, the prosecution decided to stay proceedings against Abel Esau and a new trial was therefore not held.

The fact situation in *Esau* highlights a number of issues in sexual assault trials. Often, two diametrically opposed narratives are presented to the jury—her version and his version. The main issue is usually that of consent: New South Wales Department for Women, *Heroines of Fortitude: The Experiences of Women in Court as Victims of Sexual Assault* (Woolloomooloo, November 1996), p 52; Law Reform Commission of Victoria, *Rape: Reform of Law and Procedure*, Appendixes to Interim Report No 42 (Melbourne, LRCV, 1991) Appendix 3, p 86. In the absence of witnesses, it can be very difficult for the prosecution to prove *beyond reasonable doubt* that sexual intercourse occurred without consent.

The beyond reasonable double standard and presumption of innocence means that the trial privileges the rights of the accused, and gives preference to the accused's narrative where there is no additional witness or evidence. This can be regarded as appropriate in terms of principles of criminal law. However, it is clearly a source of great distress and frustration for complainants whose competing narratives may be ultimately dismissed in what comes to be seen as a formal contest.

The fact that the prosecution decided to stay proceedings rather than proceed with a new trial of Abel Esau indicates the discretion that may be exercised in deciding not to bring those accused of sexual assault to trial. The Victorian Law Reform Commission has estimated that over a two-year period, between 1997–98 and 1998–99, only about a third of alleged rape offenders for whom a matter was reported to and recorded by police were prosecuted: *Sexual Offences: Law and Procedure*, Interim Report (Melbourne: VLRC, 2003) p 80. Further, only around 14.5 per cent of penetrative offences other than rape (such as sexual penetration of a child or incest) that are reported to and recorded by police, ultimately proceed to prosecution: Victorian Law Reform Commission, *Sexual Offences: Law and Procedure*, Interim Report (Melbourne: VLRC, 2003) p 91. Evidential problems, or an indication that the victim does not wish to proceed with the court process, may lead to decisions not to prosecute.

The term 'sexual assault' can be viewed as a broad term generally used to encompass the crimes of rape, indecent assault and incest. There are marked differences in terminology and definitions used in Australian jurisdictions. In South Australia, Queensland, Tasmania and Victoria the most serious offence is 'rape', while in the Australian Capital Territory it is 'sexual assault' and in the Northern Territory and Western Australia it is 'sexual intercourse/penetration without consent'.

There are also specific statutory provisions in Australian jurisdictions that deal with sexual offences against children and those with mental impairment. Again there are marked differences in the elements of these offences according to jurisdiction. The age of consent to sexual intercourse ranges from 16 years to 21 years. Some jurisdictions have blanket offences making it a crime to have sexual intercourse with individuals suffering from mental impairment regardless of consent; others restrict such offences to those offering medical or therapeutic services.

This chapter will use the terms 'rape' and 'indecent assault'. It will outline the issues that arise from the definitions of these crimes and will then deal briefly with other statutory sexual offences. The term 'sexual assault' will be used in its broad sense to encompass these specific crimes. There was a movement during the 1970s and 1980s away from the use of the term 'rape' in favour of 'sexual assault' in order to emphasise the violent character of the harm and to align it with the hierarchy of assault offences. This stemmed from the work of the American feminist author Susan Brownmiller, who argued that the violence associated with forced sex stemmed from man's physical capacity to rape: *Against Our Will: Men, Women and Rape* (New York: Simon and Schuster, 1975). She argued that while only some men actually carry out rapes, all men are by their potential as rapists able to keep all women in a state of fear. The violent and harmful consequences of rape, in her opinion, therefore should be highlighted. More recently, there appears to have been a return to the use of the term 'rape' perhaps because it is well understood as a description of non-consensual sexual intercourse. The Victorian Law Reform Commission pointed out in its *Rape and Allied Offences: Substantive Aspects*, Discussion Paper No 2 (Melbourne: LRCV, 1986) p 51, para 4.23: 'The main argument for retention, regardless of the form and substance of the law, is that the term "rape" is synonymous in our culture with a particularly heinous form of behaviour. The application of the term "rapist" to a person is a particularly effective and appropriate form of stigma.'

In Chapter 1, we noted that only a small proportion of crime comes to the attention of the police. The failure to report crime gives rise to what has been termed the 'dark figure' in measuring crime. This is particularly true of this area of the criminal law as most victims do not report sexual assaults: Victorian Law Reform Commission, *Sexual Offences: Law and Procedure*, Discussion Paper (Melbourne: VLRC, 2001) p 19. As mentioned briefly above, for those who do report sexual assaults, a filtering process occurs. The Australian Bureau of Statistics' Report *Women's Safety Australia 1996*, Cat No 4128.0 (Canberra: Office of the Status of Women, 1996) pp 9, 29 estimates that of *reported* sexual assault incidents, only around 22 per cent result in the perpetrator being charged by police. Of the matters going to trial, the Victorian Law Reform Commission found that on the data collected for the periods 1997–98 and 1998–99, only 24 per cent of accused were convicted or pleaded guilty to rape: Victorian Law Reform Commission, *Sexual Offences: Law and Procedure*, Discussion Paper (Melbourne: VLRC, 2001) p 47.

Recorded crime statistics indicate that victims of sexual assault are overwhelmingly women and female children. For example, in 2001, Australian statistics based on police records estimated that the reported sexual assault victimisation rate for females (139 victims per 100,000) was more than four times the male victimisation rate (28.9 victims per 100,000): Australian Bureau of Statistics, *Crimes Recorded by Police 2003*, Table 11.7, <http://www.abs.gov.au/ausstats/abs@.nsf/Lookup/E93FA3CC3D9BC5C6CA256CAE001052A3>, accessed October 2003. Sexual assault rates were particularly high for female victims in the 15–19 years age group, with the reported rate being 498 victims per 100,000 (Table 11.8). Of course, the picture may differ in reality given that sexual assaults are under-reported and there may be cultural reasons for men not reporting such assaults, but victim surveys support this overall picture. What remains true is that perpetrators of sexual assault are overwhelmingly men: ABS, *Women's Safety Survey 1996*, p 14, Table 3.7.

The previous discussion of domestic violence in Chapter 4 underlines the reality of intimate violence against women. Until recently, a husband could not be convicted of raping his wife because by 'mutual matrimonial consent the wife hath given up herself in this kind unto her husband which she cannot retract': M Hale, *The History of the Pleas of the Crown* (London: Professional Books Ltd, 1971, first published 1736) Vol 1, p 629. This marital rape immunity became the focus of feminist criticisms during the 1960s and 1970s and by the late 1980s, the immunity had been abolished by legislation in every Australian state and territory. Its status as common law was reviewed in *R v L* (1991) 174 CLR 379. The majority of the High Court (at 390) doubted whether the immunity was still in existence and stated that they 'would be justified in refusing to accept a notion that is so out of keeping with the view society now takes of the relationship between the parties to a marriage'.

While the marital rape immunity has been formally abolished, there is reason to believe that marital rape is grossly under-reported because victims are reluctant to disclose or report the matter to police: P Easteal, 'Rape in Marriage: Has the Licence Lapsed?' in P Easteal (ed), *Balancing the Scales—Rape, Law Reform and Australian Culture* (Sydney: The Federation Press, 1994); P Easteal, *Voices of the Survivors* (Melbourne: Spinifex Press, 1994). Sue Lees, in an English empirical study, found that even when marital rape is prosecuted, estranged husbands' punishments were 'frequently lower than in other rape cases': *Ruling Passions: Sexual Violence, Reputation and the Law* (Buckingham: Open University Press, 1997).

In this chapter, we will be examining current sexual offences. However, it should be pointed out that until recently, the criminal law has been used as a method of repressing and controlling sexual conduct between men conducted in private and with consent: E Henderson, 'Of Signifiers and Sodomy: Privacy, Public Morality and Sex in the Decriminalisation Debates' (1996) 20 *Melbourne University Law Review* 1023–47. Sexual conduct between women, in contrast, has largely escaped legal regulation partly because it was seen as 'unimaginable': R Ford, '"Lady-friends" and "Sexual Deviationists": Lesbians and Law in Australia, 1920s–1950s' in D Kirkby (ed), *Sex, Power and Justice: Historical Perspectives on Law in Australia* (Melbourne: Oxford University Press, 1995).

Rape and indecent assault

Background

In general, the offence of indecent assault centres upon non-consensual sexual acts that do not involve penetration whereas for the crime of rape to be made out, sexual intercourse must have occurred. Central to both crimes is the concept of consent, which has been uniquely shaped by wider community attitudes to heterosexual intercourse. Before recent legislative attempts to define consent, the courts traditionally presumed as a matter of evidence that unless a woman resisted or signalled that she did not want to be touched or sexually penetrated, she was consenting. That presumption has been challenged by recent law reform efforts and we will explore the effect of such changes below.

The *Esau* case indicates how an accused's narrative can change from 'she consented' to 'well, she may not have been consenting, but I honestly believed she was'. In the common law Australian jurisdictions of the Australian Capital Territory, New South Wales, South Australia and Victoria, the prosecution must prove that the accused intended to have sexual intercourse or to indecently touch the victim combined with a belief that the other was not consenting or being reckless as to whether or not the other was consenting. This added fault element has attracted much criticism. We shall set out the current laws relating to the physical elements of these offences before providing a critique of them. We then turn to describing the current laws relating to the fault elements and provide a critique of them.

The current law—physical elements

Sexual intercourse/indecent assault

The offence of rape requires the prosecution to prove that sexual intercourse occurred. In the past, the sexual act was referred to as 'carnal knowledge' of a woman and required penile penetration of the female genitalia. Now, rape is statutorily defined much more broadly in all jurisdictions. Sexual intercourse (or sexual penetration in Victoria and Western Australia) now encompasses:

- the penetration of vagina or anus of a person by any part of the body of another person such as the penis or finger or by an object manipulated by another person: *Crimes Act* 1900 (ACT) ss 92(a), (b); *Criminal Code* (NT) s 1; *Crimes Act* 1900 (NSW) s 61H(1)(a); *Criminal Code* (Qld) ss 6, 349(2)(a), (b); *Criminal Law Consolidation Act* 1935 (SA) ss 5(1)(a), 73(5); *Criminal Code* (Tas) ss 1, 127A; *Crimes Act* 1958 (Vic) s 35; *Criminal Code* (WA) s 319(1);
- the introduction of any part of the penis into the mouth of another person (fellatio): *Crimes Act* 1900 (ACT) ss 92(a), (b); *Criminal Code* (NT) s 1; *Crimes Act* 1900 (NSW) s 61H(1)(b); *Criminal Code* (Qld) s 349(2)(c); *Criminal Law Consolidation Act* 1935 (SA) s 5(1)(b); *Criminal Code* (Tas) ss 1, 127A (aggravated sexual assault if digital or object penetration); *Crimes Act* 1958 (Vic) s 35; *Criminal Code* (WA) s 319(1);
- the stimulation of the vulva or penetration of the vagina with the tongue (cunnilingus): *Crimes Act* 1900 (ACT) s 92(d); *Criminal Code* (NT) s 1; *Crimes Act* 1900 (NSW) s 61H(1)(c); *Criminal Law Consolidation Act* 1935 (SA) s 5(1)(c);

Criminal Code (Tas) ss 1, 127A; *Crimes Act* 1958 (Vic) s 35 (by implication); *Criminal Code* (WA) s 319(1); *Randall* (1991) 53 A Crim R 380; *DPP v M and J* (1993) 9 WAR 281; *R v JC* unreported, 18 August 2000, Supreme Court of the ACT, Higgins J, [2000] ACTSC 72; and

- the continuation of sexual intercourse: *Crimes Act* 1900 (ACT) s 92(e); *Criminal Code* (NT) s 1; *Crimes Act* 1900 (NSW) s 61H(1)(d); *Criminal Code* (Tas) s 1; *Crimes Act* 1958 (Vic) s 38(2)(b); *Criminal Code* (WA) s 319(1); *Kaitamaki v The Queen* [1985] AC 147.

In the Northern Territory and Victoria, 'vagina' includes a surgically constructed vagina meaning that non-consensual sexual intercourse with a transsexual female amounts to rape: *Criminal Code* (NT) s 1; *Crimes Act* (Vic) 1958 s 35. In Western Australia and Victoria, it is also rape where the offender forces the victim to penetrate him or her with the victim's penis: *Crimes Act* 1958 (Vic) s 38(3); *Criminal Code* (WA) s 319(1).

The physical element for the crime of rape in all Australian jurisdictions has therefore developed substantially from the old common law definition of rape being carnal knowledge of a woman. These changes have not been enacted without criticism. For example, in 1986 the Law Reform Commission of Victoria pointed out in *Rape and Allied Offences: Substantive Aspects*, Discussion Paper No 2 (Melbourne: LRCV, 1986) p 20: '[T]o alter the definition of rape to include penetration of a wider range of sexual orifices, and particularly to "de-sex" the offence, so that it is not limited to something men do to women, is to remove the law from what is a social and political reality, to a plane of almost theoretical abstraction, including the concept of women raping men.'

However, current changes to the law recognise that non-consensual oral or anal penetration can be just as traumatic as vaginal penetration, and that sexual violation of a penetrative nature can be as traumatic for men as for women. It seems inappropriate to label such acts as indecent assault rather than rape. A broad definition of sexual intercourse also aims to protect the sexual autonomy of both women and men.

An assault is an essential physical element of the crime of indecent assault in all Australian jurisdictions apart from the Australian Capital Territory: *Criminal Code* (NT) s 188(2)(k); *Crimes Act* 1900 (NSW) s 61L; *Criminal Code* (Qld) s 352(1)(a); *Criminal Law Consolidation Act* 1935 (SA) s 56; *Criminal Code* (Tas) s 127(1); *Crimes Act* 1958 (Vic) s 39; *Criminal Code* (WA) s 323. As explored in Chapter 4, an assault may involve the application of non-consensual physical force to or touching the victim's body as well as putting the victim in a situation where there is a threat that unlawful force will be applied. Thus, in *Rolfe* (1952) 36 Cr App R 4, it was held that an indecent assault was committed when the accused moved towards a woman with his penis exposed and asked her to have sexual intercourse with him.

In the Australian Capital Territory, the term 'assault' is not used: *Crimes Act* 1900 (ACT) s 92J. Instead, the statutory provision refers to an 'act of indecency without consent'. This means there does not have to be a threat to apply force for the offence to be proved. For example, in *Fairclough v Whipp* [1951] 3 Cr App R 138 it was held there was no indecent assault when a man asked a young girl to touch his penis and she complied. This was seen as not involving a threat of force, but under the terminology used in the Australian Capital Territory, this could nevertheless be seen as an act of indecency.

The Model Criminal Code Officers Committee (MCCOC) has recommended dividing the current law into offences featuring non penetrative touching and those that do not feature touching at all: *Sexual Offences Against the Person*, Report (May 1999) p 103. It recommended enacting an offence of indecent touching together with other indecent acts that do not feature penetration or touching.

At present, the law requires the assault to be indecent in itself or committed in circumstances of indecency. Indecency has not been statutorily defined, but the courts have held that 'indecent' is an ordinary English word and it is for the jury to decide whether the facts of the case amount to indecency: *R v Nazif* [1987] 2 NZLR 122 at 127. Lord Ackner in *R v Court* [1989] AC 28 at 42 referred to directing the jury as to whether 'right-minded persons would consider the conduct indecent'.

In general, the assault or act must have a sexual connotation to be considered indecent. In *Harkin* (1989) 38 A Crim R 296 at 301, the New South Wales Court of Criminal Appeal referred to the sexual connotation arising from the area of the body of the accused or victim such as 'the genitals and anus of both the male and female and the breasts of the female'.

The MCCOC has recommended statutorily defining 'indecent' as 'indecent according to the standards of ordinary people': *Chapter 5, Sexual Offences Against the Person*, Report (May 1999) p 107.

The most controversial aspect of the physical elements of both rape and indecent assault centres upon proving lack of consent and it is to the law relating to this element that we now turn.

Without consent

Prior to the nineteenth century, the crime of rape was defined as the carnal knowledge of a woman *against her will*. This necessitated proof of the use or threat of force or violence by the accused and resistance by the victim. In the mid-nineteenth century, after rape ceased to be a capital offence, English courts began to use the concept of 'lack of consent' in order to include within the definition of rape the situation where the complainant was asleep or inebriated or where the victim was deceived as to the nature of the act.

Although terminology may differ between Australian jurisdictions, the law relating to rape and indecent assault currently focuses on the question of consent: *Crimes Act* 1900 (ACT) ss 92J, 92P(2); *Crimes Act* 1900 (NSW) s 61R; *Criminal Code* (NT) ss 187, 192; *Criminal Code* (Qld) ss 245; 348; *Criminal Law Consolidation Act* 1935 (SA) s 48; *Criminal Code* (Tas) ss 182, 185; *Crimes Act* 1958 (Vic) ss 37, 38(2);

Criminal Code (WA) ss 222, 325; *Attorney-General's Reference (No 6 of 1980)* [1981] QB 715 at 718. That is, to obtain a conviction, the prosecution must prove beyond reasonable doubt that the complainant did not consent to sexual intercourse or the indecent act by the accused. This is generally classified as one of the physical elements of sexual assault in that it is proved by looking at the external or outward circumstances, rather than at the state of mind of the accused.

There is no requirement that physical resistance be proved: *Crimes Act* 1900 (ACT) s 92P(2); *Crimes Act* 1900 (NSW) s 61R(2)(d); *Criminal Law Consolidation Act* 1935 (SA) s 48; *Criminal Code* (WA) s 319(2)(b). In the Northern Territory and Victoria, judges must give a direction to the jury in rape trials that a person is not to be regarded as having consented because he or she did not protest or physically resist or sustain physical injury: *Criminal Code* (NT) s 192A; *Crimes Act* 1958 (Vic) s 37. However, as will be explored in the Critique section, evidence of physical resistance may make it easier for the prosecution to obtain a conviction.

Consent is statutorily defined in the Northern Territory and Victoria as meaning 'free agreement': *Criminal Code* (NT) s 192; *Crimes Act* 1958 (Vic) s 36 and in Tasmania and Western Australia, there is a requirement that it be 'freely given': *Criminal Code* (Qld) s 348(2); *Criminal Code* (Tas) s 2A(2); *Criminal Code* (WA) s 319(2). The different jurisdictions have developed a range of circumstances where consent may be vitiated in the case of rape such as where the consent is obtained:

- through threats of personal injury or other forms of intimidation: *Crimes Act* 1900 (ACT) ss 92P(1)(a)–(j); *Criminal Code* (Qld) s 348(2)(a)–(d); *Criminal Code* (Tas) s 2A(2)(a); *Crimes Act* 1958 (Vic) ss 36(a)–(c); *Criminal Code* (WA) s 319(2)(a); *Papadimitropoulos v The Queen* (1957) 98 CLR 249 at 255 per Dixon CJ, McTiernan, Webb, Kitto and Taylor JJ; *R v PS Shaw* [1995] 2 Qd R 97;
- through a mistake as to the nature or character of the act: *Crimes Act* 1900 (NSW) s 61R(2)(a1) (this must be induced by fraudulent means); *Criminal Code* (Qld) s 348(2)(e); *Crimes Act* 1959 (Vic) s 36(f); *R v Lock* (1872) LR 2 CCR 10; *R v Day* (1841) 9 Car & P 772; *R v Flattery* (1877) 1 QBD 410; *R v Williams* [1923] 1 KB 340;
- through a mistake as to the identity of the accused or, in Queensland, the accused inducing the victim's belief that the former is his/her sexual partner: *Crimes Act* 1900 (ACT) s 92P(1)(f); *Crimes Act* 1900 (NSW) s 61R(2)(a)(i); *Criminal Code* (Qld) s 348(2)(f); *Crimes Act* 1958 (Vic) s 36(f); *R v Dee* (1884) 15 Cox CC 579; *R v Gallienne* [1964] NSWR 919;
- through a mistaken belief that the act is for medical or hygienic purposes: *Crimes Act* 1900 (NSW) s 61R(2)(a1); *Criminal Code* (NT) s 192(2)(f); *Criminal Law Consolidation Act* 1935 (SA) s 73(5); *Crimes Act* 1958 (Vic) s 36(g);
- through fraudulent means: *Crimes Act* 1900 (ACT) s 92P(1)(g); *Criminal Code* (WA) s 319(2). Compare *Papadimitropoulos v The Queen* (1957) 98 CLR 249;
- where the victim does not understand the sexual nature of the act: *Crimes Act* 1900 (ACT) s 92P(1)(i); *Criminal Code* (NT) s 192(2)(d); *Criminal Code* (Qld) s 348(1); *Criminal Law Consolidation Act* 1935 (SA) s 73(6); *Crimes Act* 1958 (Vic) s 36(e);

- where the victim is so affected by alcohol or other drugs as to be incapable of agreeing: *Crimes Act* 1900 (ACT) s 92P(1)(e); *Criminal Code* (NT) s 192(2)(c); *Criminal Code* (Tas) s 2A(2)(c); *R v Camplin* (1845) 1 Cox CC 220; and
- where the victim is asleep: *Crimes Act* 1958 (Vic) s 36(d); *R v Mayers* (1872) 12 Cox CC 311; *R v Richard Fletcher* (1859) 8 Cox CC 131; *R v Francis* [1993] 2 Qd R 300.

Critique

The social context of consent

What constitutes and what does not constitute 'consent' is continually being debated in contemporary political, moral and legal theory: Keith Burgess-Jackson, *Rape: A Philosophical Investigation* (Dartmouth: Aldershot Publishing Company, 1996) p 91. We have already touched upon this in Chapter 4, which deals with the law relating to assault. The word 'consent' often attracts adjectives such as explicit, implicit, express, implied, presumed, informed, unwilling, reluctant, grudging, half-hearted, unreserved and so on.

The debate about meanings of consent has been deeply gendered, drawing on the dominant and competing discourses about ideas of the masculine and the feminine and about gender and sexuality. The centrality of sexuality to all people's self-identity—judges, juries, offenders and victims, members of the community—underpins the deeply-felt and entrenched nature of these concepts. This debate has failed to address gay and lesbian sexuality. Legislative changes have taken a formal equality approach by 'desexing' the parties, but no substantive changes have been made by reference to differences in sexuality or in sexual practices, or in stereotypes and discourses about homosexuality.

In rape trials, the gradual change from the prosecution having to prove that penetration occurred 'against the will' of the victim to 'without the victim's consent' did not in reality alter the presumption that unless a woman resisted or struggled in some way, the act of penetration could not amount to rape. For example, the English Court of Appeal stated in *R v Howard* [1966] 1 WLR 13: '[T]he prosecution in order to prove rape, must prove either that [the complainant] physically resisted, or if she did not, that her understanding and knowledge was such that she was not in a position to decide whether to consent or resist.'

Feminist authors such as Ngaire Naffine and Nicola Lacey have been concerned to 'deconstruct' traditional meanings of rape in order to accommodate alternative conceptions of sex and sexuality: N Naffine, *Feminism and Criminology* (St Leonards: Allen & Unwin, 1997) ch 4; N Lacey, *Unspeakable Subjects* (Oxford: Hart Publishing, 1998). By placing the law of sexual assault in its historical and cultural surroundings, a path opens up towards reconstructing sexuality and consent in terms that protect a broader range of interests than traditionally circumscribed.

The legal presumption of consent can thus be viewed as reflecting traditional masculinist social beliefs and attitudes concerning sexuality, specifically heterosexuality, in Western society: I Breines, R Connell and I Eide (eds) *Male Roles, Masculinities and Violence* (Paris: UNESCO Publishing, 2000); SP Schacht and DW Ewing, *Feminism and Men: Reconstructing Gender Relations* (New York: New York University Press, 1998).

Two main assumptions circumscribe what is generally perceived as 'normal' heterosexual behaviour. The first is that sexuality is essentially concerned with the act of penetration: Carol Smart, 'Law's Truth/Women's Experience' in Regina Graycar (ed), *Dissenting Opinions* (Sydney: Allen & Unwin, 1990) p 9. The second is that women enjoy being 'coerced' or persuaded to engage in sexual intercourse. In relation to the latter assumption, there is a general belief that the art of 'seduction' allows for any reservations on the part of the woman to be rightfully overcome by the persistence of the man: B McSherry, 'No! (means no?)' (1993) 18(1) *Alternative Law Journal* 27–30 at 27. The woman is expected both to resist sexual congress *and* to be willing to be persuaded by an artful seducer. This may have been a realistic narrative for women to accept historically when sexual activity and sexual interest by women was seen as highly inappropriate and stigmatised.

In this penetrative/coercive model of sexuality, women are viewed as submissive, as acquiescing to sexual intercourse *unless* they resist in some way, both in 'normal' sex and in rape. Following this model, physical inaction has been traditionally viewed by the courts as signalling consent. For example, in the Victorian Supreme Court case of *R v Maes* [1975] VR 541 at 548, Nelson J stated that a woman may convey her consent to a man 'by the very fact that she remains physically inactive'. In the academic field, Brent Fisse also refers to the situation where a woman 'consciously submits with passive acquiescence' as not constituting rape: *Howard's Criminal Law* (Sydney: The Law Book Company Ltd, 1990) p 179. This statement follows from Fisse's earlier comment (at 179) that '[o]utward reluctance to consent may be no more than a concession to modesty or a deliberate incitement to D [the defendant] to persuade a little harder'.

In its submission to the Victorian Law Reform Commission, the Real Rape Law Coalition summarised this point about physical inaction signalling consent: Law Reform Commission of Victoria, *Rape: Reform of Law and Procedure*, Appendixes to Interim Report No 42 (Melbourne: VLRC, 1991) Appendix 7, pp 163–4: '[There is a proposition] that in both sex and rape the woman's role consists in having something done to her, that being the male act of penetration. Consequently, no matter what she says, if she "lies there" during the assault, and does not injure the assailant or sustain extensive physical injury herself, that is consistent with a woman's part in "consensual" sexual relations.'

At the same time, the penetrative/coercive model of sexuality not only portrays women as submissive; it also views women as agents of precipitation. The very appearance of women can be portrayed as arousing men's desire: I Leader-Elliott and N Naffine, 'Wittgenstein, Rape Law and the Language Games of Consent' (2000) 26(1) *Monash University Law Review* 48–73. This explains why in a rape trial, defence counsel generally focuses on the complainant's actions to show that she was consenting. Julie Taylor suggests that men 'have placed responsibility for sexual aggressiveness on women by imputing to women a desire to be taken forcefully': 'Rape and Women's Credibility: Problems of Recantations and False Accusations Echoed in the Case of Cathleen Crowell Webb and Gary Dotson' (1987) 10 *Harvard Women's Law Journal* 59–116 at 111. This is borne out by a comment in the *Yale Law Journal* that effectively justifies the use of force in sexual penetration on the basis of women's 'needs': a 'woman's need for sexual satisfaction may lead to the unconscious desire for forceful penetration, the coercion serving neatly to avoid guilt feelings which might arise after willing participation': Anonymous, 'Forcible and Statutory Rape', Note, (1952) 62 *Yale Law Journal* 55–83 at 67. None of this of course refers to women's own experience of sex and rape.

Because of the pervasiveness of these assumptions about 'normal' heterosexual intercourse, and because they are male understandings of sexuality promulgated historically by male judges and legislators, it is little wonder that the law has traditionally stated that a woman consents to sexual penetration unless she in some way strongly resists her assailant. Even though legislative provisions now exist in the Australian Capital Territory, the Northern Territory, New South Wales, South Australia, Western Australia and Victoria stating that a failure to offer physical resistance to a sexual assault does not of itself constitute consent, it still remains difficult for the prosecution to prove beyond reasonable doubt that the complainant did not consent to sexual penetration in the absence of some form of physical signs of resistance or other evidence of corroboration.

Brent Fisse in *Howard's Criminal Law* (Sydney: The Law Book Company Ltd, 1990) p 179 explains the practicalities of proving non-consent as follows:

> [A]lthough in theory D [the defendant] is not entitled to make any presumption of consent, the fact that P [the prosecution] must prove non-consent as part of his [sic] case means in practice that if V [the victim] consciously submits with passive acquiescence, subject only to a mental reservation, D should be acquitted unless V's acquiescence is explicable in the context as arising from fear of the consequences of resistance. V must make it clear to D, up to the moment of intercourse, that she does not consent, but in so doing she is not required to incur the risk of brutality.

It appears that the legislative provisions modifying the previous requirement that the prosecution prove lack of consent through physical resistance have not resulted in any significant change to rape prosecutions because they have not displaced the presumption of consent. For example, in a study of rape prosecutions carried out in 1989 in Victoria, 85 per cent of incidents involved allegations of some form of physical coercion: Law Reform Commission of Victoria, *Rape: Law Reform and Procedure*, Appendixes to Interim Report No 42 (Melbourne: LRCV, 1991) Appendix 3, p 69. The Victorian Rape Law Reform Evaluation Project commenced in 1992 to examine, among other matters, the impact of the legislative and procedural reforms on complainants' experiences of the court process. The second report, which studied prosecutions in Victoria in 1992 and 1993, showed similar findings to that of the Law Reform Commission. In 57.5 per cent of incidents, the accused used some form of physical force and used or displayed a weapon in a further 20.9 per cent. Verbal intimidation or threats were used in another 6.1 per cent of incidents: Melanie Heenan and Helen McKelvie, *Rape Law Reform Evaluation Project*, Report No 2: *The Crimes (Rape) Act 1991: An Evaluation Project* (Melbourne: Department of Justice, 1997) p 39. These figures seem to suggest that the prosecution is more likely to proceed with cases where there is evidence of physical coercion, therefore supporting the traditional paradigm.

Peter Rush and Alison Young have argued that since it is so difficult to move away from the presumption of consent, it is worthwhile considering a new offence that omits lack of consent as an essential physical element: 'A Crime of Consequence and a Failure of Legal Imagination: The Sexual Offences of the Model Criminal Code' (1997) 9 *The Australian Feminist Law Journal* 100–33. They suggest that rape should be defined as causing serious injury with sexual penetration. They set out the following offence at 106:

(1) A person who:
  (a) voluntarily engages in the sexual penetration of another person, and
  (b) voluntarily causes that other person serious injury,
  (c) with the intention of causing serious injury or with recklessness as to causing serious injury,
 is guilty of the offence of rape.

This proposed offence challenges the traditional view of the offence of rape having circumstances as a physical element. Instead, the focus is on the consequences of the conduct, thus bringing rape into line with other result crimes such as murder and assault. There is considerable merit in an approach that places the victim's experience of trauma within the definition of rape. However, because consent is so ingrained in traditional definitions of rape, it would seem that even with a change in focus, the defence could still argue that the accused did not intend that the victim suffer serious injury because the victim consented. Consent could still be relevant in assessing the fault element. The Victorian Law Reform Commission discussed this proposal in detail in *Sexual Offences: Law and Procedure*, Interim Report (Melbourne: VLRC, 2003) ch 7, but ultimately decided not to adopt the proposed definition on the basis that the proposed offence would be unlikely to reduce victimisation of complainants in rape trials.

In Victoria there has been an attempt to go beyond the presumption of consent from physical inactivity and passive acquiescence. Section 37(a) requires a judge in a relevant case to direct the jury that 'the fact that a person did not say or do anything to indicate free agreement to a sexual act is normally enough to show that the act took place without that person's free agreement'. According to this direction, when a woman 'lies back' and does nothing to indicate free agreement, that is normally enough to show that she is *not* consenting. Physical inactivity or passive acquiescence now appears to mean non-consent rather than the opposite. The use of the word 'normally' implies that the burden is on the defence to raise evidence displacing this presumption. However, the Supreme Court of Victoria stated in *R v Laz* [1998] 1 VR 453 at 460: 'Section 37(a) does no more than require a trial judge to draw to the jury's attention the necessity, when considering the issue of consent, to have regard to the common human experience that, in general, people do not engage voluntarily in sexual activities without indicating by word or action in some way their preparedness to do so.'

This provision challenges the traditional way of viewing women as passively acquiescing to penetration; consent must be positively communicated either verbally or by unequivocal non-verbal behaviour. It makes it difficult for an accused to claim that the victim was consenting because she did not resist. This is an aspect of the common law fault element, which will be discussed in more detail later.

The Law Reform Commission of Victoria in *Rape: Reform of Law and Procedure*, Report No 43 (Melbourne: LRCV, 1991) p 16 stated that 'it is not acceptable for men to cling to outdated myths about seduction, sexual conquest and female sexuality'. It also made clear (at 8) that the jury directions should be used as an educative vehicle: 'Another benefit of expressing these directions in legislative form is that the community in general will be made aware of what type of evidence is, or is not, sufficient to prove lack of consent.'

This jury direction is therefore intended to have wider repercussions in relation to the penetrative/coercive model of sexuality. The necessity for consent rather than non-consent to be communicated opens the way for an alternative model of sexuality to come to the fore. Simon Bronitt has referred to s 37(a) as creating a positive consent standard in that 'free agreement' must be positively evidenced by words or conduct: 'The Direction of Rape Law in Australia: Toward a Positive Consent Standard' (1994) 18(5) Crim LJ 249–53. That is, a woman can no longer be presumed to be 'freely' agreeing to sexual intercourse simply because she is silent or does not resist. This 'positive' standard is based on the model of 'communicative' sexuality.

A communicative model of sexuality has been sketched out by a legal academic, Martha Chamallas, and a philosopher, Lois Pineau: M Chamallas, 'Consent, Equality and the Legal Control of Sexual Conduct' (1988) 61 *Southern California Law Review* 777–862, and L Pineau, 'Date Rape: A Feminist Analysis' (1989) 9 *Law and Philosophy* 217–43. Chamallas argues (at 836) in favour of an ideal of sexual conduct based not simply on consent, but on mutuality. She states that if it is accepted that two of the main inducements for engaging in sexual activity are emotional intimacy and physical pleasure, then the ultimate aim of sexual interaction must be the mutual experience of emotional and physical gratification. This ultimate aim is best served by the parties communicating their desires to the other.

Pineau argues (at 232) that both 'science' and women's own perceptions concur in concluding that aggressive incommunicative sex is not what women want. Where such sex takes place, the rational presumption is that it is not consensual. Pineau goes on to state (at 234):

> [I]t seems to me that there is a presumption in favour of the connection between sex and sexual enjoyment, and that if a man wants to be sure that he is not forcing himself on a woman, he has an obligation either to ensure that the encounter really is mutually enjoyable, or to know the reasons why she would want to continue the encounter in spite of her lack of enjoyment.

A communicative model of sexuality implies that there must be ongoing positive and encouraging responses by both parties. Pineau (at 235) states that sexual interaction should be looked at 'as if it were a proper conversation rather than an offer from the mafia'.

One of the main benefits of a communicative rather than a penetrative/coercive model of sexuality is that the former sees women as agents of their own sexuality rather than simply conforming to a male version of sexual pleasure. It also enables a woman's lack of consent to a man's sexual actions to be respected.

Section 37(a) reinforces this model of communicative sexuality in that it can now be presumed that where communicative sexual interaction does not occur, there is no consent. Instead of focusing on whether or not the complainant resisted or whether or not she was in a fearful or intimidated state of mind, the way is now open for the prosecution to concentrate on what actions the accused took to ensure that there was free agreement to sexual penetration. This jury direction therefore has the potential to change the way in which consent is perceived not only in the courts but also in the wider community.

In reality, however, there is some reason to believe that the penetrative/coercive model of sexuality still holds sway. The legislative equating of consent with free agreement did not receive universal support from those practising law. Most of the solicitors and magistrates interviewed in a study conducted by Melanie Heenan and Helen McKelvie were in favour of the definition of consent: *The Crimes (Rape) Act 1991: An Evaluation Report* (1997) (Melbourne: Department of Justice, 1997) pp 305–8. However, over half the judges interviewed did *not* support the introduction of a legislative definition of consent as set out in s 36 (at 306). Others thought it unnecessary because it did not add anything to the common law and two spoke about the definition being 'a salve to politician's consciences' and 'a reaction to strident feminism' (at 306). Barristers were slightly more accepting of the definition, but were not as welcoming as the solicitors or magistrates. Just over 38 per cent of barristers were in favour of consent being defined, 34 per cent were not in favour and almost 28 per cent were ambivalent about its introduction. In general, and perhaps not surprisingly, most of the barristers in favour of introducing the definition were prosecutors and most of those not in favour were defence counsel (at 302). Of those who did not support the consent definition, some were decidedly cynical. One barrister was quoted as saying: '…it's been framed by people with no experience, who are pushing a political agenda' (at 303).

Thirty per cent of barristers said that the definition had made a difference to the way they ran cases (at 308). Some defence barristers stated that the definition of consent may influence what they say to their client at their initial meeting, particularly where the client is considering pleading guilty. One defence barrister said (at 308): 'Look, its getting to the stage that unless you can demonstrate that the victim, or the main witnesses are actually telling outright lies, and discredit them, so that the jury believes nothing they say, its [sic] virtually impossible to defend.'

This is not borne out in practice: cases are still relatively easy to defend, judging by the low rate of convictions noted earlier. Prosecution barristers referred to the definition as bolstering a lack of consent case. One said the definition made it easier to prove lack of consent, which was 'clearly the intention of the amendment' (at 309).

These attitudes are perhaps understandable given that defence counsel are used to the model of consent as passive acquiescence, whereas prosecutors welcome a view that may make it easier to convict. Attitudes to s 37(a) among barristers are even more sharply dichotomised.

Heenan and McKelvie examined twenty-seven directions to the jury in rape trials in Victoria. Most of the directions involved cases where the primary issue in the trial was consent (37 per cent), the accused's belief in consent (7.4 per cent), or a combination of consent and belief in consent (25.9 per cent) at 296. (The rest of the directions were made in relation to cases where the accused denied there was sexual contact.) The authors found that most judges gave the mandatory directions on consent where relevant, but that there were trials where a small number of judges failed to direct the jury in cases where the mandatory directions arguably ought to have been given (at 298). In particular, the authors identified six trials where judges failed to direct juries that 'saying and doing nothing' ought not to be construed as an indication of consent in circumstances where this direction may have been relevant. This finding implies that the word 'relevance' referred to in s 37 may mean different things to different judges.

Heenan and McKelvie also found that some of the most negative views of judges and legal practitioners regarding the new rape provisions were expressed in relation to s 37(a). Forty-two per cent of barristers (mostly prosecutors) supported or at least had no objection to the introduction of this direction (at 316). However, just under 49 per cent of barristers (mostly defence) objected to or did not support this direction (at 317). Just over half of the judges interviewed also did not approve or had some reservations about this direction. The main criticism was that the direction did not accord with the way in which people relate to one another. One barrister said (at 317): 'I just don't think that accords with human nature and…normal interrelationship…I shouldn't assume other people's experience, but

I hazard a guess that in a vast number of sexual encounters there is nothing said one way or another about agreement or no agreement. It's all done by way of the normal messages that people give each other.'

As stated in the previous section, the communicative model of sexuality is based on an ideal of mutuality in emotional and physical gratification. This ideal may be far from the reality of how sexual intercourse occurs in a society where the penetrative/coercive model of sexuality is still pervasive.

The other criticism put succinctly by one barrister (at 318) is that the direction 'is predicated on there being two equal partners'. A communicative model of sexuality does perhaps best serve men and women who feel at ease with their sexuality and who feel comfortable enough to be able to openly express their wants and desires.

There may also be a further problem with how people perceive what is being communicated. Toni Pickard and Phil Goldman write in *Dimensions of Criminal Law* (Toronto: Emond Montgomery, 1992) p 372: 'Communication is complex, depending not only on the intention behind the words (or gestures), but also on the understanding of the recipient. What the speaker and hearer each understand will be deeply affected by each person's reading of the immediate context into which words are spoken, the larger social context that informs the transaction, the history of the relationship, and prior similar communications between them.'

Lani Anne Remick has suggested that a verbal consent standard may go some way in addressing this problem: 'Read Her Lips: An Argument for a Verbal Consent Standard in Rape' (1993) 141 *University of Pennsylvania Law Review* 1103–51. She argues (at 1144–5) that if consent rests on nonverbal signals, it may often be misinterpreted because both men and women are socialised to accept coercive male sexuality as the norm in sexual behaviour. For example, what is to prevent an accused stating that he thought consent to sexual intercourse was communicated because she accepted a cup of coffee back at his place? There is a whole range of behaviour, such as drinking at a hotel or hitch-hiking and ways of dressing, that has traditionally been viewed as signalling consent to participate in anything and everything, including sexual intercourse. Remick states (at 1148) that an affirmative verbal consent standard would alleviate these misinterpretations of behaviour: '[S]ince verbal messages are the clearest, most unequivocal variety of sexual communication, they are also most likely to lead to desirable sexual encounters.'

It is true, however, that as long as the reality of aggressive, non-communicative sexual intercourse remains, the existence of a legal presumption of non-consent may be unworkable. The question needs to be posed as to whether or not s 37(a) goes too far in trying to impose an ideal standard of consent onto the flawed reality of non-communicative sexual activity.

One of the main arguments that periodically arises against the use of law reform in relation to rape is that the criminal law should not encroach upon 'private' sexual relations between men and women. For example, the Canadian Criminal Lawyers'

Association argued that the 1992 amendments to rape law introduced by Bill C-49 and in particular the new consent provisions would 'contravene the norms of the community' and the criminal law was not the most suitable vehicle for changing sexual relations between men and women: *Submission on Bill C-49*, 1992, at 5:9.

The MCCOC in its Discussion Paper on sexual assault recommended that something akin to s 37(a) be inserted into the Model Criminal Code; *Model Criminal Code, Chapter 5: Sexual Offences Against the Person*, Discussion Paper (November 1996) p 188, cl 38.1(a). However, the Committee's suggestion does not go quite as far as the Victorian provision in establishing a presumption of non-consent, but simply emphasises that a person is not to be regarded as having consented to a sexual act just because the person remained silent or inactive. In its final report (May 1999), the Committee stated (at 265):

> The concern of the Committee is that section 37(a), as drafted, would appear to go some way to establishing a presumption of lack of consent whenever a person did not do or say anything to indicate consent. That can hardly be consistent with the onus borne by the prosecution in criminal trials of proving all elements of the offence (including, of course, the lack of consent of the complainant) beyond reasonable doubt.

A presumption of non-consent as a guide to fact-finding does not in fact challenge the burden of proof as the burden has always been on the prosecution to prove non-consent and that remains the case. It also remains the case that the defence has the evidential burden of raising evidence that there was consent. It is true that s 37(a) challenges the pervasive norms of a penetrative/coercive model of sexuality and in doing so encroaches upon 'private' sexual relations. However, if it is accepted that one of the main purposes of the criminal law is to prevent harm to individuals, then Parliament is entitled to initiate legislation that may challenge certain social attitudes in order to do so.

The main point of difference between those who advocate law reform in this area and those who believe the criminal law should not be used to encroach upon 'private' sexual relations depends upon notions of harm.

For those who believe the penetrative/coercive model of sexuality is 'normal' because it has existed for centuries and arises from some innate biological differences between men and women, which cause men to be dominant and women to be submissive, then no harm can be seen as emanating from such practices.

On the other hand, for those who believe that a penetrative/coercive model of sexuality leads to a denial of women's agency as well as to the idea of aggressive male domination of women as a natural right, the law can be seen as a vehicle for preventing harm to women by defining what is and what is not consensual intercourse.

Brenda M Baker writes that '[b]ecause sexual autonomy is intimately connected with a person's self-conception and self-respect, the importance of protecting it through respecting their [sic] consent or choice in this connection is very great': 'Consent, Assault and Sexual Assault' in Anne Bayefsky (ed), *Legal Theory Meets Legal Practice* (Edmonton: Academic Printing and Publishing, 1988) pp 223–38 at 229. See also SJ Schulhofer, 'Taking Sexual Autonomy Seriously: Rape Law and Beyond' (1992) 11 *Law and Philosophy* 35–94. On this view, acts of non-consensual sexual intercourse not only harm individual victims; they also harm society in that such acts contravene the fundamental right to sexual autonomy.

Given the benefits of a communicative model of sexuality, it should be clear that a regime of law that promotes women's sexual autonomy and freedom of choice is to be preferred. If the law is to continue to be seen and used as an appropriate avenue for controlling sexual assaults, efforts to make the law consistent with women's experiences are necessary. In this sense, the enactment of s 37(a) is a step in the right direction.

Having a standard that consent needs to be communicated benefits both men and women. The presumption that a woman's silence or inactivity is consistent with her sexual fulfilment implies that her partner intuitively knows how to discern her sexual needs correctly. Lani Anne Remick writes that '[t]he "silent is sexy" view of sexual relationships...unrealistically presupposes male sexual omniscience': 'Read Her Lips: An Argument For a Verbal Consent Standard in Rape' (1993) 141 *University of Pennsylvania Law Review* 1103–51 at 1150. Mutual sexual enjoyment requires communication and this takes the pressure away from men to have to intuit what their partners want. The communicative model of sexuality is of course not confined to heterosexual activity but is based on respect for individual sexual autonomy and mutuality in emotional and physical gratification in whatever form that may take.

Fraud and consent

Another problematic area is that of the effect of fraud on consent. In the Australian Capital Territory and Western Australia, consent is negated when obtained by fraudulent means: *Crimes Act* 1900 (ACT) s 92P(1)(g); *Criminal Code* (WA) s 319(2). As outlined previously, the other Australian jurisdictions limit fraud to situations where the victim is mistaken about the identity of the accused or the nature and character of the act. Other types of fraud will not negate consent.

In *Papadimitropoulos v The Queen* (1957) 98 CLR 249 the victim, who had recently arrived in Australia from Greece, had sexual intercourse with the accused after he fraudulently told her that they were married. In fact, they had gone to the Melbourne Registry Office where the accused had given notice of their intention to marry. There was some evidence that the victim never intended to consent to sexual intercourse outside marriage. The accused deserted the woman soon afterwards. The matter was reported to the police and the accused was charged and convicted of rape. The accused successfully appealed the conviction before the High Court.

The High Court's reasoning as to why the fraudulent procurement of sexual intercourse in *Papadimitropoulos* was not rape focused on the fact that the victim understood the nature and character of the act and knew the identity of the accused. The Court held (at 261) that consent to sexual intercourse requires 'a perception as to what is about to take place, as to the identity of the man and the character of what he is doing. But once the consent is comprehending and actual the inducing causes cannot destroy its reality and leave the man guilty of rape'.

Subsequently, this decision was reversed by statute in New South Wales where consent can now be negated if a person consents to intercourse under a mistaken belief that the other person is married to the person: *Crimes Act* 1900 (NSW) s 61R(2)(a)(ii). While sexual intercourse procured by fraudulent means in general is not considered rape in jurisdictions other than the Australian Capital Territory, New South Wales and Western Australia, the accused in *Papadimitropoulos* could now be prosecuted under a lesser offence: *Criminal Code* (Qld) s 218; *Criminal Law Consolidation Act* 1935 (SA) s 64(b); *Criminal Code* (Tas) s 129(b); *Crimes Act* 1958 (Vic) s 57; *Criminal Code* (WA) s 192. In New South Wales, the offence of procuring carnal knowledge by fraud has been abolished, but consent will be negated where the victim consents under a mistaken belief about the nature of the act induced by fraudulent means: *Crimes Amendment (Sexual Offences) Act* 2003, Sch 1.

The decision in *Papadimitropoulos* focuses on whether or not the victim made a mistake. That is, only if the victim is mistaken as to the nature and character of the act or the identity of the accused will consent be negated in most jurisdictions in relation to the crime of rape. In comparison, in Canada, the courts have continued to focus on the accused's dishonesty or deception as a basis for negating consent to sexual intercourse: *R v Cuerrier* [1998] 2 SCR 371.

The Australian approach of focusing on the victim's mistake rather than the fraud of the accused was also taken by the Victorian Supreme Court in *R v Mobilio* [1991] 1 VR 339. In that case, a radiographer used an instrument to perform internal examinations of the vaginas of a number of victims for his own gratification and not for any medical purpose. He was charged and a jury convicted him of a number of counts of rape. These convictions were overturned on appeal on the basis that each woman had understood the nature of the physical act. Again, the focus was on the victim's belief rather than the accused's fraud. Some jurisdictions have subsequently overturned the decision in *Mobilio* via statute. Consent may be negated in New South Wales, the Northern Territory, South Australia and Victoria by a mistaken belief that the act is for medical or hygienic purposes: *Crimes Act* 1900 (NSW) s 61R(2)(a1); *Criminal Code* (NT) s 192(2)(f); *Criminal Law Consolidation Act* 1935 (SA) s 73(5); *Crimes Act* 1958 (Vic) s 36(g).

The common law approach to the type of fraud that may negate consent shows how the scope and meaning of consent is affected by what one considers to be 'real' rape. If consent means free agreement to sexual intercourse, then surely there is no free agreement if the person is not fully informed about the circumstances of sexual intercourse. If a person is defrauded into consenting, that consent is not fully informed or free: V Waye, 'Rape and the Unconscionable Bargain' (1991) 16 Crim LJ 94–105. The problem of course is where to draw the line. If a person lies about their personal characteristics to procure sexual intercourse, or promises love or marriage, should consent be negated? Would giving a worthless cheque to a prostitute deem prior sexual intercourse to be rape?

The MCCOC decided to confine fraud as negating consent to situations where 'the person is incapable of understanding the essential nature of the act', or 'the person is mistaken about the essential nature of the act' (for example, the person mistakenly believes that the act is for medical or hygienic purposes): *Chapter 5, Sexual Offences Against the Person*, Report (May 1999) p 38. It is unclear as to whether an incapacity or mistake as to the 'essential nature' of the act is the same as the common law reference to the 'nature or character' of the act.

The Committee was of the view (at 49) that 'to mandate the extension of the negation of consent to consent obtained by *any* type of fraud undermines the seriousness of the offence'. Similarly, the Victorian Law Reform Commission has suggested that some types of fraudulent conduct in relation to procuring sexual intercourse should be considered 'immoral', but should not be treated as criminal: *Sexual Offences: Law and Procedure*, Discussion Paper (Melbourne: VLRC, 2001) p 61.

Legislatively setting out the types of mistake that may negate consent certainly is of benefit to juries faced with deciding whether consent existed. However, why should the fraud perpetrated in the *Mobilio* scenario negate consent and not the fraud perpetrated in *Papadimitropoulos*? What is clear is that the decision to recognise the negation of consent through fraud in some instances and not in others is heavily influenced by social and political notions of what constitutes 'real' rape.

The current law—fault elements

Intention and recklessness

As previously stated, most rape trials centre upon the construction of consent in relation to the outward or external circumstances of the crime of rape. The question of whether or not consent has occurred is generally taken as something that can be measured 'objectively' by looking at the complainant's conduct.

In New South Wales, Victoria, South Australia and the Australian Capital Territory, the prosecution must prove an added fault element: namely, that the accused intended to have sexual intercourse with the victim knowing or believing that it was without the other person's consent or being reckless as to the issue of consent: *Crimes Act* 1900 (ACT) s 92D; *Criminal Law Consolidation Act* 1935 (SA) s 48; *Crimes Act* 1900 (NSW) s 61D(2); *Crimes Act* 1958 (Vic) s 38. It is difficult to envisage a scenario where sexual intercourse was unintended once the physical element of sexual intercourse has been established. The main focus for the prosecution lies in proving knowledge of non-consent or recklessness thereto.

In the criminal codes of the Northern Territory, Queensland, Tasmania and Western Australia, there is no reference to belief, awareness or knowledge in the definitions of rape. What needs to be proved is that the accused intended to have sexual intercourse with the victim. Belief only becomes relevant if the accused argues a mistaken belief in consent.

In relation to indecent assault, in all Australian jurisdictions the prosecution must prove that the accused intentionally or recklessly touched the victim's body or intentionally or recklessly threatened that unlawful force would be applied: *R v Venna* [1975] 3 WLR 737; *R v McIver* (1928) 22 QJPR 173; *R v Vallance* [1960] Tas SR 51; *Wilkinson* (1985) 20 A Crim R 230; *Drago v The Queen* (1992) 8 WAR 488.

In the common law jurisdictions, two further matters must be established. First, as with rape in these jurisdictions, the indecent assault must have occurred with a knowledge or belief that the victim was not consenting or recklessness thereto: *R v Kimber* [1983] 1 WLR 1118; *R v Bonora* (1994) 35 NSWLR 74 at 80 per Abadee J.

Secondly, the prosecution must prove that the accused intended to commit an assault that is indecent: *R v Court* [1989] AC 28. In this regard, the act forming the charge usually has obvious sexual connotations and the question of whether the accused intended that the act should be indecent will rarely be in issue: *R v Court* [1989] AC 28 at 42–3 per Lord Ackner.

There is some discrepancy as to the meaning of recklessness in the common law jurisdictions in relation to rape and indecent assault. In Victoria recklessness for both rape and indecent assault is statutorily defined as awareness that the person *might* not be consenting, indicating that the accused must have turned his or her mind to the matter. Similarly, the South Australian requirement of 'reckless indifference' has been held to require proof that the accused 'realised the woman might not be consenting and that he, in spite of such realization, recklessly pushed on with intercourse without resolving the doubt': *Egan* (1985) 15 A Crim R 20 at 44 per White J. In *Athanasiadis* (1990) 51 A Crim R 292, King CJ held that an accused may be recklessly indifferent to the issue of consent where the accused has sexual intercourse not caring whether or not the victim has consented.

The expression 'might not be consenting' has been interpreted as meaning that the accused was aware that there was a *possibility* (not probability) that the other person was not consenting: *R v Costa* unreported, 2 April 1996, CA of SC of Vic, Phillips CJ, Callaway JA and Southwell AJA; *Helmsley* (1988) 36 A Crim R 334.

In New South Wales, recklessness goes one step further. As mentioned in Chapter 2, in *R v Kitchener* (1993) 29 NSWLR 696 and *R v Tolmie* (1995) 37 NSWLR 660, the New South Wales Court of Criminal Appeal held that a complete failure to advert to whether or not a person is consenting to sexual intercourse amounts to recklessness. Kirby P (as he then was) stated in *Kitchener* (at 697): 'To criminalise conscious advertence to the possibility of non-consent, but to excuse the reckless failure of the accused to give a moment's thought to that possibility, is self-evidently unacceptable. In the hierarchy of wrongdoing, such total indifference to the consent of the person to have sexual intercourse is plainly reckless, at least in our society today.' This broad definition of recklessness has also been applied in New South Wales to the offence of indecent assault: *Fitzgerald v Kennard* (1995) 38 NSWLR 184.

The MCCOC has recommended that recklessness include 'not giving any thought to whether or not the other person is consenting to sexual penetration': *Chapter 5, Sexual Offences Against the Person*, Report (May 1999) p 88. The Victorian Law Reform Commission has also suggested that because the level of moral culpability is similar, recklessness should cover failure to advert to whether or not the other person was consenting as well as awareness that the other person might not be consenting: *Sexual Offences: Law and Procedure*, Discussion Paper (Melbourne: VLRC, 2001) p 71. However, as the Commission points out (at 71): 'In practice, it probably has little effect on the outcome of trials. Juries are unlikely to believe an accused who says that he gave no thought to whether the complainant consented to sexual penetration.'

A mistaken belief in consent

It will be recalled from the case presented at the beginning of this chapter, that on appeal, Abel wished to argue that Jane may not have been consenting to sexual intercourse, but he honestly believed that she was. This argument, if accepted, may be raised to negate the fault element that the accused knew that the complainant was not or might not be consenting.

The main question in mistaken belief cases is whether or not the defence has the evidential burden of raising only an 'honest' but mistaken belief or should be required to produce evidence of an honest *and* reasonable but mistaken belief. In the common law jurisdictions, the defence need only raise evidence of an honest belief in order to negate the fault element. This is a purely subjective test. The question is simply: Did the accused honestly believe that the other person was consenting? In the Code jurisdictions, on the other hand, the belief must not only be honestly held, it must also be reasonable. This imposes an objective standard.

The main case that governs the law in New South Wales, South Australia, Victoria (s 37(c) of the *Crimes Act* 1958 (Vic) parallels the common law) and the Australian Capital Territory is the House of Lords decision in *DPP v Morgan* [1976] AC 182. In that case, Morgan invited three men, who were younger and more junior to him in rank in the Royal Air Force, to have sex with his wife. According to the men, Morgan had told them they must not be surprised if his wife struggled a bit because she was 'kinky' and this was the only way in which she could become 'turned on'. They admitted that the victim had indeed struggled and screamed for help to her young sons when they had held her down and each had intercourse with her, but claimed that they honestly believed she was consenting. The three men were convicted of rape, and Morgan, of aiding and abetting them. (Even though Morgan also had intercourse with his wife without her consent, he was not charged with rape as in 1976 a man could not be charged with raping his wife.)

On appeal to the House of Lords on a point of law, a majority of three to two held that if an accused honestly believes that the other person is consenting, no rape has occurred. The belief need not be reasonable. On the facts, however, the majority held that it would have been extremely unlikely that any jury would have accepted that the accused men honestly believed the victim was consenting and upheld their convictions.

In Canada, the law has developed such that the honest but mistaken belief must have 'an air of reality' to satisfy the evidentiary burden. In *R v Osolin* [1993] 4 SCR 595 at 648–9, McLachlin J stated:

> Theoretically, such a belief could be asserted in every case, even where it is totally at odds with the evidence as to what happened. So it has been held that the bare assertion of the accused that he believed in consent is not enough to raise the defence of honest but mistaken belief; the assertion must be 'supported to some degree by other evidence or circumstances': *R. v Bulmer*, [1987] 1 S.C.R. 782, at p 790. The support may come from the accused or other sources... .

Although the courts have not developed such a test in the Australian common law jurisdictions, on a practical level it would seem that an accused's claim of honest but mistaken belief in consent should have an air of reality to it for it to be accepted by a jury. For example, s 37(1)(c) of the *Crimes Act* 1958 (Vic) requires a jury to take into account reasonableness in assessing whether or not the accused had the requisite belief.

Critique

It should be kept in mind that a mistaken belief in consent is raised in sexual assault trials very rarely. In the studies of rape prosecutions in Victoria, an accused argued a mistaken belief in consent in six per cent of cases conducted in 1989: Law Reform Commission of Victoria, *Rape: Reform of Law and Procedure*, Appendixes to Interim Report No 42 (Melbourne: LRCV, 1991) Appendix 3, p 87, and only 2.2 per cent of cases conducted in 1992–93: M Heenan and H McKelvie, *Rape Law Reform Evaluation Project*, Report No 2: *The Crimes (Rape) Act 1991: An Evaluation Project* (Melbourne: Department of Justice, 1997) p 46. These percentages are perhaps so low because the accused is conceding that there was no consent. This is therefore a risky argument to run. In a further 17 per cent of cases conducted in 1989: LRCV, 1991, Appendix 3, p 87, and 3.6 per cent of cases conducted in

1992–93: Heenan and McKelvie, 1991, at 46, the defence swung between claiming that the complainant consented to claiming that even if there was no consent, the accused honestly believed the complainant was consenting.

In *R v Esau* [1997] 2 SCR 777, the majority of the Supreme Court of Canada concluded that there was enough evidence to give an air of reality to Abel's claim that he had honestly but mistakenly believed that Jane was consenting. The majority judgment was delivered by Major J who stated (at 787–8):

> [Abel] described specific words and actions on the part of the complainant that led him to believe that she was consenting. This alone may be enough to raise the defence. However there was more. The complainant's evidence did not contradict that of the respondent, as she cannot remember what occurred after she went to her bedroom. In addition there was no evidence of violence, no evidence of a struggle and no evidence of force.

Interestingly, the two female judges, L'Heureux Dubé and McLachlin JJ dissented and held that there was not a sufficient air of reality to the accused's claim of an honest but mistaken belief in consent. McLachlin J was of the view that the absence of resistance was not enough to raise evidence of such a belief. She stated (at 812) that '[a]n accused who infers consent from passivity without more makes a dishonest, irresponsible inference'. She concluded (at 812) that 'one is invited to speculatively infer a situation of ambiguity in the absence of any supporting evidence and contrary to the only existing evidence'. McLachlin J stated that the facts raised only two scenarios: that Jane was drunk and did not consent or that she was able to control her actions and did consent. These two scenarios did not allow for any situation of ambiguity or misunderstanding.

The majority and minority approaches to the facts of *Esau*'s case suggest that an honest but mistaken belief in consent may be viewed very differently according to whether or not a communicative approach to the meaning of consent is taken. Both L'Heureux Dubé and McLachlin JJ have been at the forefront of suggesting that consent must be unequivocally communicated. The evidence led that Jane was drunk suggested she had not consented and there was no ambiguity as to her lack of consent.

Both the Victorian Law Reform Commission and the MCCOC have examined the principle in *Morgan*'s case, and both bodies have accepted that this is good law: Law Reform Commission of Victoria, *Rape: Reform of Law and Procedure*, Report No 43 (Melbourne: LRCV, 1991) p 18; Model Criminal Code Officers Committee of The Standing Committee of Attorneys-General, *Model Criminal Code, Chapter 5: Sexual Offences Against the Person*, Discussion Paper (November 1996) p 75. The reasons for accepting *Morgan* are first, having a subjective fault element accords with the fundamental principles of criminal responsibility; secondly, it is too difficult to formulate an objective test of reasonableness in rape trials; thirdly, the adoption of an objective standard would have little effect on trial outcomes because so few accused raise mistaken belief as a defence; and finally, reasonableness can nevertheless be taken into account in assessing whether or not the accused in reality honestly believed the other person was consenting. In regard to the latter argument, it is said that the more unreasonable the accused's alleged mistake, the less likely a jury will accept it.

The primary argument against the principle in *Morgan* that an accused's belief in consent need only be honest is that it allows men to adhere to outdated notions about sexual behaviour and female sexuality. Following this argument, a move towards reflecting a communicative model of sexuality in the law will be impeded if it is still open to an accused to argue that he honestly believed the complainant was consenting because she failed to offer resistance or because she remained silent.

The Code jurisdictions have long accepted that the accused's belief in consent must not only be honest but also reasonable and there have been no obvious difficulties in this regard. As will be explored in the next section, statutory sexual offences against children and young people allow a defence of honest and reasonable mistake as to the age of the child. If this is allowed in relation to one category of sexual offences, why not others? Lord Simon of Glaisdale, one of the dissenting judges in *Morgan*'s case has stated (at 203) that a requirement that a belief in consent be reasonable is necessary on public policy grounds: '[I]t can be argued with force that it is only fair to the woman and not in the least unfair to the man that he take care to ascertain that she is consenting to the intercourse and be at risk of a prosecution if he fails to take care.'

Whether or not the law should restrict the mistaken view of consent to one that is reasonable will depend upon whether or not one takes a 'subjectivist' view of the law in believing that all serious crimes must have a subjective fault element. A compromise approach is to have some form of reasonableness required although not necessarily as to the belief.

One way around the subjective/objective dichotomy is to try for a midway point between the two. What the Canadian legislature has done is to enact a provision (*Criminal Code* (Can) s 273.2) stating that mistaken belief is not available where 'the accused did not take reasonable steps in the circumstances known to the accused at the time, to ascertain that the complainant was consenting'. This is one way of putting an objective gloss on mistaken belief without going as far as requiring the belief to be reasonable. As Jennifer Temkin has pointed out in *Rape and the Legal Process* (2nd edn, Oxford: Oxford University Press, 2002) p 134: 'the Canadian law goes a long way towards importing a requirement of reasonableness into the law without formally doing so'.

The Canadian approach is a compromise that, if taken with a consent standard that requires communication, may go some way in combating stereotypes of failure to resist as consent. Of course as the decision in *Esau*'s case demonstrates, how the mistaken belief will be interpreted will reflect judges' and juries' approaches to such stereotypes.

Sexual offences against children and young people

Background

When she was aged between 10 and 13, 'Toni's' father began touching her on the breasts and vagina, and on occasion inserted his finger or tongue in her vagina. When Toni's sister 'Sarah' was 12 (the complainants are referred to as T and S in the report), the father began touching her vagina. The father did not attempt penile penetration and did not persist with the sexual abuse after the girls reached puberty.

Toni was able to recall three incidents in particular and Sarah two, but the sentencing judge accepted that these incidents represented a continuing course of sexual conduct: *F* (1998) 101 A Crim R 578 at 581. There was some evidence that Toni and Sarah were also abused by another family member and it was in discussing this some twenty years after the abuse by their father, that they began talking about what their father had done. Up until then, they had avoided referring to their father's abuse of them.

When the father was confronted in 1990 with what he had done, he accepted responsibility. The matter, however, was not pursued legally until some years later and he eventually pleaded guilty to five counts of indecent assault on his two daughters that had occurred between January 1976 and February 1981.

The father was sentenced to imprisonment for a period of sixteen months with twelve months suspended upon condition that he commit no further offence involving sexual misconduct for a period of four years.

The report of the sentence in this matter hints at some of the emotional devastation wrought by the father's conduct as well as its subsequent revelation. The family unit broke down, the father attempted suicide, his daughters, still suffering from anxiety and stress, asked for 'justice' rather than retribution and expressed the hope that their father would not be given a harsh sanction. The sentencing judge, Slicer J, referred (at 580) to the daughters' 'complex and mixed emotional responses to their offending parent'.

The father in this case was charged with indecent assault. The facts would today give rise to a charge of rape. Indecent assault, as with rape, may be prosecuted where the victim is a child or young person. However, there are specific offences that aim to protect young people and that make any question of consent irrelevant. The rationale behind this is concisely expressed by the Victorian Law Reform Commission in *Sexual Offences: Law and Procedure*, Discussion Paper (Melbourne: VLRC, 2001) p 83:

> Premature involvement in sexual activity often harms children physically and psychologically. Victims of childhood sexual abuse often experience long-term effects, including low self-esteem and self-abuse, which significantly damage their lives. Where abuse involves a breach of trust by an older family member or a person in

authority over the child, its long-term consequences may be psychologically devastating. While it is expected that adolescents will be involved in some sexual activity, the current law reflects the view that there should be safeguards against sexual exploitation of adolescents by adults who take advantage of young people's immaturity and dependency. [Footnotes omitted.]

In *F*'s case, the father pleaded guilty. Cases that go to trial may be difficult to prove because of the lapse of years between the abuse and the victim's decision to report it. This is exemplified by the case of *S v The Queen* (1989) 168 CLR 266. The complainant gave evidence that her father had started sexually abusing her when she was about nine. He had begun to have sexual intercourse with her when she was about 14 and continued to do so approximately every two months until she left home at the age of 17. In her evidence, she was only able to give details of two specific occasions when her father had sexual intercourse with her. One occasion was when she was 14, but she was unsure whether it occurred in 1979 or 1980. Similarly, she remembered details of another occasion, but could not remember whether or not it occurred in 1980, 1981 or 1982. The accused was convicted, but appealed successfully to the High Court.

The High Court held that the prosecution had to identify with certainty the occasions that were alleged to give rise to the offences. Failure to do so could deprive the accused of the opportunity to defend himself adequately. The irony of this approach was pointed out in *Podinsky v The Queen* (1990) 3 WAR 128 at 136 where it was stated that 'there is a possibility that the more acts of intercourse or other acts of sexual abuse and the greater the length of time over which they occur, the more difficult it may be to establish that any one of a series of multiple offences has been committed'.

As a response to the problems associated with proving offences that may have occurred many years previously, some jurisdictions have enacted provisions making it an offence to maintain a sexual relationship with a child under a certain age. These will be referred to in the section on the current law. Other jurisdictions have relaxed evidentiary requirements regarding proof of individual events.

The main problems with sexual offences against children and young persons are the different agendas they reveal (control of adolescent sexuality as against the protection of the young from exploitation and abuse), the discrepancies that occur between jurisdictions as to the age of consent, the defences that may apply and the degree of overlap between offences. In relation to the latter, the father in *F*'s case could have been charged with indecent assault or indecent acts against a child or maintaining a sexual relationship with a child. The crime of incest also substantially overlaps with the offences of rape and sexual intercourse with a child. Choosing which offence with which to prosecute the accused may have repercussions for problems of proof and sentencing. These issues will be explored in the Critique section below.

The current law

Sexual intercourse with a young person is an offence in all Australian jurisdictions. The common physical element between this offence and that of rape is that sexual intercourse must be proven. However, the major difference is that consent is not an element of the offence.

The age at which a young person can consent to intercourse varies across Australian jurisdictions. In the Australian Capital Territory and Victoria, sexual intercourse with a person under the age of 16 is a criminal offence: *Crimes Act* 1900 (ACT) ss 2E(2), 92E(2); *Crimes Act* 1958 (Vic) s 46(1). Similar provisions in South Australia and Tasmania make it an offence to have sexual intercourse with a person under the age of 17: *Criminal Law Consolidation Act* (1935) s 49(3); *Criminal Code* (Tas) s 124.

In New South Wales, heterosexual intercourse is unlawful if the person is under the age of 16 (*Crimes Act* 1900 (NSW) s 66C). Until 2003, homosexual intercourse, including anal penetration and fellatio, was unlawful with a male under the age of 18. Schedule 1 of the *Crimes Amendment (Sexual Offences) Act* 2003 (NSW) introduced formal equality for the 'age of consent', reducing it from 18 to 16 for both heterosexual and homosexual intercourse. This legislation was voted on according to conscience rather than along party lines. In Western Australia, it is an offence to have heterosexual intercourse with a person under the age of 16 (*Criminal Code* (WA) s 321), but a male adult who penetrates a male between the age of 16 and 21 years or who allows the latter to penetrate him is guilty of a crime (s 322A).

In Queensland, it is an offence to have carnal knowledge of a girl under the age of 16 (*Criminal Code* (Qld) s 215(1)), but it is an offence to have anal intercourse with a male or female person under the age of 18 (s 208(1)). Finally, in the Northern Territory, it is an offence to have sexual intercourse with a female aged under 16 years (*Criminal Code* (NT) s 133), but an offence for a male to have sexual intercourse with another male aged under 18 (s 128(1)(a)).

In some jurisdictions, there is also a different age of consent where the accused is in a position of trust or authority in relation to the victim. For example, in South Australia and Victoria, a guardian, schoolmaster, schoolmistress or teacher or, in Victoria, one who has the 'care, supervision or authority' of the young person, must not have sexual intercourse with a person under the age of 18: *Criminal Law Consolidation Act* 1935 (SA) s 49(5); *Crimes Act* 1958 (Vic). Similarly, in New South Wales, it is now an offence for a person to have sexual intercourse with a child between the age of 16 and 18 who is under his or her 'special care'; *Crimes Act* 1900 (NSW) s 73. The victim is deemed to be under the special care of the offender where the latter is a step-parent, guardian, foster parent, school teacher, custodial officer, health professional or where he or she has an established personal relationship with the victim in connection with the provision of religious, sporting, musical or other instruction to the victim.

There are also specific provisions criminalising indecent, non-penetrative acts against children and young persons that also refer to different ages of consent: *Crimes Act* 1900 (ACT) ss 92K(1), 92K(2); *Crimes Act* 1900 (NSW) ss 61M(3)(b), 78Q; *Criminal Code* (NT) ss 128(1)(b), 129(1)(b), 132(2); *Criminal Code* (Qld) s 210; *Criminal Law Consolidation Act* 1935 (SA) s 58; *Criminal Code* (Tas) s 125B; *Crimes Act* 1958 (Vic) ss 47, 49; *Criminal Code* (WA) ss 320(4), 321(4).

There are three statutory defences to these general provisions. Consent or lack of consent is not relevant to proof of these offences. The first statutory defence concerns the similarity of age between the accused and the other young person. In the Australian Capital Territory and Victoria, where the child is aged between 10 and 16, it is a defence that the accused was not more than two years older than the child: *Crimes Act* 1900 (ACT) s 92E(2), (3); *Crimes Act* 1958 (Vic) s 46. In South Australia, it is a defence where the accused is under 17 and the other person is 16: *Criminal Law Consolidation Act* 1935 (SA) s 49(4). In Tasmania, where the young person is 15 or over, it is a defence that the accused is not more than five years older, and where the young person is aged 12 to 14, it is a defence that the accused is not more than three years older: *Criminal Code* (Tas) s 124(3).

A second defence is available in certain circumstances where the accused is married or believes on reasonable grounds that he or she is married to the young person in question. For example, in Victoria, this is a defence to sexual penetration of a young person under 18: *Crimes Act* 1958 (Vic) ss 58, 60(1). In Western Australia, the defence applies where the child is aged 13 to 16: *Criminal Code* (WA) s 321(10). In South Australia, the defence applies where the child is aged between 12 and 17: *Criminal Law Consolidation Act* 1935 (SA) s 49(8). Finally, the Northern Territory makes it an offence to 'unlawfully' have sexual intercourse with a female under the age of 16: *Criminal Code* (NT) s 129. The term 'unlawfully' is defined and means that the parties to the act are not husband and wife: *Criminal Code* (NT) s 126.

This defence is a restricted one in that s 11 of the *Marriage Act* 1961 (Cth) sets the age for marriage at 18. A person may marry at 16 with parental consent and by judicial order where there are 'exceptional circumstances': ss 11, 12.

The final defence allowable in all jurisdictions to offences of sexual intercourse and indecent assault with a child or young person is that of mistake as to the child's age. The belief must be a reasonable one. In the Australian Capital Territory and Victoria, this defence is available where the child is aged between 10 and 16 and the accused believed the child was 16 or over: *Crimes Act* 1900 (ACT) s 92E(2)–(3); *Crimes Act* 1958 (Vic) s 46. In New South Wales, the defence is available where the child was over 14 years and the accused believed he or she was 16 or over: *Crimes Act* 1900 (NSW) s 77.

In the Northern Territory, the defence applies where the accused thought the female was 16 or over: *Criminal Code* (NT) s 129(3). In Queensland, it is a defence to a charge of anal intercourse that the accused reasonably believed the other person to be aged 18 or over. It is also a defence to a charge of carnal knowledge (excluding sodomy) of a child under the age of 16 that the accused believed him or her to be 16 or older: *Criminal Code* (Qld) ss 208, 215(5). In South Australia, the defence applies where the child is aged between 12 and 17 and the accused believed the child was aged 17 or over: *Criminal Law Consolidation Act* 1935 (SA) s 49(4). In Western Australia, it applies where the child is aged between 12 and 16 and the accused believed the child was 16: *Criminal Code* (WA) s 321(9).

As outlined in the Background section, the High Court in *S v The Queen* (1989) 168 CLR 266, held that where multiple sexual assaults against children are alleged to have occurred, the prosecution must give particulars of the offences charged. Because it may be difficult for a complainant to recall exact details of when and where each act occurred, each jurisdiction has enacted offences dealing with 'persistent sexual abuse of a child': *Crimes Act* 1900 (ACT) s 92EA; *Crimes Act* 1900 (NSW) s 66EA; *Criminal Code* (NT) s 131A; *Criminal Code* (Qld) s 229B; *Criminal Law Consolidation Act* 1935 (SA) s 74; *Criminal Code* (Tas) s 125A; *Crimes Act* 1958 (Vic) s 47A; *Criminal Code* (WA) s 321A.

These provisions enable the prosecution to charge an accused with having a 'sexual relationship' with a child over a period of time. There must be a number of occasions when the sexual assaults occurred, but the prosecution need not specify the times, dates or circumstances of the acts.

A further crime that can be considered here is that of incest. All Australian jurisdictions criminalise sexual intercourse between persons who are related to one another, although the prohibited relationships vary. South Australia has the most limited provision as it prohibits sexual intercourse between parent and child and brother and sister: *Criminal Law Consolidation Act* 1935 (SA) s 72. In New South Wales, the term 'close family member' is used and it extends to grandparents and grandchildren: *Crimes Act* 1900 s 78A. The other jurisdictions generally refer to 'lineal descendants', emphasising the blood relationship between the two persons concerned: *Crimes Act* 1900 (ACT) s 92L; *Criminal Code* (NT) ss 134, 135; *Criminal Code* (Qld) s 222; *Criminal Code* (Tas) ss 133(1)–(2); *Crimes Act* 1958 (Vic) s 44; *Criminal Code* (WA) s 329. In New South Wales, Tasmania and Victoria sexual intercourse between half-brother and half-sister is prohibited: *Crimes Act* 1900 (NSW) s 78A; *Criminal Code* (Tas) s 133(4); *Crimes Act* 1958 (Vic) s 44(4). The Australian Capital Territory and Victoria go beyond the blood ties approach to also prohibit sexual intercourse with a step-child: *Crimes Act* 1900 (ACT) s 92L(7); *Crimes Act* 1958 (Vic) ss 44(1), (2).

The prosecution must prove that the accused knew of the lineal relationship at the time of the sexual intercourse. In the Australian Capital Territory, Victoria and Western Australia, there is a presumption that the accused knew of the relationship and it is up to the accused to raise evidence to the contrary: *Crimes Act* 1900 (ACT) s 92L(6); *Crimes Act* 1958 (Vic) s 44(7)(a); *Criminal Code* (WA) s 329(11)(a). The offence of incest applies to both people involved, although coercion is a defence.

Critique

The age of consent

Deciding when a young person is capable of consenting to sexual intercourse involves a balancing act between protecting the person from harm and recognising the right to sexual autonomy. Establishing an age of consent to sexual intercourse will always be difficult and the MCCOC, after initially recommending that the age of consent be sixteen in its Discussion Paper, ended up not recommending a precise age at which the age of consent should be set: *Chapter 5: Sexual Offences Against the Person*, Report (May 1999) p 123. It did state (at 123) that the age of consent should be uniform regardless of the nature of the sexual conduct, whether or not it be 'straight, male homosexual or lesbian'.

In 1977, the Royal Commission on Human Relationships recommended that where an offender had a relationship of trust or authority with the victim, the age of consent should be 17, but otherwise it should be 15: *Royal Commission on Human Relationships*, Final Report (Canberra: AGPS, 1977) Vol 5. The Commission stated at 210: 'We think this approach would be a more realistic reflection of the sexual behaviour of young people and their ability to make personal decisions. At this age children can leave school, get jobs and start playing a responsible role in society.'

Most of the submissions to the MCCOC supported 16 years as a uniform age of consent, but religious organisations such as the Social Issues Committee of the Anglican Diocese of Sydney and the Australian Christian Coalition wanted to set the age of consent at 18 and the latter wanted the age of consent for homosexual intercourse to be 21.

Sixteen is the age of consent for heterosexual intercourse in most Australian jurisdictions and since the laws have been operating in this area for some time it would seem unnecessary to lower the age to 15 or raise it to 18.

The age of consent for homosexual intercourse is always going to be a politically sensitive question, as experienced in Britain in recent years. In *Sutherland v United Kingdom* (1997) 24 EHRR CD22–CD35, the European Commission of Human Rights found the different ages for homosexual and heterosexual intercourse in the UK to be in breach of Article 8 of the European Convention on Human Rights, which sets out the right to respect for private and family life, taken in conjunction with Article 14, which prohibits discrimination. However, efforts by Tony Blair's Labour Government to reduce the age of consent for homosexual intercourse to 16 in order to conform with the heterosexual age of consent were repeatedly thwarted by the conservative House of Lords.

In November 2000, the House of Lords voted by 205 to 144 against a provision in the Sexual Offences (Amendment) Bill to lower the age of consent for homosexual intercourse. The government subsequently circumvented the House of Lords by invoking the rarely used *Parliament Acts* 1911 and 1949, and the *Sexual Offences (Amendment) Act* 2000 (UK) received Royal Assent on 30 November 2000 (ironically, the hundred year anniversary of the death of Oscar Wilde) and came into force on 8 January 2001: JP Burnside, 'The Sexual Offences (Amendment) Act 2000: The Head of a "Kiddy-Libber" and the Torso of a "Child-Saver"' [2001] Crim LR 425–34.

There does appear to be a trend towards adopting a 'neutral' stance between homosexual and heterosexual offenders. The MCCOC has proposed (at 19) that there be no special homosexual offences included in the Model Criminal Code. It would seem then that law reform efforts are leading towards a uniform age of consent. There is no logic in differentiating between heterosexual and homosexual relations in terms of what society will 'allow'. The discrepancies that currently exist are untenable and should be removed.

Defences

At present, the defences of similarity of age, belief in marriage and mistake as to the child's age do not apply when the child is under a certain age. This ranges from 10 years in Victoria and the Australian Capital Territory (*Crimes Act* 1958 (Vic) s 45; *Crimes Act* 1900 (ACT) s 92E(1)) to 16 years for females and 18 for males in Queensland (*Criminal Code* (Qld) ss 215, 208).

The MCCOC initially recommended that the age below which no defence is allowable should be 10 years: *Chapter 5: Sexual Offences Against the Person*, Discussion Paper (November 1996) p 105. This proposal received strong criticism, but on the basis that people mistakenly thought this was to be the age of consent. Consent is not a defence to these provisions and the recommendation simply meant that the three defences listed above would not be available unless the child was 10 or over. In its Final Report (May 1999 at 127) the Committee decided not to recommend a 'no defence age' in line with not recommending an age of consent. If the child is 10, it would be exceptionally difficult to accept a claim to an honest and reasonable mistake of age, and the defence of belief in marriage would be nonsensical. The real issue is whether sexual experimentation by those aged 10 to 16 should be criminalised where the ages of the parties involved are similar.

The MCCOC recommended that the Model Criminal Code follow the model of Victoria and the Australian Capital Territory in allowing a defence where the 'victim' is aged 10 to 16 and the accused is no more than two years older than the child: *Chapter 5, Sexual Offences Against the Person*, Report (May 1999) p 151. This was on the basis that it reflected the reality that consensual sexual activity does take place between those under the age of consent and that such conduct should not automatically be considered criminal. The Committee stated (at 151) that 'this defence operates to ensure the offences are used for their main purpose, aimed at paedophiles and other adults having sex with children'. While there may be disagreement as to 10 years being the age as to when such a defence may be raised, the rationale for having such a defence seems reasonable.

If the age of consent is set at 16, the defence of belief in marriage seems redundant given that the age of consent to marriage is 18, with some latitude available for those between the ages of 16 and 18. However, the MCCOC recommended (at 147) this defence be retained and that it take into account Aboriginal customary marriages where parties may be under the legal age of consent to marriage.

One recent case that touched on this defence was the case of *Hales v Jamilmira* unreported, 15 April 2003, CA of NT, [2003] NTCA 9. Jackie Pascoe Jamilmira, aged 49, was charged with unlawful sexual intercourse with a 15-year-old girl and discharging a firearm in public. He pleaded guilty to both charges before a magistrate, who sentenced him to 13 months' imprisonment, to be suspended after four months for the charge of unlawful sexual intercourse and to two months' imprisonment on the firearm charge. He appealed against sentence to the Supreme Court. Gallop J reduced the sentence to 24 hours' imprisonment on the first charge and 14 days' imprisonment on the second. Gallop J took into account Jamilmara's claim that he had done nothing wrong as the girl had been promised to him under customary law and he was under pressure from some members of her family to take her as his wife.

A majority of the Court of Appeal subsequently upheld the prosecution's appeal that this sentence was manifestly inadequate and imposed a total sentence of twelve months' imprisonment. The agreed facts made it clear that, at the very least, the girl was reluctant to have sex. Her victim impact statement said that she was sad and angry for what Jamilmara had done to her. The day after the sexual intercourse took place, she tried to leave the area. That was when Jamilmara fired his gun into the air to frighten her into remaining. Martin CJ stated (at para 28) that a distinction must be made 'between taking into account the custom which leads to an offender being punished in accordance with both the law of the Territory and by the Aboriginal community, and circumstances such as this where the custom gives rise to the commission of the offence'.

Riley J, stated that this was not a case where the defence of belief in marriage was applicable because at the time of the offence, the parties were not in a legal or traditional marriage: para [26]. However, there was evidence that under customary law, there was an arrangement of mutual obligations that had been established and that the relationship was 'in transition' and members of her family were in the area 'in case she needed comforting': para [27]. Riley J concluded (at para [33]) that '[w]hilst proper recognition of claims to mitigation of sentence must be accorded, and such claims will include relevant aspects of customary law, the court must be influenced by the need to protect members of the community, including women and children, from behaviour which the wider community regards as inappropriate'.

Mildren J, in dissent, focused on the evidence placed before Gallop J of social factors that had put pressure on Jamilmara. He viewed the sentence as light, but stated that there had not been sufficient evidence showing it was seriously inadequate.

In the majority judgments, it was revealed that Jamilmara had a previous culturally arranged marriage that was marred by domestic violence and binge drinking. In 1994, he had killed his wife and served three and a half years in jail for his conviction for manslaughter.

While there is reason to argue that the defence of belief in marriage should be available on the rare occasion when an accused believes he is married under Aboriginal customary law, it appears that the majority decision in *Jamilmara*'s case signals that a cautious approach will be taken to Aboriginal customary law in this area.

A defence based on mistaken belief in age should be available as it seems inappropriate to hold someone liable for a criminal offence where he or she honestly believed the other person to be of the age of consent. The main point of contention here is whether it should just be an 'honest' belief or an 'honest and reasonable' one. This reflects the debate as to mistaken belief in consent in rape and indecent assault.

The MCCOC, despite emphasising a subjective approach to mistaken belief in consent, recommended that a mistaken belief in age should be both honest and reasonable: at 159–61. This was on the basis that children are particularly vulnerable and that there is 'a social need to protect them from abuse and exploitation': at 159.

Another alternative is to follow that suggested in the previous part of this chapter in relation to mistaken belief in consent. A midway point between the subjective/objective dichotomy would be to enact a provision stating that the defence of mistaken belief in age is not available where 'the accused did not take reasonable steps in the circumstances known to the accused at the time, to ascertain that the complainant was of the age of consent'. This is a way of putting an objective gloss on mistaken belief without going as far as requiring the belief to be reasonable. This approach could therefore bring mistaken belief into line across sexual offences.

Overlap between offences

The main problem area in relation to the overlap between sexual offences lies with the offence of incest. Sexual intercourse between an adult and related child may be prosecuted under the provisions prohibiting sexual contact with children or under the general sexual assault provisions. It will be recalled from the case study at the beginning of this section that 'Toni's' father on occasion inserted his finger or tongue in her vagina. In most jurisdictions that would amount to rape. He could also be prosecuted for having sexual intercourse with a young person. Such acts would also amount to incest because of the direct lineal relationship. From the point of view of the prosecution, the discretion to charge age-based offences rather than rape may be justified on the basis that the former are easier to prove because there is no need to prove lack of consent.

If the father in *F*'s case can be prosecuted under the general sexual assault provisions as well as the provisions criminalising sexual intercourse with young persons, why is it necessary to also have a crime of incest?

At common law, incest was not considered a crime. Instead, it was the ecclesiastical courts that exercised power over family members and sexual relations between them. It only became a legislative offence in England in 1908 as a consequence of the efforts of Victorian moral reformers. Incest also became a statutory crime in Australian jurisdictions between 1876 and 1924: J Bavin-Mizzi, 'Understandings of Justice: Australian Rape and Carnal Knowledge Cases 1876–1924' in D Kirkby (ed), *Sex, Power and Justice: Historical Perspectives on Law in Australia* (Melbourne: Oxford University Press, 1995) pp 19–32 at 19.

The original rationale for the ecclesiastical courts' control over sexual relationships within families was to prevent inbreeding. It was believed that sexual intercourse within families would lead to the procreation of inferior populations: P Coleman, 'Incest: A Proper Definition Reveals the Need for a Different Legal Response' (1984) 49 *Missouri Law Review* 251–88. This rationale is no longer logical given that the offence now covers non-blood relations such as step-parent and step-child and is not confined to heterosexual intercourse.

More recently, the offence of incest has been seen as a mechanism for protecting children against sexual abuse within the family. The Victorian Law Reform Commission recommended retaining the offence because 'the family context is of sufficient importance to be dealt with separately from other relationships in which abuse of power occurs': *Sexual Offences Against Children*, Report No 18 (Melbourne: LRCV, 1988) p 30. The problem here is that 'incest' may not be seen in the same way as 'rape'. Toohey J stated in *R v J* (1982) 45 ALR 331 at 335–6:

> Although in one sense the term 'incest' produces an immediate reaction of disapproval, it sometimes serves to conceal the implications for the girl concerned. In an article 'Rape of Girl-Children by Male Family Members' 215 ANZJ Criminology (1982) 90, Elizabeth Ward comments: 'What other writers refer to as "father–daughter" incest, I shall call "girl-child rape". My reason for doing this is that the term "incest" focuses attention upon what is involved in "sexual activity" rather than what is happening to the girl-child. "Incest" is the label applied to sexual unions such as those between adult siblings, as well as non-consensual unions between a girl-child and an adult male. This reference to a "case of incest" serves to deny in linguistic and affective terms the fact that a form of abuse has taken place'.

Retaining a crime of incest, however, may help signify the familial nature of the sexual abuse and the breach of trust involved. Lee J stated in *P* (1997) 98 A Crim R 419 at 431:

> The move away from the notion that law is the custodian of morals; the view that sexual conduct between consenting adults does not require the intervention of the criminal law; and an emphasis upon the importance of rehabilitating the family

have all led to a climate of opinion that prison sentences may not be appropriate in some cases of incest. But the protection of young children from corruption and exploitation, especially by someone in a position of trust or authority, must remain an important and generally prevailing consideration.

In its Discussion Paper, *Sexual Offences Against the Person* (November 1996), the MCCOC recommended that there was no need for a separate offence of incest. It was focusing on consensual sexual intercourse between relatives who are adults such as occurred in the case of *R v Ball* [1911] AC 47 where a 23-year-old woman willingly lived with her brother and had a child with him. The Committee's recommendation was widely misinterpreted as meaning that it would be lawful for a parent to have sexual intercourse with his or her child who was under the age of consent. Accordingly, the recommendation met with a great deal of opposition.

In its Final Report (May 1999), the Committee explained (at 195) that it was recommending that there be no offence prohibiting adult consenting incest. However, given the weight of opinion seeking that the offence be retained, it altered its recommendation. The Committee (at 195) emphasised the submissions by those dealing professionally with sexual assault victims. The concern of these submissions was that decriminalising sexual intercourse between adult relatives might serve to legitimise continuing abuse once the child reached the age of consent. The Victorian Law Reform Commission pointed out that there may be a practical advantage in retaining the offence of incest where an accused continues to sexually abuse a relative after the latter reaches the age of consent because there may be insufficient evidence to prosecute the accused for rape or sexual intercourse with a young person: *Sexual Offences: Law and Procedure*, Discussion Paper (Melbourne: VLRC, 2001) p 87. It has since recommended that the offence of incest be retained, but renamed 'intra-familial sexual penetration': *Sexual Offences: Law and Procedure*, Interim Report (2003) p 359.

The arguments for and against the retention of the crime of incest are finely balanced, but overall, there may be practical advantages in having an overlap in statutory offences in relation to sexual abuse of children and young persons, particularly because of the problematic nature of proving non-consent to sexual intercourse for the offences of rape and indecent assault.

Sexual offences against individuals with mental impairment

Background
In 1980, a 23-year-old woman went with her sister to a fair at a country showground in South Australia. The woman was intellectually disabled and was said to have a mental age of about 10. At the fair, she was captivated by a hoopla stall and

spent a lot of time and money trying to win a large, green toy frog. While she was at the stall, a man named Beattie approached her and asked her if she wanted to 'make love'. The woman had neither any prior sexual experience nor had she received any education about sexual matters.

Beattie led her to a nearby caravan, taking with him the toy frog, which he subsequently gave to her. In the caravan, Beattie had sexual intercourse with the woman. She then went back to the fair and walked around, clutching her toy frog, and did not complain to her friends about what had occurred. She later spoke to Beattie again.

Some time after this, a second man enticed the woman into a truck, this time with a toy panda. This man also had sexual intercourse with her. Later, a third man tried to have intercourse with her, but she resisted him and bit him and ran away.

When she met her mother that evening, the woman was upset, but she denied anything was wrong. Eventually she told her parents and, subsequently, the police what had occurred: *R v Beattie* (1981) 26 SASR 481.

The facts of this case raise a number of questions concerning the law of sexual assault as it relates to those with some form of mental impairment including intellectual disabilities, mental illness, brain damage or senility.

Should Beattie be found guilty of a criminal offence in relation to his conduct towards the woman and, if so, what sort of criminal offence has he committed? Should this be considered rape or some other type of offence specifically related to sexual intercourse with an individual who is mentally impaired? Should there be scope for the possibility that the woman might in fact consent to sexual activity?

There is reason to believe that the situation experienced by the 23-year-old woman in *Beattie*'s case is not uncommon. A 1992 study of the incidence of criminal victimisation of individuals with an intellectual disability indicated significantly higher levels of victimisation with regard to offences against the person, when compared with the non-disabled population: C Wilson and N Brewer, 'The Incidence of Criminal Victimisation of Individuals with an Intellectual Disability' (1992) 27(2) *Australian Psychologist* 114–17. A New South Wales study found a high rate of sexual assault against both men and women with intellectual disabilities: M Carmody, *Sexual Assault of People with an Intellectual Disability:* Final Report (Sydney: NSW Women's Coordination Unit, 1990). One survey found that of 144 crimes against intellectually disabled clients reported to agencies, 130 involved sexual offences: K Johnson, R Andrew and V Topp, *Silent Victims: A Study of People with Intellectual Disabilities as Victims of Crime* (Melbourne: Office of the Public Advocate, 1988) fn 70.

A number of factors may lead to such a high incidence of sexual assault and exploitation of individuals with mental impairment. These include the lack of power of such individuals over resources, relationships, decision-making and information and the fact that social attitudes may stigmatise them as deviant or of little value: SC Hayes and G Craddock, *Simply Criminal* (Sydney: The Federation Press, 1992) p 75. Despite the relatively high incidence of sexual assault against individuals with mental impairment, it is rare that sexual offences are successfully prosecuted through the criminal justice system: J Phillips, 'Sexual Assault, Multiple Disabilities and the Law' (1996) 7 *Australian Feminist Law Journal* 157–62. There may be practical difficulties in prosecuting people accused of sexual offences such as rape against those with mental impairment because 'juries [may] not regard [such individuals] as credible witnesses, or are reluctant to believe a complainant who has an intellectual disability or mental illness when they give evidence that they did not consent to having sex with the accused': Victorian Law Reform Commission, *Sexual Offences: Law and Procedure*, Discussion Paper (Melbourne: VLRC, 2001) pp 113–14; see also New South Wales Law Reform Commission, *People with an Intellectual Disability and the Criminal Justice System*, Report No 80 (December 1996) Appendix B, table 3. There could also be difficulties where the accused argues that, irrespective of the absence of consent, he thought the woman was consenting.

The law in this area must balance two goals: the protection of those with mental impairment from exploitation and sexual offences and the recognition of basic human rights including the right to choose to engage in sexual activity: B McSherry and M Somerville, 'Sexual Activity Among Institutionalized Persons in Need of Special Care' (1998) 16 *Windsor Yearbook of Access to Justice* 107–16. This balancing act may be very difficult to achieve.

The current law

Beattie was charged with rape and the separate offence of having sexual intercourse with a 'mentally deficient' person. As we shall outline, some Australian jurisdictions have enacted specific provisions to protect those with mental impairment from being sexually abused.

As previously outlined, in certain jurisdictions there is no consent to sexual intercourse for the purposes of the law of rape where an individual is 'incapable of understanding' the sexual nature of the act: *Crimes Act* 1900 (ACT) s 92P(1)(i); *Criminal Code* (NT) s 192(2)(d); *Criminal Law Consolidation Act* 1935 (SA) s 49(6); *Criminal Code* (Tas) s 2A(2)(c); *Crimes Act* 1958 (Vic) s 36(e). In Queensland, the definition of consent for the purpose of the offence of rape is 'consent freely and voluntarily given by a person with the cognitive capacity to give the consent': *Criminal Code* (Qld) s 348(1).

There is little case law in this area and it is unclear how an individual's capacity to consent to sexual intercourse may be determined. In *R v Morgan* [1970] VR 337 at 341, the Supreme Court of Victoria held that there is no capacity to consent where the victim 'has not sufficient knowledge or understanding to comprehend (a) that what is proposed to be done is a physical fact of penetration of her body by the male organ or, if that is not proved (b) that the act of penetration proposed is one of sexual connexion as distinct from an act of a totally different character'. This suggests that the legal standard for capacity to consent is narrower than that, for example, relating to consent to medical treatment, where one must understand not only the nature and quality of the act to be performed, but also the risks, harms and benefits both of allowing the act and refusing it.

Section 49(6) of the *Criminal Law Consolidation Act* 1935 (SA) has a broader definition of capacity to consent than that set out in *Morgan*'s case. That section requires evidence that the complainant was unable to understand the 'nature or consequences' of sexual intercourse for the purposes of the separate offence of knowingly having sexual intercourse with a 'mentally deficient' person. The MCCOC has suggested that in relation to rape, consent be negated where 'the person is incapable of understanding the essential nature of the act': *Chapter 5: Sexual Offences Against the Person*, Report (May 1999) p 38. It is unclear what is meant by 'essential nature', but it could be taken to mean knowing that sexual intercourse may lead to pregnancy. The 'consequences' approach is more in line with the standards of capacity to consent to medical treatment. However, it has been criticised as taking protection too far as it would find more people incapable of consenting to sexual intercourse than the definition set out in *Morgan*. This point will be taken up later in the Critique section.

In most Australian jurisdictions, there are also specific laws making it an offence to have sexual intercourse with those who are mentally impaired: *Criminal Code* (NT) s 130(1) (mentally ill or handicapped person where accused provides disability support services); *Crimes Act* 1900 (NSW) s 66F(3) (person with an intellectual disability); *Criminal Code* (Qld) s 216 (intellectually impaired person); *Criminal Law Consolidation Act* 1935 (SA) s 49(6) (person with intellectual disability); *Criminal Code* (Tas) s 126(1) (person with mental impairment); *Criminal Code* (WA) s 330(1) (incapable person who is defined as someone who is mentally impaired).

In New South Wales, a person may be given a substantially heavier sentence for a sexual assault committed in 'circumstances of aggravation': *Crimes Act* 1900 (NSW) s 61J. The latter includes circumstances in which the victim has a serious physical or intellectual disability: ss 61J(2)(f) and (g). The term 'serious intellectual disability' is not defined. The policy behind this provision, which was introduced in 1989, seems to be that there should be a higher sentence in relation to crimes that the community perceives as particularly abhorrent: MCCOC, *Chapter 5: Sexual Offences Against the Person*, Discussion Paper (November 1996) p 289, para 8.11.

In New South Wales and Victoria, certain provisions prohibit sexual activity between a caregiver and a person with impaired mental functioning over whom the caregiver has authority: *Crimes Act* 1900 (NSW) s 66F(2); *Crimes Act* 1958 (Vic) ss 51, 52. The New South Wales provision prohibits sexual intercourse between one person and another who has an intellectual disability and who is under the authority of the former in connection with any facility or program providing services to those with intellectual disabilities. The Victorian provisions prohibit sexual intercourse between a person who provides medical or therapeutic services or a worker at a residential facility and a person with 'impaired mental functioning'.

Consent is not a defence to these sections. However, the Victorian provisions do not apply to those who are married or in a de facto relationship. This exemption seems to be aimed at spouses who are caregivers and who may loosely be described as providing therapeutic services.

In *R v Patterson* unreported, 29 March 1999, County Court of Vic, Mullaly J, the matters that the prosecution must prove in order to gain a conviction under s 51 of the *Crimes Act* 1958 (Victoria) were set out. Mullaly J ruled that the prosecution must prove that:

- the complainant was a person with 'impaired mental functioning';
- the accused was providing medical or therapeutic services to the complainant;
- the services related to the complainant's impairment;
- the act of sexual penetration occurred when the accused was providing the services to the complainant, although not necessarily at the exact time of giving the service;
- the accused knew that the complainant was a person with impaired mental functioning;
- the accused knew that he or she was providing medical or therapeutic services to the complainant;
- the accused knew that the services related to the complainant's impairment; and
- the acts were conscious, voluntary and deliberate.

The Victorian Law Reform Commission has expressed concern that the emphasis on the accused's knowledge in this ruling may make it difficult for this offence to be established: *Sexual Offences: Law and Procedure*, Discussion Paper (Melbourne: VLRC, 2001) p 115. They have suggested (at 116) that such an offence could be made one of strict liability so that the mental state of the accused is irrelevant, but he or she could raise a defence of honest and reasonable mistake if they believed that the victim was *not* mentally impaired.

Critique

As with rape trials in general, those involving individuals with mental impairment will centre upon the notion of consent. *Beattie*'s case was heard prior to many reforms to the law relating to rape. Perhaps not surprisingly, Beattie was not convicted of rape, although he was convicted of the lesser offence of having sexual intercourse with a 'mentally deficient' individual.

The trial judge, White J, emphasised the fact that the woman's 'clothes were not torn; her body was not bruised or marked, her hymen was not recently ruptured; she was not distressed afterwards. And she had a large toy frog as a reward for her co-operation': *R v Beattie* (1981) 26 SASR 481 at 483. Putting the evidence to the jury in such a way supports a presumption of consent; that *unless* the woman had struggled or resisted she must have consented to intercourse.

In relation to whether or not the woman had the capacity to consent to sexual intercourse, White J traced the concept of capacity back to the nineteenth-century cases of *R v Richard Fletcher* (1859) 8 Cox CC 131 and *R v Charles Fletcher* (1866) LR 1; CCR 39. In the latter case, the trial judge directed the members of the jury that the accused should be convicted of rape if they were satisfied that the complainant was incapable of expressing consent or dissent, but that a consent produced by a 'mere animal instinct' would be sufficient to prevent the act from constituting rape. In the former case, the jury had originally found the accused guilty of rape, but the Court of Criminal Appeal subsequently held that there was no evidence presented by the prosecution that what was done to the girl was against her will or without her consent and the trial judge should not have directed the jury as to rape at all.

White J in *Beattie*'s case (at 488) followed this line of reasoning, believing that 'something more must be shown by the prosecution than the facts of connection and mental deficiency of the girl'. He accordingly directed the jury (at 487) that 'consent to intercourse may be obtained in a variety of ways, by offers of marriage or money or gifts, by champagne, by flattery; or consent may be obtained, as here, by the express or implied promise of a toy frog obviously attractive to a childlike woman'. The jury accordingly acquitted Beattie of rape.

It is questionable as to whether a similar direction would now be given to a jury given that consent is meant to equal 'free agreement'. The focus in *Beattie*'s case was not so much on the capacity of the woman to consent to sexual intercourse, but more on whether she had resisted the accused in some way. White J stated (at 491): 'Rape should only be alleged in cases like this when there is some independent and reliable evidence of force or violence or threat; from which the jury can infer quite certainly both the girl's non-consent and the accused's knowledge or recklessness or lack of honest belief in relation thereto. Without such independent evidence, the prosecution for rape is likely to founder.'

Beattie's case went on appeal to the Full Court of the Supreme Court of South Australia, but it did not consider the question as to whether or not the trial judge was correct in requiring some form of resistance to be proved. Rather, the main ground of appeal concerned the interrelationship between the two provisions under which Beattie was charged.

Even if the emphasis in *Beattie*'s case had not been so much on resistance as showing lack of consent, there remains a question as to what is meant by capacity to consent. In *Beattie*'s case, the only evidence as to incapacity was gleaned from examination and cross-examination of the woman herself. It is highly likely that expert evidence would be called as to this evidence if the trial were to be heard today.

As outlined above, capacity could be defined narrowly to refer to understanding that the act is sexual in nature or more broadly to include understanding of the potential consequences of the act. More research in consultation with mental health professionals would be useful as to *how* capacity should be determined. The problem would remain, however, that a trial judge may still require something more than lack of capacity such as 'independent and reliable evidence' of some form of resistance.

Because it may be even more difficult to prove rape where the victim is mentally impaired than in other cases, prosecutors may rely on the specific provisions enacted in most jurisdictions. For example, in *Beattie*'s case, Beattie was not only charged with rape, but also with an offence under s 49(6) of the *Criminal Law Consolidation Act* 1935 (SA). That section states that 'a person who has...sexual intercourse with another person knowing that other person to be so mentally deficient as not to understand the nature or consequences of the act shall be guilty of a misdemeanour'. On appeal, the Supreme Court held in *Beattie*'s case that if rape is made out, this charge should be withdrawn from the jury: (1981) 26 SASR 481 at 494 per King CJ. This is therefore an alternative to the more serious charge of rape and one that may provide a fallback for the jury.

The jury in *Beattie*'s case convicted Beattie of this lesser offence. White J stated that it was unclear whether or not the woman understood the nature of the sexual act, but this was largely irrelevant as she did not understand the consequences of it and in particular the consequences of possible pregnancy. He stated (at 492): 'Her delight at learning where babies came from was evident during cross-examination. From the way her face lit up, it was clear that the revelation occurred there and then.'

The benefit of having specific provisions criminalising sexual acts with those with mental impairment is that they may very well lead to more convictions. Consent is not an issue and, by focusing on the accused's knowledge, a prosecution may take place without the victim having to give testimony in court. Lord Justice Applegath has stated that the purpose of an equivalent (now repealed) Canadian provision that criminalised intercourse with a woman who was 'feeble-minded, insane, or...an idiot or imbecile' was 'to punish adequately unscrupulous individuals who might take advantage of this type of female': 'Sexual Intercourse with a Feeble-minded Female Person: Problems of Proof' (1964–65) 7 *Criminal Law Quarterly* 480–4 at 480. (It is interesting to note how the language used to describe individuals with mental impairment has greatly changed since these provisions were first enacted.) Similarly, in *R v Red Old Man* (1978) 44 CCC (2d) 123 at 126, Kerans DCJ spoke of the need to protect women with mental deficiencies because of their inability to grant or withhold consent.

The problem with such provisions is that they may go too far in preventing those with mental impairment exercising any right to sexual autonomy. Many of these provisions were enacted at a time when the involuntary sterilisation of women with intellectual disabilities was justified by the theory of eugenics, their presumed inability to cope with parenthood and on hygienic grounds. In the USA, for example, as part of the 'eugenics movement' during the 1920s and 1930s, many states enacted statutes allowing for the compulsory sterilisation of those with intellectual disabilities: RK Sherlock and RD Sherlock, 'Sterilizing the

Retarded: Constitutional, Statutory and Policy Alternatives' (1982) 60 NCL Rev 943–83 at 944. The Canadian provinces of Alberta and British Columbia also had statutes providing for the sterilisation of 'mental defectives': *Sexual Sterilization Act* RSA 1970, c. 341, originally passed in 1928, repealed by 1972, c. 87; *Sexual Sterilization Act* RSBC 1960, c. 353, originally passed in 1933, repealed by 1973, c. 79. The former was one of the most extensive, enabling the involuntary sterilisation of 'psychotics', 'mental defectives', 'certain epileptics', 'neurosyphilitics' and those suffering from Huntington's chorea.

These specific provisions can thus be viewed against a background of repression towards those (mainly women) with mental impairment because of the fear that procreation among such individuals could lead to social degeneracy and because sexual behaviour 'was considered by many as a symptom and cause of mental illness': G Trudel and G Desjardins, 'Staff Reactions Toward the Sexual Behaviors of People Living in Institutional Settings' (1992) 10(3) *Sexuality and Disability* 173–88 at 176.

The Victorian Law Reform Commission has criticised these provisions on the basis that they do not allow for the sexual autonomy of individuals with mental impairment: *Sexual Offences Against People with Impaired Mental Functioning* Report No 15 (Melbourne: LRCV, 1988) pp 24–9. Similarly, the MCCOC has rejected having a blanket provision preventing sexual intercourse with such individuals: *Chapter 5: Sexual Offences Against the Person*, Discussion Paper (November 1996) p 145.

Instead, there has been a move towards more specific provisions aimed at protecting those with mental impairment from abuse by certain classes of people such as caregivers or those providing therapeutic services as outlined in the previous section. The MCCOC has recommended that it be an offence for 'a person responsible for the care of a person with a mental impairment' to sexually penetrate or to commit an indecent act with the latter: *Chapter 5: Sexual Offences Against the Person*, Report (May 1999) p 178. The definition of a caregiver is a person who 'provides medical, nursing, therapeutic or educative services to the person in connection with his or her mental impairment' (at 174). This seems overly broad, although it seems to be aimed at those providing professional services.

In its previous Discussion Paper (1996, at 145), the MCCOC justified the enactment of such provisions for 'cogent policy reasons': 'One is that a person with impaired mental functioning may not want a sexual relationship but, due to power imbalance of institutional setting, may find it difficult to refuse. Other concerns include the psychological harm which may result from such a relationship as well as the breach of trust put in the caregiver by, say, the victim's family.'

There thus seem to be two alternatives. One is to design offences aimed at caregivers and fall back on existing sexual assault laws, with appropriate definitions of consent, if a person with mental impairment is raped or assaulted by someone else. The other alternative is to have a generic provision that may go too far in interfering with the individual's right to sexual autonomy.

Margaret Somerville has argued that individual autonomy should be the starting point for any decisions in this area; that there should be a presumption that individuals with mental impairment have a right to have their autonomy respected to the greatest possible degree: 'Labels versus Contents: Variance Between Philosophy, Psychiatry and Law in Concepts Governing Decision-Making' (1994) 39(1) *McGill Law Journal* 179–99. Any interference with such individuals' expression of their sexuality can only be justified where it is shown that the interference is clearly necessary for the protection of the persons concerned.

From this perspective, blanket prohibitions on sexual intercourse with those with mental impairment seem difficult to justify. It may be better for law reform efforts to concentrate on clarifying the notion of capacity to consent in the law of rape and indecent assault and emphasising that consent means free agreement, rather than depending upon generic provisions that interfere with the right to sexual autonomy. More specific provisions prohibiting sexual conduct between those in authority positions and those with mental impairment may be justified on the basis of the protection from harm, but care must be taken that these provisions provide adequate definitions of those who should be prohibited from engaging in sexual activity.

Conclusion

Sexual assault laws must be understood in their cultural and social context, reflecting changing perspectives on sexuality in this society. The laws of rape and indecent assault developed within a dominant masculinist discourse that was focused on a penetrative/coercive and heterosexual form of sexuality. While major steps have been made in relation to law reform in this area, it remains the case that persisting presumptions about women's and men's sexuality make it easier for the prosecution to prove an offence where some resistance has occurred than otherwise. This stereotype of the submissive/provocative women who secretly 'always' consents and the aggressive/seductive/easily aroused man is of course a gendered one.

The real problem is that any step towards a legal requirement that consent to sexual activity must be communicated will be ineffective if the penetrative/coercive discourse continues to dominate understandings of 'normal' sexual relations. Legislative change in itself cannot bring about a complete overhaul in myths about sexuality. Only if legislative change goes hand in hand with a reassessment of social attitudes towards sexuality can real change come about. For example, at present there is a very broad gap between the ideal communicative model of sexuality, which forms the basis of s 37(a) of the *Crimes Act* 1958 (Vic), and the reality of the pervasiveness of penetrative/coercive sexuality.

If a fault element of knowledge or belief is to be central to sexual assault offences, mistaken belief in consent in the general sexual assault laws and mistaken belief in age in offences against young persons needs to be reassessed. A midway point between the subjective/objective dichotomy would be to enact a provision stating that mistaken beliefs are not available where the accused did not take reasonable steps in the circumstances known to the accused at the time, to ascertain that the complainant was consenting and was of the age of consent. This is a way of putting an objective gloss on mistaken belief without going as far as requiring the belief to be reasonable.

One of the benefits of having statutory offences prohibiting sexual assaults of children and young persons and individuals with mental impairment is that the prosecution need not prove non-consent. Problems still, however, remain with the scope of such offences.

Working out when a young person is capable of consenting to sexual intercourse involves a balancing act between understanding sexual development, protecting the person from harm, and recognising the right to sexual autonomy. Whatever age is chosen, it should be uniform regardless of the nature of the sexual conduct. In relation to sexual offences against individuals with mental impairment, the challenge is to balance issues of protecting those vulnerable to sexual exploitation with the right to sexual autonomy. There is perhaps a temptation to avoid the issue of capacity to consent by enacting specific provisions making it an offence to have sexual intercourse with those with mental impairment. But such blanket provisions may go too far in encroaching upon sexual autonomy.

Overall, the right to sexual autonomy should be a universal feature of sexual offences. However, this should not be seen purely in terms of ownership or control. Nicola Lacey argues that 'affective' and 'relational' values such as mutual respect, trust, love and pleasure play a significant role in how sexuality is viewed in society: *Unspeakable Subjects* (Oxford: Hart Publishing, 1998) p 116. These values, however, have played little part in the way in which sexual assault laws have been formulated. Perhaps the most difficult challenge to be faced in this area of the law lies in working towards narrowing the gap between the ideal of mutual communicative sexual activity and the continuing reality of aggressive non-communicative sexual intercourse. The time is ripe for an exploration of how a broader view of sexual autonomy and communicative sexual activity might be used in reforming sexual assault offences.

Part 3
PROPERTY OFFENCES

CHAPTER 6

Property offences involving stealing

Introduction

Frank De Stefano was a highly regarded accountant and member of his local community, having been a city councillor and Mayor of Geelong for several years. Many members of his community came to him for financial advice and entrusted him with their savings for financial management. Over almost six years he stole $8.6 million in funds entrusted to him, using it for his own business ventures and personal interests, including home renovations and school fees, and to finance his gambling activities. In one instance $4.98 million was stolen from a trust account set up to manage an award of damages paid to a client for medical negligence that resulted in the client becoming quadriplegic. This theft, as Kellam J observed in the Victorian Supreme Court, was particularly callous and cruel, taking away all possibility of independence for the client: *R v De Stefano* unreported, 13 March 2003, SC of Vic, [2003] VSC 68 at para 22. Another of De Stefano's victims, for whom the accused had acted for many years and from whom he had stolen over half a million dollars, described in a victim impact statement the stress he had suffered both from the loss of his funds and from the deception of someone he had regarded as 'a friend over the years' (at para 25).

The prosecution concluded that around $1.5 million was used to repay debts, for personal expenses, or to replace money stolen from other clients, but that the remaining money was lost through gambling. The accused said that he became addicted to gambling; the Court noted that he was 'in effect seduced by casinos', and he was 'treated like "royalty"' at Melbourne's Crown Casino, where he did much of his gambling (at para 56).

Frank De Stefano pleaded guilty to theft and was sentenced to a total of 10 years' imprisonment, with a minimum term of seven years. In sentencing, Kellam J accepted that the accused was addicted to gambling and had suffered great public humiliation. He emphasised, however, the gross breach of trust involved, particularly by a professional adviser, and the importance in such a case of general deterrence and denunciation, observing that a Court should not be distracted by the 'havoc that a custodial sentence usually [wreaks] on the lives of the white collar criminal and his or her family' in setting an appropriate sentence: at para 65.

This case illustrates a number of themes arising in this chapter and in Chapter 7 in relation to theft and other property offences. These include the challenge that property offences pose to the general sense of security in a community, the differences in types of property offences and perceptions about such offences across social classes, and the recent recognition of problem gambling as a motivation for crime. It also illustrates the similarities between activities that might be called 'theft' and those that might be seen as 'fraud', an issue to which we return in Chapter 7.

Property offences cover a wide range of behaviours, but they are essentially about taking property from others—offences involving stealing—and tricking people into giving away their property—offences involving deception. As the case of De Stefano illustrates, property offences can undermine trusting relations and confidentiality in families, communities and businesses. They can arise from a range of motivations including poverty, greed, gambling, and other addictions.

The property taken illegally may be tangible items such as jewellery, cars or cash, or it may be intangible property such as rights or entitlements, including entitlement to credit, the rights represented by cheques, and electronic transfers of money within the banking system. Property offences include such varied activities as shoplifting, passing dud cheques, misuse of money held on trust, house burglaries, and major and minor frauds. Property offences can have elements of violence or threat, as in some forms of burglary and robbery. There is also a range of associated property offences, such as receiving or handling stolen goods and conspiracy to defraud. Property offences involving stealing, together with robbery and burglary, will be examined in this chapter. Property offences involving deception will be the subject of the following chapter.

Property offences constitute the bulk of police work in Australia and comparable countries. They represented around 87 per cent of major crimes over the past five years: Australian Institute of Criminology, *Australian Crime Facts and Figures 2002* (Canberra: AIC, 2002) p 6. There were 139,943 reported motor vehicle thefts across Australia in 2001, while there were 435,524 burglaries (unlawful entry with intent) and the number of other (non-motor vehicle) thefts was 699,262: AIC, *Australian Crime Facts and Figures 2002* (Canberra: AIC, 2002) p 6. This 'other thefts' category, which includes pickpocketing, bag snatching, theft from vehicles and shoplifting, is the largest crime category included in the national statistics, and represented 55 per cent of all property-crime victims: AIC, *Australian Crime Facts and Figures 2002* (Canberra: AIC, 2002) p 6, 34. As a matter of comparison, in the same year there were 340 reported homicides and 151,733 reported assaults.

Women represented about 20 per cent of alleged offenders across all offences as recorded in police reports in Victoria, Queensland and South Australia in 2002. In the 'other theft' category, however, women accounted for 30 per cent of all offenders, representing the highest level of female participation in crime: AIC, *Australian Crime Facts and Figures 2002* (Canberra: AIC, 2002) p 38, 40.

Arie Freiberg estimated in 1997 that the value of property stolen from homes, shops, cars, factories and warehouses each year is in the vicinity of two to three billion dollars: 'Regulating Markets for Stolen Property' (1997) 30 ANZJCrim 237–58 at 237. Freiberg reports that little stolen property is either recovered and returned to its owners or retained by the thieves; most is sold or bartered in the stolen property market. Substantial sums of money are also lost through fraud, again much of it never recovered. Fraud is discussed further in Chapter 7.

House burglaries and car thefts are more likely than most other offences to be reported to the police, as this is a requirement for any insurance claim. Many other forms of theft and fraud are likely to go unreported because they are undetected or because the victim does not believe reporting to police to be useful.

Victim data shows much higher experiences of victimisation in these areas than revealed by the police statistics. For example, there were 290,000 residential burglaries and attempts recorded by police in 1997–98, while the Australian Bureau of Statistics *Crime and Safety Survey* (Canberra: ABS, 1999) reported about 800,000, involving a loss to victims estimated at $0.9 billion in 2001. While the ABS reported 27,000 recorded robbery offences, the Australian Institute of Criminology estimated that the true figure was more likely to be around 168,000: P Mayhew, 'Counting the Costs of Crime in Australia', *Trends and Issues* No 247 (Canberra: AIC, 2003) p 38.

Natalie Taylor reports surveys of businesses showing that crimes such as burglary and robbery were usually reported to police, but that other crimes such as theft by employees, employee fraud and shoplifting tend not to be reported: 'Reporting of Crime Against Small Retail Businesses', *Trends and Issues* No 242 (Canberra: AIC 2002). Businesses tended to be pessimistic about reporting the latter types of crime, as being pointless and achieving nothing. Taylor notes (at 2) that under-reporting of some crimes skews police data and popular understanding of crime in the community but also, importantly, tends to mean that resources and strategies are aimed at crimes that are frequently reported, neglecting crimes that are prevalent but less reported.

Depending on the degree of autonomy in the workplace, employees may have a degree of scope for 'fiddling' or what could be called theft from the company—from personal use of company stationery and company telephones through fiddled expense accounts to use of equipment and vehicles. Some degree of flexibility in approach to such 'fiddles' may indeed be seen as a perk or incentive, as Gerald Mars notes in his examination of workplace crime: *Cheats at Work: An Anthropology of Workplace Crime* (London: Allen & Unwin, 1982). He observes (at 42) that in some highly autonomous occupations 'fiddles and flexibility are part of the way things actually work, and indeed often the reasons *why* things work' but that (at 49) there is 'only a blurred line between entrepeneuriality and flair on the one hand and sharp practice and fraud on the other'. The recent cases of gambling-related frauds on employers illustrate the ease with which trusted and autonomous employees may carry out such 'fiddles' for extended periods of time before being detected. Self-employed professionals have even greater opportunities, as illustrated by the case of De Stefano at the start of this chapter.

Not all occupations offer this degree of access to 'fiddles', and not all companies necessarily collude in or ignore such practices. Companies often have their own internal disciplinary mechanisms, and may deal with many incidents internally, to avoid publicity or to save time. Internal discipline—from warnings and file notes to demotions and sackings—while lacking the public morality play of the criminal trial, may on occasions be more onerous on the offender than if the criminal justice system were involved: see further on 'managerial justice', D Brown, D Farrier, S Egger and L McNamara, *Criminal Laws: Materials and Commentary on Criminal Law and Process of New South Wales* (3rd edn, Sydney: The Federation Press, 2001) pp 1234–7.

During the past decade or so there has been growing awareness of the importance of thefts of information by accessing computers, and the associated problems of 'hacking' into confidential and/or commercial computer data, and using or changing data. We have also seen the growing phenomenon of 'e-crime', crime based around the Internet and electronic transactions, which has included thefts or frauds achieved by tricking people over the Internet.

At the same time there have been changing motivations for thefts. Property offences have traditionally been carried out due to hunger and poverty, as well as boredom, greed and the desire for material possessions. Poverty and marginality are clearly correlated with the 'traditional' property offences such as theft, burglary and robbery. Alan Norrie notes in *Crime Reason and History: A Critical Introduction to Criminal Law* (2nd edn, London: Butterworths, 2001) p 38 that 'Desperate social need and indignant claim of right were the motives of the poor in the seventeenth, eighteenth and early nineteenth centuries.'

Studies on contemporary criminality similarly address the implications of economic disadvantage on criminal behaviour, particularly property offending. While results vary, the research notes a range of possible effects of economic adversity including increased motivation to offend, development of disadvantaged neighbourhoods, and disrupted parenting: Kenneth Polk and Rob White, 'Economic Adversity and Criminal Behaviour: Rethinking Youth Unemployment and Crime' (1999) 32(3) ANZJCrim 284–302; Don Weatherburn, Bronwyn Lind and Simon Ku, 'The Short-Run Effects of Economic Adversity on Property Crime: An Australian Case Study' (2001) 34(2) ANZJCrim 134–48.

More recently we have become aware of the number of drug-addicted offenders who steal to sell on and maintain their drug habit. The AIC *Drug Use Monitoring Australia* project (DUMA) found in 2002 a very strong link between drug use and property crimes. Over 80 per cent of men held by police in relation to property offences and surveyed recently as part of the study tested positive for drugs; 26 per cent of men facing property charges had opiates in their system while 36 per cent tested positive for amphetamines: T Makkai and K McGregor, *Drug Use Monitoring Australia: 2002 Annual Report on Drug Use Among Police Detainees* (Canberra: AIC, 2003) pp 20–1.

Arie Freiberg reports that a New South Wales operation targeting the market in stolen goods found most offenders to be in their twenties, most with a substantial criminal history, most unemployed, and the majority supporting a drug habit: 'Regulating Markets for Stolen Property' (1997) 30 ANZJCrim 237–58. Other studies have shown that many illicit drug users, particularly users of heroin, finance their drug habit through stealing and selling goods. The finding that most heroin users commit property crimes is not, as Freiberg points out, necessarily a finding that most property crimes are committed by heroin users: at 244.

Most recently, with the relaxation of controls on gambling and indeed embracing of gambling revenue by many Australian governments, there has been a growth in thefts and frauds by people funding a gambling addiction. The case of De Stefano, outlined at the start of this chapter, illustrates the problems of gambling and the breaches of trust, as well as other social bonds, that can be triggered. It may also foreshadow the growth of a different type of crime and criminal: see Y Sakurai and R Smith, 'Gambling as a Motivation for the Commission of Financial Crime', *Trends and Issues* No 256 (Canberra: AIC, 2003).

While it is not difficult to see drug addicts and gamblers as criminals, though perhaps unfortunate and in need of help, there are other types of behaviour that are also criminal but are more difficult to identify as such. There is a significant, but still under-researched (and under-recorded) body of middle-class offenders committing property offences linked with—and sometimes merging into—acceptable (even desirable) market practices. This will be discussed further below.

A preliminary point that must be considered is why the criminal law protects interests in property at all. Unlike the protection of bodily autonomy, for example, property interests are held very inequitably across society. The French social reformer Pierre-Joseph Proudhon claimed famously in 1840 that *'La propriété c'est le vol'* (Property is theft): *Oxford Dictionary of Quotations* (4th edn, Oxford: Oxford University Press, 1992) p 530. As discussed in Chapter 1, criminal laws often reflect powerful interests. Douglas Hay has pointed out that the greatly increased number of capital offences in Britain in the eighteenth century—from about 50 in 1688 to over 200 in 1820—were almost all offences against property: D Hay, 'Property, Authority and the Criminal Law' in D Hay, P Linebaugh, JG Rule, EP Thompson and C Winslow (eds) *Albion's Fatal Tree: Crime and Society in Eighteenth-Century England* (London: Allen Lane, 1975) pp 17–63 at 18.

Andrew Ashworth argues that personal property is 'one of the basic organizing features of many modern societies, and it may be defended as an institution on grounds of individual autonomy and rights': *Principles of Criminal Law* (3rd edn, Oxford: Oxford University Press, 1999) p 374. There are obviously other ways of viewing 'rights' to property, but criminal property offences clearly enforce the existing legal framework for creating interests in property. As Hernando de Soto explains, 'Property is not a primary quality *of* assets, but the legal expression of an economically meaningful consensus *about* assets': *The Mystery of Capital* (London: Black Swan Books, 2001) p 164. Ashworth goes on (at 375) to point out that assuming agreement with the view that the law should uphold and respect property rights still leaves 'the question of proportionality: what priorities should [the law] give to them?' The question of priorities and proportionality of criminal laws to their aims will be a continuing issue in these chapters.

There are two important—although very differently focused—themes in this discussion of the operation of property offences in Australia at the start of the twenty-first century, which have already been identified. The first theme addresses who commits property crimes and why; closely related is the issue of differences in the ways that these offences are perceived, defined, prosecuted and punished. The second theme is the impact of new ways of holding information and doing business, such as computer-based information systems, on the operation of the criminal law.

An illustration of the different perceptions of property crime, and of the need to consider how different social harms are prioritised, is provided by shoplifting. Shoplifting is clearly theft. Terminology can be a useful indicator of perceptions; consider the difference between 'shoplifting' and 'shoptheft' (the term preferred by retailers). This is a difficult area in which to obtain clear data due to difficulties of terminology and to failure of retailers to identify or quantify shoptheft separately from other forms of 'leakage and shrinkage' (see discussion in D Nelson and S Perrone, 'Understanding and Controlling Retail Theft', *Trends and Issues* No 152 (Canberra: AIC, 2000)), but it has been estimated that it costs retailers in New South Wales about $700 million each year: 'Shoplifting up to $2m daily', (1996) 16(4) *Security Australia* 38. The Retail Traders' Association has a rule of thumb that 1.5 per cent of retail turnover goes on leakage and shrinkage: P Mayhew, 'Counting the Costs of Crime in Australia', *Trends and Issues* No 247 (Canberra: AIC, 2003). This covers not only shoptheft but delivery thefts, damage to goods, and burglaries. But Mayhew's calculations indicate that, applying the solidly based assumption that one in a hundred thefts is ultimately recorded by police, there were around 7.3 million shopthefts in 2001 in Australia, producing a total loss of $810 million.

Bearing in mind the factors that may lead to particular cases of shoptheft being reported to the police, it is still striking to note that, in Victoria, Police Crime Statistics record almost as many women as men in the category 'theft (shopsteal)', 8471 alleged male offenders compared with 7670 alleged female offenders: Victoria Police, *Crime Statistics 2001/02*, Table 4.1 <http://www.police.vic.gov.au/ShowContentPage.cfm?ContentPageId=484>, accessed November 2003. On the other hand, shoplifting has been popularly seen as a stereotypically female crime. It may indeed come as a surprise to some to find that men are still in the majority of offenders in this category.

Mayhew's research refers also to the under-reporting of much crime, and in particular to the under-reporting of property crimes such as shoptheft. Diana Nelson and Santina Perrone, 'Understanding and Controlling Retail Theft', *Trends and Issues* No 152 (Canberra: AIC, 2000), found that less than half of the apprehended shop thieves are reported to police, businesses being more concerned about recovering the stolen goods and avoiding adverse publicity. Shoptheft of course covers a range of activities, from one-off or occasional thefts, often of small easily concealed items, motivated by thrill-seeking, need or desire, to full-time professional shoptheft carried out to order. Many shop owners prefer not to participate in the prosecution process, on the basis that the cost of reporting shoptheft is disproportionate to the individual items stolen, or that the criminal justice system is not seen as an effective protection or deterrent: D Nelson and S Perrone, 'Understanding and Controlling Retail Theft', *Trends and Issues* no. 152 (Canberra: AIC, 2000). They may prefer to address general 'shrinkage' by increasing prices and as an insurable risk, rather than report offenders or indeed change shop design or management. Nelson and Perrone conclude that the 'competitive nature of the retail market means that businesses have to decide whether customer accessibility to goods (which is believed to increase sale) and the labour cost savings associated with fewer staff on shop floors, outweigh the costs of losses through customer theft'.

The policing and prosecution of shoptheft involves significant scope for discretion: in the initial decision whether to report the offence, or simply to focus on prevention by employment of security guards and warning of offenders; and at the prosecution stage. Prosecution is always at the discretion of the police and prosecuting agency. In the case of shoptheft there are also cautioning schemes in place aimed at adequately punishing or deterring young/first time offenders without automatically engaging them in the justice system and the stigma of conviction: see Simon Smith, 'Shoplifting Diversion in Victoria' (1985) 10 *Legal Services Bulletin* 256–61. Victoria Police reports that most (67 per cent) juvenile shopsteal offenders are cautioned, as are one-quarter of adult offenders: Department of Justice, Statistics and Research Unit Stats Flash 112, *Trends in Shopstealing*, February 2002.

Shoptheft is an area where we look again at the effectiveness of using criminal law to address social harms/practices. Preventive strategies by retailers also require consideration. Strategies such as 'target-hardening' (making theft physically more difficult and increasing identifiability of goods) are already given high priority in tackling other areas such as motor vehicle theft: D Brown, D Farrier, S Egger and L McNamara, *Criminal Laws: Materials and Commentary on Criminal Law and Process of New South Wales* (3rd edn, Sydney: The Federation Press, 2001) pp 1237–40; Karl Higgins, 'Exploring Motor Vehicle Theft in Australia', *Trends and*

Issues No 67 (Canberra: AIC, 1997). Brown et al also point out (2001, at 1236) the role played by retailers in facilitating shoptheft, in open displays aimed at increasing sales (and, one might add, encouraging 'self service'). They ask the questions (at 1236): 'Should these [marketing] pressures and the failure of particular retailers to take mechanical security measures be taken into account in assessing whether the defendant has acted "dishonestly"? Given the lack of enthusiasm of retailers for the prosecution process, and the temptations which they hold out to customers, should they be left to their civil remedies?'

The second theme in this and the following chapter is the effect of rapidly changing ways of holding property and doing business on the law's capacity to address offending behaviours. Computer-based records and electronic financial transactions, for example, and corporate structures (although these are hardly new) have posed major challenges for agencies trying to enforce the criminal law, and more generally trying to protect communities' material assets. We will return to these issues after reviewing the current law.

The criminal law on property offences across Australia is complex. There are broadly three regimes in operation. The English common law of larceny and related offences applied originally in Australia. New South Wales continues to operate under the common law, with statutory modifications. The primary offence is common law larceny, with additional statutory offences including larceny by a bailee (*Crimes Act* 1900 (NSW) s 125), embezzlement (*Crimes Act* 1900 (NSW) ss 157, 160) and fraud offences such as fraudulent misappropriation (*Crimes Act* 1900 (NSW) s 178A), obtaining by deception (*Crimes Act* 1900 (NSW) s 178BA) and obtaining by false pretences (*Crimes Act* 1900 (NSW) s 179).

Queensland, Western Australia and Tasmania retain the early 'Griffith' Codes introduced around the turn of the twentieth century. The Codes revised the common law to some extent but retain many of the common law concepts. They establish two main offences of stealing (*Criminal Code* (Qld) s 391; *Criminal Code* (WA) s 371; *Criminal Code* (Tas) s 226) and fraud (*Criminal Code* (Qld) s 408C; *Criminal Code* (WA) s 409) with a range of variants. The *Criminal Code* (Tas) is closest to the common law and includes fraud offences in ss 250, 252, 252A.

Property offences in the UK were overhauled following a report of the Criminal Law Revision Committee (CLRC), *Theft and Related Offences*, Report No 8 (London: HMSO, Cmnd 2877, 1966). The UK *Theft Act* was introduced in 1968. Victoria established a new legislative framework based on the *Theft Act* (UK) 1968 as an amendment to the *Crimes Act* 1958 (Vic) in 1973. The Victorian legislation was itself the basis for new statutory provisions in the Australian Capital Territory (*Crimes (Amendment) Act (No 2)* 1986) and is also reflected in the Northern Territory *Criminal Code*.

The Victorian legislation, following the UK legislation, essentially establishes three offences. These are theft and two fraud offences, obtaining property by deception and obtaining a financial advantage by deception. The Australian Capital Territory has merged theft and fraud into a single offence: *Crimes Act* 1900 (ACT) ss 84 and 86(1). The Australian Capital Territory with Victoria and the Northern Territory has a separate offence of obtaining a financial advantage by deception.

Property offences in South Australia were recently comprehensively revised. The legislative provisions introduced by the *Criminal Law Consolidation (Offences of Dishonesty) Amendment Act* 2002 draw on the UK *Theft Act* and the reforms proposed by the MCCOC, but in a form of 'free translation', which Ian Leader-Elliott describes as 'both radical and provincial': I Leader-Elliott, 'Offences of Dishonesty: the South Australian Version', unpublished paper presented at the South Australian Law Society Conference, 31 May 2003, at 3, 5. The amendments establish an offence of theft (*Criminal Law Consolidation Act* 1935 s 134) together with six deception offences. The main deception offence, in s 139, deals with dishonestly obtaining a benefit or causing a detriment, defined in s 130 to refer to both property and financial advantage/disadvantage.

All jurisdictions include offences in the form of burglary (breaking and entering with intent) and robbery (stealing by force/threat of force), and related offences such as receiving and handling stolen goods.

As noted above, it is understood that most stolen property is sold or bartered in the stolen property market: Arie Freiberg, 'Regulating Markets for Stolen Property' (1997) 30 ANZJCrim 237–58. Offences dealing with receiving and handling stolen goods are significant avenues for tackling this 'market' in stolen goods but will not be examined further here. Such offences, however, have been notoriously complex and may be of limited assistance due to difficulties of enforcement (see Model Criminal Code Officers Committee (MCCOC), *Chapter 3, Theft, Fraud, Bribery and Related Offences*, Report (December 1995) p 99). The new legislation in South Australia combines theft and receiving stolen goods in one offence: s 134(5). Alternative forms of regulation such as licensing of pawnbrokers and second-hand dealers, and 'target-hardening' by marking and recording valuable and electronic items, may also be important: Freiberg, 1997.

In addition there are a number of property offences in Commonwealth law. Conspiracy offences (*Criminal Code*) (Cth) ss 11.5, 135.4) are available in relation to dishonesty offences in the Commonwealth jurisdiction such as tax fraud (see Chapter 7). The common law offence of conspiracy to defraud also exists in all Australian jurisdictions including the Commonwealth: see MCCOC, *Chapter 3, Conspiracy to Defraud*, Final Report (May 1997). This is explored in Chapter 8.

Most recently, amendments to the *Criminal Code* (Cth) have incorporated a range of property offences applicable in the Commonwealth jurisdiction and broadly similar to those in Victoria, following—but not in all cases adopting—the recommendations of the MCCOC in its Report, *Chapter 3, Theft, Fraud, Bribery and Related Offences* (1995): *Criminal Code Amendment (Theft, Fraud, Bribery and Related Offences) Act* 2000 (Cth).

There are also Commonwealth provisions imposing criminal and civil penalties for breaches of corporate governance obligations and for frauds and deceptions under other pieces of substantive legislation such as the *Corporations Act* 2001 and the *Trade Practices Act* 1974, enforced by the statutory agencies the Australian Securities and Investments Commission (ASIC) and the Australian Competition and Consumer Commission (ACCC) respectively: see J Clough and C Mulhern, *The Prosecution of Corporations* (Melbourne: Oxford University Press, 2002) p 158 ff on civil penalties. The significance of the growing Commonwealth regulatory structure cannot be ignored in a discussion of the role of the criminal law in this area.

Commentators have been critical of the variation and complexity of property offences across the Australian jurisdictions. CR Williams has observed: 'There is no reason why conduct which is criminally dishonest should not be conceived and defined uniformly throughout Australia. Certainly there is no justification for continued toleration of the complexity and extreme technicality of the common law in this area': *Property Offences* (3rd edn: Sydney: LBC Information Services, 1999) p 1.

The MCCOC reviewed property offences as part of its wide-ranging examination of the criminal law and reported in 1995. It concluded in *Chapter 3, Theft, Fraud, Bribery and Related Offences*, Report (December 1995) p 1, that 'Clearly the choice for model theft and fraud provisions must be one which reduces the complexity of the common law and its *Griffiths Code* variants.'

The MCCOC proposed a model based principally on the Victorian provisions. The approach of the MCCOC informs the structure and analysis of this and the following chapter.

Theft

Background

Lopatta had worked loyally for an oil company for two years, when he was abruptly sacked. His former employer owed him holiday and other pay but fobbed him off when he tried to discuss payment of the amount he believed to be owing. Lopatta then broke into the ex-employer's warehouse in northern Adelaide with a rented truck and took twenty large drums of oil, worth about $5000. He was charged with warehouse-breaking and larceny. He claimed that he had not acted dishonestly, but had honestly believed he had a claim to the value of the drums, which he intended to sell to obtain the money he believed was owed to him. He did subsequently concede that, looking at the incident with hindsight, he had been 'foolish and wrong-headed' but said he had at the time honestly believed in his claim of right: *R v Lopatta* (1983) 35 SASR 101.

Theft is the traditional property offence. It comprises a taking of property belonging to another, acting dishonestly and intending to keep the property or use it in ways that exclude the true owner. All jurisdictions have an offence of this type.

The case of *Lopatta* illustrates the focus of larceny (and theft) on taking property. It also raises the question of when someone who takes another's property can nonetheless claim to have acted honestly, a point we will return to.

The common law developed over several centuries around the offence of larceny. George Fletcher in 'The Metamorphosis of Larceny' (1976) 89(3) *Harvard Law Review* 469–530 at 474 outlines the earliest approach to larceny, up to the late eighteenth century, pointing out that the traditional view of theft focused as much on the social harm it caused (as noted at the start of this chapter) as on any harm to personal property interests: 'In the traditional view, the thief upset the social order not only by threatening property, but by violating the general sense of security and well-being of the community; in this broader sense, theft was feared as a socially unnerving event.' [Footnote omitted.]

According to Fletcher (at 472) the key principles of traditional larceny involved distinguishing when the criminal process should be involved, and when the individual should be left to their private law rights. One element in this distinction was the principle of possessorial immunity, that is, the rule that once the owner of property transferred possession to another, the recipient was not subject to the criminal law. The harm being addressed by the use of the criminal law was the unauthorised taking of identifiable goods. If the owner was persuaded—even by a deception—to hand over the goods in such a way as to transfer ownership there was no larceny. The harm was left to the civil law for resolution. The modern law of theft has moved away from fine distinctions about whether ownership or merely possession have been transferred (concepts that still complicate the common law and to some extent the Codes). However, we continue to grapple with the proper distinction between criminal and civil processes and when the criminal law should be employed to regulate harmful behaviour.

As refined in the nineteenth century, the common law offence of larceny entailed taking property fraudulently and with an intention to permanently deprive; the focus of the common law offence, however, continued to be on the physical act of taking property. Notions of ownership and property meant that the original offence focused on the taking away of a physical object from another person, as discussed earlier. It had to be something literally capable of being taken and carried away.

The *Crimes Act* 1900 (NSW) adopts the common law of larceny in s 116 to which a maximum penalty of five years applies: s 117. There is no statutory statement of the components of the offence. Brown et al outline the elements as including a taking and a carrying away, at the time of which the accused must intend to permanently deprive the possessor, and must be acting fraudulently without any genuine claim of entitlement: D Brown, D Farrier, S Egger and L McNamara, *Criminal Laws: Materials and Commentary on Criminal Law and Process of New South Wales* (3rd edn, Sydney: The Federation Press, 2001) pp 1154–8. The *Larceny Act* 1916 (UK) embodied the common law of larceny in the UK. It provided in s 1(1) that: 'A person steals who, without the consent of the owner, fraudulently and without claim of right made in good faith, takes and carries away anything capable of being stolen with intent, at the time of such taking, permanently to deprive the owner thereof.'

In New South Wales additional statutory offences were created to deal, for example, with fraudulently keeping goods that were already in the thief's possession, with intangible property, and with different types of property and different types of victims, such as employers and landlords. New South Wales has large numbers of such specific offences, as did the previous South Australian legislation (see *Crimes Act* 1900 (NSW) ss 124–162). The MCCOC pointed out (MCCOC, *Chapter 3, Theft, Fraud, Bribery and Related Offences*, Report (December 1995) p 1) that:

> Since the early part of the industrial revolution in the eighteenth century, judges and legislatures have been struggling to adapt the law of larceny to the needs of societies with more and more complex and abstract notions of property rights: the idea that there can be a division of interests—ownership, possession, control—of the same object; the creation of abstract rights by special documents like cheques and credit cards. These adaptations have produced a patchwork of judicial decisions and statutory provisions. [Footnote omitted.]

The Codes introduced a single offence of stealing but many of the common law elaborations still apply. The Queensland Code, for example, provides for a penalty of five years' imprisonment for 'basic' theft, while it is seven years in Western Australia. There are higher and different penalties for stealing where:
- the object stolen is one of a list of animals, or a will, or property over a prescribed value, or a vehicle, or a firearm;
- the theft occurs in particular circumstances such as theft from a vehicle in transit or a vehicle in distress; or
- the theft is committed by particular classes of persons—public servants, clerks, directors or officers of companies, agents, tenants or lodgers (*Criminal Code* (Qld) s 398; *Criminal Code* (WA) s 378).

The UK *Theft Act* and the Victorian, Australian Capital Territory, Northern Territory and South Australian provisions shift the focus of the offence from the physical to the fault element—from the taking of property to the dishonesty of the offender's action. The offences carry a high maximum penalty (10 years in Victoria, the Australian Capital Territory and South Australia). Differences in the nature and value of the property taken, and the status and vulnerability of the victim, are addressed in sentencing. The Northern Territory legislation provides for a maximum penalty of seven years for theft (*Criminal Code* (NT) s 210(1)) but this is increased to a maximum of 14 years if the item stolen was 'a testamentary instrument' or something worth $100,000 or more (s 210(2)).

The offence of theft is defined as meaning 'stealing' (*Crimes Act* 1958 (Vic) s 72(2)), defined in s 72(1) of the *Crimes Act* 1958 (Vic) and in similar terms in s 84 of the *Crimes Act* 1900 (ACT) as follows:

> A person steals if he [or she] dishonestly appropriates property belonging to another with the intention of permanently depriving the other of it.

The *Criminal Code* (NT) uses the term 'unlawfully' in place of 'dishonestly' but otherwise is in similar terms. In South Australia, theft is defined as dealing with property '(a) dishonestly; and (b) without the owner's consent; and (c) intending (i) to deprive the owner permanently of the property; or (ii) to make a serious encroachment on the owner's proprietary rights': *Criminal Law Consolidation Act* 1935 (SA) s 134(1).

The components of theft will be outlined here using the Victorian and Australian Capital Territory theft provisions as the framework, noting jurisdictional differences as they arise. See S Bronitt and B McSherry, *Principles of Criminal Law* (Sydney: LBC, 2001) pp 667–9 for an overview table of theft/larceny offences across Australia (but noting South Australian changes).

The physical elements will be discussed first. These relate to the existence of 'property', which belongs to someone other than the offender, and which has been 'appropriated' or 'taken'.

Physical elements

Property

As previously discussed, the common law limited the types of 'things' that could be stolen to objects having a physical existence that were capable of being taken and carried away. The Codes and Victorian, Australian Capital Territory and Northern Territory provisions define property more widely, with specific limitations for the purpose of theft.

In Victoria 'property' is defined in s 71(1) for the purposes of all property offences as including 'money and all other property real or personal including things in action and other intangible property': see also *Crimes Act* 1900 (ACT) s 83; *Criminal Law Consolidation Act* 1935 (SA) s 130. These definitions obviously cover physical items; they also cover intangible items such as rights, debts and trademarks. This broad definition is then cut back in relation to specific offences. For example, land (real property) is generally not property that can be stolen, and there are only specific circumstances in which animals can amount to 'property' that can be the subject of a theft charge: *Crimes Act* 1958 (Vic) s 73(6) and (7); *Crimes Act* 1900 (ACT) s 83. The definition in s 130 *Criminal Law Consolidation Act* 1935 (SA) includes 'real or personal property' including money, intangible property, electricity and wild animals in captivity; land is specifically excluded as a subject of theft (s 135).

The Codes in Queensland, Tasmania and Western Australia define 'property' as referring to 'every thing animate or inanimate capable of being the subject of ownership'. The Queensland Code also refers to 'money...electrical or other energy...[animals that have been in some way 'owned' by people], any other property real or personal, legal or equitable, including things in action and other intangible property': (*Criminal Code* (Qld) s 1; *Criminal Code* (Tas) s 1; *Criminal Code* (WA) s 1). The Codes also, however, limit the objects of theft more narrowly than is the case in Victoria, the Australian Capital Territory and the Northern Territory to items that are moveable, consistent with the continuing common law influences on the Codes: *Criminal Code* (Qld) ss 390, 391; *Criminal Code* (WA) ss 370, 371.

Theft of land
A person cannot be charged with theft of land at common law or under the Codes, given the focus on moveable items that can be taken and carried away. At common law this extends to things attached to the land such as trees and crops and minerals, although the focus on moveability does not necessitate this. The approach is also continued in Victoria and the Northern Territory with particular exceptions: see, for example, *Crimes Act* 1958 (Vic) s 73(6); *Criminal Code* (NT) s 209(2); see also *Criminal Law Consolidation Act* 1935 (SA) s 135(1). It will, however, often be possible to charge a person who obtains an interest in land by deception with a fraud offence such as obtaining property by deception or obtaining a financial advantage by deception. Such issues are also, of course, addressed under relevant civil property laws. In New South Wales a number of related items are covered under specific statutory provisions, such as parts of buildings and fences (*Crimes Act* 1900 (NSW) s 139), trees and plants (ss 140 and 521A), and rocks, gravel and soil (s 521A).

The Criminal Law Revision Committee considered, but rejected, making 'land thieves' amenable to the new UK theft law, other than in the exceptional cases noted in the previous paragraph: *Theft and Related Offences*, Report No 8 (London: HMSO, Cmnd 2877, 1966) paras 41–4. The failure of Australian courts and governments to address the 'land theft' of the British colonisers of this country is highlighted by D Brown, D Farrier, S Egger and L McNamara, *Criminal Laws: Materials and Commentary on Criminal Law and Process of New South Wales* (3rd edn, Sydney: The Federation Press, 2001) p 1166. They argue that 'the common law concept of native title recognised in [*Mabo v Queensland (No 2)* (1992) 175 CLR 1] represents a legal validation of the theft'.

Financial transactions as property
At common law there had been a view that for an item to be the subject of larceny it had to have some value. Some early writers indicated that paper money, although evidence of a chose in action, had no intrinsic value and could not be the subject of larceny. This was the rationale for the definition of property in *Crimes Act*

1958 (Vic) s 71(1) as including 'things in action'. The *Cheques Act* 1986 (Cth) and common law developments such as *Parsons v The Queen* (1999) 195 CLR 619, which is discussed below, may have moved to recognition of the intrinsic value of security documents.

Developments in the electronic movement of funds have further challenged the traditional concepts of property offences. The question of how banking transfers fit within the idea of 'property' has been considered recently in two important cases, one in England and one in Victoria in a case that went on appeal to the High Court of Australia. These cases are also relevant to the following question of what amounts to 'property belonging to another'.

The House of Lords considered the character of electronic funds transfers in *R v Preddy* [1996] 3 WLR 255. John Preddy and others had been charged with obtaining property by deception after they obtained loans or advances from various lenders by providing false information. Some of these advances were transferred electronically to the conspirators' bank accounts and some were paid by cheque. The Court concluded that the electronic transfers of loan funds were 'property'—the credit entries that arose from the electronic funds transfer (EFT) were a chose in action, that is, a debt—but were not property 'belonging to another'. This was because the chose in action was only created when the funds were credited to the applicant's account.

The House of Lords in *Preddy* also made some comments about cheques (but in passing as the case only raised the nature of the electronic transfers) and similarly concluded that a cheque could not be the subject of theft, whether as a piece of paper or as a chose in action. The chose in action represented by the cheque was not 'property belonging to another' and there could be no intent to permanently deprive in relation to the physical cheque. Lord Goff of Chieveley observed (at 266) that:

> [W]hen the cheque was obtained by the payee from the drawer, the chose in action represented by the cheque then came into existence and so had never belonged to the drawer. When it came into existence it belonged to the payee, and so there could be no question of his having obtained by deception 'property belonging to another'...[The cheque form does belong to the drawer but] there can have been no...intention on the part of the payee permanently to deprive the drawer of the cheque form which would on presentation of the cheque for payment be returned to the drawer via the bank.

The status of cheques was considered recently in Australia in *Parsons v R* (1999) 195 CLR 619. The High Court rejected the House of Lords' approach in *Preddy*. Roumald Charles Parsons worked for a company selling stationery products, primarily imported pens, to newsagents in the Melbourne metropolitan area. He was the main employee of the company, and the directors of the company left him with the day-to-day running of the business. Parsons invited a number of local newsagents to purchase cheap photocopying paper from him, which he said he would obtain from a supplier in South-East Asia and which they would easily be able to resell in Victoria at a profit. He even showed the newsagents faked contractual documents 'proving' that he had secured outlets for the sale of the paper with large local companies. Parsons persuaded them to give him cheques addressed to the company he worked for. In all, he obtained cheques totalling over $160,000. In fact no orders for copy paper were made, and no paper was delivered to the newsagents. The cheques were paid into the company's bank account. Some of the proceeds were used to pay the company's business expenses but otherwise the funds were dissipated.

Parsons was charged with a number of counts of obtaining property by deception. We will be discussing this offence in Chapter 7. The issue of 'property belonging to another' is, however, common to both theft and obtaining property by deception.

Parsons pleaded guilty to the offences of obtaining property by deception, leading to the prosecution agreeing to withdraw a number of other charges. However, he then appealed his conviction to the Victorian Court of Appeal on the basis—citing *Preddy*'s case—that there could be no offence where cheques were involved as there was no 'property belonging to another' and therefore no convictions possible at law.

It was unusual to hear an appeal in such circumstances, where the accused had originally pleaded guilty, but the Court agreed that the case raised special issues: [1998] 2 VR 478. The judges also noted the practical implications of the argument, which they recognised needed resolution. Cheques are of course often the vehicle for frauds and as the Court noted, many cases in Victoria and elsewhere have led over the years to convictions in just such situations.

The Supreme Court rejected Parsons' argument that a cheque was not property belonging to another and affirmed the conviction. The Supreme Court, and the High Court of Australia, which confirmed the decision, concluded that a cheque in itself—the piece of paper—is tangible 'property' and not simply a 'chose in action' or intangible property. The High Court noted that it is Australian banking practice for banks to retain the cheque document unless specifically requested to return it, so there is no difficulty in showing intent to permanently deprive. Therefore, the Court held that the accused had properly been convicted of obtaining the cheque itself by deception.

The High Court also rejected the House of Lords approach to the cheque as not creating property 'belonging to another'. At least since the passing of the *Cheques Act* 1986 (Cth) the cheque represents an existing chose in action, an agreement as between the bank and the cheque drawer that the bank will pay the nominated amount to whomever was entered as drawee on the cheque. The cheques here were clearly property belonging to another, which had been dishonestly obtained by deception. The case does not, however, address the question of electronic funds transfers, and their status remains unclear. The implications of the decision are discussed further in the Critique section.

Information as property
The common law has refused to treat information as 'property' that can be the subject of theft (or fraud). The key case of *Oxford v Moss* (1978) 68 Cr App R 183 involved a civil engineering student at Liverpool University, Paul Moss, obtaining a copy of a forthcoming examination paper. He read it and returned the copy. He was charged with theft of confidential information. The magistrate dismissed the case. On appeal the Court held that information did not fall within the term 'intangible property' under the UK equivalent of s 71(1) *Crimes Act* 1958 (Vic).

Body parts as property
It is unclear whether body parts are regarded in law as property. This is relevant to whether they can be the subject of theft or fraud. It may also be relevant to medical, ethical and legal issues of rights in body parts such as blood and other tissue, upon which medical researchers may conduct research and make commercial gains, and ownership of body organs that may be in demand for transplant. Useful writings on the medical issues include M Davies and N Naffine, *Are Persons Property? Legal Debates About Property and Personality* (Aldershot: Dartmouth Publishing Company, 2001); H McKelvie, 'Property in the Body' (1998) 6(1) *Journal of Law and Medicine* 16–18; and L Griggs, 'The Ownership of Excised Body Parts: Does an Individual Have the Right to Sell?' (1994) 4(1) *Journal of Law and Medicine* 223–8.

The common law traditionally stated that there was no property in a corpse. There could be no offence of theft from the activities of grave-robbers (unless gravecloths were also stolen, being the property of the estate): M Davies and N Naffine, *Are Persons Property? Legal Debates About Property and Personality* (Aldershot: Dartmouth Publishing Company, 2001) pp 106–7. On the other hand, enforceable rights to ownership of a corpse have also been recognised. In the early case of *Doodeward v Spence* (1908) 6 CLR 406 the High Court of Australia upheld the right of the plaintiff to the return of a bottle containing the preserved corpse of a stillborn two-headed baby, where the bottle had been confiscated by the police. The decision does not, however, clearly determine the question whether there are property rights in body parts. One of the majority judges, Griffith CJ (at 414), concluded that there could be property in a body where someone has exercised 'work or skill' such that the body has acquired 'attributes differentiating it from a mere corpse awaiting burial'. The other majority judge, Barton J (at 416), did not consider that the usual principles regarding corpses applied to such a 'dead-born foetal monster'. More recently, Anthony-Noel Kelly, a sculptor, was convicted in England of theft on similar grounds to those adopted by Griffith CJ when he removed body parts from the Royal College of Surgeons in London without authorisation for use in his art works: *R v Kelly* [1998] 3 All ER 741.

A very different approach has, however, been employed regarding rights to tissues that have been medically removed and subsequently used for commercial purposes. In the American case of *Moore v Regents of the University of California* 271 Cal Rptr 146 (Cal 1990) the Court rejected an action brought by John Moore against his physicians and a hospital for commercial use they had made of biopsied tissues taken from him over several years, ostensibly as part of treatment for leukaemia. The Court held (at 162) that there were no property rights in the human body, and that no such rights should be recognised in such a case, as this would 'destroy the economic incentive to conduct important medical research'. The Court preferred to rely on imposing an obligation on surgeons to obtain informed consent from the patient. The implications of the case are usefully discussed in M Davies and N Naffine, *Are Persons Property? Legal Debates About Property and Personality* (Aldershot: Darmouth Publishing Company, 2001) chs 1 and 7; see more generally L Andrews and D Nelkin, 'Whose Body is it Anyway? Disputes Over Body Tissue in a Biotechnology Age' (1998) 351 *The Lancet* 53–7. Medical researchers appear currently to be adopting the approach endorsed in *Moore*'s case, dealing with questions of ownership of body parts by seeking prospective consent from the patient: see McKelvie at 17.

Belonging to another

The Victorian, Australian Capital Territory and Northern Territory provisions include a requirement that the property, to be stolen, must have belonged to another: *Crimes Act* 1958 (Vic) s 72(1); *Crimes Act* 1900 (ACT) s 84; *Criminal Code* (NT) s 209. This requirement is further defined in *Crimes Act* 1958 (Vic) s 71(2) and *Crimes Act* 1900 (ACT) s 85(1) to extend to property in another's possession or control, or where another has any proprietary interest in it. Under the South Australian legislation, theft requires a dealing with property 'without the owner's consent' (*Criminal Law Consolidation Act* 1935 (SA) s 134(1)(b)), and an 'owner' is defined as including any person with any proprietary interest, together with any person 'entitled to possession or control' (s 130).

This addresses the traditional common law distinction between ownership and possession. Larceny was originally an offence against possession, as was highlighted in the earlier discussion about the focus of the offence on the taking away of moveable property. It has, however, come to be recognised both at common law and in its statutory forms as an offence that can be committed where the victim has any of possession, or control, or ownership of the property: see CR Williams, *Property Offences* (3rd edn, Sydney: LBC Information Services, 1999) p 16. A person has 'possession' of property if they intend to possess the property and if they at some stage had physical control of the property, even if they are not currently in physical control: see *Hayes v Fries* (1988) 49 SASR 184. Property can continue to be in the 'possession' of one person while another has physical control over the property, such that a taking from the person who merely has control can amount to theft. This was found to have occurred in *Smith v Desmond* [1965] AC 960, when the House of Lords concluded that employees working at a bakery at night had been robbed of the contents of a safe which, while not in their immediate 'possession', was held to be under their physical control, despite being inaccessible to them in a locked room. Usually the owner of property will have both possession and physical control. However, a person can be the owner, with full title to the property, who has neither possession nor control, for example where the property has been lost: *R v Thurborn* (1849) 169 ER 293.

This broad definition of property 'belonging to another' means that a person can be guilty of theft from several people, each holding a different proprietary interest in the property. Indeed, individuals may be guilty of theft of property in which they themselves have a proprietary interest. For example, an accused was held by the English Court of Appeal to have been guilty of theft when he removed his car from a car mechanic's yard after it had been repaired, to avoid paying for the repairs: *R v Turner (No 2)* [1971] 1 WLR 901. However, in a subsequent case the opposite conclusion was reached, when the accused retrieved his car from a police yard, where it had been placed by the police, who had towed it away as it was causing an obstruction: *R v Meredith* [1973] Crim LR 253. JC Smith, commenting on *Meredith*, suggested that it was 'correct in principle' and that *Turner* was probably explicable on the basis that the Court in *Turner* had taken into account the fact that the accused still owed the repairer for the work done on the car, despite stating that the existence of this 'repairer's lien' was irrelevant to the question of whether the property could be said to 'belong to another': JC Smith, 'Case Comment: R v Meredith' [1973] Crim LR 253–4 at 254. In any event, it may be difficult to prove the separate element of dishonesty, where the accused takes back property to which he or she has an immediate right to possession. In *Turner* dishonesty was clear: the accused intended to avoid paying the repair fee.

A person cannot be found guilty of theft if the property is in fact in his or her possession and control already. Some types of property can more readily be said to have passed into the possession and control of the accused, such as petrol once poured into the petrol tank of a car. For example, Greenberg filled his car's tank with petrol at a self-serve petrol station, and went to pay at the cashier's desk. The cashier was busy, and Greenberg then decided not to wait. He left and drove away. At trial it was held there was no case to answer on the charge of theft: *R v Greenberg* [1972] Crim LR 331. The Court confirmed that when he drove away with the petrol, with the dishonest intent, the petrol already belonged to him. The difficulty for the prosecution was that no other charge was available since, when Greenberg put the petrol in the tank, when it was still 'property belonging to another', he did not have any dishonest intention, and indeed he assumed the right of an owner with consent, on the assumption that he would pay.

The concept of property 'belonging to another' has required further definition to allow for a conviction for theft where someone misuses property they hold on trust or on account of another person, or where they obtain property due to another's mistake: see *Crimes Act* 1900 (ACT) s 85; *Criminal Code* (NT) s 209(3)–(5); *Criminal Law Consolidation Act* 1935 (SA) s 134(3); *Crimes Act* 1958 (Vic) s 73(8)–(10).

The definition of property in s 71(2) *Crimes Act* 1958 (Vic) already includes the interest of a beneficiary under a trust; s 73(8) extends the definition to situations where there is no identifiable beneficiary. It provides:

> Where property is subject to a trust, the persons to whom it belongs shall be regarded as including any person having a right to enforce the trust…

If a person receives property under an obligation to hold it for a particular purpose, it 'belongs to' the person who was to benefit: *Crimes Act* 1958 (Vic) s 73(9); *Crimes Act* 1900 (ACT) s 85(3) (a 'legal obligation'); *Criminal Code* (NT) s 209(4); *Criminal Law Consolidation Act* 1935 (SA), see definition of 'owner' in s 130. Common law principles will be applied to determine where such an obligation exists. In *R v Hall* [1973] QB 126 the Court concluded on the facts that there had been no obligation to deal with the clients' money in a particular way where a travel agent had been given money for flights that ultimately were not taken (although the Court commented that this was 'scandalous conduct': at 131). The courts have, however, confirmed that a legal obligation is required, and have found such an obligation to exist even in circumstances where the 'obligation' could never have been legally enforced (in this case involving a cheque obtained by fraud), on the basis that the obligation arises from the relationship between the recipient and the deliverer of the property, irrespective of any rights in a third party: *R v Meech* [1974] QB 549.

At common law it was not clear whether a person who keeps property given to him or her as a result of the giver's mistake commits an offence. If an accused is overpaid by mistake, and the accused immediately realises when receiving the money that it is an overpayment, he or she is guilty of theft under general principles and has appropriated property belonging to another: *R v Middleton* (1873) LR 2 CCR 38. However, what of the situation where the accused only sees later that the payment is excessive and decides then to keep it? In *Middleton* the accused requested payment of one amount of money but the bank clerk, relying on documentation regarding another customer, paid the accused a larger amount. The accused had in that case immediately realised the error, but the Court commented that whether the mistake was recognised immediately or later, the accused has committed theft, on the basis that where such a mistake is made property does not pass. Effectively a fundamental mistake vitiates the owner's consent to transfer the goods. Fundamental mistakes are 'mistakes about the identity of the defendant, the essential nature of the property, [and] the quantity of the goods (but not the amount of money)': MCCOC, *Chapter 3, Theft, Fraud, Bribery and Related Offences*, Report (December 1995) p 49. *Middleton*'s case can be analysed as involving a fundamental mistake as to the identity of the person being paid.

Australian courts have rejected the approach in *Middleton*, although it does not in fact appear that the distinction between fundamental and non-fundamental mistakes has necessarily been rejected. *R v Potisk* (1973) 6 SASR 389 involved a bank teller in Coober Pedy applying the wrong conversion rate when he exchanged traveller's cheques for Australian currency, such that the recipient was paid more than double the correct amount. The recipient only realised the mistake when he got home. He was convicted of larceny. On appeal a majority of two to one held that whether an offender was aware of the mistake at the time or realised it later, he was not guilty of larceny. Bray CJ in the South Australian Supreme Court did not regard the case of *Middleton* as binding in Australia, a view criticised by CR Williams, *Property Offences* (3rd edn: Sydney: LBC Information Services, 1999) p 32.

However, as the High Court observed in *Ilich v The Queen* (1987) 162 CLR 110 it was not necessary to decide whether *Middleton* should be followed or distinguished in either *Potisk* or *Ilich*. In *Middleton* the mistake was a fundamental one—as to the identity of the recipient—while in *Potisk* the mistake was not fundamental and so would not have vitiated the teller's consent. The High Court similarly concluded that there had been no offence under s 371 of the *Criminal Code* (WA) in *Ilich*. A vet returned to his practice and, angry with the state of the premises, threw the locum vet's pay at him and ordered him out. By mistake he threw down three envelopes instead of the two he intended. When the locum vet reached his home he realised he had been overpaid. He was still deciding what to do when he was charged with stealing and convicted. The High Court concluded that there was no theft under the *Criminal Code* (WA), as there had been no fundamental mistake. Property had passed and the money was therefore not 'property belonging to another' at the time the guilty intent had been formed. Wilson and Dawson JJ at 129 stated that the only mistakes that will be regarded as 'fundamental' will be mistakes as to the identity of the transferee, the identity of the thing delivered, or the quantity of the thing delivered (but not including the amount of money where money is knowingly transferred). No such mistake was made here.

Section 73(10) *Crimes Act* 1958 (Vic) provides that if the accused obtains property due to another person's mistake, and is under an obligation to restore the property, the property will be regarded as 'belonging to' the person entitled to its return, and intention not to restore will be regarded as intent to permanently deprive; and see *Crimes Act* 1900 (ACT) s 85(4); *Criminal Code* (NT) s 209(5). The common law still applies in determining whether the provision is required—that is, whether property passed at all. Where there has been a fundamental mistake (as above), property will not have passed, as the consent of the owner is vitiated by the mistake, and theft will have occurred under general principles as the property still 'belonged to another'. There are, however, complications regarding the types of mistake that have this effect: see MCCOC, *Chapter 3, Theft, Fraud, Bribery and Related Offences*, Report (December 1995) p 53 ff.

It is also necessary to turn to the common law to determine when a person is 'under an obligation to make restitution' when obtaining property by a non-fundamental mistake. This will be a matter for the law of contract, turning on whether the contract is void or voidable: see *Attorney-General's Reference (No 1 of 1983)* [1985] QB 182, applying *Norwich Union Fire Insurance Society Ltd v Williams H Price Ltd* [1934] AC 455.

A legal obligation to make restitution will be required: *Crimes Act* 1900 (ACT) s 85(4). In *R v Gilks* [1972] 1 WLR 1341 a bookmaker paid £106 in the mistaken belief that Gilks had backed the winner. Gilks knew this was not correct but kept the money. It was held that he was guilty of theft under general principles: this was property 'belonging to another' when he accepted it with the guilty intent. The Court confirmed that had the UK equivalent of s 73(10) been relied on, any 'obligation' would have to be a legal obligation. Here there would have been an argument that there was no 'obligation' because gaming transactions were not legally enforceable under the then-applicable UK legislation.

Neither the Codes nor the new South Australian legislation include the requirement that the property 'belong to another'. Under the Codes, property capable of being stolen is defined as 'anything that is the property of any person…' (*Criminal Code* (Qld) s 390; *Criminal Code* (WA) s 370). The Queensland Code provides an extended meaning of ownership covering 'any person having possession or control': s 391(7); in both Queensland and Western Australia any person in possession of property has a form of proprietary right, which if violated can lead to a theft charge: see E Colvin, S Linden and J McKechnie, *Criminal Law in Queensland and Western Australia* (3rd edn, Sydney: Butterworths, 2001) p 136. As in Victoria, there are additional specific sections dealing with the criminal liability of people misusing funds held for others (for example *Criminal Code* (Qld) ss 393–396). The new South Australian legislation focuses on dishonestly dealing with property 'without the owner's consent'. This is extended to misuse of fiduciary obligation: s 134(1)(b) and (3)(b).

Taking or appropriating the property

What does the offender have to do to be regarded as 'taking' or 'appropriating' the property? The legislation of Victoria, the Australian Capital Territory, the Northern Territory and the UK uses 'appropriation' as the key concept. 'Appropriation' is defined in the *Crimes Act* 1958 (Vic) s 73(4) (and see *Criminal Code* (NT) s 209(1)) as follows:

In New South Wales an alternative verdict of fraudulent appropriation (carrying a lesser penalty) is available if a person is charged with larceny and is found not to have taken the property with fraudulent intent, but to have subsequently 'fraudulently appropriated' it: *Crimes Act* 1900 (NSW) s 124.

> Any assumption by a person of the rights of an owner amounts to an appropriation, and this includes, where he [or she] has come by the property (innocently or not) without stealing it, any later assumption of a right to it by keeping or dealing with it as owner.

The Australian Capital Territory legislation gives a definition of appropriation that covers both the concept of assumption of the rights of an owner, *and* the notion of obtaining by deception, which in the other jurisdictions—Victoria, Northern Territory and UK—is the basis for the separate offence of obtaining by deception. Section 86(1) of the *Crimes Act* 1900 (ACT) states that a person will have appropriated property if:

> a) he or she obtains by deception the ownership, possession or control of the property for himself or herself or for any other person; or
> b) he or she adversely interferes with or usurps any of the rights of an owner of the property.

There is no separate requirement in any of these jurisdictions that the appropriation be without the owner's consent, a factor that has caused ongoing problems in the courts, as we shall see. By contrast, the new South Australian legislation refers to dishonestly 'dealing with' property without the owner's consent (s 134(1)(b)). 'Deal' is defined (s 130) to include taking, obtaining, receiving, retaining or converting the property, or dealing with it 'in any other way'.

The test under the Australian Capital Territory, Northern Territory, Victorian and UK legislation is whether the offender 'assumed' or 'usurped' the rights of an owner. The phrase was considered in *Stein v Henshall* [1976] VR 612. Henshall drove a car that he knew to be stolen. The Victorian Supreme Court held that, whether the thief had given him the car, or had loaned it to him, his use of the car amounted to appropriation. The Court said that the question was 'whether the offender acted in relation to the car in a manner in which the owner would have the right to act'. It was not necessary to show that the offender intended, for example, to exclude all others.

The proviso as to any later assumption of a right covers the situation of finding an item, or having it delivered by mistake. At common law, if the finder believed the owner could be discovered but decided to keep the property anyway, they would be guilty of larceny, but if they only decided to keep the property later they could not be convicted of larceny as the guilty intent did not exist at the time of the finding: *Thompson v Nixon* [1966] 1 QB 103. A similar situation applies if the property was obtained by mistake as discussed above. The statutory provisions in Victoria and the Northern Territory mean that a person can be guilty of theft if she or he later dishonestly assumes the rights of an owner over the property: *Crimes Act 1958* (Vic) s 73(4); *Criminal Code* (NT) s 209.

The High Court confirmed the centrality of consent to the common law concept of larceny in *Croton v The Queen* (1967) 117 CLR 326. Croton withdrew money from an account he held jointly with his de facto partner consisting of her salary cheques, and put the money into an account in his own name without her knowledge or consent. His conviction for larceny was quashed in the High Court. When Croton's partner put the money into the account she consented to it going into a joint account, in relation to which the Court found no clear agreement limiting which of the partners could withdraw funds. The money paid out by the bank was also considered, at least by Barwick CJ (at 331), to be different 'property' from that deposited, and was clearly also handed over with the bank's consent.

The common law offence of larceny has a range of variations relating to the basis of the owner's consenting to hand over the goods. For example, where a person hands over goods to another there will not have been an offence of larceny as the owner has consented to transferring (at least) possession of the property. However, if the transfer is for a specific purpose such as repair, and the repairer then steals the goods, he or she will have committed 'larceny as a bailee' (*Crimes Act 1900* (NSW) s 125). On the other hand, if the recipient intended from the start to keep the goods, there will have been no bailment, and he or she will then be guilty of the separate offence of larceny by a trick. Where consent is induced by trick or deception the offence falls into one of the fraud categories. It will be larceny by a trick if it results in possession being gained, or obtaining property by false pretences or fraudulent misappropriation if it results in ownership passing (*Crimes Act 1900* (NSW) s 179): see summary in D Brown, D Farrier, S Egger and L McNamara, *Criminal Laws: Materials and Commentary on Criminal Law and Process of New South Wales* (3rd edn, Sydney: The Federation Press, 2001) p 1214. The difference matters in New South Wales as an accused in that state can only be convicted of larceny as a bailee if specifically charged with that offence.

There is no specific requirement that the taking be without the owner's consent in the Queensland or Western Australian Codes. The Codes employ the common law expression 'taking', covering a range of common law larceny offences in the one Code offence. The Western Australian and Queensland Codes refer to 'fraudulently takes...or fraudulently converts to [his] own use or to the use of any other person' (*Criminal Code* (WA) s 371(1), *Criminal Code* (Qld) s 391(1)). The Tasmanian Code refers to 'takes' or 'converts to his own use or to the use of any person other than the owner' (*Criminal Code* (Tas) s 226(1)). It also includes a requirement that any taking be 'without the consent of the owner'. 'Taking' involves obtaining possession of the property; conversion is a common law concept that involves a person, already being lawfully in possession (for example as a bailee), who then deals with the property in a way that is inconsistent with the rights of the owner: see E Colvin, S Linden and J McKechnie, *Criminal Law in Queensland and Western Australia* (3rd edn, Sydney: Butterworths, 2001) pp 136–7.

Under the Tasmanian Code 'taking' includes 'obtaining possession (i) by a trick; (ii) by intimidation; (iii) by a mistake on the part of the owner, if the taker knows of such mistake; or (iv) by finding, if at the time of the finding the taker believes that the owner can be discovered by reasonable means': *Criminal Code* (Tas) s 226(2).

Appropriation and consent
It is central to common law larceny that the taking and carrying away be without the owner's consent. This is also reflected in the new South Australian legislation. However, neither the Queensland and Western Australian Code provisions, nor the Australian Capital Territory, Northern Territory or Victorian legislation, addresses the issue of consent. It is not clear whether lack of consent is an element of the offence, and if so whether it operates to prevent there having been a 'theft' irrespective of how it was obtained, for example if obtained by a deception. The issue of consent is of course also relevant to the requirement of dishonesty as part of the fault element of the offence, a point to which we will return.

The offence of stealing in the Criminal Codes of Queensland and Western Australia refers to a fraudulent taking or conversion. The term 'fraudulent' is defined broadly to mean with intention to permanently deprive, or to use or borrow in an equivalent manner: *Criminal Code* (Qld) s 391; *Criminal Code* (WA) s 371. This component of the offence is discussed further below. A fraudulent taking includes situations where the owner of the property handed it over, but their consent was vitiated by deception or duress: CR Williams, *Property Offences* (3rd edn, Sydney: LBC Information Services, 1999) p 167. The distinction under the Codes and also at common law turned on whether the owner intended only to pass possession of the property, or to pass property also. In the former case the offence was stealing; in the latter it was obtaining by false pretences. The stealing offence therefore only applies where the deception persuaded the owner to part only with possession of the property. There is now an offence of fraud in the Queensland and Western Australian Codes that replaces the offence of obtaining by false pretences: *Criminal Code* (Qld) s 408C; *Criminal Code* (WA) s 409. This applies whether the owner intended to part with ownership or to part only with possession: *Criminal Code* (Qld) s 408C(3)(f); *Criminal Code* (WA) s 1 'obtains'.

The question whether there can be a criminal 'appropriation' when the owner consented to handing the goods over has been considered in a series of English and Victorian cases. The concept has been sufficiently challenging and unclear that it has gone to the House of Lords, and the Supreme Court in Victoria. The Victorian and English courts have reached very different conclusions.

A key early English case involved an appeal by Alan Lawrence, a taxi driver, who was charged with theft for taking more money from a passenger than was warranted. The passenger, Mr Occhi, was an Italian visitor in London for the first time. He spoke little English and did not know the correct fare, so he opened his wallet and held out £1 to the driver. Lawrence took out £6 from the open wallet. The regular fare would have been less than £1. Lawrence argued that the passenger had consented and that therefore there was no appropriation: *Lawrence v Commissioner of the Police for the Metropolis* [1972] AC 626.

The House of Lords confirmed that this was theft. Their lordships were not convinced that the facts actually showed that Mr Occhi had 'consented', but in any event they took the view that Parliament had deliberately omitted any words such as 'without the consent of the owner' from the theft legislation. The prosecution therefore was not required to show that the taking was without consent—this was not an ingredient of the offence. The Court held that there had clearly been an appropriation. Consent to the taking is relevant, but only to the defence of dishonesty (see below).

A different approach was taken in *R v Morris* [1984] AC 320. The accused was convicted of theft for swapping price tags on items in a self-service store and paying the lower price at the check-out. The House of Lords confirmed the convictions. The Court held that the concept of appropriation involves an element of adverse interference with or usurpation of some right of the owner. It stated that consent is relevant; there can be no 'appropriation' if the offender has the owner's consent and acts within the scope of that consent, but the key concept is the adverse interference with any of the owner's rights. Mere removal of an item from the shelf would not amount to appropriation, but removal from the shelf together with switching the labels is an adverse interference with a right of the owner—to ensure that the goods are sold and paid for at proper prices—and amounts to appropriation.

The relevance of consent to appropriation was reconsidered 10 years later in the House of Lords in *R v Gomez* [1993] AC 442. The Court preferred to follow the decision in *Lawrence*, concluding that the consent of the owner is irrelevant to a finding that 'appropriation' has taken place. In this case the consent had clearly been obtained by deception. Gomez was an assistant manager at an electrical goods shop. He agreed on a scam with a customer to help the customer purchase over £15,000 worth of electrical goods with stolen cheques. Gomez assured his manager that the cheques were valid, and thereby obtained his manager's authorisation to accept the cheques. Gomez was originally convicted of theft of the electrical goods. The House of Lords confirmed that the consent of the owner is irrelevant to the question whether there has been an appropriation. Any consent, or belief in consent, is only relevant to proof of dishonesty. So here there had been an appropriation.

Commenting on the supermarket cases, such as *Morris*, Lord Keith at 461–2 thought the assumption of any right of an owner could amount to appropriation, and this included switching labels (whether intending to steal or as a joke). He observed that it would probably amount to appropriation simply to put the item in the trolley. Usually of course this would not be accompanied by any guilty intent so it would not be an offence.

The law in England as reflected in *Gomez* and *Lawrence*, therefore, is that any taking can amount to an appropriation, if the necessary fault element is found, even where the owner consented to the taking. This is apparently not limited to situations where the consent was induced by deception, and has the rather surprising result of making normal practices such as picking up items at self-service retailers—behaviour that is not only condoned but required by the owner of the goods—amount to an appropriation.

The position has recently been confirmed in *R v Hinks* [2000] 4 All ER 833. Karen Hinks was a friend and carer of John Dolphin, an older man of limited intelligence. John Dolphin gradually transferred most of his life savings, a total of over £60,000, into Karen Hinks' bank account. Hinks was in due course convicted of theft of that money. The prosecution case was that Hinks had influenced and coerced Mr Dolphin to transfer the money to her. The House of Lords rejected her argument, on appeal, that the money was a gift, that property in the money had passed, and that it could not therefore have been 'appropriated'. The House of Lords affirmed by a majority the conclusion in *Lawrence* and *Gomez* that an appropriation can occur even where the giver of the property consented to handing over the property. Any belief in consent will be relevant to the question of dishonesty. Lord Steyn, giving the majority judgment, observed that there was no evidence that the ruling in *Lawrence* and *Gomez* had caused injustice, and that there was therefore no compelling reason to reconsider the question. He concluded (at 843) that 'in practice the mental requirements of theft are an adequate protection against injustice'.

The Victorian cases on the other hand support the view that there will be no appropriation if there was consent given by the owner. However, they accept that such 'consent' is irrelevant—and appropriation can be proven—if it was obtained by deception. In the majority of cases the outcome will therefore be equivalent to that in the UK, but there is scope for differences in result where the consent was obtained other than by deception. The obtaining of consent by unfair, but not deceptive, means as arose in *Hinks* has been specifically addressed in South Australia where a new s 142 creates the offence of dishonestly exploiting a position of advantage, carrying the same penalty (10 years) as theft.

The key case outlining the position in Victoria is the decision of the Victorian Supreme Court in *R v Baruday* [1984] VR 685, decided after *Morris* but before *Gomez*. George Baruday was an insurance broker who had sent out bogus accounts to clients, asking for extra premiums (which the insurance company had in fact already paid on the clients' behalf). His conviction for theft was upheld on appeal. When he received the cheques and paid them into his account, he was appropriating them. Although the cheques were sent with the consent of the owner, the consent was vitiated because it was induced by deception.

Morris and *Baruday* were subsequently followed by the Victorian Supreme Court in *R v Roffel* [1985] VR 511. Roffel and his wife were sole shareholders and directors of a company. While the company was undoubtedly a separate legal entity, Roffel had the sole day-to-day control of the company's affairs. Roffel, with intent to defraud creditors, drew cheques on the company's account for his own use. He was convicted of theft.

On appeal his convictions were quashed on the ground that there had been no appropriation. Although the company was a separate legal entity, Roffel's consent was effectively the company's consent, and there was no adverse interference with or usurpation of the rights of an owner. This was one case where consent was not induced by deception, and therefore was effective.

While the question has not squarely been decided, the current situation in Victoria appears to be as held in *Baruday* that there is no appropriation where there is consent, except where the consent is vitiated by deception. This appears to be consistent with *Roffel* and *Morris*, although the Court in *Baruday* said it was also applying *Lawrence*.

Critique—physical elements

Property the subject of theft

The House of Lords approach in *Preddy* was clearly not consistent with the reality of everyday banking practices, particularly with the increase in 'virtual' banking and use of electronic and other indirect transactions for both commercial and domestic financial arrangements. The House of Lords has been strongly criticised for its approach to cheques and to electronic funds transfers: see for example JC Smith, 'Obtaining Cheques by Deception or Theft' [1997] Crim LR 396–405. Jacqueline Lipton commented that the result 'leads to an apparent inconsistency between payments in cash and those made by electronic funds transfer': 'Property Offences in the Electronic Age' (1998) *Law Institute Journal* 54–8, 55. The MCCOC observed that it can obviously be argued that a cheque itself is a valuable security, one which people take steps to protect from loss. Once drawn upon, a cheque is fundamentally changed—whether returned to the original owner or not. This was the view taken in *Parsons*. So the physical cheque itself should be seen as included in the definition of 'property', of which the accused intends to permanently deprive the owner.

Following the decision in *Preddy*, the Law Commission for England and Wales reported urgently on the problem in *The Law of Dishonesty: Money Transfers*, Report No 243 (London: HMSO, 1996) and the UK Parliament in December 1996 passed amendments to the *Theft Act* 1968 to establish a specific offence of obtaining money transfers by deception (see s 15A *Theft Act* 1968 (UK)).

The new South Australian legislation may have aimed to address some of these problems by framing the theft offence as dealing with property (including money and things in action) without the owner's consent: *Criminal Law Consolidation Act* 1935 (SA) s 134. The latter element may still cause difficulties, however, if it is concluded that a new 'chose' comes into being when an electronic transfer occurs, such that the person defrauded was not at that point the 'owner' of the chose in action.

The status of electronic funds transfer in Australia is unclear. Problems may be avoided by charging an offender with obtaining a financial advantage by deception, where there is no requirement to identify 'property belonging to another', or with offences such as dishonesty by a deception procuring the execution of a valuable security, or a general offence of dishonestly obtaining a benefit by deception (such as *Criminal Law Consolidation Act* 1935 (SA) s 139): J Lipton, 'Property Offences into the 21st Century' (1999) 1 *Journal of Information Law and Technology*, <http://elj.warwick.ac.uk/jilt/99-1/lipton.html>, accessed 9 November 2003; more generally see P Grabosky, R Smith and G Dempsey, *Electronic Theft: Unlawful Acquisition in Cyberspace* (Cambridge: Cambridge University Press, 2001) ch 2.

New technologies are giving rise to new challenges to the concept of 'property' that might be dishonestly appropriated. Jacqueline Lipton highlights the issues that may be raised by new forms of intangible property such as electronically registered shares, computer software, and trade secrets and other confidential information: 'Property Offences into the 21st Century' (1999) 1 *Journal of Information Law and Technology*, <http://elj.warwick.ac.uk/jilt/99-1/lipton.html>, accessed 9 November 2003.

Existing limitations are discussed in Chapter 7 under the heading 'Computer Fraud'. One key issue has been the failure to conceptualise information as property. The case of *Oxford v Moss* (1978) 68 Cr App R 183 has been followed in Canada on the basis that the criminal law cannot recognise proprietary rights in information as the civil law has not yet taken such a step: *Stewart v The Queen* (1988) 41 CCC (3d) 481: see Winifred Holland, *The Law of Theft and Related Offences* (Scarborough, Ontario: Thomson Canada, 1998) p 374; see also Gordon Hughes, 'Computers, Crime and the Concept of "Property"' (1990) 1 *Intellectual Property Journal* 154–63.

This limitation on the concept of property has, however, been seriously challenged in the reviews and reforms that have taken place across Australia in response to growing concerns about computer misuse and access to electronically recorded confidential information. Civil actions such as breach of copyright might be available in some situations but criminal liability would not apply.

The MCCOC reviewed these issues in a separate report: *Chapter 4, Damage and Computer Offences*, Report (January 2001). It was recognised that the special character of computer technology made it necessary to introduce specific offences. These are discussed further in Chapter 7. The Northern Territory Code specifically establishes an offence of 'unlawfully obtaining confidential information': s 222. Statutory offences of unauthorised dealing with information held on a computer have been enacted in several jurisdictions.

Another obstacle to pursuing computer-based offending, at least indirectly, has been the common law view that electricity was not 'property' capable of being stolen. This was also the conclusion in the English case of *Low v Blease* [1975] Crim LR 513. This situation continues in the Codes and in the Victorian and Australian Capital Territory provisions. It appears to preclude a charge of theft where someone, for example, bypasses an electricity meter to avoid paying for the electricity used, or misuses a computer or phone.

The Codes have incorporated separate offences of misuse of electricity (*Criminal Code* (Qld) s 408; *Criminal Code* (Tas) s 233; *Criminal Code* (WA) s 390) as have the Australian Capital Territory (*Crimes Act* 1900 (ACT) s 106 'dishonest abstraction') and the Northern Territory (*Criminal Code* (NT) s 221 'unlawful appropriation of power'). The MCCOC recommended that electricity should clearly amount to 'property' for the purposes both of theft and obtaining property by deception. This approach has been adopted in the new South Australian provisions (*Criminal Law Consolidation Act* 1935 (SA) s 130).

Property belonging to another

The case of *Greenberg* highlighted problems with self-service retailers such as petrol stations, where ownership of goods passes immediately. This would appear to apply equally under the South Australian legislation, provided the dishonest intent only arose after the petrol had been placed (with the owner's consent) in the petrol tank and ownership had therefore passed to the purchaser. Thefts and frauds from service stations now represent a significant problem. The New South Wales Bureau of Crime Statistics and Research reported in June 2002 that recorded fraud offences in that state rose 16 per cent between 2000 and 2001, and that much of this increase was caused by cases of people filling up their cars with petrol and driving off without paying: Marilyn Chilvers, 'What Lies Behind the Growth in Fraud?', NSW Bureau of Crime Statistics and Research (July 2002). The Bureau found that there was a 38 per cent increase in service station frauds, from 4624 in 2000 to 6366 in 2001. Many of these cases would of course involve a person having the necessary dishonest intent at the time of putting the petrol in the tank, but this may not always be easy to prove. A possible solution was to require pre-payment of petrol, at least at times when the offence is particularly prevalent, an approach already being trialled in other states. This solution neatly resolves both the legal and practical problems.

The effect of mistake on the receiver's criminal liability still appears problematic. In particular, the law has been complicated by the requirement to ascertain, using civil law principles, when an obligation to make restoration arises in such cases. Subject to the operation of special statutory provisions, the result differs depending when the receiver realised the mistake, and depending on whether the mistake was one that could be categorised as 'fundamental'. The MCCOC discussed these issues in detail in *Chapter 3, Theft, Fraud, Bribery and Related Offences*, Report (December 1995) pp 49–61. It concluded that, to avoid inappropriately extending criminal liability, the decision in *Illich v The Queen* (1987) 162 CLR 110 should be confirmed. As the Committee pointed out (at 57), the culpability of the offender who has been unexpectedly overpaid is lower than for other thefts because 'the defendant has had temptation thrust upon him or her. To make a defendant like Illich, or the recipient of a social security overpayment, guilty of theft in these cases [where the mistake was only realised later] is to cast a duty to act in relation to innocently acquired property on pain of committing theft'. Fundamental mistakes should continue to negate the intention to transfer ownership, and such mistakes should be defined as mistakes as to the essential nature of the subject matter or as to the identity of the transferee, or as to the amount of any money provided the receiver was aware of the mistake at the time of the overpayment. This formulation has been incorporated in s 131.7 of the *Criminal Code* (Cth) as amended in 2000. Where there has been a fundamental mistake, the property will still belong to the victim, and the receiver will be guilty of theft, provided they have the relevant intent, whenever they become aware of the mistake. Where a non-fundamental mistake was made, the victim would be left to their civil remedies: see MCCOC, *Chapter 3, Theft, Fraud, Bribery and Related Offences*, Report (December 1995) p 59.

The meaning of appropriation

The English cases on the meaning of 'appropriation' have expanded the concept to cover almost any act dealing with property, even with the owner's apparent consent. Australian cases similarly have not dealt thoroughly or unambiguously with the relevance of consent to criminal appropriation. The extension in the UK to picking up items in a supermarket suggests that this expansive interpretation may be becoming disconnected from the 'real world'. Support for the *Gomez* approach may arise from the view that consent is irrelevant at least where it can be said to be vitiated by deception: see, for example, CR Williams, *Property Offences* (3rd edn, Sydney: LBC Information Services, 1999) p 338. The question of when a fraud does vitiate consent is however not entirely clear. The MCCOC rejected the *Gomez* approach as a basis for dealing with the question of consent in theft: MCCOC, *Chapter 3, Theft, Fraud, Bribery and Related Offences*, Report (December 1995) p 35. The Committee (at 35) argued that as property passes irrespective of fraud or mistake (except of a fundamental kind), it is inconsistent to say that a non-fundamental fraud or mistake vitiates consent for the purpose of finding appropriation.

The effect of adopting the approach in *Gomez* is to place considerable weight on the concept of dishonesty, which becomes the key element in differentiating thefts from non-criminal takings. The meaning of dishonesty has itself been controversial, with very different paths being taken by the English and Victorian courts, as will be discussed in more detail below.

R v Roffel [1985] VR 511 was criticised in the House of Lords in *Gomez*. Lord Browne-Wilkinson reiterated that the issue of consent was irrelevant at the time of deciding whether there had been an appropriation. This had also been the view of the dissenting judge, Brooking J, in *Roffel*. Whether or not the company could be said to 'consent', the defendant will be found to have appropriated the property: the question will then be whether the accused acted dishonestly and with intent to permanently deprive. Lord Browne-Wilkinson observed [1993] AC 442 at 497: 'I am glad to be able to reach this conclusion. The pillaging of companies by those who control them is now all too common. It would offend both common sense and justice to hold that the very control which enables such people to extract the company's assets constitutes a defence to a charge of theft from the company.'

Roffel appeared to leave small companies exposed to the frauds of their directors, although as CR Williams points out (*Property Offences* (3rd edn: Sydney: LBC Information Services, 1999) p 123), such frauds can still be prosecuted under the corporations legislation. The decision in *Roffel* has recently been rejected in principle in the High Court decision of *Macleod v The Queen* (2003) 197 ALR 333 by McHugh J at 351 and Callinan J at 358–9. The decision was in any event later restricted to cases where the consent could *in law* be said to be that of the victim company, looking at the memorandum and articles of association. This will in practice be rare. As an example, in *Clarkson and Lyon* (1986) 24 A Crim R 54 it was held that, due to the terms of incorporation of the Building Society, a director could not give valid consent to acts that benefited him.

The Victorian approach, where consent means there has been no appropriation *but* the consent may be negated by any fraud, blurs the distinction between theft and obtaining property by deception. It has the effect that obtaining property by a deception that induces 'consent' could be prosecuted as either theft or obtaining property by deception, and that almost every obtaining of property by deception could be a theft (although not vice versa).

The *Crimes Act* 1900 (ACT) was amended in 1985 and now differs from the Victorian and English legislation in relation to the definitions of appropriation and of dishonesty. As noted earlier, the definition of appropriation has two alternative parts, combining the notions of usurping the rights of owner and obtaining by deception, reflecting the approach in *Gomez*: s 86. The legislation thereby removes the traditional distinction between theft and obtaining property by deception. This is also the effect of the South Australian reforms. Section 134(1) *Criminal Law Consolidation Act* 1935 (SA) requires proof of a 'dealing with property' without the owner's consent for there to be an offence of theft; s 132(3) provides that 'a person who knows that another's consent was obtained by dishonest deception is taken to act without consent'. There is therefore some overlap with the South Australian deception offence; as in Victoria the two offences carry the same penalty.

The MCCOC concluded that this blurring of the offences is unsatisfactory. It argued that there is a socially understood difference between 'theft' and 'fraud' (that is, obtaining property by deception). The issue of the overlap between theft and obtaining property by deception will be examined in more detail in Chapter 7. The MCCOC proposed a definition of appropriation as any 'assumption of rights of an owner without consent'. Deception therefore would not vitiate consent but would lead to using a charge of obtaining property by deception in the alternative. This definition appears in the 2000 amendments to the Commonwealth *Criminal Code*, s 131.3(1). MCCOC argued strongly that under current civil law principles a non-fundamental fraud will not vitiate consent, and that cases such as *Baruday* are in error in taking this approach: MCCOC, *Chapter 3, Theft, Fraud, Bribery and Related Offences*, Report (December 1995) p 35.

We agree with the Committee's preferred approach of asking whether there was consent to the taking; if there was, there should not be an offence of theft but an obtaining by deception (if deception was used). The only exception would be for consent induced by fundamental mistake or fraud. Again it seems likely that the general public would see consent as having been given in cases such as *Baruday* and *Gomez*, albeit induced by fraud. It appears reasonable then to say that this is obtaining property by deception but not theft.

To avoid problems where the prosecutor chose the 'wrong' offence, theft and fraud/deception should be alternative verdicts for the jury, carrying the same maximum penalty (provided there was no risk of an offender being ambushed at the trial and not knowing that both offences were open to being found by the jury). Provision for alternative verdicts appears in the amended Commonwealth *Criminal Code*: s 134.1(15) and (16), together with a requirement that the accused be accorded 'procedural fairness' in relation to the operation of the alternative charges.

The current law—fault elements

We will now look at the fault elements for the traditional stealing offences. These are an intention to permanently deprive the owner, and an additional element of moral blameworthiness, such as acting 'fraudulently' or acting 'dishonestly' or 'unlawfully'.

Intention to permanently deprive

Borrowing is not theft. There must be intention to substantially or permanently deprive. This component of the offence is fundamental to the common law of larceny and is retained under both the Criminal Codes of Queensland (s 391(2)), Tasmania (s 226(1)), Western Australia (s 371(2)) and the Northern Territory (s 209), and in the Australian Capital Territory (*Crimes Act* 1900 s 84), South Australia (*Criminal Law Consolidation Act* 1935 (s 134(1)(c)) and Victoria (*Crimes Act* 1958 s 72(1)).

This does not mean that it must be shown that there was actual permanent deprivation. What is being punished is having the 'guilty intent'. It merely requires proof beyond reasonable doubt of the intention to permanently deprive.

Further, the requirement to show an intent to permanently deprive only means showing intention to effect a deprivation that is 'permanent' relative to the original owner's right to the property.

It therefore seems to be generally accepted, both at common law and in terms of social understanding of property crimes, that borrowing something, even without consent, is not theft. However, where are we to draw the line between borrowing and theft? The concept of intent to permanently deprive is an attempt at making such a distinction. It will therefore only be theft if the accused person's claimed intention to return the property is so loose, or extends for so long, as to be equivalent to an outright taking.

The concept is extended in the new South Australian legislation to refer both to intent to permanently deprive and intent 'to make a serious encroachment on' proprietary rights (s 134(1)(c)). It is further developed in *Crimes Act* 1958 (Vic) s 73(12); see also *Crimes Act* 1900 (ACT) s 87, *Criminal Code* (NT) s 209(1) and *Criminal Law Consolidation Act* 1935 (SA) s 134(2). An intention to permanently deprive is deemed where the accused intends to treat the property as his or her own to dispose of regardless of the owner's rights, and a borrowing may amount to this if it is 'for a period and in circumstances making it equivalent to an outright taking or disposal': *Crimes Act* 1958 (Vic) s 73(12).

The *Crimes Act* 1958 (Vic) s 73(12) is itself developed further, s 73(13) (and see also ACT s 87; NT s 209(1); SA s 134(2)(b)) providing that:

> where a person, having possession or control (lawfully or not) of property belonging to another, parts with the property under a condition as to its return which he [or she] may not be able to perform, this (if done for purposes of his [or her] own and without the other's authority) amounts to treating the property as his [or her] own to dispose of regardless of the other's rights.

This is intended to deal with the case where the accused (for example) pawns the property of another as security for a loan, intending to redeem the property and return it to the owner. If the accused's circumstances are such that there is some risk that he or she will not be able to redeem the property, it may fall within this extension of 'intent to permanently deprive'.

In the Code jurisdictions the notion of intent to permanently deprive is given an extended reading by the concept of taking or converting property 'fraudulently'. The *Criminal Code* (Qld) s 391(1) provides that stealing involves 'fraudulently' taking or converting property. A taking or conversion is deemed to be fraudulent if done with any of a series of intents, including:

- intent to permanently deprive the owner of it: s 391(2)(a);
- intent to use the thing as a pledge or security: s 391(2)(c);
- 'intent to part with it on a condition as to its return which the person taking or converting it may be unable to perform': s 391(2)(d);
- 'intent to deal with it in such a manner that it cannot be returned in the condition in which it was at the time of the taking': s 391(2)(e);

and in relation to money,

- intent to use it 'at the will of the person who takes or converts it' even if the person intends to repay the amount later: s 391(2)(f).

The *Criminal Code* (WA) includes identical sections in s 371(2); see also *Criminal Code* (Tas) s 228.

In New South Wales the term 'fraudulently' is used in its common law sense but, as the MCCOC notes, the common law cases have been confused. While some cases virtually equated 'fraudulently' with intention to permanently deprive, others considered it also to introduce an additional element of moral wrongfulness: MCCOC, *Chapter 3, Theft, Fraud, Bribery and Related Offences*, Report (December 1995) p 11. We will come back to this point when discussing the meaning of dishonesty.

The *Theft Act* 1968 (UK) replaced the term 'fraudulently' with 'dishonestly': the framers regarded this as a vital concept in the offence of theft, more readily understood than, but equivalent to, the common law term 'fraudulently'. The UK *Theft Act* and the Australian equivalents, however, also include the component of intention to permanently deprive.

The common law of larceny requires proof that the accused assumed ownership of the property, intending to permanently deprive the owner: *Foster v The Queen* (1967) 118 CLR 117 at 121. The High Court said in relation to the offence of larceny under s 118 *Crimes Act* 1900 (NSW) that this fault element is made out by showing either the intent to deprive the owner permanently of *possession* of the goods, or to deprive him or her of *property* in the goods. *Crimes Act* 1900 (NSW) s 118 provides that an offender will not be entitled to an acquittal simply where they argue that they intended to restore the property to the owner, or, in the case of money, to return an equivalent amount. The High Court in *Foster* in examining that provision stated that where the accused only intends to deprive the owner of *possession* for a limited time, this will not amount to larceny but larceny will have been committed where there is intent to deprive of ownership, even if there is an intent to return the goods later. Intention to use the property as a pledge or security, even in the hope of being able later to return it, will therefore still amount to 'intent to permanently deprive'.

The English and Victorian courts have maintained the distinction between borrowing and theft, even where the defendant was clearly engaged in some sort of criminal enterprise. In *Warner* (1970) 55 Cr App R 93 the accused had been annoyed by neighbours and took a box of their tools to hide them. When he was charged with theft he said he had intended to return the box in an hour or so. He was convicted of theft, but his conviction was quashed on appeal. Edmund Davies LJ said that the aim of s 73(12) was to ensure that it was no excuse for an accused person to plead absence of intent to permanently deprive 'if it is clear that he appropriated another's property intending to treat it is as his own, regardless of the owner's rights'. It did not extend to the sort of borrowing in question here.

Similarly, in *R v Lloyd* [1985] 3 WLR 30 the English Court of Appeal held that the unauthorised borrowing of feature films for a few hours, for the purpose of making large numbers of pirate copies, did not fall within the theft legislation. In that case, the whole enterprise depended on returning the films as quickly as possible so that their absence was not noticed. There may of course have been civil remedies available arising out of the cinema's contract, or in relation to infringing copyright:

the Court in fact noted (at 38) that there was potentially a conspiracy to contravene the UK copyright legislation. Conspiracy to defraud could be charged in such circumstances: *Scott v Metropolitan Police Commissioner* [1975] AC 819. The possibility that behaviours such as occurred in *Scott* and *Lloyd* require establishment of new criminal offences based on general dishonesty is discussed further in Chapter 7.

Section 73(12) *Crimes Act* 1958 (Vic) does include cases where the offender 'borrows' property intending to return it to the owner when it is no longer of value. For instance, he or she might 'borrow' someone's tram ticket, or ticket to the football, intending to return it at the end of the day, when it is no longer of any value. This would constitute theft, either under the general definition, or at least under s 73(12). It is borrowing 'for a period and in circumstances making it equivalent to an outright taking or disposal' (and see *Criminal Code* (Qld) s 391(2)(c)–(e) and *Criminal Code* (WA) s 371(2)(c)–(e)). The new South Australian legislation specifically provides that the relevant intent will be found where the offender deals with the property in a way that creates a substantial risk that 'when the owner gets it back, its value will be substantially impaired': *Criminal Law Consolidation Act* 1935 (SA) s 134(2)(b)(ii).

For example, the English case of *R v Duru* [1974] 1 WLR 2 held that a scam that resulted in cheques being provided by a city council on false information amounted to the offence of obtaining property (the cheques) by deception, with intention to permanently deprive. While under English banking practice the cheque itself would ultimately be returned—once drawn upon by the conspirators—it had clearly totally changed in its nature by the time the piece of paper returned to the drawer. The Court in *Duru* considered this to fall within the general definition of intent to permanently deprive, without requiring reference to s 73(12), but agreed that s 73(12) also applied here—that the accused had intended to treat the property as though it had been their own, to dispose of regardless of the owner's rights.

A further twist in this discussion is the situation where the offender had—or claimed to have—intended to return the property if it was not what had been wanted. This is referred to as 'conditional intention'. The cases have turned on how the court interpreted the particular facts. *R v Easom* [1971] 2 QB 315 involved John Easom, who was sitting in the theatre and who picked up a handbag belonging to the person in front of him. He looked in the handbag but only found a purse, tissues and such items. He put the handbag back under the seat. Unfortunately for Easom it belonged to a female police officer, who had attached it to her wrist with thread, and was therefore aware of his actions. Easom was charged with theft of the handbag, and of a purse, notebook, some tissues and cosmetics and a pen.

The English Court of Appeal held (at 319) that Easom had not committed theft, because he had only intended to deprive the owner of anything found, on examination, to be valuable. This 'conditional appropriation' did not amount to intention to permanently deprive, particularly not of the specified items.

On the other hand, something more than conditional intent was found in the Victorian case of *Sharp v McCormick* [1986] VR 869. In this case the accused,

McCormick, had taken a motor car coil from his employer, dishonestly, intending to fit it to his car. McCormick said in the police interview that if it turned out to be the wrong size he would have returned it. The magistrate dismissed the theft charge on the basis that the accused had no case to answer, following *Easom*. The Supreme Court disagreed. It concluded, hearing an application for an order to review the magistrate's decision, that McCormick could be guilty of theft in either of two ways:

- if it were said that, at the time of the appropriation, he intended to keep the coil *unless* it did not fit this is sufficient intention for theft under the general definition in s 72(1);
- alternatively if it was decided that he intended, at the time of appropriation, to return the coil *unless* it fitted and he then decided to keep it this came within the first part of 73(12), intending to treat the thing as his own to dispose of regardless of the owner's rights (discussed at 872).

Here the Court considered (at 872–3) that '[w]hen the respondent took the coil he was quite clearly treating the coil as his own to dispose of as he saw fit and he was paying no regard to the rights of the true owner'. The case went back to the magistrate for a hearing of the theft charge.

Stealing cars, boats and planes
Most jurisdictions include special provisions to deal with unauthorised use of cars, planes and other vehicles. Such provisions effectively remove any requirement to prove intent to permanently deprive, on the basis that such behaviour seriously inconveniences owners but that most 'joyriders' only intend to 'use' and will not in fact intend to permanently deprive the owner (or to make a financial gain) so that in practice it will often be difficult to prove such an intent.

Most jurisdictions provide that the use of motor vehicles without consent or without authority is an offence. The *Criminal Code* (WA) s 371(1) simply states that such a person 'is said to steal' the motor vehicle; *Crimes Act* 1900 (NSW) s 154A states (in relation to any 'conveyance') that such a person is deemed to be guilty of larceny. New South Wales also creates specific offences: *Crimes Act* 1900 (NSW) ss 154AA, 154B. The legislation in the Australian Capital Territory, Northern Territory, Queensland and South Australia similarly creates separate offences for such behaviour: *Crimes Act* 1900 (ACT) s 111; *Criminal Code* (NT) ss 216, 217, 218; *Criminal Code* (Qld) s 408A (dealing with 'vessels'); *Criminal Law Consolidation Act* 1935 (SA) s 86A. The Victorian provision operates by deeming unauthorised use of a motor vehicle or aircraft to be conclusive evidence of intent to permanently deprive: *Crimes Act* 1958 (Vic) s 73(14)(a).

The problem of fungibles
The requirement to prove intent to permanently deprive creates a problem where the goods taken are fungible, that is, are interchangeable. Examples include

money or a borrowed cup of sugar. A borrower of money will usually not intend to return the precise coins or notes, although they may have every intention of 'repaying' the amount. The sugar-borrower may intend to return replacement sugar. Because of their nature, intent to permanently deprive will exist even though the offender may 'really' only be borrowing: *R v Cockburn* [1968] 1 WLR 281 at 284. This means that the taking (borrowing) of fungibles is dealt with differently from other items. Whether the accused will be guilty of theft turns on whether they were dishonest.

The Queensland Code provides for a rebuttable presumption of fraud where fungibles are taken without payment (s 391(2A) and (2B)).

Section 87(4) of the *Crimes Act* 1900 (ACT) specifically provides that where money is taken, intention to permanently deprive is not automatically found only on the basis that there was no intention to return the specific money taken. It does not directly address other fungibles. However, the revised definition of dishonesty included in the Australian Capital Territory legislation in 1985, whereby a person will not be regarded as dishonest who intends not to cause any significant practical detriment to the owner, could lead to an acquittal in relation to fungibles such as the borrowed cup of sugar, a point discussed further below in relation to the meaning of dishonesty.

Acting dishonestly

Langham bought a crossbow from a sports store in Adelaide for $675: *R v Langham* (1984) 36 SASR 48. He subsequently found it did not 'meet his purposes' and he returned it. The shop would not give him a cash refund, but gave him credit for another purchase. Langham needed the cash, and a few weeks later he returned to the store and used part of his credit to buy a shotgun. He pointed the gun at the store manager and demanded the balance of his credit in cash, $301, from the shop manager. The manager handed over $300; Langham then demanded and received the remaining dollar to use up his credit.

Taking another's property with intent to permanently deprive is likely to be morally wrong. However, most jurisdictions also include explicit reference to a requirement of moral culpability in terms of the offender having acted 'dishonestly' or 'fraudulently'. In cases such as *Langham*, above, and *Lopatta*, discussed earlier in this chapter, the courts have had to decide when a taking with intent to permanently deprive is and is not 'dishonest' or 'fraudulent'.

'Dishonesty' is a key concept in the Victorian, Australian Capital Territory, South Australian and English frameworks. It is a requirement in obtaining property by deception (*Crimes Act* 1958 (Vic) s 81; *Crimes Act* 1900 (ACT) s 84), obtaining a financial advantage by deception (*Crimes Act* 1958 (Vic) s 82; *Crimes Act* 1900 (ACT) s 95) and in the South Australian deception offence (*Criminal Law Consolidation Act* 1935 s 139) as well as in theft. In fact the focus of the theft offence shifted significantly, from an action-oriented offence as at common law to an offence defined primarily by the existence of the dishonest state of mind. In Tasmania the expression 'fraudulently and without claim of right' was replaced in 1975 with the term 'dishonestly'. Dishonesty now carries a substantial part of the meaning of the offence in these jurisdictions.

Dishonesty is, however, not statutorily defined, other than in the new South Australian legislation (s 131). The English Criminal Law Revision Committee, in the report which formed that basis for the English (and then Victorian) legislation, thought that dishonesty was 'something which laymen [and laywomen] can easily recognise when they see it': *Theft and Related Offences*, Report No 8 (London: HMSO, Cmnd 2877, 1966) p 20.

The UK, the Australian Capital Territory and Victorian legislation provide definitions of mental states that do not amount to dishonesty, but only in relation to theft. These are:

- a claim of right or entitlement (s 73(2)(a) *Crimes Act* 1958 (Vic));
- belief that the owner would have consented (s 73(2)(b) *Crimes Act* 1958 (Vic)); and
- belief that the owner cannot be discovered (s 73(2)(c) *Crimes Act* 1958 (Vic)).

The offences of obtaining property and obtaining financial advantage by deception contain no elaboration of the meaning of dishonesty. Section 86(4) *Crimes Act* 1900 (ACT) provides equivalent definitions, with the addition of belief that no detriment will be caused to the owner.

Section 131(1) of the *Criminal Law Consolidation Act* 1935 (SA) provides that a person's conduct is dishonest if 'the person acts dishonestly according to the standards of ordinary people and knows that he or she is so acting'. The legislation also provides that a person does not act dishonestly who finds property and believes the owner cannot be discovered (s 131(4)), or who acts under a belief as to their legal or equitable right to the property (s 131(5) and (6)).

The Northern Territory legislation makes no reference to dishonesty, instead defining the offence as 'unlawfully' appropriating property. This is defined in s 1 as 'without authorization, justification or excuse'. The only express exclusion from the offence is for a person appropriating abandoned property believing that the owner cannot be discovered, in similar terms to *Crimes Act* 1958 (Vic) 73(2)(c): *Criminal Code* (NT) s 209(1). Claim of right is a general defence set out earlier in the *Criminal Code* (NT) s 30(2).

There is no separate requirement of 'dishonesty' under the common law or the Queensland and Western Australian Codes. However, New South Wales, Queensland and Western Australia use the term 'fraudulently'. In Queensland and Western Australia a taking is deemed to be fraudulent if carried out with any of the listed intentions noted earlier, which comprise forms of 'intent to permanently deprive': *Criminal Code* (Qld) s 391(2); *Criminal Code* (WA) s 371(2). Claim of right is a separate general defence. It is also specifically provided that the intention to repay money taken does not prevent the taker from being found to have acted fraudulently: *Criminal Code* (Qld) s 391(2)(f); *Criminal Code* (WA) s 371(2)(f).

The framers of the UK *Theft Act* regarded 'fraudulently' as equivalent to the new term 'dishonesty': Criminal Law Revision Committee, *Theft and Related Offences*, Report No 8 (London: HMSO, Cmnd 2877, 1966) pp 19, 20. This was also the view of the New South Wales Court of Appeal in *R v Glenister* [1980] 2 NSWLR 597.

Some case law limits the term 'fraudulently' to an equivalent to intent to permanently deprive: see the discussion on that concept above. Other authorities require proof both of intent to permanently deprive and some dishonesty or moral obloquy. The three negative definitions of dishonesty in the Victorian legislation will be discussed in turn, before we consider, in the Critique section, the debate about broader understandings of the meaning of dishonesty.

Claim of right

Herbert Walden was an elder of the Gungalida people from the country around Burketown in Queensland. When he was growing up he had hunted with his father for bush tucker—emus, plain turkeys, kangaroos, goannas and snakes—which the family ate. He later married and went to live with his wife and children in Mt Isa. During this time he would still leave the town to hunt in the bush for bush tucker every week or so. One Sunday in February 1984 Walden, his wife and children were in the bush hunting, having obtained permission from the station owner. Walden shot a plain turkey and took it home to eat, and his son Peter caught a turkey chick and carried it home to keep as a pet, both practices they believed they were entitled to do, and which were consistent with Aboriginal traditions. Plain turkeys were, however, protected fauna under the *Fauna Conservation Act* 1974 (Qld)—a matter of which Walden was unaware—and he was charged with and convicted of taking and keeping protected fauna, receiving a substantial fine.

If a person honestly believes they have a legal right to take goods they will not be held to have acted fraudulently or dishonestly. Claim of right is a central defence at common law (see, for example, *R v Love* (1989) 17 NSWLR 608) and under the Codes, as well as by express statutory provision in Victoria, the Australian Capital Territory, the Northern Territory and South Australia. Section 73(2)(a) of the *Crimes Act* 1958 (Vic) states that a person will not act dishonestly:

> if he [or she] appropriates the property in the belief that he [or she] has in law the right to deprive the other of it, on behalf of himself [or herself] or of a third person...

The *Criminal Code* (Cth) provides a general defence of claim of right in s 9.5. The same general principles appear to apply in all jurisdictions on the availability of this defence. For example, the Codes provide that a person is not criminally responsible (*Criminal Code* (NT) s 30(2); *Criminal Code* (Qld) s 22(2); *Criminal Code* (WA) s 22):

> ...for an act done or omitted to be done by the person with respect to any property in the exercise of an honest claim of right and without intention to defraud.

The Queensland section was in issue in *Walden v Hensler* (1987) 163 CLR 561. The members of the High Court differed on how they interpreted Walden's belief in his entitlement to take plain turkeys according to Aboriginal law and traditions. His claim was ultimately dismissed, although the Court (perhaps uncomfortable about the political implications of its decision) varied the outcome of his charge from conviction with a substantial fine to an absolute discharge. Brennan J observed (at 578) that: 'To deprive an Aboriginal without his knowledge of his traditional right to hunt for bush tucker for his family on his own country and then to convict and punish him for doing what Aborigines had previously been encouraged to do would be an intolerable injustice. It adds the insult of criminal conviction and punishment to the injustice of expropriation of traditional rights.'

Three of the six judges (Brennan, Toohey and Gaudron JJ) concluded that Walden's belief did amount to an honest claim of right, confirming also that it is no obstacle that a right claimed is not a right recognised by the law of Queensland. Brennan J, however, went on (at 569) to decide that the defence was not available here. On his interpretation, the *Criminal Code* (Qld) limited such claims to offences 'with respect to any property' and he concluded that the conservation offences were not property offences. Toohey and Gaudron JJ (at 603, 609) disagreed with this view of the operation of the legislative provision and would have supported Walden's appeal. Deane J (at 582) regarded the claim as merely a claim to ignorance of the criminal law, which could provide no defence and Dawson J (at 594) concluded that claim of right was not available in the context of the particular legislative provision.

Pre-*Theft Act* 1968 (UK) cases suggested that the term 'fraudulent' effectively meant 'without claim of right'. This was the position also adopted by the Victorian Supreme Court when considering the meaning of 'dishonesty' in the offences of obtaining property and obtaining a financial advantage by deception under the Victorian legislation: see *R v Salvo* [1980] VR 401, *R v Brow* [1981] VR 783 and *R v Bonollo* [1981] VR 633. However, at common law and in the Code states it appears that 'fraudulent' cannot simply mean 'without claim of right'. Absence of any claim of right is a separate component of the offence, as noted in the earlier discussion of larceny and a separate defence in the Code states.

The English courts in the key cases of *R v Feely* [1973] 1 QB 530 and *R v Ghosh* [1982] 1 QB 1053 and the New South Wales Court of Criminal Appeal in *R v Glenister*

[1980] 2 NSWLR 597 have certainly adopted a broader test of the meaning of fraudulent or dishonest. This has also been the approach of Gaudron and Toohey JJ in the High Court in *Peters v The Queen* (1998) 192 CLR 493, and this broader reading of dishonesty is embodied in the new s 131(1) *Criminal Law Consolidation Act* 1935 (SA). These lines of case law are discussed further below in the Critique section.

The claimed belief in entitlement—claim of right—must be genuinely held but need not be reasonable, although reasonableness will be a factor in deciding whether the belief was genuinely or honestly held. This was considered in the case of *R v Lopatta* (1983) 35 SASR 101, which was discussed earlier. Lopatta had broken into his ex-employer's warehouse with a hired truck and had taken twenty large drums of oil, worth about $5000, which was approximately the amount Lopatta claimed he was owed in back pay. He was charged with warehouse-breaking and larceny. He claimed that he had not acted dishonestly, but had honestly believed he had a right to the value of the drums, which he intended to sell to obtain the money he believed owing to him. White J observed (at 107–8) when allowing Lopatta's appeal from his conviction:

> If the accused was to have any chance of acquittal, the jury had to take a reasonably favourable view of his general honesty and his credibility as a witness because his conduct was unlawful and even bizarre. Nevertheless, an accused person charged with a crime of dishonesty may be heard to say that he honestly believed in a claim of right even if there is no foundation in fact or law for that wrong-headed belief. …Whatever the merits of the defence…insistence upon reasonableness in the grounds as well as honesty in the belief is not and never has been the law.

The defence is available where the accused acts on behalf of a third party whom the accused believes is entitled to the property: see *Crimes Act* 1958 (Vic) s 73(2)(a).

The claim must be of a legal right not simply a claim to a moral right. Murphy J in *R v Salvo* [1980] VR 401 at 420 roundly asserted that 'a sincere belief entertained by the accused that Karma required that he should retake the car would not prevent the retaking from being dishonest. But a sincere belief that the law of the land allowed him to do so would'.

In *Walden v Hensler* (1987) 163 CLR 561 the Court stated that if Walden's only claim was a moral or ethical claim it would not be sufficient to enliven this defence. This requirement has been modified in South Australia where the legislation refers to a 'legal or equitable right' (*Criminal Law Consolidation Act* 1935 s 131(5) and (6)).

The claim of legal right need not, however, relate to any known or existing law: *R v Lopatta* (1983) 35 SASR 101; *Walden v Hensler*. It also need only be a belief in entitlement to *possession*, not a belief in a right to the method of taking away. This was the conclusion in *R v Langham* (1984) 36 SASR 48, outlined earlier. Langham had used a shotgun to obtain money he believed he was owed. He gave evidence that he believed he was entitled to the cash and needed it urgently. Langham was convicted of armed robbery, that is, stealing, using force or threat of force to achieve the theft. On appeal his conviction was quashed. The South Australian Supreme Court held that provided an accused honestly believes he or she has a legal right to the money this is a good defence to a theft or robbery charge—however the right is enforced. The belief need not be reasonable; and it need not be a belief that the particular method of obtaining the property is lawful. Such a belief will prevent the taking being theft.

The new South Australian legislation specifically provides that conduct is not dishonest if the person 'honestly but mistakenly believes that he or she has a legal or equitable right to act in that way' (*Criminal Law Consolidation Act* 1935 s 131(5)), and that a person who asserts a legal or equitable right to property does not act dishonestly if they honestly believe that right exists (s 131(6)). This addresses both the claim to take the property, and also the accused's belief (even if mistaken) that he or she is entitled to act in the way he or she did to retrieve the property. These exceptions do not, however, prevent the accused being charged with a separate offence addressed to the method of enforcing the claim of right, such as assault where the property is forcibly taken from another.

Belief in the owner's consent
It is not dishonest to appropriate property if the accused believes the owner would have consented if he or she had known of the appropriation. For example, an accused may have forgotten her wallet when leaving for work. She borrows five dollars from petty cash at work to get home, believing the employer will not mind, and intending to repay the money the next day. A taking will not be dishonest if the taker 'appropriates the property in the belief that he [or she] would have the other's consent if the other knew of the appropriation and the circumstances of it' (*Crimes Act* 1958 (Vic) s 73(2)(b) and see *Crimes Act* 1900 (ACT) s 86(4)(c)). In South Australia lack of consent must be proven as an element in the offence of theft (*Criminal Law Consolidation Act* 1935 s 134): s 132(2) provides that the element is negated if the offender 'honestly believes, from the words or conduct of [the owner], that he or she has [the owner's] consent'.

The test is whether the belief is honest. If so, dishonesty cannot be proven. Again, reasonableness will still be relevant to whether the fact finder believes there was an honest belief. A jury might query whether there was a genuine belief in consent in the example given earlier if the employer had explicitly prohibited any borrowings from petty cash.

This does not appear to be a specific defence at common law or under the Codes. Given the definition of larceny as being 'fraudulent and without claim of right' (as discussed earlier) it may be argued that a person who takes property, genuinely believing the owner would have consented had they known, will not be regarded as acting fraudulently and may in addition be seen as exercising an honest claim of right. A belief in consent should similarly provide a defence under the South Australian provision, which defines theft as dealing with property dishonestly and without the owner's consent, intending to permanently deprive, but provides that a claim of right negates a finding of dishonesty (*Criminal Law Consolidation Act* 1935 s 131(5) and (6)). This broader interpretation of claim of right was spelt out by Gleeson, Gummow and Hayne JJ in *Macleod v The Queen* at 342, where they adopted the general principle spelt out by Dawson J in *Walden v Hensler* (1987) 163 CLR 561 at 591: that it is '…always necessary for the prosecution to prove the intent which forms an ingredient of a particular crime and any honestly held belief…which is inconsistent with the existence of that intent will afford a defence.'

Belief that the owner cannot be found
Ordinarily, lost property—as distinct from abandoned property—still belongs to the owner. But if an accused believes he or she cannot find the owner by taking reasonable steps, he or she will not ordinarily be regarded as acting dishonestly if they keep it. This is the common law position. It is also reflected in the Victorian, Australian Capital Territory, Northern Territory and South Australian legislation. For example, under s 73(2)(c) *Crimes Act* 1958 (Vic) a person will not be regarded as dishonest:

> (except where the property came to him [or her] as trustee or personal representative) if he [or she] appropriates the property in the belief that the person to whom the property belongs cannot be discovered by taking reasonable steps.

This 'defence' covers cases of finding lost or abandoned property. It also covers the situation where an accused obtains property by another's mistake, for example where property comes to her address by mail, with no return address, and the receiver does not know how, using reasonable means, the owner could be traced.

Willingness to pay
The fact that the person is willing to pay for the goods taken does not in itself negate the fault element for theft: *Crimes Act* 1900 (ACT) s 86(3); *Crimes Act* 1900 (NSW) s 118; *Criminal Law Consolidation Act* 1935 (SA) s 131(3); *Crimes Act* 1958 (Vic) s 73(3). It is clearly undesirable that people think they can take what they want from someone else, and be safe from criminal punishment because they are willing to pay.

This does not mean that willingness to pay is no defence. It may show lack of dishonesty in some cases, such as the petrol station cases. When putting petrol in the car, an accused may be appropriating property belonging to another with intent to permanently deprive, but not dishonestly, provided he or she intends to go into the office and pay. An accused in this situation believes or assumes that they have the owner's consent, as required, for example, under *Crimes Act* 1900 (ACT) s 86(4) and *Crimes Act* 1958 (Vic) s 73(2)(b). This would apply in the supermarket scenarios envisaged by the English cases on the meaning of 'appropriation' where someone takes an item from a supermarket shelf intending to pay at the checkout. Indeed people not only have the owner's consent in self-serve situations: they are required to act in this way, as supermarket and petrol-station owners minimise their staffing and other costs by shifting such tasks to the customer.

Critique—fault elements

The meaning of dishonesty

The question remains whether 'dishonest' and 'fraudulent' only mean 'without claim of right' (leaving aside the additional specific statutory provisions regarding finding and consent in *Crimes Act* 1900 (ACT) s 86(4) and *Crimes Act* 1958 (Vic) s 73(2)). Are there any other situations where a person can argue that they were not dishonest, even though they did not make any claim of right? Or to put it another way, does 'dishonesty' have a positive meaning, separately from the negative 'defence' aspects already discussed?

Consider the case of the cook employed in the Canadian Air Force who took home left-over raisin loaf cake for his children, rather than see it thrown out: *R v Pace* [1965] 3 Can CC 55. Was this dishonest? Was it morally wrong? Lorne Pace was in fact convicted of theft of the raisin loaf (valued at 50 cents); the Court fined him $1 in recognition of the trivial nature of the offence. What of the situation where a person takes someone's cheap pen, intending to replace it later with another pen, or takes a $1 coin to buy chocolate, intending to replace it with two 50-cent coins? The taker would argue there was no dishonesty here—that he or she had no intention of causing any detriment or loss to the owner of the goods. As a third hypothetical, a well-intentioned person might take away from a heavily intoxicated friend the bottle of spirits he or she plans to drink or the firearm he or she is threatening to use. Should this amount to dishonesty?

Kirby J pointed out in *Peters v The Queen* (1998) 192 CLR 493 at 534 that the meaning of the terms 'dishonest' and 'dishonesty' has been unclear, despite the importance of the concept, and the fact that it is raised in a large proportion of criminal charges. Judges have preferred to leave the term undefined, and this approach was essentially adopted by the CLRC and the legislators when introducing the UK and Victorian theft legislation. As King CJ observed in *R v Kastratovic* (1985) 42 SASR 59 at 62 in relation to defining 'intent to defraud':

> Human ingenuity in devising dishonest schemes designed to produce an advantage to one person at the expense of another or of the community at large is notoriously fecund. The courts have been understandably reluctant to place themselves

in the position of being unable to punish conduct which should by commonly accepted standards be stigmatized as fraudulent by reason of the constraints of an a priori definition framed without thought of conduct of that particular kind.

In the pre-*Theft Act* case of *R v Williams* [1953] 1 QB 660, the English Court of Criminal Appeal stated that the word 'fraudulently' does mean something more than simply 'without claim of right', but rejected the appeals of the two accused convicted of larceny, who had claimed that they had intended to repay the money taken. They had further argued that they had not intended to act to the detriment of the owner, and that they therefore could not be said to have acted 'fraudulently'. These claims were held by the Court not to negate a finding of fraudulent actions on their part.

A narrow approach to interpreting the moral component of theft has been adopted in Victoria in the trio of cases discussed below, *Salvo*, *Brow* and *Bonollo*, which effectively limit the definition back to claim of right. By contrast, the approach in *R v Williams* [1953] 1 QB 660 and the Victorian cases has been explicitly rejected in the English cases of *R v Feely* [1973] 1 QB 530 and *R v Ghosh* [1982] 1 QB 1053, and in cases on conspiracy to defraud such as the High Court in *Peters v The Queen* (1998) 192 CLR 493. In these areas it will be up to the jury to decide— in the rare fact situation where the accused makes no claim of right, but argues that they were not acting 'dishonestly'/fraudulently—whether the behaviour of the accused was dishonest/fraudulent by the standards of 'ordinary decent people'.

We will examine the two approaches and consider their merits.

The 'ordinary' or 'community standard' approach
The English courts have held in relation to the *Theft Act* 1968 (UK) that the word 'dishonestly' does have a meaning beyond the negative definition in s 2 of that Act. They have said that its meaning is to be determined by the jury, or magistrate, expressing the standards of the ordinary person. Two key cases for this interpretation are the decisions of the Court of Appeal in *R v Feely* [1973] 1 QB 530 and in *R v Ghosh* [1982] 1 QB 1053.

Feely was a branch manager in a firm of bookmakers. His employer had sent around a circular saying that borrowings from the till were to stop. A month later, the accused took £30 from the firm's safe to give to his father. He said he intended to return the money, and that the firm owed him £70 in wages and commission. Feely was convicted of theft. The judge had in fact virtually directed the jury to convict, saying (at 537) 'if someone does something deliberately knowing that his employers are not prepared to tolerate it, is that not dishonest?'

The Court of Appeal held that the notion of dishonesty does involve 'moral obloquy' and the application of moral blame. It stated (at 538) that the jury should be allowed to decide as a question of fact whether the accused was dishonest, applying the 'current standards of ordinary decent people'. Juries decide such questions in ordinary life and do not need a judge to direct them on the meaning of the term. (The Court of Appeal in this case, however, considered that the dishonesty of the accused in this case would have been obvious in any event.)

This approach was modified by the Court of Appeal in *R v Ghosh* [1982] 1 QB 1053. The Court emphasised that dishonesty refers to a state of mind, and not to a course of conduct. It must be assessed by reference to the knowledge and belief of the accused (at 1063). While the Court of Appeal doubted (at 1064) that the Court in *Feely* meant to create an objective test, it reframed the test as follows:

> [The] jury must first of all decide whether according to the standards of reasonable and honest people what was done was dishonest. If it was not dishonest by those standards, that is the end of the matter and the prosecution fails. If it was dishonest by those standards, then the jury must consider whether the defendant himself must have realized that what he was doing was by those standards dishonest. It is dishonest for a defendant to act in a way which he knows ordinary people consider dishonest...For example, Robin Hood or those ardent anti-vivisectionists who remove animals from vivisection laboratories are acting dishonestly, even though they may consider themselves to be morally justified in doing what they do, because they know that ordinary people would consider these actions to be dishonest.

The accused person's understanding of the honesty or dishonesty of his or her actions turns on his or her *honest* or *genuine* belief. The understanding of the situation need not be 'reasonable' although reasonableness does of course tend to help in proving the existence of a genuine belief or state of mind: *R v Waterfall* [1970] 1 QB 148.

The narrow approach to dishonesty in Victoria
The Victorian courts have taken a different track, and have concluded that there are no additional meanings for dishonesty beyond claim of right, and (in relation to theft) the two additional 'defences' contained in *Crimes Act* 1958 s 73(2)(b) and (c). The Victorian Supreme Court worked through the issues in three cases heard close together in 1980 and 1981, although as will be seen it is not at all clear that the court is of one mind as to the reasoning behind this position. While the High Court has moved recently towards the English approach, the Victorian courts' position regarding the *Crimes Act* 1958 (Vic) provisions is legally clear. It might well, however, be open to challenge on an appropriate appeal, given the developments following the English line, and given the differences in judicial opinion in those three cases.

The three cases all involved offences of obtaining property by deception. But in deciding the scope of 'dishonesty' for that offence, the decisions are also relevant to the meaning of 'dishonesty' for theft.

R v Salvo [1980] VR 401 involved a car dealer, Salvo, charged with obtaining a Ford Falcon Coupe by deception from Erich Kapaufs. Kapaufs had traded in his Valiant Charger to buy the Ford from the accused Salvo. Salvo did not realise that the Valiant was subject to a bill of sale to a finance company: he sold it on to a third party, and then the finance company repossessed it from the third party. To protect his business reputation Salvo paid off the money owing to the finance company and restored the car to the purchaser. This left him substantially out of pocket. Salvo subsequently heard that Kapaufs wanted to sell the Ford. He gave Kapaufs a cheque for the Ford, which he then had stopped by his bank once he had possession of the Ford.

Salvo was charged with obtaining the Ford by deception. He admitted to the police that when he gave Kapaufs the cheque he did not intend to honour it. He argued that he believed he was entitled to take back possession of the Ford, because Kapaufs had obtained it by offering in exchange a car to which Kapaufs had not had good title.

The trial judge, following *Feely*'s case, left it to the jury to decide whether Salvo had acted 'dishonestly'. He was convicted of obtaining property by deception. His appeal from conviction, however, was upheld and the case sent for retrial. Murphy and Fullagar JJ made up the majority. They stated (at 423, 424) that *Feely* should not be followed. They held that the jury should be given a direction by the judge as to the meaning of dishonesty. An appropriation will not be dishonest if the accused took the property believing he or she had a legal right to the property, that is, with a claim of legal right, as provided under the common law and in the context of theft in Victoria by s 73(2)(a) *Crimes Act* 1958. The decision was not in this respect controversial. Fullagar J (at 432) regarded claim of right as the sole defence to dishonesty. It was not, however, necessary for the Court to decide whether other defences might be available given that the case in question only raised the issue of claim of right. Murphy J, who agreed with Fullagar J's decision, did not expressly find that claim of right was the only way of negativing dishonesty. Nonetheless in the subsequent case of *R v Brow* [1981] VR 783 the Court assumed that he did take this view.

Both judges, however, were quite clear that 'dishonestly' is used in a special sense in the Victorian legislation, and is a term about which the judge must direct the jury. It cannot be left to the intuitive reactions of a jury.

McInerney J was in the minority. He agreed that dishonesty includes, at least, the idea that the person had no belief that he or she was entitled in law to do what he or she did, that is, no claim of right. But he considered (at 411) that it was proper to leave the meaning of dishonesty to the jury. In the later case of *R v Bonollo* [1981] VR 633 McInerney J still preferred that view, but bowed to the majority position in the interests of certainty.

The next year, the cases of *Brow* and *Bonollo* came up for decision. *R v Brow* [1981] VR 783 also concerned a second-hand car dealer. Adam Brow was convicted on a number of counts of theft and obtaining property by deception. The charges of obtaining property by deception related to arrangements he entered into, representing himself as the owner of various cars, free of encumbrances, whereby he obtained cheques and money from customers. Brow was not in fact the owner of the vehicles, which were subject to encumbrances, but he claimed he intended to pay off the amounts owing so that the new buyers would not suffer any loss. The theft charges related to his appropriation of cheques given to him by purchasers of cars for the owners of the cars who had put the cars in for sale. Brow claimed that he always meant to account to the owners for the amounts paid by purchasers, as soon as he could afford it.

Brow's argument was that he had not acted 'dishonestly'. He did not argue that he believed he had a legal right to do as he did. But he claimed that dishonesty could be negated, not only by a claim of right, but also if one acted with the intention that the victims suffer no ultimate loss.

This argument was rejected by the Supreme Court, and Brow's appeal from his convictions was dismissed. The Court unanimously held that an intention not to cause loss did not negative dishonesty, and that on facts such as these, the only defence would be a legal claim of right. The Court (at 790) did seem to leave open, however, the possibility of other 'defences' to 'dishonesty'.

A differently constituted Full Court (but with Chief Justice Young sitting in each) in *R v Bonollo* [1981] VR 633, however, decided just after the decision in *Brow* that dishonesty in obtaining property by deception means, and only means, without bona fide claim of legal right. The members of the Court said that they reached this conclusion in reliance on *Brow* but this was arguably not a correct reading of that case.

Maria Bonollo had set up a scam by which she fraudulently received loans from finance companies ostensibly to purchase furniture and fittings she actually already owned. The accused was convicted of eight counts of obtaining property by deception. On her appeal she argued that she had not acted dishonestly, because she intended to make the payments to the finance companies as they fell due and the companies would therefore suffer no loss.

Her appeal was dismissed by the Full Court of the Supreme Court, which confirmed the trial judge's understanding of the law of dishonesty as limited to situations where there was a claim of right, but each judge had different reasons for doing so.

Young CJ (at 635) held that, in view of the decisions in *Salvo* and *Brow*, the word 'dishonestly' in relation to obtaining property by deception is used in a special sense and requires judicial direction. It does not allow for the acceptance of 'anything less than a sincere belief in an entitlement to do what he [or she] did without infringement of the law' as a defence.

McInerney J (at 642–3) felt that the cases had not decided that this was the only way of rebutting the 'dishonesty' component, and would have preferred to leave the matter to the jury in other cases. However, he considered that to attempt to redefine again the meaning of dishonesty would bring the law into disrepute and be contrary to the doctrine of precedent, and so accepted the approach of Young CJ.

McGarvie J had written a draft decision coming to a different conclusion, when the decision in *Brow* was delivered. He then accepted the meaning of dishonesty put forward by Young CJ on the basis that he was bound to do so.

He nonetheless published his intended decision, in which he concluded that an accused might have a defence of lack of dishonesty in cases not covered by s 73(2). McGarvie J (at 656) considered that a person acts dishonestly if 'he [or she] is conscious that by obtaining [property by deception] he [or she] will produce a consequence affecting the interests of the person deprived of it; and if that consequence is one which would be detrimental to those interests...in a significant practical way'. This would be a matter of fact for the jury. He considered, however, that the judge should explain the meaning of dishonesty to the members of the jury, not leave it to them, as was proposed in *Feely*. The second limb of the formulation would require the jury to decide whether the consequence would be detrimental by asking whether an 'ordinary person' would have regarded the consequence as detrimental in a 'significant practical way'. This definition would have applied in this case, as the finance company would be incurring a greater risk than it had understood itself to be taking on.

In summary, then, the narrow legalistic reading of dishonesty in Victoria means that where theft is charged, the element of dishonesty can be rebutted only by proof of any of the defences in s 73(2)—claim of right, belief in consent, or abandonment. If offences of obtaining property or obtaining a financial advantage by deception are charged, dishonesty can only be rebutted by claim of right.

The High Court's approach to dishonesty in Peters's case
The Victorian approach has been rejected in recent Australian decisions dealing with other statutory and common law offences. The Victorian Supreme Court itself refused to follow it when interpreting the Commonwealth *Crimes Act* offence of fraudulent misappropriation: *R v Lawrence* [1997] 1 VR 459. Instead the Court (at 470) adopted the community standard test of dishonesty established by *Ghosh*, although referring only to the 'touchstone...of the ordinary standards of reasonable and honest people'. The majority of the High Court came to the same conclusion in *Peters v The Queen* (1998) 192 CLR 493 in relation to a charge of conspiracy to defraud.

Philip Peters was a solicitor who acted for Larry Spong, a drug trafficker. Peters assisted his client to set up various sham mortgage arrangements the object of which was essentially to conceal the true amount of Spong's income, thereby depriving the Commissioner of Taxation of tax payable on the income. He was convicted of conspiracy to defraud the Commonwealth pursuant to ss 86(1)(e) and 86A of the *Crimes Act* 1914 (Cth). His first appeal was unsuccessful and he appealed to the High Court. Peters claimed that he knew that the transactions were a sham, but that he was not part of any agreement to conceal Spong's income or to deprive the Commissioner of Taxation, but was merely acting as Spong's solicitor.

An aspect of the case concerned whether 'dishonesty' was a part of the statutory Commonwealth offence of conspiracy to defraud, and if so, how the jury should be directed when considering whether Peters acted 'dishonestly' (an issue also examined in Chapter 8). The trial judge (at 493) had directed the jury in line with *Ghosh*'s case that the jury should decide whether what he intended was 'dishonest according to the standards of ordinary reasonable and honest people in the community' and also whether 'the accused knew that what was intended was dishonest by those standards'. The High Court concluded, for reasons that differed between the judges, that this direction was erroneous. It was, however, unduly favourable to the accused, such that there had been no miscarriage of justice, and the appeal failed.

The majority in the High Court (Toohey, Gaudron and Kirby JJ) said that there is a component of dishonesty in the offence of conspiracy to defraud, although it is not a separate element of the offence and a jury direction as to its meaning would only be necessary in borderline cases (Toohey and Gaudron JJ at 509–510). McHugh and Gummow JJ concluded (at 532, 533) that there was no requirement to prove dishonesty as a separate fault element in this offence and that no jury direction as to dishonesty was required, even in borderline cases. The Court further held, by a slim majority, that the question whether what the accused intended was dishonest was to be decided by the jury applying the standards of 'ordinary, decent people'. Toohey and Gaudron JJ adopted this view (at 504) and were ultimately supported by Kirby J, although he had concluded (at 553) that dishonesty should be seen as a subjective fault element. His Honour endorsed the finding in *Salvo*'s case that dishonesty in that case could be disproved if the accused believed he had a legal right to act as he did. He went on to find (at 553), however, that a wider interpretation was possible where claim of right did not arise, but where dishonesty could be found from an intent to produce 'a consequence which was in some sense detrimental to a lawful right, interest, opportunity or advantage of the person to be defrauded' (quoting King CJ in *Kastratovic* at 62–3). Nonetheless, to permit a decision to be reached his Honour put aside his opinion on this point. This majority therefore endorsed the first limb of the UK test for the offence of conspiracy to defraud. McHugh and Gummow JJ, dissenting, took the view that the jury has no role to play in determining the meaning of the term 'dishonesty'.

Toohey and Gaudron JJ (at 502) observed that in Victoria 'dishonestly' is given a special meaning under the theft and fraud provisions of the *Crimes Act* 1958, which did not apply in Victoria in relation to other offences involving dishonesty, and which they did not intend to apply here. It was also seen as different from the UK provisions, where dishonesty was given its 'ordinary' meaning. This is a distinction that has been made in other cases and commentary but is difficult to follow, given that the Victorian sections are identical on this point to those in the UK *Theft Act*. The UK legislation was, however, seen to give dishonesty its 'ordinary' meaning, which was to be decided by the jury, applying the standards of ordinary decent people. This was the approach adopted by the High Court in this instance in relation to the Commonwealth provision. Toohey and Gaudron JJ rejected, however, the additional requirement developed in the UK that the jury consider whether the accused knew his or her behaviour was dishonest by the standards of ordinary decent people. The test proposed was stated at 504:

> ...the proper course is for the trial judge to identify the knowledge, belief or intent which is said to render that act dishonest and to instruct the jury to decide whether the accused had that knowledge, belief or intent and, if so, to determine whether, on that account, the act was dishonest. ...if the question is whether the act was dishonest according to ordinary notions, it is sufficient that the jury be instructed that that is to be decided by the standards of ordinary, decent people.

The view that fraud or dishonesty is a question for the jury to decide, applying the standards of ordinary decent people to the state of mind or knowledge of the accused, has recently been clearly endorsed by the High Court in *Macleod v The Queen* (2003) 197 ALR 333 at 342, 353, 360 in relation to the offence of fraudulent use of company property by a company director, contrary to *Crimes Act* 1900 (NSW) s 173.

The meaning of dishonesty in other Australian jurisdictions
CR Williams points out that the early common law commentaries on larceny stressed the necessity for the 'taking' to be morally wrongful, and argues that the English approach, adopted by the High Court in relation to the offence of conspiracy to defraud, is equally applicable to common law larceny: *Property Offences* (3rd edn: Sydney: LBC Information Services, 1999) p 48. The approach in *Ghosh* has been rejected in New South Wales in relation to *Crimes Act* 1900 (NSW) s 178BA (which is similar to s 81 *Crimes Act* (Vic), the section discussed in *Salvo*'s case) in *R v Love* (1989) 17 NSWLR 608 at 614 and *Condon* (1995) 83 A Crim R 335 at 346. It has, however, been adopted in New South Wales in relation to s 173 *Crimes Act* 1900 (NSW) in *R v Glenister* [1980] 2 NSWLR 597 and most recently in *Macleod*, in the modified form established in *Peters*.

There is no scope for such a flexible reading of the requirement of 'fraudulently' in the Criminal Codes of Queensland and Western Australia. As noted earlier, the Codes provide an exhaustive definition of the fault element for theft. The English formulation has, however, been adopted in relation to other offences of dishonesty in Queensland (see *Harvey* [1993] 2 Qd R 389) and Western Australia (*Clark* (1991) 52 A Crim R 180).

The Tasmanian legislature in 1975 substituted the term 'dishonestly' for 'fraudulently' in the *Criminal Code* 1924 (Tas). In a 1980 decision the Tasmanian Supreme Court adopted the English approach to the meaning of dishonesty: *Fitzgerald* (1980) 4 A Crim R 233 at 235. However, J Blackwood and K Warner, *Tasmanian Criminal Law: Text and Cases* (Hobart: University of Tasmania Law Press,

1997) p 965, note that given the subsequent developments in Victoria the meaning of dishonesty in Tasmania cannot be regarded as settled.

The Northern Territory Code theft provision is similar to the Victorian provision, but uses the term 'unlawfully' instead of 'dishonestly'. It provides explicitly that it will be a defence if the person reasonably believed the property had been lost and the owner could not be discovered: *Criminal Code* (NT) s 209(1). This is equivalent to the Victorian provision in s 73(2)(c). The Code also provides a general defence of legal claim of right: s 30(2), and a definition of 'unlawfully' as meaning 'without authorization, justification or excuse'. CR Williams suggests that this means only a justification or excuse provided by the Code will be regarded as taking behaviour outside the meaning of 'unlawful', and that there is therefore no scope for the broader UK approach to 'dishonesty' here: *Property Offences* (3rd edn: Sydney: LBC Information Services, 1999) p 100. It may, however, be arguable that if 'unlawfully' means no more than without the legislated defences, it is superfluous in the provision. To give it meaning, it may be that there is scope for a broader reading, allowing for some further meaning to be given to the notion of not-unlawful as, for example, the approach adopted in the UK.

The *Crimes Act* 1900 (ACT) as amended in 1985 includes in its negative definition of dishonesty (along with three definitions paralleling those in the Victorian legislation) a provision based on that proposed by McGarvie J in *Bonollo*: a person's appropriation of property in the Australian Capital Territory is not to be regarded as dishonest if '...he or she appropriates the property in the belief that the appropriation will not cause any significant practical detriment to the interests of the person to whom the property belongs in relation to that property': s 86(4)(b).

In reality there will be few cases where the accused had intent to permanently deprive and no claim of right but still makes a genuine claim not to have acted dishonestly. This discussion is about these unusual cases. However, the discussion is also important as part of an examination of the whole scope of the offence of theft, and by extension of the offences of obtaining property or financial advantage by deception. This is especially important if dishonesty carries the main work of the offence, since appropriation (as discussed earlier) arguably has a minimal role in identifying moral responsibility. The debate is also important in relation to the question of whether or not the test for dishonesty addresses the accused person's perspective on his or her own behaviour, or an external 'community standard'.

The Court of Appeal in *Feely* stated that judges should not define 'dishonesty' but leave the question whether a particular appropriation was dishonest to the jury. Kirby J points out in *Peters v The Queen* (1998) 192 CLR 493 at 545 that the Court was in fact not establishing an objective test for dishonesty, but describing the mechanism for reaching a decision in a particular case. The phrase was, however, adopted in the subsequent case of *R v Ghosh* [1982] 1 QB 1053 in which the Court stated (at 1064) that juries should be directed to apply such standards, and then to consider whether the defendant 'must have realised that what he was doing was by those standards dishonest'. This was at once an attempt to introduce a subjective component to the test, and at the same time an unusual formulation involving a jury deciding what a defendant 'must have realised'.

Dishonesty: where to from here?
The English *Feely/Ghosh* position on leaving the question of 'dishonesty' to the jury has been criticised on a number of grounds. Fundamentally, the criticism is that if the meaning of the term is left to juries, different juries will decide differently. As Edward Griew observed after the decision in *Ghosh* in 'Dishonesty: The Objections to Feely and Ghosh' [1985] Crim LR 342–54, 344: '[The test] implies the existence of a relevant community norm. ...It is simply naïve to suppose—surely no one does suppose—that there is, in respect of the dishonesty question, any such single thing as "the standards of ordinary decent people"'. See also DW Elliott, 'Dishonesty in Theft: A Dispensable Concept' [1982] Crim LR 395–410; A Halpin, 'The Test for Dishonesty' [1996] Crim LR 283–95.

It is also not clear that people will 'properly' understand the dishonesty of their own conduct. Robin Hood might indeed believe that the general community would agree with him that it is socially desirable, and not dishonest, to take from the rich in order to assist the poor.

It can be argued that the judge should define dishonesty for the jury. Otherwise it is being left to the jury to decide what the criminal offence of theft constitutes: that it is an offence 'to do something dishonestly'. Where complex commercial practices are involved, the line between 'sharp practice' and dishonesty may be particularly unclear, and not readily ascertained by a jury: see A Halpin, 'The Test for Dishonesty' [1996] Crim LR 283–95 at 290. The judge should direct on the legal parameters of the criminal offence, and the jury then decide whether the particular facts fall within that definition.

The English approach can also be criticised for applying an objective standard in determining an aspect of the fault element of a serious offence, where this is usually determined on a subjective basis. Kirby J in *Peters v The Queen* (1998) 192 CLR 493 at 555 reiterated that, consistent with general criminal law principles regarding serious crimes, the fault element of dishonesty requires attention to the accused's actual state of mind: 'Dishonesty of its essential nature connotes conscious wrongdoing. It is not dishonesty by the standards of other persons but by the appreciation and understanding of the accused personally.' Kirby J (at 553) expressed support for the broad formulation of King CJ in *R v Kastratovic* (1985) 42 SASR 59 at 62–3, that dishonesty includes an intention to produce a consequence that is 'in some sense detrimental to a lawful right, interest, opportunity or advantage of the person to be defrauded'. As mentioned earlier, Kirby J abandoned his preferred test of dishonesty and supported that of Gaudron and Toohey JJ to facilitate a clearer outcome in *Peters*. The case was also dealing with a specific offence, in which the application of the notion of dishonesty was itself in dispute. The case thus stands as something less than the guiding beacon that is needed in the application of the law of dishonesty in Australia, despite being expressly endorsed by the High Court of Australia in *Macleod v The Queen* at 344, 353, 360.

The Victorian approach steers a clear legalistic path. It is also appropriately subjective, giving attention to what the accused actually believed. It is, however, open to the criticism that it wrongly provides no scope for acquitting the person who was not morally blameworthy for some other reason, such as the cook in *Pace*'s case, the genuine borrower of fungibles, and the person removing the firearm from its drunken and dangerous owner.

The approach taken in *Peters* is supported by CR Williams, 'The Shifting Meaning of Dishonesty' (1999) 23 Crim LJ 275–84 at 283–4 as providing scope for finding something is not dishonest, beyond the legal exemptions for claim of right, belief in consent, and abandonment. He argues (at 284) that this better handles the issue of taking of fungibles with intent to return an equivalent, and with other potential situations where the accused lacks moral blameworthiness. The MCCOC in its Final Report in 1995 considered the problems in this area and ('in apparent resignation, rather than with enthusiasm', as Kirby J concluded in *Peters* (1998) 192 CLR 493 at 548) recommended a definition of dishonesty consistent with the English cases. The MCCOC proposed a two-part definition of dishonesty as follows: 'cl 14.2 (1) In this chapter, 'dishonest' means dishonest according to the standards of ordinary people and known by the defendant to be dishonest according to the standards of ordinary people.'

The Commonwealth *Criminal Code* already incorporates a general defence of claim of right (s 9.5(1)). It was proposed in addition to include a provision to aid the interpretation of the term 'dishonesty', permitting reference to some of the factors in the UK and Victorian definitions of dishonesty. It would not be dishonest to appropriate property believing the owner could not reasonably be discovered (cl 15.2(1)), and willingness to pay would not of itself negate dishonesty (cl 15.2(2)).

A provision along the lines proposed by the MCCOC in cl 14.2 is included in the recent addition of s 130.3 to the *Criminal Code* (Cth), introduced by the *Criminal Code Amendment (Theft, Fraud, Bribery and Related Offences) Act* 2000 (Cth).

The formulation has, however, been criticised in view of the subsequent rejection of the two-stage approach by the majority of the High Court in *Peters v The Queen* (1998) 192 CLR 493 and the criticisms of the *Ghosh* approach in the English Law Commission's *Legislating the Criminal Code: Fraud and Deception*, Consultation Paper No 155 (London: HMSO, 1999) pp 52–9. Nonetheless, a provision adopting the MCCOC recommendation was also recently enacted in s 131(1) *Criminal Law Consolidation Act* 1935 (SA).

The Law Commission in its Consultation Paper No 155 (1999) (at 121) rejected reliance on a 'unified conception of dishonesty which we do not think is workable in modern society'. It proposed that there be no reference to dishonesty in the deception offences but that the offences include a 'negative' dishonesty component, similar to that already applying in the UK (and Victorian) theft provisions, simply establishing a defence of belief in legal entitlement. This was widely opposed during the subsequent consultation. In its 2002 Report the Law Commission then revised its view, proposing a reformulated fraud offence but concluding that the *Ghosh* formulation was workable, was not likely to give rise to highly inconsistent jury decisions, and should be retained for the new offence. The jury would, for example, be able to test a defendant's claim of right by reference to both the community standard and whether the defendant recognised this community standard: Law Commission, *Fraud*, Report No 276 (London: HMSO, 2002 para 7.69).

Alex Steel has argued that both the *Peters* decision (insofar as a clear position can be identified) and the MCCOC models are inadequate, and proposes a definition of dishonesty based on the formulation of McGarvie J in *Bonollo*: 'The Appropriate Test for Dishonesty' (2000) 24 Crim LJ 46–59, 57; and see DW Elliott, 'Dishonesty in Theft: A Dispensable Concept' [1982] Crim LR 395–410. Steel argues that this approach would deal with the hypotheticals such as the well-intentioned remover of a friend's alcohol or firearm. At the same time it would make easy acquittals unlikely for 'the famous Robin Hoods and anti-vivisectionists of Lord Lane CJ's judicial nightmare' (at 57) as such accused would know that their actions would be significantly practically detrimental to the victim's interests.

We would support a formulation along the lines proposed by McGarvie J in *Bonollo*'s case, and employed (expressed in negative terms) in the *Crimes Act* 1900 (ACT) in addition to the traditional exceptions for claim of right and belief in consent. The positive formulation of McGarvie J would include in the definition of dishonesty an obtaining where the accused 'is conscious that by obtaining...[he or she] will produce a consequence affecting the interests of the person deprived...and if that consequence is one which would be detrimental to those interests in a significant practical way': [1981] VR 633 at 656. This approach also reflects the formulation of King CJ in *Kastratovic*, cited by Kirby J in *Peters*'s case. We agree with the MCCOC that a consistent approach to key elements of property offences is vital. We differ from the Committee's conclusion on this point in favour of the UK formulation: MCCOC, *Chapter 3, Theft, Fraud, Bribery and Related Offences*, Report (December 1995) pp 21, 23. The meaning of dishonesty does require elaboration to address the residual cases excluded by the Victorian formulation, but we consider that the *Ghosh* and *Peters* approaches are limited by their objective focus and by the uncertainty they engender. A formulation such as that proposed by McGarvie J makes the accused person's awareness of the harm they will cause correctly the central question for the jury. It allows the jury to consider broadly whether what is intended or known to be a consequence amounts to a significant detriment to the interests of the victim. It allows the jury to address the significance of the taking of fungibles and trivial borrowings, such as the taking of unused cake as in *Pace*, and to consider the honesty of the accused assisting his or her drunken and dangerous friend.

Detriment would not be limited to financial loss. The owner of property has an interest in choosing how he or she uses his or her property, which may be adversely affected by the accused's actions irrespective of any economic harm: see DW Elliott, 'Dishonesty in Theft: A Dispensable Concept' [1982] Crim LR 395–410 at 408. Concern that a person might be acquitted because he or she concluded that a wealthy victim would not notice the loss could be addressed by an inclusion along the lines of the second limb of McGarvie J's formulation, that in determining whether the consequence would be detrimental the jury would consider whether an ordinary person would have regarded the particular consequence as detrimental 'in a significant practical way'. As DW Elliott points out, this approach is already used elsewhere in the criminal law: 'the jury asks what the accused himself [or herself] intended or foresaw, and then find the category of gravity of that': 'Dishonesty in Theft: A Dispensable Concept' [1982] Crim LR 395–410 at 408.

The requirement of intent to permanently deprive

Glanville Williams argued in 1981 for the abolition of the requirement that there be proof of an intention to permanently deprive: 'Temporary Appropriation Should be Theft' [1981] Crim LR 129–41. He asserted that intention to use temporarily can at times be at least as injurious, citing illustrations such as the 'borrowing' without consent of major art works from galleries or valuable books from libraries, and the taking of items with the intention of returning them shortly, but only when they are no longer of use or value. He was also highly critical of the notion of conditional intent outlined in *R v Easom* [1971] 1 QB 315. Glanville Williams considered that the UK equivalent of s 73(12) *Crimes Act* 1958 (Vic) was not always effective in borrowing cases, and proposed deletion of 'permanently' from the definition of the fault element, and insertion of a clause to protect people simply holding properly borrowed or hired items beyond the agreed time. He suggested that this could have a benefit for public morality in stating that dishonest taking is theft. He suggested (at 137): 'Just as supermarkets now exhibit notices saying that "shoplifting is theft", so libraries could announce that "unauthorised removal of books is theft".'

Section 322 of the Canadian *Criminal Code* refers to fraudulent takings with intent to deprive 'temporarily or absolutely'. Section 118 of the *Crimes Act* 1900 (NSW) states that the intention to return property, or to return an equivalent amount of money where money was taken, does not of itself ensure acquittal. This has not been interpreted as removing the common law requirement to show intention to permanently deprive (a point noted with some disappointment by Glanville Williams, 'Temporary Appropriation Should be Theft' [1981] Crim LR 129–41). The High Court held in *Foster v The Queen* (1967) 118 CLR 117 at 121 that proof of intent to permanently deprive includes intent to assume ownership of the goods, to 'deal with them as his [or her] own' or to deprive the owner of property (as distinct from mere possession) in the item. If the accused has such an intent, an intention to restore the property to the owner later does not prevent a finding of larceny.

The MCCOC in its 1995 Report considered arguments for and against abolishing the requirement of intent to permanently deprive. In support of simply abolishing the requirement, the MCCOC noted the effective abolition of the requirement in the case of joyriding and of theft of fungibles. It is also arguable that extending the definition of intent to permanently deprive to cover borrowings, as effected by s 73(12) *Crimes Act* 1958 (Vic), takes it so far that it could be abolished.

Competing arguments include the serious nature of the offence, and the high maximum penalty it attracts. The MCCOC ultimately gave significant weight to the argument that dishonest borrowing, without intention to more seriously deprive the owner, should not be theft. The Committee recommended retention of intent to permanently deprive in the Victorian form.

In relation to fungibles, the MCCOC also recommended a provision that appropriation of a fungible does not automatically show intent to permanently deprive, merely because the person does not intend to return the precise item (for example money). We agree that intent to permanently deprive continues to be a significant element of the moral blameworthiness of this offence, and support its continued inclusion, extended to the blameworthy forms of borrowing covered by the Victorian, Australian Capital Territory, Northern Territory and South Australian legislation. A provision dealing with fungibles is also desirable, in the interest of fairness, in the form recommended by the MCCOC.

Robbery

The property offences seen as most personally threatening are probably robberies (thefts with violence) and burglaries (house-breakings). We will look at the elements of robbery and its more serious form, armed robbery, in this section. Burglary will be examined in the following section.

The Australian Institute of Criminology reported that in 2001 there were 340 homicides recorded by police across Australia. In the same year there were 26,565 robberies: AIC, *Australian Crime Facts and Figures 2002* (Canberra: AIC, 2002), 24. These comprised 15,509 unarmed robberies and 11,056 armed robberies. Almost three-quarters of the unarmed robberies occurred in community locations such as streets, while almost half of the armed robberies occurred in retail premises. Men, especially young men, were more than twice as likely as women to be a victim of robbery. Offenders were also most likely to be male: AIC, *Australian Crime Facts and Figures 2002* (Canberra: AIC, 2002), 25–9, 48. Women comprised a little over 10 per cent of alleged offenders recorded by the Victoria Police in 2001–02 (305 female and 2353 male offenders: Victoria Police, *Crime Statistics 2001/02*, <http://www.police.vic.gov.au/ShowContentPage.cfm?ContentPage=484>, accessed November 2003). See also Natalie Taylor, 'Robbery Against Service Stations and Pharmacies: Recent Trends', *Trends and Issues* No 223 (Canberra: AIC, 2002).

Robbery is an aggravated or more serious category of theft: it involves using violence or the threat of violence in order to carry out a theft, including preventing resistance to theft and effecting an escape. The offence of robbery is broadly similar across all Australian jurisdictions.

The provisions in Victoria (*Crimes Act* 1958 s 75(1)) and the Australian Capital Territory (*Crimes Act* 1900 s 91(1)) are in the following terms: a person will be guilty of robbery who:

> steals, and immediately before or at the time of doing so, and in order to do so, he [or she] uses force on any person or puts or seeks to put any person in fear that he [or she] or another person will be then and there subjected to force.

The penalty in Victoria is 15 years, and 14 years in the ACT.

Section 137(1) of the *Criminal Law Consolidation Act* 1935 (SA) refers to use of force or the threat to use force, to commit theft or in order to escape from the scene of the offence.

The common law and Codes use the term 'violence' rather than 'force' and have slightly wider operation. The Code states specify that robbery has occurred where a theft takes place and violence (*Criminal Code* (Tas) 240(1); *Criminal Code* (WA) s 392) or 'actual violence' (*Criminal Code* (Qld) s 409 is used or threatened towards 'any person or property' in order to steal or to prevent or overcome resistance.

Section 94 of the *Crimes Act* 1900 (NSW) provides for offences of 'robbery or stealing from the person' carrying a maximum penalty of 14 years. Robbery is defined at common law as a violent assault upon another, putting him or her in fear in order to take money or other goods from his or her person: E Coke, *Institutes of the Laws of England: Third Part* (London, 1680) 3 Inst 68.

Most jurisdictions have other related theft and violence offences, some carrying lesser penalties, such as assault with intent to steal/rob, for example: *Crimes Act* 1900 (ACT) s 91(2); *Crimes Act* 1900 (NSW) s 94(1); *Criminal Code* (Qld) s 413; *Criminal Law Consolidation Act* 1935 (SA) s 270B; *Crimes Act* 1958 (Vic) 75(2); *Criminal Code* (WA) s 393. All jurisdictions also have a range of related offences based on using threats to make demands for money, such as blackmail and offences relating to extortion. These will not be discussed in this chapter.

The current law: physical elements

Steals

The offence of robbery turns on the offender stealing, that is, committing a theft. It will usually be possible for an offender to be convicted of theft/larceny even though charged with robbery if, for example, the super-added elements of robbery cannot be proven.

If any element of theft is not proven, there can be no offence of robbery. For example, if the accused believed he or she was entitled in law to take the property, or if the accused did not have an intention to permanently deprive, there would be no robbery. In *R v Langham* (1984) 36 SASR 48 the accused used a gun to intimidate the shopkeeper into returning money he had spent on the item he had returned. The South Australian Supreme Court (at 51) confirmed that Langham's claim of right—the claim that he was entitled to the money—need only be a claim to *entitlement* to the goods. In this case Langham's claim of right provided a good defence both to the charge of theft and of robbery.

Common law robbery also requires the element of taking and carrying away, as required for larceny, together with proof that the stealing was 'from the person', meaning directly from the victim's body or from the victim's protection or control: this was discussed in *Smith v Desmond* [1965] AC 960 at 985 and 991, the facts of which were noted earlier.

Uses force/violence

As previously stated, the Australian Capital Territory, South Australian and Victorian provisions use the term 'force'. The common law and Code states use the expression 'violence' (*Criminal Code* (Tas) s 240(1); *Criminal Code* (WA) s 391) or 'actual violence' (*Criminal Code* (Qld) s 409).

It is not clear whether 'force' and 'violence' are the same. The UK, Victorian, Australian Capital Territory and South Australian legislatures presumably intended to clarify or change the law by replacing 'violence' with 'force'. JC Smith in *The Law of Theft* (8th edn, London: Butterworths, 1997) p 88 suggests that the difference between the terms is 'elusive' but that 'force' is probably slightly wider than 'violence'. He concludes (at 88) that '...simply to hold a person down is not violence but it certainly involves the use of force against the person. Force denotes any exercise of physical strength against another whereas violence seems to signify a dynamic exercise of strength as by striking a blow'.

It will clearly be robbery where, for example, the offender punches the victim to knock him or her out, in order to steal a wallet or handbag. It will not amount to 'force' merely to pick a pocket, but may if the wallet becomes stuck or if a struggle follows: MCCOC, *Chapter 3, Theft, Fraud, Bribery and Related Offences*, Report (December 1995) p 71. 'Force' may involve quite slight amounts of physical pressure. It has been held to extend to nudging someone to put them off-balance and enable an offender to take their wallet. In *Dawson and James* (1976) 64 Cr App R 170 a sailor on shore leave in Liverpool was waiting at the docks to catch a boat back to his ship. He was approached by three men. One stood on each side of him and one behind. The men at each side started nudging the sailor, so that he was trying to keep his balance and was not able to stop the third man from taking his wallet. The police, however, gave chase and caught two of the men. They had clearly committed a theft; the only question was whether what had happened amounted to 'using force for the purposes of stealing' so as to be a robbery.

The accused were convicted of robbery, and an appeal to the Court of Appeal was unsuccessful. The Court of Appeal accepted that the mere act of jostling was capable of amounting to the use of force in the relevant sense. This was a question for the jury, and the jury had obviously thought it was so.

The question of the meaning of 'force' was considered in Victoria in *R v Butcher* [1986] VR 43, discussed in Chapter 3 above. The case involved an accused who threatened a milkbar proprietor with a knife, demanding money. The milkbar proprietor was stabbed, according to the accused man's unsworn evidence, because he walked towards and onto Butcher's knife. The Court concluded that holding out a knife demanding money constituted both force/threat of force (for the purpose of robbery) and also 'violence' (for the purposes of the felony murder rule under s 3A *Crimes Act* 1958 (Vic)).

This was a felony murder case, where the death arose in the course of an attempted robbery. The question was whether a killing in the course of robbery came within s 3A, as 'a crime a necessary element of which is violence'. The Victorian Supreme Court held that robbery is, by definition, a crime 'a necessary element of which is violence'. The Court stated (at 50) that:

> if actual force is not used, then the menace or threat must either be such as to cause personal intimidation, or be intended to cause intimidation or submission...if force is used there can be no debate but that this is actual violence. If threats are made personally to intimidate or seeking to intimidate, this is also in our opinion violence...It may be put that the latter is constructive violence...

The Code states require 'actual' violence. It is not clear whether this requires a more serious level of force or violence than at common law. The Queensland case of *R v Jerome* [1964] Qd R 595 accepted that removal of a victim's boots did not amount to 'actual violence' under the Queensland Code. On the other hand, a conviction for robbery was upheld in Western Australia in a case where the accused picked up cash that the victim had put down after obtaining it from an automatic telling machine; the victim grabbed the accused by the shirt and held on as the accused ran away, but fell to the ground when the accused's shirt came off: *Hood* (2000) 111 A Crim R 556.

In the Australian Capital Territory, South Australia, Tasmania and Victoria, for robbery to have been committed, it is sufficient to show that force or violence was applied to anyone, not only the owner of the property: *Crimes Act* 1900 (ACT) s 91(1); *Criminal Law Consolidation Act* 1935 (SA) s 137(1)(a); *Criminal Code* (Tas) s 240(1); *Crimes Act* 1958 (Vic) s 75(1). Provided it is applied in order to steal or prevent resistance or to assist escape (see below) it can still be robbery. For example, it would be robbery to overpower a neighbour, or nightwatchman, if this was done to facilitate carrying out a theft from a house or factory. In Queensland and Western Australia it will also be robbery where there is violence against property: *Criminal Code* (Qld) s 409; *Criminal Code* (WA) s 392.

Threatens violence/seeks to put any person in fear of immediate force

It is not necessary for the prosecution to prove that force or violence was actually used; it is sufficient if the accused 'threatened' violence (*Criminal Code* (Tas) s 240(1); *Criminal Code* (Qld) s 409) or 'put/sought to put' any person in fear of being subjected to force (*Crimes Act* 1958 (Vic) s 75) or 'uses force or threatens to use force' (*Criminal Law Consolidation Act* 1935 (SA) s 137(1)(a)).

The case of *Butcher* provides a gloss on the meaning of 'threat of force' in the Victorian, Australian Capital Territory and South Australian legislation. The term means that the menace or threat must either be such as to cause personal intimidation, or be intended to cause intimidation or submission.

Under the Victorian and Australian Capital Territory legislation the accused can be guilty either for putting the victim in fear, or for seeking to put them in fear. Both limbs of this component of the offence seem to require some level of fault (intentionality) on the part of the accused; the first limb, but not the second, also requires attention to the state of mind of the victim.

Under the first limb, the accused must be shown to have intentionally or knowingly caused the victim to fear the application of force or violence. Under the second limb the intention of the accused is central; he or she must have intended to cause the victim to fear the application of force. It is not necessary under this second limb to show that the victim was in fact afraid. Even if the person is very brave or recognises that the weapon is not dangerous and is not frightened by the threats, but has the property taken anyway, this will be a robbery.

This reading may also be applicable by inference from the phrase 'threaten' in Queensland, South Australia, Tasmania and Western Australia. That is, the accused must intentionally carry out 'threatening' behaviour and do all he or she can to try to put the victim in fear, irrespective of whether the victim actually felt fear. On the other hand, the mere fact that the victim was afraid does not automatically mean the accused is guilty of robbery. He or she must have intended to threaten or put the victim in fear of force, and this must have been in order to steal, prevent resistance or escape.

The threat of force may be express or implied. The Court in *Butcher* observed that threats made to remove a person's resistance constitute the use of force, for example where the victim is surrounded by thugs and a demand is made that he or she hand over money. Even though the victim is not touched, and no express threat is made, this will constitute robbery. The Supreme Court said (at 54): 'These cases are simply illustrative of the fact that violence must be interpreted to include threats such as in common experience would be expected or likely to take away resistance.' The Codes provide for threats of violence to property as well as to any person.

Immediately before, after or at the time of stealing

The violence or threats must occur before or at the time of the stealing under the Victorian and Australian Capital Territory legislation. The common law and the Code states require that these occur immediately before, after or at the time of the stealing: *Criminal Code* (NT) s 211; *Criminal Law Consolidation Act* 1935 (SA) s 137(1)(b); *Criminal Code* (Qld) s 409; *Criminal Code* (Tas) s 240(1); *Criminal Code* (WA) s 391. In all jurisdictions the violence/force and threats must be shown at the same time to have occurred 'in order to' steal.

Use of force separately from the theft, whether before or after, will simply allow an assault offence to be charged along with the theft. For example, in *McConville* (1989) 44 A Crim R 455 Mark McConville was convicted of the murder, with others, of a husband and wife; he was also convicted of robbery, having been found to have the deceased man's gold watch in his possession. The Victorian Court of Criminal Appeal heard McConville's appeal from his convictions and observed that the facts did not warrant a trial for robbery given that there was no evidence whether the theft occurred before or after the victim's death, nor whether the theft and killings were related as required by s 75(1) *Crimes Act* 1958 (Vic).

One problem in Victoria and the Australian Capital Territory is ascertaining when the theft has been completed, in particular deciding when the property has been appropriated. This is less of a problem in the common law and Code states and South Australia, given their broader time frame, but it is still necessary to determine, in all jurisdictions, precisely the time limits of 'before' and 'after' the stealing.

Read most strictly, for Victoria and the Australian Capital Territory, once the property has been taken or appropriated (with the necessary intention) any later force cannot convert the offence into robbery—for instance, force used to help the offender escape. By contrast, it was held in the Western Australian case of *Hood* (2000) 111 A Crim R 556 at 559 (discussed earlier) that the actual violence of the victim grabbing the accused man's shirt, the accused dragging the victim along on his shirt and the victim then falling to the ground had occurred 'at or immediately after' the stealing and in order to obtain the thing stolen.

There may be some flexibility in the notion of 'appropriation' in jurisdictions where this is an element of theft or of 'dealing with' property as in South Australia. The courts may be prepared to see the appropriation as involving some continuity so as to bring the use of force within the time frame of the theft, making it therefore a robbery, provided it can still be said to have been carried out 'in order to steal'.

This flexible approach to appropriation is illustrated in the case of *Hale* (1978) 68 Cr App R 415. Hale and another man broke into the victim's home. One stayed downstairs and held his hand over the owner's mouth to stop her from screaming, while the other was upstairs stealing a box of jewellery. The offender who had been upstairs came down and demanded to know where the rest of the property was. The owner took them upstairs, and when they came down they tied her up and left, telling her not to call the police. Hale was convicted of robbery. He appealed, arguing that the appropriation of property upstairs had been completed before any force was used downstairs.

The Court of Appeal concluded that appropriation could here be regarded as a continuing act, which was going on until the offenders left the house. There was clearly force applied for the purpose of carrying out the theft when Hale put his hand over the owner's mouth to stop her screaming and this occurred before or during the theft, but the Court said the jury could also have concluded that the tying up of the owner also occurred while the theft was continuing, enabling the thieves to assume the rights of an owner and permanently to deprive her of the goods.

The issue of what is 'immediately before' will also have to be interpreted in the light of 'in order to steal'. A threat made earlier may continue to operate on the mind of the victim up to the moment of stealing. Provided this is what the accused intended, the subsequent taking will still be robbery. It will be an ongoing threat intended to have effect 'immediately before' the intended stealing.

In *Donaghy and Marshall* [1981] Crim LR 644 the two accused had got into a taxi in Newmarket and demanded the driver take them to London. The driver protested but they threatened his life, with Donaghy, in the rear of the cab, poking his finger into the driver's back to simulate a gun. When they got to London, Marshall stole £22 from the driver, without any further specific threats being made. The case is reported at first instance. The judge's direction was that the offenders could be convicted jointly of robbery if there had been threats, the effect of the threats was continuing, the defendants knew the effect was continuing, they deliberately made use of the effect of the threats in order to obtain the money, and by their manner they gave the impression they were continuing the threats at the time of the theft. The jury acquitted.

The current law—fault elements

Each component of the fault element of the relevant theft or larceny offence must be shown before there can be a conviction for robbery.

In addition, it must be shown that the force or violence used, or threatened, was intended by the accused to facilitate the theft. Assault and theft do not necessarily amount to a robbery, as noted in *McConville* (1989) 44 A Crim R 455 above. In addition, the fact that someone present when property was being stolen was frightened does not of itself convert the theft into a robbery.

The common law form of this additional intent is the requirement that the violence have been inflicted or threatened in order to prevent or overcome resistance to the stealing: see CR Williams, *Property Offences* (3rd edn: Sydney: LBC Information Services, 1999) p 200. In Victoria and the Australian Capital Territory the force or threat of force must have occurred 'in order to steal'. In the Code states the necessary additional intent is 'to obtain the thing stolen or to prevent or overcome resistance to its being stolen': *Criminal Code* (Qld) s 409; *Criminal Code* (Tas) s 240(1); *Criminal Code* (WA) s 392. The Northern Territory includes in addition 'to prevent or hinder...pursuit': *Criminal Code* (NT) s 211(1).

The terminology proposed by the MCCOC in cl 16.1 was 'with intent to commit theft or to escape from the scene'. This formulation was employed, with modifications, in the new s 137(1) *Criminal Law Consolidation Act* 1935 (SA).

It will usually be possible for a jury to bring in a verdict of theft on a robbery charge, that is, where the jury is satisfied the theft/larceny occurred but is not satisfied of the further elements of robbery. For example, s 421(2) *Crimes Act* 1958 (Vic) states that a jury can find any other included offence. Thus, on a charge of robbery, a jury could find theft proven if not satisfied of the use of force in order to steal.

Critique—the law of robbery

Degree of force or violence
Cases such as *Dawson* suggest that the force used may be fairly slight; its meaning will ultimately be a question of fact for the jury. Courts should not be too ready, however, to shift a theft into the more serious category of robbery. If the degree of force/violence to be used in the 'taking' of the item is defined widely, the risk is that what might be seen as quite minor thefts come to be classified as robberies, with the heavier penalty and stigma this entails.

CR Williams argues that the decision in *Dawson* went too far in finding nudging to amount to the use of force, and that 'force on any person' must connote more than mere physical contact: *Property Offences* (3rd edn: Sydney: LBC Information Services, 1999) p 208. The MCCOC also considers that the 'force' must be 'more force than is necessary merely to remove the object from the victim's person': *Chapter 3, Theft, Fraud, Bribery and Related Offences*, Report (December 1995) p 71.

The CLRC said in their report that they did not regard 'mere snatching of property, such as a handbag, from an unresisting owner as using force for the purpose of the definition' although it might amount to force if the owner resisted: *Theft and Related Offences*, Report No 8 (London: HMSO, Cmnd 2877, 1966) p 32. We agree that the degree of force or violence necessary to turn a theft into a robbery should be defined restrictively.

Timing of the use of force
The MCCOC recommended inclusion of force or threats before, at the time of, or after the theft: MCCOC, *Chapter 3, Theft, Fraud, Bribery and Related Offences*, Report (December 1995) p 71. This would be consistent with the Codes and common law states, and has been adopted in South Australia. It would slightly extend the Victorian and Australian Capital Territory provisions. The aim of this variation was to

avoid the fine distinctions needed in deciding whether the theft had ended when the force was applied. This seems to provide an adequate solution, and would mean that the creative approach of the court in cases like *Hale* would be unnecessary.

Nature of the threats

The Victorian and Australian Capital Territory legislation includes reference to putting any person in fear that he or she *or any other person* will be subjected to force (*Crimes Act* 1958 (Vic) s 75; *Crimes Act* 1900 (ACT) s 91(1)). CR Williams notes that the expression was added in Victoria in 1977 after the trial of an accused who had pretended to threaten the life of an innocent bystander to persuade a shopkeeper to hand over money: *Property Offences* (3rd edn: Sydney: LBC Information Services, 1999) p 209. The ostensible hostage was in fact a confederate. The accused was acquitted; the element of 'putting in fear or seeking to put in fear' could not have been shown.

This would not appear to be a problem in jurisdictions using expressions such as 'using or threatening to use violence to any person' (*Criminal Code* (NT) s 211; *Criminal Code* (Qld) s 409; *Criminal Law Consolidation Act* 1935 (SA) s 137(1)). In these jurisdictions there is no need to show either that the 'threatenee' was in fear, or that the accused genuinely meant that he or she be afraid. This was the preferred approach of the MCCOC: *Chapter 3, Theft, Fraud, Bribery and Related Offences,* Report (December 1995) cl 16.1.

The MCCOC proposed that only a threat of immediate use of force to a person should be sufficient for a conviction. Threats to property, or to embarrass the victim, should not be included (though they might be punished as blackmail): MCCOC, *Chapter 3, Theft, Fraud, Bribery and Related Offences,* Report (December 1995) p 73. The MCCOC proposals were adopted in the Commonwealth *Criminal Code* amendments in 2000; see s 132.2 and *Criminal Law Consolidation Act* 1935 (SA) s 137.

Armed/aggravated robbery

Each jurisdiction includes aggravated versions of robbery. The aggravated character of the offence usually lies in the commission of the offence with weapons; it may also include commission of the offence in company, and acts of violence while committing the offence. These are perceived as factors heightening the gravity of the offence, and are reflected in a higher maximum penalty than for the 'head' offence.

Over half of armed robberies in Australia (55 per cent) involve knives or other sharp instruments. The next most common weapon is firearms (19 per cent): see J Mouzos and C Carcach, *Weapon Involvement in Armed Robbery,* AIC Research and Public Policy Series No 38 (Canberra: AIC, 2001).

Armed or aggravated robbery entails commission of a robbery with weapons, including imitation weapons (*Crimes Act* 1900 (ACT) s 92; *Crimes Act* 1900 (NSW) s 97; *Criminal Code* (Qld) s 411; *Criminal Law Consolidation Act* 1935 (SA) s 137(2)(b);

Crimes Act 1958 (Vic) s 77; *Criminal Code* (WA) s 392(c)). In some jurisdictions it also includes robbery in company with other persons (*Crimes Act* 1900 (NSW) s 97; *Criminal Code* (Qld) s 411(2); *Criminal Law Consolidation Act* 1935 (SA) s 137(2)(a); *Criminal Code* (WA) s 391) and where personal violence is used (*Crimes Act* 1900 (NSW) ss 95, 96, 98; *Criminal Code* (Qld) s 411(2); *Criminal Code* (WA) s 391). The *Criminal Code* (Tas) provides for aggravated robbery (in company or where bodily harm is caused: s 240(2)), armed robbery (armed with a firearm: s 240(3)), and aggravated armed robbery (s 240(4) combining the two previous categories).

Armed/aggravated robbery carries a higher penalty than robbery on its own: Australian Capital Territory 25 years; New South Wales 20 or 25 years; Queensland (s 411) life imprisonment; South Australia life imprisonment; Victoria 25 years; Western Australia life if 'armed', 20 years in company/with violence (ss 391, 392).

The Codes and New South Wales *Crimes Act* refer to the offender being 'armed' with the offensive weapon. In Victoria and the Australian Capital Territory a person is guilty of armed robbery if they commit a robbery and at the time they have with them a 'firearm, imitation firearm, offensive weapon, explosive or imitation explosive' (*Crimes Act* 1958 (Vic) s 75A(1); *Crimes Act* 1900 (ACT) s 92) or in South Australia 'an offensive weapon' (*Criminal Law Consolidation Act* 1935 s 137(2)(b)). The offence is committed if the accused 'has with' them the arms at the time of the offence. In *R v Kolb and Adams* unreported, 14 December 1979, the Full Court of the Victorian Supreme Court considered the use of the word 'armed' together with 'has with him' to show that 'the possession of the weapon must be for the purpose of the robbery' and that the 'weapon must be available to the accused for use for the purpose of the robbery'.

The accused can only be said to 'have the weapon with him [or her]' if he or she knows of its presence: *R v Cugullere* [1961] 1 WLR 858. A person has been held to 'have with him a firearm' where the firearm was in a locked car outside the auction room in which the accused intended to commit the robbery, on the basis that it was readily accessible to the offender: *R v Pawlicki and Swindell* [1992] 1 WLR 827.

The weapons referred to are defined in *Crimes Act* 1958 (Vic) s 77(1A) and *Crimes Act* 1900 (ACT) s 84. 'Offensive weapon' means an article made for causing injury or incapacitating a person (such as a knuckleduster: *Miller v Hrvojevic* [1972] VR 305), an article adapted to cause injury or incapacitate (such as a sharpened piece of metal) and any other article that is being carried with the intention of using it, or threatening to use it, to injure or incapacitate. This last category has been held to include a small plastic soft drink bottle used to threaten staff in a pharmacy: *R v Nguyen* [1997] 1 VR 551. It has also been held to include a belt. In *Considine v Kirkpatrick* [1971] SASR 73 once the accused formed the intention to use his belt as an offensive weapon the Court said (at 87) it 'ceased to be a lawful instrument for keeping up his pants which it was previously, and came within the ambit of the section because he formed a new intention…and the overt act of twirling the belt like a bolo simply indicated outwardly what that new intention was'.

An item will only be an offensive weapon under this section if it is being carried for this purpose. In *Ohlson v Hylton* [1975] 1 WLR 724 the accused, a carpenter, was on his way home from work with his bag of tools, which included a hammer. There was a shortage of trains, due to an industrial dispute, and the trains were very full. When he tried to get into a crowded train he got into an argument with another passenger and hit the person on the head with the hammer. He was convicted of assault and of having an offensive weapon.

His conviction in relation to the offensive weapon was quashed in the Crown Court, on the ground that there was only an offence if the person was carrying the weapon with the intent to use it as an offensive weapon. That intent had to be found at some prior time, not just as he used it.

This decision has been followed in Victoria in *Wilson v Kuhl* [1979] VR 315. Kuhl and the victim Matthews were in adjoining toilet cubicles in a public toilet. There was a hole in the wall between them and the victim tried to block the hole, out of modesty. The accused then stuck a carving knife through the hole because the victim 'was annoying him' (at 317). Kuhl was found not guilty of the offence of being in possession of an offensive weapon. A carving knife is not an offensive weapon per se; it only becomes an offensive weapon if the person carrying it had the intention of using it for an aggressive purpose. Here the accused claimed he carried the knife in case he needed to defend himself (which on the facts the Court conceded could be believed); see also *Freundt v Hayes* (1992) 59 A Crim R 430.

Critique—armed robbery

The elements of aggravation that constitute armed robbery vary between jurisdictions. The MCCOC (*Chapter 3, Theft, Fraud, Bribery and Related Offences*, Report (December 1995)) recommended (at 70) that the aggravated form of robbery should be that the offender had an offensive weapon with him or her, or that the robbery took place in company with one or more people. This is consistent with the current law in several jurisdictions. The aggravated offence would be called 'aggravated robbery' rather than merely 'armed robbery' given its broader definition. The offence is formulated in these terms, with a definition of 'offensive weapon' similar to that in the Victorian legislation, in the amended Commonwealth *Criminal Code* s 132.3. The recent amendments to the South Australian legislation similarly establish an offence of aggravated robbery, carrying a maximum penalty of life imprisonment, where a robbery is committed in company or where the offender had an offensive weapon with him or her: *Criminal Law Consolidation Act* 1935 s 137. The previous legislation also included wounding or using other personal violence in the course of a robbery, but this component was not included in the new provisions.

The MCCOC noted a submission suggesting that wounding in the course of a robbery should count as aggravated robbery, but was of the view that it would be more appropriate to charge the relevant assault offence, which could be charged in addition to robbery.

It would be desirable to provide consistency in the application of such serious offences across jurisdictions. Circumstances of aggravation, leading to liability for substantially higher penalties, should only be those that clearly heighten the seriousness of the offence. Where an assault or other criminal harm takes place in the course of a robbery it should be charged and punished separately, allowing proper recognition of that harm. It can be argued that committing a robbery in company could be addressed adequately in sentencing for the base robbery offence. However, the contributions of the MCCOC and the South Australian legislature suggest that there may be a level of concern warranting inclusion in an aggravated offence of committing a robbery either in company with other persons or with offensive weapons.

Burglary

Background

Burglary involves unlawful entry into a house or other building with the intention of committing an offence such as theft. These offences are a key subject of public concern. Burglary was found to be the most feared crime among all respondents to the British Crime Survey, closely followed by rape: M Hough, *Anxiety About Crime: Findings from the 1994 British Crime Survey*, Home Office Research Study No 147 (London: Home Office, 1995). It should be noted that levels of fear of crime in any community do vary with gender, age, experience of victimisation and other factors: see, for example, C Carcach and S Mukherjee, 'Women's Fear of Violence in the Community', *Trends and Issues* No 135 (Canberra: AIC, 1999).

The Australian Institute of Criminology statistics on housebreaking showed the figure to be far larger than for robberies, but relatively stable since 1995: *Australian Crime Facts and Figures 2002*, 8. It reported that in 2001 there were 435,524 incidents of 'unlawful entry with intent' (including both offences where property is taken and those where no property is taken) recorded by police in Australia, most (64 per cent) from private dwellings: AIC, *Australian Crime Facts and Figures 2002* 29, 30. This represented approximately fifty recorded incidents of unlawful entry with intent every hour in 2001: AIC, *Australian Crime Facts and Figures 2002* (Canberra: AIC, 2002), 31 <http://www.aic.gov.au/publications/facts/2002/index.html>, accessed November 2003. When Pat Mayhew factored in the rates of under-reporting of such crime she concluded that there were in fact an estimated 819,000 residential and 176,000 non-residential burglaries in 2001, giving rise to an overall loss of $1.3 billion: P Mayhew, 'Counting the Costs of Crime in Australia', *Trends and Issues* No 247 (Canberra: AIC, 2003).

A national survey of businesses addressing crime and costs of crime to business found that in 1992 burglary was the most common crime, experienced by over a quarter of all businesses surveyed, followed by some form of theft (by customers, staff or others). Total costs of burglaries to business in that year were calculated to be $435 million: John Walker, *First Australian National Survey of Crimes Against Businesses* (Canberra: AIC 1995). Walker observes (at 6) that a 'saving grace, at least as far as the businesses were concerned, is the fact that almost two-thirds are insured for the full amount of any loss through burglary'. This is reflected in the assumptions of Mayhew's research that virtually all non-residential burglaries are reported (a requirement for making an insurance claim). Her research indicated that only about one in three residential burglaries are reported. D Brown, D Farrier, S Egger and L McNamara (*Criminal Laws: Materials and Commentary on Criminal Law and Process of New South Wales* (3rd edn, Sydney: The Federation Press, 2001) p 1252) point out the significance of the reliance on insurance and 'target-hardening' strategies in this area:

> What we are seeing in practice is a de facto privatisation of regulation in this area, with insurance companies placing increasing pressure on policyholders to use mechanical security devices and the police placing greater emphasis on the role of Neighbourhood Watch Schemes, staffed primarily by the householders themselves, in the prevention of housebreaking. In this environment, it is the poor and those living in areas of high mobility who end up being disadvantaged.

All jurisdictions include one or more offences based around housebreaking and entering with the intention of committing an offence such as theft. The main such offence is burglary, involving entry onto premises as a trespasser with an intent to steal or to commit another crime. Generally it is not necessary to prove that anything unlawful actually occurred on the premises; the offence is specifically of entry with a proscribed *intent*. There may be additional offences of actually committing the offences on private premises.

The common law defined the felony of burglary as 'the breaking and entering of the dwelling house of another at night with intent to commit a felony'. The same behaviour done in the daytime was the misdemeanour of housebreaking: CR Williams, *Property Offences* (3rd edn: Sydney: LBC Information Services, 1999) p 214. The common law focus on a nocturnal crime was not retained in New South Wales when these offences were given statutory form (see ss 109–113 *Crimes Act* 1900 (NSW)) or in the new South Australian provisions dealing with what is now called 'serious criminal trespass' (*Criminal Law Consolidation Act* 1935 (SA) ss 168–170A), but persists less directly in some jurisdictions. The Code in Queensland s 419 provides that if the offence of burglary is committed at night, or involves other elements of aggravation (with a weapon; being in company; using or threatening violence), the maximum penalty is life imprisonment instead of 14 years. The New South Wales legislation has removed the references to 'night' but includes in its offence of 'being armed with intent to commit an indictable offence' the offence of having one's face 'blackened or otherwise disguised' with intent to commit an indictable offence: *Crimes Act* 1900 (NSW) s 114(1)(c); see also *Criminal Code* (Tas) s 248(c); *Criminal Code* (Qld) s 425(1)(e).

The Codes also have a range of burglary-type offences drawing on the common law offences but differing in a number of ways. Differences include the scope of the concept of 'entry', the nature of the building, and whether the offence involves mere entry or extends to remaining in the building, with or without a relevant intent: see generally CR Williams, *Property Offences* (3rd edn: Sydney: LBC Information Services, 1999) pp 226–31.

It should be noted that some jurisdictions include in this offence not only entry with intent, but entry accompanied by the commission of a prescribed offence: for example *Crimes Act* 1900 (NSW) s 109; *Criminal Code* (Qld) s 421.

Victoria, the Australian Capital Territory, the Northern Territory and Tasmania have a single burglary offence— *Crimes Act* 1958 (Vic) s 76; *Crimes Act* 1900 (ACT) s 93; *Criminal Code* (NT) s 213; *Criminal Code* (Tas) s 244—while in South Australia parallel offences deal with serious criminal trespass in a place of residence (*Criminal Law Consolidation Act* 1935 (SA) s 170) and in a non-residential building (s 169). The focus in these jurisdictions is on the trespass involved (or unlawful entry: Northern Territory), rather than the breaking and entering element. The offence involves entry to a building as a trespasser with intent to steal, to assault someone, or to damage property (*Crimes Act* 1958 (Vic) s 76(1); *Crimes Act* 1900 (ACT) s 93(1); *Criminal Law Consolidation Act* 1935 (SA) s 168); or with intent to commit a crime (*Criminal Code* (Tas) s 244; *Criminal Code* (NT) s 213). The *Crimes Act* 1900 (ACT) s 93(1) includes the broader concept of entering *or remaining* on the premises.

In recent times media and public concerns, and anxiety about drug-related property crime, have led to the enactment of 'home invasion'–type offences. In New South Wales, for example, the *Home Invasion (Occupants Protection) Act* 1998 (NSW) in s 11 provided immunity from criminal liability to householders acting in defence of self or property against an intruder, with the legislated policy statement (s 5):

> [I]t is the public policy of the State of NSW that its citizens have a right to enjoy absolute safety from attack within dwelling-houses from intruders...

The Act was repealed in 2001, but the policy statement was expressly restated, in the *Crimes Amendment (Self Defence) Act* 2001 (NSW) s 4. The *Criminal Code* (NT) provides in s 226B for an offence titled 'home invasion and invasion of business premises', effectively an aggravated form of burglary. It comprises entering a dwelling house or business premises and unlawfully damaging the premises or property, and carries a maximum sentence of seven years. The penalty is increased to 10 years if there is serious damage or loss, the seriousness of the damage to be determined by considering 'any physical, psychological or emotional harm' or 'any apprehension, fear, distress or revulsion' caused to a person by the damage: s 226A(2). Amendments in Victoria in 1997 show similar concerns. A further element was added to 'aggravated' burglary, attracting a heavier sentence than simple burglary, where there is, to the accused's knowledge, a person present in the building; see also s 77(1)(b) *Crimes Act* 1958 (Vic) and s 170(2)(c) *Criminal Law Consolidation Act* 1935 (SA). As part of the recent amendments to property offences in South Australia, s 170A *Criminal Law Consolidation Act* 1935 (SA) introduces a new offence of criminal trespass in a place of residence carrying a maximum penalty of three years and requiring no other ulterior intent beyond knowledge that the person was present.

The focus on violating people's homes is also clearly present in the Code states, where the penalty for housebreaking-type offences is more severe where the building is a dwelling house (*Criminal Code* (NT) s 213(6); *Criminal Code* (Qld) s 419) or where the place is ordinarily used for human habitation (*Criminal Code* (Tas) s 245(a)(iii); (*Criminal Code* (WA) s 401(1)(b)). The new South Australian legislation provides for a more severe penalty where the serious criminal trespass occurs in a 'place of residence' (*Criminal Law Consolidation Act* 1935 (SA) s 170(1): 15 years) rather than a non-residential building (s 169(1): 10 years).

Burglary is in statutory form in New South Wales, but retains its common law complexity. The main offences are *Crimes Act* 1900 (NSW) s 109 entering with intent to cause serious indictable offence and breaking out: 14 years; s 110 breaking and entering and assaulting with intent to murder: 25 years; s 111 entering with intent to commit a serious indictable offence: 10 years; s 112 breaking and entering and committing a serious indictable offence: 14 years.

The Code states of Queensland and Western Australia focus on the concepts of 'entry' and 'breaking', drawing essentially on the common law of burglary. The main provision under the *Criminal Code* (Qld) is s 419(1) (entry to another's dwelling with intent to commit indictable offence); see also ss 421 and 425. The *Criminal Code* (WA) provides for burglary (s 401) and being armed with intent to enter a place to commit a crime (s 407). Offences differ in terms of whether there was a mere entry or a breaking and entering and on the seriousness of the intended crime.

We will focus the discussion here on the Victorian/Australian Capital Territory model, in view of the adoption of that model by the MCCOC.

The current law—physical elements

Entry

'Entry' is a concept used in most jurisdictions, and common law definitions apply. Entry is made when any part of the accused, or of an instrument used to effect entry, is in the building: *Criminal Code* (Qld) s 418(2); *Criminal Code* (Tas) s 243(8). The early case of *R v Davis* (1823) 168 ER 917 involved a prosecution where the accused's finger was inside the window of a jeweller's shop, when he was in the course of breaking in. This was held to be sufficient 'entry'.

In section 243(8) of the *Criminal Code* (Tas) 'entry' of instruments applies to those used to gain entry, to take anything from the building, or to commit any crime in the building. The Queensland Code is broader, simply referring to 'any part of the person's body or any part of an instrument used by the person' (*Criminal Code* (Qld) s 418(1)).

In the case of 'entry' by instruments, CR Williams suggests that at common law it may only be regarded as being 'entry' for the purpose of the offence of burglary if the instrument was inserted for the purpose of committing the intended crime: *Property Offences* (3rd edn: Sydney: LBC Information Services, 1999) p 219.

Entry as a trespasser

As noted above, Victoria, Australian Capital Territory, South Australia and Tasmania focus on the concept of 'entering as a trespasser'. This will be examined first. The approach of other jurisdictions based on the common law concepts of 'breaking and entering' will be discussed later.

A case in which the High Court considered the meaning of 'entering as a trespasser' is *Barker v The Queen* (1983) 153 CLR 338. Richard Barker had been asked by a neighbour to keep an eye on the neighbour's house while he was away. The neighbour told Barker where he kept a hidden key, should he need to enter. While the neighbour was away Barker did in fact enter the house and used a truck to remove furniture and domestic equipment (most of which he later returned, on being charged). Barker was convicted of burglary. The High Court confirmed his conviction. The Court reiterated the application of the common law of trespass: that trespass is an entry without right or authority by a person into a building or part of a building in the possession of another.

Obviously a person breaking a window and climbing into the house of a stranger will usually be 'entering as a trespasser', that is, without 'right or authority'. What about the situation that arose on these facts, where someone had *some* authority to enter the premises. Can he or she be said nonetheless to have 'entered as a trespasser'?

Mason J stated (at 346) that it is simply a question of determining the scope of the authority to enter: 'If a person enters for a purpose outside the scope of the authority then he stands in no better position than a person who enters with no authority at all'. In the present case, Mason J stated (at 348) that Barker had entered for a purpose 'quite unrelated to the invitation or licence which he had' and clearly entered as a trespasser. Barker had argued at his trial that he had removed the goods for their protection, a claim that was obviously rejected by the jury. If this claim had been accepted it may well have been found that Barker was acting within the terms of the authority given by the neighbour.

There are two aspects of 'entering as a trespasser' that must be proven: the fact that the accused was a trespasser—addressed in *Barker*—and the further requirement that the accused *knew* that he or she was a trespasser. This separate fault element can be understood also by reference to the doctrine of honest claim of right. A person cannot be said to enter premises as a trespasser who honestly believes he or she is entitled to enter. Brennan and Deane JJ stated in *Barker* (at 366) that such a person cannot be convicted of burglary unless 'the jury is satisfied also that he [or she] knew or was reckless as to the existence of the facts which made him [or her] a trespasser and that he [or she] did not enter in assertion of an honest claim of right to do so'.

Some of these issues had been considered in the English case of *R v Collins* [1973] 1 QB 100. Stephen Collins had been drinking heavily and visited a house where he knew a girl lived. Seeing a light in her upstairs bedroom, he found a stepladder and climbed to the girl's bedroom, where she was asleep. Collins did not know the girl. Nonetheless, when he climbed the ladder he had—according to his police interview—the intention to have sex with the girl who lived there, irrespective of her consent. He climbed onto the windowsill. As he did so, the girl woke up and, assuming in the dark that it was her boyfriend, invited him in. Collins said he was surprised, but he climbed in the window and they had intercourse. It was only afterwards that she realised it was not her boyfriend. She hit him and he fled. Collins was charged with and convicted of burglary with intent to rape.

Collins appealed, and the Court of Appeal held (at 105) that a person cannot be convicted of burglary unless they enter 'knowing that [they are] a trespasser…or…reckless as to whether or not [they are] entering the premises of another without the other party's consent'. In this case the question then turned on where he was when he was invited in. If he was still outside the window, then he could not be said to have knowingly or recklessly entered as a trespasser. If he was already climbing into the house before the invitation was given, he could be guilty. Since it was uncertain where the accused was at the critical moment, he could not be convicted of burglary.

What is the law in relation to entry to places with general public access and an apparent general licence to enter, such as a department store or supermarket? If a person enters intending to shoplift is he or she guilty of burglary when they enter? Again, it is a question of the scope of the authority. If the person enters the premises beyond the scope of the permission granted, he or she will be entering as a trespasser. In the case of shops it can be said that what is given is a general permission to enter. The permission is not limited by reference to purpose. Although the customer who takes goods from the shelves may be guilty of theft, he or she will probably not be guilty of burglary.

The High Court discussed this in *Barker v The Queen* (1983) 153 CLR 338. Brennan and Deane JJ concluded (at 357–8) that if there is a general permission to enter, it is not legitimate to try to cut that back by saying that, had the grantor been asked, they would probably have excluded from the scope of the permission any entry for the proposed unauthorised purposes.

Breaking and entering
The other Australian jurisdictions use the common law concepts of 'breaking and entering'. The Queensland Code simply refers to entering (the dwelling of another) with intent to commit an indictable offence (s 419(1)); entry by breaking carries the more severe penalty of life imprisonment (s 419(2)).

The common law concept of breaking involves some degree of forced entry to the premises. For example, entry through an open door or window does not amount to breaking but opening a closed, though unlocked, door or window is breaking: CR Williams, *Property Offences* (3rd edn: Sydney: LBC Information Services, 1999) pp 217–18. Section 418(1) of the Queensland Code defines breaking a dwelling or premises as breaking 'any part…of a dwelling or any premises, or [opening] by unlocking, pulling, pushing, lifting, or any other means whatever, any door, window, shutter, cellar…'. It is also extended to 'constructive breaking', which at common law and under the Tasmanian Code extends to obtaining admission by an artifice or intimidation: *R v Boyle* [1954] 2 QB 292; *Criminal Code* (Tas) s 244.

It will be seen that the complexities of such concepts are obviated in the Victorian model under which attention is on the trespasser rather than on entry. Entry will obviously amount to trespass when a window is broken to enter with permission; it can also be a trespass to enter by an open door without needing to show any 'break in'.

Entry to a building or part of a building
The Victorian and Australian Capital Territory provisions refer to entering 'any building or part of a building'. The meaning of 'building' is extended (by s 76(2) *Crimes Act* 1958 (Vic) and s 93(2) *Crimes Act* 1900 (ACT)) to include inhabited vehicles or vessels, whether or not they were inhabited at the time. This would include a caravan or ship, at least while inhabited. The Tasmanian provision refers to 'any building or conveyance' further defined in *Criminal Code* (Tas) s 243(3) and (4) to include any 'structure or erection' and 'any vehicle, vessel, or aircraft', and specifically a caravan and a tent (s 243(6)).

To be a building, there must be a solid structure with some degree of permanence. A tent, for instance, is not a building. A structure can be a building although it is a number of distinct sets of premises, for example a block of flats. The outbuildings of a house are also buildings. A structure can also be a building while it is still under construction—whether a particular incomplete structure is a building will be a question of fact, depending on the extent to which it is completed: CR Williams, *Property Offences* (3rd edn: Sydney: LBC Information Services, 1999) p 236.

The Adelaide Central Market, a roofed area covering roadways and stalls, some of which were open and some of which could be locked, was held to be a 'building' in *R v Wilson Flanders* [1969] SASR 218.

Sections 109–113 *Crimes Act* 1900 (NSW) use the expression 'dwelling house', which is defined in s 4(1) as including 'any building or other structure intended for occupation as a dwelling…although it has never been so occupied', 'a boat or vehicle in or on which any person resides', and 'any building or other structure within the same curtilage as a dwelling house, and occupied therewith…'.

Section 419 *Criminal Code* (Qld) refers only to entering a 'dwelling' in relation to burglary (entry with intent). This is defined in s 1 to include any building or structure, or part of a building or structure, which is being kept as a residence. The Western Australian provisions go further, referring to entry to 'the place of another person'. This is defined to mean a 'building, structure, tent, or conveyance, or a part of [such]' (*Criminal Code* (WA) s 400(1)); it is stated to include uninhabited or empty places. The new South Australian provisions create separate offences for criminal trespass in non-residential buildings (*Criminal Law Consolidation Act* 1935 (SA) s 169) and in a 'place of residence', defined in s 170(3).

The provisions in *Crimes Act* 1958 (Vic) s 76, *Crimes Act* 1900 (ACT) s 93(2), *Criminal Code* (Qld) s 418(4), *Criminal Law Consolidation Act* 1935 (SA) ss 169(3), 179(3), *Criminal Code* (Tas) s 243(7) and *Criminal Code* (WA) s 400(1) also include 'part of a building'. This would cover the situation where the offender entered the building with authority to enter, but then went into a 'part' of the building as a trespasser. For example, the owner of a flat may, without authority, enter another flat in the same block: this will amount to entering a part of a building as a trespasser.

A 'part' of a building may include an area that is simply delineated as separate, as discussed in the English case of *R v Walkington* [1979] 1 WLR 1169. Walkington was seen wandering about a department store at the end of the day, watching the activity around the tills. He entered an area enclosed by three moveable counters and looked into the till. It was empty and he slammed it shut. He was convicted of burglary and appealed. One issue was whether he had entered a 'part of a building' as a trespasser. The Court of Appeal affirmed his conviction. It said that the counter area could be regarded as constituting 'part' of a building. There was a physical partition, and it was open to the jury to decide that the public were clearly excluded, and that the defendant knew that this was a separated area.

The current law—fault elements

With intent to commit another offence
The Victorian and Australian Capital Territory provisions require for a conviction of burglary that the entry have occurred with intent to steal or to commit any assault

on a person in the building or any property damage, where either intended offence is punishable by imprisonment for five years or more. Other jurisdictions provide different criteria for the intended offences: *Criminal Code* (Qld) s 419(1) refers to 'indictable offence'; *Criminal Code* (Tas) s 244 'a crime'; *Crimes Act* 1900 (NSW) s 109 'serious indictable offence'; *Criminal Code* (NT) s 213 provides for different penalties depending on the seriousness of the intended offence; *Criminal Law Consolidation Act* 1935 (SA) s 168 refers to offences involving theft, offences against the person, and offences involving damage to property attracting penalties of three years or more.

'Intent to steal' in s 76(1)(a) *Crimes Act* 1958 (Vic) means intent to commit theft contrary to s 72. If the planned offence does not come within s 72, there is not the necessary intent. In the English case of *Low v Blease* [1975] Crim LR 513 the accused entered premises as a trespasser and made a phone call. He was convicted of burglary on the basis of theft of the electricity used to make the call. His appeal was successful. The Divisional Court held that electricity is not 'property' capable of being stolen and so he could not be guilty of theft (as discussed earlier in this chapter) and therefore was not guilty of burglary either.

In Victoria and the Australian Capital Territory most assault offences carry a penalty of five years or more (see *Crimes Act* 1958 (Vic) ss 16–18; *Crimes Act* 1900 (ACT) ss 19–24, 27) as do most offences involving damage to buildings or to property: see *Crimes Act* 1958 (Vic) s 197; *Crimes Act* 1900 (ACT) ss 116, 117. Summary assault and property damage offences fall outside the category of prescribed offences as they carry lesser penalties. Rape is clearly an assault and carries a penalty of more than five years' imprisonment. The South Australian provisions include some common and all more serious assaults (see *Criminal Law Consolidation Act* 1935 (SA) Part 3, Division 9).

The intent must exist at the time of entry in New South Wales, Northern Territory, Victoria and Tasmania. If the person entered as a trespasser, and then decided to commit a theft or assault or property damage, he or she could only be charged with that substantive offence. Of course, the fact that an offence was committed is strong evidence of the pre-existing intent. The offence is defined more broadly in the Australian Capital Territory, South Australia, Queensland and Western Australia where a person can be guilty of burglary who enters 'or remains in' (*Crimes Act* 1900 (ACT) s 93(1); *Criminal Law Consolidation Act* 1935 (SA) s 168) or 'is in' the building (*Criminal Code* (Qld) s 419(1); *Criminal Code* (WA) s 401(1)) with the relevant intent.

In addition, since it is the offender's intention that is of interest, it is irrelevant if the offence could not in fact have been carried out. In *Walkington*'s case, for instance, the till in the shop was empty. Theft would have been impossible. But the Court of Appeal reiterated that this did not take away the accused's undoubted intention, when he entered the prohibited area of the shop, to steal any money that he found in the till.

Critique—the law of burglary

Burglary as defined in Victoria, the Australian Capital Territory, South Australia and Tasmania provides a major simplification of the common law (and Code) offence of burglary and the associated offences developed to fill in the gaps in the basic offence. It also does away with the traditional distinctions between night and day, dwellings and buildings, and so on: see MCCOC, *Chapter 3, Theft, Fraud, Bribery and Related Offences*, Report (December 1995) p 75.

The MCCOC proposed a similar burglary offence. The proposed offence refers to entering or remaining in a building as a trespasser, with intent to commit either theft or an offence involving harm to a person or damage to property and punishable by at least five years' imprisonment: cl 16.3

Specific elements were varied to address some of the difficulties that the UK and Victorian model has encountered. First, as discussed above, it is sometimes difficult to ascertain whether the offender actually entered as a trespasser, where they had authority to enter the property for one purpose but not for their actual unlawful purpose. There has also been some debate about the desirable scope of the law of burglary: *should* the concept of 'entry as a trespasser' be read so widely that the shoplifter would be charged as a burglar?

The High Court in *Barker v The Queen* (1983) 153 CLR 338 explored the civil law of trespass to determine whether on the facts in the case the entry could be said to have been a trespass. They concluded that where Barker had permission to enter to look after the neighbour's house, but entered to steal his property, there was a trespass as the action went beyond the authority to enter. The Court also explored questions of entry to more public spaces, by people such as shoplifters. Brennan and Deane JJ (at 362) concluded that if there was a general authority to enter, the offender did not then become a trespasser simply because they would not have been permitted to enter had the owner known of the unlawful purpose. They would also be unlikely to have known that they were entering as a trespasser. Murphy J observed (at 353) that it was inappropriate to introduce complex civil law concepts into the criminal law, concluding emphatically that 'Parliament could never have intended that guilt of an offence carrying fourteen years imprisonment would depend on such fine points in regard to everyday circumstances, such as intended pilfering, by house or office cleaners, repairers, office workers, shop assistants and customers in shops'.

The MCCOC agreed that such cases should not be included in the offence of burglary, as they lack the degree of physical violation of the victim's possessory rights to restrict entry that the offence envisages: MCCOC, *Chapter 3, Theft, Fraud, Bribery and Related Offences*, Report (December 1995) p 77. It proposed that the burglary offence should provide that a person is not a trespasser merely because they were 'permitted to enter or remain in the building for a purpose that is not the person's intended purpose'. These recommendations have been adopted in the Commonwealth *Criminal*

Code amendments, s 132.4. This limitation does not of course prevent the prosecution charging the offender with a substantive offence once it is committed, such as theft.

Section 244 of the *Criminal Code* (Tas), which otherwise generally mirrors those in Victoria and the Australian Capital Territory, includes other ways in which an apparent consent or authority can be exceeded, referring to entering as a trespasser 'or by means of any threat, artifice, or collusion' (s 244), as does the *Criminal Law Consolidation Act* 1935 (SA) s 168(3). Bearing in mind the problems around arguments that fraud 'vitiates' consent (discussed earlier), the MCCOC (at 81) did not recommend extending the notion of entry as a trespasser to include entry obtained by fraud, preferring to leave such offences to be prosecuted as theft.

The focus in some jurisdictions on '*entry* as a trespasser' can give rise to problems in determining whether the offender entered with the relevant intent, or only formed the intent once in the building. The attention to 'entry' also means that a person cannot be charged with burglary who enters with permission, but then remains on the premises when the permission has expired (for example remaining in a building after closing time) with the relevant intent. As discussed above, the Australian Capital Territory, Queensland, South Australia and Western Australia use a broader time frame, and MCCOC recommended extension of the offence from merely 'entering' to 'entering or remaining': MCCOC, *Chapter 3, Theft, Fraud, Bribery and Related Offences*, Report (December 1995) cl 16.3(1).

Different jurisdictions cover entry into different types of buildings and structures in their burglary offences. Burglary is about the violation of possessory rights, particularly of places used as dwellings. The MCCOC proposed a broad definition of 'building' to include a part of a building and any structure (whether moveable or not), vehicle or vessel that is 'used, designed or adapted for residential purposes': cl 16.3(3). This would include tents, caravans and cars in which people are living, as well as empty buildings or structures intended for residential use.

The MCCOC proposal, embodied in the 2000 amendments to the Commonwealth *Criminal Code* 1995, addresses the problems that have arisen around the different formulations of burglar. We consider that it strikes an appropriate balance in reflecting the nature of the harm represented by an offence of burglary.

Aggravated burglary

The aggravated form of burglary, similar to that of armed/aggravated robbery, involves factors such as being armed, committing the offence in company, and burglary where actual injury or damage is caused. The offence of aggravated burglary carries a severe penalty, considerably higher than for simple burglary.

The prosecution must prove the offence of burglary with the element of aggravation. In Victoria, the Australian Capital Territory and the Northern Territory this is shown where the person has with them 'any firearm or imitation firearm, any offensive weapon or any explosive or imitation explosive' (*Crimes Act* 1958 (Vic) s 77(1)(a); *Crimes Act* 1900 (ACT) s 94; *Criminal Code* (NT) s 213(6)). The definition of the relevant weapons in *Crimes Act* 1958 (Vic) s 77(1A) has already been discussed in relation to armed robbery, above.

In Victoria it is also shown if when they entered the building there was a person present in the building and the offender 'knew that a person was then so present or was reckless as to whether or not a person was then so present' (*Crimes Act* 1958 (Vic) s 77(1)(b)); the penalty is higher again in the Northern Territory where the offence occurs in a dwelling house.

The Code states refer to such aggravating factors as being armed with, or pretending to be armed with, items such as dangerous or offensive weapons, instruments or noxious substances, or explosives, use or threat of actual violence, and acting in company: see *Criminal Code* (Qld) s 419(3); *Criminal Code* (Tas) s 245; *Criminal Code* (WA) s 400(1). The South Australian provisions also include as aggravating factors having an 'offensive weapon' in possession and acting in company (*Criminal Law Consolidation Act* 1935 (SA) s 169(2); s 170(2)(a),(b)); where the criminal trespass involves a place of residence it will also be an aggravating factor if there was another person lawfully in the property and the accused knew or was reckless as to their presence (s 170(2)(c)).

Critique—aggravated burglary

Consistent with its approach to armed/aggravated robbery, the MCCOC (*Chapter 3, Theft, Fraud, Bribery and Related Offences*, Report (December 1995)) recommended that the elements of the aggravated form of burglary should be that the offender had an offensive weapon with him or her, or that the burglary took place in company with one or more people: cl 16.4 (and see s 132.5 *Criminal Code* (Cth)). The Committee noted that some submissions suggested additional aggravating factors for burglary such as occurring at night, or in a dwelling house, but it concluded that these would be adequately addressed in sentencing.

The insertion of *Crimes Act* 1958 (Vic) s 77(1)(b) in 1997 has been criticised. It appears to be a response to community fears about 'home invasion' burglaries where someone is at home at the time, but would obviously apply also where the accused entered an office building or factory where it was likely people would be present, but where the accused had every intention of not being discovered. CR Williams argues that extending the offence in this way seems to 'devalue the significance of the distinction between aggravated burglary and burglary': *Property Offences* (3rd edn: Sydney: LBC Information Services, 1999) p 239. The new South Australian legislation also includes such an extension of liability, although limited to criminal trespass in a place of residence.

We agree that the South Australian and Victorian provisions extend the offence too far. We would, however, endorse an approach that provided for consistency across jurisdictions in defining aggravating factors for both burglary and robbery, as discussed by the MCCOC and earlier in this chapter.

Conclusion

Property offences involving stealing constitute a significant proportion of the community's experience of crime. In this chapter we have examined the offences of theft, robbery and burglary. Beginning with the case of Frank De Stefano, we have seen that property offences can involve tangible and intangible property and can arise from a range of motivations. The criminal laws dealing with offences against property ownership have developed from the common law and, in Australia, are still highly complex and lacking in uniformity. We might not go so far as Winifred Holland, who has said that 'The law of theft in Canada is in a mess': W Holland, *The Law of Theft and Related Offences* (Scarborough, Ontario: Thomson Canada, 1998) p 376. It is obvious, however, that much needs to be done to reduce the complexity of the common law and Code regimes, and to address problems of uniformity across Australia. We will return to this point after looking at the current picture of fraud offences in the next chapter.

The Victorian theft legislation adopted the UK reforms and restructured the common law of theft by introducing the new concept of 'dishonest appropriation' and by employing more abstract notions of property and ownership. This model has provided the framework for the legislation in the Australian Capital Territory and, to a degree, the new South Australian provisions, as well as for the uniform theft laws proposed by the MCCOC, and many of the provisions now included in the Commonwealth *Criminal Code*.

As the MCCOC observed in the introduction to their 1995 report at iii: 'The vast majority of the submissions [on this report] endorsed the adoption of the [UK] *Theft Act* model and the goal of uniformity in this area of the law.'

Nonetheless, while the reforms brought about by the English and Victorian theft legislation were significant, there are still areas that need review and modification to take account of technological and social change. Some of these areas are discussed in Chapter 7. A number of these issues also raise broader questions about the appropriate uses of criminal and civil laws, which are revisited at many points in this book.

The new concepts introduced in the English and Victorian legislation have also brought their own complications. Appropriation has caused a number of problems; the meaning of dishonesty continues to cause difficulty despite recent judicial and legislative attempts at clarifying it. While the model adopted in the *Criminal Code* 1995 (Cth) is intended to address these problems it is arguable that, at least in relation to the central concept of 'dishonesty', the law is still uncertain. The ongoing debate about the correct formulation of the meaning of dishonesty in the English Law Commission, noted earlier, underscores the difficulties in this area.

Property offences based on deception are the subject of the next chapter. Many of the issues discussed in this chapter in relation to stealing will also be relevant to the critical analysis of fraud offences.

CHAPTER 7

Property offences involving deception

Introduction

Shiralee Ann Lambie had a £200 limit on her Barclays Bank credit card. When her debt reached £533 the bank requested return of the card. She agreed to return it the next day but continued to use it for another two weeks, running up a total debt of £1005.26, before returning the card to the bank. One of her last transactions involved shopping at Mothercare, a shop selling babyclothes, to buy goods worth £10.35. When she presented her credit card to buy the goods, the shop manager checked that the card was not expired, that the signature was the same as that on the card, and that the card did not appear on the current stop-lists, as she was required to do by her employer. Everything was in order, and she handed over the goods. In her evidence, the manager said she knew that if she carried out the necessary checks, as she had done, the contract with the Bank had been observed and the shop would be paid by the Bank. Shiralee Lambie was convicted of obtaining a financial advantage by deception: *R v Lambie* [1982] AC 449.

Lambie's case illustrates a particularly common form of fraud. It also raises a number of questions about the law relating to fraud—questions about the nature of the deception and the identity of the victim when credit cards are misused, and about how the criminal law deals with fraudulently obtaining property and less tangible benefits. These are some of the issues examined in this chapter.

More than two decades on from *Lambie*'s case, the most common types of fraud still involve credit cards and cheques. A recent study of 155 completed serious fraud files from Australian and New Zealand prosecution agencies reported that the main categories of prosecuted fraud involved obtaining finance or credit by deception (21 per cent of offence types), followed by fraud involving cheques (15 per cent): Australian Institute of Criminology and PricewaterhouseCoopers,

333

Serious Fraud in Australia and New Zealand (Canberra: AIC and PricewaterhouseCoopers, 2003). Offenders most frequently disposed of the proceeds of their crime by purchasing luxury goods and services such as motor vehicles or travel. The next largest categories involved spending on gambling and personal living expenses: *Serious Fraud in Australia and New Zealand* (Australian Institute of Criminology and PricewaterhouseCoopers, 2003) pp 2–3. The authors examined the motivations of the accused, reflected in evidence from various sources at the trial, and concluded (at 44) that greed was the primary motivation of over a quarter of all offenders (27 per cent of offenders), followed by gambling (16 per cent). The significance of gambling as a motivation for property offences has been discussed in Chapter 6.

The seriousness of fraud for Australian business is underlined by the number of recent inquiries into the issue. In addition to the AIC/PricewaterhouseCoopers study, the Victorian Drugs and Crime Prevention Committee has released a Discussion Paper, *Inquiry into Fraud and Electronic Commerce* (March 2003), and the management firm KPMG Australia has released its *Fraud Survey 2002* (April 2002). The AIC/PricewaterhouseCoopers study found recorded losses of $260.5 million, of which only $13.5 million was recovered at the time of sentencing. The Victorian Committee summarised a range of data—including Victorian police statistics on offences of deception, which showed losses close to $3 million in 2000–01—and concluded that crimes of dishonesty are likely to involve many hundreds of millions of dollars in Victoria alone each year: Victorian Drugs and Crime Prevention Committee, *Inquiry into Fraud and Electronic Commerce*, Discussion Paper (March 2003) pp 58, 61.

A study of prosecuted frauds can only provide a partial picture. It is believed that much fraud goes undetected, is unreported, or is not prosecuted: Victorian Drugs and Crime Prevention Committee, Inquiry into Fraud and Electronic Commerce, Discussion Paper (March 2003), 37. Pat Mayhew, in a recent attempt to quantify the cost of crime in Australia, concluded that the overall fraud bill (noting the difficulties of defining fraud and the lack of reliable data in this area) for 2001 could be put at $5.88 billion: 'Counting the Costs of Crime in Australia', *Trends and Issues* No 247 (Canberra: AIC, 2003). This figure was reached by multiplying the number of recorded state and federal fraud offences by their average value, and then multiplying this by three on the basis that research indicates that there are three undetected frauds for every one recorded; see also Russell Smith, 'Measuring the Extent of Fraud in Australia', *Trends and Issues* No 74 (Canberra: AIC, 1997).

KPMG Australia carries out a biennial Fraud Survey. Its 2002 survey of Australian and New Zealand public and private sector organisations found that fraud was thriving, committed both by people external to the organisation and internally by management and other employees: KPMG, *Fraud Survey 2002* (April 2002). There were 361 respondents to the survey; 55 per cent reported at least one fraud incident over the two-year period, suffering total losses of $273 million, or an average of $1.4 million per organisation. KPMG reported that, outside the financial services sector, the highest proportion of losses (40 per cent of losses by fraud) originated internally, coming from dishonest managers. Across all sectors, theft of inventory and plant was the most common form of internal fraud, representing more than 40 per cent of internal frauds. The most common types of fraud committed by external parties were credit card fraud and obtaining services and benefits by false information: *Fraud Survey 2002* (April 2002), 9. The authors observed that many organisations exacerbated the problem of internal fraud by treating fraudsters with undue leniency, for example dismissing them without reporting the fraud to the police, presumably to minimise publicity. This then enables the offender to move on to other organisations and to reoffend: see further M Levi, *Regulating Fraud: White Collar Crime and the Criminal Process* (London: Tavistock Publications, 1987). Issues relating to corporations and fraud and to computer-based frauds are discussed further below.

Another perspective on fraud can be gained by the ways in which the criminal justice system handles frauds by economically vulnerable members of the community: see Dee Cook, *Rich Law Poor Law: Different Responses to Tax and Supplementary Benefit Fraud* (Milton Keynes: Open University Press, 1989). Welfare recipients who obtain benefits to which they are not entitled may be guilty of fraud, and may be dealt with in a number of ways. The discretions exercised in this area underline the differing political and justice agendas: protection of the limited welfare dollar/taxpayer's money and deterrence of fraud, particularly systemic fraud. The Commonwealth government, which provides most social welfare payments, has administrative means of obtaining repayment of overpayments. It can also prosecute summarily under the *Social Security Act* 1991 (Cth) s 1230C, or on indictment under the *Criminal Code* (Cth) s 135.1.

Welfare fraud is an area with a high proportion of female offenders, perhaps not surprisingly given the number of women reliant on welfare benefits. In 1998–99 one benefit, the single parent payment, was received by 384,000 people, of whom 93 per cent were women. In this period, 393 women and 44 men were prosecuted for fraudulently receiving this benefit: Patricia Easteal, *Less than Equal* (Sydney: Butterworths Australia, 2001) p 61; see also Meredith Wilkie, *Women Social Security Offenders: Experiences of the Criminal Justice system in Western Australia* (Nedlands, WA: Crime Research Centre University of Western Australia, 1993) ch 3. The departmental guidelines on prosecuting in welfare matters include consideration of the degree of the person's involvement, whether the person is a first offender, and the need to provide a deterrent to similar offenders: see Springvale Legal Service, *Lawyers Practice Manual* (Melbourne: Law Book Co) 1.5.402. Considerable publicity is given to the rigorous pursuit of welfare fraud. While it appears that many cases are dealt with administratively or by a summary prosecution, rather than being directed to the Director of Public Prosecutions, this is an area where political and other factors may also be relevant to the discretion whether and how to prosecute: Mayuran Sivapragasam, 'For whose benefit anyway?' (1997) 22(4) *Alternative Law Journal* 170–2. A number of writers have noted the high levels of public disapproval and pursuit of welfare frauds compared with approaches to tax or medicare frauds: see Dee Cook, *Rich Law Poor Law: Different Responses to Tax and Supplementary Benefit Fraud* (Milton

Keynes: Open University Press, 1989); Patricia Easteal, *Less than Equal* (Sydney: Butterworths Australia, 2001) p 73.

Theft and fraud can be seen as aspects of the same sort of dishonest behaviour—taking property from another without being entitled to do so, either by persuading the owner to hand over the goods by a deception or trick, or by simply taking the goods without the owner's consent. It would be possible to have a single offence of dishonest acquisition to cover all such offences: this was discussed (but rejected) in the Model Criminal Code Officers Committee (MCCOC), *Chapter 3, Theft, Fraud, Bribery and Related Offences*, Report (December 1995). At the other extreme it would be possible to deal separately with dishonest acquisition of tangible and intangible property; with property and financial benefit; with taking the property and with deceiving the owner into handing the property over, and so on. The Australian jurisdictions all sit at various points along this spectrum.

The *Crimes Act* 1900 (ACT) as amended in 1985 defines theft as covering both usurping the rights of owner and obtaining property by deception: s 86. The legislation thereby removes the traditional distinction between theft and fraud (obtaining property by deception). All other Australian jurisdictions maintain the distinction in some form.

The common law offences dealing with fraudulently obtaining property turned on the distinction between obtaining mere possession of the goods, and obtaining full ownership or property in the goods. If the owner only intended to transfer possession, the offence is common law larceny by trick. If the owner intended to transfer property in the good then the offence is obtaining by false pretences. As CR Williams observes, '[i]t is relatively easy to state the distinguishing criterion in a coherent fashion....it is much more difficult to apply it in practice': *Property Offences* (3rd edn, Sydney: LBC Information Services, 1999) p 144. Section 179 of the *Crimes Act* 1900 (NSW) creates the statutory offence of obtaining property by false pretences, and applies whether possession or ownership was obtained: *R v Petronius-Kuff* [1983] 3 NSWLR 178.

Other related statutory offences in New South Wales include fraudulent misappropriation (*Crimes Act* 1900 (NSW) s 178A), obtaining money by deception (s 178BA), obtaining money by false statements (s 178BB) and obtaining credit by fraud or false pretences (s 178C).

South Australia, Queensland and Western Australia have a single main fraud offence. The Queensland and Western Australian offences were introduced in 1997. The offence is defined as comprising a range of dishonest behaviours including dishonestly obtaining property, use of property belonging to another, or gaining of an advantage ('pecuniary or otherwise') or causing of detriment, including making off without payment: *Criminal Code* (Qld) s 408C. The focus in the Queensland Code provisions is on *dishonesty* as distinct from *deception*. The West Australian Code similarly has a single fraud offence, with a similar breadth in terms of obtaining property, or gaining a benefit pecuniary or otherwise, but defined as obtaining such property or advantage 'with intent to defraud, by deceit or any fraudulent means': *Criminal Code* (WA) s 409(1). The terms 'dishonestly', 'with intent to defraud' and 'by any fraudulent means' are not defined in the legislation but are arguably equivalent. The English Criminal Law Revision Committee (CLRC) considered that 'fraudulently' meant 'dishonestly': *Theft and Related Offences*, Report No 8 (London: HMSO, Cmnd 2877, 1966). Kirby J in *Peters* certainly regarded the terms as 'interchangeable' ((1998) 192 CLR 493 at 542).

As discussed in Chapter 6 in the context of theft offences, the offence of stealing in Queensland and Western Australia (fraudulently taking property) covers situations where the owner of the property handed it over, but his or her consent was induced by deception or duress: *Criminal Code* (Qld) s 391(1); *Criminal Code* (WA) s 371(1): and see CR Williams, *Property Offences* (3rd edn, Sydney: LBC Information Services, 1999) p 167. This stealing offence applies where the deception persuaded the owner to part only with possession of the property. The fraud offences in *Criminal Code* (Qld) s 408C and *Criminal Code* (WA) s 409(1), on the other hand, replace the common law offence of obtaining by false pretences and similar offences, and apply whether the owner intended to part with property or to part only with possession: *Criminal Code* (Qld) s 408C(3)(f); s 1 'obtains' *Criminal Code* (WA).

The single fraud offences in *Criminal Code* (Qld) s 408C and *Criminal Code* (WA) s 409(1) encompass property and financial fraud. The offence explicitly includes gaining 'a benefit or advantage, pecuniary or otherwise' *Criminal Code* (Qld) s 408C(1)(d); and see *Criminal Code* (WA) s 409(1)(c).

In Queensland, property is further defined in *Criminal Code* (Qld) s 408C(3)(a) to include 'credit, service, any benefit or advantage...right to incur a debt or to recover or receive a benefit'. These parallel the concepts covered in the Victorian notion of 'financial advantage'. Section 408C(1)(a) *Criminal Code* (Qld) also includes an offence of dishonestly applying property belonging to another to one's own use, an offence not found in the Western Australian Code and having a wider application than stealing: see E Colvin, S Linden and J McKechnie, *Criminal Law in Queensland and Western Australia* (3rd edn, Sydney: Butterworths, 2001) p 141.

The new South Australian provisions establish a single main offence of deception, where a person deceives another and 'by doing so (a) dishonestly benefits him/herself or a third person; or (b) dishonestly causes a detriment...': *Criminal Law Consolidation Act* 1935 (SA) s 139. Benefit and detriment are defined in s 130 to refer to proprietary benefits/detriments, and financial advantages/disadvantages.

The *Criminal Code* (Tas) similarly includes in theft 'larceny by a trick' (s 226(1)), which applies where the deception persuaded the owner to part only with possession of the property. There are several other fraud offences, including obtaining goods by false pretences (s 250), cheating (s 252) and obtaining a financial advantage by deception (s 252A), an offence that parallels s 82 of the Victorian *Crimes Act* 1958.

There are still a number of specific offences around fraudulent practices in the Code jurisdictions, such as fraudulently dealing with minerals (*Criminal Code* (Qld) s 405; *Criminal Code* (WA) s 385), fraudulent disposition of mortgaged goods (*Criminal Code* (Qld) s 407), and fraudulent appropriation of electrical or other power (*Criminal Code* (Qld) s 408; *Criminal Code* (WA) s 390; *Criminal Code* (Tas) s 233).

There are three fraud offences under the Northern Territory Code: obtaining property by deception (s 227), which is similar to s 81 of the *Crimes Act* 1958 (Vic), obtaining credit by deception (s 227(3)) and by deception inducing a person to engage in any conduct for the purposes of gain to the offender (s 227(4)). The last is an extremely broad offence. The appropriateness of introducing such general dishonesty offences is considered further at the end of this chapter. An offence of doing 'anything with the intention of dishonestly obtaining a gain from another person' has recently been included in the Commonwealth *Criminal Code* s 135.1 by the *Criminal Code Amendment (Theft, Fraud, Bribery and Related Offences) Act* 2000 (Cth).

In Victoria there are two fraud-type offences: obtaining property by deception (s 81 *Crimes Act* 1958 (Vic)) and obtaining a financial advantage by deception (s 82). While the Australian Capital Territory combines theft and obtaining property by deception in one offence (s 86 *Crimes Act* 1900 (ACT)), it maintains a separate offence of obtaining a financial advantage by deception: s 95.

A general offence of conspiracy to defraud exists at common law in all jurisdictions and existed in statutory form in s 86 of the Commonwealth *Crimes Act* 1914 (repealed in 2001). These have been discussed earlier in relation to recent cases such as *Peters v The Queen* (1998) 192 CLR 493 and will not be considered further here, but see Chapter 8 below.

As in the discussion about theft, we will use the framework employed by the MCCOC in outlining the components of fraud-type offences. We will then look critically at the operation of these offences.

Obtaining property by deception

Background

Stephanie Kovacs had a cheque account and cheque card from the local branch of the National Westminster Bank. Kovac's account became overdrawn, and the Bank wrote and told her not to draw any more cheques. A bank official called to collect the cheque book and card, but she said she did not have them with her. Kovacs later used cheques from the cheque book to buy a railway ticket and a Pekinese dog. The Bank honoured the cheques, and Kovac's overdraft thereby increased. Kovacs was convicted of obtaining a financial advantage by deception, the deception being the representation that she was entitled to use the cheque card: *R v Kovacs* [1974] 1 WLR 370.

The offences to be examined in this section involve obtaining property by deception. Some or all of the elements of deception, dishonesty and intention to permanently deprive appear in the offences in all jurisdictions. Most also differentiate between the obtaining of property and of other types of advantage. The case of Stephanie Kovacs appears to involve obtaining property—the Pekinese dog and the train ticket—by deception. However, at the time the case was decided it was regarded as unclear whether property obtained by a deception concerning the accused's entitlement to use the cheque or credit card could be regarded as being 'obtained' by the deception. We will examine the complications around cheques and credit cards, the meaning of deception, and the requirement for a causal connection between the obtaining and the deception raised by this case later in this chapter.

Section 81(1) of the *Crimes Act* 1958 (Vic) provides that the offence is committed where 'A person...by any deception dishonestly obtains property belonging to another, with the intention of permanently depriving the other of it'. The penalty is equivalent to that for theft: 10 years' maximum imprisonment. The provisions in Victoria and the Northern Territory are similar in requiring obtaining of property of another by deception. The Victorian provision, however, also requires proof of dishonesty and intention to permanently deprive. The Northern Territory section has much broader application, with no such additional requirements; it is proven where any person 'by any deception (a) obtains the property of another [or obtains a benefit]': *Criminal Code* (NT) s 227(1).

The Code states differ in their approach, as already noted. Section 408C of the *Criminal Code* (Qld) requires proof of dishonesty but no requirement of deception while s 409 of the *Criminal Code* (WA) refers to 'with intent to defraud, by deceit or any fraudulent means'. The *Criminal Code* (Tas) covers larceny by trick (s 226(1)) and obtaining goods by false pretences (s 250). The latter offence requires proof of the use of a false pretence (further defined in s 249), with intent to defraud.

The common law provisions also vary. Section 179 of the *Crimes Act* 1900 (NSW) creates the offence of obtaining by false pretences, and provides that 'Whosoever, by any false pretence or by any wilfully false promise...obtains from any person any property, with intent to defraud, shall be liable to imprisonment for five years'. Section 178BA(1) *Crimes Act* 1900 (NSW) refers to 'Whosoever by any deception dishonestly obtains...any money or valuable thing or any financial advantage of any kind...'. Section 178BB *Crimes Act* 1900 (NSW) deals with making a false statement for the purpose of obtaining a valuable thing. Section 139 of the *Criminal Law Consolidation Act* 1935 (SA) requires proof of deception and dishonesty in obtaining a benefit or causing a detriment.

The elements of these offences are discussed in turn.

The current law—physical elements

Deception

For offences using this concept there must be proof of a deception. The meaning of 'deceive' has been defined at common law as 'to induce a [person] to believe that a thing is true which is false, and which the person practicing the deceit knows or believes to be false': *In re London and Globe Finance Corporation Limited* [1903] Ch 728 at 732.

The meaning of deception is elaborated in s 81(4)(a) *Crimes Act* 1958 (Vic), and s 83 *Crimes Act* 1900 (ACT) in similar terms; see also *Criminal Law Consolidation Act* 1935 (SA) s 130 'deception'. Victorian s 81(4)(a) provides that deception:

> means any deception (whether deliberate or reckless) by words or conduct as to fact or as to law, including a deception as to the present intentions of the person using the deception or any other person...

Section 179 of the *Crimes Act* 1900 (NSW), obtaining by false pretences, uses the phrase 'by any false pretence or by any wilfully false promise': this is understood to be equivalent to deception and largely overlaps with s 178B, obtaining property by passing a cheque: see Brown et al (3rd edn, Sydney: The Federation Press, 2001) p 1210 for a review of New South Wales offences. For the offence of obtaining money, a valuable thing or any financial advantage by deception under s 178BA *Crimes Act* 1900 (NSW), 'deception' is defined very similarly to the Victorian definition in s 81(4) *Crimes Act* 1958 (Vic) (including the provision discussed below dealing with deceiving a computer).

A basic form of what would commonly be understood to be fraud was considered in the case of *R v Gilmartin* [1983] QB 953. Gilmartin used post-dated cheques to pay for goods for resale through his stationery business. His account was heavily overdrawn and he did not pay any money into the account to cover the cheques. The cheques were dishonoured and he was charged with obtaining property by deception. The conviction was affirmed. By giving a cheque, the drawer impliedly represented that the account was in a state whereby the cheque would be met on or after the date on the cheque.

Deception can be by words or conduct. Conduct might include taking a taxi, which amounts to a representation that the fare will be paid: *R v Waterfall* [1970] 1 QB 148. Actions that began honestly but became false can still constitute deception if characterised as a 'continuing' representation. For example, a group of people go to a restaurant and order a meal, intending to pay at the end of the meal as is the common practice. After eating the meal the group decides to leave without paying. They continue to sit and maintain 'the demeanour of ordinary customers' until the waiter goes out to the kitchen, when they leave without paying. This occurred in the case of *DPP v Ray* [1974] AC 370. One of the diners was charged with obtaining a pecuniary advantage by deception, being the evasion of the debt for the cost of the meal (47 pence).

There was no doubt by the time the case reached the House of Lords that the offender had obtained a financial (pecuniary) advantage, and had done so dishonestly. The only question was whether he had obtained the advantage by a deception. The majority of the House of Lords held that there had been a deception by conduct; that by simply looking like a normal honest customer, when the accused was not intending to be one, there had been a deception. The analysis was complicated by the fact that the dishonest intent only arose during the course of the meal, and was not reflected in any change in the party's conduct. The initial representation led the waiter to treat them as honest customers; the later change of mind falsified that representation so that it became a deception. Lord Morris of Borth-y-Gest (at 386) observed that '[t]he essence of the deception was that the waiter should not know of it or be given any sort of clue that it [the change of intention] had come about'.

Ray's case can be seen as an example of a continuing representation by conduct. When the customer orders a meal in a restaurant, he or she is representing that the bill will be paid at the end. If the intent at that point was dishonest, there is then a deception. If the intent was initially to pay, but the customer changes his or her mind and leaves before the bill comes, it could be said that the representation, which was originally true, has become false. If it deceives the waiter, it can be relied upon by the prosecution as a deception.

The deception can be 'deliberate or reckless'. To be guilty of this offence by carrying out a deception, the accused has to know that his or her representation is false or that there is a risk that the statement was untrue at the time of making it, and to be indifferent to the risk. For example, Smith had an overdraft with no fixed limit. He ran an earthmoving business, and wrote a large number of cheques on his account. Some were honoured and some were dishonoured—it was not clear why. There was evidence that could have satisfied a jury beyond reasonable doubt that whenever the accused drew a cheque he adverted to the probability that the bank would dishonour it, but he was either indifferent to the consequence, or willing to run the risk. He was convicted of obtaining a financial advantage by deception: *Smith* (1982) 7 A Crim R 437. His appeal failed. The Victorian Supreme Court said he had practised a reckless deception. The trial judge (at 441) considered that Smith had acted recklessly, in that he 'either knew or recognised that there was a substantial risk' that the cheques would be dishonoured.

The concept of recklessness in obtaining offences therefore seems to be less fully developed than in, for example, murder. It clearly requires a subjective, more than careless or negligent, awareness (*Staines* (1975) 60 Cr App R 160) but foresight of 'substantial risk' seems to have been accepted as adequate.

Obtains

The prosecution must be able to show a causal connection between the deception and the obtaining of the property: that the accused obtained the property *by reason of* the deception. Section 81(2) of the *Crimes Act* 1958 (Vic) is elaborated to provide that 'obtaining' includes obtaining ownership, possession or control. It also includes 'obtaining for another or enabling another to obtain or to retain'. The same definition applies in s 227(2) of the *Criminal Code* (NT). The concepts of ownerships and possession are discussed in more detail in Chapter 6.

Section 408C(3)(e) of the Queensland Code states that 'obtain' includes getting, gaining, receiving or acquiring. The Queensland and Western Australian fraud offences include 'induc[ing] any person to deliver property to any/another person': *Criminal Code* (Qld) s 408C(1)(c); *Criminal Code* (WA) s 409(1)(b); see also *Criminal Code* (Tas) ss 250, 252. The new South Australian provision refers simply to deceiving and 'by doing so' dishonestly benefiting oneself or causing detriment to another: *Criminal Law Consolidation Act* 1935 (SA) s 139.

If the accused is to be found to have 'obtained' property by the deception, the deception must have operated on the mind of the victim and caused him or her to part with the property or confer the financial advantage. It follows that if the victim did not believe the representation, or did not part with the property because of the representation, there can be no offence.

The early case of *R v Perera* [1907] VLR 240 involved an accused who claimed to be able to communicate with spirits of the dead. Romel Perera advertised on a notice outside his house 'Indian Clairvoyance Trance Reader'. The 'victim' (in fact a plain clothes police officer, presumably investigating a complaint) visited the house and asked if Perera could advise him about a (fictitious) robbery and if he could also help him communicate with his (fictitious) deceased first wife. Perera placed his hand on the police officer's, warned him that the voice coming from him would change, and closed his eyes. He then gave information on these matters, purportedly from 'the spirits'. He opened his eyes as if coming out of a trance and accepted the agreed payment. As the police officer did not in fact believe Perera's claims, it was held that Perera could not be convicted of the common law offence of obtaining money by false pretences. He was, however, convicted of attempting to commit this offence.

Particular issues about causation are raised by the use of credit cards, as the usual contract between retailer and bank provides that the bank will pay the retailer irrespective of the shopper's authority. More generally, the issue of causation arises if the ostensible victim did not care whether the accused's representation was true or false. It can then be argued that the deception was not an effective cause of the obtaining. Unlike the misuse of credit cards, the presentation of a bad cheque is likely to have a negative effect on the retailer; if the goods are handed over and the cheque bounces the retailer has to pursue the customer for payment. The presentation of a cheque when the presenter knows there are no funds to support it, can therefore be said to 'induce' or lead to the obtaining of the goods.

Cheques are thus obviously risky; in England cheque cards are issued by banks to customers so that retailers will accept cheques. When a bank issues a cheque card to a customer they guarantee to cover the cheque to the prescribed maximum. They are therefore equivalent to credit cards in this respect.

In the early days of the *Theft Act* 1968 (UK) it was unclear whether there was actually any causal connection between the deception and the obtaining in such cases, given that the retailer was not directly affected by whether or not the shopper was authorised to use the card. There was also uncertainty whether a person could be said to have obtained property, or a financial advantage, by deception when a cheque card, or credit card, was used.

In *R v Lambie* [1982] AC 449, the facts of which appear at the start of this chapter, the unauthorised use of a credit card was found to have been a deception that induced the shop employee to part with goods. The Court was perhaps concerned about the wider implications of a different conclusion. The case of *R v Kovacs* [1974] 1 WLR 370, discussed at the start of this section, also confirmed that a deception of person A constitutes the offence even if the loss is felt by person B (perhaps a bank). These cases, and the broader issues around the use of credit cards, are discussed further in the Critique section.

The deception must occur prior to the obtaining of the property, as it must induce or lead to the handing over of the goods. Where a person enters a restaurant, sits down and orders a meal, intending all along to leave without paying, the deception will be immediately effective in enabling the customer to obtain the meal, that is, obtaining property by deception. However, as previously discussed, in a case such as that of *DPP v Ray* [1974] AC 370, where the customer at the restaurant leaves at the end of the meal without paying, after initially intending to pay, the property (the meal) was obtained without any deception. The only possible charge would be obtaining a financial advantage (evading a debt). The House of Lords in *Ray* considered the deception to be staying in the restaurant looking like an ordinary honest customer even after his intention became to escape without paying. The House of Lords also thought it could be said that the deception 'caused' the obtaining of the financial advantage because you could say that the waiter was 'put off his guard' by the deception, and did not watch the diner carefully, enabling him to slip out unnoticed and to evade his debt.

Property

In Victoria the definition of property in relation to theft applies also to the fraud offences: s 71(1) *Crimes Act* 1958 (Vic). The only difference from theft is that the limitations in s 73 do not apply. It is possible, for instance, to obtain an interest in land by deception.

The single fraud offence in Queensland *Criminal Code* s 408C and Western Australia *Criminal Code* s 409 refers to both 'property' and any benefit or advantage. The general definition of property applies, but is extended in Queensland to include such financial benefits as credit or services: s 408C(3)(a). The deception offence in *Criminal Law Consolidation Act* 1935 (SA) s 139 refers to 'benefits' and causing 'detriment': both broadly refer to proprietary or financial benefits/

disadvantage (s 130). The coverage of the equivalent offences in other jurisdictions has been outlined above.

Belonging to another

The Victorian offence of obtaining property by deception requires proof that the property obtained by deception belonged to another. This has been discussed in Chapter 6 in relation to theft.

Section 71(2) of the *Crimes Act* 1958 (Vic) applies: property is regarded as belonging to any person having possession or control of it, or any proprietary right or interest. It is therefore possible for a person to be guilty of obtaining his or her own property by deception, where someone else has lawful possession or control of it. For instance, a person who has pledged an item as security to a pawnbroker, and uses a bad cheque to recover the goods—that is, represents that the cheque will be honoured when presented—has obtained the property by deception. If the accused simply took the item from the pawnbroker, while the pawnbroker was not looking, he or she would clearly be guilty of theft.

The Code provisions are not limited to dealing with property belonging to another. *Criminal Code* (WA) s 409 includes no requirement that the property or benefit belong to another person, referring to 'obtains property from any person'. The same provision appears in *Criminal Code* (Qld) s 408C(1)(b), although s 408C (1)(a) includes applying to the offender's 'own use...property belonging to another'; and s 408C(1)(b) 'obtains property from any person'. *Criminal Code* (Qld) s 408C(3)(d) elaborates the concept of property 'belonging to' another. This includes the owner, any joint or part owner, any person with a legal or equitable interest in the property, and any person who 'immediately before the offender's application of the property, had control of it'.

Critique—physical elements

Obtaining by deception

Lord Reid, the dissenting judge in *DPP v Ray* [1974] AC 370, found (at 380) the 'continuing representation' approach to be artificial and considered there should not have been a conviction. He concluded that no 'conduct' could be identified in such cases, where there has simply been a change of mind: 'But what did the accused do here to create such a [deceptive] situation? He merely sat still'. CR Williams observes (at 174) that the willingness of the majority to find the element of deception satisfied indicates that a broad view of this concept is likely to be taken by courts: *Property Offences* (3rd edn, Sydney: LBC Information Services, 1999). In response to such cases, and to the petrol station cases discussed in Chapter 6, several jurisdictions now have offences of making off without paying, to address this particular form of conduct (for example *Crimes Act* 1900 (ACT) s 98; *Criminal Code* Qld s 408C(1)(h); *Criminal Law Consolidation Act* 1935 (SA) s 144).

The cases dealing with credit card frauds confirm that there must be a causal link between the deception and the obtaining. The courts' conclusion in such cases that causation had been shown, where the accused represented that they were authorised to use the card, also demonstrates a generous judicial attitude to the issue, presumably because of the practical consequences of finding otherwise.

It will be recalled that in *R v Lambie* [1982] AC 449 the accused was convicted of obtaining a financial advantage by deception. The conviction was affirmed by the House of Lords. The shop manager's evidence had been that having checked the expiry date, signature and stop-lists and finding everything was in order, she had not in fact been influenced by Lambie's deception in deciding to hand over the goods, because of the terms of the credit card contract. Nonetheless, the House of Lords held that the deception *had* led to the obtaining of the goods. They considered that, had the employee known the truth, she would not have gone on with the transaction: see also *Commissioner of Police v Charles* [1977] AC 177.

However, it was clear on the evidence that the employee proceeded with the transaction because she was satisfied that her employer would be paid, rather than because she believed the purchaser was an authorised user of the card. This is the rationale for the development of credit cards. The fact that she might not have been prepared to accept the card if she had known—for example because she did not want to become involved in a fraud—does not mean the representation induced the passing over of the property, or the obtaining of the financial advantage.

The House of Lords was clearly concerned about the possibilities for fraud using credit cards and cheque cards. This may explain the very wide interpretations of the evidence in these cases—decisions made 'in the teeth of' the evidence according to JC Smith, *Smith and Hogan Criminal Law* (10th edn, London: Butterworths, 2002) p 588. But the Court clearly stated, or assumed, that the deception must cause the obtaining. Presumably if the retailer knew that the customer was not entitled to use the credit or cheque card, but proceeded with the sale, this might amount to an offence of conspiracy to defraud the bank: see MCCOC, *Chapter 3, Theft, Fraud, Bribery and Related Offences*, Report (December 1995) pp 127–9.

The cases on cheque cards and credit cards also take further the requirement that the deception must be directly connected to the obtaining. In such cases the courts have concluded that the deception need not operate on the mind of the person from whom the property is being obtained in order to be 'causally connected'. The deceptive use of cheque and credit cards operates on the mind of the retailer to produce the loss suffered by the bank when credit or property is provided. For example, in the case of *Kovacs*, the facts of which are outlined earlier, the accused knew she was not entitled to use her cheque account but nonetheless used it to buy a railway ticket and a dog. Kovacs was convicted of obtaining a financial advantage by deception, the deception being the representation that she was entitled to use the cheque card. She argued in her appeal to the House of Lords that she had deceived the pet-shop owner and railway booking clerk, not the bank. The financial advantage had, however, been obtained as against the bank. Therefore, she claimed, there had been no causal relationship between the deception and the obtaining of the advantage.

The Court agreed that she had practised a deception and obtained the financial advantage by persuading the sellers to believe she was entitled to use the cheque card, as a result of which deception they accepted her cheques, which the bank was bound to honour. Thus the loss suffered by the bank was causally connected to Kovac's deception: see also *Commissioner of Police v Charles* [1977] AC 177; *R v Clarkson* [1987] VR 962 at 980.

This could presumably have been charged as obtaining property (the dog and ticket) by deception. However, the case was heard in 1974, before *Lambie*. At this time it was generally considered that if the shop employee was not specifically interested in the authority of the customer to use the credit card or cheque card, it could not be said that the deception as to the customer's authority was causal. It is now clear that such use of credit cards does amount to obtaining by deception, at least using the expansive interpretation above. As noted at the start of this chapter, these are the main types of frauds that arise.

Fault elements

Intention to permanently deprive

The requirement of an intention to permanently deprive is a part of the Victorian offence of obtaining property by deception and the Australian Capital Territory theft offence but not (probably logically) of the Victorian and Australian Capital Territory offences of obtaining a financial advantage by deception. It has already been discussed earlier in relation to theft.

Section 81(3) *Crimes Act* (Vic) incorporates the definitions in s 73(12) and 73(13): the accused is regarded as having an intention to permanently deprive if his or her intention is to treat the thing as his or her own to dispose of regardless of the other's rights, and this includes a borrowing if the circumstances make it equivalent to an outright taking; see also *Crimes Act* 1900 (ACT) s 87.

Intention to permanently deprive is an element in the common law offence of larceny by a trick, but not in the statutory offences of obtaining by false pretences (*Crimes Act* 1900 (NSW) s 179; see also *Criminal Code* (Tas) s 250) or of deception (*Criminal Law Consolidation Act* 1935 (SA) s 139). The intent to permanently deprive is not a component of fraud in Queensland, Western Australia or the Northern Territory.

Dishonesty

Proof both of deception and dishonesty is required in the Australian Capital Territory, Tasmania and Victoria, and in New South Wales and South Australia. There is no definition of dishonesty in s 81 *Crimes Act* 1958 (Vic), and s 73(2) is stated not to apply. The Courts are therefore left with a straightforward exercise in statutory interpretation as to the meaning of the word. Here we can refer to the meaning of dishonesty discussed in Chapter 6 in relation to theft.

Section 227 of the *Criminal Code* (NT) requires proof of deception but not dishonesty. *Criminal Code* (Qld) s 408C(1) requires proof of dishonesty for the offence of fraud but has no separate requirement of any deception. The legislation states that actions or omissions *may* be dishonest even if the offender is willing to pay or intends to restore the property, or if the owner consents, or if another's mistake was involved (s 408C(3)(b)). It also provides that an act will not be taken to be dishonest where the person does not know and cannot ascertain who the owner is (s 408C(3)(c)). Similar tests for 'negative' dishonesty apply to the *Crimes Act* 1900 (ACT) s 86(4) with the addition of the belief that there will be no 'significant practical detriment' caused. This provision is discussed further in Chapter 6. In *Criminal Law Consolidation Act* 1935 (SA) s 131, for conduct to be found to be 'dishonest' it must be found to be so 'according to the standards of ordinary people' and the accused must in addition be shown to know that he or she is so acting, a formulation proposed by the MCCOC, *Chapter 3, Theft, Fraud, Bribery and Related Offences*, Report (December 1995).

In New South Wales and Tasmania it is necessary to prove 'intent to defraud' in addition to deception (false pretences): *Crimes Act* 1900 (NSW) s 179; *Criminal Code* (Tas) s 250. The common law concept of 'intent to defraud' has given rise to some difficulties of definition. An English case early in the twentieth century concluded that intent to defraud incorporated an element of deception—it was a 'deceitful deprivation': '[T]o deceive is by falsehood to induce a state of mind; to defraud is by deceit to induce a course of action': *In re London and Globe Finance Corporation Limited* [1903] Ch 728 at 733.

There may, however, also be situations where the behaviour was dishonest, but did not involve deception. Where an offender bribed employees of a cinema to temporarily provide films so that pirate copies could be made before the films were returned, there was arguably a dishonest agreement to defraud, but no deception. The House of Lords in *R v Scott* [1975] AC 819 at 839 developed the 'dishonest deprivation' test: 'If..."fraudulently" means "dishonestly", then to "defraud" ordinarily means...to deprive a person dishonestly of something which is his...'

As examined in detail in Chapter 6 in relation to theft, common law dishonesty means at least without any claim of right, a defence that is also incorporated in the Code states. Beyond that, as we know, the English courts have established the view that dishonesty is a matter to be identified by the jury, applying the standards of reasonable and honest people: *R v Ghosh* [1982] 1 QB 1053

In Victoria, however, a narrower interpretation has been arrived at in relation to the *Crimes Act* provisions. The Supreme Court in *R v Salvo* [1980] VR 401, *R v Brow* [1981] VR 783 and *R v Bonollo* [1981] VR 633 concluded that the common law defence of claim of legal right was still available for obtaining property or financial advantage by deception, but that this was the only way to rebut dishonesty under these provisions. The Victorian Supreme Court approach in *Salvo* was adopted in New South Wales in *R v Love* (1989) 17 NSWLR 608 at 615 in relation to correctly addressing the jury on a defence based on claim of right and in *Condon* (1995) 83 A Crim R 335 at 344 in relation to a Commonwealth statutory fraud charge.

The Victorian approach has, however, been distinguished in recent cases to apply in Victoria only to the specific statutory provisions in the *Crimes Act*. The High Court in *Peters v The Queen* (1998) 192 CLR 493 held that the term 'dishonestly' is used in a 'special sense' in these statutory provisions, but that in other situations it has its 'ordinary' meaning, to which the UK approach applies. The High Court, however, modified the UK approach. It held by a three to two majority that the question whether what the accused intended was dishonest was to be decided by the jury applying the standards of 'ordinary, decent people' (see Toohey and Gaudron JJ at 504), but rejected the additional requirement developed in the UK that the jury consider whether the accused knew his or her behaviour was dishonest by the standards of ordinary decent people. *Peters* involved Commonwealth statutory fraud offences. The UK/*Peters* approach has also been preferred and endorsed in Victoria, at least in requiring the question to be left to the jury to determine in accordance with the 'standards of reasonable and honest people', in relation to common law conspiracy to defraud cases: *R v Lawrence* [1997] 1 VR 459; *Walsh* (2002) 131 A Crim R 299.

Critique—fault elements

Intention to permanently deprive
As discussed in Chapter 6 above in relation to theft, the MCCOC considered whether intent to permanently deprive should be retained as an element both of theft and of obtaining property by deception. It reported that a clear majority of submissions favoured retention in each case: *Chapter 3, Theft, Fraud, Bribery and Related Offences*, Report (December 1995) p 131.

Dishonesty
Usually the fact that there has been a deception makes it likely that there is also dishonesty. However, there may be cases where the deception is more justifiable and not necessarily 'dishonest'—to regain a piece of property that you believe to be rightfully yours; or persuade a heavily intoxicated friend to hand over the bottle of spirits they plan to drink or the firearm they are threatening to use. The MCCOC (*Chapter 3, Theft, Fraud, Bribery and Related Offences*, Report (December 1995) p 129) also notes the more morally (and legally) problematic scenario of a company with a temporary cash flow crisis providing false information to obtain a loan to return them to a sound financial position.

This leaves the question, discussed in Chapter 6 in relation to theft, of whether the notion of dishonesty is broader than a belief in a claim of right.

As mentioned earlier, the MCCOC proposed the adoption of the UK approach whereby dishonesty is determined by the jury applying the standards of ordinary people, and where it is known by the accused to have been dishonest by the standards of ordinary people. This is now embodied in s 130.3 of the *Criminal Code* (Cth) and in the new South Australian s 131. The High Court in *Peters* and most recently in *Macleod*, however, has endorsed the modified test outlined above.

McGarvie J in *Bonollo* proposed an alternative test of dishonesty in terms of whether the accused was 'conscious that by obtaining [the property or advantage] he [or she] will produce a consequence affecting the interests of the person deprived...and if that consequence is one which would be detrimental to those interests in a significant practical way': *R v Bonollo* [1981] VR 633 at 653. Section 86(4)(b) of the *Crimes Act* 1900 (ACT) incorporates similar wording. This approach was examined in detail in Chapter 6. Alex Steel has argued that this would be preferable to the approach of the English courts and the Commonwealth Code in ensuring consistency of meaning and certainty in a key component of a serious criminal offence: 'The Appropriate Test for Dishonesty' (2000) 24 Crim LJ 46–59 at 56. This might excuse the troubled company providing false information, discussed by the MCCOC. However, the facts of *Bonollo* were considered by McGarvie J to be such that the accused would in reality be conscious that she would be detrimentally affecting the interests of the bank, increasing their exposure to risk, and this analysis could also lead to the conviction of the troubled company. A legislative amendment would clearly be needed to reflect such an approach to the meaning of dishonesty.

Obtaining a financial advantage by deception

Background
Horrie Matthews had employed a personnel consultant in his business. The agreement was that she would receive $100 per week together with commission. At the end of two weeks he gave her a cheque for $200, which was not honoured. Matthews knew that there were no funds to meet the cheque, and that he had reached the limit of his overdraft. The employee continued to work for the accused for another four weeks, while asking repeatedly for both the $200 originally owed and her later wages. Matthews explained that he was in financial difficulties but promised that he would be in a position to pay imminently. The employee left the job after six weeks without receiving any of the money owing. Matthews was convicted of obtaining a financial advantage by deception.

On a case stated to the Supreme Court it was argued for the defence that a person who knowingly proffers a valueless cheque to discharge a debt does not obtain a financial advantage, because he or she might not have been able to pay the debt in any event. Gray J in *Matthews v Fountain* [1982] VR 1045 rejected this argument. He said that, however 'penniless' the debtor might be, there is still a financial advantage in evading a debt, for however short a period. He stated (at 1049–50) that by the deception the debtor obtains an extension of time within which to pay, and a temporary relief from harassment by the creditor. In this instance the accused not only put off the payment of the first two weeks' wages, but also persuaded the employee to stay on by appearing to intend to pay her.

The second main form of fraud offences involves dishonestly obtaining a financial advantage. Most of the components of this offence have been considered in relation to obtaining property by deception; the main area of possible uncertainty involves what constitutes a 'financial advantage'. This was the issue in *Matthews*'s case. As we shall explore, it has been decided differently in the Australian and UK courts.

This offence addresses obtaining credit or services dishonestly by deception; the key distinction from theft and obtaining property by deception is that no 'property' is being obtained. This is a separate offence in Victoria and the Australian Capital Territory. Section 82(1) of the *Crimes Act* 1958 (Vic) provides that 'A person who by any deception dishonestly obtains for himself or another any financial advantage is guilty of an indictable offence'. The penalty (10 years' maximum imprisonment) is the same as the penalty for theft and obtaining property by deception. Section 95 of the *Crimes Act* 1900 (ACT) is in the same terms, with a further definition of 'financial advantage', which will be discussed later.

The general Queensland and Western Australian fraud offences include dishonestly 'gaining a benefit or advantage, pecuniary or otherwise': *Criminal Code* (Qld) s 408C(1)(d); and see *Criminal Code* (WA) s 409(1)(c). Section 408C(1)(h) of the Queensland Code, of which there is no equivalent in the Western Australian Code, refers to making off without payment. Colvin et al, *Criminal Law in Queensland and Western Australia* (3rd edn, Sydney: Butterworths, 2001) note at 142 that this type of offending would probably fall under the other provisions relating to obtaining a benefit or property anyway. *Criminal Law Consolidation Act* 1935 (SA) s 139 similarly refers to dishonestly benefiting oneself or causing detriment to another, defined in s 130 to include both proprietary and financial advantage.

Specific statutory offences have been enacted in New South Wales. Section 178BA(1) of the *Crimes Act* 1900 (NSW) refers to 'whosoever by any deception dishonestly obtains...any money or valuable thing or any financial advantage of any kind...'; the offence is similar to the Victorian provision. Section 178BB of the *Crimes Act* 1900 (NSW) deals with making a false statement for the purpose of obtaining a valuable thing. *Crimes Act* 1900 (NSW) s 179 deals with obtaining 'property' by false pretences. 'Property' is defined very broadly to include valuable securities and debts in the definition section *Crimes Act* 1900 (NSW) s 4(1). Also relevant is *Crimes Act* 1900 (NSW) s 178C, obtaining credit by false pretences.

Most of these components have been discussed in detail in relation to obtaining property by deception and/or theft.

The current law—physical elements

Deception

In Victoria the definition of deception in s 81(4) *Crimes Act* 1958 applies to obtaining financial advantage by deception too: deception means 'any deception (whether deliberate or reckless) by words or conduct as to fact or as to law, including a deception as to the present intentions of the person using the deception or any other person'. Section 83 *Crimes Act* 1900 (ACT) is in similar terms. This includes the extension in s 81(4)(b) *Crimes Act* 1958 (Vic) regarding deceiving a machine, for example using another's debit or credit card, having discovered their Personal Identification Number (PIN), to obtain cash or credit. This may constitute obtaining property by deception (money) and obtaining financial advantage by deception (a financial benefit such as credit). An equivalent definition is found in s 178BA *Crimes Act* 1900 (NSW). Section 130 *Criminal Law Consolidation Act* 1935 (SA) defines deception in similar terms; a separate offence is created, however, to deal with 'dishonest manipulation of machines' (s 141).

The case of *DPP v Ray* [1974] AC 370, discussed previously, illustrates the concept of deception by conduct. The accused was charged with obtaining a financial advantage by deception, the deception being his conduct in continuing to behave as an ordinary honest diner.

Deception can be deliberate or reckless. Writing cheques knowing there is a real risk that the cheques will be dishonoured is an example of reckless deception producing a financial advantage, as occurred in *Smith* (1982) 7 A Crim R 437.

Obtains

The obtaining must be a result of the deception, as discussed in relation to the offence of obtaining property by deception. In Queensland, the benefit is to be 'gained' dishonestly; there should be a causal connection then between the dishonesty and the benefit gained.

An example is *Lambie*'s case, discussed earlier, where a credit card was used to obtain property from shops. The House of Lords held that the implied representation that the offender had authority to use her card was a deception that induced the employee to hand over the goods. There had therefore been an obtaining of a financial advantage—credit or a deferral of the time to pay—by deception.

The obtaining can be for the offender or for another; so it would not be a defence for the accused to argue that the financial advantage was not for him or herself: *Crimes Act* 1958 (Vic) s 82(1); *Crimes Act* 1900 (ACT) s 95; *Criminal Code* (Qld) s 408C(1)(d); *Criminal Law Consolidation Act* 1935 (SA) s 139.

Where the deception did not induce the handing over of the property (obtaining property by deception) or provision of the financial advantage (obtaining financial advantage by deception)—for example where the person did not believe the representation or did not care—the accused might be charged with an attempt. The law of attempts and other inchoate offences is explored in Chapter 8.

Financial advantage

The term 'financial advantage' or 'pecuniary advantage/benefit' is not generally defined in the jurisdictions in which it appears, with the exception of the Australian Capital Territory (and the UK). It would include deferring or avoiding a debt, obtaining credit, obtaining services (such as hairdressing or a train trip, or access to the theatre) without paying, and probably obtaining the opportunity to receive a salary (for example by use of faked qualifications).

The offence of obtaining a financial advantage by deception may be used where the facts preclude charging theft or obtaining property by deception. For example, if the use of property is obtained by deception, but there is no intention to permanently deprive the owner, there will not be an offence of obtaining property or theft, but it may amount to obtaining financial advantage by deception.

There was a definition in s 16 of the *Theft Act* 1968 (UK) of 'pecuniary advantage', which does not seem conceptually different from 'financial advantage', and is noted below in the Critique section. The first part of the definition, covering reducing, evading or deferring debts, caused so much difficulty in the courts that it was repealed in 1978, and replaced with three new, separate, offences: obtaining services by deception; evasion of liability by deception; and making off without payment: ss 1–3 *Theft Act* 1978 (UK). Financial advantage is defined in s 95(2)(a) and (b) *Crimes Act* 1900 (ACT) in provisions similar to s 16(2)(b) and (c) *Theft Act* 1968 (UK) covering access to borrowing and the opportunity to earn remuneration. Additional offences equivalent to the UK amendments are included in ss 96–98 *Crimes Act* 1900 (ACT). The separate offence of dishonestly making off without payment (*Crimes Act* 1900 (ACT) s 98) would avoid the problems in situations such as that in *DPP v Ray* [1974] AC 370.

Moves in this direction in the UK and Australia will be discussed further in the Critique section below.

The other two provisions in s 16(2) remain in the English legislation (referring to being able to borrow, and obtaining the opportunity to earn remuneration), and have led to divergence between English and Victorian decisions on financial advantage.

The main difference arises from the finding of English courts that once a case falls within one of the definitions of financial advantage, a financial advantage is deemed to have occurred, whether or not in fact the accused gained any actual financial advantage. The legislation provides that a pecuniary advantage 'is to be regarded as obtained' in the specified situations.

In Victoria, it has been held—in view of the non-existence of an equivalent definition section—that it is necessary to show that a financial advantage actually occurred: *Matthews v Fountain* [1982] VR 1045. This has also been the view of the Australian Capital Territory provision: *Fisher v Bennett* (1987) 85 FLR 469. Gray J in

Matthews refused to offer a definition of financial advantage but Miles CJ in *Fisher* ventured a definition of financial advantage (at 472) as involving 'a situation which from the financial aspect is more beneficial than another situation'.

The most common form of obtaining a financial advantage by deception involves bad cheques. The House of Lords held (definitively for UK purposes) that using a bad cheque to pay for a taxi fare is obtaining a financial advantage: *R v Turner* [1974] AC 357. It is an advantage to evade or at least defer a debt. A debt is 'evaded' even if the evasion falls short of being final or permanent, and is only for the time being. This has also been recognised in Victoria in such cases as *Smith* (1982) 7 A Crim R 437.

Critique—physical element

The meaning of 'financial advantage'

As already noted, the *Theft Act* 1968 (UK) defines 'pecuniary advantage' in s 16. It originally contained three sub-sections:

- s 16(2)(a)—reducing, evading or deferring a debt;
- s 16(2)(b)—being allowed to borrow, or to obtain improved terms for borrowing; and
- s 16(2)(c)—obtaining the opportunity to earn remuneration in employment, or to win money in betting.

The first part of the definition was repealed in 1978 and replaced with three more specific offences: obtaining services by deception; evasion of liability by deception; and making off without payment.

In both the UK and the Australian Capital Territory, obtaining a financial advantage by deception is punishable at a lower tariff than theft, with a maximum of five years' imprisonment. Both also have a five-year maximum for the offences of obtaining services by deception and evasion of liability, and a two-year penalty for making off without payment (or six months where the goods or services were worth less than $1000: *Crimes Act* 1900 (ACT) s 98(2)). Victoria previously also provided for a lower sentence for obtaining a financial advantage by deception. However, the penalty was increased to equate with theft and obtaining property by deception in 1991 as part of a general review of penalties: R Fox and A Freiberg, *Review of Statutory Maximum Penalties* (Melbourne: Victorian Government Publishing Office, 1989).

The MCCOC recommended an offence of obtaining a financial advantage by deception in the same terms as the Victorian provision. It rejected the UK and Australian Capital Territory direction of increasing definition and specificity, noting that the definitions had become a 'judicial nightmare' in the UK: MCCOC, *Chapter 3, Theft, Fraud, Bribery and Related Offences*, Report (December 1995) p 135. The Victorian provision was regarded as covering at least the same conduct as the UK provisions, with the extended offences of obtaining a service and evading a liability.

By requiring proof of an actual advantage, in financial terms, the provision was seen to be adequately delimited. The broader provisions of Queensland (s 408C) and Western Australia (s 409), which extend to dishonestly obtaining any benefit or causing any detriment, financial or otherwise, were regarded as permitting too wide an application for a 'property offence': MCCOC, *Chapter 3, Theft, Fraud, Bribery and Related Offences*, Report (December 1995) pp 135–6. The new South Australian legislation defines 'benefit' more narrowly, essentially limited to proprietary or financial advantage: s 130.

The Court of Appeal in *R v Turner* [1974] AC 357 suggested that the person who writes a bad cheque purporting to pay a debt but who has no money in the account, and no likelihood of having money—what is referred to as the 'penniless debtor'— might not be said to have obtained a financial advantage by using the cheque. The House of Lords did not have to decide this point because it concluded that, in view of the wording of the statute, a financial advantage was deemed to have arisen. However, Lord Reid commented (at 365) that if a financial advantage had had to be shown this might have been difficult in the case of the penniless debtor.

This is not the approach that the Victorian and Australian Capital Territory courts have taken.

The issue of the 'penniless debtor' was considered in Victoria in *Matthews v Fountain* [1982] VR 1045, the facts of which are outlined at the start of this section. Matthews had argued that a person who knowingly proffers a valueless cheque, in the belief that he or she may never be able to finance it, does not obtain a financial advantage. Gray J rejected this argument. He stated (at 1049) that, however 'penniless' the debtor might be, there is still a financial advantage by evading a debt. By the deception, the debtor obtains an extension of time within which to pay, and a temporary relief from harassment by the creditor.

The case therefore confirmed that actual financial advantage does have to be shown (at 1048) and that giving a bad cheque does usually confer a financial advantage, even where the giver of the cheque would not in fact ever be in a position to cover the payment.

The meaning of 'financial advantage' in the Australian Capital Territory, which has similar legislation to that in Victoria, was considered in *Fisher v Bennett* (1987) 85 FLR 469. The accused borrowed $10,000 from Langridge, as bridging finance for a property deal. He promised to repay Langridge within a few days. Despite requests, he did not repay the money, though he did pay interest due. Eventually he gave Langridge a cheque purportedly in payment of the full amount owing. It was dishonoured at the bank. The accused was convicted of obtaining a financial advantage by deception. The magistrate considered that he had used a deception to obtain a financial advantage.

Miles CJ in the Australian Capital Territory Supreme Court (at 471) held that in the Australian Capital Territory (and Victoria) an actual advantage has to be shown: it is not deemed when the behaviour falls into a particular class. The definition in s 95(2) *Crimes Act* 1900 (ACT) does not operate, as it does in the UK, to deem a financial advantage to exist. Miles CJ held that the mere presentation of a valueless cheque does not, without more, constitute the obtaining of a financial advantage. Here there was no evidence that the accused's financial position was improved by his representing to Langridge, by a valueless cheque, that he had sufficient funds to discharge his debt. His Honour agreed that there might be cases where a debtor does obtain a financial advantage by deferring the payment of a debt by means of a deception. This was, however, not one of them.

Miles CJ did not agree that the deception induced Langridge to defer suing for the money owing, this being a financial advantage. Interest continued to accrue while the debt remained unpaid. There was no indication that Langridge had forborne to sue. Miles CJ also rejected the argument that presenting the cheque gave the accused a financial advantage in the continued use of the money Langridge had previously lent him.

Fisher's case may be authority for the view that there is no financial advantage obtained when a debt is deferred by a person who is likely to have difficulty paying it anyway. This puts it in conflict with *Matthews*'s case. It may be, however, that *Fisher* can be distinguished simply on its facts. Miles CJ certainly admitted (at 472) that there might be circumstances where passing a bad cheque did give rise to a financial advantage. He did not consider that his decision was necessarily in conflict with that in *Matthews*. The Australian Capital Territory offence of evading liability by deception states (*Crimes Act* 1900 (ACT) s 97(2)) that a person induced to accept a cheque is deemed to have been induced to wait for payment.

The MCCOC endorsed the approach in *Matthews*, agreeing that the terms 'financial' and 'advantage' are ordinary words and should not be legislatively defined, but that evasion of a debt for even a short time, even by someone who is penniless, will be a financial advantage as it amounts to a form of credit or time to pay: *Chapter 3, Theft, Fraud, Bribery and Related Offences*, Report (December 1995) p 137. The simplicity of the concept of 'financial advantage' has, however, been doubted by Brown et al (3rd edn, Sydney: The Federation Press, 2001) p 1211 in its discussion of the equivalent New South Wales provision s 178BA *Crimes Act* 1900 (NSW).

The *Crimes Act* 1900 (ACT) now has a separate offence in s 99 of obtaining goods or benefit, or discharging a debt, by passing a valueless cheque, where the accused had intent to defraud or had no reasonable grounds to believe the cheque would be paid. The offence carries a lesser penalty than the other fraud offences but may be a simpler approach to the problem.

Can it be said that a person has gained a financial advantage when he or she has, by deception, evaded a debt or obtained a service for which he or she was not legally obliged to pay? An example is sexual services provided by a prostitute. Depending on the current law in the jurisdiction these may not be debts that could be recovered by civil action. In Victoria, provision of sexual services in licensed brothels is itself lawful and any debt incurred in a licensed brothel should be enforceable. However, this may not apply in other less clear legal circumstances. Enforcement of drug debts would presumably cause difficulties. CR Williams notes the argument that the criminal law should not be used to protect interests that are not recognised by the civil law: *Property Offences* (3rd edn, Sydney: LBC Information Services, 1999) p 187. On the other hand, he points out, something of value clearly has been obtained. People who dishonestly evade such debts should not be permitted to escape criminal sanction simply because they are not legally enforceable.

Section 97 of the *Crimes Act* 1900 (ACT) creating the offence of evasion of liability by deception is limited to evading a 'legally enforceable liability'. Similarly the offence of making off without payment (s 98) excludes the application of the offence to '(a) the supply of goods or the provision of a service where that supply or provision is contrary to law; or (b) payment for the provision of a service where that payment is not legally enforceable': s 98(3)(a) and (b) *Crimes Act* 1900 (ACT). The equivalent South Australian offence (*Criminal Law Consolidation Act* 1935 s 144) excludes liability where the activity was unlawful or 'unenforceable as contrary to public policy'.

The current law—fault element

Dishonesty

This concept has been discussed in detail in Chapter 6 in relation to theft and in this chapter in relation to obtaining property by deception. Dishonesty is the sole fault element in Victoria, the Australian Capital Territory, New South Wales, Queensland and South Australia. Section 409(1) *Criminal Code* (WA) refers to 'intent to defraud'; as discussed earlier, this has been regarded as equivalent to 'dishonesty'.

It is clear that on the basis of the cases of *R v Salvo* [1980] VR 401, *R v Brow* [1981] VR 783 and *R v Bonollo* [1981] VR 633 the only way to negative dishonesty for obtaining financial advantage by deception in Victoria is by a legal claim of right. Section 178BA of the *Crimes Act* 1900 (NSW) is formulated in the same terms as s 82 of the *Crimes Act* 1958 (Vic); the approach in *Salvo* has been endorsed in *R v Love* (1989) 17 NSWLR 608 and *Condon* (1995) 83 A Crim R 335. The High Court's re-formulation in *Peters* of the UK approach to determining dishonesty appears to apply in most other jurisdictions, as discussed in Chapter 6.

Notions such as 'intention to permanently deprive' are less relevant in the context of financial advantage. As the MCCOC has observed, the 'abstract nature of a financial advantage does not easily lend itself to permanence'; further, even a temporary financial advantage [for example deferral of debt] can lead to other gains. MCCOC recommended that intent to permanently deprive not be included in the definition of this offence: MCCOC, *Chapter 3, Theft, Fraud, Bribery and Related Offences*, Report (December 1995) p 137.

Critique—fault element

The MCCOC recommended an offence similar to s 82 of the *Crimes Act* 1958 (Vic), with dishonesty to be defined, as for the other offences against property, in terms of the direction in *Ghosh*: MCCOC, *Chapter 3, Theft, Fraud, Bribery and Related Offences*, Report (December 1995) p 134. The Commonwealth Criminal Code amendments inserted in 2000 in fact include two relevant offences, neither of them in the terms of the MCCOC proposals. There is the general dishonesty offence in s 135.1 of doing anything with the intention of dishonestly obtaining a gain from or causing a loss to another person (penalty five years) and s 135.2 obtaining a financial advantage 'knowing or believing that he or she is not eligible to receive that financial advantage'. The latter offence makes no reference to 'dishonesty' but the alternative fault element and the relatively low penalty of 12 months suggests the provision is aimed at welfare frauds. The notion of (not being) 'eligible' does not sit well with the range of definitions of financial advantage discussed earlier, such as deferral of debts and non-payment of services. The issue of a general dishonesty offence is discussed further at the end of this chapter.

Should fraud and theft be separate offences?

There is a considerable degree of overlap between theft and offences of obtaining property by deception. One clear difference between theft and obtaining is that land is capable of being the subject of obtaining property by deception, but not of theft. The difference is greater in the Code states and South Australia, where broader concepts such as obtaining a 'benefit' are included in the definition of the deception offences. But otherwise, is there a difference in principle between the offences? Should there be?

The key difference in the legal formulation in Victoria and the UK is that theft involves an 'appropriation' of property while the obtaining offence involves 'obtaining property by deception'. As we discussed in Chapter 6, there has been a significant blurring of the distinction between these concepts in both England and Victoria, turning on the relevance of the owner's consent to the question whether 'appropriation' has occurred. The offences have been combined in the Australian Capital Territory: s 86 *Crimes Act* 1900 (ACT).

Several cases have confirmed the overlap between the offences. In the case of *Lawrence v Commissioner of the Police for the Metropolis* [1972] AC 626, where a taxi driver took more money from the passenger's wallet than was justified by the ride, the House of Lords agreed (at 633) that there was clearly a considerable overlap between theft and obtaining property by deception, but that theft had properly been charged, as there may have been an argument that there had been no deception when the driver obtained the money from the wallet.

In *R v Gomez* [1993] AC 442 at 495 the House of Lords held that consent is irrelevant to whether the accused has 'appropriated' property, and confirmed that virtually all obtainings by deception were theft. Lord Browne-Wilkinson (at 496) noted that the decision that it was possible for a person to have 'appropriated' even with the consent of the owner did not make obtaining property by deception entirely redundant because it could cover interests in land. Lord Lowry dissented in *Gomez*. He argued that there was a significant difference between theft and obtaining property by deception, and that calling it appropriation where someone obtains the property by deceiving the owner into consenting made the obtaining offence irrelevant. He pointed out (at 474–5) that the CLRC in *Theft and Related Offences*, Report No 8 (London: HMSO, Cmnd 2877, 1966) had initially considered combining the offences, but ultimately concluded that the offences of theft and obtaining property dishonestly (at that time the common law offence of obtaining by false pretences) should be maintained as separate offences.

The CLRC concluded in its *Theft and Related Offences*, Report No 8 (London: HMSO, Cmnd 2877, 1966) para 38: 'Obtaining by false pretences is ordinarily thought of as different from theft, because in the former the owner in fact consents to part with his [or her] ownership; a bogus beggar is regarded as a rogue but not as a thief...To create a new offence of theft to include conduct which ordinary people would find difficult to regard as theft would be a mistake.'

The overlap has, however, been accepted in Victorian cases. *Heddich v Dike* (1981) 3 A Crim R 139 involved a prosecution arising when the accused Dike went to a shop in Clayton that made offset printing plates, and told the assistant that he had come to collect all the old printing plates as arranged with the employer. She, believing that the employer must have asked him to collect the plates, allowed him to take all the old plates. In fact the employer had not given Dike permission to remove the plates. Dike was charged with theft. He argued that he could not be guilty of theft, since he had obtained the plates with the consent of the person in possession, and there had there been no 'appropriation'. The magistrate accepted the submission and held that there was no case to answer on the charge of theft. He refused to allow the prosecutor to amend the information to charge the accused with obtaining property by deception. The prosecutor took the matter to the Supreme Court on an order to review.

Justice Gobbo in the Victorian Supreme Court concluded that Dike could have been convicted of theft on these facts: there can be an appropriation under s 73(4) even though the person in lawful possession consented. Later Victorian cases have confirmed this approach, looking at the relevance of consent to 'appropriation': see *R v Baruday* [1984] VR 685. The South Australian theft offence (*Criminal Law Consolidation Act* 1935 (SA) s 134) requires proof that the property was dealt with 'without the owner's consent', but states that the dealing will have been without consent where the accused knew that the consent was obtained by dishonest deception: s 132(3). The overlap between theft and deception in the South Australian legislation is supported by s 330 of the Act, which provides that 'no objection to a charge...can be made on the ground that the defendant might, on the same facts, have been charged with...some other offence'.

The result is that most obtaining offences in Victoria and South Australia can be prosecuted as theft. Every taking by deception would now appear to amount to appropriation or to dealing without consent, although there are some limits to the degree of overlap. As noted, land cannot be the subject of theft but can be obtained by deception. On the other hand, not all appropriations or dealings are 'deceptive'. Simply taking something from someone's house does not amount to obtaining property by deception. In the South Australian context, the benefits/detriments that can be the subject of a deception offence are also wider than the reference to 'property' in the theft offence.

Blurring the distinction between theft and obtaining property by deception places considerable pressure on the dishonesty component of the offences, as discussed earlier. It also shifts significant discretion onto the prosecution in deciding which charges to lay. Theft and obtaining property by deception carry the same maximum penalty. There may, however, be situations where it is useful to be able to choose the charge. Where there was effectively an obtaining by deception, it may nonetheless be easier to prosecute for theft. There might in some cases be problems proving the act of deception, so that it is easier to show that there was an appropriation. It may be difficult to establish a causal link between the deception and the obtaining, for example if on the facts it is not clear whether the victim relied on the deception.

There is no provision in the *Crimes Act* 1958 (Vic) for alternative verdicts in this area, so the prosecutor's choice matters. It can mean that the case fails, if the wrong choice was made. By contrast, s 183 of the *Crimes Act* 1900 (NSW) allows for an alternative verdict of larceny in cases charged as particular fraud offences.

The Australian Capital Territory merged the offences in 1985. This approach was recommended by the Gibbs Committee's *Review of the Commonwealth Criminal Law* (Canberra: Australian Government Publishing Service, 1990). The MCCOC considered arguments for and against keeping theft and fraud offences (that is, obtaining by deception) separate in its Discussion Paper 1992. It stated that it was clear that obtaining a financial advantage by deception would have to be a separate offence, but less clear whether separate offences of obtaining property by deception and theft were necessary. In its 1995 Final Report, *Chapter 3, Theft, Fraud, Bribery and Related Offences*, the Committee said (at 119) that it recognised that the community sees fraud and theft as different and that it can confuse juries and undermine public acceptance of the law to merge disparate forms of criminal behaviour. On the other hand, the case law has virtually merged the offences already, and there can be problems for the prosecution in choosing the correct charge, given that there is no option for a jury to consider one charge as an alternative to the other.

The MCCOC ultimately recommended retention of separate offences, noting in its Final Report (at 123) that the vast majority of submissions favoured this approach, including some submissions from the Australian Capital Territory. The Committee included provision for the jury to return an alternative verdict where the facts supported this in draft clause 17.2(6). This is now embodied in *Criminal Code* (Cth) s 134.1(15) and (16) and stated to be subject to the defendant being 'accorded procedural fairness'.

We agree that there is still a strong case for dealing separately with the thief and the fraudster, and retaining separate offences. The proviso would be that the practical prosecution difficulties were addressed and there was provision for alternative verdicts and for informing the accused of this option, and parity of penalties.

Computer fraud

Background

Business transactions are increasingly being conducted electronically. It has been estimated that global business-to-business online commerce could amount to anywhere between US$2.7 and US$7 trillion by 2004 (research cited in P Grabosky, R Smith and G Dempsey, *Electronic Theft: Unlawful Acquisition in Cyberspace* (Cambridge: Cambridge University Press, 2001) p 1. Grabosky, Smith and Dempsey comment (at 1–2): 'One might expect the growth of electronic commerce to be reflected in the growth of electronic misappropriation. The fundamental principle of criminology is that crime follows opportunity, and opportunities for theft abound in the Digital Age.'

Computers have clearly given rise to problems for the application of traditional criminal law concepts of property offences. The focus of the law of larceny on property that could be physically carried away, and related decisions applying across jurisdictions that 'property' did not extend either to information (*Oxford v Moss* (1978) 68 Cr App R 183) or to electricity (*Low v Blease* [1975] Crim LR 513), has meant that conventional property offences are virtually irrelevant to many computer-based misappropriations.

Specific offences relating to the misuse of electricity have recently been enacted (*Criminal Code* (NT) s 221; *Criminal Code* (Qld) s 408; *Criminal Code* (Tas) s 233; *Criminal Code* (WA) s 390). In South Australia 'property' is defined to include electricity: s 130. There is, however, something artificial about using such an offence to prosecute what may be substantial computer-based crimes.

Offences such as obtaining property and obtaining financial advantage by deception have also been used, although these have also had some limitations, for instance around the notion of 'deceiving' or obtaining consent from a machine. A problem with the notion of 'deception' is that it requires a person—a human mind—to have been deceived or misled. What happens where the offender obtains property, such as money, by 'deceiving' a machine such as an automatic teller or using another person's password to access a computer?

Kennison v Daire (1985) 38 SASR 404 involved the accused using a card dishonestly to withdraw money from a closed account at an off-line ATM. The Supreme Court accepted (at 416) that a person cannot 'obtain by deception' from a machine. The deception must have operated on a human mind. But the Court upheld the accused's conviction for larceny and rejected his argument that the machine had 'consented' to handing over the money (at 408).

In 1987 the Standing Committee of Attorneys-General of all Australian states and the Commonwealth agreed that there should be a coordinated strategy and uniform legislation to deal with computer crime. In 1988 the *Review of Commonwealth Criminal Law: Interim Report on Computer Crime* (the Gibbs Report) (Canberra: Attorney-General's Department and AGPS, 1988) recommended the creation of specific computer offences. Disagreements over the form of such legislation have, however, prevented implementation of the agreement to develop uniform legislation. The reality of state-based criminal law has meant that responses have been varied.

The current law

Following the Gibbs Report, the New South Wales parliament enacted Part 6 'Computer Offences' (see now *Crimes Act* 1900 (NSW) ss 308–308I) and the Commonwealth enacted ss 76A–76F *Crimes Act* 1914 (Cth) (repealed in 2001: see now *Criminal Code* (Cth) ss 476.1–478.4). Similar legislation was enacted in Tasmania and the Australian Capital Territory to deal with causing damage to computer data or obstructing the lawful use of computers.

In 1988, Victoria introduced what the MCCOC called 'perhaps the most elaborate Australian example of legislation aimed at computer fraud': MCCOC, *Chapter 4, Damage and Computer Offences,* Report (January 2001) p 87. The *Crimes (Computers) Act* 1988 (Vic) introduced key provisions on criminal liability for extra-territorial offences (s 80A) and on deception of machines (s 81(4)(b)). As discussed earlier, s 81(4)(b) extends the definition of deception, for purposes of obtaining property or a financial advantage, to include doing something with the intention of causing a computer or similar machine to make a response that the offender is not authorised to make the computer do, for example by using a stolen ATM card or PIN, or using someone's password to get into a computer system to obtain information. The MCCOC (*Chapter 3, Theft, Fraud, Bribery and Related Offences,* Report (December 1995) p 124) proposed a similar provision in the definition of deception for the offence of fraud, now enacted in *Criminal Code* (Cth) s 133.1.

A further separate series of offences was created by the addition of s 9A *Summary Offences Act* 1966 (Vic) (computer hacking: repealed in 2003, now see ss 247A–I *Crimes Act* 1958 (Vic)) and s 83A *Crimes Act* 1958 (Vic). The latter offence deals with falsification of documents, and would include falsification or misuse of computer records, credit cards and ATM cards. Entering false instructions on a computer disk has been held to involve creation of a false instrument: *R v Governor of Brixton Prison; Ex parte Levin* [1997] QB 65. A similar offence now appears in *Criminal Law Consolidation Act* 1935 (SA) s 140.

The *Crimes Act* 1900 (NSW) was amended by the inclusion of s 178BA, which is virtually identical to s 81(4)(b) *Crimes Act* 1958 (Vic), and applies to the offence of obtaining money, valuable things or any financial advantage by deception. Other jurisdictions have related computer hacking and misuse offences: for example *Criminal Code* (NT) ss 276 ff; *Criminal Code* (Qld) s 408D; *Criminal Law Consolidation Act* 1935 (SA) s 141; *Criminal Code* (Tas) s 257A–F; *Criminal Code* (WA) s 440A; and see generally Olujoke Akindemowo, *Information Technology Law in Australia* (Sydney: LBC Information Services, 1999) ch 5.

Critique

Not all of these responses will in fact make a significant difference to the capacity to prosecute people who misuse computers using conventional property offences. For example, where the other components of the fraud offences—property, intention to permanently deprive—remain, the traditional limitations still apply. In Victoria, if the computer misuse provision (s 81(4)(b)) is applied in relation to obtaining property by deception it still requires subject matter that falls into the definition of 'property', together with proof of intent to permanently deprive. *Oxford v Moss* (1978) 68 Cr App R 183 limits the meaning of property in relation to information; *R v Lloyd* [1985] 3 WLR 30 (which involved cinema employees making pirate copies of films) maintains a narrow interpretation of 'intending to permanently deprive'. If charged with obtaining a financial advantage by deception these limitations do not apply.

Section 178BA of the *Crimes Act* 1900 (NSW) would appear to have wider application, being an offence the subject of which can be 'any money or valuable thing or any financial advantage'.

The MCCOC also recommended the inclusion of provisions dealing with forgery by 'false documents', which deal with the use of computers for dishonest gain, where a 'document' includes any paper with words, marks or symbols 'capable of being given a meaning by qualified persons or machines' (cl 19.1(1)(a)) discs or tapes from which 'sounds, images or messages are capable of being reproduced' (cl 19.1.(1)(b)), and credit and other electronically readable cards. These provisions have been given legislative form by ss 143.1 to 144.1 of the *Criminal Code* (Cth) introduced by the *Criminal Code Amendment (Theft, Fraud, Bribery and Related Offences) Act* 2000 (Cth). The legislation also includes (s 133.1) provisions in the obtaining by deception and receiving offences for dishonest conduct inducing automatic electronic money transfers.

Criminal misuse of computers of course goes beyond the specific use of computers to carry out the property and fraud offences being considered in this chapter. The Gibbs Report provided a Commonwealth template for legislation protecting computer-based data from disclosure or corruption. This has been adopted in the Australian Capital Territory, New South Wales, Tasmania and the Commonwealth: for background see MCCOC (2001) p 87 ff; Alex Steel, 'Vaguely Going Where No-one has Gone: The Expansive New Computer Access Offences' (2002) 26 Crim LJ 72–97. In 2001 the MCCOC published a report on the area, *Chapter 4, Damage and Computer Offences*, Report (January 2001). The MCCOC has consistently taken the position that general criminal law provisions should be used wherever possible rather than developing specialised offences. Submissions were received supporting separate offences of fraud and forgery on the Internet but the Committee concluded (MCCOC, *Chapter 4, Damage and Computer Offences*, Report (January 2001) p 100) that in general the conventional offences do cover the field even where a computer or electronic communications system was used. However, the area of data protection was one where the Committee reached the view that the principle should not apply, stating (at 6): '[t]here are few areas of current legislative concern in which the need for uniformity of approach in the formulation of criminal offences is more desirable or more pressing'. The MCCOC recommended a code of offences addressing the misuse of computers and damage to computer data, including unauthorised access, unauthorised modification of data, and unauthorised impairment of electronic communications. This has now been enacted in the *Criminal Code* (Cth) ss 476.1–478.4, in the *Criminal Code* (ACT) part 4.2, and see ss 247A–I *Crimes Act* 1958 (Vic).

The MCCOC saw the proposed computer offences as complementing the offences dealing with misuse of computers for purposes of dishonest gain covered in the 1995 Report. As the latter form of criminality is the subject of this chapter, the range of computer and damage offences discussed in MCCOC, *Chapter 4, Damage and Computer Offences*, Report (January 2001) will not be taken further here. See for additional discussion: Clare Sullivan, 'The Response of the Criminal Law in Australia to Computer Abuse' (1988) 12 Crim LJ 228–50; P Grabosky and R Smith, *Crime in the Digital Age: Controlling Telecommunications and Cyberspace Illegalities* (Leichardt, NSW: The Federation Press, 1998); J McConville, 'Computer Trespass in Victoria' (2001) 25 Crim LJ 220-7; Alex Steel, 'Vaguely Going Where No-one has Gone: The Expansive New Computer Access Offences' (2002) 26 Crim LJ 72–97; YF Lim, *Cyberspace Law* (Melbourne: Oxford University Press, 2002).

Grabosky, Smith and Dempsey discuss a range of measures for reducing computer-based or e-crime: P Grabosky, R Smith and G Dempsey, *Electronic Theft: Unlawful Acquisition in Cyberspace* (Cambridge: Cambridge University Press, 2001). Situational responses to e-crime are broadly aimed at preventing crime by increasing the effort required to commit offences (for example target hardening and access controls), creating greater risk of apprehension of offenders (for example, increased surveillance), and decreasing the potential for reward (for example, removing targets and identifying property). These may in their turn, however, lead to crime displacement—that is, to offenders moving on to easier targets or different offences: see Russell Smith, Nicolas Wolanin and Glenn Worthington, 'e-Crime Solutions and Crime Displacement', *Trends and Issues* No 243 (Canberra: AIC, 2003).

Jurisdictional limits on state-based criminal law were discussed in Chapter 1. Technological change has made the state-based jurisdictional limits on fraudulent behaviour in particular more problematic in recent years. The *Crimes Act* 1958 (Vic) was amended by the inclusion of s 80A, which extends the application of the fraud offences to cover actions occurring outside Victoria but having a 'real and substantial link' (defined further in s 80A(2)) with Victoria. This is one approach to ensuring that prosecutions will not fail for want of jurisdiction.

Offences involving corporations

Background

Some theft and fraud offences by corporations fall clearly within the traditional notions of property offences, the only difference being the corporate nature of the offender. This brings with it issues of ascribing corporate responsibility, discussed earlier in Chapters 1 and 3. Otherwise, the traditional offences will apply.

Notably, however, offences committed by corporations are likely to be connected to changing technologies, in particular to actions around computers, and around data and information. The issues raised by computers and by the nature of information as property have already been examined.

Corporations are also victims of theft and fraud crimes, both from within and externally, as discussed earlier: KPMG Australia, *Fraud Survey 2002* (April 2002); Australian Institute of Criminology and PricewaterhouseCoopers, *Serious Fraud in Australia and New Zealand* (Canberra: AIC and PricewaterhouseCoopers, 2003); Victorian Drugs and Crime Prevention Committee, *Fraud and Electronic Commerce*, Discussion Paper (March 2003). The frauds reported in the KPMG Survey were most frequently carried out internally, except those occurring in the financial sector. Internal management committed frauds involving the largest dollar losses, while non-management employees committed the greater number of internal frauds: *Fraud Survey 2002*, 6. Major frauds were perpetrated internally in 73 per cent of cases; frauds by managers constituted 51 per cent of the total dollar value of major frauds, compared with non-management employee frauds, which accounted for 16 per cent of value: *Fraud Survey 2002*, 11. The report's authors pointed to three factors affecting the level of corporate fraud (and no doubt the high levels of internal fraud), which were (a) the flattening of organisational structures and reduction in middle management, which had traditionally enforced internal controls, leading to poor internal controls; (b) the tendency to treat internal fraudsters leniently; and (c) the increase in fraud motivated by gambling, which they saw as reflecting the increased accessibility of gambling in the community: *Fraud Survey 2002*, ii, 14.

The current law

Traditional criminal laws will generally apply to offences involving corporations, once modifications are incorporated to deal with computer and electronic-based offending, and provided corporate responsibility can be identified.

Some deception offences by corporations are, on the other hand, unique to the corporation. One example arises from the relationship with investors and shareholders. Specific offences of making false statements to such stakeholders exist in most jurisdictions: *Crimes Act* 1900 (ACT) s 102; *Crimes Act* 1900 (NSW) s 176; *Criminal Code* (Qld) s 438; *Criminal Code* (Tas) s 282; *Crimes Act* 1958 (Vic) s 85; *Criminal Code* (WA) s 420. There is considerable overlap between the criminal law and laws dealing with corporate governance such as the *Corporations Act* 2001 (Cth) and the *Trade Practices Act* 1974 (Cth) (ss 53–53C): see discussion in J Clough and C Mulhern, *The Prosecution of Corporations* (Melbourne: Oxford University Press, 2002) p 158 ff. The recent inquiry into the disastrous collapse of the insurer HIH highlights the importance of supervision of standards of corporate governance using the regulatory system and reinforcing internal controls and processes, as well as the criminal process: HIH Royal Commission, *The Failure of HIH Insurance*, Vol 1 (Canberra: Commonwealth of Australia, 2003).

Critique

The Commonwealth Director of Public Prosecutions (DPP) called for a separate fraud offence in the Corporations Law to address gaps in prosecutorial jurisdiction. The DPP noted in a submission to the MCCOC the problem of fraud cases that were initially investigated under state law but then handed over to the Commonwealth DPP, where the latter has no power to charge under state or territory criminal law, or where the Commonwealth agency discovers conduct that amounts to state fraud offences: MCCOC, *Chapter 3, Theft, Fraud, Bribery and Related Offences*, Report (December 1995) p 171. The MCCOC was strongly of the view that separate offences for corporate fraud were inappropriate. The simplest solution would appear to be providing the Commonwealth DPP with power to lay charges under state criminal laws where necessary.

Frauds by corporations raise the fundamental question of the appropriate role of the criminal law—whether criminal or civil mechanisms are more appropriate to dealing with the corporate offender. Richard Quinney argues that corporate crime is not seen as truly criminal because corporate practices are central to the functioning of capitalist society: 'Class, State and Crime' in J Jacoby (ed), *Classics of*

Criminology (New York: Waveland Press Inc, 1994, first published 1980) pp 106–15 at 110. See also H Glasbeek, *Wealth by Stealth: Corporate Crime, Corporate Law and the Perversion of Democracy* (Toronto: Between the Lines, 2002).

This is correct both in the sense that some corporate practices that include deception may be regarded within the dominant culture as 'normal' business practice (although they would be seen differently if committed by individuals), and also in the sense that civil mechanisms may be seen as more appropriate, or at least more practical, for the corporate entity. There can be difficulties in allocating moral responsibility to the corporate entity. This has been another issue in the recent HIH Insurance inquiry: HIH Royal Commission, *The Failure of HIH Insurance*, Vol 1 (Canberra: Commonwealth of Australia, 2003) p xvi ff. Sentencing may also be problematic; imprisonment will not be available unless individual managers or directors are made liable, and fines may slip into the category of the 'price' the corporation is to pay for particular practices.

Existing civil/regulatory corporate regimes are well established, administered by independent statutory agencies such as the Australian Competition and Consumer Commission and the Australian Securities and Investments Commission, which have a range of powers of investigation and civil sanctions.

The financial and corporate environment in Australia and elsewhere has changed radically in recent decades, with withdrawal of the state and of direct government controls leading to new regulatory structures, all with their own membership requirements, compliance obligations, and enforcement mechanisms. Regulatory regimes use a carrot and stick approach to ensuring good corporate behaviour, encouraging compliance but always with the threat of enforcement should compliance not be achieved: see Peter Grabosky and John Braithwaite, *Of Manners Gentle: Enforcement Strategies of Australian Business Regulatory Agencies* (Melbourne: Oxford University Press and Australian Institute of Criminology, 1986); I Ayres and J Braithwaite, *Responsive Regulation: Transcending the Deregulation Debate* (New York: Oxford University Press, 1992).

These regulatory schemes rely on scrutiny by regulatory agencies. They also provide, ultimately, for criminal sanctions, although it is assumed these will generally remain abstract threats. Allan Fels, the former President of the main corporate regulator and 'watchdog', the ACCC, called for stronger criminal sanctions for breaches of the *Trade Practices Act* 1974 (Cth): Allan Fels, 'The Trade Practices Act and World's Best Practice: Proposals for Criminal Penalties for Hard-Core Collusion', *Current Issues in Regulation: Enforcement and Compliance*, (Melbourne: AIC/Regnet Conference, September 2002). The recent Dawson review of the Trade Practices Act has endorsed this approach, recommending criminal sanctions, including jail terms for company executives for 'hard-core cartel conduct' (perhaps extending the conventional notions of 'criminal' behaviour) and increases in civil penalties to the greater of $10 million or 10 per cent of the company's turnover: Trade Practices Act Review Committee, *Review of the Competition Provisions of the Trade Practices Act* (Canberra: Commonwealth of Australia, January 2003) p 163.

Criminal penalties imposed on individuals carry the stigma of a criminal record, and the risk of loss of liberty, factors widely recognised as 'focusing the mind' of managers, against which the corporation cannot provide protection.

Justice Neville Owen in his report on the failure of HIH Insurance concluded that 'HIH is not a case where wholesale fraud or embezzlement abounded' but he identified major malfeasance producing a deficiency of several billion dollars, and referred fifty-two matters involving thirteen senior officers for civil or criminal charges: *Australian Financial Review*, 17–21 April 2003.

The question recurs: when is corporate behaviour 'criminal'? The somewhat arbitrary nature of the label should by now be obvious. There is a choice, and Western societies have preferred to treat corporate offenders more gently than individual offenders, for the reasons outlined by Richard Quinney and others. Not all corporate misbehaviour should automatically be criminal: much can effectively be managed using a regulatory approach. There are, however, situations where the criminal law should be invoked, on the same lines as its use for individuals. As J Clough and C Mulhern argue: 'The fact that corporate illegality is treated civilly, when it would be regarded as criminal if performed by an individual, tends to legitimise that conduct. ...The imposition of criminal law therefore plays an important role in shaping public perception of certain wrongs by stating, unequivocally, that the relevant conduct will not be tolerated': *The Prosecution of Corporations* (Sydney: Oxford University Press, 2002).

Conclusion

In this chapter we have examined the operation of fraud offences in Australia, noting again the jurisdictional differences and limitations of the current criminal law.

The analysis raises the question whether a general offence of dishonesty might be introduced. Such an offence might not require proof either of deception or intent to permanently deprive. General dishonesty/fraud offences are fairly recent arrivals, but included s 29D *Crimes Act* 1914 (Cth). There are such provisions in Western Australia (s 409 *Criminal Code* (WA)) and in Canada (s 380 *Criminal Code* (Canada)). The operation of these provisions is outlined in MCCOC, *Chapter 3, Theft, Fraud, Bribery and Related Offences*, Report (December 1995) pp 143–7. A general dishonesty offence was introduced in the *Criminal Code* (Cth) amendments in 2000. Section 135.1, which replaces s 29D *Crimes Act* 1914 (Cth), provides that a person is guilty of an offence if 'the person does anything with the intention of dishonestly obtaining a gain from another person' (s 135.1(a)) or 'the person does anything with the intention of dishonestly causing a loss to another person' (s 135.1(3)(a)). The offence is limited to offences against 'Commonwealth entities'. The new South Australian legislation provides in s 142 for a more targeted general offence of dishonestly exploiting a position of advantage (defined in s 142(1)) in order to benefit or cause detriment to another.

A general dishonesty offence addresses cases that have been found to fall outside the traditional theft/fraud offences. An example would be the person making a secret profit at work, such as the projectionist copying the films at work and selling the copies. The accused who acted in this way in *Scott v Metropolitan Police Commissioner* [1975] AC 819 was charged with conspiracy to defraud, in the absence of a deception, of appropriation, and of an intent to permanently deprive. It could cover the person obtaining social security payments who continues to receive payment because they fail to notify the department of a material change in circumstances where there is no deception but there is clearly a financial advantage and there *may* be dishonesty. It could also include people obtaining benefits not amounting to property or a financial advantage such as a visa: see MCCOC, *Chapter 3, Theft, Fraud, Bribery and Related Offences*, Report (December 1995) p 149.

Depending on the breadth of the offence it could extend to the 'theft' of information, and electronic benefits. It might also cover some corporate misbehaviour where there is no 'deception' but there are clear breaches of corporate governance obligations. The offence would parallel the 'conspiracy to defraud' offences and cases without the need to prove conspiracy, or indeed the involvement of more than one person.

The MCCOC ultimately recommended against the introduction of a general offence of dishonesty, on the grounds that it inappropriately extended the reach of the criminal law, even perhaps to the person hiding when the debt collector comes, or sneaking into the picture theatre without paying: MCCOC, *Chapter 3, Theft, Fraud, Bribery and Related Offences*, Report (December 1995) p 153. Any extension of criminal liability to practices not currently clearly criminal needs very careful thought. This is particularly salient in the context of business practices, where 'so much commercial activity is directed toward inflicting loss or obtaining gain from competitors': S Bronitt and B McSherry, *Principles of Criminal Law* (Sydney: LBC Information Services, 2001) p 703.

The breadth of the new Commonwealth Criminal Code provision and the *Criminal Code* (WA) s 409 make any form of dishonesty that leads to gain, or loss against another, an indictable offence. Its implications for business transactions that might in any way be construed as dishonest are uncertain. Many actions that currently contravene the misleading and deceptive practices provisions of the *Trade Practices Act* 1974 (Cth) would also fall foul of a general dishonesty offence: MCCOC, *Chapter 3, Theft, Fraud, Bribery and Related Offences*, Report (December 1995) p 153.

Such an offence would give rise to considerable prosecutorial discretion and probably makes prosecutions more likely to succeed, if indeed we want to see the reach of the criminal law so extended.

In submissions regarding the amendments to the *Criminal Code* (Cth) in 2000 to deal with theft and fraud, the DPP indicated that, in relation to prosecution of social security fraud, their guidelines would treat the general dishonesty offence as a last option. The *Social Security Act* 1991 (Cth) offences would be the first avenue, and where the summary offences were regarded as inadequate the preference would be for using the conventional obtaining property by deception offence, before considering the new general offence: see *Advisory Report on the Criminal Code Amendment (Theft, Fraud, Bribery and Related Offences) Bill 1999*, House of Representatives 2000.

Andrew Ashworth described a proposed UK general offence (in terms of dishonestly causing another person to suffer financial prejudice or dishonestly to make a gain for oneself) as 'an offence of staggering breadth' and a 'blunderbuss': *Principles of Criminal Law* (3rd edn, Oxford: Oxford University Press, 1999) p 419. He was particularly critical of the uncertainty engendered by such general provisions, but conceded that they may be useful in preventing the broader commercial abuses. In some situations, as he notes, a highly specific law can in fact be misused by 'those with resources to manipulate, to slip between its provisions, and to draw fine distinctions' (at 419–20). On recent UK proposals for a general dishonesty offence, see Law Commission for England and Wales, *Fraud*, Report No 276 (London: HMSO, 2002); Jessica Holroyd, 'A New Criminal Law of Fraud: The Recent Proposals of the Law Commission of England and Wales' (2003) *The Journal of Criminal Law* 67(1) 31–6.

The MCCOC (*Chapter 3, Theft, Fraud, Bribery and Related Offences*, Report (December 1995) p 155) concluded:

> No doubt there is a strong concern to weed out dishonest practices in business and elsewhere, but to turn every shady business practice into theft or fraud runs the risk of over-criminalisation and selective prosecutions. Not every case of dishonesty does amount to theft or fraud. Apart from theft or fraud, there are a number of offences in legislation such as the *Corporations Law* and the *Trade Practices Act* making specific forms of dishonest or misleading conduct an offence. The price of this specificity is that occasionally innovative forms of dishonest conduct will elude the scope of the existing offences. In the Committee's view, this price is worth paying in order to stay within the important rule of law that criminal offences should be certain and knowable in advance.

The Commonwealth *Proceeds of Crime Act* 1987 included an offence of 'organised fraud': s 83 (repealed in 2003). The offence was introduced following the revelations about organised frauds, particularly tax frauds, in the 1980s. It was apparently not widely used: MCCOC, *Chapter 3, Theft, Fraud, Bribery and Related Offences*, Report (December 1995) pp 159, 161. The MCCOC considered whether to recommend such a provision in the Model Criminal Code. In the face of opposition from the vast majority of submissions, and strong arguments against the necessity for such a separate provision, it ultimately recommended against inclusion of such an offence, preferring to leave sanctioning of more highly organised and more serious criminal behaviour and 'organisation' to the sentencing discretion: *Chapter 3, Theft, Fraud, Bribery and Related Offences*, Report (December 1995) p 169. An organised fraud offence appeared in the Bill to amend the Commonwealth Criminal Code 1995 but was again opposed and does not appear in the legislation as passed: see *Advisory Report on the Criminal Code Amendment (Theft, Fraud, Bribery and Related Offences) Bill 1999* (Canberra: House of Representatives, June 2000).

Fraud offences in Australia currently address 'traditional' frauds, together with frauds employing computers and other new technologies and the e-environment. The criminal law is being called on increasingly to deal with e-crime and with corporate practices. Its appropriateness, however, certainly as the sole mechanism of prevention, is unclear. Prevention strategies such as increased surveillance and decreased ease of access are also important. The use of civil and regulatory mechanisms to deal with corporate behaviour also offer considerable advantages. Criminal sanctions should also be available, however, as recognised by the Dawson inquiry.

Lawyers and governments may need to rethink the community priorities currently reflected in the treatment of fraud. It is arguable that some types of dishonest behaviour are *over*-criminalised, and that a shift towards civil mechanisms is desirable, for example in relation to minor frauds, shoplifting, and welfare frauds. In other areas re-evaluation may be needed to challenge the traditionally 'civil' perceptions of the behaviour and reconceptualise criminal processes and sanctions, for example in what has been termed 'crime in the suites': see Brown et al (3rd edn, Sydney: The Federation Press, 2001) pp 1247–9.

Fraud offences now take place both locally and globally. This and the previous chapter have identified the complexity (particularly in the Code and common law states) and lack of uniformity of state-based legislation. State-based criminal justice agencies at the same time can have significant difficulties responding to offences crossing domestic borders (let alone offences crossing national borders). The importance of providing for prosecution of offences across borders has been noted earlier, and some legislative changes have been made along these lines. There must also be clearer coordination of state, territory and Commonwealth agencies. This has been the goal of the MCCOC since the Standing Committee of Attorneys-General gave priority to fraud as the first substantive offence for consideration by MCCOC. The Committee stated: 'More than most offences, fraud knows no jurisdictional boundaries and, in view of what has come to be termed "the excesses of the 80s", the need for a uniform and principled approach to the problems of fraud and these related offences has never been greater': MCCOC, *Chapter 3, Theft, Fraud, Bribery and Related Offences*, Report (December 1995) p iii.

Despite the political difficulties in addressing state-based differences, and state-federal issues, we agree that the importance of uniformity in this area is beyond doubt.

Part 4
EXTENDING CRIMINAL RESPONSIBILITY

CHAPTER 8

Inchoate offences

Introduction

In November 1983, the *National Times* reported that there were tapes of telephone conversations between a Sydney solicitor, Morgan Ryan, and a number of people including a judge. On 2 February 1984, the *Age* reprinted extracts from an alleged conversation between a judge and Ryan. In March 1984 it was stated in the Queensland Parliament that the judge was Justice Lionel Murphy of the High Court of Australia. Jenny Hocking writes that the *Age* extracts 'established a tone of sinister intrigue, double-dealing, sexual profligacy and dissolute corruption': *Lionel Murphy: A Political Biography* (Cambridge: Cambridge University Press, 1997) p 289.

It was alleged that Lionel Murphy had spoken to Clarence Briese, the Chief Magistrate in New South Wales, seeking to have him use his influence over another magistrate, Kevin Jones, to secure a favourable result for Morgan Ryan in committal proceedings for forgery and conspiracy. As a result of evidence presented before two Senate Committees inquiring into the matter, in November 1984, Lionel Murphy was charged with two counts of attempting to pervert the course of justice under s 43 of the *Crimes Act* 1914 (Cth). The first count related to conversations he had had with the Chief Magistrate Clarence Briese. The second count related to alleged pressure placed on Paul Flannery, a judge of the District Court, in relation to the trial of a count of conspiracy against Morgan Ryan.

Lionel Murphy pleaded not guilty to each count, but stood down from his position as a justice of the High Court pending his trial. At Lionel Murphy's first trial, Michael Kirby, now a justice of the High Court, was called as a character witness, while another current High Court justice, Ian Callinan, was the prosecutor. The jury found him guilty on the first count, but not on the second. In November 1985, the New South Wales Court of Criminal Appeal found that Judge Cantor had misdirected the jury, quashed Murphy's conviction and ordered a new trial: *R v Murphy* (1985) 4 NSWLR 42.

The retrial, which took place in early 1986, resulted in a finding of not guilty. After an 18-month hiatus, Murphy returned to his position on the High Court. Allegations against Murphy, however, continued to be made. Parliament, by resolution of both houses, appointed three retired Supreme Court judges as Commissioners under the *Parliamentary Commission of Inquiry Act* 1986 (Cth) to consider and report on the allegations. The Commission commenced its hearings, but in August 1986 Lionel Murphy announced he was suffering from advanced cancer and would not attend any further hearings. He died in October of that year. Understandably, the trials and inquiries resulted in widespread media coverage and raised issues concerning the powers of Parliament to dismiss justices of the High Court for misconduct. A Report by the Advisory Committee on the Australian Judicial System, David Jackson, Chairman (Canberra: Constitutional Commission, 1987) p 83 found that the system had operated in a 'prolonged, uncertain, repetitious, and unsatisfactory way...amid a continued blaze of publicity and speculation'.

The trials also raised questions about the nature of the charge, attempting to pervert the course of justice. Perverting the course of justice was recognised by the common law as a substantive offence independent of conspiracy in the case of *R v Grimes* [1968] 3 All ER 179. However, Lionel Murphy was charged under s 43 of the *Crimes Act* 1914 (Cth) with *attempting* to pervert the course of justice. The Model Criminal Code Officers Committee (MCCOC) has pointed out that perverting the course of justice is generally charged as an 'inchoate' offence in the sense of attempting, inciting or conspiring to pervert the course of justice: *Chapter 7, Administration of Justice Offences*, Report (July 1998) p 111. The term 'inchoate' stems from the Latin *inchoare*, which means to 'start work on'.

The Australian jurisdictions treat inchoate offences as substantive crimes in themselves, separate from the completed offences at which they are aimed. The three main inchoate offences are attempts, conspiracy and incitement. In *Rowell* (1977) 65 Cr App R 174 at 180, the Court of Appeal pointed out that a charge of attempting to pervert the course of justice is misleading as the general law relating to attempts is not directly in point. Rather, it is viewed as a separate offence.

In Murphy's first trial, Cantor J reserved twenty-one questions for the consideration of the High Court. The Attorney-General for the State of New South Wales also brought an application concerning the proper construction of s 43 of the *Crimes Act* 1914 (Cth). These questions were heard together and, among other matters, the High Court held that attempting to pervert the course of justice applies to committal proceedings concerning indictable offences against the laws of the Commonwealth: *R v Murphy* (1985) 158 CLR 596.

Attempting to pervert the course of justice is but one of a range of 'inchoate' offences. In general, the common thread among these crimes is that there can be a conviction even though the substantive offence that was intended is not completed and no apparent harm is caused. One of the reasons inchoate offences exist is to aid the police and law enforcement officials to intervene before the commission of the offence. The main point of contention is that these offences have the potential to greatly broaden the scope of the criminal law and to be used for political reasons. Evidential rules also enable more character evidence to be introduced than in trials for substantive offences. Jenny Hocking writes (at 302) in relation to Lionel Murphy's first trial:

> It is in the nature of an 'attempt' charge, as with a conspiracy charge, that the rules of evidence are broad, allowing the introduction of evidence concerning the reputation, the 'known character', of the accused. For Murphy to be shown as likely to act in such a way as to pervert the course of justice could be evidenced, it would be argued, by his past activities including even his policy decisions as Attorney-General, which were once again raked over, although he had not been charged with an offence in relation to any of them.

Inchoate offences are defined broadly in abstract terms and have required a high degree of judicial interpretation. The doctrine of attempts is designed to punish those who intend to commit a crime and who do some acts that are more than merely preparatory to the crime, but are unsuccessful in carrying it out. Conspiracy serves to criminalise an agreement between two or more persons to commit an unlawful act where there is an intention to commit that unlawful act. Incitement is somewhat similar to conspiracy in its time frame for criminalisation, but covers circumstances where one person tries to persuade another to commit a crime that the inciter intends to have committed.

The origins of attempts, conspiracy and incitement can be traced back to the authority of common law courts to create offences, but the treatment of them as substantive crimes in themselves is of comparatively recent origin: IP Robbins, 'Double Inchoate Crimes' (1989) 26(1) *Harvard Journal on Legislation* 1–116 at 9–10, 25–6, 30–2; FB Sayre, 'Criminal Attempts' (1928) XLI (7) *Harvard Law Review* 821–59. Ira Robbins points out (at 9) that 'despite the independent origins and developments of the three offences, conspiracy and [incitement] can be viewed as early stages of an attempt to commit a completed offense'.

The traditional division of crimes into 'physical' and 'fault' elements does not sit well with the notion of inchoate crimes. In attempts, for example, there is a set fault element, but a loosely defined physical element, and in conspiracy, the requirement that an agreement to commit an offence must be identified overlaps with proving an intention to commit the substantive offence.

The CLOC has noted that incitement is rarely charged: Criminal Law Officers Committee, *Chapters 1 and 2, General Principles of Criminal Responsibility*, Final Report (December 1992) p 93. While there have been difficulties in defining what constitutes an attempt, conspiracy is perhaps the vaguest and most problematic of the inchoate crimes. This crime, unlike an attempt, does not require conduct that is proximate to the completion of the substantive offence. This enables criminal responsibility to be proved on the basis of a preliminary plan or consensus between the parties. Gallop J observed in *Nirta v The Queen* (1983) 10 A Crim R 370 at 377 that '[a]n indictment alleging conspiracy has become an increasingly important weapon in the prosecutor's armoury'. The problem is that there is a danger that the crime of conspiracy may be abused if there are unclear limitations on its scope.

Prosecutors and the courts tend to take a policy-oriented approach to inchoate crimes by first identifying whether the accused's acts are sufficiently dangerous to merit punishment and then identifying which inchoate crime can be charged to best suit the facts: IP Robbins, 'Double Inchoate Crimes' (1989) 26(1) *Harvard Journal on Legislation* 1–116 at 115.

From a procedural perspective, a conviction for an attempt as well as for the substantive offence is procedurally impermissible because it is viewed as contrary to the rule against double jeopardy: *Wesley-Smith v Balzary* (1977) 14 ALR 681 (SC NT) at 685 per Forster J; *R v Lee* (1990) 1 WAR 411 at 426 per Malcolm J, at 434 per Kennedy J; *Criminal Code* (Tas) s 342(3). However, currently, there is no legal barrier to enabling a conviction both for conspiracy to commit a crime and actually committing the offence. The situation is unclear with respect to incitement, probably because it is rarely charged.

In *R v Hoar* (1981) 148 CLR 32, Gibbs CJ, Mason, Aickin and Brennan JJ stated (at 38) that it was 'undesirable' for conspiracy to be charged when a substantive offence had been committed. This is because inclusion of a conspiracy count adds to the length and complexity of trials and, in particular, complicates the task of summing up to a jury. In addition, convicting a person of both conspiracy and the substantive crime is akin to punishing a person twice for what is substantially the same offence.

On the other hand, the ability to charge both conspiracy and the crime intended may be attractive to the prosecution because it enables it to allege a wide-ranging scheme of criminal activity without having to pinpoint the accused's precise role. It provides a 'fall back' charge for the jury if the substantive elements of the full offence cannot be proven beyond reasonable doubt: Law Commission for England and Wales, *Criminal Law: Report on Conspiracy and Criminal Law Reform*, Report No 76 (London: HMSO, 1976) pp 27–8.

Overall, it is very difficult to identify consistent principles with regard to inchoate offences. The following three sections deal with each of the inchoate offences in turn. We then examine the law relating to inchoate crimes and the impossibility of committing the substantive offence.

Attempts

Background

In 1974, John Stonehouse, aged 49, a well-known English politician and Privy Councillor, was suffering from severe financial difficulties. On 20 November of that year, his clothes were found piled on a beach in Miami, where he was on a business trip, but there was no sign of him. He was presumed to have accidentally drowned while swimming.

On 24 December 1974, police arrested Stonehouse in Melbourne. He gave a false name and, interestingly, the police thought at first that they had caught the missing Lord Lucan, who was wanted in England for murder. The police soon established that Stonehouse had arrived in Australia on a forged passport.

Stonehouse had taken out life insurance with five different companies, naming his wife, Barbara, who was unaware of the plan to fake his death, as the beneficiary. The policies totalled £125,000 payable to Barbara Stonehouse upon the death of her husband within five years. Stonehouse was convicted of a number of dishonesty offences and, in relation to the life insurance, *attempting* to obtain property by deception. Under s 15(2) of the *Theft Act* 1968 (UK) the word 'obtain' includes 'enabling another to obtain'. Thus, the charge concerned Stonehouse attempting, by deceiving the authorities as to his death, to enable his wife Barbara to obtain the insurance money.

On appeal to the House of Lords, the accused argued that his acts were too remote from the commission of the offence of obtaining property by deception to constitute an attempt: *DPP v Stonehouse* [1978] AC 55. That is, the mere disappearance did not enable Barbara Stonehouse to obtain the property. She would have had to decide to make a claim and communicate that claim before the full offence could be carried out.

The House of Lords dismissed Stonehouse's appeal for reasons we will explore in the section on the physical elements. Despite initially hiring Richard du Cann QC and the then junior barrister, Geoffrey Robertson, as his defence team, Stonehouse decided at the last moment to conduct his own defence: G Robertson, *The Justice Game* (London: Vintage, 1999) p 70. He was sentenced to seven years' imprisonment, which was upheld on appeal. Subsequently, Stonehouse lived with his secretary, Sheila Buckley, who had stuck by him throughout the trial. He died of a heart attack a few years after his release.

Stonehouse's conviction for attempting to obtain property by deception shows that the law is prepared to punish an unconsummated substantive offence. The law in this area stems from the latter part of the seventeenth century when it was a misdemeanour to have a felonious intent manifested by an overt act. In the case of *R v Scofield* (1784) Cald Mag Rep 397, the accused was charged with placing combustible material together with a lighted candle near another's house with intent to burn it down. The Court established that it was unnecessary for the house to have caught fire and burnt down for a crime to have occurred. Today, the facts of this case would probably give rise to a conviction for attempted arson.

The offence of attempt differs from substantive offences in that it combines the fault element of intention with a loosely defined physical element. The law has been criticised for being too vague as to the physical element and therefore unworkable: P Glazebrook, 'Should We Have a Law of Attempted Crime?' (1969)

85 *Law Quarterly Review* 28–49. However, it appears that the response of law reformers has not been to abandon the law of attempts, but to try to produce legislative answers instead: GJ Moloney, 'Attempts' (1991) 15 Crim LJ 175–85.

Generally, no harm or damage will have occurred in relation to an attempt. As set out in Chapter 1, John Stuart Mill argued that state intervention into individual liberty could only be justified to prevent harm to others: *On Liberty* (London: Harmondsworth, Penguin, 1974, first published 1859). If no harm occurs in an attempt, how then can punishment be justified?

Various answers have been suggested to this question. First, the 'harm' of attempts and the other inchoate offences could be viewed broadly as the *potential* to cause harm. Secondly, as Francis Sayre points out: '[t]hat those should not be allowed to go free who attempt to commit some crime but fail, is a feeling deep rooted and universal': 'Criminal Attempts' (1928) XLI (7) *Harvard Law Review* 821–59 at 821. That is, the criminal law should not concentrate on outcomes, but rather focus on culpability instead. Thirdly, the law of attempts can be justified from a crime-prevention approach. The police should be able to step in to *prevent* harm rather than have to wait until after harm has been done. The criminal law should thus punish those who are trying to commit harm as well as those who succeed in so doing.

The punishment for an attempted offence varies between jurisdictions. Penalties range from half that of the completed indictable offence (*Criminal Code* (NT) ss 278, 279; *Criminal Code* (Qld) ss 536–578; *Criminal Code* (WA) ss 554, 555A) to two-thirds of the completed offence (*Criminal Law Consolidation Act* 1935 (SA) s 270A(3); *Crimes Act* 1958 (Vic) s 321P) to the same penalty as if the offence had been completed (*Crimes Act* 1914 (Cth) s 7; *Crimes Act* 1900 (NSW) s 344A). David Lewis has argued that it is difficult to find a rationale for leniency in punishing attempts compared to the crime attempted: 'The Punishment That Leaves Something to Chance' (1989) 18(1) *Philosophy and Public Affairs* 53–67. For example, imagine two assassins intend to kill a public figure. One shoots at her and misses. The other shoots and hits and kills her. Both assassins have the same intention to kill and their conduct is equally dangerous. Why should 'failure' mean a more lenient punishment?

In Chapter 2, we explored the differences between the subjectivist and objectivist approaches to fault. Antony Duff argues against the strict subjectivist approach to the criminal law in stating that consequences should have a role to play in determining criminal responsibility. He argues that lesser punishment for such an attempt marks the fact that the assassin who missed the target failed to produce the intended effect in the real world: *Criminal Attempts* (Oxford: Oxford University Press, 1996) ch 4 and at 351–4.

If the potential assassin had a gun in a public place and was caught prior to getting near the target, an argument can perhaps more strongly be made out for a lesser punishment. Andrew Ashworth writes (at 483) that in such a case a more lenient punishment may be justified 'because of the possibility of voluntary abandonment of the attempt, because it takes greater nerve to consummate an offence, and because it may be prudent to leave some incentive (i.e. reduced punishment) to the incomplete attempter to give up rather than to carry out the full offence': *Principles of Criminal Law* (3rd edn, Oxford: Oxford University Press, 1999) p 483.

As well as differences in punishment between the Australian criminal law jurisdictions, there are also differences in the definitions of what constitutes attempt. General statutory provisions exist in all Australian jurisdictions that establish that attempts to commit certain offences are themselves offences. In Queensland, Tasmania and Victoria, criminal responsibility is limited to attempting to commit indictable offences: *Criminal Code* (Qld) s 535; *Criminal Code* (Tas) s 299; *Crimes Act* 1958 (Vic) s 321M. In New South Wales, criminal responsibility pertains to those attempting to commit offences listed under the *Crimes Act* 1900: s 344A. In contrast, at the Commonwealth level, s 7 of the *Crimes Act* 1914 (Cth) applies to all offences under Commonwealth and Territory laws, not only to offences under the Act.

In the Australian Capital Territory, the Northern Territory, South Australia and Western Australia, criminal responsibility pertains to attempting any offence: *Criminal Code* (ACT) s 44; *Criminal Code* (NT) s 277(1); *Criminal Law Consolidation Act* 1935 (SA) s 279A(1); *Criminal Code* (WA) ss 552, 555A. There are also statutory offences relating to specific crimes such as attempted murder: *Crimes Act* 1900 (NSW) ss 27–30; *Criminal Code* (NT) s 165; *Criminal Law Consolidation Act* 1935 (SA); *Criminal Code* (Qld) s 306; *Criminal Code* (WA) s 283.

In this section, we will be concentrating on the general doctrine of attempt. Despite variations, the actual substance of the statutory definitions and the common law definition are similar. An attempt involves both physical and fault elements, but as pointed out above, the physical element is loosely defined. Without the requisite fault element, the conduct alone may appear inoffensive. Accordingly, the fault element for an attempt generally differs from that of the completed offence in that a higher standard must be satisfied. A definition of an attempt at common law was set out by Murphy J in *Britten v Alpogut* [1987] VR 929 at 938:

> [A] criminal attempt is committed if it is proven that the accused had at all material times the guilty intent to commit a recognised crime and it is proven that at the same time he [or she] did an act or acts (which in appropriate circumstances would include omissions) which are seen to be sufficiently proximate to the commission of the said crime and not seen to be merely preparatory to it.

The same requirements of an intention to commit the completed offence and conduct that is more than merely preparatory are common to all the various statutory definitions of attempt. We will set out the requirements for the physical and fault elements in turn and provide critiques of each.

The current law—physical elements

A distinction has generally been drawn between *preparing* to commit a crime and *attempting* to commit it. Only the latter is considered punishable. In *Britten v Alpogut* [1987] VR 929 at 938, Murphy J spoke of conduct being 'sufficiently proximate' and not 'merely preparatory'. The latter term is mentioned in the Commonwealth legislation and in Victoria and Western Australia: *Crimes Act* 1914 (Cth) s 7(2); *Crimes Act* 1958 (Vic) s 321N(1); *Criminal Code* (WA) s 4. The Victorian provision adds a requirement that the conduct be 'immediately and not remotely connected' to the commission of the offence. In the Northern Territory and Queensland, the phrase used is 'by means adapted to [the crime's] fulfilment': *Criminal Code* (NT) s 4; *Criminal Code* (Qld) s 4. What this means is unclear, but the courts have applied common law decisions on proximity to the Queensland section: *R v Williams* [1965] Qd R 86 at 102 per Stable J; *R v Chellingworth* [1954] QWN 35 (Circuit Court); *R v Edwards* [1956] QWN 16. In Tasmania, the conduct must not be too remote and part of a series of events that, if not interrupted, would constitute the actual commission of the crime: *Criminal Code* (Tas) s 2.

All of the statutory provisions and the common law are thus concerned with the notion of proximity. Whether conduct is considered sufficiently proximate to the actual offence is generally a matter for the jury to determine: *DPP v Stonehouse* [1978] AC 55; *R v Gullefer* [1990] 3 All ER 882 at 884; (1990) 91 Cr App R 356 at 357 per Lord Lane CJ. In Tasmania, however, the question of whether or not conduct was too remote to constitute an attempt is a matter of law for the trial judge to determine: *Criminal Code* (Tas) s 2. Once the trial judge decides that the conduct was not too remote, then it is up to the jury to decide whether the accused would have committed the completed offence if not interrupted.

The difficulty in all jurisdictions lies in determining when conduct is sufficiently proximate to qualify as an attempt. The courts have referred to whether the conduct is 'too remote', 'more than merely preparatory', 'sufficiently proximate', 'the last act', 'a substantial step', 'on the job' or 'unequivocal'.

A number of different approaches have been evident in the case law. The *first stage* approach posed criminal responsibility for the first overt act performed with the intention to commit a specific crime. This seems to have been the approach taken during the eighteenth century when the law relating to attempts was in its infancy: FB Sayre, 'Criminal Attempts' (1928) XLI(7) *Harvard Law Review* 821–59 at 834 ff. Such an approach has been rejected as concentrating too much on the fault element: G Niemann, 'Attempts' (1991) 2(3) *Criminal Law Forum* 549–67 at 550.

At the other end of the spectrum, the *last act* theory found favour for a brief time during the nineteenth century. In *R v Eagleton* (1855) 6 Cox CC 559, the accused made a contract with a local Poor Law authority to supply bread for an agreed weight to the poor. He was to be paid a certain amount per loaf by the authority. The accused supplied underweight loaves, but his conduct was discovered before he was paid. He was charged with attempting to obtain money by false pretences. The case went to the Court for Crown Cases Reserved on the question of law as to whether the accused's activity constituted an attempt. The Court held that there had been an attempt. Parke B (at 571) in delivering the judgment of the Court stated: 'Acts remotely leading towards the commission of the offence are not to be considered as attempts to commit it; but acts immediately connected with it are...[O]n the statement in this case, no other act on the part of the defendant would have been required. It was the last act depending on himself towards the payment of the money, and therefore it ought to be considered as an attempt... .'

The last act approach was taken up in *R v Robinson* [1915] 2 KB 342. In that case, the accused was a jeweller who insured his goods against theft. He faked a robbery by tying himself up and calling for help. He told the police that he had been knocked down and jewellery taken from the safe. The police later found the jewellery in the shop and the accused admitted he intended to put in a false claim to the insurers. The accused's conviction for attempting to obtain money by false pretences was quashed by the Court of Criminal Appeal on the basis that his acts were too remote in that he had not taken the last step of communicating with the insurers and making a false claim.

The last act test subsequently fell into disfavour by the courts on the basis that some offences may be committed in stages over a period of time: *DPP v Stonehouse* [1978] AC 55 at 86 per Lord Edmund-Davies; *Jones* (1990) 91 Cr App R 351. For example, the last act test is not useful in situations involving guns. If a person buys a rifle, loads it, aims it at the victim and is seized before firing it, this would seem to be sufficient conduct for attempted murder: L Waller and CR Williams, *Criminal Law: Text and Cases* (9th edn, Sydney: Butterworths, 2001) p 537. According to the last act test, the accused would have to pull the trigger as well, before an attempt could be made out. The *Criminal Codes* of the Northern Territory, Queensland and Western Australia expressly state that whether or not the accused has done all that is necessary on his or her part for completing the intended offence is immaterial: *Criminal Code* (NT) s 4; *Criminal Code* (Qld) s 4; *Criminal Code* (WA) s 4.

An alternative approach is that of *unequivocality*. This requires there to be conduct that unequivocally indicates that the accused intended to commit the offence. Lord Salmond set out this test in *R v Barker* [1924] NZLR 865 at 874:

> [An] act done with intent to commit a crime is not a criminal attempt unless it is of such a nature as to be itself sufficient evidence of the criminal intent with which it is done. A criminal attempt is an act which shows criminal intent on the face of it. The case must be one in which res ipsa loquitur [the thing speaks for itself] applies...That [an accused's] unfulfilled criminal purposes should be punishable, they must be manifested not by his [or her] words merely, or by acts which are themselves of innocent or ambiguous significance, but by overt acts which are sufficient in themselves to declare and proclaim the guilty purpose with which they are done.

This approach enables an acquittal if the accused's conduct can be associated with an innocent motive as well as an intention to commit an offence. It has received only limited support in Australia: *R v Williams* [1965] Qd R 86 at 100 per Stable J. It was expressly rejected as a definitive test by the Tasmanian Court of Appeal in *Nicholson* (1994) 76 A Crim R 187 at 190–2 per Underwood J and at 199 per Wright J. It has been criticised because, on a practical level, 'determining whether or not something unequivocally demonstrates an intention to commit an offense is difficult in itself to discern': G Niemann, 'Attempts' (1991) 2(3) *Criminal Law Forum* 549–67 at 550. However, an admitted intention or an act that unequivocally indicates an intention will be highly persuasive in establishing an attempt.

An alternative approach is to focus on whether the accused's acts were *sufficiently proximate* to the crime attempted: *R v Cline* [1956] OR 539 at 551 per Laidlaw J (Can Ont CA). This tries to provide a point for criminal responsibility somewhere between the first act and the last act approaches. However, it is vague and its application has led to opposite decisions on almost identical facts: for example, *R v Robinson* [1915] 2 KB 342 (outlined above) compared with *Comer v Bloomfield* (1971) 55 Crim App R 305.

Another approach that is similar to that of the *sufficiently proximate* approach is one that concentrates on whether or not the accused has made *substantial progress* towards the commission of the substantive offence. This approach focuses on what has been done as well as what remains to be done. For example, in *Jones* (1990) 91 Cr App R 351, the victim was in a relationship with the accused's ex-girlfriend. The accused got into the victim's car with a loaded sawn-off shot gun. The victim managed to disarm the accused and the latter was charged with attempted murder. Lord Justice Taylor (at 356), in delivering the judgment of the Court of Criminal Appeal, focused on the conduct that had already been committed:

> Clearly his actions in obtaining the gun, in shortening it, in loading it, in putting on his disguise, and in going to the school could only be regarded as preparatory acts. But, in our judgement, once he had got into the car, taken out the loaded gun and pointed it at the victim with the intention of killing him, there was sufficient evidence for the consideration of the jury on the charge of attempted murder.

In comparison, the Court of Criminal Appeal in *R v Campbell* [1991] Crim LR 268, focused on the steps that needed to be taken before substantial progress had been made. In that case, the police arrested the accused when he was close to a post office, carrying an imitation firearm and a threatening note. His appeal against conviction for attempted robbery was successful on the basis that he had not entered the post office. This decision seems to imply that the police have to wait until a person is inside a bank or post office and has shown a weapon before an arrest can be made. The substantial progress step test is necessarily vague, being adapted to the facts of each case and providing considerable leeway in determining criminal responsibility.

To complicate matters further, sometimes the courts seem to merge the approaches. For example, in *DPP V Stonehouse* [1978] AC 55, the facts of which were outlined at the beginning of this section, Lord Edmund-Davies seemed to combine the substantial progress approach with that of the last act approach, despite his disapproval of the latter. He pointed out (at 87) that not only did Stonehouse's faking of his death go a substantial distance towards the attainment of the complete offence, it was also the final act that *he* could perform. In comparison, Lord Diplock (at 70) cast the question in terms of sufficient proximity while Lord Salmon (at 77) resorted to 'ordinary common sense' to hold that an attempt had occurred.

There is therefore no single approach that definitively enables a court to say that an attempt has occurred. This, as we shall explore in the Critique section, has led PR Glazebrook to argue for the abolition of this offence: 'Should We Have a Law of Attempted Murder?' (1969) 85 *Law Quarterly Review* 28–49.

One further matter that falls within the consideration of the physical element of attempts is that of 'desistance'. That is, there is a general rule that when an accused 'desists' or decides not to go ahead with an offence, he or she may still be found criminally liable for an attempt if the conduct performed is considered sufficiently proximate to the completed offence: *R v Page* [1933] VLR 351; *R v Collingridge* (1976) 16 SASR 117; *Criminal Code* (NT) s 4(2); *Criminal Code* (Qld) s 4(2); *Criminal Code* (WA) s 4; *Criminal Code* (Tas) s 2(2). There is no mention of desistance in the Victorian provisions and it would seem that the common law still applies.

For example, in *R v Page* [1933] VLR 351, the accused kept watch while another man, Partridge, put a lever under a window in order to break into a shop. Before opening the window, Partridge had a change of heart and decided that he would not 'continue with the job'. He dropped the lever and descended and the two men were arrested. The Full Court of the Supreme Court of Victoria held that what was done by Partridge amounted to an attempt and the fact that he had 'desisted of his own volition' made no difference.

In the Northern Territory and Queensland, desistance may be taken into account in reducing the penalty for an attempt: *Criminal Code* (NT) s 279(1); *Criminal Code* (Qld) s 538.

The policy for allowing desistance to exculpate an accused obviously makes more sense the further back the conduct is from the substantive offence. A change of mind at a very early stage may be seen as 'undoing' the original blameworthy state of mind. Allowing desistance to be taken into account may also show the deterrent effect of criminalising an attempt. In practice, desistance is rarely raised presumably because of the difficulty in arguing that a change of mind was truly voluntary and not merely an opportunistic claim made after the event.

Critique

Justice Salmond described the problem with finding a workable approach to the physical element of attempts in *R v Barker* [1924] NZLR 865 at 874: '[T]o constitute a criminal attempt, the first step along the way of criminal intent is not necessarily sufficient and the final step is not necessarily required. The dividing line between preparation and attempt is to be found somewhere between these two extremes; but as to the method by which it is to be determined the authorities give no clear guidance.'

In 1980, the Law Commission for England and Wales produced a Report (No 102) reviewing the law of criminal attempts. The Commission concluded that the last act test fixed the point of intervention for criminal liability too late. The Law Commission in an earlier Working Paper (No 50) had provisionally favoured the adoption of the substantial progress approach, but abandoned this on the grounds that it was too imprecise and took the threshold of liability too far back.

In its 1980 Report the Law Commission adopted a formulation based on 'acts more than merely preparatory to the commission of the offence'. This was then enacted in s 1(1) of the *Criminal Attempts Act* 1981. The Law Commission rejected the use of the terms 'proximate', 'closely connected' and 'immediately connected' because of the danger that these terms suggest that only the last act could be an attempt.

Using the words 'more than merely preparatory' does appear to avoid notions of unequivocality or substantial progress. However, as with the other approaches, this formulation has been criticised as being too imprecise: I Dennis, 'The Criminal Attempts Act 1981' [1982] Crim LR 5–16. Ian Dennis has also suggested that the statutory test could have been 'fleshed out' by a clear statement that certain specific types of acts amount to more than preparatory acts: I Dennis, 'The Law Commission Report on Attempt and Impossibility in Relation to Attempt, Conspiracy and Incitement: (1) The Elements of Attempt' [1980] Crim LR 758–79.

The 'more than merely preparatory' formulation has been adopted at the Commonwealth level and in Victoria and Western Australia: *Crimes Act* 1914 (Cth) s 7(2); *Crimes Act* 1958 (Vic) s 321N(1); *Criminal Code* (WA) s 4. Section 11.1(2) of the *Criminal Code* (Cth) has similarly adopted this more than merely preparatory formula. Whatever words are used in legislation, a completely clear formulation for pinpointing the physical element of an attempt appears to lie in the realm of fantasy.

PR Glazebrook has argued that the primary objection to having an attempt as an offence in itself is that any 'definition' is inescapably vague and uncertain: 'Should We Have a Law of Attempted Crime?' (1969) 85 *The Law Quarterly Review* 28–49. He writes (at 39):

> No one has ever supposed that some single formula might, given a clever enough lawyer, be devised which would embrace the *actus reus* of, for instance, the offences of murder, obtaining property by deception, and the commission of acts of gross indecency between males. Why, then, should it be supposed that a single

formula might, when combined with the definitions of those very different crimes, serve to identify the *actus reus* of such disparate offences as attempting to murder, attempting to obtain property by deception, and attempting to commit an act of gross indecency?

Glazebrook proposes that instead of a general offence of attempt, the legislature should criminalise conduct that is intended to facilitate the future commission of an offence. For example, there could be a crime of 'going equipped with the instruments of housebreaking'.

It certainly seems a noble dream to expect that one single formula can be devised to cover all types of blameworthy preparatory conduct related to the commission of such disparate offences as murder, assault or theft. Glazebrook's suggestion makes sense, but it seems that the general doctrine of attempts is now too intractable for it to be abolished. There is little doubt that the courts will continue to struggle with finding an appropriate approach to the physical element for this inchoate offence.

The current law—fault element

In all jurisdictions, the requisite fault element for an attempt is an *intention* to commit the requisite offence: *Britten v Alpogut* [1987] VR 929; *Knight* (1988) 35 A Crim R 314; *Criminal Code* (NT) s 4; *Criminal Code* (Qld) s 4; *Crimes Act* (Vic) s 321N(2); *Criminal Code* (Tas) s 2(1); *Criminal Code* (WA) s 4.

In Chapter 2, we set out how the narrow interpretation of intention known as direct intention 'connotes a decision to bring about a situation so far as it is possible to do so—to bring about an act of a particular kind or a particular result': *He Kaw Teh v The Queen* (1985) 157 CLR 523 at 569 per Brennan J. This is the form of intention that is generally referred to in the context of attempts. Oblique intention or recklessness is not considered sufficient for attempts to commit offences where the physical element refers to the results or consequences of conduct.

In *Giorgianni v The Queen* (1985) 156 CLR 473, Wilson, Deane and Dawson JJ stated (at 473):

> For the purposes of many offences it may be true to say that if an act is done with foresight of its probable consequences there is sufficient intent in law even if such intent may more properly be described as a form of recklessness. There are, however, offences in which it is not possible to speak of recklessness as constituting a sufficient intent. Attempt is one and conspiracy is another... Intent is required and it is an intent which must be based upon knowledge or belief of the necessary facts.

This approach that only a direct intention will suffice for an attempted result crime has been followed in subsequent cases. In *Knight v The Queen* (1992) 175 CLR 495, the High Court held that in relation to attempted murder, only an intention to kill would suffice. Mason CJ, Dawson and Toohey JJ explained this as follows (at 501): '[A]n accused is not guilty of attempted murder unless he [or she] intends to kill... An intention to cause grievous bodily harm may constitute the malice aforethought for murder when death ensues, but for there to be attempted murder there must be an intention to cause the death which is an essential element of the completed crime of murder.'

Brennan J also reinforced this approach in *McGhee v The Queen* (1995) 183 CLR 82 at 85–6. This high standard for the fault element in relation to result offences also carries over to attempted strict and absolute liability offences: *Trade Practices Commission v Tubemakers of Australia Ltd* (1983) 47 ALR 719 at 737 per Toohey J. Following Brennan J's approach in *McGhee*'s case, the emphasis is on an intention to commit the physical element of the offence. The fault element, or lack thereof, for the completed offence is irrelevant.

While the fault element therefore appears straightforward in relation to attempted result crimes, the position is less clear regarding attempted crimes where the physical element requires conduct to be performed in certain specified circumstances.

There are some cases that support a lower fault standard for attempted rape. While the Code jurisdictions require an intention to commit the offence and do not refer to recklessness, in *R v Bell* [1972] Tas SR 127, Neasey J stated (at 131-2) that awareness of the possibility of non-consent would be sufficient for the purpose of attempted rape under the Tasmanian *Criminal Code*.

In *R v Evans* (1987) 48 SASR 35, the South Australian Court of Criminal Appeal held that attempted rape may be committed when the accused intended to sexually penetrate another, being recklessly indifferent as to the absence of consent. King CJ (at 41) pointed out that the difference between result crimes and crimes involving circumstances led to a difference in fault elements:

> The state of facts, the existence of which renders the act of sexual penetration criminal, is the non-consent of the person penetrated. The mental state of the accused in relation to that state of facts, required by the definition of the crime...includes reckless indifference to its existence. There cannot be an attempt to commit a crime involving particular consequences where those consequences are not intended, because the notion of unintended consequences is inconsistent with the notion of attempt to bring about those consequences. That reasoning does not apply, however, to an accused's state of mind as to the existence of circumstances which render an act criminal.

Special leave to appeal against *Evan*'s case was refused by the High Court and its reasoning was followed by the English Court of Appeal in *R v Khan* [1990] 2 All ER 783. However, Russell LJ noted in *Khan*'s case (at 819) that the reasoning that explained the inclusion of recklessness in the fault element for attempted rape did not apply equally to all offences. Whether the lower fault element applies to other crimes that include circumstances is unclear.

Critique

Setting a standard of intention as the fault element for attempted result crimes has attracted criticism. For example, Arnold Enker has pointed out that it is anomalous to hold a person guilty of attempted murder for conduct intended to cause death, but not for highly dangerous conduct known to the actor to risk death or grievous bodily harm: 'Mens Rea and Criminal Attempt' (1977) 845(4) *American Bar Foundation Research Journal* 845–79 at 847. There are, however, lesser statutory offences that may apply to such a situation and setting the high fault standard of intention for attempts goes some way towards restricting its scope. To attempt something, by contrast to accidental behaviour, also implies that the accused has a purpose in mind.

What then of the fault standard for attempted crimes of circumstance? Jonathan Clough and Carmel Mulhern are of the opinion that a lower fault standard for attempted rape is difficult to reconcile with the clear requirement that the fault element of an attempt is an intention to commit an offence: *Butterworths Tutorial Series: Criminal Law* (Sydney: Butterworths, 1999) p 209. They are not convinced that the distinction between result crimes and crimes of circumstance set out in *Evan*'s case justifies a lower fault standard. Brent Fisse also points out that because there are no definitive tests for the physical element in attempts, relaxing the fault element may be 'dangerous': *Howard's Criminal Law* (5th edn, Sydney: The Law Book Company Limited, 1990) pp 388–9.

The English Law Commission recommended in 1973 that there be a difference in the fault elements for attempted result crimes and attempted crimes involving circumstances: Working Paper No 50, *Codification of the Criminal Law, General Principles: Inchoate Offences: Conspiracy, Attempt and Incitement* (London: HMSO, 1973) pp 59–61. This recommendation was based on the difference in the focal point for the harm involved in these two different types of offences. For result crimes, it is the specific intention that is seen as the source of potential criminal harm. The focus is on the accused's state of mind. In comparison, with crimes that involve circumstances as a physical element, it is not so much the state of mind of the accused, but the existence or non-existence of specific circumstances that makes the conduct harmful. For example, in rape, what is harmful is intentional sexual intercourse *without consent*. That remains harmful regardless of whether or not the accused knew the other person was not consenting or was reckless as to consent.

This is a fine distinction between the two types of crimes, but one that can be justified in terms of policy. For example, Andrew Ashworth points out in *Principles of Criminal Law* (3rd edn, Oxford: Oxford University Press, 1999) pp 464–5, that if 'two men set out to have sexual intercourse with two women, not caring whether they consent or not, it would be absurd if the one who achieved penetration was convicted of rape, while the other, who failed to achieve penetration despite trying, was not even liable for attempted rape'. It would seem that this 'absurdity' should provide a policy exception to the general principle that only intention should suffice.

Conspiracy

Background

Between October 1991 and December 1992, John Walsh worked out a plan with three others to induce the Nauru Phosphate Royalties Trust to put money into a purported investment scheme. In fact the investment scheme was a method for channelling part of the money to Walsh and the three men for their own use and benefit. More than US$60 million was 'invested' by the trust. It was able to recover US$50 million, but the rest was lost and Walsh was found with US$838,400. Walsh claimed that he believed the investment was genuine and that he was entitled to the money he obtained. He admitted that there was a conspiracy by the three others to defraud the trust, but that he had not been a party to it. The trial lasted for ninety-nine days and the judge's charge to the jury took seven days to complete. The jury did not believe Walsh and he was convicted of one count of the common law offence of conspiracy to defraud.

There was also evidence that Walsh had made at least twenty-three false documents with the intent of impeding and frustrating a police investigation and he attempted to persuade two other men who managed the trust to provide false information to the police. He was also convicted of three counts of perverting the course of public justice in relation to these matters.

The Supreme Court of Victoria dismissed an application for leave to appeal against conviction and sentence: *Walsh* (2002) 131 A Crim R 299.

Conspiracy to defraud forms one sub-category of conspiracy in general. It has been used in a number of high profile tax and corporations law cases and it extends beyond agreements to commit *criminal offences* into agreements to inflict economic loss on another, to endanger the economic interests of another and to influence the exercise of public duty. It includes dishonest conduct that would not be criminal if committed by an individual.

The MCCOC has pointed out that conspiracy to defraud 'supplies an important weapon in the prosecution armoury against major crimes of dishonesty': *Chapter 3, Conspiracy to Defraud*, Final Report (May 1997) p 26. Conspiracy in general also forms an important part of the 'prosecution armoury' because it does not require conduct that is proximate to the completion of the substantive offence. In this area, perhaps more so than with attempts, there is a need to provide a balance between enabling convictions for preliminary plans to commit crimes and preventing possible abuse of this offence if there are too few limitations in its scope.

The first statutory reference in England to the crime of conspiracy dates back to the thirteenth century to the reign of Edward I. James Wallace Bryan in his book on the development of the law of conspiracy refers to the first Ordinance of Conspirators, anno 21 Edward 1, as providing a remedy against 'conspirators, inventors and maintainers of false quarrels and their abettors and supporters...and brokers of debates': JW Bryan, *The Development of the English Law of Conspiracy* (New York: Da Capo Press, 1970) p 9. Its non-statutory origins may, however, be much older.

In its early years of development, the law relating to conspiracy required there to be some act that followed the agreement: JW Bryan, *The Development of the English Law of Conspiracy* (New York: Da Capo Press, 1970) p 14. By the early seventeenth century, the law had altered to the more modern conception of simply requiring an agreement to be established. In the *Poulterers' Case* (1611) 9 Co Rep 55b; 77 ER 813, the Court of Star Chamber held that mere agreement was enough to constitute the offence. Francis Bowes Sayre writes that after the abolition of the Star Chamber, the Court of Kings Bench 'began to extend the offense so as to cover combinations to commit all crimes of whatsoever nature, misdemeanours as well as felonies': FB Sayre, 'Criminal Conspiracy' (1922) 35 *Harvard Law Review* 393–427 at 400.

Conspiracy was subsequently broadened at common law to include a number of heads such as conspiracy to commit a crime, conspiracy to defraud, conspiracy to pervert the course of justice and conspiracy to corrupt public morals. Until the decision in *Director of Public Prosecutions v Withers* [1975] AC 842, which restricted the development of conspiracy, it seemed that this offence had the potential for continuous expansion. The House of Lords in *Withers* made it clear that only Parliament and not the courts can add new heads to the offence of conspiracy.

A number of rationales has been proffered as to why an agreement to commit a crime should be punished. The first is that, as with the other inchoate offences, conspiracy serves a crime-prevention function. It is also seen as a useful way of supplementing the law of attempt in this regard. For example, Lord Tucker stated in *Board of Trade v Owen* [1957] AC 602 at 626: '[I]t seems to me that the whole object of making such agreements punishable is to prevent the commission of the substantive offence before it has even reached the stage of an attempt, and that is all part and parcel of the preservation of the Queen's peace within that realm.'

Ian Dennis points out that this rationale is insufficient. He writes that '[b]y itself, it does not explain what it is about an *agreement* that permits the law to step in to prevent crime where it could not do so without such agreement': 'The Rationale of Criminal Conspiracy' (1977) 93 *The Law Quarterly Review* 39–64 at 41.

Some social psychology research suggests that people in groups will conform to normative pressure: GM Vaughan and MA Hogg, *Introduction to Social Psychology* (2nd edn, Sydney: Prentice Hall Australia Pty Ltd, 1998) pp 142 ff. An anonymous piece entitled 'Developments in the Law—Criminal Conspiracy' (1959) 72 *Harvard Law Review* 920–1008 at 924 follows this social science suggestion in arguing that it is necessary to intervene to prevent a crime occurring at such an early stage because members of a group will be more likely to go ahead with a crime than an individual given time to consider the implications. On the other hand, Robert Hazell argues that the larger the number of people involved, the more likely the agreement will be leaked and dissension likely to grow: *Conspiracy and Civil Liberties* (London: Bell, 1974) p 94.

Perhaps a stronger rationale is the notion that the offence of conspiracy is 'a vital legal weapon in the prosecution of "organized crime," however defined': PE Johnson, 'The Unnecessary Crime of Conspiracy' (1973) 61(5) *California Law Review* 1137–88. Lord Bramwell stated in *Mogul Steamship Company v McGregor, Gow & Co* [1892] AC 25 at 45:

> It has been objected by capable persons, that it is strange that that should be unlawful if done by several which is not if done by one…I think there is an obvious answer, indeed two; one is, that a man [or woman] may encounter the acts of a single person, yet not be fairly matched against several. The other is, that the act when done by an individual is wrong though not punishable, because the law avoids the multiplicity of crimes…while if done by several it is sufficiently important to be treated as a crime.

In practice, conspiracy functions differently from its rationale as an inchoate offence. Usually some overt acts following the agreement have taken place before conspiracy is charged. This is because it may be difficult for the prosecution to prove what occurred in a private meeting between conspirators.

Phillip Johnson argues that conspiracy is more than an inchoate offence because it invokes several procedural and evidential doctrines: 'The Unnecessary Crime of Conspiracy' (1973) 61(5) *California Law Review* 1137–88 at 1139. For instance, there are certain evidential rules that are specific to conspiracy. The statements of one co-conspirator, for example, are admissible in evidence against another where there is other reasonable evidence of the participation of the latter: *Ahern v The Queen* (1988) 165 CLR 87; *R v Masters* (1992) 26 NSWLR 450. In *Walsh's* case outlined above, two of the accused's co-conspirators were called to give evidence and in the course of doing so, they gave evidence that they had pleaded guilty to conspiracy to defraud. The admissibility of such evidence is an exception to the general rule that admissions of one accused cannot be admitted in evidence: B Hocking, 'Commentary on *Dellapatrona and Duffield*' (1995) 19 Crim LJ 164–71.

Phillip Johnson argues that the crime of conspiracy should be abolished: 'The Unnecessary Crime of Conspiracy' (1973) 61(5) *California Law Review* 1137–88. His views will be canvassed in the Critique section following an outline of the physical elements of conspiracy.

The current law—physical elements

New South Wales and South Australia rely on the common law to criminalise conspiracy. Willes J in *Mulcahy v The Queen* (1868) LR 3 HL 306 at 317 set out the following definition: 'A conspiracy consists not merely in the intention of two or more, but in the agreement of two or more to do an unlawful act, or to do a lawful act by unlawful means.'

The first part of this definition subsumes the second. An agreement to use unlawful means is in itself an agreement to do an unlawful act. This definition therefore appears to be setting out two ways of saying the same thing. It has been endorsed in Australia by Blair CJ in *R v Campbell* [1933] St R Qd 123 at 133 and by Brennan and Toohey JJ in *R v Rogerson* (1992) 174 CLR 268 at 281.

In the other jurisdictions, legislative provisions have established liability for conspiracy to commit certain crimes: *Criminal Code* (ACT) s 48; *Criminal Code* (NT) ss 282–289; *Criminal Code* (Qld) ss 541–543; *Criminal Code* (Tas) s 297; *Criminal Code* (WA) ss 558, 560. Only Victoria and the Commonwealth have attempted to legislatively define the scope of conspiracy: *Crimes Act* 1958 (Vic) s 321; *Crimes Act* 1914 (Cth) s 86. The common law is still relevant in the other jurisdictions, including the Code jurisdictions, in determining what constitutes conspiracy.

In an attempt to limit charges for conspiracy, certain jurisdictions have statutory provisions preventing the commencement of proceedings without the consent of a person such as the Director of Public Prosecutions or Attorney-General: *Crimes Act* 1914 (Cth) s 86(9); *Crimes Act* 1958 (Vic) s 321(4); *Criminal Code* (Qld) ss 541(2), 542(2), 543(2). This provides a rare example of control over prosecutorial discretion, in this case, because of the recognition of the risks and attraction of conspiracy charges for prosecutors.

At common law, the physical elements of conspiracy consist of:
- an agreement
- between two or more persons
- to commit an unlawful act.

The fault element, which will be dealt with in a later section, is an intention to commit the unlawful act. The Victorian and Commonwealth provisions are stated in similar terms.

In practice, conspiracy to commit crimes, conspiracy to defraud and conspiracy to pervert the course of justice are the usual forms of conspiracy charged in Australia.

We introduced the section on conspiracy with a brief overview of *Walsh*'s case in which the accused was charged with conspiracy to defraud. The common law offence of conspiracy to defraud is well established: *Scott v Metropolitan Police Commissioner* [1975] AC 819; *R v Hersington* [1983] 2 NSWLR 72; *R v Walsh and Harney* [1984] VR 474; *Wai Yu-tsang v The Queen* [1992] 1 AC 269; *R v Battisti and Wilson* unreported, 13 September 1995, NSW CCA, 60284/9.

Section 321F(2) of the *Crimes Act* 1958 (Vic) retains this head of the common law and there are statutory provisions in the Northern Territory, Queensland and Tasmania setting out this offence: *Criminal Code* (NT) s 284; *Criminal Code* (Qld) s 430; *Criminal Code* (Tas) s 297(1)(d). The common feature of these provisions and the offence at common law is that liability is extended to fraudulent acts that do not involve theft or any other crime. Conspiracy to defraud does not exist as a statutory offence at the Commonwealth level or in Western Australia. Instead, s 409 of the *Criminal Code* (WA) makes it an offence for a person with intent to defraud, by deceit or any fraudulent means to gain property or any benefit pecuniary or otherwise. There need be no agreement as one person may be punished under this provision.

The word 'defraud' raises the question as to whether or not the prosecution has to prove dishonesty. The majority of members of the High Court in *Peters v The Queen* (1998) 192 CLR 493 have held that dishonesty is not a separate element of conspiracy to defraud, but is descriptive of the means used in order to achieve the design of the conspiracy. This is taken up in the ensuing section on the fault element for conspiracy to defraud, and *Peters*'s case was also explored in Chapter 6.

Conspiracy to defraud is not confined to causing economic loss. In *Allsop* (1976) 64 Cr App R 29, the accused was a sub-broker for the victim, a hire-purchase finance company. The accused agreed with others to enter false particulars on the hire-purchase application forms so that the company would enter agreements with purchasers whom they would otherwise have rejected. The accused expected that the company would suffer no economic loss because the creditors would maintain payments. The Court of Appeal upheld the accused's conviction for conspiracy to defraud on the basis that the hire-purchase company was being induced into taking a financial or economic risk that it would not have taken but for the false particulars. It was no excuse that the accused believed the company would suffer no loss: See also *R v McGrath and Simonidis* [1983] 2 Qd R 54; (1983) 8 A Crim R 316; *Wau Yu-tsang v The Queen* [1992] 1 AC 269.

Conspiracy to pervert the course of justice is another related offence at common law: *R v Grimes* [1968] 3 All ER 179; *R v Baba* [1977] 2 NSWLR 502; *R v Murphy* (1985) 158 CLR 596; *R v Rogerson* (1992) 174 CLR 268. It also exists in statutory form at the Commonwealth level and in the Code jurisdictions: *Crimes Act* 1914 (Cth) s 42; *Criminal Code* (NT) s 286; *Criminal Code* (Qld) s 132; *Criminal Code* (Tas) s 297(1)(2); *Criminal Code* (WA) s 135. Interestingly, s 321F(1) of the *Crimes Act* 1958 (Vic) appears to abolish this head of conspiracy. In New South Wales the common law offence has been abolished: *Crimes Act* 1900 (NSW) s 341 as amended by the *Crimes (Public Justice) Amendment Act* 1990. In its place, s 319 creates an offence of doing an act with the intention of perverting the course of justice and s 342 confirms that a person may be charged with conspiracy to commit this offence.

The rationale for retaining conspiracy to pervert the course of justice lies in the policy that 'the purity and integrity of the course of justice' needs to be maintained: *R v Baba* [1977] 2 NSWLR 502 at 504 per Street J. Its ambit is very broad. In *R v Rogerson*

(1992) 174 CLR 268, the High Court held that there could even be a conspiracy to pervert the course of justice where no relevant police investigation had commenced or judicial proceedings contemplated. There is also some authority that conspiracy to pervert the course of justice may apply to decisions after sentence. In *R v Machirus* [1996] 6 NZLR 404, the New Zealand Court of Appeal held that conspiracy to pervert the course of justice encompassed an agreement to try to affect by deceit the decision of the Parole Board. Jeremy Finn writes that this case significantly extends the scope of the offence in New Zealand, 'not merely by extending the "course of justice" to include events occurring after sentence has been imposed, but in determining that the offending conduct need not be concerned with proceedings that are judicial in character': 'Case and Comment: *Machirus*' [1997] 21 Crim LJ 51–3 at 52.

Both conspiracy to defraud and conspiracy to pervert the course of justice build upon the foundations of conspiracy at common law. We now turn to examining each of the physical elements of conspiracy in general.

The agreement

As with the law relating to attempts, the traditional division of a crime into physical and fault elements does not fit well with the notion of a conspiracy. The requirement for an agreement between two or more persons may be difficult to separate out from the requirement that there be an intention to commit an unlawful act. Matthew Goode states in *Criminal Conspiracy in Canada* (Toronto: Carswell, 1975) p 16: '[T]he concept of actus reus is an elusive one, particularly in the area of criminal conspiracy; so much so, in fact, that it may well be possible to say that the crime has no distinguishing mental and physical elements.'

Cussen J stated in *R v Orton* [1922] VLR 469 at 473 that an agreement for the purposes of conspiracy is satisfied where there is a 'conscious understanding of a common design'. There is no liability where a person is merely talking about the *possibility* of committing an unlawful act, unless they have reached the stage of agreeing to do that act. The courts distinguish between cases where the parties have *agreed to do something* and where the parties are *merely negotiating*.

Lord Parker CJ in *Mills* (1963) 47 Cr App R 49 held that determining whether the parties are merely negotiating or whether they have reached an agreement to do something may involve subtle distinctions. He stated at 54:

> [I]t may be that those cases will be decided largely on the form of the reservation. If the reservation is no more than if a policeman is not there, it would be impossible to say there had not been an agreement. On the other hand, if the matters left outstanding and reserved are of a sufficiently substantial nature, it may well be that the case will fall on the other side of the fence, and it will be said that the matter is merely a matter of negotiation.

If there is an agreement, the crime of conspiracy has been committed: *R v Gunn* (1930) 30 SR(NSW) 336 at 338. It is sufficient if there is evidence from which it may be inferred that two or more persons are pursuing the same unlawful purpose and doing so in combination.

Section 86(3)(c) of the *Crimes Act* 1914 (Cth) now requires that one party must have committed an overt act pursuant to the agreement and, in practice, evidence of overt acts will certainly aid the prosecution's case. One example where the prosecution case failed due to lack of evidence of overt acts is the English case of *O'Brien* (1974) 59 Cr App R 222. The accused was charged with conspiring to release two of the 'Luton Three' from Bedford Prison and the other member from Winson Green Prison. The members of the 'Luton Three'—Campbell, Mealey and Sheridan—had been jailed for robbery. It was alleged that they had robbed a bank to gain proceeds for their support of Irish nationalism.

The evidence upon which the prosecution proceeded was that the accused was found taking photographs outside the Winson Green Prison. A search of his house in Luton found literature of a kind that might be associated with those supporting the cause of Irish nationalism. There were annotated maps of Bedford and the prison, and a drawing that may have been some crude attempt to prepare a plan of the interior of Bedford Prison. The Court of Appeal held that there was insufficient evidence to entitle the jury to draw the inference that the accused had agreed *with others* to break into prison. The evidence at the most showed that he had been formulating a plan himself.

Except at the federal level, once the agreement has been made, a subsequent change of mind or withdrawal from the agreement does not make a difference: *R v Aspinall* (1876) 2 QBD 48. Section 86 (6) of the *Crimes Act* 1914 (Cth) states:

> A person cannot be found guilty of conspiracy to commit an offence if, before the commission of an overt act pursuant to the agreement, the person:
> (a) withdrew from the agreement; and
> (b) took all reasonable steps to prevent the commission of the offence.

As previously stated, s 86(3)(c) of the *Crimes Act* 1914 (Cth) requires evidence of the commission of an overt act. This explains why a withdrawal may be allowed.

It is not necessary that all the parties to the agreement should have been in communication with each other, provided they entertained a common design communicated at least to one other party, expressly or tacitly, in relation to the object of the conspiracy: *Gerakiteys v The Queen* (1984) 153 CLR 317; *Lee* (1994) 76 A Crim R 271; *R v Griffiths* [1966] 1 QB 589 at 597 per Paull J for the Court; *R v Chrastny (No 1)* [1991] 1 WLR 1381.

The prosecution may sometimes be faced with a series of connected but separate conspiracies and therefore may find it difficult to establish a conspiracy with a common design. There is some reason to believe, however, that the courts will take a flexible approach to such a difficulty. For example, in *Meyrick and Ribuffi* (1929) 21 Cr App R 94, the accused were nightclub owners operating unlicensed nightclubs in London's West End. They bribed a police officer to turn a blind eye to the operation of their respective nightclubs. The accused, together with the police officer, were convicted of conspiracy to contravene the provisions of the Licensing Acts and to effect a public mischief by obstructing and corrupting police officers. There was no evidence that the two accused knew each other, or had met each other, or had consulted together.

The Court of Criminal Appeal held that the accused had been rightfully convicted. The Court held that the prosecution need not establish that the individuals were in direct communication with each other, or directly consulting together, but that they entered into an agreement with a common design. On the facts, the 'common design' was to evade the licensing laws. Hewart CJ stated at (101–2):

> [I]t was necessary that the prosecution should establish, not indeed that the individuals were in direct communication with each other, or directly consulting together, but that they entered into an agreement with a common design. Such agreements may be made in various ways. There may be one person…round whom the rest revolve. The metaphor is the metaphor of the centre of the circle and the circumference. There may be a conspiracy of another kind, where the metaphor would be rather that of a chain; A communicates with B, B with C, C with D, and so on to the end of the conspirators. What has to be ascertained is always the same matter: is it true to say…that the acts of the accused were done in pursuance of a criminal purpose held in common between them.

However, the decision in *Meyrick*'s case may be questioned in the light of subsequent cases. For example, in *R v Griffiths* [1966] 1 QB 589, the two accused were convicted of conspiring to defraud a government department by claiming false agricultural subsidies on behalf of farmers. The accused brought each farmer into the conspiracy, but none of the farmers knew one another. The prosecution charged one general conspiracy against the accused and the farmers. The Court of Criminal Appeal held that the evidence disclosed not one general conspiracy, but a number of them. That is, there was one general conspiracy between the two accused and several smaller conspiracies involving the accused and each farmer. The accuseds' appeals against conviction were therefore allowed on the basis that there was no evidence of a conspiracy between all those convicted as opposed to a number of separate conspiracies.

The importance of charging specific conspiracies rather than one general one was apparent in the High Court decision of *Gerakiteys v The Queen* (1984) 153 CLR 317. In this case the first accused, a doctor, was charged with conspiring with the second accused, an insurance agent and nine others (the claimants) to defraud a number of insurance companies. The prosecution case was that the first and second accused had arranged the conspiracy. The different claimants had agreed with the first and second accused to defraud a particular insurance company with whom each claimant was insured. Gibbs J stated at 320:

> The jury in this case could not have found that the applicant and [the insurance agent] and any one or more of the nine claimants were guilty of the conspiracy alleged, because the evidence did not show that the claimant had a common purpose with the applicant and [the insurance agent] to defraud divers insurance companies. Each claimant had only the purpose of defrauding his own insurer. The case resembles *Reg v Griffiths*...[A]ssuming the correctness of the Crown evidence, the claimants were parties to a number of different conspiracies, not to one common conspiracy.

The first accused's conviction was quashed. It is therefore essential for the prosecution to consider whether a general conspiracy has taken place rather than a series of connected but separate conspiracies.

Agreement between two or more persons

The general rule at common law is that the agreement must be between two or more parties: *Gerakiteys v The Queen* (1984) 153 CLR 317 at 334 per Deane J; *R v Alley; Ex parte Mundell* (1886) 12 VLR 13; *Phillips* (1987) 86 Cr App R 18. There are two major exceptions to it.

First, at common law and under statute in Queensland and Tasmania, a husband and wife cannot be criminally responsible for a conspiracy between themselves alone: *DPP v Blady* [1912] 2 KB 89; *R v McKechie* [1926] NZLR 1; *Kowbel v The Queen* [1954] 4 DLR 337; *Mawji v The Queen* [1957] AC 126; *Criminal Code* (Qld) s 33; *Criminal Code* (Tas) s 297(2). This rule has been abolished in the Northern Territory and Western Australia and for conspiracy to commit murder or treason in Victoria: *Criminal Code* (NT) s 291; *Criminal Code Amendment Act (No 2)* 1987 (WA) s 6.; *Crimes Act* 1958 (Vic) s 339(1). The rationale for this rule is that historically, a husband and wife have been viewed in law as forming one personality. This is of course highly questionable today and remains an anomaly in those jurisdictions where the rule has not been abolished.

Secondly, it has been held that a corporation cannot be liable for conspiracy with a person who is acting as its 'directing mind and will': *R v McDonnell* [1966] 1 QB 233. This rule echoes the problems associated with holding a corporation criminally responsible that were explored in Chapters 1 and 3. The rule has been abolished at the federal level: *Crimes Act* 1914 (Cth) s 86(4)(b). If a company director conspires with other persons in the course of company business, then criminal liability will exist: *R v ICR Haulage Ltd* [1944] KB 551.

The general rule is that one party to a conspiracy can still be found liable even where the other party is exempt from liability or is acquitted or is an undercover agent. For example, in *R v Duguid* (1906) 94 LT 887, the accused agreed with a child's mother, to take the child from the possession of her lawful guardian. The child's mother could not herself be convicted of child stealing as the *Offences Against the Person Act* 1861 (UK) exempted parents who took their own children. It was held that the mother's exemption from liability was no bar to the accused being convicted for conspiracy. This common law rule has been legislatively enacted in the Northern Territory for cases of conspiracy where the other person lacks the capacity to commit the substantive offence: *Criminal Code* (NT) s 292(e).

This rule reflects the Australian laws relating to primary liability in the area of complicity and the doctrine of acting in concert. In Chapter 9, we will explore how a person who has assisted or encouraged a crime pursuant to a preconceived plan or who is considered a joint principal offender will still be held liable if the perpetrator is exempt from prosecution or where a defence is available to the perpetrator.

In *Gerakiteys v The Queen* (1984) 153 CLR 317, Deane J stated at 334: '[A]s a matter of common law principle, an accused may be convicted of conspiring "with a person or persons unknown" to commit an unlawful act.'

In *R v Sayers* [1943] SASR 146 it was held that one person could be convicted of conspiracy even where the other person was within the jurisdiction and was not charged. This ruling also covers those situations where one party has been given immunity from prosecution in exchange for giving evidence against the other: see also *Criminal Code* (NT) s 292.

But what if the other person has in fact been acquitted of conspiracy? In *R v Darby* (1982) 148 CLR 668, the accused and another man called Thomas were tried together on a charge of conspiring to rob. Both were found guilty, but Thomas successfully appealed to the Supreme Court of Victoria, which quashed his conviction and ordered that a verdict and judgment of acquittal be entered. The accused Darby subsequently argued before the High Court that the essence of conspiracy was an agreement of minds and therefore the effect of an acquittal of one party is to deny the very existence of the conspiracy itself.

This argument was rejected by a majority of the High Court. Gibbs CJ, Aickin, Wilson and Brennan JJ (at 677) referred to Lord Salmon's observations in *DPP v Shannon* [1975] AC 717. They quoted Lord Salmon's statement (at 772): 'A verdict of not guilty may mean the jury is certain that the accused is innocent, or it may mean that, although the evidence arouses considerable suspicion, it is insufficient to convince the jury of the accused's guilt beyond reasonable doubt…The only effect of an acquittal, in law, is that the accused can never again be brought before a criminal court and tried for the same offence.'

The majority of the High Court explained that the phenomenon of inconsistent verdicts in joint trials for conspiracy resulted from the jury's obligation to consider separately the guilt of the two accused on the basis of the evidence admissible against each. Gibbs CJ, Aickin, Wilson and Brennan JJ declared the common law of Australia as follows (at 678):

[T]he conviction of a conspirator whether tried together with or separately from an alleged co-conspirator may stand notwithstanding that the latter is or may be acquitted unless in all circumstances of the case his [or her] conviction is inconsistent with acquittal of the other person. In our opinion such a determination will focus upon the justice of the case rather than upon the technical obscurities that now confound this subject.

This rule is now found in statutory form in s 321B of the *Crimes Act* 1958 (Vic) and s 86(5)(a) of the *Crimes Act* 1914 (Cth). Section 292 (d) of the *Criminal Code* (NT) simply states that it is not a defence that the person with whom the accused is alleged to have conspired has been acquitted.

In *Yip Chiu-Cheung v The Queen* [1995] 1 AC 111, the Privy Council held that an accused may be convicted of conspiracy even where the other person was an undercover drug enforcement agent. In that case, the accused was convicted in Hong Kong of conspiracy to traffic in heroin. He had agreed with another man, Needham, to take five kilograms of heroin from Hong Kong to Australia. Needham was in fact an American undercover drug enforcement agent. The plan was that Needham would fly to Hong Kong, pick up the heroin and fly to Australia. Needham had kept the authorities in Hong Kong and Australia informed of the plans and they agreed that he would not be prevented from carrying the heroin to Australia, with the aim of identifying both the suppliers and distributors of the drug. In fact, Needham's original flight to Hong Kong was delayed and he missed the rescheduled flight. The accused was arrested at Hong Kong airport and admitted that he was there to meet Needham.

The accused argued on appeal to the Privy Council that he should not have been convicted of conspiracy as Needham was not a co-conspirator because he lacked the fault element for the crime. Lord Griffiths in delivering the judgment of the Privy Council held that Needham had in fact the intention to commit the criminal offence of trafficking and therefore could be regarded as a co-conspirator. Lord Griffiths stated (at 118): 'Naturally, Needham never expected to be prosecuted if he carried out the plan as intended. But the fact that in such circumstances the authorities would not prosecute the undercover agent does not mean that he did not commit the crime albeit as part of a wider scheme to combat drug dealing.'

Lord Griffiths distinguished the facts from the situation where the undercover agent has no intention to commit the offence but pretends to join a conspiracy in order to gain information that would frustrate it. In the latter case, there would be no conspiracy.

These cases therefore show that the courts are prepared to hold one party to a conspiracy criminally liable even where the co-conspirator is exempt from liability or acquitted.

The unlawful act

Historically at common law, the definition of an 'unlawful act' has been broadly interpreted to include not only crimes, but also agreements to defraud, to commit a tort with intent to cause injury, to corrupt public morals, to commit a public mischief, and to pervert the course of justice. In 1976, the Law Commission recommended that conspiracy be restricted to agreements to commit criminal offences: Law Commission, *Criminal Law: Report on Conspiracy and Criminal Law Reform*, Report No 76, (London: HMSO, 1976). As a consequence, the *Criminal Law Act* 1977 (UK) was enacted. Part I of the Act created a statutory offence of conspiracy limited to committing one or more criminal offences. However, conspiracy to defraud and conspiracy to corrupt public morals remain offences at common law in England.

As mentioned earlier, in practice, conspiracy to defraud, conspiracy to commit crimes and conspiracy to pervert the course of justice are the usual forms of conspiracy charged in Australia. In Victoria, s 321(1) of the *Crimes Act* 1958 confirms this limitation. While most of the legislative provisions deal with conspiracies to commit offences in general, there also exist legislative provisions specifying the crime such as conspiracy to commit murder: *Criminal Code* (NT) s 287; *Criminal Code* (Qld) s 309.

Critique

The offence of conspiracy has been criticised for being overly broad and having the potential for abuse. During the 1960s in England, the courts were criticised for judicial law-making in relation to conspiracy. In *Shaw v DPP* [1962] AC 220, the accused published *The Ladies' Directory*, which advertised the names and addresses of prostitutes and the sexual acts they were willing to practise. He was convicted of conspiracy to corrupt public morals.

On appeal to the House of Lords, the accused argued that he should only be convicted of conspiracy to commit a crime and that corrupting public morals was not an established crime. The House of Lords upheld the accused's conviction on the basis that conspiracy to corrupt public morals was an independent offence in itself. They did not decide as to whether there was a substantive offence of corrupting public morals.

Lord Reid in dissent saw the majority as inventing an offence. He stated (at 275):

> [T]here are wide differences of opinion today as to how far the law ought to punish immoral acts which are not done in the face of the public. Some think that the law already goes too far, some that it does not go far enough. Parliament is the proper place...to settle that. When there is sufficient support from public opinion, Parliament does not hesitate to intervene. Where Parliament fears to tread it is not for the courts to rush in.

The decision in *Shaw*'s case was affirmed by majority in the later House of Lords case *Knuller (Publishing & Printing Promotions) Ltd v DPP* [1973] AC 435. In that case, the accused had agreed to publish advertisements to facilitate homosexual acts. At the time, homosexual acts conducted in private between adult men were no longer considered criminal. Nevertheless, the House of Lords upheld the accused's conviction for conspiracy to 'outrage public decency'.

The extension of conspiracy into the realms of immoral or antisocial behaviour was put to an end by the House of Lords in *DPP v Withers* [1975] AC 842. In that case, the Court quashed convictions of conspiracy 'to effect a public mischief' on the basis that no such general offence was known at law. It was of the view that criminal conspiracy should not be extended any further than what was already established. This provided a forerunner to the recommendations of the Law Commission's Report No 76 on *Conspiracy and Criminal Law Reform*. The subsequent *Criminal Law Act* 1977 (UK) created a statutory offence of conspiracy, but did not completely abolish the existing common law heads. Thus *Shaw*'s case and *Knuller*'s case still remain authorities in England for conspiracy to corrupt public morals and outrage public decency.

Interestingly, these two cases have never been followed in Australia. In *R v Cahill* [1978] 2 NSWLR 453, an argument was run that the agreements of three Chinese men and three Australian women to marry in order to increase the chances of permanent residency for the men were offensive to public morality. Street CJ made it clear that only Parliament should create new offences involving matters of public morality. He stated (at 455): '[R]eligious precepts do not in this country affect the application of the ordinary criminal law unless and until such precepts find expression through a validly made law of the Commonwealth or State.'

Section 321F(1) of the *Crimes Act* 1958 (Vic) also makes it clear that conspiracy to corrupt public morals or to outrage public decency are not offences in that state. In relation to the ability of the courts to make new offences, McHugh J stated categorically in *R v Rogerson* (1992) 174 CLR 268 at 305 that they 'are no longer able to create criminal offences'.

Phillip Johnson has taken the most radical perspective in arguing that the offence should be abolished: 'The Unnecessary Crime of Conspiracy' (1973) 61(5) *California Law Review* 1137–88. He argues (at 1140) that the essential problem lies with the use of 'a single abstract concept to decide numerous questions that deserve separate consideration in light of the various interests and policies they involve'. Johnson argues (at 1164) that conspiracy adds overly broad criminal liability to attempt provisions and therefore should be abolished. In *Chapters 1 and 2, General Principles of Criminal Responsibility*, Final Report (December 1992), the Criminal Law Officers Committee (CLOC) did consider the possibility of abolishing conspiracy, but dismissed it because of its long history and general acceptance at common law.

In contrast to Johnson's approach, Ian Dennis argues for a reformulated view of conspiracy based on its only adequate rationale—namely, viewing conspiracy as a criminal partnership: (1977) 93 *The Criminal Law Quarterly* 39–64. He quotes (at 51) Holmes J's version of conspiracy in *US v Kissel* 218 US 601 (1910) at 608: 'A conspiracy is constituted by an agreement, it is true, but it is the result of the agreement, rather than the agreement itself, just as a partnership, although constituted by a contract, is not the contract, but is a result of it. The contract is instantaneous, the partnership may endure as one and the same partnership for years. A conspiracy is a partnership in criminal purposes.'

Given that it seems overly optimistic for law reformers to advocate abolishing the inchoate offence of conspiracy, it seems more practical to concentrate on how best to limit the scope of the offence. The Review Committee of Commonwealth Criminal Law in its Interim Report, *Principles of Criminal Responsibility and Other Matters* (July 1990) stated (at 361):

> Conspiracy is a crime which is regarded by many criminal lawyers with suspicion and distaste, not only because of the wide and imprecise scope of the offence itself, but also because the evidentiary rules peculiarly applicable to the offence may cause unfairness in particular cases. However, all the submissions received by the Review Committee express the opinion that the offence of conspiracy is one that must be retained, although one submission, that of the New South Wales Bar Association, reached this conclusion with reluctance. The Review Committee has no doubt that conspiracy should be retained in the law of the Commonwealth as an offence.

Major law reform efforts in Australia have thus concentrated on reformulating conspiracy rather than abolishing it.

For example, s 86(3)(c) of the *Crimes Act* 1914 (Cth) now requires that one party must have committed an overt act; a mere agreement to commit a crime is not enough. The CLOC recommended this approach in its *Chapters 1 and 2, General Principles of Criminal Responsibility*, Final Report (December 1992). Section 11.5(2) of the *Criminal Code* (Cth) now reads:

> (2) For the person to be guilty:
> (a) the person must have entered into an agreement with one or more other persons; and
> (b) the person and at least one other party to the agreement must have intended that an offence would be committed pursuant to the agreement; and
> (c) the person or at least one other party to the agreement must have committed an overt act pursuant to the agreement.

The CLOC further agreed (at 101) that it was impossible to resist the conclusion that there should be a defence of withdrawal or disassociation, for there would be time between the agreement and the commission of the overt act for that to take place.

The requirement for there to be an overt act as well as an agreement appears at first glance to limit the scope of conspiracy. However, Phillip Johnson points out that in jurisdictions that have this added requirement, '[p]ractically any act will do, including seemingly innocent conduct that carries the conspiracy no closer to accomplishing its object than the agreement itself': 'The Unnecessary Crime of Conspiracy' (1973) 61(5) *California Law Review* 1137–88 at 1142–3.

Moving on to more conceptual matters, there have been concerns about the general rule that if a co-conspirator is acquitted, the other co-conspirator may still be found guilty. The majority of the High Court in *R v Darby* (1982) 148 CLR 668 in finding that an acquittal was no bar to a conviction for another co-conspirator, were influenced by s 5(8) of the *Criminal Law Act* 1977 (Eng). This provides that the acquittal of all the other parties is not a ground for quashing the conviction of the person accused of conspiring with them 'unless under all the circumstances of the case his [or her] conviction is inconsistent with the acquittal of the other person or persons'. Gibbs CJ, Aickin, Wilson and Brennan JJ (at 678) encouraged the practice of separate trials where the evidence against one party was significantly different from the evidence against the other.

There was a very strong dissent from Murphy J, affirming the old common law position that had been set out in *Dharmasena v The King* [1951] AC 1. In that case, the Privy Council held that the acquittal of one co-conspirator necessitated the acquittal of the other because one person alone cannot commit a conspiracy. Murphy J argued in *R v Darby* (1982) 148 CLR 668 at 683 that the members of the majority were degrading the effect of an acquittal:

> In Australia there are no degrees of acquittal. As between the State and the accused, either every judgment of acquittal is conclusive of evidence or none is. The doctrine that acquittal does not mean innocence is unacceptable in a free society.
>
> It is irrelevant that persons may hold private reservations about the acquitted person's innocence. It is irrelevant that remedies may be available in tort or other branches of private law arising out of the conduct of the acquitted person. The relationship between the State and the accused is not to be assimilated to private law relations.

The High Court's ruling in *Darby*'s case has been subsequently followed in *R v Brown* [1990] VR 820, *Catalano* (1992) 61 A Crim R 323 and *R v Rogerson* (1992) 174 CLR 268. Nevertheless, Peter Sallmann and John Willis argue that the majority decision in *Darby*'s case is 'indubitably wrong': 'Editorial: Criminal Conspiracy: Takes One to Tango?' (1982) 15 *Aust and NZ Journal of Criminology* 129–30 at 130. Primary liability for complicity whereby differing verdicts may be reached can be differentiated from conspiracy because in the former, a criminal act has occurred. As Sallmann and Willis emphasise, the essence of conspiracy is an *agreement* rather than criminal conduct in itself. To try one accused for conspiracy when the other accused has been acquitted makes a mockery of the acquittal process. If one of the main rationales for conspiracy is to deal with dangerous criminal groups, then it does appear anomalous to hold one person guilty where the co-conspirator has been acquitted.

Another question related to the scope of conspiracy is whether or not there should be a separate offence of conspiracy to defraud. This was considered by the MCCOC in its *Chapter 3, Conspiracy to Defraud*, Report (May 1997). The arguments in favour of its abolition (at 25) concerned the breadth of the law allowing conduct to be rendered criminal after the event and the fact that the uncertainty surrounding the issue of dishonesty rendered 'the criminal law applicable to a number of relationships previously thought to be in the realm of civil remedies'. All the submissions received by the MCCOC, however, were in favour of retaining the offence. The MCCOC reached the conclusion that the offence should be retained, stating at 27: '[I]t may not be that conspiracy to defraud is justified on the basis of gaps in the existing law (all of which could be addressed through specific legislation) but on the basis that human ingenuity is such that there is a need to have an offence which can be used in relation to newly-devised gaps. Addressing them with specific legislation after the event may be too late.'

The MCCOC has noted that there is also a substantive offence of perverting the course of justice independent of conspiracy and has recommended that this be codified: *Chapter 7, Administration of Justice Offences*, Report (July 1998) pp 111–19.

Overall then, most of the criticisms of conspiracy have concerned its breadth, and law reform efforts have concentrated on narrowing the scope of its physical elements. We turn now to considering the fault element of this offence.

The current law—fault element

In *Churchill v Walton* [1967] 2 AC 224, the House of Lords held that for conspiracy to be made out, there must be an *intention* to be a party to an agreement to do an unlawful act. This raises the question as to whether or not there simply has to be an intention to be *a party* to the agreement or whether or not there must also be an intention to bring about the unlawful act.

The High Court in *Gerakiteys v The Queen* (1984) 153 CLR 317 held that there must be proof of an intention, shared by all the parties, to commit the unlawful act alleged. As outlined above, in this case, the first accused, a doctor, was charged with conspiring with the second accused, an insurance agent and nine others (the claimants) to defraud a number of insurance companies. Gibbs CJ (at 320), Wilson J (at 323) and Brennan J (at 330) referred to there being a 'common purpose' to commit the offence occurring by implication where two or more persons have agreed to commit an offence.

On the facts, the accused's conviction was quashed as the evidence failed to disclose that there was a common purpose to defraud because the claimants had only the purpose of defrauding their own insurance company.

In *Giorgianni v The Queen* (1985) 156 CLR 473, Wilson, Deane and Dawson JJ stated (at 473): 'There are...offences in which it is not possible to speak of recklessness as constituting a sufficient intent. Attempt is one and conspiracy is another...

Intent is required and it is an intent which must be based upon knowledge or belief of the necessary facts.'

Thus, conspiracy will not be made out where an objective is seen as a probable or possible outcome of carrying out an agreement to achieve some other objective. As with attempts, the high fault standard for conspiracy means that an accused must act with an intention to commit the offence even where it is one of strict liability, negligence or recklessness: *Giorgianni v The Queen* (1985) 156 CLR 473; *Kamara v DPP* [1974] AC 104.

As with conspiracy in general, the fault element for conspiracy to pervert the course of justice requires an intention to achieve the unlawful act. The leading High Court decision dealing with the fault element in conspiracy to pervert the course of justice is that of *R v Rogerson* (1992) 174 CLR 268. Roger Rogerson, a police officer, Morris Nowytarger and Nicholas Paltros had been convicted of conspiracy to pervert the course of justice. The charge arose out of an alleged agreement to fabricate evidence in order to hinder a police investigation into the possible commission of a crime. The New South Wales Court of Appeal set aside the convictions: *R v Rogerson* (1992) 174 CLR 268. The prosecution then applied to the High Court for special leave to appeal, which was granted. The appeal was dismissed in relation to Nowytarger, but allowed for Rogerson and Paltros with orders that the matter be remitted to the Court of Criminal Appeal.

Brennan and Toohey JJ stated (at 281): 'The prosecution [has] to prove that the conspirators intended that, if the relevant act was done pursuant to the conspiracy and in the circumstances contemplated by the conspirators, it would have the effect of perverting the course of justice.'

Mason CJ agreed (at 278) that an intention to achieve the result of perverting the course of justice was necessary. McHugh J went somewhat further (at 311) in stating that the offence requires 'not merely an intention to pervert the course of justice but an agreement to do something which has the tendency to pervert it'. These judgments imply that recklessness will not be sufficient as a fault element.

In the subsequent High Court decision of *Meissner v The Queen* (1995) 184 CLR 132, Brennan and Toohey JJ (at 144) pointed out that an intention to do acts that have the effect of perverting the course of justice may be established even if the conspirator has never heard the expression 'perverting the course of justice'.

The fault element for conspiracy to defraud has proved a little more elusive. It seems relatively settled that the accused must intend to bring about a situation in which there is a risk of economic loss to or an imperilment of the economic interests of another: *R v Karounos* (1994) 63 SASR 451. Alternatively, it must be proved that the accused intended to prejudice another person's performance of public duty. This is broader than an intention to prejudice another person's right or interest in that no economic loss need be intended: *R v Howes* (1971) 2 SASR 293; *Scott v Metropolitan Police Commissioner* [1975] AC 819; *R v Horsington* [1983] 2 NSWLR 72; *R v McGrath and Simonidis* [1983] 2 Qd R 54; *Peters v The Queen* (1998) 192 CLR 493.

There has been some debate as to whether or not dishonesty amounts to a separate fault element. In *Scott v Metropolitan Police Commissioner* [1975] AC 819 at 839, Viscount Dilhorne stated that the word 'defraud' means 'to deprive a person dishonestly of something which is his [or hers]'. This raises the question as to whether or not dishonesty is a state of mind or something that attaches to the physical element of conspiracy to defraud.

In *Peters v The Queen* (1998) 192 CLR 493, the accused was a solicitor who had been retained by his client, a drug trafficker, to launder money through a series of sham mortgage transactions. He was convicted of conspiracy to defraud the Commonwealth Commissioner of Taxation, but was acquitted of a charge of conspiracy to pervert the course of justice on the basis that he did not know his client's source of income and was simply acting as his solicitor.

All the members of the High Court dismissed the accused's appeal against conviction, but on different grounds. Toohey and Gaudron JJ (at 506–7) took the view that it was superfluous to have a separate direction to the jury as to the meaning of dishonesty. Toohey and Gaudron JJ (at 509) stated:

> [T]he offence of conspiracy to defraud involves dishonesty at two levels. First, it involves an agreement to use dishonest means…And quite apart from the use of dishonest means, the offence involves an agreement to bring about a situation prejudicing or imperilling existing legal rights or interests of others. That too, is dishonest by ordinary standards.

They went on to state (at 510):

> [I]t will ordinarily be sufficient to instruct the jury as to the facts they must find if the agreed means are to be characterised as dishonest. Alternatively, it will be sufficient to instruct them that, if satisfied as to those facts, they will be satisfied that the agreed means were dishonest. Only in the borderline case will it be necessary for the question whether the means are to be so characterised to be left to the jury.

In those borderline cases, Toohey and Gaudron were of the view that 'dishonesty' is a question of fact to be determined by the jury, applying the current standards of ordinary decent people. This was the test set out in *R v Feely* [1973] QB 530 at 537–8 per Lawton LJ and by Lord Lane CJ in *R v Ghosh* [1982] 1 QB 1053 at 1064. This was discussed in Chapter 6.

McHugh and Gummow JJ went further in holding that dishonesty was not a separate element of conspiracy to defraud and no direction as to dishonesty need be given even in borderline cases. McHugh J (with whom Gummow J agreed) stated (at 527):

> The authors of *Archbold* [*Criminal Pleading, Evidence and Practice* (1996), vol 2, par 17-102] seem to have been voices in the wilderness in robustly maintaining the view that it is 'superfluous' to direct a jury as to dishonesty. In my opinion, how-

ever, the authors of *Archbold* are right. A successful prosecution for conspiracy to defraud does not require proof that the accused knew that he or she was acting dishonestly either in a *Ghosh* sense or a wholly subjective sense.

Kirby J regarded dishonesty as a separate fault element, but in order to provide 'clear instruction to those who have responsibility for conducting criminal trials' (at 556) he withdrew his own opinion and concurred with the views expressed by Toohey and Gaudron JJ that conspiracy involves dishonesty at two levels. In Kirby J's opinion (at 555): 'Dishonesty of its essential nature connotes conscious wrongdoing. It is not dishonesty by the standards of other persons but by the appreciation and understanding of the accused personally.'

It would seem then as a result of *Peters*'s case there must be an intention to use dishonest means to prejudice another person's right, interest or performance of public duty. There is no requirement for dishonesty to be a separate element above and beyond these concepts.

The intention to prejudice another person's right or interest was interpreted in *Scott v Metropolitan Police Commissioner* [1975] AC 819 by Lord Diplock as meaning an intention to cause *economic loss* by depriving the other person of some property or right to which he or she was or might be entitled. This interpretation limits the fault element quite substantially as often those involved in fraud want to make a profit for themselves rather than causing an economic loss to others. Toohey and Gaudron JJ pointed out in *Peters*'s case (at 506–7) that there are difficulties associated with Lord Diplock's approach and stated that the offence of conspiracy to defraud is not limited to an agreement involving an intention to cause economic loss. It is sufficient that the accused intended to bring about a situation in which there is *a risk* of economic loss. This latter approach was taken by the Supreme Court of South Australia in *R v Karounos* (1994) 63 SASR 451. In that case, Olsson J stated at 458: 'If the action embarked upon imperils the economic interest of the victim, that is enough to constitute fraud, even though, in the event, no actual loss may be suffered and loss may not even be intended.'

It would seem then that Lord Diplock's narrow approach to the fault element does not hold sway in Australia.

Critique

The fault element in conspiracy is difficult to divorce from the physical element of an agreement. The word 'agree' in itself seems to indicate a mental state. Viscount Dilhorne remarked in *Churchill v Walton* [1967] 2 AC 224 at 237: 'In cases of this kind, it is desirable to avoid the use of the phrase "mens rea", which is capable of different meanings, and to concentrate on the terms or effect of the agreement made by the alleged conspirators. The question is, "What did they agree to do?".'

The fault element does not sit easily with subjective notions of intention because liability does not depend solely on the accused's state of mind, but also on that of the other parties to the conspiracy.

In England, there is a lower fault standard applied for conspiracy. The House of Lords in *R v Anderson* [1986] AC 27 held that a person is guilty of conspiracy under s 1 of the *Criminal Law Act* 1977 (UK) irrespective of whether he or she intended that the offence would be committed. It is sufficient that the parties agree to embark on a course of conduct, being reckless as to whether or not the offence may occur.

The CLOC recommended that intention must be established and recklessness should not suffice for the offence of conspiracy: *Chapters 1 and 2, General Principles of Criminal Responsibility*, Final Report (December 1992) p 99. At present, s 86(3)(b) of the *Crimes Act* 1914 (Cth) requires that the accused and at least one other party to the agreement must have intended that an offence would be committed pursuant to the agreement. Similarly, s 321(2) of the *Crimes Act* 1958 (Vic) requires that there is an intention that the offence be committed and an intention or belief that any fact or circumstance the existence of which is an element of the offence will exist. Section 11.5(2)(b) of the *Criminal Code* (Cth) also requires an intention that an offence would be committed pursuant to the agreement. The CLOC stated (at 99) that '[t]he concept of recklessness is foreign to an offence based wholly on agreement'.

This approach aids in restricting the scope of conspiracy and should remain the law in Australia. What the law should be in relation to the fault element for conspiracy to defraud is perhaps more complex.

The MCCOC stated in its May 1997 Report on *Conspiracy to Defraud* at 33: 'The fault element of common law conspiracy to defraud is an intent to defraud. As has been seen, this phrase has been interpreted to include within it the concept of dishonesty and an intent to cause a loss, imperil a person's economic interests, or to influence the exercise of a public duty.'

The MCCOC recommended that the Model Criminal Code provision should include a fault element of dishonesty based on the test set out in *R v Feely* [1973] QB 530 at 537–8 per Lawton LJ and by Lord Lane CJ in *R v Ghosh* [1982] 1 QB 1053 at 1064. This was discussed more fully in Chapter 6.

In *Peters v The Queen* (1998) 192 CLR 493, Toohey and Gaudron JJ were highly critical of the MCCOC's recommendation. They took the view that it was superfluous to have a separate fault element of dishonesty because the notion of dishonesty was attached to the agreed means to be used or to the agreement itself. Generally, it is therefore unnecessary for the judge to direct the jury as to the meaning of dishonesty. The decisions in *Peters*'s case as discussed above led to the conclusion that dishonesty is not a separate fault element of conspiracy to defraud. This again shows how what may be considered a fault element overlaps with the physical element of an agreement.

Overall, the current law relating to the fault element of conspiracy in general appears workable despite this overlap. The offence of conspiracy to defraud is perhaps more disturbing because it extends to an agreement to commit an act that is not in itself criminal. Whether or not dishonesty is seen as a separate fault element, conspiracy to defraud remains an overly broad inchoate offence, but one that will undoubtedly continue to exist given the belief that human ingenuity is such that there is a need to have an offence to cover gaps in the law: MCCOC, *Chapter 3, Conspiracy to Defraud*, Report (May 1997) p 27.

We turn now to examine the least used inchoate offence, that of incitement.

Incitement

Background

In 1985, Angelo Dimozantos started a business with Anthony Williams in order to purchase a property on which to conduct a brothel. Over the next four years, the business arrangements became very complicated and resulted in ill feeling developing between the two men and others involved. In 1989, Dimozantos made an appointment to see a man named Sui and asked him whether he could find someone to 'knock off' Williams. Sui said he needed time to think about it. He then asked an acquaintance to tell the police. It was arranged for a police officer, Senior Constable Steven Martin to play the part of a contract hit man. Several conversations took place between Dimozantos and Martin, who had a tape recorder concealed on his body. Dimozantos asked Martin to kill Williams and dispose of his body in a way that could not be found. He offered Martin $10,000.

On 26 September 1989, Martin told Dimozantos that the matter had been dealt with and Dimozantos handed him the money. Dimozantos was arrested shortly afterwards.

On 26 July 1991, the jury found the applicant guilty of incitement to murder. He was sentenced to 12 years' imprisonment with a minimum of 10 years before he could be eligible for parole.

On appeal to the Victorian Court of Criminal Appeal, Dimozantos' counsel argued that for incitement to have been made out, the person incited had to have acted on the inciter's urgings. This argument was rejected as was an application for leave to appeal against sentence: *Dimozantos* (1991) 56 A Crim R 345. A further appeal to the High Court against sentence was upheld on the basis that the sentencing judge and the members of the Court of Criminal Appeal had acted on a mistaken view of the maximum penalty for incitement to murder: *Dimozantos v The Queen* (1992) 174 CLR 504.

The matter was returned to the Court of Criminal Appeal for resentencing. On 17 December 1992, the Court sentenced Dimozantos to nine years' imprisonment with a minimum period of seven years before being eligible for parole. Dimozantos appealed once more to the High Court against sentence, but this appeal was dismissed: *Dimozantos v The Queen (No 2)* (1993) 178 CLR 122.

Dimozantos's case gives an example of this seldom-used inchoate offence. The existence of the offence can be dated back to the case of *R v Higgins* (1801) 2 East 5, where a conviction for inciting a person to steal another person's property was upheld. At common law, incitement to commit any offence is a summary offence and this has been retained in New South Wales and South Australia. Statutory provisions now exist in the Australian Capital Territory, Tasmania, Victoria, Western Australia and at the Commonwealth level: *Criminal Code* (Cth) s 11.4; *Criminal Code* (ACT) s 47; *Criminal Code* (Tas) ss 2, 298; *Crimes Act* 1958 (Vic) ss 321G–321I; *Criminal Code* (WA) ss 1, 553, 555A. In the Northern Territory and Queensland, incitement is not an offence, but there are equivalent provisions of attempting to procure the commission of an offence: *Criminal Code* (NT) s 280; *Criminal Code* (Qld) s 539. The offence of attempted procurement also exists in Western Australia: *Criminal Code* (WA) s 556. For incitement to be made out, there must be conduct amounting to incitement and an intention that the offence be committed. We will first examine the physical element and provide a critique of it before turning to the fault element.

The current law—physical element

Incitement involves seeking to encourage or persuade another person to commit an offence: *Invicta Plastics Ltd v Clare* [1976] Crim LR 131. It can be seen as analogous to accessorial liability, which will be explored in Chapter 9, in the sense that both forms of liability depend upon the doing of an act in furtherance of a crime. Except in the Northern Territory and Queensland, it is an offence to incite another person to commit an offence, even if that offence is not carried out and even if the incitement has no effect on the other person: *R v Higgins* (1801) 2 East 5; *Crimes Act* 1914 (Cth) s 7A(a); *Criminal Code* (ACT) s 47(4); *Criminal Code* (Tas) s 298; *Crimes Act* 1958 (Vic) ss 321G–321I; *Criminal Code* (WA) ss 553, 555A. In comparison, accessorial liability, being a derivative form of liability, is dependent on the commission of the offence.

Liability for incitement exists in relation to all offences, whether indictable or summary. At common law, the inchoate offence of incitement is viewed as a summary offence. In comparison, in Victoria, incitement is an indictable offence and this remains the case even where the offence intended is only a summary one: *Crimes Act* 1958 (Vic) s 321G(1). In Western Australia, there is a graded approach so that there is a higher punishment for inciting an indictable offence and a lower punishment for inciting a 'simple' offence: *Criminal Code* (WA) ss 554, 555A.

Section 1 of the *Criminal Code* (WA) refers to the word 'incite' as encompassing 'solicits and endeavours to persuade' and s 2A(1) of the *Crimes Act* 1958 (Vic) refers to 'incite' as including 'command, request, propose, advise, encourage or authorise'.

The prosecution must prove that there was some form of persuasion or encouragement; a mere intent to commit an offence is insufficient: *R v Chrichton* [1915] SALR 1; *Invicta Plastics Ltd v Clare* [1976] Crim LR 131. As well as positive encouragement, incitement encompasses negative threats or pressure: *Race Relations Board v Applin* [1973] QB 815. The encouragement or persuasion must be communicated to the other person: *R v Krause* (1902) 66 JP 1902. If it fails to be communicated, there may still be liability for attempted incitement: *R v Ransford* (1874) 13 Cox CC 9. The encouragement may be directed towards the world at large rather than a specified person. For example, in *R v Most* (1881) 7 QBD 244, the accused published an article in a London newspaper encouraging readers to kill their Heads of State. The accused was convicted of incitement to murder and this was upheld by the Court for Crown Cases Reserved.

The person incited need not act on the incitement for the physical element to be made out. Providing the accused incited the other person it is irrelevant that the latter is not influenced or unwilling to commit the offence: *R v Higgins* (1801) 2 East 5; *R v Krause* (1902) 66 JP 1902. In Victoria, s 321G(1) of the *Crimes Act* 1958 refers to incitement being an offence 'if the inciting is acted on in accordance with the inciter's intention'. This would seem to substantially narrow the scope of the offence. However, the Victorian Court of Criminal Appeal held in *Dimozantos* (1991) 56 A Crim R 345 at 349 that this section should not be interpreted 'as meaning that the offence is only complete if the person incited takes steps towards doing something that is impossible'. The general rule that the person incited need not act on the incitement therefore also applies to Victoria.

Critique

The CLOC has suggested that the word 'urges' should be used in preference to 'incites': *Chapters 1 and 2, General Principles of Criminal Responsibility*, Final Report (December 1992) p 93. In the Committee's opinion, the word 'incites' could be interpreted as only requiring the accused to have *caused* rather than *advocated* the offence. This reflects the principle that at common law an incitement can occur without the need for the offence to have been committed.

There is some lack of clarity as to the law concerning inciting a person, such as a child, who is exempt from criminal responsibility for the substantive offence. In Victoria, incitement in these circumstances will still attract criminal responsibility: *Crimes Act* 1958 (Vic) s 321G(1). However, at common law, there is some suggestion that the accused will not be criminally responsible in such circumstances.

For example, in *R v Whitehouse* [1977] QB 868, the Court of Appeal upheld the accused's appeal against his convictions on two counts of inciting his 15-year-old daughter to commit incest with him. Under s 1(1) of the *Sexual Offences Act* 1956 (UK), a girl under the age of 16 could not be convicted of an offence by permitting a man to commit incest with her. This decision contrasts with the position taken in the law relating to conspiracy. In *Burns* (1984) 79 Cr App R 173, it was held that there can be liability for conspiracy with a party excused from criminal responsibility. In addition, we will explore in Chapter 9 how a person who has taken part in a crime pursuant to a preconceived plan may be convicted even where the perpetrator has died, is unknown, has not been arrested or has been acquitted. It therefore seems that the Victorian approach reflects that taken in the law relating to conspiracy and acting in concert. The decision in *Whitehouse*'s case may not therefore be good law in Australia.

In Chapter 9 we will explore the law relating to complicity, which is not considered a separate crime in the way that the inchoate offences are. Accessorial liability (aiders, abettors, counsellors and procurers) is considered derivative in that the liability of an accessory is dependent upon the commission of the principal offence. It requires the prosecution to prove that the person who was assisted, or encouraged, committed, or at least attempted to commit, the offence. Consequently, accessorial liability is often described as a form of 'secondary liability'. However, incitement is viewed as a form of primary liability since the accused will be held liable for what he or she does, regardless of whether the crime incited is committed. This leads to the peculiar situation that a person will be criminally responsible if he or she *incites* another who fails to commit the crime, but will not be criminally responsible for *aiding* another who fails to commit the crime.

A further area of concern is how broad the scope of incitement is in relation to the other inchoate offences. JC Smith has pointed out that it may be technically possible to incite an attempt to commit an offence: JC Smith, *Smith and Hogan Criminal Law* (10th edn, London: Butterworths, 2002) p 293. They refer to the example of an accused giving another person a substance that the accused knows to be harmless. The accused says that it is poison and urges the other person to give it to the 'victim'. Smith and Hogan state that the accused cannot be convicted of attempted murder, but may be guilty of inciting an attempt to murder. It seems that such a 'double inchoate' offence extends the boundaries of the criminal law too far.

Section 321F(3) of the *Crimes Act* 1958 (Vic) specifically abolishes inciting a conspiracy, but this may be an offence at common law. The CLOC has rightly recommended that it should not be possible to incite a conspiracy or an attempt because '[t]here has to be some limit on preliminary offences': *Chapters 1 and 2, General Principles of Criminal Responsibility*, Final Report (December 1992) p 95; See further IP Robbins, 'Double Inchoate Crimes' (1989) 26(1) *Harvard Journal on Legislation* 1–116.

Another problem lies in the Victorian approach to treating incitement as an indictable offence even when the offence incited is a summary one. It seems anomalous that an incitement should be treated more seriously that the offence intended, and the Western Australian approach of having different penalties for incitement to commit indictable as opposed to simple offences is preferable.

The Law Commission for England and Wales has proposed the creation of a non-derivative crime of encouraging and assisting crime: Law Commission, *Assisting and Encouraging Crime*, Consultation Paper No 131 (London: HMSO, 1993). Such a provision would not be dependent upon the commission of a crime and therefore would serve to encompass both incitement and accessorial liability. This could serve to simplify an overly complex area of law.

However, there appears to be no sign that incitement will be replaced by any other offence. The MCCOC has pointed out that while incitement is rarely charged, 'circumstances may arise that are so serious that an appropriate offence is required': *Chapters 1 and 2, General Principles of Criminal Responsibility*, Final Report (December 1992) p 93.

The current law—fault element

The case law is silent as to the fault element for incitement. In *Giorgianni v The Queen* (1985) 156 CLR 473, Wilson, Deane and Dawson JJ stated (at 473) in relation to the other inchoate offences of attempt and conspiracy that 'Intent is required and it is an intent which must be based upon knowledge or belief of the necessary facts.'

From this, it can be inferred that the fault element for incitement will also be an intention to commit the substantive offence. Section 321G(2) of the *Crimes Act* 1958 (Vic) clearly sets out a high fault element for incitement that is in line with the fault element for attempts:

> For a person to be guilty...of incitement the person
> (a) must intend that the offence the subject of the incitement be committed; and
> (b) must intend or believe that any fact or circumstance the existence of which is an element of the offence in question will exist at the time when the conduct constituting the offence is to take place.

Critique

The CLOC has pointed out that recklessness as a fault element could lead to a threat to free speech: *Chapters 1 and 2, General Principles of Criminal Responsibility*, Final Report (December 1992) p 95. Accordingly, s 11.5(2) of the *Criminal Code* (Cth) requires an intention that the offence incited be committed.

The lack of case law on incitement and the fact that it is rarely charged leaves open what is meant by intention. It would seem that the narrow interpretation of intention that 'connotes a decision to bring about a situation so far as it is possible to do so—to bring about an act of a particular kind or a particular result' will be relevant here: *He Kaw Teh v The Queen* (1985) 157 CLR 523 at 569 per Brennan J.

As with the other inchoate offences, having intention as a fault element aids in restricting the scope of incitement and should remain the law in Australia.

Impossibility

Background

On 18 September 1971, there was a burglary at a Liverpool warehouse and a large quantity of corned beef was stolen. On 28 September, the police intercepted a large van because it was obviously overloaded. When they opened the van the police saw cartons of corned beef that were part of the proceeds of the Liverpool theft. The police took the driver and his companion to the police station. There, the police decided to allow the van to proceed with two police officers installed inside. They then arrested the accused, Roger Smith, when he met the van in order to unload the goods. Because the goods ceased to be stolen when the police intercepted them, the accused was charged with and convicted of attempting to handle stolen goods. This was on the basis that s 24(3) of the *Theft Act* 1968 (UK) stated that goods were not considered stolen 'after they have been restored to the person from whom they were stolen or to other lawful possession or custody'.

Smith was convicted of the attempt and appealed to the Court of Appeal. The Court quashed the accused's conviction on the basis that it was physically impossible for the accused to commit the completed offence as the goods were no longer stolen: *Haughton v Smith* [1975] AC 476. A further appeal was made to the House of Lords by James Haughton, the Chief Constable of Liverpool and Bootle Constabulary. The House of Lords agreed with the approach taken by the Court of Appeal and dismissed the appeal.

Lord Morris, stated (at 501) that the 'goods that [the accused] had, in fact, handled were not stolen', and posed the question: 'How then, can it be said that he attempted to handle stolen goods?'

As we will explore in the Critique section, the decision of the House of Lords in *Haughton v Smith* has been the subject of much criticism. It raises the question as to what the law should be in relation to criminal responsibility for inchoate crimes when the substantive offence is 'impossible' to achieve. This may occur in a number of different situations:

- *The conduct itself is not in fact a crime.* For example, the accused may mistakenly believe that importing foreign currency is an offence or committing adultery is a crime. There is thus a belief in an 'imaginary crime' and this is generally referred to as *legal* impossibility.
- *The means of carrying out the offence is defective.* For example, the poison used was too little to kill or the victim was out of range of the rifle.
- *The person or thing aimed at does not exist.* For example, the accused stabs a corpse believing it to be a living person or there is no money in the pocket or safe.

- The circumstances or facts accompanying the conduct are such that an element of the offence is absent. For example, as in *Haughton v Smith*, the goods received were not stolen or the sexual partner was not under 16.

The third and fourth categories are often referred to as *factual* or *physical* impossibility. In *R v Donnelly* [1970] NZLR 980, Turner J stated (at 990–1) concerning this category:

> [The accused] may find what he [or she] is proposing to do is after all impossible— not because of insufficiency of means, but because it is for some reason physically not possible, whatever means be adopted. He [or she] who walks into a room intending to steal, say a specific diamond ring, and finds that the ring is no longer there, but has been removed by the owner of the bank, is thus prevented from committing the crime which he [or she] intended, and which, but for the supervening physical impossibility imposed by events he [or she] would have committed.

The first category of legal impossibility has traditionally permitted the accused to escape criminal responsibility for inchoate crimes. Where the most debate has occurred is between insufficiency of means and the third and fourth categories of factual impossibility. In England, evidence of factual impossibility is considered a defence to a charge of attempt, conspiracy or incitement, whereas insufficiency of means is not. This distinction no longer exists in Australian jurisdictions except in South Australia, which follows the approach taken in *Haughton v Smith* [1975] AC 476. We will outline the current laws in relation to the categories of legal and factual impossibility before providing a critique of them.

The current law

Legal impossibility in relation to inchoate crimes refers to evidence of an intention to commit an imaginary crime such as importing an object believing it to be illegal to do so when it is not in fact prohibited. In this situation, the accused can escape criminal responsibility for an inchoate crime. For example, in *R v Taaffe* [1984] AC 539, the accused brought some packages into England, believing them to contain foreign currency and believing this was prohibited. The packages actually contained cannabis, the importation of which was illegal, but the importation of currency was not prohibited. He was convicted of being 'knowingly concerned in [the] fraudulent evasion' of the prohibition of certain goods. The Court of Appeal in *Taaffe* (1983) 77 Crim App R 82 at 85 upheld his appeal on the basis that he should be judged on 'the facts as he believed them to be'. That is, the accused believed he was importing currency and he mistakenly believed this was illegal. Lord Lane CJ (at 85) said that the accused's mistake of law '[n]o doubt made his actions morally reprehensible. It did not…turn what he…believed to be the importation of currency into the commission of a criminal offence'.

It would seem unlikely that a case concerning an imaginary crime would ever get to court. Antony Duff in his book *Criminal Attempts* (Oxford: Oxford University Press, 1996) p 93 points out that an adulterer who turned up at a police station to report his or her 'crime' would be told to go home. The cases on impossibility primarily deal with factual impossibility and whether or not this should serve to exculpate an accused from criminal responsibility for an inchoate crime. We will deal with the law relating to each inchoate crime in turn.

Attempts

In relation to attempts, all Australian jurisdictions except South Australia criminalise all cases of impossibility apart from legal impossibility, providing the accused's conduct is sufficiently proximate to the offence: *Crimes Act* 1914 (Cth) s 7(3)(a); *Criminal Code* (NT) s 4(3); *Criminal Code* (Qld), ss 4, 4(3); *Criminal Code* (Tas) s 2(2); *Crimes Act* (Vic) s 321N(3); *Criminal Code* (WA) s 4; *Britten v Alpogut* [1987] VR 929 at 938 per Murphy J; *R v Mai* (1992) 26 NSWLR 371 at 381–4 per Hunt CJ; *R v Lee* (1990) 1 WAR 411 at 423 per Malcolm CJ; *R v Prior* (1992) 91 NTR 53.

The decision in *Haughton v Smith* gave rise to much discussion. Section 1(2) of the *Criminal Attempts Act* 1981 (UK) was subsequently enacted enabling a conviction for an attempt 'even though the facts are such that the commission of the offence is impossible'. This section was central to the decision of *R v Shivpuri* [1987] AC 1. In that case, the accused believed that he was importing heroin and cannabis into the UK. After his arrest, a chemical analysis proved that the substance imported was in fact dried cabbage leaves. The House of Lords held that he had been rightly convicted of attempted importation of a prohibited substance despite the substantive offence being factually impossible.

This decision was followed by the Victorian Supreme Court in *Britten v Alpogut* [1987] VR 929. The accused believed he was importing cannabis. Upon analysis, the substance was discovered to be an anaesthetic, procaine, which is not a prohibited drug. The Supreme Court held that the accused had been rightly convicted under s 233B of the *Customs Act* 1901 (Cth) because impossibility was no answer to a charge of attempt unless it was the accused's intention to commit an 'imaginary crime'.

The Full Court of the Supreme Court of South Australia has taken a different approach. It followed the House of Lords decision in *Haughton v Smith* [1975] AC 476 in *R v Collingridge* (1976) 16 SASR 117. South Australia therefore distinguishes between allowing factual impossibility to exculpate an accused and insufficiency of means or the non-existence of a person or thing that does not. In *R v Collingridge* (1976) 16 SASR 117, the accused was charged with the attempted murder of his wife. He had thrown the bare end of a live wire into the bath while she was in it. There was evidence that the victim could have been killed if the wire had made contact with her body, but the accused claimed he did not intend to touch the victim's body with the wire. The Supreme Court found that this was a case of insufficient means rather than factual impossibility and upheld the accused's conviction.

The Code jurisdictions make it clear that factual impossibility is no bar to a conviction for attempt: *Criminal Code* (NT) s 4(3); *Criminal Code* (Qld) s 4(3); *Criminal Code* (WA) s 4. For example, the third paragraph of s 4 of the *Criminal Code* (WA) states that it is immaterial that by reason of circumstances not known to the offender, it is impossible in fact to commit the offence. Section 2(2) of the *Criminal Code* (Tas) states that an attempt may be committed whether under the circumstances it was possible to commit the crime or not. Section 321N(3) of the *Crimes Act* 1958 (Vic) enables a conviction despite the existence of facts of which the accused is unaware that make the commission of the substantive offence impossible.

In 1990, the Review Committee of Commonwealth Criminal Law recommended that future law should contain a statutory provision to the effect that a person may be convicted of an attempt, even though the facts are such that the commission of the offence is impossible: *Principles of Criminal Responsibility and Other Matters*, Interim Report (Canberra: AGPS, 1990) p 349. This recommendation was followed by the insertion of s 7(3)(a) into the *Crimes Act* 1914 (Cth). This section states that a person can be found guilty even if committing the attempted offence is impossible. Given that the term 'impossibility' is not qualified, this section may be interpreted as meaning that neither legal nor factual impossibility will be a barrier to conviction.

Conspiracy

It is clear that in Victoria and federally there will still be liability for conspiracy in situations of insufficiency of means as well as factual impossibility. Section 321(3) of the *Crimes Act* 1958 (Vic) states that there will be liability where an accused enters an agreement to commit acts that, unknown to the person at the time of the agreement, make the commission of the offence impossible. Section 86(4)(a) of the *Crimes Act* 1914 (Cth) goes further than the Victorian provision in enabling a conviction for conspiracy even if committing the offence is impossible. Legal impossibility therefore does not appear to be a barrier to a conviction for a federal offence.

The common law is relevant in the other jurisdictions, including the Code jurisdictions in determining what constitutes conspiracy. Just what the common law position is in relation to conspiracy and factual impossibility is unclear.

In *DPP (UK) v Nock and Alsford* [1978] AC 979, the House of Lords followed *Haughton v Smith*'s division between insufficiency of means and factual impossibility, holding that there is no liability for conspiracy in the latter situation. In *Nock*'s case, the two accused men agreed to produce cocaine from a substance in their possession. Cocaine could not in fact be produced from the substance. They were convicted of conspiracy to produce a controlled drug contrary to the *Misuse of Drugs Act* 1971 (UK). The House of Lords quashed their convictions on the basis that factual impossibility in conspiracy should be treated in the same way as factual impossibility in attempt. The House of Lords viewed both conspiracy and attempt as being criminal because they allowed the police to intervene to prevent the substantive offence being committed.

In contrast, in *R v Sew Hoy* [1994] 1 NZLR 257, the Court of Appeal of New Zealand held that factual impossibility is not a bar to a conviction for conspiracy. In that case, the accused agreed to produce falsified documents in order to have Customs officers wrongly classify men's clothing as women's clothing, the latter carrying a lower duty. There was evidence that this was bound to fail as Customs officers did not rely on documents, but on inspections of the goods. In the District Court, the jury was directed to return a verdict of not guilty on the basis that there could be no liability in circumstances of factual impossibility. The Crown then appealed on a reserved point of law.

The Court of Appeal ordered a retrial. While the Court thought that the facts could be interpreted as insufficiency of means, they based their decision on the broader basis that factual impossibility was not a 'defence' to conspiracy: GF Orchard, 'Impossibility and Inchoate Crimes—Another Hook in a Red Herring' [1993] *New Zealand Law Journal* 426–7. The Court of Appeal declined to follow *Nock*'s case because it was based on *Haughton v Smith*, which they found was of little persuasive value because the latter decision had been rejected in Australia (except in South Australia) and legislatively overturned in England. The Court of Appeal was also of the opinion that conspiracy should not be viewed in the same way as attempt, but should be seen as 'inherently culpable' rather than as an 'auxiliary' crime. The Court stated at 267: 'It is the making of the agreement itself that is seen as inimical to the public good, whether it proceeds further or not. It should therefore be irrelevant that it may not be possible in fact to carry out the agreement.'

There has not been a definitive Australian case on this issue. The decision in *R v Barbouttis* (1995) 37 NSWLR 256 seems to hint at factual possibility not being a bar to liability for conspiracy. In that case, the accused was charged with conspiracy to receive stolen property. It was alleged that he and others agreed to buy fifty boxes of cigarettes, believing them to be stolen. In circumstances reminiscent of the facts in *Haughton v Smith*, the boxes were in fact in the lawful possession of the police for the purpose of an undercover operation designed to catch the accused. The person from whom the boxes were to be bought was in fact an undercover policeman. The indictment was quashed in the District Court on the basis that there could not be a conspiracy where it was factually impossible to commit the substantive crime. The prosecution appealed on a point of law. A majority of the Court of Criminal Appeal of New South Wales rejected the appeal.

Dunford and Smart JJ in the majority based their decision on the agreement being one to purchase cigarettes, in itself not an unlawful act. The accused's belief that the cigarettes were stolen was therefore irrelevant. Dunford J stated (at 278): '[T]he conspiracy alleged in this case was not an agreement to do an unlawful act because the act agreed to be done, that is, receive the cigarettes, was not an unlawful act; nor was it an agreement to do a lawful act by unlawful means; and so it was not, in my view, a criminal conspiracy.'

The decision therefore was not based on there not being criminal responsibility due to factual impossibility. Gleeson CJ and Dunford J were in fact in agreement that factual impossibility could no longer be a bar to criminal responsibility for conspiracy. In contrast, Smart J (at 277) appeared to suggest that there may still be room for a 'defence' of factual impossibility.

An application by the Solicitor-General for New South Wales to the High Court for leave to appeal was originally granted, but later revoked: *R v Single, Barbouttis and Dale* unreported, 15 March 1996, HC, S134/1995, Dawson, Gaudron and Gummow JJ; *R v Barbouttis, Dale and Single* unreported, 2 October 1996, HC, S51/1996, Brennan CJ, Dawson, Toohey, Gaudron and McHugh JJ. The application was originally couched in terms of whether or not a crime of conspiracy can encompass an agreement to do that which is factually impossible. The High Court took the approach of Gleeson CJ and Dunford J in the Court of Criminal Appeal decision, that no question of impossibility arose on the facts. The real problem was with the agreement charged in the indictment.

Incitement

As with conspiracy, in Victoria factual impossibility is no bar to a conviction for incitement: *Crimes Act* 1958 (Vic) s 321G(3). Interestingly, the *Crimes Act* 1914 (Cth) does not include a provision dealing with impossibility in relation to this inchoate crime.

The situation at common law in relation to incitement and factual impossibility is unclear in Australia. The English decisions seem to suggest that factual impossibility can operate as a bar to liability for incitement. In *McDonough* (1962) 47 Cr App R 37, the accused was convicted of three counts of inciting another to receive stolen lamb carcasses. On one of the counts, there was no evidence that at the time of the incitement the carcasses existed. On the other two counts there was clear evidence that there were no stolen lamb carcasses in existence. His appeal against conviction was dismissed.

McDonough's case would seem to imply that factual impossibility is not a bar to conviction. However, in *DPP (UK) v Nock and Alsford* [1978] AC 979, Lord Scarman at 999 referred to the physical element in *McDonough*'s case as being the making of the incitement. The offence was complete at the time even though there were no stolen goods or no goods at all. Michael Cohen writes that what Lord Scarman is saying here is that at the time of incitement it was still possible to receive stolen lamb carcasses because some lamb carcasses (if not the specific ones originally aimed at) could be stolen subsequent to the incitement: 'Inciting the Impossible' [1979] Crim LR 239–44 at 241. In Cohen's opinion, *McDonough*'s case does not stand for the proposition that factual impossibility is irrelevant to criminal responsibility.

This approach seems to be borne out in the subsequent case of *R v Fitzmaurice* [1983] QB 1083 in which the English Court of Appeal held that factual impossibility may excuse an accused from criminal responsibility for incitement. In that case, the accused's father thought up an elaborate scheme whereby he would be given a reward for informing a security firm that there was a plan to rob a security van. He asked the accused to arrange a robbery of a woman who was meant to be carrying wages from her company to the bank. The accused organised for three men to carry out the robbery. The accused and the three men did not know that the woman was part of the charade and a security van was going to be in the vicinity at the time the three men were meant to be robbing the woman. On the accused father's tip-off, the three men were arrested for conspiracy to rob and the father subsequently received payment from the security firm for his information.

The accused was convicted at the Central Criminal Court of having incited the three men to commit a robbery. On appeal, he argued that he could not be convicted of inciting other men to commit a crime that in fact could not be committed.

The Court of Appeal emphasised Lord Scarman's opinion in *DPP v Nock* [1978] AC 979 at 995 that the focus must be on evidence of the offence that was to be the outcome of the conspiracy or incitement in order to see whether the offence was in fact impossible to achieve.

On the facts, the Court of Appeal held that the offence of robbery could have been achieved. Neill J, in delivering the judgment of the Court, stated (at 1092):

> [T]he appellant believed that there was to be a wage snatch and he was encouraging Bonham [one of the three men] to take part in it…It is to be remembered that the particulars of offence in the indictment included the words 'by robbing a woman in Bow'. By no stretch of the imagination was that an impossible offence to carry out and it was that offence which the appellant was inciting Bonham to commit.

While the Court of Appeal therefore agreed that factual impossibility could bar a conviction for incitement, they were nevertheless able to find on the facts that this was not a case of factual impossibility.

There has not been an equivalent case on incitement and factual impossibility in Australia and the situation at common law remains unclear.

Critique

From a subjectivist fault-based perspective, there is little moral distinction between the person who intends to commit a crime and succeeds, and the person who intends to commit a crime but is frustrated because of ineptitude or physical impossibility. On a subjectivist approach, both a mistake about insufficiency of means and physical impossibility will be irrelevant to criminal responsibility. If the accused believed that the offence could be committed in circumstances when it could not be, his or her state of mind is just as blameworthy as if the offence were able to be carried out. Andrew Ashworth writes in his book *Principles of Criminal Law* (3rd edn, Oxford: Oxford University Press, 1999) p 469:

> [W]e are justified in convicting the person who smuggles dried lettuce leaves in the belief that they are cannabis, and the person who puts sugar in someone's drink in the belief that it is cyanide, and the person who handles goods in the belief that they are stolen. In all these cases there is no relevant difference between their culpability and the culpability in cases where the substances *really* are cannabis, cyanide and stolen goods.

From an objectivist or consequentialist approach to the criminal law, however, factual impossibility should act as a bar to conviction. This approach emphasises the lack of harm or danger in circumstances where an offence cannot be carried out. That is, the criminal law should not be used to criminalise conduct that does not have the potential to cause harm: J Temkin, 'Impossible Attempts: Another View' (1976) 39 *Modern Law Review* 55–69. Otherwise, there is a danger that convictions might be based on confessions that have been extracted through police pressure. It can be a backdoor method of convicting on the evidence of intention alone. As Andrew Ashworth in *Principles of Criminal Law* (3rd edn, Oxford: Oxford University Press, 1999) points out (p 469): '[I]t is argued that there is a risk of oppression if the law criminalizes people in objectively innocent situations. Part of the concern here is that convictions might be based on confessions which are the result of fear, confusion or even police fabrication. Without the need to establish any objectively incriminating facts, the police might construct a case simply on the basis of remarks attributed to the accused person.'

In jurisdictions where impossibility no longer bars a conviction, prosecutorial discretion is assumed to play a significant role. The Law Commission, in *Criminal Law: Attempt and Impossibility in Relation to Attempt, Conspiracy and Incitement*, Report No 102 (London: HMSO, 1980), noted that factual impossibility could provide a fall-back position for an attempt to be charged. Paragraph 2.97 of the Report notes:

> If it is right that an attempt should be chargeable (even though it is impossible to commit the crime intended) we do not think that we should be deterred by the fact that such a charge would also cover such extreme and exceptional cases...an example would be where a person is offered goods at such a low price that he [or she] believes they are stolen, when in fact they are not; if he [or she] actually purchases them...he [or she] would be liable for an attempt to handle stolen goods.

Although in such cases the accused would be guilty in theory, the Commission concluded that it would be unlikely that a complaint would be made or that a prosecution would follow.

The decision in *Haughton v Smith* attracted much academic criticism due to the difficulty in dividing situations into factual and other sorts of impossibility and because of its lack of clarity in distinguishing between an attempt and the substantive offence: see, for example, G Williams, *Textbook of Criminal Law* (2nd edn, London: Stevens & Sons, 1983) pp 406–10; RA Ribeiro, 'Criminal Liability for Attempting the

Impossible—Lady Luck and the Villains' (1974) 4(2) *Hong Kong Law Journal* 109–32 at 131; HLA Hart, 'The House of Lords on Attempting the Impossible' (1981) 1 *Oxford Journal of Legal Studies* 149–66 at 164. The decision may have served some practical value as a means of controlling police behaviour during criminal investigation. Limiting criminal responsibility to insufficiency of means prevents the reliance upon proof of criminal intent alone, which in turn leads to reliance on confession evidence or other circumstantial evidence.

However, the decision in *Haughton v Smith* is indefensible at a conceptual level. Eugene Meehan in *The Law of Criminal Attempt—A Treatise* (Calgary: Carswell Legal Publications, 1984) points out at 191: 'The Lords confused liability for an attempt and liability for the completed crime, and in the process eliminated attempt. Smith *did* attempt to receive the stolen goods; he was not in London to see the sights, he was there to direct the distribution of the previously stolen corned beef, which he was actually doing.'

The English Law Commission conducted a major review of impossibility and inchoate crimes and recommended that factual impossibility should be irrelevant to criminal responsibility: Law Commission, *Attempt and Impossibility in Relation to Attempt, Conspiracy and Incitement*, Report No 102 (London: HMSO, 1980). Subsequently, the *Criminal Attempts Act* 1981 (UK) was enacted. As referred to above, s 1(2) of that Act provides that a person may be guilty of an attempt 'even though the facts are such that the commission of the offence is impossible'.

Since all Australian jurisdictions apart from South Australia now hold that factual impossibility is no bar to a conviction for attempt, it seems logical to bring the law relating to factual impossibility in conspiracy and incitement in line with it. The approach in *Sew Hoy*'s case should hold sway. In South Australia, the decision in *Nock* will probably still be relevant given that *Haughton v Smith* still applies. However, this may be reconsidered in the future. The Review Committee of Commonwealth Criminal Law recommended 'for practical reasons' that physical impossibility should not defeat a prosecution: Review [Committee] of Commonwealth Criminal Law, *Principles of Criminal Responsibility and Other Matters*, Interim Report (July 1990) (Canberra: AGPS, 1990) p 398. It gave the following example at 398–9: 'A conspiracy to defeat the taxation laws or otherwise defraud the revenue may in fact be impossible to succeed because the Commissioner happens to know all the relevant circumstances; again the criminality of the conspiracy would seem to be just as great as if it had been possible of success.'

Sections 11.1(4), 11.4(3), 11.5(3)(a) of the *Criminal Code* (Cth) (which deal with inchoate offences) state that a person may be found guilty even if commission of the substantive offence is impossible. Similarly, the provisions dealing with attempts and conspiracy in the *Crimes Act* 1914 (Cth) enable a conviction where the substantive offence is impossible: *Crimes Act* 1914 (Cth) ss 7(3)(a), 86(4)(a). No such provision appears in s 7A dealing with incitement. These provisions appear to go further than the usual statutory ones that refer to impossibility in relation to circumstances or facts. Legal impossibility would also seem to be encompassed by this provision. In fact, the CLOC stated in 1992 in relation to attempts, that 'impossibility arising by reason of matters of fact *or law* should no longer be a bar to conviction' [emphasis added]: CLOC, *Chapters 1 and 2, General Principles of Criminal Responsibility*, Final Report (December 1992) p 81.

The Committee, however, did not explain why a conviction would be appropriate in cases where it is legally impossible for the defendant to commit the offence. Charging individuals with imaginary crimes would extend the criminal law much too far. It would be oppressive and ultimately unworkable. For example, many people believe that trespassing is a crime rather than a tort, and signs on property reinforce this. If legal impossibility is no longer a bar to conviction for inchoate crimes, this conduct would be deemed criminal despite it not being an offence. Such an approach raises questions as to how a judge would go about determining the sentence for an imaginary crime.

There are solid conceptual reasons for why insufficiency of means and factual impossibility should not act as a bar to conviction for inchoate offences. However, these do not carry over to situations of legal impossibility. The current law at the Commonwealth level thus goes too far in its ambit.

Conclusion

The common thread among inchoate offences is that they are committed even though the substantive offence that was intended is not completed and no harm is caused. As we have pointed out in the Critique sections, the main point of contention about these offences is that they have the potential to greatly broaden the scope of the criminal law. The trials of Lionel Murphy mentioned at the beginning of this chapter suggest the potential use of such offences for political reasons.

In relation to attempts, it seems unlikely that one single formula will ever be devised to cover all types of blameworthy preparatory conduct related to the commission of such disparate offences as murder, assault or theft. It could be possible to devise separate offences to cover specific situations now considered attempts. However, it seems that the general doctrine of attempts is too firmly established for it to be abolished. In relation to conspiracy, there is a need to provide a balance between enabling convictions for preliminary plans to commit crimes and preventing possible abuse of this offence if there are too few limitations to its scope.

There is also a need to rethink the conceptual basis of primary and derivative liability as it relates to incitement and aiding and abetting. It was previously pointed out that a person will be criminally responsible if he or she *incites* another who fails to commit the crime, but will not be criminally responsible for *aiding* another who fails to commit the crime. In the next chapter we will discuss the movement towards viewing accessorial liability as non-derivative. If this course were taken, it could make incitement redundant. This may make practical sense given that incitement is rarely charged and there is little case law as to its scope.

In relation to impossibility and the inchoate offences, insufficiency of means and factual impossibility should be irrelevant to criminal responsibility. Attention should be focused on restricting the scope of these crimes in ways other than through the device of factual impossibility.

Because the law relating to inchoate offences has often developed on an ad hoc basis, there is a need for a more restrictive approach to be followed as to the ambit of inchoate offences. Confining the fault element to an intention to commit the substantive offence has been one step in the right direction, although there are obvious policy reasons for enabling recklessness to be the fault element for attempted rape. Another way of restricting inchoate offences would be to confine them to preparatory conduct for indictable offences rather than for indictable *and* summary offences.

The elements of inchoate offences do not fit neatly into physical and fault elements and these offences are exceptional in imposing criminal responsibility in the absence of any harm being caused. What remains clear is that the three inchoate offences remain firmly in place in Australian jurisdictions despite criticisms of their breadth.

CHAPTER 9

Complicity

Introduction

Heather Osland and her son, David Albion, were charged with the murder of Frank Osland, Heather Osland's husband and David Albion's stepfather. Frank Osland had a long history of violence towards his wife and stepson. On 30 July 1991, Heather and David dug a large 'hole' in the bush near Bendigo. That evening, Heather mixed sedatives into Frank's dinner. David then waited until Frank was lying unconscious in bed and, while Heather assisted by holding Frank down, fatally struck him on the head with an iron pipe. David then placed a plastic bag around Frank's head and placed the body in the boot of Heather's car. They drove into the bush and buried the body in the grave they had prepared. For the next three and a half years, they acted as though Frank Osland had simply disappeared, including reporting him as a missing person.

Rumours began circulating that Frank had been killed after David confessed to his brother Paul, who then told his wife. The latter reported the matter to the police after she had split up from Paul. The police then placed telephone intercepts on the telephones of Heather and her youngest daughter, Erica. A large number of conversations was recorded and in some of them, Heather expressed her anger against Paul for breaking ranks and suggested to Erica that Paul should be 'knocked'.

Heather was arrested on 12 January 1995. She confessed that she had participated with David in killing Frank. At their trial for the murder of Frank Osland, both Heather Osland and David Albion relied on the defences of self-defence and provocation. A clinical and forensic psychologist, Dr Ken Byrne, gave evidence concerning battered woman syndrome. This was to support the defences of self-defence and provocation in relation to Heather. The concept of battered woman syndrome is discussed more fully in Chapter 10. The evidence showed that for 13 years, Frank had physically and mentally tormented Heather and her children and had reduced Heather to a state of servility. He was also extremely controlling of Heather's social interactions. There were times when Heather would leave Frank, but she would inevitably return to him after persistent efforts by him to get her back with promises of better conduct.

By July 1991, Heather regarded herself as totally under Frank's control and stated that there was hardly a day when she was not abused for failing to do something in the way in which Frank wanted it done. David gave evidence that on the night of the killing, he was working on his car when he heard Heather scream. He rushed into the room to see her against the wall with Frank standing over her. He yelled at Frank. Frank then turned on him and told him to 'get the fuck out of the house'. When David said he would not leave without his mother, Frank screamed 'I'll kill you' after which he punched David in the head.

On 2 October 1996, Heather Osland was convicted of murder, but the jury could not reach a verdict in relation to David. He was later re-tried and was acquitted on 12 December 1996. Heather was sentenced to 14 years and six months' imprisonment with a minimum term of nine years and six months before becoming eligible for parole.

An application for leave to appeal to the Victorian Court of Appeal was dismissed: *R v Osland* [1998] 2 VR 636. Heather then appealed to the High Court: *Osland v The Queen* (1998) 197 CLR 316. Just before the special leave application commenced, the High Court directed counsel for Heather that it wished to hear argument on the point as to the possible inconsistency of the verdicts. This had not been raised previously.

Accordingly, counsel for Heather argued first, that Heather's conviction was inconsistent with the jury's failure to convict her son and, secondly, that it was inconsistent with David's subsequent acquittal. All the members of the High Court dismissed the second point on the basis that different evidence may lead to different outcomes. However, the members of the High Court split three to two as to the first ground concerning the alleged inconsistency between Osland's conviction and the jury's failure to convict her son at their joint trial.

To those unfamiliar with the intricacies of the law relating to primary and derivative criminal responsibility, an acquittal for the person who actually did the killing and a sentence of 14 years and six months' imprisonment for the person who assisted seems incomprehensible. The justification for this outcome is that Heather's actions in digging the grave, drugging Frank's meal and holding him down while David struck him over the head are viewed as her 'acting in concert' with David. This means that she may be treated as a principal offender regardless of David's criminal responsibility, and whether he had a defence specific to himself.

The term 'complicity' refers to involvement or partnership in crime. It includes both primary and derivative liability. Primary liability encompasses three scenarios. First, it refers to those who act as joint principal offenders such as where two people attack another and the effects of their combined blows cause death. Secondly, the High Court decision in *Osland* means that primary liability also encompasses those who act in concert where the acts are performed in the presence of each other according to a preconceived plan. Thirdly, primary liability encompasses situations where an 'innocent agent' is used to carry out a crime. Derivative liability generally refers to those who aid or abet, counsel or procure the commission of an offence. These are all concepts that are analysed in this chapter.

A majority of the High Court in *Osland* held that acting in concert is a form of primary rather than derivative liability such that a person acting pursuant to a preconceived plan may be convicted even where the perpetrator is not. As will be explored in this chapter, the conceptual basis for acting in concert as a form of primary liability is controversial and the English approach differs from that of the High Court of Australia.

If Heather had simply aided David in some way outside of a preconceived plan, she would have been considered an accessory, which is a form of derivative criminal responsibility. This form of criminal responsibility depends upon the existence of criminal behaviour by the perpetrator upon which the accessory's liability is based. David's acquittal on this scenario would have meant that Heather would not have been held criminally responsible.

The rationale for the doctrine of complicity is that a person who promotes or assists the commission of a crime is just as blameworthy as the person who actually commits the crime. There is a tension in this area of the law because of the need to discourage acts that assist the commission of crime without imposing excessive sanctions on a much broader class of persons than those who directly commit a crime. As a consequence, some of the areas encompassed by the doctrine of complicity have developed in a haphazard and inconsistent fashion. In 1993, the Law Commission for England and Wales called for a new structure of statutory offences to replace the common law of complicity in order to clarify this complex area: Law Commission, *Assisting and Encouraging Crime*, Consultation Paper No 131 (London: HMSO, 1993). This recommendation has, unfortunately, not been heeded.

The common law distinguished between modes of complicity based on the *nature* of the offence assisted or encouraged. In relation to felonies, the law identified several 'degrees' of participation: the perpetrator of the offence was designated 'principal in the first degree', whereas parties who were assisting or encouraging during the commission of the perpetrator's crime were described as 'principals in the second degree'. Parties who were not physically present during the commission of the offence were divided into 'accessories before the fact' (assisting or encouraging *before* the commission of the perpetrator's crime) or 'accessories after the fact' (assisting *after* the commission of the perpetrator's offence). In relation to misdemeanours, however, the law deemed all accessories, irrespective of their precise participation, to be principals.

In the sixteenth century, the courts deemed accessories, who were present at the scene, aiding and abetting the commission of the offence, to be principal offenders for procedural purposes: *R v Griffith* (1553) 75 ER 152. This rule eventually found its way into legislation via the *Accessories and Abettors Act* 1861 (UK). This Act affirmed the common law principle of eligibility for equal punishment for all parties in that a person who aided, abetted, counselled or procured an offence was liable to be tried, indicted, and punished as a principal offender. Similar statutory provisions have been enacted in all Australian jurisdictions: *Criminal Code* (ACT) s 45; *Criminal Code* (Cth) s 11.2; *Crimes Act* 1914 (Cth) s 5; *Crimes Act* 1900 (NSW) ss 249F, 346; *Criminal Code* (NT) s 12; *Criminal Law Consolidation Act* 1935 (SA) s 267; *Criminal Code* (Qld) s 7; *Criminal Code* (Tas) s 3; *Crimes Act* 1958 (Vic) s 323; *Criminal Code* (WA) s 7.

The terms 'principals in the first and second degree' and 'accessories before and after the fact' are now irrelevant given that these terms have been superseded by legislation. Nevertheless, lawyers and judges sometimes refer to terms such as 'accessories before and after the fact' despite their obsolescence. In this chapter we will refer simply to 'principal offenders' and 'accessories'.

Deeming accessories to be principal offenders for procedural purposes did not alter the derivative nature of accessorial liability. The historical linking of accessorial liability to the perpetrator's offence has had conceptual as well as procedural consequences. Rather than being viewed as an extension of criminal responsibility like the inchoate offences of incitement or conspiracy, accessorial liability is a *mode of participation* in the perpetrator's offence. The consequences of linking the culpability of the accessory to the perpetrator have proved problematic. As we shall explore, the connection between perpetrator and accessory has fuelled controversy over the fault required for accessorial liability.

Another problematic area is associated with the development of the doctrine of 'common purpose', which is generally regarded as a special form of accessorial liability. It serves to hold those who embark on a joint criminal enterprise or plan to commit an offence liable for any further crime committed by other group members in the course of that joint criminal enterprise or plan. The nature and scope of the fault required of individuals who commit offences that are foreseen but not necessarily intended pursuant to a common purpose or joint criminal enterprise remain controversial.

In this chapter, we will explore the notion of primary liability through an analysis of principal offenders, acting in concert and innocent agency. We will then turn to derivative liability in the form of aiding and abetting crime and how this has been broadened through the doctrine of common purpose.

Principal offenders and acting in concert

Background

We outlined above how primary liability covers three situations. Here we deal with the first two situations of joint principals and acting in concert. In the next section, we will turn to the example of primary liability where an innocent agent is used to commit a crime.

The term principal offender refers to the person who directly performs the physical elements of the criminal offence. In most cases there is little dispute over who is the principal offender. However, on occasion, there may be more than one perpetrator of a crime and it will be difficult to determine whether parties should be termed joint principals or principal offender and aider or abettor. This may arise because of evidential difficulties in identifying the precise role of each participant. The law has developed a way of holding accessories liable through the doctrine of common purpose. This will be explored after we analyse derivative liability. However, it is sometimes important to distinguish between joint principal offenders and accessorial liability because liability as an aider and abettor is derivative and is therefore dependent upon the conviction of the principal offender.

The following section outlines the current law relating to joint principals and acting in concert. We then turn to a critique of the conceptual difficulties associated with acting in concert.

The current law

Two or more persons can be joint principals if they are closely connected to the occurrence of the physical element of the offence: *Macklin and Murphy's* case (1838) 2 Lew CC 225; *R v Bingley* (1821) Russ & Ry 446. For example, in *R v Macdonald* [1904] QSR 151 the victim, a young girl, died of starvation and lack of medical care after the two accused brutally mistreated and neglected her. The accused were both convicted of wilful murder on the basis that they were jointly responsible for the victim's death.

Two or more persons may be joint principal offenders where each has the requisite fault element and together perform all the physical elements of the crime: *R v Clarke and Wilton* [1959] VR 645; *R v Wyles; Ex parte Attorney-General (Qld)* [1977] Qd R 169; *R v Webb; Ex parte Attorney-General* [1990] 2 Qd R 275; *Russell and Russell* (1987) 85 Cr App R 388. The Law Commission for England and Wales gives as an example the situation where, during a robbery, one party holds a gun or holds down the victim while the other grabs the victim's property: Law Commission, *General Principles, Parties, Complicity and Liability for the Acts of Another*, Working Paper No 43 (London: HMSO, 1972) p 33, illustration *b*. The use of force and stealing are two separate physical elements of the offence of robbery and both have been made out in this situation.

Primary liability now also encompasses the situation set out in *Osland*'s case where the criminal act is performed in the presence of both accused and pursuant to a preconceived plan. This is known as acting in concert. In *Lowery v King (No 2)* [1972] VR 560 Smith J stated (at 560):

> The law says that if two or more persons reach an understanding or arrangement that together they will commit a crime and then, while that understanding or arrangement is still on foot and has not been called off, they are both present at the scene of the crime and one or other of them does, or they do between them, in accordance with their understanding or arrangement, all the things that are necessary to constitute the crime, they are all equally guilty of that crime regardless of what part each played in its commission.

However, as shown by *Osland*'s case, the concept of acting in concert has been used to hold such a person liable even where the perpetrator is not. That is, a person who has assisted or encouraged a crime pursuant to a preconceived plan may be convicted even where the perpetrator has died, is unknown, has not been arrested or has been acquitted: *King v The Queen* (1986) 161 CLR 423; *R v Darby* (1982) 148 CLR 668; *Murray v The Queen* [1962] Tas SR 170; *R v Lopuszynski* [1971] QWN 33; *R v Daniels* [1972] Qd R 323; *O'Sullivan v Thurmer* [1955] SASR 76. A person acting in concert can also still be held liable if the perpetrator is exempt from prosecution: *R v Austin* [1981] All ER 374. By contrast, the derivative offences of counselling, procuring, aiding and abetting depend upon the commission of the principal offence and the liability of the principal offender: *R v Demirian* [1989] VR 97; *Osland v The Queen* (1998) 197 CLR 316 at 324 per Gaudron and Gummow JJ, at 342 per McHugh J.

An example of the operation of the doctrine of acting in concert occurred in *King v The Queen* (1986) 161 CLR 423. The accused, King, together with a man named Matthews, were jointly charged as principals in the murder of King's wife. The prosecution claimed at the trial that Matthews had actually killed the victim. He was acquitted, presumably on the basis that there was a possibility that some other person had killed the victim. King, however, was convicted of murder. On appeal, the majority of the High Court stated that there was no inconsistency between the conviction of King and the acquittal of Matthews. On the facts, the accused had encouraged someone to kill the victim and the offence had been carried out. Dawson J stated at 433–4: '[W]here two persons are tried jointly upon the one charge as participants in the same degree, it does not inevitably follow that both must be convicted or both must be acquitted… The evidence may be sufficient to prove the case against one accused beyond reasonable doubt, but be insufficient to prove the case against the other.'

In *Matusevich v The Queen* (1977) 137 CLR 633 the accused who had been jointly charged with murder was found guilty despite the principal offender being found not guilty of murder on the ground of insanity. The members of the High Court, however, differed in their reasons for this conclusion. The majority appeared to have supported the principle that it is the acting in concert that grounds liability. The accused could be found liable provided that the principal offender knew the nature and quality of the act but did not know that it was wrong. Aickin J specifically referred to acting in concert in this regard (at 633–64) and Mason and Murphy JJ agreed with this (at 645 and 648 respectively). Gibbs and Stephen JJ appear to have gone further in extending liability to the situation where the principal offender did not know the nature and quality of the act. Gibbs J, however, went on to say (at 638) that this fact situation could also be analysed via the doctrine of innocent agency. Gibbs J pointed out (at 638) that the law on this issue was unsettled.

In *R v Demirian* [1989] VR 97, McGarvie and O'Bryan JJ took the view that the theoretical distinction between primary liability for those acting in concert and derivative liability as an aider and abettor is of little practical significance. They stated (at 123): 'When the evidence is that the accused were present acting in concert when the crime was committed it is seldom necessary for a jury to find, or to be concerned, whether individually they were principal offenders or accessories at the crime. They will all fall within one or other of those categories. They may all be convicted of the crime.'

This approach can be seen in the facts of *Mohan v The Queen* [1967] 2 AC 187 where both accused simultaneously attacked the victim with cutlasses and inflicted two severe injuries. The victim subsequently died and it was possible that only one of the injuries was fatal and it was not proved which of the accused inflicted the one fatal injury. On appeal against conviction, the accused argued that because it could not be proved who inflicted the fatal wound, their conviction should be quashed. The Privy Council held it irrelevant that it was unknown who struck the fatal blow; since the two accused attacked the victim at the same time with the same intention, they were assisting each other and thus were equally guilty.

McGarvie and O'Bryan JJ went on to state in *R v Demirian* [1989] VR 97 at 124 that in previous cases, those who were acting in concert were not treated as principals in the first degree. Two of the judges of the High Court in *Osland v The Queen* (1998) 197 CLR 316 expressly disapproved of this statement. Callinan J stated at 402: 'With respect, the passage in *Demirian* overlooks that it is an important aspect of concert that it does not depend upon derivative liability. This is because those who act in concert are to be treated as being causatively jointly responsible for the commission of the crime.'

McHugh J also stated in *Osland* (at 350) that McGarvie and O'Bryan JJ's statement in *Demirian* was inconsistent with previous authority and Callinan J (at 402) pointed out that it overlooks the fact that acting in concert does not depend upon derivative liability.

Returning to the facts of *Osland*'s case, the prosecution argued at the joint trial that Osland and Albion were acting pursuant to an understanding or arrangement and they were both liable as principal offenders. No issue was taken to this approach by the defence at trial. The defence accepted the prosecution case that Osland was equally responsible for the acts of Albion and never raised the argument that Osland's conviction was dependent upon the conviction of Albion. Heather's own interview with the police emphasised joint responsibility. Part of the interview is mentioned in *Osland v The Queen* (1998) 197 CLR 316 at 397:

> Right. Can you tell me exactly what happened?
> We just hit him with a bar.
> What sort of bar was it, Heather?
> Just a round bar. Just a piece of pole.
> And where did you get that from?
> Down the shed.
> Who actually hit him?
> Well, we—it's together. I'm not saying David did. He—I wanted to do it but I wasn't strong enough, David said. Poor David.
> How many times did you hit him?
> Just once, I think. Just once, might be twice.
> So, in fact, David hit him with the steel pole?
> We hit him together, it's joint responsibility. I know it is, it's not fair that David's got to take that blame.
> What happened after he was hit?
> (No audible reply)
> Was he dead?
> Yeah. He was dead.
> How did you know?
> Well, he wasn't movin'.

The defence's acceptance of the prosecution approach to acting in concert meant that ultimately Heather Osland could be convicted and sentenced to jail yet David be acquitted. In the High Court, McHugh, Kirby and Callinan JJ held that there was no inconsistency between the verdicts at trial. Where two or more people act in concert, the verdict in relation to each offender may differ. McHugh J said (at 360) that because this was a case of presence at the scene and acting in concert, the jury was entitled to convict Osland and fail to reach a verdict on Albion because the issue of their criminal responsibility was independent. The evidence supporting the defences differed in the case of each accused and was capable of giving rise to different verdicts.

Kirby J expressly agreed with McHugh J on this point in relation to those acting in concert and stated at 384:

> [T]he appellant made it plain that she was the moving force: contributing the idea, the methodology and the disposal of the body. She seemed to express regret for involving her son at all, a view which might well have been shared by the jury.

When Mr Albion struck the blows that killed the deceased, she accepted that he was doing so for her. She made the death possible by administering the sedative and holding the deceased whilst he twitched his last mortal movements. Far from objecting to the tender of the evidence of [the] interview at the trial, the appellant's counsel took the appellant through it.

Similarly, as quoted above, Callinan J said (at 402) that where two or more people act in concert they are causatively jointly responsible for the commission of the crime.

Gaudron and Gummow JJ in the minority agreed (at 324–5) that there is no necessary inconsistency between the conviction of a person who substantially contributed to the death of another and the acquittal of a person whose act is the immediate cause of death.

However, Gaudron and Gummow JJ went on to say (at 326) that on the facts, the only act done by Heather Osland that might be thought to have contributed to the death of her husband was the mixing of sedatives into his dinner. This was not a substantial contribution given that the judge directed the jury that it could only be the blow that was the operative and substantial cause of death.

Gaudron and Gummow JJ then separated the causation issue from the question of whether or not Heather and David acted in concert. They stated (at 333) that the only way in which Heather could be convicted was if David had acted pursuant to an understanding or arrangement that they would kill Frank Osland. They were of the view that there could not have been any understanding or arrangement unless the prosecution had negatived self-defence and provocation in relation to David. Because these defences had not been negatived, there could not have been an agreement.

This reasoning is very difficult to follow. As McHugh J points out (at 360), there is no inconsistency in finding that David was acting in self-defence or under provocation and at the same time acting pursuant to an understanding or arrangement. Nor does it seem logical to divorce the causation issue from that of acting in concert. It seems that Callinan J's view, that where two or more people act in concert they are causatively jointly responsible for the commission of the crime, is to be preferred here.

In all, the significant principles to be derived from *Osland*'s case are that the doctrine of acting in concert is a form of primary rather than derivative liability, and where two or more people act in concert, the verdict in relation to each offender may differ.

Critique

The conceptual basis for the doctrine of acting in concert has proved problematic. In England, unlike Australia, the weight of academic opinion favours the view that joint enterprise liability is a type of accessorial or derivative liability: see CMV

Clarkson, 'Complicity. Powell and Manslaughter' [1998] Crim LR 556–61 and JC Smith, 'Criminal Liability of Accessories' [1997] 113 *Law Quarterly Review* 453–67 at 462. The idea that a person who jointly agrees to the commission of an offence but does not actually commit the physical elements may be deemed to 'participate' as a principal offender is viewed as illogical. John Cyril Smith is strongly critical of the trend to view joint enterprise as a separate form of liability and a means of participating in another person's offence as opposed to simply being an application of ordinary principles of accessorial liability. He observed (at 462): 'If D and P set out together to rape (or to murder), how does D "participate" in P's act of sexual intercourse with V (or P's pulling of the trigger and shooting V) except by assisting him [or her] or encouraging him [or her]…It is submitted that there is no other way.' Smith distinguished joint enterprise liability from joint principal liability where each person's action forms part of the physical element.

On the other hand, it may be appropriate for those who act as the result of a preconceived plan to be held liable for each other's acts: G Hubble, 'Osland v The Queen' (1999) 23 Crim LJ 109–13. The emphasis should then be on the scope of what was decided. It is significant that all members of the High Court in *Osland* were prepared to hold that acting in concert was a form of primary rather than derivative liability. This seems to settle the matter once and for all.

In hindsight, perhaps it could have been argued that Heather Osland was simply aiding and abetting the killing of her husband. That would have left open the possibility of her acquittal because David had been acquitted. However, as McHugh J stated at 364–5:

> It is, in my view, unremarkable that at the trial counsel for Mrs Osland was not prepared to raise the issue that she could not be convicted of murder unless her son was convicted of the charge…
>
> Mrs Osland by her own admission played a significant part in the sequence of events that brought about Frank Osland's death. She administered the drugs that rendered him unable to defend himself against the fatal blow or blows. She went into the bedroom to see whether he was asleep so that he could be hit with the pipe. She told her son that she would use the pipe. She plainly encouraged her son when he said that he could not do it. She was present as he struck the blow or blows that killed her husband. The fact that she held his body down on the bed during his death throes was also evidence which, combined with other evidence, indicated that she could be regarded as a principal in the first degree in her own right rather than simply as an accessory… .

Perhaps the real problem lies in the practicalities of determining who was acting according to a preconceived plan and who was aiding and abetting a principal offender. As we shall explore later, derivative liability and the doctrine of common purpose bring with them other problems. We turn first to an exploration of innocent agency as a means of assigning primary liability.

Innocent agency

Background

In *Osland v The Queen* (1998) 197 CLR 316, the prosecution predominantly focused on Heather Osland's acting in concert with her son to kill Frank Osland. However, the prosecution also argued that David could be seen as an 'innocent agent' in that Heather's conviction was consistent with the jury's failure to convict her son on the basis that he was her innocent agent. Gaudron and Gummow JJ (at 326) rejected this argument on the basis that it had not been raised at trial and a guilty verdict cannot be upheld on a basis not left to the jury. The other judges apart from McHugh J did not consider innocent agency.

McHugh J pointed out (at 348) that in many cases, it is better to describe the actual perpetrator as a 'non-responsible' rather than an 'innocent' agent. As we outline the current law in this area, this should be kept in mind.

The doctrine of innocent agency converts an apparent 'aider and abettor' into a principal offender. It attributes criminal responsibility to a person who has not personally performed the physical elements of a crime. That is, if a person uses an 'innocent agent' to commit a crime, it is that person and not the innocent agent who is the principal offender, regardless of whether he or she was present at the scene of the crime.

Peter Alldridge portrays the doctrine as arising out of the constraints of the procedural and substantive law of accessorial liability: 'The Doctrine of Innocent Agency' (1990) 2(1) *Criminal Law Forum* 45–83 at 48. The early cases characterised 'innocence' as that of infancy or ignorance. This was gradually extended to situations where the agent was considered not responsible by reason of some defence.

The current law

An innocent agent is one who is not considered criminally responsible by reason of infancy, mental impairment, lack of knowledge of the true facts or belief that the act is not unlawful. Innocence refers to the agent's lack of criminal responsibility rather than lack of moral fault: *Hewitt* (1996) 84 A Crim R 440 at 450 per Winneke P.

An extensive range of offences has been listed as having been committed by an innocent agent, including:
- **murder**: *Coombes* (1785) 1 Leach 388; *Tyler and Price* (1838) 1 Mood CC 428; *Michael* (1840) 9 C & P 356;
- **administering poison**: *Harley* (1830) 4 C & P 369;
- **forgery**: *Palmer* (1804) 2 Leach 978; *Giles* (1827) 1 Mood CC 166; *Mazeau* (1840) 9 C & P 676; *Clifford* (1845) 2 Car & K 202; *Bull* (1845) 1 Cox 281; *Valler* (1844) 1 Cox 84; *Bannen* (1844) 1 Car & K 295;

- **theft**: *Pitman* (1826) 2 C & P 423; *Manley* (1844) 1 Cox 104; *Welham* (1845) 1 Cox 192; *Bleasdale* (1848) 2 Car & K 765; *Flatman* (1880) 14 Cox 396; *Adams* (1812) R & R 225; *Kay* (1857) Dears & B 231; *Paterson* [1976] NZLR 394;
- **offences involving fraud**: *DPP v Stonehouse* [1978] AC 55; *Mutton* (1793) 1 Esp 62; *Brisac and Scott* (1803) East, *PC* iv. 164, 102 ER 792; *Butcher* (1858) Bell 6; *Dowey* (1868) 11 Cox 115; *Butt* (1884) 15 Cox 564; *R v Oliphant* (1905) 2 KB 67;
- **libel**: *Johnson* (1805) 29 St Tr 81; *Cooper* (1846) 8 QB 533; and
- **rape**: *R v Cogan and Leak* [1976] 1 QB 217; *Hewitt* (1996) 84 A Crim R 440.

An example of when the agent was innocent of any wrongdoing and the accused was regarded as the principal offender is exemplified by *White v Ridley* (1978) 140 CLR 342. In that case, the accused employed an airline carrier to unwittingly import cannabis into Australia. On appeal against conviction, a majority of the High Court held that the accused could be found liable for the importation of drugs via an innocent agent. This is an unusual example of the doctrine in that the 'innocent agent' was the airline carrier rather than a person. The majority found (at 354 per Stephen J) that a person can be properly convicted of an offence when an innocent agent is used to perform the physical elements of the crime, providing the requisite intent is present and no other cause has intervened to displace the accused's actions as a continuing legal cause of the crime's physical elements.

The doctrine of innocent agency may apply even where the accused is personally unable to commit the crime as a principal offender. For example, in *R v Cogan and Leak* [1976] QB 217 the accused, Leak, persuaded Cogan, his 'drunken friend', to have sexual intercourse with Leak's wife. The latter submitted to sex with Cogan out of fear of her husband. She did not struggle with Cogan, but sobbed throughout the ordeal and tried to turn away from him. Cogan was convicted of rape and Leak was convicted of aiding and abetting the rape.

On appeal, Cogan argued that he honestly believed the victim had been consenting. His appeal was allowed and his conviction quashed. Leak then appealed on the ground that he could not be convicted of aiding and abetting Cogan because the latter had been acquitted of the crime of rape. When the case of *Cogan and Leak* was heard, a husband could not be found guilty of raping his wife. Nevertheless, the Court of Appeal upheld Leak's conviction on the basis that he had possessed the necessary fault element for raping his wife and had used Cogan as an 'instrument' for the necessary physical act.

The Court of Appeal clearly viewed Leak as a principal offender rather than an aider and abettor. The Court stated (at 223):

> The modern law allowed Leak to be tried and punished as a principal offender. In our judgment he could have been indicted as a principal offender. It would have been no defence for him to submit that if Cogan was an 'innocent' agent, he was

necessarily in the old terminology of the law a principal in the first degree, which was a legal impossibility as a man cannot rape his own wife during cohabitation. The law no longer concerns itself with niceties of degrees in participation in crime; but even if it did Leak would still be guilty. The reason a man cannot by his own physical act rape his wife during cohabitation is because the law presumes consent from the marriage ceremony...There is no such presumption when a man procures a drunken friend to do the physical act for him.

This decision has been criticised on the ground that the 'bodily connotations' of rape are so strong that it is incongruous to hold that the offence can be perpetrated by another's act: G Williams, *Textbook of Criminal Law* (2nd edn, London: Stevens & Sons, 1983) p 371. The Victorian Court of Appeal has stressed, however, that the physical element of rape can be satisfied by an accused sexually penetrating a person who is not consenting or by *causing* such a person to be sexually penetrated: *Hewitt* (1996) 84 A Crim R 440. See further G Hubble, 'Rape by Innocent Agent' (1997) 21(4) Crim LJ 204–12.

Critique

The Criminal Law Officers Committee (CLOC) took the view that a provision for innocent agency should be included in the Model Criminal Code: Criminal Law Officers Committee, *Chapters 1 and 2, General Principles of Criminal Responsibility*, Final Report (December 1992) p 93. Section 11.3 of the *Criminal Code* (Cth) reads as follows:

> A person who:
> (a) has, in relation to each physical element of an offence, a fault element applicable to that physical element; and
> (b) procures conduct of another person that (whether or not together with conduct of the procurer) would have constituted an offence on the part of the procurer if the procurer had engaged in it;
> is taken to have committed that offence and is punishable accordingly.

This section is based on s 7 of the *Criminal Code* (WA), which refers to procuring another to commit an act or omission that would have been an offence if the procurer had done the act or made the omission. The significance of these provisions is that they serve to deem the procurer a principal offender regardless of the responsibility of the perpetrator. This is not the case with a procurer under accessorial liability, which is dependent upon the perpetrator of the criminal act being found criminally responsible.

The term 'procure' in the Commonwealth legislation is not defined, but presumably has the same meaning as at common law. As we shall explore in the next section, a 'procurer' is one who causes the offence to be committed: *R v Beck* [1985] 1 All ER 571.

In practice, the use of these provisions could lead to anomalous situations. For example, if an accused is charged under s 11.3 for procuring a child to commit theft, the accused can be found liable because the child will be considered an innocent agent. However, where another accused is charged as an accessory under s 11.2 for procuring an adult to commit theft and the latter claims he or she was acting under duress and is afforded a defence, the latter cannot be found liable because of the derivative nature of accessorial liability.

Peter Alldridge argues that the doctrine of innocent agency is unnecessary: 'The Doctrine of Innocent Agency' (1990) 2(1) *Criminal Law Forum* 45–83. An accused either commits the crime, is an accessory to it or not. Alldridge argues that the current rule that a perpetrator must be convicted before an accessory can be explains why the doctrine of innocent agency has developed. His solution (at 65) is to legislate 'a provision to the effect that the nonconvictability of the perpetrator of an act that contravenes a norm laid down by the criminal law should not bar the liability of accomplices to that act'. That solution depends upon a move away from viewing accessorial liability as derivative. The Law Commission has suggested abolishing accessorial liability as it now stands and replacing it with two new offences of encouraging crime and assisting crime: Law Commission, *Assisting and Encouraging Crime*, Consultation Paper No 131 (London: HMSO, 1993). The merits of this approach will be considered later in this chapter.

Accessorial liability

Background

In the Introduction to this chapter, we outlined how the common law evolved distinctions between modes of complicity based on the nature and seriousness of the offence assisted or encouraged. The older terminology of 'principal in the first and second degree' and 'accessories before and after the fact' have now evolved into counsellors, procurers, aiders and abettors. In this section, we will concentrate on what is meant by these terms as well as accessories 'after the fact'.

All parties to a crime, except for accessories after the fact, face prosecution for the substantive crime itself and therefore face the same punishment or range of punishments. For example, s 323 of the *Crimes Act* 1958 (Vic) reads:
Complicity is therefore not a distinct crime in the way that an attempt, conspiracy or incitement is. Rather, complicity is a way of committing a substantive offence and is dependent upon the commission of that offence. It should by now be clear that accessorial liability is considered derivative in that the liability of an accessory

> A person who aids, abets, counsels or procures the commission of an indictable offence may be tried, indicted or presented and punished as a principal offender.

is dependent upon the commission of the principal offence. It requires the prosecution to prove that the person who was assisted, or encouraged, committed, or at least attempted to commit, the offence. Consequently, accessorial liability is often described as a form of 'secondary liability'. The fault required for this mode of complicity is complex because it has 'two points of reference rather than one—the wrongful act of the accessory as well as the wrongful act of the principal': I Dennis, 'The Mental Element for Accessories' in P Smith (ed), *Criminal Law: Essays in Honour of JC Smith* (London: Butterworths, 1987) p 58. Accessorial liability thus gives rise to questions as to the state of mind that an accessory must possess in order to be guilty of an offence: that is, what level of knowledge or foresight of the offence is required.

The derivative nature of accessorial liability, which links the liability of the accessory to the *guilt* of the principal offender, has been a major source of academic dissatisfaction. We have foreshadowed in the previous section that there is a suggestion that if this approach is abandoned, the law would be greatly clarified in this area. That option will be explored further after we examine the doctrine of common purpose.

We shall outline the current law relating to the physical elements of aiding, abetting, counselling and procuring and then consider in the Critique section the problems associated with accessorial liability by inactivity and whether withdrawal by an accused is enough to negate criminal liability. We will then provide an overview of the law relating to the fault element and provide a critique of recent decisions in this area.

The current law—definitions and physical elements

Although there are some differences in terminology, every Australian jurisdiction has legislative provisions that treat aiders, abettors, counsellors and procurers as well as accessories after the fact to be tried and punished as if they were a principal offender: *Criminal Code* (Cth) s 11.2; *Crimes Act* 1914 (Cth) s 5; *Criminal Code* (ACT) s 45; *Crimes Act* 1900 (NSW) s 346; *Criminal Code* (NT) s 12; *Criminal Code* (Qld) s 7; *Criminal Law Consolidation Act* 1935 (SA) s 267; *Criminal Code* (Tas) s 3; *Crimes Act* 1958 (Vic) ss 323, 324; *Criminal Code* (WA) s 7.

Traditionally, aiders and abettors refer to those present when the offence is committed while counsellors and procurers are those who are absent: *Thambiah v The Queen* [1966] AC 37; *Ferguson v Weaving* [1951] 1 KB 814 at 818–19; *Bowker v Premier Drug Co Ltd* [1928] 1 KB 217; KJM Smith, *A Modern Treatise on the Law of Criminal Complicity* (Oxford: Clarendon Press, 1991) p 32. In *Attorney-General's Reference (No 1 of 1975)* [1975] QB 773 at 779, it was suggested that these terms, which were set out in s 8 of the *Accessories and Abettors Act* 1961 (UK), should be given their 'ordinary meaning'. The Court held that each term has a different shade of meaning and therefore describes a distinct form of accessorial liability. An 'aider' is one who helps, supports or assists the principal offender: *Thambiah v The Queen* [1966] AC 37. An 'abettor' has been held to be a person who incites or encourages the principal to commit the offence: *Wilcox v Jeffery* [1951] 1 All ER 464. In *R v Giorgi* (1983) 31 SASR 299 at 311, Zelling J stated that 'abet' requires encouragement whereas 'aid' does not.

A 'counsellor' is one who advises or encourages the principal offender prior to the offence: *R v Calhaem* [1985] QB 808. A 'procurer' is one who causes the offence to be committed: *R v Beck* [1985] 1 All ER 571. Lord Widgery held in *Attorney-General's Reference (No 1 of 1975)* [1975] QB 773 at 779 that 'procure' means '[t]o produce by endeavour. You procure a thing by setting out to see that it happens and [by] taking the appropriate steps to produce that happening'. By contrast to the word 'procure', the term 'aids' does not imply a causal connection between the assistance given and the commission of the crime. In other words, a person may aid the commission of the crime, without the perpetrator being aware of the assistance offered. The word 'abets' connotes encouragement, implying that the words or conduct must influence the perpetrator's decision to commit a crime, and therefore there must be a causal connection between the acts of encouragement and the crime. Although in 'ordinary language' each word may have a different shade of meaning, the preferable view is that the phrase 'aids, abets, counsels or procures' is merely descriptive of a general concept. Mason J stated in *Giorgianni v The Queen* (1985) 156 CLR 473 at 493: 'While it may be that in the circumstances of a particular case one term will be more closely descriptive of the conduct of a secondary party than another, it is important that this not be allowed to obscure the substantial overlap of the terms at common law and the general concept which they embody.'

In relation to the physical elements of accessorial liability for aiding, abetting, counselling or procuring, an accessory's influence on the commission of an offence may range from a minor to a major role. It may involve encouraging by words or supplying materials or information for use in committing an offence: *National Coal Board v Gamble* [1959] 1 QB 11. It may also encompass driving the principal offender to the scene of the crime, keeping watch, or holding the victim so that the principal offender can commit the offence: *R v Clarkson* [1971] 1 WLR 1402; *Betts and Ridley* (1930) 22 Cr App R 148. The main limitation to the liability of an accessory via the doctrine of complicity is that the prosecution must prove that the accessory showed his or her assent to the principal offender's actions in a manner that promoted their performance.

In general, there does not have to be a causal connection between the accessory's assistance and the commission of the crime: *O'Sullivan v Truth and Sportsman Ltd* (1957) 96 CLR 220; *R v Calhaem* [1985] QB 808. For example, if two persons are involved in a fight and a passer-by cheers them on, the passer-by cannot be said to have caused the fight, but may be criminally responsible in the sense that he or she has encouraged the fight: *R v Coney* (1882) 8 QBD 534; *Wilcox v Jeffrey* [1951] 1 All ER 464. In relation to procuration, however, a causal link may be required: *Attorney-General's Reference (No 1 of 1975)* [1975] QB 773. The procuration need not be the sole or dominant cause of the commission of the offence: *R v Solomon* [1959] Qd R 123 at 129 per Philp J; *Murray v The Queen* [1962] Tas SR 170 at 199 per Crawford J; *Attorney-General v Able* (1984) QB 795.

Those who assist offenders after a crime has been committed are generally referred to as accessories after the fact. The crime that the accessory commits is quite separate from the offence committed by the principal offender and any doctrine relating to participation in a crime. Each jurisdiction apart from New South Wales has statutory provisions dealing with accessories after the fact: *Crimes Act 1914* (Cth) s 6; *Crimes Act 1900* (ACT) s 346; *Criminal Code* (NT) s 13; *Criminal Code* (Qld) s 10; *Criminal Law Consolidation Act 1935* (SA) s 241; *Criminal Code* (Tas) ss 6, 161, 300; *Crimes Act 1958* (Vic) s 325; *Criminal Code* (WA) s 10 and there is a provision in New South Wales dealing with matters of penalty and procedure: *Crimes Act 1900* (NSW) s 347.

Liability as an accessory after the fact is also derivative in that it arises only if the principal offence has been committed: *Dawson v The Queen* (1961) 106 CLR 1. It is a slightly different form of derivative liability to that of other accessories in that the emphasis is on the offence having taken place rather than the principal offender being found criminally responsible. If the principal offender is acquitted, the accessory after the fact can only be convicted if there is sufficient evidence that the accessorial offence took place: *R v Carter* [1990] 2 Qd R 371; *R v Williams* (1932) 32 SR(NSW) 504; *Mahadeo v The King* [1936] 2 All ER 813; *R v Dawson* [1961] VR 773 (Revised on other grounds: *Dawson v The Queen* (1961) 106 CLR 1). If the principal offender has been convicted, the accessory may still argue that the principal offence has not been proved as against him or herself: *Mahadeo v The King* [1936] 2 All ER 813. Obviously proof of the conviction of the principal offender is admissible and constitutes evidence that the accessory committed the accessorial offence: *R v Dawson* [1961] VR 773; *Carter and Savage; Ex parte Attorney-General* (1990) 47 A Crim R 55.

An accessory after the fact must have performed an act that assisted or had the potential to assist the principal offender escape from the administration of justice: *R v Tevendale* [1955] VLR 95; *R v McKenna* [1960] 1 QB 411. Examples of such acts include:

- driving the principal offender away from the scene of the crime: *R v Holey* [1963] 1 All ER 106;
- impersonal assistance such as altering the engine number and repainting a stolen car: *R v Tevendale* [1955] VLR 95;
- helping dispose of stolen property: *R v Butterfield* (1843) 1 Cox CC 39; *R v Williams* (1932) 32 SR(NSW) 504;

- the removal of incriminating evidence after the principal offender has been arrested: *R v Levy* [1912] 1 KB 158; and
- buying a car and clothes for the principal offender: *R v Solomon* [1959] Qd R 123 at 129 per Philp J; *Murray v The Queen* [1962] Tas SR 170 at 199 per Crawford J; *Attorney-General (UK) v Able* [1984] QB 795.

Indirect assistance may also be sufficient to establish liability: *R v McKenna* [1960] 1 QB 411. For example, a person who employs another to aid the principal offender may be convicted as an accessory: *R v Jarvis* (1837) 2 Mood and R 40. Liability may also attach where there is no personal assistance given to the principal offender, but the accessory performs an act such as altering the engine number of a stolen car: *R v Tevendale* [1955] VLR 95; *R v Chapple* (1840) 9 Car and P 355.

To be found criminally responsible, an accessory after the fact must have performed a positive act. For example, in *R v Ready* [1942] VLR 85 the accused passed a message from an abortionist to the woman operated upon, returning the money paid for the operation in return for the latter's silence. The Victorian Supreme Court held that passing on a message was not sufficiently active assistance to constitute the accused as an accessory. Similarly, merely enjoying the proceeds of the crime will not be sufficient: *R v Barlow* (1962) 79 WN(NSW) 756. Visiting a place where stolen property has been brought with a view to a possible purchase is also not enough to constitute liability as an accessory after the fact: *R v Rose* [1962] 3 All ER 298.

Critique

There is no reason why arcane terminology such as aiding, abetting, counselling, procuring and accessories after the fact needs to be retained. Sanford Kadish suggests that accessorial liability should draw a distinction between two forms of conduct—assistance and encouragement—and that only these two forms of liability should be criminalised: S Kadish, 'Complicity, Cause and Blame: A Study in the Interpretation of Doctrine' (1985) 73 *California Law Review* 324–410; *Blame and Punishment; Essays in the Criminal Law* (New York: Macmillan, 1987). JC Smith speculates that it may be necessary to recognise a third category of conduct, 'causing another person to commit an offence': JC Smith, 'Criminal Liability of Accessories: Law and Law Reform' (1997) 113 *The Law Quarterly Review* 453–67 at 453, footnote 3. This latter approach would render obsolete the need for a separate doctrine of innocent agency, which was discussed above. The 'plain language' approach would greatly assist juries to understand the types of conduct giving rise to accessorial liability.

Two major questions associated with the physical elements of accessorial liability are:
- Should a person be held liable as an accessory by merely being present, that is, by simply doing nothing or supplying goods or advice while being indifferent to the commission of a crime; and

- Should a person be held liable as an accessory where he or she has had a change of heart before the commission of the offence?

Mere presence, omissions and supplying goods and advice

The individual who is present during the commission of a crime, but who does not intervene, poses a dilemma for the criminal law. This dilemma has not arisen in relation to accessories after the fact where a positive act is required.

The principles governing accessorial liability by 'mere presence' have been developed in a series of spectator liability cases. In these cases, the courts have held that accessorial liability depends on whether the conduct amounts to encouragement. In general, mere presence at the scene of the crime will not be sufficient for criminal responsibility. For example, in *R v Coney* (1882) 8 QBD 534 Hawkins J stated (at 557–8): 'It is no criminal offence to stand by, a mere passive spectator of a crime, even of a murder. Non-interference to prevent a crime is not itself a crime.'

However, if a person is *deliberately* present at the scene of a crime, this may be taken as evidence that he or she intended to promote or assist the commission of the crime: *R v Coney* (1882) 8 QBD 534; *R v Russell* [1933] VLR 59; *R v Clarkson* [1971] 1 WLR 1402; *R v Bland* [1988] Crim LR 41; *R v Allan* [1965] 1 QB 130. In *Coney*'s case, the accused was among a crowd of spectators who watched two men participate in an illegal prize-fight. The prosecution was unable to prove that the accused took part in the management, or said, or did anything during the prize-fight. The accused was tried for common assault as an accessory.

At trial, the judge held that, as a matter of law, spectators at a prize-fight were guilty of assault. The majority of the Court for Crown Cases Reserved on appeal rejected the assertion that voluntary presence was, as a matter of law, enough to be guilty as an accessory. Hawkins J held (at 557) that the previous authorities established that 'some active steps must be taken by word or action, with intent to instigate the principal, or principals'. However, the Court held that mere presence may in certain circumstances amount to proof of participation. Cave J distinguished (at 540) between accidental presence at the scene of a crime and deliberate presence that might amount to evidence of aiding and abetting. He observed (at 540) that '[w]here presence is prima facie not accidental it is evidence, but no more than evidence, for the jury [of abetting the assault]'.

Coney's case sets out the general principle that an accessory must assist or encourage the principal offender through a positive act, although how this encouragement is manifested will be for the jury to decide. For example, in *R v Clarkson and Carroll* [1971] 1 WLR 1402 the Courts Martial Appeal Court considered whether or not presence during the commission of a rape could give rise to liability as an accessory. A young woman went to a party at an army barracks. At about midnight, she went to the room of a soldier that she knew well. He was not there. In the room, there were a number of gunners in the Royal Artillery some of whom attacked the woman and subjected her to a gang rape. The two appellants, David

Clarkson and Joseph Carroll, did not participate in the rapes. At first, they simply stood outside the room, listening to what was happening. Later they entered the room and remained there while the girl was raped. There was no evidence that the accused had done or said anything to assist or encourage the perpetrators. The Courts Martial Appeal Court, affirming *Coney*, held that being voluntarily and purposely present witnessing the commission of a crime and offering no opposition or dissent, provides cogent evidence that the accused wilfully encouraged the crime or activity and so aided and abetted. The Courts Martial Appeal Court stressed that it is important that the presence *in fact* encouraged the principal offenders and that this is a question for the jury.

In Chapter 2, we explored how there has been a traditional reluctance to use the criminal law to punish those who omit to act in the absence of a legal duty. Nevertheless, an omission to act may give rise to criminal responsibility if the person concerned is under a duty to prevent the crime committed by the principal offender or if the person concerned has a duty of control over the principal offender but deliberately refrains from preventing the principal offender committing the offence.

In *R v Russell* [1933] VLR 59, the accused had committed bigamy. He told his wife of the bigamous relationship. The wife and two children were found drowned in a public pool. The accused claimed that his wife had drowned the children and then committed suicide by drowning herself. The accused claimed that he tried unsuccessfully to save them and failed to report the drowning because he was frightened. The accused was charged with murder and convicted of manslaughter.

The trial judge directed the jury on two possible scenarios. First, if the accused were merely a silent observer, who stood by and did nothing, then he would be guilty on the basis of negligent manslaughter. His omission could give rise to liability because as a parent he was under a duty to care for his children and hence must prevent his wife murdering his children. Alternatively, if the accused actively encouraged or persuaded his wife to kill the children, he was guilty of murder in that he would be taking part in the crime of murder committed by her. The jury returned a verdict of manslaughter on all three charges.

The first scenario based the accused's liability on his omission to act as a form of primary liability for manslaughter in perpetrating the deaths of his children. The second scenario based his liability on being an accessory to the killings committed by his wife. Cussen A-CJ considered the liability on the basis of secondary participation—that is, accessorial liability—and so did not focus on the question of parental duty. He reviewed the authorities governing complicity by mere presence, and the earlier decision of *Coney*. Cussen A-CJ stated (at 67) that if a person was present at the scene of a crime, assent to the crime could sometimes be made out by the 'absence of dissent, or the absence of what may be called effective dissent'. Mann J agreed with Cussen A-CJ, but went even further to say (at 75) that the accused's liability arose from a father's duty to save his children. McArthur J, however, stated that mere non-interference was insufficient for liability as an aider and abettor.

It is difficult to glean any principle regarding complicity from *Russell*'s case, but it appears that it stands for the proposition that 'manifest assent' is necessary in cases where the person is present but does nothing to prevent the commission of a crime. This seems to merge physical and fault elements because it requires evidence that individuals knew or intended that their conduct would assist or encourage the principal offender, a matter that will be considered below.

The duty to prevent a crime may go beyond the bounds of blood ties. In *Ex parte Parker: Re Brotherson (1957)* 57 SR (NSW) 326 the accused was an employee who allowed the principal offender to steal property from the accused's employer. There was some evidence of positive encouragement, but Walsh J stated (at 330) that in some circumstances a failure to carry out a duty to protect arising from a contract could amount to encouragement of the commission of a crime.

Imposing liability for complicity on the basis of omissions places a heavy burden on individuals to control the criminal conduct of others, constituting 'in one sense a policy of conscripting "controllers" into the ranks of crime prevention authorities': KJM Smith, *A Modern Treatise on the Law of Criminal Complicity* (Oxford: Clarendon Press, 1991) p 46. For example, there is some precedent for requiring owner-passengers of cars to prevent another's dangerous driving: *Dennis v Plight* (1968) 11 FLR 458; *R v Harris* [1964] Crim LR 54. It can easily be imagined that this rule could be extended to require those serving alcohol to take steps to prevent intoxicated persons under their control from driving: HR Weinert, 'Social Hosts and Drunken Drivers: A Duty to Intervene?' (1985) 133 *University of Pennsylvania Law Review* 867–94. While it is obviously important as a matter of public policy to prevent dangerous conduct, criminalising the conduct of those who fail to prevent the commission of a crime significantly extends the reach of the criminal law.

The Law Commission for England and Wales has proposed that accessorial liability should be limited to positive acts. This, however, could be offered by mere presence during the commission of the crime, provided that the presence is intended and does, in fact, encourage the crime: Law Commission, Consultation Paper No 131, *Assisting and Encouraging Crime* (London: HMSO, 1993) p 134. The *Criminal Code* (Cth) is silent as to whether mere presence or omissions will constitute accessorial liability. Section 11.2(2)(a) requires the person's conduct to have in fact aided, abetted, counselled or procured the commission of the offence by the other person. Arguably, this requires something more than a mere omission.

A related question to that of accessorial liability by inactivity is whether or not a person may be guilty as an accessory for supplying goods or advice that subsequently makes possible the principal offender's offence. This is exemplified by a shopkeeper or assistant who supplies the 'tools of the trade' while being indifferent to the customer's subsequent use of the goods or advice supplied.

Glanville Williams has argued that '[t]he seller of an ordinary marketable commodity is not his [or her] buyer's keeper in criminal law unless he [or she] is specifically made so by statute. Any other rule would be too wide an extension of criminal responsibility': *Criminal Law—The General Part* (2nd edn, London: Stevens & Sons, 1961) p 373.

The extension of criminal responsibility to include omissions to act and those supplying goods or advice may not be as problematic in Australia as it is in other countries. Simon Bronitt suggests that the radical step of abolishing or restricting accessorial liability by omission is not required in Australia since the fault requirements are more stringent than in England: 'Defending Giorgianni—Part Two: New Solutions for Old Problems in Complicity' (1993) 17 Crim LJ 305–18 at 311. Fault element requirements are discussed further below. The High Court in *Giorgianni v The Queen* (1985) 156 CLR 473 held that an accessory must possess an intention to assist or encourage the principal offender's conduct based on the 'knowledge of the essential matters'. Mere recklessness or wilful blindness will not suffice. Omitting to act may therefore not be enough to establish intention and knowledge. Similarly, following *Giorgianni v The Queen* (1985) 156 CLR 473, suppliers will only be liable as an accessory where they have an intention to assist or encourage the crime based on knowledge of the essential matters that constitute the crime. Suppliers who know that a customer intends to use their goods or services in the commission of a crime must decline to serve that customer to avoid liability as an accessory.

Withdrawal by an accessory

In relation to accessorial liability, there may be a period of time between assisting or encouraging the crime and its actual commission. Considerations of social policy have led to the acceptance of the proposition that if an accessory has a change of heart and clearly makes this known, he or she should be acquitted. KJM Smith refers to an incentive justification for the doctrine: 'Withdrawal in Complicity: A Restatement of Principles' [2001] Crim LR 769–85 at 772. That is, that providing a method of avoiding criminal liability through withdrawal will increase the chances of accessories doing so, thereby leading to a reduced risk of the offence being carried out. Such a policy also enables a person the opportunity for redemption.

Because of its derivative nature, an accessory is not liable until a crime is in fact committed or attempted by the principal offender. Thus, if a person withdraws from assisting or encouraging the crime *before* its commission, then there is no accessorial liability.

Withdrawal generally requires some positive act that gives unequivocal notice of a complete withdrawal to the principal offender. A mere change of mind or secret repentance will not be enough: *R v Jensen and Ward* [1980] VR 194 at 201 per the court; *White v Ridley* (1978) 140 CLR 342; *Becerra* (1975) 62 Cr App R 212; *R v Menniti* [1985] 1 Qd R 520; *R v Saylor* [1963] QWN 14; *R v Solomon* [1959] Qd R 123; *R v Croft* [1944] 1 KB 295. Repentance without a positive act is insufficient because, although the accessory may not possess the requisite fault element at the time of the commission of the crime, he or she will have possessed it at the time of assisting or encouraging the principal offender.

While the law recognises that withdrawal may enable an accused to escape liability as an accessory, 'there is a remarkable area of doubt about the precise limits of the defence': D Lanham, 'Accomplices and Withdrawal' (1981) 97 *The Law Quarterly Review* 575–92. Indeed, there is some conflict as to whether it is in fact a defence at all. This is borne out by the different approaches to withdrawal by the High Court in *White v Ridley* (1978) 140 CLR 342. As previously discussed in the section on innocent agency, the accused employed an airline carrier to unwittingly import cannabis hidden in a stereo receiver from Singapore into Australia. Before the plane took off, the accused was questioned by Customs officers. He then tried to get the airline to cancel delivery of the box containing the drug. The accused claimed that he had withdrawn from the enterprise and therefore was not criminally liable. Gibbs, Stephen and Aickin JJ rejected this argument, with Jacobs and Murphy JJ dissenting. Four of the judges, however, differed as to the nature of withdrawal as an exculpatory factor.

Stephen (at 354) and Aickin JJ (at 363) were of the opinion that withdrawal could not exculpate an accused from criminal responsibility unless it broke the chain of causation. They held that the accused's initial acts had started the chain of causation and that his ineffective attempts to cancel delivery of the box did not break the chain of causation. Gibbs J, on the other hand, held (at 350–1) that withdrawal is a defence in its own right, requiring a timely countermand and such action as is reasonably possible to counteract the effect of the previous conduct. Murphy J (at 363) went one step further than Gibbs J in requiring that the secondary party take such action as is reasonably possible to *prevent* the commission of the offence planned.

The New South Wales Court of Criminal Appeal has followed the approach of Gibbs J in treating withdrawal as a defence in its own right: *Tietie* (1988) 34 A Crim R 438. This approach requires both a timely countermand and action to counteract the effect of previous conduct. An example of such action is informing the police of the proposed crime: *R v Jensen and Ward* [1980] VR 194 at 201.

The differing views in *White v Ridley* show that the conceptual basis for withdrawal is somewhat confused. Gibbs J's approach sees withdrawal as a defence because of the 'reasonable steps' that must be taken to frustrate the commission of crime and because of the reduced culpability of the accessory. Another approach is that evidence of withdrawal negates key ingredients of accessorial liability. As such, withdrawal is not a defence in itself; rather it is merely evidence that the physical and fault elements of accessorial liability are not fulfilled. On Stephen and Aickin JJ's approach, withdrawal means that the accessory's conduct had no causative influence on the subsequent criminal conduct of the principal offender. This evidence may also support the inference that the accessory lacked the intention to assist or encourage the principal offender.

The real problem occurs when the desistence is very close to the commission of the crime. For example, in *Becerra* (1976) 62 Cr App R 212 the accused and two other men broke into a house with intent to steal. The accused gave one of the men a knife to use if they were interrupted by anyone. The accused heard the victim coming down the stairs and told the other two men to leave. Instead of himself confronting the victim, the accused jumped out of the window and the man holding the knife stabbed the victim and killed him. The accused was convicted of murder. An appeal against conviction was dismissed by the Court of Appeal on the basis that the accused's countermand was ineffective and did not amount to withdrawal. The Court stated (at 218):

> Where practicable and reasonable there must be timely communication of the intention to abandon the common purpose from those who wish to dissociate themselves from the contemplated crime and those who desire to continue in it. What is timely communication must be determined by the facts of each case but where practicable and reasonable it ought to be such communication, verbal or otherwise that will serve unequivocal notice upon the other party to the common unlawful cause that if he [or she] proceeds upon it he [or she] does so without the further aid and assistance of those who withdraw.

It would seem that in such a situation nothing short of a physical act on the part of the accused would have stopped the murder occurring. In this sense, the requirement for withdrawal comes very close to Murphy J's analysis in *White v Ridley*.

The law regarding withdrawal aims both to clearly define when a person has continued to be an accessory and so is criminally responsible for the outcome, and when he or she has truly withdrawn. It also recognises the reality that many defendants are likely to claim to have withdrawn, after the event. The law therefore tends to look for some external evidence of withdrawal, which may otherwise amount to no more than a claimed change of mind.

The CLOC followed *Becerra*'s case in placing the onus on the accused to try to prevent the commission of the offence: Criminal Law Officers Committee, *Chapters 1 and 2, General Principles of Criminal Responsibility*, Final Report (December 1992) p 91. Section 11.2(4) of the *Criminal Code* (Cth) now reads as follows:

> A person cannot be found guilty of aiding, abetting, counselling or procuring the commission of an offence if, before the offence was committed, the person:
> (a) terminated his or her involvement; and
> (b) took all reasonable steps to prevent the commission of the offence.

The CLOC stated (at 91) that what will constitute reasonable steps will vary, 'but examples might be discouraging the principal offender, alerting the proposed victim, withdrawing goods necessary for committing the crime (eg a getaway car) and/or giving a timely warning to the appropriate law enforcement authority'.

It appears that the degree and type of assistance rendered by the accessory, together with the proximity in time to the commission of the offence will have a bearing on what will constitute an effective withdrawal. It should, for example, be somewhat easier to show withdrawal after encouraging the commission of an offence than assisting it. If the accessory has only encouraged or advised the perpetrator then it may be enough for him or her to tell the perpetrator to desist in unequivocal terms: *R v Saunders and Archer* (1576) 2 Plowd 473; 75 ER 706; *R v Croft* [1944] 1 KB 295; *R v Fletcher* [1962] Crim LR 551. For example, in *R v Grundy* [1977] Crim LR 543 the accessory supplied information to the perpetrator in relation to a burglary, but substantial attempts to stop the perpetrator breaking in during the two weeks leading up to the offence were held to be sufficient evidence of a valid withdrawal for the jury to consider. A person who does assist a crime should be able to extricate him or herself by a clear countermand without having to take further action to prevent it. Far more will be required if the accessory supplies the means for committing the crime as the situation in *Becerra* attests.

The current law—fault elements

Assisting and encouraging crime

The High Court decision in *Giorgianni v The Queen* (1985) 156 CLR 473 helped clarify the fault element for accessorial liability, but, as we shall explore in the Critique section, there are some associated issues that remain unclear. In *Giorgianni*'s case, Giorgianni leased and operated a prime-mover and trailer. He employed a driver, Renshaw, who lost control of the prime-mover when it suffered a brake failure while heavily laden with coal. The prime-mover crashed into two cars, killing five people and seriously injuring another. Giorgianni was charged with five counts of culpable driving causing death and one count of culpable driving causing grievous bodily harm contrary to s 52A of the *Crimes Act* 1900 (NSW). Section 52A is an offence of strict liability. As explored in Chapter 2, this means that the prosecution need only prove the physical elements of the crime, but a defence of honest and reasonable mistake of fact is open to the accused. The prosecution argued that Giorgianni had procured the act of culpable driving and that he was aware of the prime-mover's brake problems following maintenance work that he had recently undertaken.

The trial judge directed the jury that in order for Giorgianni to have procured the act of culpable driving, he must or *ought to have known* that the brakes were defective. The trial judge went on to direct that it would equally suffice if Giorgianni had acted recklessly, not caring whether or not the brakes were defective. Giorgianni was convicted and he eventually appealed to the High Court on the basis of the trial judge's directions to the jury.

The High Court overturned Giorgianni's convictions and the majority set out the test for the fault element of complicity. The particular facts of the case required specific consideration of the fault required of an accessory when assisting or encouraging an offence of strict liability. However, the High Court took the opportunity to clarify, in general terms, the fault required for *all* accessories, irrespective of the type of offence assisted or encouraged.

There are two aspects to the fault element. The first deals with intentional assistance or encouragement. The second deals with knowledge of the essential facts of the offence.

All the members of the High Court apart from Mason J stated that an accessory must intentionally assist or encourage the principal offender: *Giorgianni v The Queen* (1985) 156 CLR 473 at 482 per Gibbs CJ; at 500 per Wilson, Deane and Dawson JJ. Wilson, Dawson and Deane JJ stated (at 505): 'Aiding, abetting, counselling or procuring the commission of an offence requires the intentional assistance or encouragement of the doing of those things which go to make up the offence.' Recklessness will therefore be insufficient.

The second question for the High Court in *Giorgianni* was whether or not an accessory to the offence of culpable driving under s 52A had to possess actual knowledge of the 'essential matters' (on the facts, knowledge of the defective state of the vehicle), or whether some lesser mental state would suffice.

Prior to *Giorgianni*, the degree of awareness required of an accessory about the factual ingredients of the principal offender's crime was unclear. Some cases took a broad approach, supplementing actual knowledge with recklessness or wilful blindness. In *R v Glennan* (1970) 91 WN (NSW) 609 at 614, the New South Wales Court of Criminal Appeal held that: '[I]t must be shown that [the accessory] either knew or suspected the existence of facts which would constitute the commission of the offence or, perhaps, that he [or she] acted recklessly, not caring whether the facts existed or not.'

The Court of Criminal Appeal further explained (at 614) that knowledge encompassed wilful blindness: that is, 'a failure to make an inquiry which is of such a kind as to suggest that the defendant has deliberately abstained from acquiring knowledge because he [or she] suspected the existence of a fact which would have been ascertained on inquiry'.

The majority of the High Court (Wilson, Deane and Dawson JJ at 506–7) in *Giorgianni* emphatically rejected that recklessness as to the existence of the essential ingredients of the principal offender's offence would suffice: 'It is not sufficient if [the accessory's] knowledge or belief extends only to the possibility or even probability that the acts which he [or she] is assisting or encouraging are such, whether he [or she] realises it or not, as to constitute the factual ingredients of a crime.'

Gibbs CJ (at 487) and Mason J (at 495) agreed with the majority that actual knowledge was required, and that recklessness could never be enough to constitute a person as an accessory. They were prepared (at 482 and 495 respectively), however, to equate wilful blindness with knowledge.

Applied to the facts, Giorgianni would only be an accessory to the strict liability offence of culpable driving committed by Renshaw, if he had *actual* knowledge of the defective state of the vehicle. Since recklessness did not suffice, a belief that the brakes were possibly (or even probably) defective would be insufficient for liability as an accessory. Therefore, the trial judge's direction to the jury in terms of recklessness amounted to a misdirection, and on that basis the majority of the High Court allowed the appeal.

Accessories after the fact

In relation to accessories after the fact, the prosecution must prove beyond reasonable doubt that the accessory:
- knew or believed the principal offender was guilty of the principal offence; and
- intended to assist the principal offender to escape from the administration of justice.

In the past, it appears that the common law required the accessory to have knowledge of the precise principal offence that had been committed before he or she could be found criminally responsible: *R v Tevendale* [1955] VLR 95; *R v Stone* [1981] VR 737 at 741 per Crockett J. Most of the statutory provisions reflect this requirement: *Crimes Act* 1900 (ACT) s 346; *Crimes Act* 1914 (Cth) s 6; *Criminal Code* (NT) s 13; *Criminal Code* (Qld) s 10; *Criminal Code* (Tas) s 6; *Criminal Code* (WA) s 10.

However, the South Australian and Victorian provisions have extended the fault element such that it is not necessary for the prosecution to prove that the accessory knew the precise offence or even the particular kind of offence: *Criminal Law Consolidation Act* 1935 (SA) s 241(1); *Crimes Act* 1958 (Vic) s 325(1). In Victoria, it is sufficient if the accessory simply believes that the principal has committed a serious indictable offence. The South Australian provision also extends to a belief that some other offence was committed in the same, or partly in the same, circumstances. In South Australia and Victoria, it is a defence that the accessory's act was done with lawful authority or reasonable excuse: *Criminal Law Consolidation Act* 1935 (SA) s 241(2); *Crimes Act* 1958 (Vic) s 325(1).

The prosecution must further prove that the accessory intended to assist the principal offender to evade justice in some way. If the accused does an act solely for his or her own benefit, he or she will not be held liable as an accessory: *R v Jones* [1949] 1 KB 194; *R v Barlow* (1962) 79 WN (NSW) 756; *Middap* (1992) 63 A Crim R 434 (Vic CCA). If, however, the accused acted partly for his or her own benefit *and* partly in order to assist the principal offender, as may occur in the situation of receiving stolen goods, he or she will be considered liable as an accessory: *R v Reeves* (1892) 13 LR (NSW) 220; *Leaman v The Queen* [1986] Tas R 223 at 231 per Cox J.

Critique

In Chapter 2, we referred to Alan Norrie's suggestion that the law has recognised three different and conflicting meanings of intention: 'Criminal Law to Legal Theory:

The Mysterious Case of the Reasonable Glue Sniffer' (2002) 65(4) *Modern Law Review* 538–55 at 539. These are:
- intention as purpose in the sense of meaning to perform the conduct;
- intention as purpose plus foresight of virtually certain side-effect; and
- intention as purpose plus foresight of probable consequence.

What is meant by intentional assistance or encouragement is therefore open to question. It could mean a 'specific intent' in the sense of meaning to promote the commission of the offence. Alternatively, it could mean foresight of the probable consequence that the accused's conduct will encourage or assist the principal offender to commit the offence.

The majority in *Giorgianni* referred to the fact that 'intention' had a variable meaning in the criminal law. Wilson, Dawson and Deane JJ stated at 506:

> For the purposes of many offences it may be true to say that if an act is done with foresight of its probable consequences there is sufficient intent in law even if such intent may more properly be described as a form of recklessness. There are, however, offences in which it is not possible to speak of recklessness as constituting sufficient intent. Attempt is one and conspiracy is another. And we think the offences of aiding and abetting and counselling and procuring are others. Those offences require intentional participation in a crime by lending assistance or encouragement.

Wilson, Dawson and Deane JJ (at 506) clearly favoured a requirement of specific intent—requiring that the accessory's acts of assistance or encouragement '…be intentionally aimed at the commission of the acts which constitute [the principal offender's offence]'. They also observed (at 507) that if an alternative, less stringent fault element is permitted, 'a person might be guilty of aiding, abetting, counselling or procuring the commission of an offence which formed no part of his [or her] design'. Gibbs CJ held (at 487–8) that the natural meaning of the words 'aiding, abetting, counselling or procuring' suggests a more restrictive fault standard based on intent. This certainly helps confine the scope of accessorial liability.

In relation to the second part of the fault elements, it is still unclear what will constitute knowledge of the essential facts of an offence. Is it knowledge of the elements of the crime? Will it be enough for an accessory to know that the principal offender will commit a type of crime rather than a specific crime or simply that the perpetrator intends to commit a crime? What happens if the perpetrator's offence differs from the crime that the accessory contemplates?

One approach to these questions emerges from the facts of *Stokes and Difford* (1990) 51 A Crim R 25. In that case, Stokes was convicted as a principal offender of maliciously inflicting grievous bodily harm with intent to inflict grievous bodily harm. Difford was convicted as an accessory of maliciously inflicting grievous bodily harm. On appeal, the New South Wales Court of Criminal Appeal quashed Difford's conviction. Hunt J, in delivering the judgment of the Court stated (at 38):

In relation to [accessories]...it seems to me, it is usually more appropriate to speak of the accessory's knowledge (or awareness) of the principal offender's *intention* to do an act with a particular state of mind at the time when the accessory aids, abets, counsels or procures the principal offender to commit the crime in question than it is to speak of the accessory's knowledge of the act *done* by the principal offender with that state of mind. [Emphasis in original.]

On the facts, it was held that the prosecution had failed to establish that Difford knew of the intention of Stokes to hit the victim and that Stokes intended to inflict some physical injury or realised the possibility that some such injury might result but nevertheless intended to go ahead and hit the victim.

The case of *Stokes and Difford* therefore stands for the proposition that the knowledge of the principal offender's *intention* will be enough to satisfy this limb of the fault element.

Another approach to what is meant by this part of the fault element is to require proof that the accessory had knowledge of the physical elements of the crime. It appears that it will be sufficient if the secondary party had knowledge of the type of crime to be committed. For example, in *R v Bainbridge* [1960] 1 QB 129, the accused supplied oxygen-cutting equipment to others who used the equipment to break into a bank and steal cash. The Court of Appeal held that the accused was liable as he knew, when supplying the equipment, that it would be used for a breaking and entry offence. The Court of Appeal held that an accessory only needed to know the general type of crime to be committed, rather than the specific crime, for criminal responsibility to be made out. Similarly, in *DPP (Northern Ireland) v Maxwell* [1978] 3 All ER 1140, the House of Lords held that an accessory would be liable if he or she knew that the crime to be committed was one from a limited range of offences.

The approach set out in *Bainbridge* runs the risk of over-criminalisation: Law Commission, Working Paper No 43, *General Principles, Parties, Complicity and Liability for the Acts of Another* (London: HMSO, 1972) pp 73–7. The *Bainbridge* decision means that an accessory who assists or encourages a person to commit a particular crime is theoretically liable for all crimes subsequently committed by the perpetrator provided those subsequent crimes are of the same *type* as the crime that the accessory originally contemplated.

JR Spencer points out that the decision in *Bainbridge* must be seen in the context of having to tie the liability of the accessory to the commission of the perpetrator's offence: 'Trying to Help Another Person Commit a Crime' in PF Smith (ed), *Criminal Law: Essays in Honour of JC Smith* (London: Butterworths, 1987) pp 148–69 at 148. The derivative nature of accessorial liability again is the cause of problems in this area.

Bainbridge's case was decided prior to the decision in *Giorgianni*, whereas *Stokes and Difford* was decided afterwards. It may be that the High Court had in mind *Bainbridge*'s case so that liability would attach to an accessory who intended to assist or encourage a type of offence committed by the perpetrator. This version has been adopted by the CLOC: Criminal Law Officers Committee, *Chapters 1 and 2, General Principles of Criminal Responsibility*, Final Report (December 1992) p 86. Section 11.2(3)(a) of the *Criminal Code* (Cth) now states that for a person to be guilty, he or she must have intended that 'his or her conduct would aid, abet, counsel or procure the commission of the offence (including its fault elements) *of the type* the other person committed' [emphasis added].

The Law Reform Commission of Canada has made an alternative recommendation: Working Paper No 45, *Secondary Liability: Participation in Crime and Inchoate Offences* (1985) p 36. It has proposed that there should be no criminal liability as an accessory where there is a difference between the crime the accessory intends to promote and the crime actually committed by the perpetrator, *except* where that difference relates to the 'identity of the victim or to the degree of harm'.

Perhaps the better approach is to reconsider the derivative nature of accessorial liability. If it is the assistance or encouragement of an offence that is sought to be criminalised, then the focus should be on workable ways of doing just that. We shall return to this point once we have examined the doctrine of common purpose in the next section.

The doctrine of common purpose

Background

Sean McAuliffe, who was aged 17, and his brother David McAuliffe, who was aged 16, spent the evening of Friday, 20 July 1990 with their friend Matthew Davis consuming a large amount of alcohol and smoking marijuana. At some stage, they decided to 'roll', 'rob' or 'bash' someone near Bondi Beach. Both of the McAuliffes had considerable expertise in Tae Kwon Do and Davis was described as an experienced street fighter.

Sean McAuliffe armed himself with a hammer and Davis armed himself with a baton or stick. There was no direct evidence that David McAuliffe knew of this fact before they arrived at a park near the beach, which was near cliffs and lookout areas. Two men, Sullivan and Rattanajaturathaporn, were walking near a lookout at the top of a cliff. These two men were not in each other's company, but were not far apart.

Sean McAuliffe threatened Sullivan with a hammer and told him to hand over his jacket. He then punched and kicked him and left him on a bench. In the meantime, David McAuliffe and Davis attacked Rattanajaturathaporn—McAuliffe punching and kicking him and Davis beating him with a stick. Davis chased the victim on to an elevated footpath that ran along the top of the cliff. Sean McAuliffe then kicked the victim in the chest. He said by that stage, Rattanajaturathaporn had been severely bashed and he kicked him to finish the bashing. As a result of the kick, the victim fell onto a slightly elevated footpath into a puddle, which was three metres from the edge of the cliff. The McAuliffes and Davis then left the scene.

The next day, Sullivan reported the attack to the police. The day after, the body of Rattanajaturathaporn was found at the base of the cliff. It was obvious that he had been bashed, but the direct cause of death was either the fall from the cliff or drowning. All three youths were charged with the murder of Rattanajaturathaporn. Matthew Davis pleaded guilty to murder and did not give evidence at the trial of the McAuliffes.

The two brothers pleaded not guilty, but were convicted of murder and this was upheld by the Supreme Court of New South Wales. The matter then went on appeal to the High Court: *McAuliffe and McAuliffe v The Queen* (1995) 183 CLR 108.

The facts of this case raise a number of questions. The three men had agreed to assault someone, but had not agreed to kill anyone. The situation therefore differed from that of *Osland v The Queen* (1998) 197 CLR 316 where there was evidence that Heather and David *had* agreed to kill Frank Osland. Further, the McAuliffe brothers argued that they may have intended to cause harm, but they did not intend to inflict *grievous* bodily harm and therefore could not be found guilty of murder.

The High Court, in a joint judgment, dismissed the McAuliffe's appeal against conviction for murder. In the process, the Court set out the common law rules for what is referred to as the 'doctrine of common purpose'.

The 'common purpose' refers to an understanding or arrangement between one person and another or others that they will commit a crime. The doctrine of common purpose is generally regarded as a special form of accessorial liability. It serves to hold those who embark on a joint criminal enterprise or plan to commit an offence, liable for any further crime committed by other group members in the course of that joint criminal enterprise or plan.

The doctrine of common purpose at common law thus imposes accessorial liability in relation to the commission of crimes that are not within the scope of the original criminal agreement *but are contemplated as a possible consequence*. In the Australian context, where ordinary liability for 'aiding, abetting, counselling or procuring' requires the accessory to assist or encourage with intention based on knowledge of the essential matters, this doctrine considerably widens the scope of complicity.

In *McAuliffe*'s case, the prosecution argued at trial that each of the youths contemplated the intentional infliction of grievous bodily harm as a *possible* consequence in carrying out a 'common purpose' to assault someone. This argument found favour with the High Court. Thus for an accused to be found liable under the doctrine of common purpose at common law:

- there must be an understanding or agreement to commit a crime (in *McAuliffe*'s case an assault);
- the crime must be carried out in accordance with the understanding or agreement.

If these two criteria are fulfilled, then an accused can be found liable (at 115) for 'the possible consequences...which were within the contemplation of the parties to the understanding or arrangement'.

The position in the Code jurisdictions, as we shall explore, is slightly different, emphasising an objective rather than a subjective component of the doctrine.

'Acting in concert', which was explored earlier, needs to be distinguished from the doctrine of 'common purpose'. The High Court in *Osland v The Queen* (1998) 197 CLR 316 held that acting in concert is a form of primary liability and it means that it will be enough to establish liability as a principal offender if the acts were performed in the presence of all and pursuant to a preconceived plan. The doctrine of common purpose, on the other hand, imposes secondary liability for foreseen but unintended offences committed by other members who are also participating in the original criminal agreement. There is clearly the potential for these two doctrines to overlap on the same facts and this may help explain why there has been so much conceptual confusion in the law of complicity.

John Smith describes the doctrine of common purpose as 'parasitic accessory liability': 'Criminal Liability of Accessories: Law and Law Reform' (1997) 113 *The Law Quarterly Review* 453–67 at 455. That is, it depends upon the existence of what Smith terms 'basic accessorial liability'. The rationale for having such an extension of accessorial liability relates to the risk of joint criminal enterprises escalating into the commission of more serious offences. From a public policy perspective, there is a perceived need to provide effective protection to the public caused by criminals operating in gangs: *R v Powell*; *R v English* [1997] 3 WLR 959 at 966, per Lord Steyn and at 976, per Lord Hutton.

While the doctrine of common purpose is generally seen as a method of extending accessorial or 'parasitic' liability, the High Court in *R v Barlow* (1997) 188 CLR 1 has ruled that an accessory can be found guilty of a different offence to that of the perpetrator's. This is in sharp contrast to the situation in England where the House of Lords in *R v Powell*; *R v English* [1997] 3 WLR 959 refused to permit differential verdicts, affirming a principle of exact equivalence for accessorial and principal offender culpability.

The High Court in *Barlow*'s case reviewed authority from various Commonwealth jurisdictions and concluded that an accessory participating in a common purpose may be liable for manslaughter even where the perpetrator is guilty of murder. Although the case concerned the interpretation of the statutory provisions dealing with the liability of secondary parties who share a 'common intention to prosecute an unlawful purpose' contrary to s 8 of the *Criminal Code* (Qld), Brennan CJ, Dawson and Toohey JJ held (at 14) that s 8 operates in the same way as the common law.

Brennan CJ, Dawson and Toohey (at 10) posed the question raised by the appeal thus: 'Does Barlow avoid liability for manslaughter because the striker of the fatal and unjustified and unexcused blow had an intention that made him liable to punishment for murder?' Such an interpretation, in their view, would be 'perverse'.

Brennan CJ, Dawson and Toohey (at 11) considered that the effect of s 8 is to 'deem' the secondary party to have committed the acts of the perpetrator. This approach to liability echoes the approach taken in 'acting in concert' cases, although liability under s 8 was viewed as a form of secondary participation rather than primary liability. In such cases, the culpability of the secondary parties is determined by two reference points: first, the parties' original 'common intention to prosecute an unlawful purpose' and secondly, the precise mental state of the secondary party at the relevant time. In relation to the latter, the mental state of the accessory could extend to either lesser or greater offences committed by the perpetrator, thus leaving open the possibility of differential verdicts. Brennan CJ, Dawson and Toohey JJ stated at 14:

> If, at the time that the act was done or the omission was made, the secondary party had a state of mind which, in combination with an act or omission of the nature which s 8 deems him [or her] to have done or made, renders him [or her] guilty of a more serious offence than the offence of which the principal offender is guilty, the secondary party is liable to conviction of the more serious offence. Thus, the mastermind who, having greater knowledge of the circumstances or the likely result of a minor criminal offence which he [or she] and a comparatively innocent principal offender agree to commit, or who has an evil intent not shared by the principal offender, will be liable according to his [or her] (the secondary party's) state of mind, although the common plan was merely to commit the minor offence.

Kirby J agreed with the judgment of Brennan CJ, Dawson and Toohey JJ, pointing out the wide array of legal authority, both statutory as well as common law, that supported differential verdicts. In addition to legal authority, Kirby J pointed out (at 40) that differential verdicts allow the trier of fact 'to distinguish between the culpability of the accused and to avoid artificial consequences which may offend the sense of justice'. The option of having differential verdicts also helps avoid practical problems in cases where secondary parties and perpetrators are tried separately. In such cases, the trial judge of 'the common purpose offender could not finally know the conviction entered against the principal. Yet, on this theory, it is needed in order to define the offence of the co-offender'.

McHugh J dissented, basing his judgment on a narrow interpretation of the Code provision. He held that the common law had no bearing on the matter as the legislation, properly construed, required the party of an unlawful common purpose to be acquitted or convicted of the *same offence* as that for which the principal offender was convicted.

The possibility of having differential verdicts seems to be at odds with accessorial liability's derivative foundations. This paves the way for abandoning the difference between primary and derivative liability and this will be taken up further in the Conclusion.

There have been calls for the abolition of the doctrine of common purpose: see, for example, S Gray, '"I Didn't Know, I Wasn't There": Common Purpose and the Liability of Accessories to Crime' (1999) 23 Crim LJ 201–17. As we shall explore in the Critique section, the CLOC at first decided to abolish the doctrine of common purpose, but after submissions on the matter, decided to retain common purpose in a modified form based on the general definition of recklessness used in the Code: Criminal Law Officers Committee, *Chapters 1 and 2, General Principles of Criminal Responsibility*, Final Report (December 1992) p 89.

The current law

As stated above, the High Court in *McAuliffe and McAuliffe v The Queen* (1995) 183 CLR 108 set out the common law approach to the doctrine of common purpose. An accused can be liable for those criminal acts that were *within the contemplation* of the parties to the original understanding or arrangement. Liability for incidental offences committed pursuant to a common purpose is therefore determined by reference to the subjective state of mind of the parties. Section 8(1) of the *Criminal Code* (NT) follows the common law approach.

The other Code jurisdictions, however, take a different approach. An accessory will be liable for any crime committed by the principal offender that *was a probable consequence* of the pursuit of the unlawful purpose: *Criminal Code* (Qld) s 8; *Criminal Code* (Tas) s 4; *Criminal Code* (WA) s 8. This must be determined objectively: *Stuart v The Queen* (1974) 134 CLR 426.

The word 'probable' has been held to mean a 'real' or 'substantial' possibility: *Hind and Harwood* (1995) 80 A Crim R 105 at 117, 142, 143. In *Stuart v The Queen* (1974) 134 CLR 426 at 443, Gibbs J set out the objective test in relation to s 8 of the Queensland *Criminal Code*: 'Under s 8 it is necessary for the jury to consider fully and in detail what was the unlawful purpose and what its prosecution was intended to entail and what was the nature of the actual crime committed, and then to decide whether the crime was of such a nature that its omission was a probable consequence of the prosecution of that purpose.'

The test to establish the existence and scope of the common purpose is the same in the Code jurisdictions as at common law. That is, the original agreement to commit an offence must be operating when the incidental offence is committed. The rationale for this is based on the idea that this form of accessorial liability is 'parasitic' upon the original criminal purpose of the parties.

For example, in *Heaney et al* (1992) 61 A Crim R 241 the Victorian Court of Criminal Appeal held that crimes committed *after* the original plan had been executed or where the party has effectively withdrawn from the original plan are not within the scope of the common purpose. In *Heaney's* case, two sisters, Karen and Donna Randall, and Rhona Heaney and Ian Gillin were involved in a plot to kill Paul Snabel, who had been ill-treating Karen. Snabel was lured to Heaney's home and the plan was to mix up amphetamines with battery acid and give it to the victim, who was a drug user. However, the injection failed to work. Another person present clubbed the victim to death. The Randall sisters had left the house before the clubbing was either discussed or inflicted. The Court of Criminal Appeal allowed the appeals of Karen and Donna Randall against conviction for murder on the ground that the jury had not been directed that the common purpose or design between the parties must be continuing during the commission of the crime.

The main point of difference between the common law and the Code jurisdictions is that the former's emphasis on the contemplation of possible consequences of the scope of the common purpose extends the scope of complicity quite substantially. That is, *McAuliffe*'s case extends the scope of the doctrine of common purpose to include the commission of an offence that occurred *outside* the scope of the original understanding or agreement, but was nevertheless contemplated as a possibility. There are therefore two situations encompassed by the doctrine at common law. The High Court in *McAuliffe*'s case holds that an accessory will be liable where he or she contemplates:

- possible consequences occurring *within* the scope of the common purpose; as well as
- possible consequences occurring *outside* the scope of the common purpose.

As we shall examine in the next section, some commentators have argued that this second limb goes too far in extending the scope of accessorial liability.

In reaching this conclusion, the High Court in *McAuliffe*'s case first approved the previous High Court decision of *Johns v The Queen* (1980) 143 CLR 108. In that case, the Court held that it is sufficient that the secondary party contemplate that the principal offender *might* commit the crime in the furtherance of the common purpose. That is, the accessory need only contemplate the possibility rather than the probability of an incidental crime occurring. Mason, Murphy and Wilson JJ in *Johns v The Queen* (1980) 143 CLR 108 at 131 set out the rationale for the acceptance of a lower threshold test of contemplation as follows:

> Suppose a plan made by A, the principal offender, and B, the accessory before the fact, to rob premises, according to which A is to carry out the robbery. It is agreed that A will carry a loaded revolver and use it to overcome resistance in the unlikely event that the premises are attended, previous surveillance having established that the premises are invariably unattended at the time when the robbery is to be carried out. As it happens, a security officer is in attendance when A enters the premises and is shot by A. It would make nonsense to say that B is not guilty merely because it was an unlikely or improbable contingency that the premises would be attended at the time of the robbery, when we know that B assented to the shooting in the event that occurred.

The High Court in *McAuliffe* (at 115, 117) approved the decision in *John's* case, but then went one step further:

The Court [in *Johns*] did not consider the situation in which the commission of an offence which lay outside the scope of the common purpose was nevertheless contemplated as a possibility in the carrying out of the enterprise by a party who continued to participate in the venture with that knowledge... There was no occasion for the Court to turn its attention *to the situation where one party foresees, but does not agree to, a crime other than that which is planned, and continues to participate in the venture*. However, the secondary offender in that situation is as much a party to the crime which is an incident of the agreed venture as he [or she] is when the incidental crime falls within the common purpose. [Emphasis added.]

The facts in *McAuliffe*'s case fell within this second scenario of the McAuliffe brothers contemplating the possible consequences that could occur *outside* the scope of the common purpose. The original agreement was to 'roll', 'rob' or 'bash' someone near Bondi Beach. They did not set out to kill anyone. However, the High Court held that there was sufficient evidence that the McAuliffe brothers had contemplated the intentional infliction of grievous bodily harm (the fault element for murder) as a *possible* consequence in carrying out a 'common purpose' to assault someone. They had therefore been rightly convicted of murder.

If the principal offender deliberately acts outside the scope of the common purpose and commits an act that was not foreseen as a possibility, then no liability will attach to the accessory: *Sharah v The Queen* (1992) 30 NSWLR 292; *Duong* (1992) 61 A Crim R 140; *R v Anderson and Morris* [1966] 2 QB 110; *R v Smith* [1963] 3 All ER 597; *Reid* (1975) 62 Cr App R 109; *Varley v R* (1976) 12 ALR 347; *Markby v R* (1978) 140 CLR 108. In *Duong* (1992) 61 A Crim R 140 at 149–50, the New South Wales Court of Criminal Appeal stated:

> It is important...to recognise the distinction between unexpected incidental acts of a principal and unexpected consequences of the principal's actions. The law has long provided for accessorial liability in relation to unforeseen and unusual consequences, so long as they are caused during the carrying out of the common design. But it has never created liability in respect of acts (and therefore the consequences of those acts) which fall entirely outside the ambit of the common design.

In *Duong*, the accused believed that the victim had instigated a break-in at his home and he discussed this with a friend who agreed to go over and 'have words' with the victim. The friend and four other men, one of whom was carrying a knife, went to the victim's home and an altercation ensued in which the victim was stabbed to death. There was no evidence that the accused knew that one of the men had a knife.

The accused was convicted of manslaughter as an accessory before the fact. The New South Wales Court of Criminal Appeal quashed the accused's conviction on the basis that while he may have foreseen that violence might be used against the victim, he foresaw that it would be no more than a minor 'punch-up' or assault.

Critique

The main criticisms of the doctrine of common purpose have focused on whether or not the common law has gone too far in its subjectivist approach. It does appear intuitively unjust to have different fault elements for accessorial liability and for the doctrine of common purpose. As explored above, the High Court in *Giorgianni v The Queen* (1985) 156 CLR 473 set out the requirement that an accessory must intentionally assist or encourage the principal offender and must know of the matters that constitute the physical elements of the offence. The fault element set out in *McAuliffe* for liability based on contemplation of possible consequences is much more extensive than the standard of the fault element set out in *Giorgianni*.

The traditional approach has been to have the same fault element for common purpose as for aiding, abetting, counselling or procuring: B Fisse, *Howard's Criminal Law* (5th edn, Sydney: The Law Book Company Ltd, 1990) pp 340–3. Stephen Odgers, who appeared for one of the appellants in *McAuliffe*'s case, has argued that the High Court decision in that case has created 'reckless accessoryship', which goes against the tenor of the decision in *Giorgianni*: 'Criminal Cases in the High Court of Australia: McAuliffe and McAuliffe' (1996) 20 Crim LJ 43–7. He writes at 46: 'Why should the accessory who does not kill and does not intend or agree to the intentional infliction of serious injury be treated in the same way as someone who did?…If recklessness for murder by the principal requires foresight of the likelihood or probability that death will result, why is it sufficient that an accessory need only foresee the intentional killing or infliction of serious harm as a "possibility"?'

The House of Lords considered the discrepancy between fault elements in *R v Powell; R v English* [1997] 3 WLR 959. In that case, the House of Lords considered whether or not an accessory participating in an agreement to carry out a crime must share the perpetrator's *specific intent* for murder (that is, to kill or cause serious bodily injury) or whether recklessness would suffice. In England, the fault element for murder does not include recklessness and there is mandatory life imprisonment for murder.

In the first appeal concerning Powell, three men went to buy drugs in the course of which one of them shot and killed the drug dealer. The Crown could not prove who was the perpetrator but it was contended that each could be liable for murder on the basis of joint enterprise if they realised that the perpetrator *might* kill in the course of buying the drugs. On appeal against Powell's conviction for murder, the appellant argued that if recklessness were enough, it would result in a form of constructive criminal liability that was contrary to principle.

The House of Lords held that the relevant authorities establish that the accessory who is party to a common purpose must foresee or contemplate the possibility that the perpetrator may commit the physical element of the incidental crime with the relevant fault element. Lord Steyn approved John Cyril Smith's summary of the principles governing accessorial liability for murder (at 964–5): 'The accessory to murder, however, must be proved to have been reckless, not merely whether death might be caused, but whether murder might be committed: *he [or she] must have been aware not merely that death or grievous bodily harm might be caused, but that it might be caused intentionally, by a person whom he [or she] was assisting or encouraging to commit a crime.*' [Emphasis added.]

Lord Steyn held (at 966) that requiring parties to a common purpose to possess the 'specific intention' for murder would be impractical because proof of an intention to kill or cause serious bodily injury would be 'well nigh impossible in the vast majority of joint enterprise cases'. He also referred to the public interest in deterring group-based criminal activity and stated that experience had shown that joint criminal enterprises could easily escalate into the commission of greater offences. In Lord Steyn's view, the logical elegance of requiring 'strict equivalence' of culpability between the accessory and the perpetrator gave way to the practical needs of the criminal justice system. He acknowledged the potential unfairness of imposing a mandatory life sentence for accessories to murder who merely foresee the possibility of serious injury being inflicted by the perpetrator, but was not prepared to change what he perceived to be the ordinary principles of accessorial liability to ameliorate this unfairness.

Lord Hutton referred also (at 976–7) to similar policy considerations:

> [T]he secondary party who takes part in a criminal enterprise (for example the robbery of a bank) with foresight that a deadly weapon may be used, should not escape liability for murder because he [or she], unlike the principal party, is not suddenly confronted by the security officer so that he [or she] has to decide whether to use the gun or knife or have the enterprise thwarted and face arrest.

In its Discussion Paper, the CLOC recommended abolition of the doctrine of common purpose: Criminal Law Officers Committee, *Chapters 1 and 2, General Principles of Criminal Responsibility*, Discussion Paper (July 1992) pp 79–81. This was on the basis that it was unjust as well as confusing to juries for an accessory to be convicted on the basis of contemplation of a possibility in cases of collateral offences, but not for other offences, nor, in fact, for the planned offence. The Committee instead recommended a fault element for accessorial liability that encompassed recklessness as well as intention.

After receiving submissions on the matter, in its Final Report, the CLOC decided to drop recklessness as a fault element and retain the doctrine of common purpose in a modified form based on the general definition of recklessness used in the Code: Criminal Law Officers Committee, *Chapters 1 and 2, General Principles of Criminal Responsibility*, Final Report (December 1992) p 89. Section 11.2(3) of the *Criminal Code* (Cth) now reads as follows:

> For the person to be guilty, the person must have intended that:
> (a) his or her conduct would aid, abet, counsel or procure the commission of any offence (including its fault elements) of the type the other person committed; or
> (b) his or her conduct would aid, abet, counsel or procure the commission of an offence and have been reckless about the commission of the offence (including its fault elements) that the other person in fact committed.

Section 5.4 of the Act refers to recklessness in terms of awareness of a substantial risk that a result will occur. This 'solution' echoes that recommended by the South Australian Criminal Law and Penal Methods Law Reform Committee: *The Substantive Criminal Law*, Fourth Report (1977) p 303. It recommended a redefinition of the doctrine of common purpose in terms of recklessness so that an accessory would be held liable for an offence committed by the principal offender if he or she knew that there was a 'substantial risk' that the offence would be committed.

This approach seems to be simply putting *McAuliffe*'s case into statutory form rather than truly modifying the doctrine. Stephen Gray argues that it is best to abolish the doctrine completely: '"I Didn't Know, I Wasn't There": Common Purpose and the Liability of Accessories to Crime' (1999) 23 Crim LJ 201–17. Gray argues that accessorial liability should be seen as an independent form of liability. The question whether or not an accessory possesses a culpable mental state should be seen independently of the principal offender's mental state. The physical elements are counselling, procuring, aiding or abetting. The fault element should focus on what the accessory contemplated the act and its consequences to be.

In the *McAuliffe* case, Gray argues (at 213) that the question for the jury should be whether the offence committed was within the contemplation of the accessories as a possibility. The McAuliffe brothers foresaw an assault and contemplated that grievous bodily harm was a possible result; therefore they should be found guilty of murder.

This approach may serve to simplify the law somewhat, but the conceptual basis for accessorial liability still needs to be assessed. Gray argues that accessorial liability should be dependent upon the commission of an offence, but not on the liability of the accused. This seems to accept the traditional view of accessorial liability as being derivative. Perhaps it is time to reassess this view as well as the problems associated with the extension of accessorial liability through the doctrine of common purpose.

Conclusion

Stephen Gray has pointed out that behind all the problems associated with complicity, lies 'the issue of whether the law of accessorial liability in Australia has become so complicated that juries are unlikely, in a trial, to be able to make sense of it': '"I Didn't Know, I Wasn't There": Common Purpose and the Liability of Accessories to Crime' (1999) 23 Crim LJ 201–17. There is also some reason to believe that trial judges find it exceptionally difficult to direct juries on this area of the law. For example, some recent appeal court judgments have discussed the problems with jury directions given on complicity: *R v Helene* unreported, 28 July 1999, CCA of NSW, [1999] NSW CCA 203, Ireland, Kirby JJ, Carruthers JA; *R v Chai* unreported, 25 August 2000, CCA of NSW, [2000] NSW CCA 320, Mason P, Sperling and Bergin JJ; *R v Chai* (2002) 187 ALR 436 (HC); *Franklin* (2001) 119 A Crim R 223. Certainly there is a real need to clarify some of the complexities associated with the scope of primary and derivative liability. We have already identified specific difficulties such as whether an omission to act should give rise to accessorial liability and what constitutes knowledge of the essential facts of an offence. But perhaps the most important conceptual difficulties stem from the derivative nature of accessorial liability.

There are two ways of approaching accessorial liability. The first way of viewing accessorial liability is to posit that the liability of an accessory is dependent upon the commission of the offence and the guilt of the principal offender. On this approach, it is unjust for an accessory to be found guilty of an offence that was merely contemplated as an abstract possibility or where the principal offender has a defence to the crime. Liability depends upon what actually occurred. This has, until recently, been the pervasive way of viewing accessorial liability: that it was derivative in nature.

The second way of approaching accessorial liability is to view assisting or encouraging a crime as separate from the actual commission of the crime. On this view, the principal offender need not be found guilty of the offence for which the accessory is found liable. This is the rationale behind the doctrine of acting in concert and explains why Heather Osland was held liable for murder when her son was acquitted. This approach also seems to lie behind the High Court decision on the doctrine of common purpose in *R v Barlow* (1997) 188 CLR 1, which held that an accessory can be found guilty of a different offence to the perpetrator's offence.

This second approach is based on an 'independent' basis of accessorial liability. From the perspective of moral culpability, it can be argued that a person who promotes the commission of an offence may be as great a danger to society as the person who actually performs it. It is therefore irrelevant in assessing the moral culpability of those who assist or encourage another to commit the offence that the actual perpetrator has, for example, a personal defence.

The disadvantages that flow from the derivative framework for complicity have prompted calls, from both academics and law reformers, for the creation of a non-derivative criminal facilitation offence: R Buxton, 'Complicity in the Criminal Code' (1969) 85 *The Law Quarterly Review* 252, at 268–9, and JR Spencer, 'Trying to Help Another Person Commit a Crime', in PF Smith (ed), *Criminal Law: Essays in Honour of JC Smith* (London: Butterworths, 1987). The Law Commission of England and Wales has proposed the creation of the non-derivative crime of encouraging and assisting crime: Law Commission, Consultation Paper No 131, *Assisting and Encouraging Crime* (London: HMSO, 1993).

Such an offence would help to resolve the conceptual strains clearly apparent in the present framework of complicity. It would also help to bring complicity into line with the inchoate offences. JR Spencer has drawn attention to the fact that although the present law contains an inchoate version of complicity by encouragement (namely incitement), there is no inchoate equivalent of complicity by assisting crime: 'Trying to Help Another Person Commit a Crime' in PF Smith (ed), *Criminal Law: Essays in Honour of JC Smith* (London: Butterworths, 1987) p 149. The absence of such an offence provides a powerful disincentive for the police to intervene to apprehend the person assisting until the perpetrator has committed, or at least attempted, the principal crime.

While both academics and law reformers alike have canvassed the creation of a non-derivative form of accessorial liability, the courts have not, until recently, considered it. There are signs, however, that the judiciary may be moving towards such an approach. For example, Callinan J in *Osland v The Queen* (1998) 197 CLR 316 reviewed the history of accessorial liability. He concluded (at 402) that the purpose of the statutory provisions dealing with accessorial liability adopted in England and Australian jurisdictions 'seems to have been to do away with derivative liability'. He stated (at 402):

> If it were necessary to decide the point I would be inclined to hold that the practical effect of the section [s 323, *Crimes Act* 1958 (Vic)] is to make it irrelevant to decide whether the accused actually struck the blow or did a final act to complete a crime. The section appears to eliminate the need for a trial of a person formerly thought to be an accessory only, to await and depend upon the attainment or conviction of the principal.

Callinan J takes the view that these statutory provisions have substantive as well as procedural effects. In moving away from the derivative nature of accessorial liability, Callinan J focuses instead on what he sees as the primary question in this area, namely whether or not the assistance or encouragement *caused* another person to commit the offence.

This approach appears to pave the way for a statutory offence of criminal facilitation that does not require the commission of a principal offence. Indeed, there are already signs that the derivative nature of accessorial liability that links the liability of an accessory to the *guilt* of the principal offender is being questioned. Section 11.5(5) of the *Criminal Code* (Cth) states:

> A person may be found guilty of aiding, abetting, counselling or procuring the commission of an offence even if the principal offender has not been prosecuted or has not been found guilty.

The law of complicity has thus far developed randomly without regard to the conceptual complexities underlying the doctrines of acting in concert, innocent agency and common purpose. The Law Commission for England and Wales has called for a new structure of statutory offences relating to complicity in order to clarify this increasingly complex area: Law Commission, *Assisting and Encouraging Crime*, Consultation Paper No 131 (London: HMSO, 1993). It seems that now is the time to heed this call.

Part 5
DEFENCES

CHAPTER 10

Self-defence and provocation

Introduction

Leo Tolstoy wrote in *Anna Karenina* (New York: Signet, 1961, first published 1875) p 1 that 'all happy families resemble one another, every unhappy family is unhappy in its own way'. According to the evidence of Mary Sandra Falconer at her trial for the wilful murder of her husband, the unhappiness of the Falconer family stemmed from the violence of Gordon Robert Falconer.

Mary Falconer stated that during the 30 years they had been married, her husband struck her many times, often around the head and 'once with a strap with a buckle on'. She also stated that she had been kicked in the head 'with his Alcoa boots on with steel caps in them' (*Falconer* (1989) 46 A Crim R 83 at 100, CCA of WA). Her hearing subsequently became impaired.

There had been a history of separations and reconciliations, but Mary Falconer permanently separated from her husband after she was told by two of her daughters that their father had sexually assaulted them over a period of years.

Criminal proceedings were preferred against Gordon Falconer in relation to these allegations and Mary Falconer became increasingly fearful that he would harm her daughters. She obtained a non-molestation order pursuant to the *Family Law Act* 1975 (Cth). The affidavit for the order revealed Mary Falconer's knowledge of her husband's incest and the fact that she was terrified as to what he might do. There was also evidence that while Gordon Falconer had been violent towards his wife quite frequently, the last occasion had been 'four or five years ago'.

Despite the order, in the months that followed the separation, Gordon Falconer appeared at the premises where she was staying and on two separate occasions hit her.

A friend gave evidence that Mary Falconer was 'emotional and very frightened'. She was half her normal weight and could not stop trembling (p 102). Finally, on 9 October 1988, Gordon Falconer entered Mary Falconer's house unexpectedly. Later, at her trial for the murder of her husband, Mary Falconer gave the following account (at 105–7) of what happened in her evidence in chief:

> [He said:] 'It doesn't have to be like this,' that he loved me and I was still his wife. He was worrying what would happen if he goes to Fremantle [prison]…'You know what they'd do to me in there'. I said—I don't know the exact words but I said I couldn't help him this time; 'I believe my girls; I know they're telling the truth'…He got a bit angry. I went to pass him; he went to hit me and I don't know whether I slipped or what but I caught the glancing blow on my shoulder. I was shocked and I just stood there for a minute, and then he just seemed to have disappeared. I just took it that he must have gone outside, or something.
>
> Q. Was there any paper or document that he had spoken to you about that he wanted.
> A. He wanted some papers. I was doing the tax papers, and he wanted some papers.
> Q. Where were they kept? A. In a green, flat briefcase type of thing.
> Q. Where was the briefcase normally kept? A. We normally kept that in our en suite, in the wardrobe section…
> Q. Did you go into the bedroom[?] A. I went into the bedroom.
> Q. And? A. I went to reach for my glasses—I went to turn—he was there. Oh god.
> Q. Did he say anything or do anything[?] A. He put his hand between my legs. I fell against the bed. I don't know what I had on my feet but I was slipping; and then I must have swore [sic] at him and called him names.
> Q. I'm sorry. I realise that it is difficult for you…you said he—you were in the bedroom; he was there. You said he put his hands between your legs and you slipped, as I understood you to say, and fell back on the bed. Is that right? A. Partly on to the bed…
> Q. How did you feel when he put his hands between your legs? A. I felt so disgusted and dirty.
> Q. Did he say anything to you at all? A. He just kept saying he loved me.
> Q. He kept saying he loved you. What next can you remember? A. He hit me across the face, side of the face.
> Q. What else? A. I just—*I just went all funny*. He was laughing at me.
> Q. Was he saying anything when he was laughing. A. He said that 'Nobody's going to believe you or the girls,' and then he mentioned Erin's name.
> Q. Did he say anything about the [sexual assault] case? He mentioned Erin. Who was Erin? A. A little nine-year-old girl I had in my care. My son went up on charges for interfering with [her]—three years ago…
> Q. When he said: 'Remember Erin,' did that have any significance to you? A. I went very cold and I was feeling very sick.
> Q. Why was that? A. All I could think of: 'How many more children?'

Q. Why did you think your husband had anything to do with Erin? A. If he'd done it to his own daughters, he must have done it to her too…The last thing I remember is—I think I was reaching down to get—to look for the papers and the next thing Gordon was still there.

Q. Was he doing anything? A. He was just coming at me.

Q. Where was your shotgun? A. The shotgun should have been kept in the wardrobe behind the clothes, where the clothes are hung.

Q. Do you remember picking up the shotgun? A. No.

Q. The shotgun was obviously loaded. Do you remember if you loaded it at any time? A. I don't remember when I loaded it.

Q. Did you load it at the time? A. I don't remember ever loading that gun.

Q. What is the next thing you can remember? You have told us about how he was there, that he was—I think the expression was, he was coming at you. He was coming at you. What is the next thing you can remember, Mrs Falconer? A. I was slumped up against that archway, or near that archway, because my head and neck were hurting…I think it was the archway of the bedroom…Gordon was still there. I was standing or crouching. I seen [sic] the gun near me. By my feet, or maybe across my foot on the floor. [Emphasis in original.]

The prosecution argued that according to Mary Falconer's previous affidavit, there had been no violence in the marriage for four or five years. She said under cross-examination that she had lied in this affidavit as she still loved her husband, but there had been violence in the years leading up to the killing. The prosecution also gave evidence that Mary Falconer had bought shotgun ammunition shortly after hearing that her husband was going to be charged with sexual offences, there were two shotgun cartridges by the vanity basin in the en suite bedroom and that she intended to kill him.

In a criminal trial, the prosecution and the defence present very different narratives. In the Canadian case of *R v Beharriell* (1995) 130 DLR (4th) 422 at 450, L'Heureux-Dubé J stated that the 'principal aim of our adversarial trial process is the search for the truth'. It has thus been traditionally presumed that the 'truth' behind a particular legal problem may ultimately be found by a judge or jury through a process of weighing competing narratives.

The term 'narrative' is taken here to refer to a connected account of events which produces a story. Narratives in legal trials derive, in the main, from witnesses. In a trial such as Mary Falconer's, witnesses will often have rehearsed their story with themselves, with family and friends, with police and with other professionals. Their tale will probably have been re-fashioned later when told to solicitors, 'brushed up' in conference prior to trial, led out in chief, then recast in cross-examination.

The sequence and version of events presented at the trial by both parties will be summarised by the judge in his or her 'charge' to the jury. Counsel and judges may then recast the events on appeal. This adversarial presentation and retelling of stories is important to note because 'the truth' of what occurred when a crime is committed is dependent upon the perceiver. Mary Falconer's story, presented above in examination-in-chief, would undoubtedly have been told in different ways many times before the trial. What makes it even more difficult to uncover what occurred at the time of the killing is Mary Falconer's inability to recollect the shooting. It is not uncommon for those who kill or commit serious crimes to have little recollection of the event. This will be explored further in Chapter 11.

Accepting for the moment Mary Falconer's narrative, a number of defences may have been open to her such as provocation, self-defence, automatism or, if the killing had occurred in the Australian Capital Territory, New South Wales, the Northern Territory or Queensland, diminished responsibility. At her trial, provocation was raised but was not accepted by the jury. An application by the defence to have evidence of automatism put before the jury was not successful. On 14 July 1989, Mary Falconer was convicted of the wilful murder of her husband and sentenced to life imprisonment. Under s 278 of the *Criminal Code* (WA), the fault element for wilful murder is that the accused intended to cause death.

An appeal to the Court of Criminal Appeal (WA) on the basis that automatism should have been left for the jury to decide was successful and a new trial ordered. The Crown then appealed against this decision to the High Court concerning the admissibility of evidence concerning automatism. The High Court dismissed the Crown's appeal and the matter was set down for a re-trial: *R v Falconer* (1990) 171 CLR 30. What happened next will be explored in Chapter 11.

It may appear unusual that self-defence was not raised in the *Falconer* trial and that provocation was unsuccessful. This chapter will explore the difficulties associated with the current laws of self-defence and provocation, using the scenario of women who kill as a way of highlighting these difficulties.

Self-defence

Background

Self-defence is a total defence to murder as well as to assault in that it leads to a complete acquittal. The defence of self-defence arose out of the regulation of duels and other forms of combat. It developed in the context of fights between two men, the traditional scenario being a bar-room brawl or a one-off duel: I Leader-Elliott, 'Battered But Not Beaten: Women Who Kill in Self-Defence' (1993) 15 *Sydney Law Review* 403–60 at 405. This is not surprising given that 'violence in general, and homicide in particular, are masculine phenomena': Jenny Mouzos, *Homicidal Encounters: A Study of Homicide in Australia 1989–1999* (Canberra: Australian Institute of Criminology, 2000) p 103.

In Chapter 4 we explored how the 'typical' assault involves males fighting in a public place after alcohol has been consumed. In her study on homicides over a 10-year period, Jenny Mouzos found (at 114) that three out of five victims of homicide and about seven out of eight homicide offenders in Australia were male. Male-on-male homicides accounted for approximately fifty per cent of all homicides and are most likely to occur on a Friday, Saturday or Sunday evening during the early hours of the morning and as a result of an argument, usually alcohol precipitated. The empirical data dealing with homicide was explored in Chapter 3.

Lethal force was traditionally seen as justifying killing when the accused was responding to an imminent *life-threatening* attack. This scenario has made it difficult for women to use the defence where they have killed a previously violent partner in circumstances when there is not an immediate attack or the force used is not overtly life-threatening.

We suspect that self-defence was not raised in the *Falconer* trial because in 1989 it was (and still remains) difficult to show that a woman's lethal reaction to violence was 'reasonable'. On the narrative presented in court by Mary Falconer, she had been struck a glancing blow on the shoulder, had been indecently assaulted and then hit on the face. On one view, these events were not life-threatening enough to justify the use of lethal force. The Prosecution would probably have argued that Mary Falconer's reaction of shooting her husband dead was disproportionate to being indecently assaulted, hit twice and taunted. That is, subjectively, she may have believed that it was necessary to do what she did, but objectively, this belief was not based upon reasonable grounds or it was not reasonably necessary to use fatal force. Ironically, the evidence of violence in the past might have been used to show that the violence on this occasion was not life-threatening. Peter Alldridge points out in *Relocating Criminal Law* (Aldershot: Ashgate Dartmouth, 2000) p 94 that the 'more evidence there is of previous attacks which did not actually cause serious bodily harm, or which, in any event, the defendant was apparently able to tolerate and live through, the smaller will be her chance of establishing that the occasion of the killing was unique, so as to justify a lethal response'.

As we shall explore a little later in our critique of self-defence, one challenge for law reformers has been to find ways in which to admit evidence to explain why a woman's lethal response to violence was reasonable.

The current law

Self-defence is open-ended in its formulation in the sense that there are not many rigid rules limiting its scope and it is very much a matter of fact for the jury to decide: *DPP Reference (No 1 of 1991)* (1992) 60 A Crim R 43 at 46. At common law, Wilson, Dawson and Toohey JJ set out the requirements for the defence in *Zecevic v DPP (Vic)* (1987) 162 CLR 645 at 661 as follows:

The question to be asked in the end is quite simple. It is whether the accused believed upon reasonable grounds that it was necessary in self-defence to do what he [or she] did. If he [or she] had that belief and there were reasonable grounds for it, or if the jury is left in reasonable doubt about the matter, then he [or she] is entitled to an acquittal. Stated in this form, the question is one of general application and is not limited to cases of homicide.

Wilson, Dawson and Toohey JJ went on to state (at 662) that a threat does not ordinarily call for a fatal response 'unless it causes a reasonable apprehension on the part of [the accused] of death or serious bodily harm'. This formulation of self-defence applies in New South Wales and Victoria. This test is an amalgamation of subjective and objective elements. It is not wholly subjective because the accused's belief must be tested by reference to reasonable grounds. There is, however, no requirement that the accused's belief be tested against that of the ordinary person; the question is what the accused might reasonably have believed in all the circumstances. The statutory defence of self-defence that exists in the Australian Capital Territory and at the Commonwealth level is couched in similar but slightly simplified terms: *Criminal Code* (ACT) s 42; *Criminal Code* (Cth) s 10.4.

In South Australia and Tasmania, the legislation gives the defence slightly more of a subjective emphasis. Section 46 of the *Criminal Code* (Tas) states that a 'person is justified in using, in defence of himself [or herself] or another person, such force as, in the circumstances as he [or she] believes them to be, it is reasonable to use'. Similarly, s 15(1) of the *Criminal Law Consolidation Act* 1935 (SA), which was amended in 1997, now allows an accused to use force if that person believes that the force is necessary and reasonable for self-defence and the conduct was reasonably proportionate to the threat that the accused genuinely believed to exist.

The Queensland, Northern Territory and Western Australian *Criminal Codes* are more complex and supplement the core element of 'reasonable necessity' with additional rules that limit the use of permissible force. Section 283 of the *Criminal Code* (Qld) and s 260 of the *Criminal Code* (WA) distinguish between self-defence as it relates to provoked and unprovoked attacks. In relation to an unprovoked attack, 'it is lawful for [the accused] to use such force to the assailant as is reasonably necessary to make effectual defence against the assault, provided that the force used is not intended and is not such as is likely, to cause death or grievous bodily harm'. Here, the test is objective in determining whether or not the force used by the accused was reasonably necessary.

The use of lethal force may be used in certain prescribed circumstances such as where the attack is of such a nature as to cause reasonable apprehension of death or grievous bodily harm. This is also reflected in s 28(f) of the *Criminal Code* (NT). As a defence to homicide then, the test of self-defence is both subjective and objective. The jury must consider whether the accused apprehended death or grievous bodily harm and then assess on an objective basis whether the apprehension was a reasonable one.

Critique

Mark Kelman has pointed out in his article 'Interpretive Construction in the Substantive Criminal Law' (1981) 33 *Stanford Law Review* 591–673 that the time-frame adopted by the criminal law is usually a very short one: it is that of a photo rather than a video. The fault and physical elements must be concurrent: the accused is judged by his or her actions at a particular instant. This has very much been the case with self-defence: a necessary response is traditionally viewed as an instantaneous act against immediate or imminent aggression. Cynthia Gillespie in *Justifiable Homicide* (Columbus, OH: Ohio State University Press, 1989) p 80 writes ironically about the reasonable male response to aggression:

> A real man, a brave man, faces his adversary in a fair fight. He does not sneakily lie in ambush or shoot an enemy in the back or kill him while he is asleep. He does not panic and kill someone who is just blustering and making threats. He does not avoid a showdown by indulging in a pre-emptive strike, getting his adversary before the latter can get him. These are the acts of cowards and villains, and the law has always declined to excuse or justify them.

The unreasonable reactions mentioned here, such as killing the 'adversary' while he sleeps, are of course reactions that have been taken by women who have been subjected to a history of abuse. The requirement that the accused's belief be based upon reasonable grounds has thus drawn criticism for setting an underlying male standard of response: E Sheehy, J Stubbs and J Tolmie, 'Defending Battered Women on Trial: The Battered Woman Syndrome and Its Limitations' (1992) 16 Crim LJ 369–94 at 372, 374. The challenge has been to show that the male response to aggression is not necessarily the only reasonable response.

Criticisms of the current law of self-defence have been focused on three main areas that overlap to some extent:

1. the move away from a mid-way point of lesser responsibility for an accused whose reaction to an assault or threat is disproportionate to the attack;
2. the failure of the law to encompass the reaction of a woman to a violent partner; and
3. how to attain the correct balance between subjective and objective elements in the defence.

The following section deals with these three areas in more detail and provides an overview of reform suggestions.

Excessive self-defence

In the past, at common law, if there was disproportionate force used in self-defence, under the doctrine of excessive self-defence, murder could be reduced to manslaughter: *Viro v The Queen* (1978) 141 CLR 88 at 147. This doctrine was subsequently rejected by a five to two majority of the High Court in *Zecevic v DPP (Vic)* (1987) 162 CLR 645. Wilson, Dawson and Toohey JJ stated (at 654):

> [T]he use of excessive force in the belief that it was necessary in self-defence will not automatically result in a verdict of manslaughter. If the jury concludes that there were no reasonable grounds for a belief that the degree of force used was necessary, the defence of self-defence will fail and the circumstances will fail to be considered by the jury without reference to that plea. There is some force in the view, adopted by Stephen, Mason and Aickin JJ in *Viro*, that this may result in a conviction for murder of a person lacking the moral culpability associated with that crime. Experience would suggest, however, that such a result is unlikely in practice.

In all jurisdictions apart from New South Wales and South Australia, proportionality may now only be taken into account as a relevant circumstance of the case, for example in showing reasonableness of the accused's belief, rather than as a separate rule of law or determinative element. In the Northern Territory, if excessive force was believed to be necessary, the killing may be excused under s 32 of the *Criminal Code* (NT), which deals with a reasonable mistake of fact.

In 1991, South Australia reintroduced excessive self-defence for those situations where the accused's belief as to the nature or extent of the necessary force used was grossly unreasonable and was accompanied by criminal negligence. This subjective test of excessive self-defence was amended in 1997 to a partly objective one: s 15(2) *Criminal Law Consolidation Act* 1935 (SA). In New South Wales, the doctrine of excessive self-defence was reintroduced by the *Crimes Amendment (Self-defence) Act* 2001 and came into force on 22 February 2002. Section 421 of the *Crimes Act* 1900 (NSW) now enables a verdict of manslaughter where the conduct is not a reasonable response, but the accused believed the conduct was necessary.

The main argument in support of a doctrine of excessive self-defence is based on a moral distinction between intentional killing and a killing based on an error of judgment. Mason J stated in *Viro v The Queen* (1978) 141 CLR 88 at 139:

> The underlying rationale…is to be found in a conviction that the moral culpability of a person who kills another in defending himself [or herself] but who fails in a plea of self-defence only because the force which he [or she] believed to be necessary exceeded that which was reasonably necessary falls short of the moral culpability ordinarily associated with murder. The notion that a person commits murder in the circumstances should be rejected on the ground that the result is unjust. It is more consistent with the distinction which the criminal law makes between murder and manslaughter that an error of judgment on the part of the accused which alone deprives him [or her] of the absolute shield of self-defence results in the offence of manslaughter.

Stanley Yeo has argued that there is also support for the doctrine of excessive self-defence among lawyers and members of the general public: 'Revisiting Excessive Self-Defence' (2000) 12(1) *Current Issues in Criminal Justice* 39–57. The Model Criminal Code Officers Committee (MCCOC), however, has recommended that excessive self-defence should not be reintroduced: *Chapter 5, Fatal Offences Against the Person*, Discussion Paper (June 1998) p 113. The Committee was concerned that excessive self-defence is 'inherently vague' and that a sufficient test has not been promulgated. Certainly the test set out by Mason J in *Viro v The Queen* (1978) 141 CLR 88 at 146–7 was overly complex because it attempted to incorporate the substantive law of excessive self-defence as well as the law in relation to the burden of proof.

However, the Committee went on to state that if excessive self-defence is reintroduced it should be a subjective test along the lines suggested by Deane J in *Zecevic*. He stated (at 681) that self-defence would be made out if the accused 'reasonably believed that what he [or she] was doing was reasonable and necessary in his [or her] own defence against an unjustified attack which threatened him [or her] with death or serious bodily harm'. If the accused *unreasonably* believed this to be the case, he or she should be convicted of manslaughter. This test found favour with Professor Fisse in *Howard's Criminal Law* (5th edn, Sydney: Law Book Company Ltd, 1990) p 103.

Deane J's test is very much a subjective one because it concentrates on what the accused believed. The Law Reform Commission of Victoria recommended a similar subjective test in its Report No 40, *Homicide* (Melbourne: LRCV, 1991), but as the basis for a separate offence. It suggested (at 98) that the following offence be enacted: 'A person who kills another in self-defence on the basis of a belief that was grossly unreasonable either in relation to the need for force or in relation to the degree of force that was necessary should be guilty of the offence of culpable homicide. Penalty: 7 years or 150 penalty units or both.'

An alternative approach is to have a partly subjective/partly objective test as currently exists in South Australia and New South Wales. For example, s 15(2) of the *Criminal Law Consolidation Act* 1935 (SA) now provides for a verdict of manslaughter where the accused genuinely believed the conduct to be necessary and reasonable for a defensive purpose, but the conduct was not, in the circumstances as the accused genuinely believed them to be, reasonably proportionate. Stanley Yeo has argued in 'Revisiting Excessive Self-Defence' (2000) 12(1) *Current Issues in Criminal Justice* 39–57 that this direction is readily comprehensible to juries and therefore can be supported on a practical basis. Yeo writes at 49 that having a purely subjective model, while theoretically attractive, may be more difficult to apply: 'How, for instance, is a juror to determine the reasonableness of an intoxicated or a partially blind person's belief in the need for certain force to be applied in self-defence?'

The partly subjective/partly objective test of excessive self-defence appears to be workable in practice. It seems anomalous that a person who kills under provocation is seen as less morally culpable than a murderer, yet a person who has 'over-reacted' in a situation where entitled to use self-defence is seen as equally culpable as a person who has killed without any circumstances of self-defence. Reintroducing the doctrine of excessive self-defence may also go some way towards taking into account women's reactions to violence. This criticism of self-defence will be explored in the next section.

Women's reactions to violence

As stated above, the defence of self-defence developed at a time when women were not expected to avail themselves of the defence. The failure of the law to encompass the reaction of a woman to a violent partner has been addressed in recent years through the use of evidence of 'battered woman syndrome'. Phyllis Crocker in 'The Meaning of Equality for Battered Women Who Kill Men In Self-Defense' (1985) 8 *Harvard Women's Law Journal* 121–53 at 149 explained the use of such evidence as follows: 'The issue in a self-defence trial is not whether the defendant is a battered woman, but whether she justifiably killed her husband. The defendant introduces testimony to offer the jury an explanation of reasonableness that is an alternative to the prosecution's stereotypic explanations. It is not intended to earn her the status of a battered woman, as if that would make her not guilty.'

The role of this expert evidence is therefore to help support the claim that the accused believed *on reasonable grounds* that it was necessary to do what she did or that the force used was reasonably necessary.

'Battered woman syndrome' was first mentioned in a book published in 1979 by psychologist Dr Lenore Walker: *The Battered Woman* (New York: Harper & Row, 1979). She subsequently wrote a follow-up book, *The Battered Woman Syndrome* (New York: Springer Pub Co, 1984) detailing a study of 403 battered women. She stated that a 'cycle of violence' was characterised by three stages: tension building, the acute battering incident and loving contrition. She defined a battered woman as one who had gone through the cycle at least twice.

Walker emphasised that a battered woman finds it difficult to break out of this cycle because of 'learned helplessness'. This theory was based on earlier unsavoury experiments by Martin Seligman concerning the effect of electric shocks on two groups of dogs: MEP Seligman and SF Maier, 'Failure to Escape Shock' (1967) 74 *Journal of Experimental Psychology* 1–9; MEP Seligman, *Helplessness: On Depression, Development and Death* (San Francisco: Freeman, 1975).

In Australia, the first case to recognise the role of this type of evidence in a case of self-defence to murder was *R v Kontinnen* (1992) 16 Crim LJ 360. The accused shot and killed her de facto husband while he slept. The victim lived with the accused and another woman and her child. The accused claimed that the victim had abused her over many years, and that on the night of the shooting, threatened to kill her, the other woman and the child. The accused had been hospitalised 10 times in two years as a result of the beatings she suffered at the hands of her de facto husband.

At her trial, the defence raised both self-defence and provocation. Evidence of battered woman syndrome was led to allay the possible doubt of jurors that the accused's shooting the victim while he was asleep was necessary by way of self-defence. The evidence was admitted without objection by the Crown or the trial judge. The latter treated this evidence as relevant to two issues: first, it was relevant to whether or not the accused believed that it was necessary to shoot the victim and, secondly, it was relevant to the question as to whether the belief was based on reasonable grounds. The jury acquitted the accused.

The New South Wales Supreme Court considered similar evidence in *R v Hickey* (1992) 16 Crim LJ 271. This again concerned a de facto relationship that had been abusive for several years. Mervyn Priestley was violent not only towards the accused but also towards their children, usually when he was intoxicated. The accused had separated from Priestley and at the time of the killing, was living with family and friends in a close-knit Aboriginal community. She visited Priestley with the children at the home of a mutual friend, believing it to be a safe environment. After some time spent drinking and after the accused refused to allow the children to stay overnight, Priestley became violent. He threw the accused on the bed, headbutted her and tried to strangle her. When Priestley stopped the attack and sat up and turned his back on the accused, she grabbed a knife and fatally stabbed him.

During the trial for murder, expert psychological evidence on battered woman syndrome was admitted without objection either by the Crown or the trial judge to support self-defence. The jury acquitted Hickey.

In his commentary on the case, Yeo points out (at 273) that it is conceivable that Hickey could have been acquitted without the use of expert psychological evidence because there had been escalating violence in the relationship and a violent assault. Yeo also states that many women who remain in violent relationships do so not because they are experiencing battered woman syndrome. There are often other more mundane social factors at play in these relationships, such as financial dependence and lack of sympathy and help from family members, social services or the police. According to Yeo, battered woman's syndrome should not be unduly emphasised.

Yeo's comments mirror a movement towards treating evidence of battered woman syndrome with prudence. In *Osland v The Queen* (1998) 197 CLR 316 at 370–3, Kirby J referred to a number of controversies with battered woman syndrome and stressed the need for caution in the reception of such evidence. In general, criticisms of the use of battered woman syndrome have concentrated on:
- the inadequacy of evidence to support a 'syndrome';
- its limited assistance to a claim of self-defence; and
- the way in which it medicalises a social problem.

The following is an overview of these criticisms.

Inadequacy of evidence to support a 'syndrome'
The 'syndrome' itself and Walker's research methodology have been the subject of much criticism. Walker herself admitted in 1995 that there is a definitional vagueness

in the syndrome: LE Walker, 'Understanding Battered Woman's Syndrome' (1995) 31(2) *Trial* 30–4.

Walker's initial findings were based on a non-random sample of 'more than 120' battered women and caseworkers. Her subsequent study was based on a sample of 403 women who had responded to advertisements or had been referred from women's refuges, hospitals, medical centres and the like. In both studies, the information was obtained from 'self-report data from a self-referred and voluntary sample': LE Walker, *The Battered Woman Syndrome* (New York: Springer, 1984) p 228. Marilyn McMahon has criticised this methodology because there were no control groups, because most of the reporting of abuse was retrospective and because the samples were skewed towards professionally employed women who left their abusive partner after experiencing moderate levels of abuse: 'Battered Women and Bad Science: The Limited Validity and Utility of Battered Woman Syndrome' (1999) 6(1) *Psychiatry, Psychology and Law* 23–49. There were also problems with interviewer expectancies, rating of open-ended questions and discrepancies in the data reported.

McMahon also points out that subsequent empirical research has not supported Walker's model. She concludes (at p 43): '[S]ubstantial deficiencies in the methodological basis of relevant empirical research, poor conceptualisation of the notions of learned helplessness and the cycle of violence, internal inconsistency in the theory, and confusion of findings legitimately derived from original research with those derived from the research of others, indicate that the scientific basis of battered woman syndrome is inadequate.'

Limited Assistance to a Claim of Self-Defence
In *Osland v The Queen* (1998) 197 CLR 316 at 378, Kirby J stated that evidence of battered woman syndrome might be relevant to explaining the following:

> (1) why a person subjected to prolonged and repeated abuse would remain in such a relationship; (2) the nature and extent of the violence that may exist in such a relationship before producing a response; (3) the accused's ability, in such a relationship, to perceive danger from the abuser; and (4) whether, on the evidence, the particular accused believed on reasonable grounds that there was no other way to preserve herself or himself from death or grievous bodily harm than by resorting to the conduct giving rise to the charge.

One problem with the use of battered woman syndrome in relation to self-defence is that it may explain why the accused didn't leave the relationship, but it is difficult to link 'learned helplessness' with finally breaking out and killing an abusive partner. R Emerson Dobash and Russell Dobash in a study of 109 women who had suffered abuse found that the majority responded to a violent attack by remaining physically passive: *Violence Against Wives* (London: Open Books, 1980) pp 108–9. Women who wait until their partners are unarmed or asleep before retaliating do not appear to be exhibiting learned helplessness.

Rather, Charles Ewing argues that retaliation does not result from learned helplessness, but from a realisation or turning point where the abused woman begins to see the danger she is in. This may result from a serious escalation in violence, the discovery that her children have also been physically and/or sexually abused by her partner or an incident that makes the abuse visible to others outside the relationship: *Battered Women Who Kill: Psychological Self-Defense as Legal Justification* (Massachusetts: Lexington Books, 1987). See also P Easteal, 'Battered Woman Syndrome: What is "Reasonable"?' (1992) 17(5) *Alternative Law Journal* 220–3 at 220.

Walker herself has altered her approach to learned helplessness since her initial study to decrease the emphasis on passivity. In her more recent research, she has pointed to selective behavioural responses on the part of battered women such as avoiding novel responses that would 'launch them into the unknown': LE Walker, *Terrifying Love* (New York: Harper Perennial, 1989) p 51. Even on this reading, women who kill violent partners cannot be said to be engaging in a restricted repertoire of behaviours.

Medicalising a social problem

A further problem with evidence of battered woman syndrome lies in medicalising women's behaviour by the use of a 'syndrome'. Ian Freckelton has pointed out that it is difficult to translate a field of endeavour that has therapy as its purpose into a forensic context: 'When Plight Makes Right: The Forensic Abuse Syndrome' (1994) 18 Crim LJ 29–49.

Freckelton explains that in the medical context, the term 'syndrome' is used to denote a collection of symptoms that occur together where the cause of the symptom is not known. There is therefore some confusion between the medical use of the term 'syndrome' meaning that the cause of the symptoms is not identifiable and the legal and evidential use of the term that assumes that a cause can be identified. Freckelton points out that the advantage for the defence of using the term 'syndrome' is that it cloaks the social and psychological explanation of the accused's conduct in a veneer of medical respectability to make it more acceptable to the jury.

There are dangers in this medicalisation of women's experiences and behaviour. First, women who do not exhibit these symptoms will find it difficult to convince a jury that their reactions were reasonable: the use of battered woman syndrome means that women must now conform to a medical model for their evidence to be credible. Second, in crude terms, syndrome evidence suggests that the woman is not bad, but mad. This may suggest that the more appropriate defences are those of mental impairment or diminished responsibility. Again this pathologises the experience of battered women and takes their situation out of a social context.

Because of these three main problems raised by the use of battered woman syndrome, some authors have argued that it is more useful to turn the focus back on the law of self-defence and other ways of accommodating women's experiences. Ian Leader-Elliott writes that the *Zecevic* model of self-defence is more accommodating to defensive acts impelled by necessity than other models: I Leader-Elliott, 'Battered But Not Beaten: Women Who Kill in Self Defence' (1993) 15 *Sydney Law Review* 403–60 at 460. Certain cases such as *Hickey*'s case, which was discussed earlier, clearly raise a self-defence narrative, at least on the basis of how events were perceived by the woman concerned.

Gail Hubble, however, has warned that the expansion of the scope of self-defence may interfere with the traditional reluctance of the law to accept that the choices of individuals are determined by their personal histories. She argues that if there is too much of a focus on past experiences as an explanation for a woman's violence, this 'determinism' could have repercussions for the way in which the conduct of male criminals is explained: G Hubble, 'Feminism and the Battered Woman: The Limits of Self-Defence in the Context of Domestic Violence' (1997) 9(2) *Current Issues in Criminal Justice* 113–23. Julie Stubbs and Julia Tolmie argue against this view, that new constructions of self-defence that reflect women's experiences do not have to be based on determinism: 'Feminisms, Self-Defence, and Battered Women: A Response to Hubble's "Straw Feminist"' (1998) 10(1) *Current Issues in Criminal Justice* 75–84 at 81.

The challenge remains to find ways in which to take into account the circumstances leading to an abused woman killing her partner without medicalising her reactions. The use of battered woman syndrome to do this is a two-edged sword. It may very well help explain why the woman stayed in the abusive relationship, but the very existence of such a syndrome can be questioned and if the circumstances do not readily 'fit' the cycle of violence, it can be used against the accused.

Subjective/objective elements

It was stated above that in all jurisdictions, the defence of self-defence has both subjective and objective elements. In its report on homicide, the Law Reform Commission of Victoria recommended that self-defence be made a fully subjective defence: *Homicide*, Report No 40 (Melbourne: LRCV, 1991) p 96. The Commission stated that this was 'consistent with the emphasis on moral culpability and on the subjective mental state of the defendant': p 96.

In *Zecevic v DPP (Vic)* (1987) 162 CLR 645 the High Court unanimously rejected the argument that the test for self-defence be purely subjective. Deane J (at 673) was of the opinion that there was 'simply no warrant for such a wholesale reversal' of what he termed 'settled law' relating to self-defence. Wilson, Dawson and Toohey JJ (at 658) referred to the traditional rationale for the defence to support a partly objective test. They perceived that self-defence was not concerned 'with the execution of justice but with the necessary and reasonable response to the preservation of life and limb'. This implies a shift from justification to excuse as the basis for the defence.

A purely subjective test does appear problematic. From a theoretical perspective, a subjective test fails to distinguish between the elements of an offence and the elements of a defence. Generally, if an offence requires a particular mental state as part of its definition, then a subjective test can be applied. However, a mental state forming part of a defence requires an objective test. This distinction is based on societal values. That is, before a society decides to exercise compassion by exculpating an accused from criminal liability, it is entitled to demand that the accused lacked any blameworthiness in relation to the plea relied on. As Stanley Yeo in *Compulsion in the Criminal Law* (Sydney: Law Book Co Ltd, 1990) p 200 points out, '[a]n unreasonable or negligently held belief would constitute blameworthiness denying the accused the excuse'.

On a practical level, without some form of objective limitation such as reasonableness, it would seem that an accused who may be excessively fearful or apprehensive would be able to react violently towards others with perfect impunity. While a purely subjective defence may aid abused women who kill their partners, it may also mean that more men would be afforded an acquittal on the basis of unreasonable mistaken beliefs that they were being threatened.

The MCCOC has suggested instead a 'simplified' test of self-defence as a defence to both murder and assault. Section 10.4(2) of the *Criminal Code* (Cth) states:

> A person carries out conduct in self-defence if and only if he or she believes the conduct is necessary:
>
> to defend himself or herself or another person; or
>
> to prevent or terminate the unlawful imprisonment of himself or herself or another person; or
>
> to protect property from unlawful appropriation, destruction, damage or interference; or
>
> to prevent criminal trespass to any land or premises; or
>
> to remove from any land or premises a person who is committing criminal trespass;
>
> and the conduct is a reasonable response in circumstances as he or she perceives them to be.

Section 42 of the *Criminal Code* (ACT) is couched in similar terms. As with s 46 of the *Criminal Code* (Tas), the test focuses on the belief of the accused, but there is an objective component in relation to whether the conduct was a reasonable response. This appears to be an adequate test for self-defence. Its emphasis on the subjective belief of the accused allows for sufficient account to be taken of an accused's personal characteristics such as sex, ethnicity, age and religion. The objective element provides for limitations on behaviour deemed appropriate by society as represented by members of the jury.

Provocation

Background

One defence that was put to the jury in the *Falconer* trial, but which was unsuccessful, was that of provocation. This defence, like the defence of diminished responsibility, which will be discussed in Chapter 11, is a partial one in that it reduces murder to manslaughter rather than leading to a complete acquittal. It only becomes relevant where the prosecution proves or the defence concedes that the fault element for murder existed at the time of the killing. Provocation operates as a defence to offences that have assault as a defined element in the Northern Territory, Queensland and Western Australia: *Criminal Code* (NT) s 34; *Criminal Code* (Qld) s 269; *Criminal Code* (WA) s 246. This was discussed in Chapter 4.

The nature and role of provocation is best understood in its historical context. The development of the defence can be traced back to seventeenth-century England: Bernard J Brown, 'The Demise of Chance Medley and the Recognition of Provocation as a Defence to Murder in English Law' (1963) 7 *American Journal of Legal History* 310–18; Jeremy Horder, *Provocation and Responsibility* (Oxford: Clarendon Press, 1992). In the sixteenth century, drunken brawls and fights arising from 'breaches of honour' were commonplace. Killings that occurred as a result of a sudden affray were termed *chaud mêlée*, which was corrupted into 'chance medley'. During the seventeenth century, the law began to distinguish between the most serious types of killing, which required proof of malice aforethought, and killings that were unpremeditated and occurred on the spur of the moment in response to an act of provocation. Sir William Holdsworth wrote in *A History of English Law* (London: Sweet & Maxwell, 1966) Vol 8, p 302: '[T]he readiness with which all classes resorted to lethal weapons to assert their rights, or to avenge any insult real or fancied, gave abundant opportunity for elaborating the distinctions between various kinds of homicide.'

The need to draw such distinctions followed from the fact that murder at this time was a capital felony. The accused could escape capital punishment only if he or she lacked malice aforethought. Manslaughter was only available where the killing had occurred 'suddenly', and in 'hot blood' in response to an act of provocation by the deceased. Thus, provocation emerged as a way of avoiding mandatory capital punishment: G Coss, '"God is a righteous judge, strong and patient: and God is provoked every day": A Brief History of the Doctrine of Provocation in England' (1991) 13 *Sydney Law Review* 570–604. When capital punishment was abolished, provocation was still important as a way to avoid the mandatory life sentence for murder.

The early decisions relating to provocation sought to identify the fact situations where the defence could operate. Four categories developed: a grossly insulting assault; attack upon a relative or friend; the sight of an Englishman unlawfully deprived of his liberty and seeing a man in the act of adultery with one's wife: J Horder, *Provocation and Responsibility* (Oxford: Clarendon Press, 1992) ch 2.

The law at this stage imposed a suddenness requirement; where there was an opportunity for the 'blood to cool', the defence was not available. Aspects of this early law have survived through to the current law. Suddenness and the absence of delay or premeditation are no longer substantive rules, but they may provide evidence that an ordinary person faced by that degree of provocation could have acted in the way in which the accused did.

As outlined in Chapter 1, the common law underwent significant changes during the nineteenth century partly in response to the philosophical currents of liberal theory and positivism. The concepts of free will and autonomy led to the use of morally neutral terms such as 'intention' and 'recklessness' rather than 'malice' or a 'wicked' or 'evil mind'. This changed understanding of criminal responsibility made an impact on the defence of provocation in several ways.

First, the focus of the defence became, and remains, the accused's 'loss of self-control' rather than justifiable retribution. The defence's rationale became the recognition that an individual may suffer a temporary loss of self-control in certain circumstances: Alex Reilly, 'Loss of Self-Control in Provocation' (1997) 21 Crim LJ 320 at 320.

Secondly, as a means of controlling the scope of the defence, the courts developed and applied an objective test by examining what a 'reasonable man' would have done in the circumstances. In *R v Welsh* (1869) 11 Cox 336, Keating J stated (at 338): 'The law contemplates the case of the reasonable man, and requires that the provocation shall be such as that such a man might naturally be induced, in the anger of the moment, to commit the act.'

In recent times, the reasonable man developed into the ordinary person. Barwick CJ in *Moffa v The Queen* (1977) 138 CLR 601 at 606 noted that it is preferable to characterise the objective standard in terms of an ordinary rather than a reasonable person because the use of the term 'reasonable' might be taken as excluding severe emotional reactions from consideration.

Thirdly, the courts began to apply a test of proportionality that required some correlation between the act of provocation and the accused's retaliation. This is no longer a separate requirement under the common law, but it may be relevant to the question as to whether or not the provocation was sufficient to have induced an ordinary person to have lost self-control and acted in the way in which the accused did.

This short history of provocation shows how it can be viewed as containing elements of both excuse and justification. It is excusatory in its focus on the accused's lack of self-control and justificatory in its focus on the provocative conduct of the victim and the acceptability of the accused's actions. Because of this combination of elements of excuse and justification, the conceptual basis for the defence of provocation is often confused. Its lack of a clear rationale has led to the MCCOC calling for its abolition: *Chapter 5, Fatal Offences Against the Person*, Discussion Paper (June 1998) p 83. This will be considered in the Critique section.

The current law

The elements of the defence of provocation are set out by the common law that is followed in South Australia and Victoria and reflected in the statutory provisions of the Australian Capital Territory, New South Wales and the Northern Territory: *Crimes Act* 1900 (ACT) s 13(2); *Crimes Act* 1900 (NSW) s 23(2); *Criminal Code* (NT) s 34. The defence of provocation has recently been abolished in Tasmania by the *Criminal Code Amendment (Abolition of Defence of Provocation) Act* 2003. There is no mention of provocation in the current *Criminal Code* (ACT), but it could be that defences to homicide will appear in a future Chapter of the Code. The common law has been held to apply to the interpretation of provocation under s 304 of the *Criminal Code* (Qld), which sets out provocation as a partial defence to murder: *Van Den Hoek v The Queen* (1986) 161 CLR 158 at 168 per Mason J; *R v Johnson* [1964] Qd R 1; *Kaporonovski v The Queen* (1973) 133 CLR 209.

It seems, however, that the definition of provocation that applies as a defence to assault also applies to the partial defence to murder set out in s 281 of the *Criminal Code* (WA): *Sreckovic v The Queen* [1973] WAR 85; *Censori v The Queen* [1983] WAR 89; *Roche v The Queen* [1988] WAR 278. Section 245 of the *Criminal Code* (WA) defines 'provocation' as any wrongful act or insult as to be likely, when done to an ordinary person, to deprive him or her of the power of self-control.

In general, the test for provocation contains both subjective and objective elements. There must be some evidence that the accused was in fact acting under provocation. The content and extent of the provocative conduct is assessed from the viewpoint of the particular accused. This is the subjective element of the defence. In addition, however, there is an objective requirement that the provocation be of such a nature that could or might have moved an ordinary person to act as the accused did.

The defence can thus be divided into three fundamental requirements:
- there must be provocative conduct;
- the accused must have lost self-control as a result of the provocation; and
- the provocation must be such that it was capable of causing an ordinary person to lose self-control and to act in the way the accused did.

Provocative conduct

Before an accused can rely on the defence of provocation, there must be evidence of some form of conduct that caused the accused to lose self-control. In the past, the case law referred to the existence of a clearly identifiable triggering incident or series of incidents: *R v Croft* [1981] 1 NSWLR 126 at 140 per O'Brien J. That requirement has been lessened to some degree in recent years. In *Chhay* (1994) 72 A Crim R 1, Gleeson CJ stated (at 13): '[T]imes are changing, and people are becoming more aware that a loss of self-control can develop even after a lengthy period of abuse, and without the necessity for a specific triggering incident.'

What is important is the cumulative effect of all the circumstances including the background and history leading up to the accused's loss of control. An incident or words that may seem inoffensive may amount to provocation when placed in the context of an abusive relationship. In *R v R* (1981) 28 SASR 321 the accused killed her husband with an axe after he had stroked her arm and cuddled up to her in bed telling her that they would be one happy family and two of their daughters would not be leaving. The accused had recently been informed that her husband had sexually abused each of their five daughters. She gave evidence that while he slept, she sat smoking one cigarette after another, thinking about her daughters before going to the shed and getting the axe. The trial judge did not allow provocation to go to the jury. On appeal, the majority of the South Australian Supreme Court (King CJ and Jacobs J) allowed an appeal against conviction and ordered a re-trial. They held that the victim's conduct had to be placed against a background of brutality, sexual assault, intimidation and manipulation. Zelling J dissented in holding that there wasn't a specific provocatory act. Interestingly, at the re-trial, the jury acquitted the accused altogether despite this not being a possible verdict under the defence of provocation: VLRC, Report No 40, *Homicide*, p 86, fn 153. This suggests the jury had great sympathy towards the accused given the circumstances leading to the killing.

It appears unlikely that insulting words alone constitute provocation. The *Criminal Codes* of the Northern Territory and Western Australia require that there be a 'wrongful act or insult'. The Queensland Court of Appeal in *Buttigieg* (1993) 69 A Crim R 21 held that words alone, no matter how insulting or upsetting, cannot amount to sufficient provocation to murder.

Mason J in *Moffa v The Queen* (1977) 138 CLR 601 at 620–1 pointed out the rationale for excluding words alone as provocation: '[A] case of provocation by words may be more easily invented than a case of provocation by conduct, particularly when the victim was the wife of the accused. There is, therefore, an element of public policy as well as common sense requiring the close scrutiny of claims of provocation founded in words, rather than conduct.'

In *Holmes v DPP* [1946] AC 588 at 600, Viscount Simon stated that 'a sudden confession of adultery without more can never constitute provocation of a sort which might reduce murder to manslaughter'. In *Moffa v The Queen* (1977) 138 CLR 601, Barwick CJ, Gibbs, Stephen and Mason JJ accepted that *Holmes* was still good law (at 605, 616, 619, 620–2). In *R v Parsons* [2000] 1 VR 161, the Victorian Court of Criminal Appeal held that the trial judge had been correct in withdrawing provocation from the jury where the accused killed his de facto wife in the midst of an adjournment of a Family Court hearing after she allegedly said to him 'we have got you now, you bastard'. Similarly, in *R v Leonboyer* unreported, 7 September 2001, CA of the SC of Vic, [2001] VSCA 149, the Victorian Court of Criminal Appeal held that the trial judge had been correct in withdrawing provocation from the jury where the accused had killed his girlfriend after she allegedly admitted to having sex with another man, stating 'he did it better than what you did'. In addition, in *R v Kumar* [2002] 5 VR 193, a majority of the Court of Appeal of Victoria held that the victim's alleged swearing and taunts that she would 'take another man' in front of the accused did not amount to enough evidence of provocation for the defence to be left to the jury.

If we return to *Falconer*'s case, Mary Falconer being hit, indecently assaulted and being told that her daughters would not be believed seen against the background of the charges laid against Gordon Falconer would appear to be sufficient for provocative conduct. Her daughters' claims concerning sexual assault on their own would not be enough as there is some support for the notion that the provocation must take place in the sight or hearing of the accused. For example, in *R v Arden* [1975] VR 449 the accused's de facto wife, who was two months' pregnant, told him that she had been raped by a man who was asleep in another room of the house. She showed the accused her torn pantyhose and pants. The accused confronted the man, who denied the allegation. The accused attacked and killed him with an iron pipe. Menhennit J excluded the defence of provocation on the basis that being told by a third person of an incident is an insufficient basis for the defence. He stated (at 452):

> The rationale of this rule appears to me to be as follows. If a person actually sees conduct taking place in respect to a third person and he [or she] is provoked thereby, it is understandable that he [or she] may be provoked to the extent of taking the other person's life and in circumstances which would reduce murder to manslaughter. Where, however, all that happened is that the accused is told something by a third person there enters immediately the element of belief, and there is nothing tangible upon which the accused can be said to have acted.

The accused's loss of self-control

For the defence of provocation to be successful, the accused must have lost the power of self-control as a result of the provocative conduct. This loss of self-control may be the result of anger or fear or panic: *Van Den Hoek v The Queen* (1986) 161 CLR 158 at 168 per Mason J.

It used to be the case that the reaction had to be sudden or immediate. This was the case in Western Australia at the time of the *Falconer* trial. The Commissioner in the original trial stated the law in his charge to the jury as follows ((1989) 46 A Crim R 83 at 114–15):

Our *Criminal Code* says that where a person unlawfully kills another in circumstances which would normally constitute wilful murder or murder but does the act which causes death in the heat of passion caused by sudden provocation and before there is time for his or her passion to cool, he or she is guilty of manslaughter. So you will see the essential ingredients are: first, the person has done the act which caused death in the heat of passion. Secondly, the passion has been caused by sudden provocation. Thirdly, the killing occurred before there was time for the passion to cool.

Suddenness is no longer a separate requirement in the defence of provocation. However, the jury may consider the significance of any time-delay in assessing whether or not the accused lost self-control. Any evidence of a 'cooling-off period' will merely be a factor that the jury can consider: *Parker v The Queen* (1963) 111 CLR 610 at 630 per Dixon CJ.

In any case, on Mary Falconer's narrative, her reaction was sudden. But did she lose self-control? Her inability to recall the events makes this difficult to assess. In finding her guilty of wilful murder, the jury must have accepted that she intended to kill her husband. The prosecution's emphasis that she bought cartridges and had loaded the gun before her husband arrived at her home may lend credence to the notion that she had pre-planned the shooting and therefore did not lose self-control. The Court of Appeal of Western Australia heard an appeal partly based on the Commissioner's charge to the jury. That centred on the 'ordinary person' part of the test of provocation and this is discussed in the next section. In relation to the accused's loss of self-control, the Commissioner directed the jury as follows (1989) 46 A Crim R 83 at 116:

> As I said before, bear in mind that the Crown must prove beyond reasonable doubt that this was not a killing under provocation. You might say, 'What is the evidence', then you might find some of it in the evidence which came from Detective Sergeant Migro when he told you what the accused said after he interviewed her some time later on the day of the shooting. He said: 'What happened at home today?' and she said: 'He just kept laughing at me, saying nobody would believe me or the girls.' You will see there the taunt, the insult, I suppose. It is for you to judge whether it is the type of insult which would constitute provocation as I have defined it; the effect it would have on the ordinary person. Although, I must say that you must bear in mind too, of course, that to Migro she said this: Migro said, 'Did you shoot him because he laughed at you?' and she said: 'No.' So she actually disclaimed that she shot him for that reason. Migro said: 'Why did you shoot him?' and she said: 'He was coming at me.' Migro said: 'How was he coming at me [sic]?' and she said: 'He reached out for my hair. I stepped back. I don't remember; it all happened so suddenly. I didn't mean to shoot him.' So you see, if you accepted that evidence and took the view that this is what really happened then it might be difficult to find it was a killing under provocation because she is not saying: 'I shot him because he provoked me.' It would be different if the accused woman had come into the court and said: 'Yes, I shot him. I

pointed the rifle at him and I pulled the trigger and I shot him and it was because he had been taunting me and taunting me to death and I could stand no more.' She hasn't said that but you have to decide, on the evidence, irrespective of what she said, whether, in the circumstances, there is evidence which would constitute provocation which would reduce wilful murder or murder to manslaughter.

In finding that Mary Falconer committed wilful murder, the jury must have accepted that she intended to kill her husband and this was not a provoked killing. From the judge's directions, the fact that she said she hadn't shot her husband because he laughed at her was significant. There was no evidence that she had lost control because of his taunts. It is interesting that there is no mention of the indecent assault in this passage. That omission will be taken up a little later when the situation facing Mary Falconer is compared with that of Malcolm Green.

The ordinary person test

The defence of provocation will only be successful where the provocation was of such a nature as to be 'capable of causing an ordinary person to lose self-control and to act in the way the accused did': *Masciantonio v The Queen* (1995) 183 CLR 58 at 66 per Brennan, Deane, Dawson and Gaudron JJ; *Stingel v The Queen* (1990) 171 CLR 312 at 325–7. The ordinary person test involves two questions:

1   given that the accused actually lost self-control, was the provocation of such a nature as to be capable of causing an ordinary person to lose self-control? This is usually referred to as assessing the gravity of the provocation; and
2   given that the ordinary person would have lost self-control, was the provocation such as could cause an ordinary person to act in the way in which the accused did?

The first part of the ordinary person test involves an assessment of the content and the extent of the provocation; the second involves an assessment of whether the provocation would have caused an ordinary person to kill another. Peter Rush explains this in *Criminal Law* (Sydney: Butterworths, 1997) p 353 as follows: 'The possibility being envisaged here by the judiciary is that, although the ordinary person would have lost their self-control to the same extent the [accused] did, the ordinary person would have laughed it off or told the victim to go jump in the lake whereas the actual accused killed the victim.'

Different personal characteristics may be taken into account in applying the ordinary person test in these two ways.

In assessing the gravity of the provocation, any relevant characteristic of the accused may be attributed to the ordinary person: *Stingel v The Queen* (1990) 171 CLR 312 at 325–7.

Brennan, Deane, Dawson and Gaudron JJ provided a rationale for this requirement in *Masciantonio v The Queen* (1995) 183 CLR 58 (at 67): 'Conduct which might not be insulting or hurtful to one person might be extremely so to another because of that person's age, sex, race, ethnicity, physical features, personal attributes, personal relationships or past history. The provocation must be put into context and it is only by having regard to the attributes or characteristics of the accused that this can be done.'

With regard to the second question as to whether or not the ordinary person could or might have lost control in the way the accused did, the High Court has ruled that no personal characteristic apart from age may be taken into account: *Stingel v The Queen* (1990) 171 CLR 312 at 326–7, at 330–1 per the Court.

In *Masciantonio v The Queen* (1994–95) 183 CLR 58 Brennan, Deane, Dawson and Gaudron JJ (at 67) spoke of the ordinary person test as follows:

> The test involving the hypothetical ordinary person is an objective test which lays down the minimum standard of self-control required by the law. Since it is an objective test, the characteristics of the ordinary person are merely those of a person with ordinary powers of self-control. They are not the characteristics of the accused, although when it is appropriate to do so because of the accused's immaturity, the ordinary person may be taken to be of the accused's age.

At the time of Mary Falconer's trial, the objective test was not so divided. In *Johnson v The Queen* (1976) 136 CLR 619 at 636, Barwick CJ set out the test as whether or not '…the provocation of the accused was such as would have caused an ordinary man [sic], placed in all the circumstances in which the accused stood, to have lost his [sic] self control to the point of doing an act of the kind and degree of that by which the accused killed the deceased.'

One of the grounds of appeal to the Supreme Court of Western Australia, was that the Commissioner had failed to direct the jury that the ordinary person was the ordinary person in the position of Mary Falconer at the time of the killing with regard to all the circumstances. The Court of Appeal dismissed this ground of appeal. The Commissioner had said at the trial ((1989) 46 A Crim R 83 at 115):

> What is a reasonable person you might ask me? What is the ordinary person, who is he? Well, he [sic] is probably not me…but it has been said that an ordinary person is a person of either sex, not exceptionally excitable, not the real hothead, or pugnacious, a person who wants to hit everybody, but possessed of such powers of self-control as everyone would be entitled to expect from our fellow citizen as they would exercise it in society today.

The jury later asked for further directions as to provocation. What happened next is reported at 117–18:

> When dealing with provocation the learned Commissioner further charged the jury as follows:

'When you are looking at provocation I said that it was once said for the purposes of the law of provocation a reasonable person means an ordinary person of either sex, not exceptionally excitable or pugnacious but possessed of such powers of self-control as everyone is entitled to expect from his [sic] fellow citizen in society today. Essentially, ladies and gentlemen, I think that is it. I know it is hard to wrap your mind around that because it has so many different components but you are looking first at did the woman kill under provocation, herself? Then you are looking at the question of was death caused—did she do the act which caused death in the heat of passion? Was that passion caused by sudden provocation? Did the killing occur before there was time for the passion to cool? Then provocation itself—a wrongful act or insult of such a nature as to be likely when done to an ordinary person, to deprive him or her of the power of self-control and to induce him or her to do what they did. Do you think that covers the question you were asked?'

Counsel for the appellant then put it to the learned Commissioner:

'I think with respect, sir, that it should be made clear, as I understand the law, that when we are talking about an ordinary person, we are talking about an ordinary person in the circumstances of which the accused found herself, that is, with the history of, leading up to and on that occasion.'

This was said in the presence of the jury to which the learned Commissioner commented:

'That is a good point. Mr Singleton reminded me. Earlier I said to you, and I didn't say on this occasion but I should say it again, that provocation—in looking at provocation you can look at the past history of the relations between the deceased man and his wife and where you have a long history of wrongful acts or insults you could have a final wrongful act or insult which finally broke the accused's self-control and caused her to act in the heat of passion. That is the last straw aspect which I addressed you on earlier and I had forgotten to address on this time until Mr Singleton reminded me, so I agree with that.'

As pointed out above, the jury rejected provocation as a defence. Given that the law has now changed to imbuing the ordinary person only with age in assessing whether or not the provocation could have caused an ordinary person to act in the way in which the accused did, it would appear that it is somewhat easier for the prosecution to disprove provocation in a situation like that of *Falconer*'s case. Would a 52-year-old ordinary person with no assigned sex or history have done what Mary Falconer did in the face of being laughed at, hit and touched 'between the legs'? Responding by shooting someone may seem an over-reaction, but if the accused is male and the provoker is male, it would seem that judges and juries are now willing to accept that an ordinary person would react in such a way.

In *Green v The Queen* (1997) 191 CLR 334, the 22-year-old accused, Malcolm Green, killed the 36-year-old male victim, one of his 'best friends' after the latter had gently touched the accused's side, bottom and groin area. The accused punched the deceased about thirty-five times, banged his face against the wall and stabbed him with a pair of scissors about ten times. In attempting to establish provocation at his trial, the accused sought to admit evidence that he was particularly sensitive to matters of sexual abuse as a result of being told by his sisters and mother that his father had sexually abused four of his sisters and after witnessing violent assaults by his father upon his mother. The trial judge directed the jury that this evidence was not relevant to the issue of provocation and the accused was convicted of murder.

On appeal to the New South Wales Court of Criminal Appeal, the Crown conceded that the trial judge had erred in law in determining that this evidence was not admissible in relation to the question as to whether or not the accused had in fact been provoked, but a majority of the Court (Priestley JA, Ireland J concurring, Smart J dissenting) dismissed the appeal on the basis that there was no miscarriage of justice. On a further appeal to the High Court all five judges agreed that there had been a misdirection but a majority of three judges, Brennan CJ, Toohey and McHugh JJ with Gummow and Kirby JJ dissenting, held that there had been a miscarriage of justice and ordered a retrial. At his retrial, Green was convicted of manslaughter and sentenced to imprisonment for ten and a half years. An appeal against sentence was dismissed: *Green v The Queen* unreported, 18 May 1999, CCA of NSW, [1999] NSW CCA 97.

Section 23(2)(b) of the *Crimes Act* 1900 (NSW) states that the provocation must be such 'as could have induced an ordinary person in the position of the accused to have so far lost self-control as to have formed an intent to kill, or to inflict grievous bodily harm upon, the deceased'. The appellant argued that the words 'in the position of the accused' requires the ordinary person to be imbued with all the attributes or characteristics of the accused. Toohey J stated (at 673) that these words simply mean that in determining the *gravity* of the provocation to the accused, it is relevant to take into account the accused's own circumstances. Both Toohey and Gummow JJ referred (at 693) with approval to a statement made by Samuels JA in *Baragith* (1991) 54 A Crim R 240 (at 244) that 'the words "in the position of the accused" so far as they make relevant attributes or characteristics of a particular accused do so only in assessing the gravity of the alleged provocation and are to be ignored in deciding whether the accused's response was or was not that of an ordinary person'.

Similarly, McHugh J stated (at 682) that the words 'in the position of the accused' 'require that the hypothetical person be an ordinary person who has been provoked to the same degree of severity and for the same reasons as the accused'. Kirby J appears (at 716) to have taken a slightly different view of the meaning of the words 'in the position of the accused', holding not that they deal with the gravity of the provocation, but rather, the 'consideration to be given to the age and maturity of the accused person'. The end result of these judgments is that, in relation to the ordinary person test, the two-tiered approach taken by the High Court in *Stingel* and *Masciantonio* still holds sway.

Should a non-violent sexual advance constitute provocation? The Attorney-General's Department (NSW) had previously released a Discussion Paper (No 18) in 1996 entitled *Review of the 'Homosexual Panic Defence'*. It concluded (paras 56–7) that a non-violent homosexual advance should not constitute sufficient provocation to incite an ordinary person to lethal violence. Kirby J referred to this Paper and stated at 408–9:

> In my view, the 'ordinary person' in Australian society today is not so homophobic as to respond to a non-violent sexual advance by a homosexual person as to form an intent to kill or to inflict grievous bodily harm. He or she might, depending on the circumstances, be embarrassed; treat it at first as a bad joke; be hurt; insulted. He or she might react with the strong language of protest; might use as much physical force as was necessary to effect an escape; and where absolutely necessary assault the persistent perpetrator to secure escape. But the notion that the ordinary 22-year-old male (the age of the accused) in Australia today would so lose self-control as to form an intent to kill or grievously injure the deceased because of a non-violent sexual advance by a homosexual person is unconvincing. It should not be accepted by this court as an objective standard applicable in contemporary Australia.

In comparison, Brennan CJ (at 345–6) quoted Smart J's judgment in the Court of Appeal decision:

> The provocation was of a very grave kind. It must have been a terrifying experience for the appellant when the deceased persisted. The grabbing and persistence are critical.
>
> Some ordinary men would feel great revulsion at the homosexual advances being persisted in the circumstances and could be induced to so far lose their self-control as to form the intention to and inflict grievous bodily harm. They would regard it as a serious and gross violation of their body and person.

Brennan CJ (at 346) then went on to decide that the matter should be up to the jury to decide: 'A juryman or woman would not be unreasonable because he or she might accept that the appellant found the deceased's conduct "revolting" rather than "amorous".'

These are obviously two very different views of homosexual advances. Kirby J (at 416) made the point that any unwanted sexual advance, homosexual or heterosexual, may be offensive. But, if it were a non-violent heterosexual advance, would a lethal response be considered acceptable? The fact that in his charge, the Commissioner in the *Falconer* trial emphasised Gordon Falconer's laughter and taunts and failed to mention the indecent assault or being hit as evidence of provocation seems to indicate that in a heterosexual relationship, such acts are not seen as sufficiently provocative to the ordinary person.

From this overview of the current law, it is perhaps not surprising that commentators have concentrated on the ordinary person test as most in need of reform in the law of provocation. It is to criticisms of this defence and possible reforms that we now turn.

Critique

Criticisms of the current law of provocation have centred on the following issues:
1 What characteristics of the ordinary person should be taken into account in assessing the gravity of the provocation and what the accused did?
2 Should there be an ordinary person test at all?
3 Should there be a defence of provocation at all?

The following sections deal with these three areas in more detail and provide an overview of reform suggestions.

Characteristics of the ordinary person

Assuming that there should be an objective standard in provocation, there has been debate as to the characteristics with which the 'ordinary person' should be imbued. Alex Reilly refers to this as '[o]ne of the most intractable debates surrounding the defence': 'Loss of Self-Control in Provocation' (1997) 21 Crim LJ 320–35 at 326.

Up until *Stingel*'s case, the trend was for the courts to imbue the ordinary person with many of the accused's characteristics. As outlined above, *Stingel*'s case decided that in assessing the gravity of the provocation, any relevant characteristic of the accused may be attributed to the ordinary person. However, in assessing whether or not an ordinary person could or might have lost control in the way the accused did, only age may be taken into account.

Some authors and judges have called for other characteristics as well as age to be taken into account in the second tier of the test. Two important characteristics that have been discussed in this regard are sex and cultural background.

The ordinary woman

In England, the sex of the accused is a relevant characteristic to be taken into account in assessing an ordinary 'person's' response to provocation: *DPP v Camplin* [1978] AC 705; *R v Morhall* [1996] AC 90. In Australia and Canada, the courts have resisted taking the sex of the accused into account in assessing loss of self-control on the basis that it would violate the principle of equality to hold men and women to different standards of self-control: *R v Hill* [1986] 1 SCR 313; *Stingel v The Queen* (1990) 171 CLR 312.

Some authors such as Elizabeth Sheehy, Julie Stubbs and Julia Tolmie have argued that the sexless ordinary person is really a male: 'Defending Battered Women on Trial: The Battered Woman Syndrome and its Limitations' (1992) 16 Crim LJ 369–94. The challenge has therefore been to demonstrate that the male response to provocation is not necessarily the only reasonable response or ordinary reaction.

In the past, the use of the defence of provocation proved difficult for women who had killed their abusive partners. The common law traditionally required suddenness and a proportionate relationship between the provocation and the conduct undertaken. Since these two requirements are no longer separate rules, but are matters to be taken into account overall, there has been a freeing up of the availability of the defence.

For example, as previously discussed, in *R v R* (1981) 28 SASR 321 the accused killed her abusive husband with an axe while he was sleeping. The lack of suddenness in the provocative conduct was not a bar to provocation. The Supreme Court of South Australia accepted that the words and conduct of the deceased had to be seen in the context of the history of the relationship between the two.

Similarly, in *Hill* (1981) 3 A Crim R 397 the New South Wales Court of Criminal Appeal took a contextual approach to the traditional suddenness requirement and held that the accused's loss of self-control had to be seen in the context of a history of domestic violence. In that case, there was evidence that the husband had a propensity for violent conduct when he was drunk. On the day of the killing, he returned home from the pub drunk, swearing and 'screaming his head off'. The accused, who was holding a rifle, warned him not to come near her. She claimed she fired three shots, trying to frighten him away. One of the shots hit and killed her husband. The Court substituted a verdict of manslaughter and sentenced the accused to four and a half years in prison.

Evidence of 'battered woman syndrome' may be relevant to the questions as to whether or not the accused lost self-control and the gravity of the provocation. However, such evidence has no bearing on the powers of self-control expected of the ordinary person. Stanley Yeo points out in 'Battered Woman Syndrome in Australia' (1993) 143 *New Law Journal* 13–14:

> [F]or the purposes of provocation, battered women are regarded as possessing normal levels of self-control and are not to be distinguished in this respect from the ordinary woman in the community. What the syndrome does do is to present the latest provocative incident in the light of a history of provocation, and contribute to the jurors' comprehension of how a person with such a history could have viewed the latest provocation.

Because of the difficulties of 'fitting' the circumstances of battered women within the provocation defence, an accused who kills her partner after years of abuse may still be liable for murder. However, a man who kills his partner after discovering her in an act of adultery may be liable for manslaughter. There is some slight empirical evidence suggesting, however, that in practice, women who raise the defence of provocation are more 'successful' than men who do so. This will be explored a little later.

Cultural background

In *Masciantonio v The Queen* (1995) 183 CLR 58 McHugh J recanted his previous approach in *Stingel*'s case and stated (at 74) that 'unless the ethnic or cultural background of the accused is attributed to the ordinary person, the objective test of self-control results in inequality before the law. Real equality before the law cannot exist when ethnic or cultural minorities are convicted or acquitted of murder according to a standard that reflects the values of the dominant class but does not reflect the values of those minorities'.

In reaching this conclusion, McHugh J stated that he was influenced by Professor Yeo's criticisms of the objective test in his article 'Power of Self-Control in Provocation and Automatism' (1992) 14 *Sydney Law Review* 3 at 12–13.

Interestingly enough, Yeo subsequently altered his position after reading the work of Leader-Elliott: see for example I Leader-Elliott, 'Sex, Race and Provocation: In Defence of Stingel' (1996) 20 Crim LJ 72–96. In 1996, Professor Yeo wrote that imbuing the ordinary person with the accused's ethnic or cultural background may give rise to essentialist views of various cultures and thereupon give rise to racism: S Yeo, 'Sex, Ethnicity, Power of Self-Control and Provocation Revisited' (1996) 18 *Sydney Law Review* 304–22.

There are certainly dangers associated with the present test in that by excluding cultural and ethnic background as a relevant consideration, discrimination against minority groups may be concealed and perpetuated. Objective standards of behaviour are predicated on the existence of a 'community consensus' about what constitutes reasonable and ordinary behaviour. However, where minority groups are not adequately represented either on juries or on the bench, objective standards will be determined exclusively by the values of the dominant Anglo-Saxon-Celtic culture: Australian Law Reform Commission, *Multiculturalism and the Law*, Report No 57 (Sydney: ALRC, 1992) pp 183–4.

On the other hand, the adoption of an ordinary person standard that is sensitive to cultural background may also be problematic. In determining the reactions of an ordinary person of a particular cultural background, there is also a risk that judges and juries may draw on discriminatory generalisations about the cultures of minority groups of which they have little or no understanding. It would be very difficult to gather empirical evidence of cultural practices in this regard. Further, such a modified standard could accommodate cultural claims about the use of domestic violence to discipline women and children.

It may be that the difficulties associated with the ordinary person test are so intractable that it might be worthwhile considering other more radical solutions than attempting to modify it. Such alternatives are considered next.

Should there be an ordinary person test?

If it is so difficult to frame an ordinary person test, why bother having one at all? The rationale for having an objective standard was expressed by Wilson J in *R v Hill*

[1986] 1 SCR 313 at 324 as follows: 'The objective standard...may be said to exist in order to ensure that in the evaluation of the provocation defence there is no fluctuating standard of self-control against which accuseds are measured. The governing principles are those of equality and individual responsibility, so that all persons are held to the same standard notwithstanding their distinctive personality traits and varying capacities to achieve the standard.'

The ordinary person test in provocation has drawn much criticism from both judges and academic commentators. In *Moffa v The Queen* (1977) 138 CLR 601 Murphy J (at 625–6) called for its abolition:

> The objective test is not suitable even for a superficially homogeneous society, and the more heterogeneous our society becomes, the more inappropriate the test is. Behaviour is influenced by age, sex, ethnic origin, climatic and other living conditions, biorhythms, education, occupation and, above all, individual differences. It is impossible to construct a model of a reasonable or ordinary South Australian for the purpose of assessing emotional flashpoint, loss of self-control and capacity to kill under particular circumstances...The same considerations apply to cultural sub-groups such as migrants. The objective test should not be modified by establishing different standards for different groups in society. This would result in unequal treatment...The objective test should be discarded. It has no place in rational criminal jurisprudence.

Peter Brett in his article 'The Physiology of Provocation' reviewed the sociological and physiological studies that demonstrate that the old common law was grounded on a number of fallacies about human nature: [1970] Crim LR 634–40. He examined the judicial view of 'controllable anger'—that is, the idea that individuals who have lost self-control are in a position to control the degree of retaliation. This conception was embodied in the requirement of proportionality between the insult and the retaliation. Brett noted that the human body under stress prepares for strenuous action, a phenomenon known as the 'fight or flight' reaction. The changes that occur have something of an 'all or nothing' quality; the reaction is not nicely proportioned to the threat that is expected of the ordinary person. Brett concluded (at 638) that 'the all or none quality of the reaction make[s] it pointless to draw a distinction of nicety between different types of provocative act'. He also showed that how individuals cope with stress varies from one individual to another in that some individuals 'are highly vulnerable to stress, others are strikingly resistant to it': at 637. This provides another reason why it is difficult to identify the response of an ordinary person.

If the ordinary person test is abandoned, how might a test of provocation be phrased? In 1978, the Irish Court of Appeal abandoned the objective test in *People v MacEoin* (1978) 112 ILTR 43. Subsequent cases in Ireland have followed a subjective test that examines whether the accused, given his or her temperament, character and circumstances, in fact killed under provocation. This approach has been criticised in going too far in favour of the accused. Finbarr McAuley and Paul McCutcheon pose the example of a white supremacist killing a black person who speaks to him. The supremacist is enraged because he believes that it is the gravest insult for a black person to speak to a white person unless spoken to first: *Criminal Liability* (Dublin: Round Hall Sweet & Maxwell, 2000) p 877. According to the Irish approach, such a person would be afforded a defence.

Does an objective standard have to incorporate the 'ordinary person'? The Law Reform Commission of Victoria in *Homicide*, Report No 40 (Melbourne: LRCV, 1991) proposed abandoning the ordinary person test in favour of emphasising the circumstances under which the accused should be partially excused for losing self-control and killing. They proposed the following test (at 84):

> Where a person suffers a loss of self-control as a result of provocation (whether by things done or words said and whether by the deceased or someone else) and intentionally kills or is a party to the killing of another, he or she is not guilty of murder but guilty of manslaughter if, in all the circumstances, including any of the defendant's personal characteristics, there is a sufficient reason to reduce the offence from murder to manslaughter.

It is certainly tempting to consider abandoning the ordinary person test given the problems associated with identifying the characteristics of the ordinary person. But having a purely subjective test as in Ireland brings its own problems. While stressing the accused's personal situation and characteristics, the Law Reform Commission of Victoria test does have somewhat of an objective gloss in requiring the jury to consider whether there is 'a sufficient reason' to reduce murder to manslaughter.

The LRCV test avoids the pitfalls of working out what characteristics should imbue an ordinary person. Whether or not the wording of the proposed test is sufficiently clear is another matter, but perhaps it is better to leave the jury with sufficient discretion in relation to provocation than to direct it on a two-tiered ordinary person test.

Should there be a defence of provocation at all?
In 1992, after a thorough examination of the history and social background of the doctrine of provocation, Jeremy Horder concluded that the defence of provocation should be abolished and evidence of provocation be considered as a matter for mitigation in sentence: *Provocation and Responsibility* (Oxford: Clarendon Press, 1992). He questioned why the emotion of anger should merit more indulgence in terms of reducing moral culpability than other emotions such as envy, lust or greed.

More recently, the MCCOC, in its Discussion Paper, *Chapter 5, Fatal Offences Against the Person*, has also recommended that the defence of provocation be abolished: (June 1998) pp 87 ff. As with Horder, the Committee argued that evidence of provocation can be reflected in sentencing.

Both Horder and the Committee were concerned that the doctrine of provocation predominantly excuses male anger and violence against women. The Committee stated (at 89):

> Why is a husband who kills his wife because he found her committing adultery morally less guilty than a murderer? Why is a conservative Turkish Muslim father partially excused when he stabs his daughter to death because she refuses to stop seeing her boyfriend? [Referring to *R v Dincer* [1983] VR 460.] Why do we partially excuse a man who kills another man who has made a homosexual advance on him? [Referring to *Green v The Queen* (1997) 191 CLR 334.] Why is deadly violence mitigated in these cases?

These arguments proved persuasive in leading the Tasmanian Parliament to abolish the defence of provocation: Second Reading, *Criminal Code Amendment (Abolition of Defence of Provocation) Bill* 2003, *Hansard*, Tasmanian Legislative Council, <http://www.hansard.parliament.tas.gov.au/ISYSquery/IRL7C7.tmp/1/doc>, accessed November 2003. As explored above, there are certainly problems with condoning violence perpetrated through a loss of self-control. If, however, provocation is to be abolished, what becomes of those women who do benefit from such a defence? The Law Reform Commission of Victoria and the Judicial Commission of New South Wales have conducted research that suggests that while the provocation defence is used more frequently by men who kill women than women who kill men, the women who raise provocation seem more 'successful' with the provocation defence than men: Law Reform Commission of Victoria, *Homicide*, Report No 40 (Melbourne: LRCV, 1991) pp 75–6; H Donnelly, S Cumines and A Wilczynski, *Sentences for Homicides in New South Wales 1990–1993: A Legal and Sociological Study* (Judicial Commission of NSW, Monograph Series No 10, 1995) ch 5. Helen Brown has argued that even with all its faults, abolition of provocation is not warranted because 'there is an attendant risk that more women who kill a chronically violent spouse will be convicted of murder and sentenced accordingly'; 'Provocation as a Defence to Murder: To Abolish or to Reform' (1999) 12 *Australian Feminist Law Journal* 137–41 at 138.

If the consideration of explanations for violent conduct are shifted to the sentencing stage, judges would still have to ascertain the basis for the killing. This undermines the role of the jury in apportioning criminal responsibility and raises the potential for inconsistent dealings with those who kill after losing self-control.

Andrew Ashworth has also pointed out, in *Principles of Criminal Law* (3rd edn, Oxford: Oxford University Press, 1999) p 284, that whether provocation should exist as a defence is closely related to issues of stigma and labelling. He writes (p 284): '[T]he label "murder" should be reserved for the most heinous of killings, and most people would accept that provoked killings are not in this group.'

The rationale for the defence lies in the recognition that there is a difference between intentional killings that are committed in 'cold blood' or for revenge and those that occur in an extreme emotional state and that are unpremeditated: see Alex Reilly, 'Loss of Self-Control in Provocation' (1997) 21 Crim LJ 320–35 at 320. It is unsettling at the very least to label a person who kills in the latter fashion a 'murderer' with all the stigma that label invokes. The better approach may be to concentrate on developing a workable test of provocation rather than wiping the slate clean.

Conclusion

In this chapter, we have outlined the history, current law and main criticisms of the defences of self-defence and provocation. The main criticisms of self-defence revolve around the excessive use of force, the reactions of women to violence and how the defence should be framed. We have also considered the main criticisms of provocation relating to the characteristics of the ordinary person test, whether there should be an ordinary person test at all and whether provocation as a defence should be retained.

We have argued that the MCCOC's proposed test for self-defence appears adequate and if the doctrine of excessive self-defence is reintroduced at common law and introduced in the Code jurisdictions, a half-way point in a verdict of manslaughter for those who use excessive force will be available.

In relation to provocation, we have outlined the intractable problems concerning the characteristics of the ordinary person in the current version of the defence. We would advocate retaining the defence, but not in its existing form. The Law Reform Commission of Victoria test stresses the accused's personal situation and characteristics, while retaining somewhat of an objective gloss in requiring the jury to consider whether there is 'a sufficient reason' to reduce murder to manslaughter.

Both defences continue to be the subject of debate and law reform endeavours. In relation to Mary Falconer's trial, the defence of provocation was rejected by the jury and self-defence not raised. Evidence of 'automatism' was also sought to be raised at the original trial to cast doubt on whether Mary Falconer's actions were truly voluntary. This brings us into the realm of mental states and it is to the defences concerning abnormal states of mind that we now turn. In the next chapter we will outline what happened to Mary Falconer after the High Court decision.

CHAPTER 11

Mental state defences

Introduction

On 12 November 1990, Andre Chayna, aged 31, stabbed her sister-in-law, Cheryl Najim, to death while Cheryl was sitting at the kitchen table, reading a letter. Later that same day, Chayna went into the bedroom of her daughter Sandy and asked her to close her eyes while she read her a story. Chayna then stabbed her daughter in the throat, killing her. The bodies remained undiscovered until three days later when Chayna stabbed to death her second daughter, Suzanne, who had been away at camp when the first two killings occurred.

At her trial for murder, the prosecution argued that Chayna was motivated by jealousy and hostility to kill her sister-in-law and that she then killed her daughters to prevent her husband, with whom she had a problematic relationship, from having custody of them when she was in jail.

Seven psychiatrists were called to give evidence at the trial. All had examined Chayna and all agreed that she was in a floridly psychotic state when she arrived in jail. She was given medication and responded to treatment. However, the psychiatric evidence as to her state of mind at the time of the killings differed markedly.

Three psychiatrists testified that Chayna was in a psychotic state at the time of the killing such that she did not know that what she was doing was wrong for the purposes of the insanity defence. Another said she was suffering from a dissociative state that could support either a defence of insanity or diminished responsibility. Two others said she was suffering from a depressive illness that could support the defence of diminished responsibility, but not insanity. Chayna's treating psychiatrist, who was called by the prosecution, said Chayna had not been suffering from a mental illness at all at the time of the killing.

The jury convicted Chayna of murder. The Court of Criminal Appeal of New South Wales subsequently upheld the accused's appeal against conviction and substituted a verdict of manslaughter: *Chayna* (1993) 66 A Crim R 178.

The case of Andre Chayna raises a number of questions as to how to take into account mental impairment in assessing criminal responsibility. The usual way in which mental impairment is taken into account is through the separate defence of mental impairment. This is traditionally known as the insanity defence, but we will use the modern terminology in this chapter except where the case law deals with the traditional defence. In the Australian Capital Territory, New South Wales, the Northern Territory and Queensland, mental impairment may also be taken into account through the defence of diminished responsibility. If one of Chayna's children had been under the age of 12 months, she could also have raised infanticide as a defence in New South Wales and Victoria.

Less commonly, mental impairment may be taken into account in assessing whether the accused's actions were voluntary (relating to the physical element of the crime) or intentional (relating to the fault element of the crime).

This area of the criminal law is exceptionally complex partly because of the different aims of the mental health professions and the law. For lawyers involved in prosecuting or defending a case such as Andre Chayna's, the essential question is whether or not she should be excused for her actions because of mental impairment. Put simply, the trial revolves around whether or not she can be said to be criminally responsible.

For mental health professionals, the emphasis is on treatment of disorders rather than on concepts of responsibility for behaviour. Consequently, difficulties can occur because the focus of lawyers and mental health professionals are so divergent. The criminal trial where mental impairment is in issue deals in absolutes in trying to determine whether there was mental impairment at the time the crime was committed, the categorisation of the type of mental impairment and the effect it had on the accused's behaviour. This occurs despite there being no general definition of mental disorder that is acceptable in all countries. Psychiatric and psychological notions of mental disorder are constantly changing because forms of mental disorder may be culturally or socially determined and diagnosis inevitably contains a subjective element. This is exemplified by the fact that in *Chayna*'s case the seven mental health professionals differed in their diagnoses. John Ellard, a psychiatrist, has written that diagnoses 'are this year's shorthand for this year's hypotheses about the nature of things that interest us. The only thing certain about them is that they will be found wanting and will change as the years change': 'New White Elephants for Old Sacred Cows: Some Notes in Diagnosis' (1992) 26(4) *Australian and New Zealand Journal of Psychiatry* 546–9 at 548.

There are thus a number of tensions between the law and the mental health professions. The criminal law centres on proving matters beyond a reasonable doubt; the mental health professions are concerned with possibilities and probabilities of diagnostic criteria. The criminal law is concerned with questions of guilt and punishment; the mental health professions are concerned with relieving suffering. This needs to be kept in mind as we outline how the law in this area sometimes conflicts with the often amorphous categorisations of mental disorders used by mental health professionals.

The other thread that runs through this area of the criminal law is the question of what to do with someone who has been found not criminally responsible due to mental impairment. There appears to be a widely held assumption in the community that those with mental illness are predisposed to acting violently. Psychiatrist Paul Mullen writes that the origin of this assumption probably lies in the 'unease which acutely mentally disturbed individuals produce in those around them…When we experience fear we all too readily attribute that fear to dangerousness in the exciting object, rather than considering whether our reactions may not be excessive or misplaced': 'The Dangerousness of the Mentally Ill and the Clinical Assessment of Risk' in W Brookbanks (ed), *Psychiatry and the Law* (Wellington: Brooker's Ltd, 1996) pp 93–116 at 93.

As pointed out above, the definition of mental disorder is by no means clear and it is a myth to say that all those with mental disorder are predisposed to violence. The empirical literature has concentrated on whether or not there is an association between severe psychotic disorders such as schizophrenia and violence. Symptoms of schizophrenia may include delusions, hallucinations, disorganised speech, grossly disorganised behaviour and 'negative' symptoms such as unresponsive behaviour, diminished emotional expressiveness or little interest in participating in work or social activities.

The recent literature suggests that there does appear to be a modest association between schizophrenia and violent and fear-inducing behaviour, but this does not mean that severe schizophrenia *causes* violent behaviour. It may be that those with severe schizophrenia are brought into contact with the police more often because of social isolation or homelessness. Those with schizophrenia who do act violently often act on the prompting of their delusions. Adequate treatment and follow-up can prevent such violence. It should be noted that substance abuse appears to be a stronger predictor of an increased probability of violence: P Mullen, 'Dangerousness, Risk and the Prediction of Probability' in MG Geldner, JJ Lopez-Ibor and N Andreason (eds), *New Oxford Textbook of Psychiatry* (London: Oxford University Press, 2000) pp 2066–78. In this chapter, we also touch on how intoxication has been taken into account in assessing criminal responsibility.

While the perception that mental disorder equals violence has always been strong, it was only in England in 1800 that the *Criminal Lunatics Act* introduced a 'special verdict' of not guilty on the ground of insanity. This resulted in the court being required to make an order detaining the person so found until 'His Majesty's pleasure shall be known'. Prior to 1800, the verdict in insanity cases was 'not guilty' and the acquittee was entitled to an unconditional acquittal. This, however, meant that the accused was usually forced to live in brutal conditions in the community or join the streams of beggars that wandered the streets: E Shorter, *A History of Psychiatry* (New York: John Wiley & Sons Inc, 1997) p 2.

Australian jurisdictions adopted the special verdict for insanity acquittees, usually enabling indefinite detention at the 'Governor's Pleasure'. The traditional justification for such detention has been based on the notion of preventing further harm to the public. While treatment may have been incidentally involved, it was never the dominant objective of Governor's Pleasure orders. Many of those detained were kept in prisons rather than in hospitals. For example, in 1988, 66 per cent of Governor's Pleasure detainees in Victoria were kept in G Division at Pentridge Prison: A Freiberg, 'The Disposition of Mentally Disordered Offenders in Australia' (1994) 1(2) *Psychiatry, Psychology and Law* 97–118 at 103.

The prospect of indefinite detention has affected not only the rarity of use of the defence of mental impairment—at least if a mentally impaired accused pleads guilty, he or she is given a time limit to the sentence—but also the content of the defence. Only very serious long-standing illnesses such as psychotic disorders (*Bratty v Attorney-General for Northern Ireland* [1963] AC 386 at 412 per Lord Denning) and cerebral arteriosclerosis (*R v Kemp* [1957] 1 QB 399) have been considered forms of mental impairment that give rise to a separate defence, presumably because the individuals suffering from them are viewed as warranting indefinite detention. A wider range of disorders including severe depression (*R v Whitworth* [1989] 1 Qd R 437), post-traumatic stress disorder (*R v Nielsen* [1990] 2 Qd R 578) and personality disorders (*Byrne* [1960] 2 QB 396) may give rise to the diminished responsibility defence, which operates to reduce murder to manslaughter in some jurisdictions. The consequence of a successful defence of diminished responsibility is a determinate sentence on the level for manslaughter.

More flexible dispositional options apart from indefinite detention are gradually being enacted in Australian jurisdictions along with the introduction of reformulated defences of mental impairment: B McSherry, 'Criminal Detention of Those with Mental Impairment' (1999) 6 *Journal of Law and Medicine* 216–21. It is to be hoped that these changes will aid in reforming the overly complex law in this area.

The consequences for those accused considered mentally ill and the difficulties caused by the disparate aims of the criminal law and the mental health professions need to be kept in mind while exploring the current law. Before starting the latter enterprise, it is worthwhile now taking a step back and thinking of why mental impairment operates to excuse those accused of serious offences.

The ability to reason is central to why we have mental state defences. As explored in Chapter 1, the notion that children and those with some form of mental illness or disorder lack the ability to reason has long been found in laws excusing them from responsibility for criminal acts.

We outlined in Chapter 2 how a model for serious offences can be visualised, as shown again here in Figure 11.1.

506 Defences

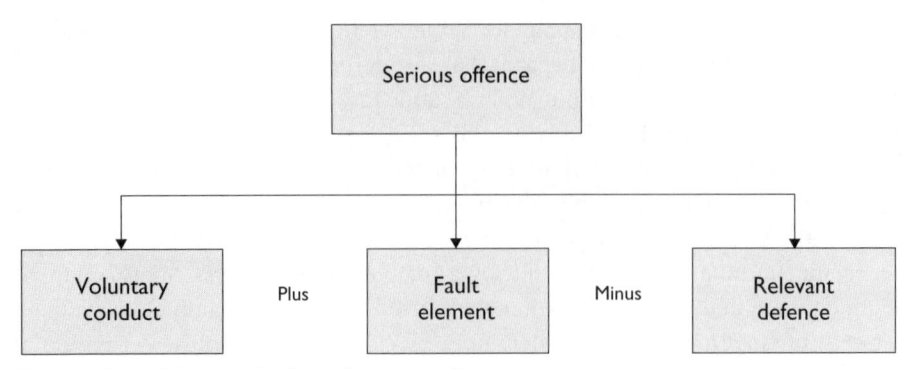

```
                    ┌─────────────────┐
                    │ Serious offence │
                    └─────────────────┘
                             │
        ┌────────────────────┼────────────────────┐
        ▼                    ▼                    ▼
┌───────────────┐    ┌───────────────┐    ┌───────────────┐
│   Voluntary   │Plus│     Fault     │Minus│   Relevant   │
│    conduct    │    │    element    │    │    defence    │
└───────────────┘    └───────────────┘    └───────────────┘
```

Figure 11.1 Modern division of serious offences

Mental impairment, however, may not only be taken into account as the basis for separate defences such as infanticide, diminished responsibility and the defence of mental impairment; it may also be relevant to negating voluntary conduct and, occasionally, whether or not the accused's actions were intentional. Stephen Morse has suggested that the legal concept of criminal responsibility, which requires voluntariness and a fault element, means that the individual must have acted rationally and without compulsion: 'Craziness and Criminal Responsibility' (1999) 17 *Behavioral Sciences and the Law* 147–64. He suggests that irrationality is the primary excusing condition produced by mental impairment. Using mental impairment as evidence of involuntary conduct has proved problematic. Morse rightly points out (at 153) that situations 'involving "unconsciousness" from sleepwalking or similar dissociative states often cause confusion in the law'.

The case law in this area demonstrates that evidence of mental impairment has been used to show that the individual did not act 'rationally' for the purpose of the traditional defences as well as to show that the act was involuntary or was not intentional. This can be illustrated as shown in Figure 11.2.

In this chapter, we will follow this model by first dealing with how mental impairment may lead to involuntary conduct. Secondly, we will examine a High Court decision dealing with mental impairment and unintentional conduct and, thirdly, we will outline how intoxication as a form of mental impairment 'fits' into the notion of involuntary or unintentional conduct. The defences of mental impairment, diminished responsibility and infanticide will then be examined.

If involuntary or unintentional conduct is not disproved beyond reasonable doubt, the accused will be acquitted of the offence charged. This obviously has its attractions for defence counsel, but there are only a handful of cases where mental impairment has been raised in this way. This is because once the defence raises evidence of mental impairment, it is open to the prosecution in most jurisdictions to raise the separate defence of mental impairment with the prospect of indefinite detention.

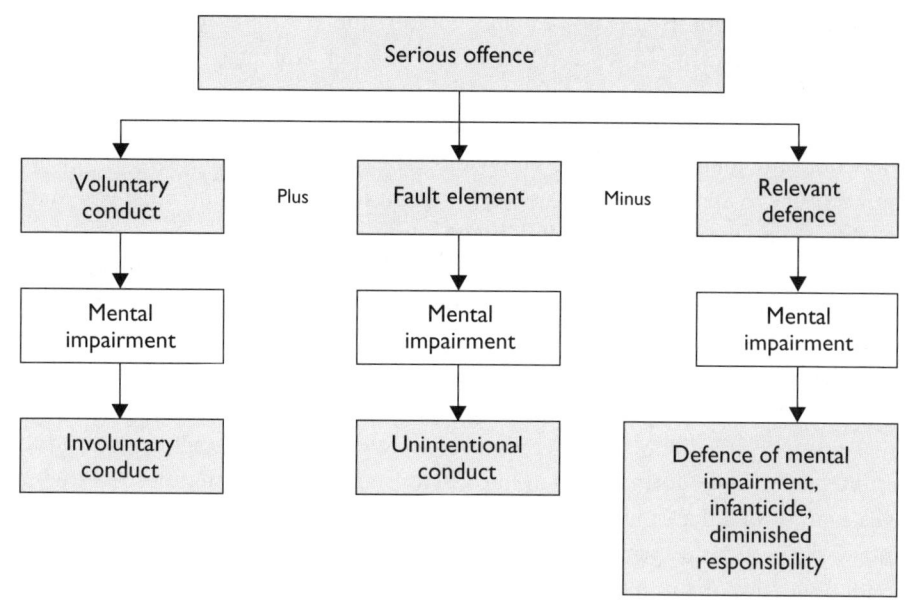

Figure 11.2 Mental impairment and criminal responsibility

Mental impairment and involuntary conduct

Background

In the previous chapter, we explored how Mary Falconer gave evidence that she did not remember picking up the gun, loading it or shooting her estranged husband. All she could remember was being slumped near the archway of the bedroom and looking at the dead body of Gordon Falconer: *R v Falconer* (1990) 171 CLR 30.

Many of those accused of homicide or serious violent crimes claim that they do not remember the actual killing or assault. Findings of memory impairment for criminal offences vary from anywhere between 10 per cent and 70 per cent of offenders, with that figure being higher in violent offenders, and highest in homicide cases: S Porter, AR Birt, JC Yuille, HF Herve, 'Memory for Murder: A Psychological Perspective on Dissociative Amnesia in Legal Contexts' (2001) 24 *International Journal of Law and Psychiatry* 23–42. In 1979, one study found that nearly two-thirds of a sample of thirty convicted murderers reported some form of amnesia for the killings: JW Bradford and SM Smith, 'Amnesia and Homicide: The Padola Case and a Study of 30 Cases' (1979) 7 *Bulletin of the American Academy of Psychiatry and Law* 219–31.

Should those who report some form of amnesia for their crimes be excused from criminal responsibility? The initial response may be a negative one because of the danger of false reports of amnesia. While amnesia is often linked to involuntary conduct, amnesia of itself is not a defence to a crime: *R v Hartridge* (1966) 57 DLR (2d) 332; *R v Matchett* [1980] 2 WWR 122 at 134 per Walker DCJ, Saskatchewan District Court.

There are, however, some forms of altered states of consciousness that may affect not only memory, but also behaviour. The law developed during the twentieth century to allow some concession for forms of impaired consciousness. Mary Falconer's case in fact led to the key High Court decision in this area.

As explored in Chapter 2, in a criminal trial, the prosecution must prove beyond reasonable doubt that the accused's conduct was voluntary. This requirement is quite separate from any consideration of a defence of mental impairment: the defence can raise evidence that the accused's conduct was involuntary in the absence of raising a defence of mental impairment.

Automatism is the term generally used to refer at law to involuntary conduct resulting from some form of impaired consciousness. While sometimes referred to as a separate 'defence', the accused only need raise evidence that the act was involuntary and then the prosecution must rebut that evidence beyond reasonable doubt. Evidence of automatism only began to be accepted in England in the 1950s as a way around the narrowness of the insanity defence and the prospect of indefinite detention: CR Williams, 'Development and Change in Insanity and Related Defences' (2000) 24(3) *Melbourne University Law Review* 711–36 at 717–18. Accordingly, the law in this area is still developing, which may explain why this particular area relating to mental impairment is somewhat confused.

The current law

There is no practical difference between the Australian jurisdictions in relation to the requirement that the prosecution prove that the accused's conduct was voluntary: *Criminal Code* (Qld) s 23; *Criminal Code* (Tas) s 13(1); *Criminal Code* (WA) s 23; *R v Falconer* (1990) 171 CLR 30. A number of conditions have been accepted by the courts as giving rise to involuntary conduct such as a blow to the head, sleep disorders, the consumption of alcohol or other drugs, neurological disorders, hypoglycaemia, epilepsy or dissociation arising from extraordinary external stress. It does not matter what the cause of automatism is, providing that the accused's actions are rendered involuntary: *Jiminez v The Queen* (1992) 173 CLR 572 at 581.

Because automatism is related to the concept of involuntariness rather than consciousness, a degree of awareness or cognitive function is not necessarily fatal to automatism being accepted by the trier of fact. In *Ryan v The Queen* (1967) 121 CLR 205 at 217, Barwick CJ stated:

> [I]t is important...not to regard [automatism] as of the essence of the discussion, however convenient an expression automatism may be to comprehend involuntary deeds where the lack of concomitant or controlling will to act is due to diverse

causes. It is that lack of will which is the relevant determinant...It is of course the absence of the will to act or, perhaps, more precisely, of its exercise rather than lack of knowledge or consciousness which...decides criminal liability.

The law has become particularly complex in relation to automatism because the courts have divided certain conditions as falling within either 'sane' automatism or 'insane' automatism. If an accused is acquitted on the basis of sane automatism, he or she is entitled to a complete acquittal because the criminal act is considered involuntary. If, however, the automatism arose from something 'internal' to the accused, it is considered 'insane' automatism and the defence of mental impairment is brought into play with the result that the accused generally becomes subject to indefinite detention.

In the previous chapter, we outlined how Mary Falconer made a successful appeal to the Western Australian Court of Criminal Appeal on the basis that automatism should have been left for the jury to decide: *Falconer* (1989) 46 A Crim R 83. The Crown then appealed against this decision to the High Court concerning the admissibility of evidence concerning automatism. The High Court dismissed the Crown's appeal and the matter was set down for a re-trial: *R v Falconer* (1990) 171 CLR 30.

What evidence was there that Mary Falconer's actions were involuntary? At her initial trial, counsel for the defence sought to call evidence from two psychiatrists to show that the accused was in a state of automatism such that her actions were unwilled and thus involuntary. The Commissioner presiding at the trial conducted a *voir dire* (a hearing in the absence of the jury) to test the admissibility of the evidence. Both psychiatrists gave evidence that the circumstances leading up to and surrounding the shooting could have produced a dissociative state where, according to one of the psychiatrists, 'part of her personality would be sort of segmented and not functioning as a whole and she became disrupted in her behaviour, without awareness of what she was doing': *Falconer* (1989) 46 A Crim R 83 at 109.

The following narrative (at 110–11) was presented by one of the psychiatrists called by the defence, Robert Astley Finlay-Jones:

> From my interview with her, there was evidence of more than just psychological stress; there was evidence of conflict. I am referring in particular to these things: the evidence that she was under considerable stress I accept to be that she learnt in January 1988 that her husband had been unfaithful not just once but repeatedly and yet she took him back as she had done on previous occasions. Then she learnt in about June or July or August 1988 that he for many years had behaved in a sexual way with at least two of her daughters and she told me in my interview with her what her evidence was for being totally sure from his own mouth that he had done that (the witness was referring to the telephone conversation between her daughter Debbie and the deceased which she overheard on an extension line). Then there was a third factor which came out, I think, only minutes before he was

dead...She told me as background to this news that she received just minutes before Gordon's death that her adopted son had been charged some years before with sexually interfering with a girl who was in her custody, from Community Welfare and for whom she felt responsible. She said to me that the girl, Erin, had always claimed at the time that there were two men involved; not just one but two—and that the identity of the second man was not known...She had referred in her interview with me repeatedly to the fact that she loved [her husband] and I have heard this afternoon that she stated the same thing. I think she was faced with an intolerable dilemma at that moment, that on the one hand it is undeniable that he is, to use her words: 'a filthy bastard and yet I love him. Possibly, by extension that makes me filthy too.' She is faced with what I would call a psychological conflict. I think it is that setting of psychological conflict that a person is capable of losing control of the mind, of acting—quite briefly—in an automatic way. I think that her inability to remember what happened next is consistent with that.

According to Dr Finlay-Jones, it was this psychological conflict that caused Mary Falconer to go into a dissociative state. The legal use of dissociation as a subset of automatism is controversial and will be discussed further in the Critique section. From a mental health perspective, dissociative disorders are defined in the *Diagnostic and Statistical Manual of Mental Disorders* as 'a disruption in the usually integrated functions of consciousness, memory, identity, or perception of the environment': American Psychiatric Association, (4th edn Text Revision, Washington, DC: APA, 2000) p 477.

Marlene Steinberg writes that '[d]uring a dissociative episode, the mental contents that are dissociated from full consciousness remain on some peripheral level of awareness; from this perspective dissociation can also be defined as a fragmentation of consciousness': *Handbook for the Assessment of Dissociation: A Clinical Guide* (Washington: American Psychiatric Press, 1995) p 23.

At Mary Falconer's trial, the Commissioner ruled the psychiatric evidence inadmissible. When the matter went to the High Court, all seven judges agreed that the Commissioner had erred in rejecting the evidence of dissociation.

In Western Australia, s 23 of the *Criminal Code* provides that 'a person is not criminally responsible for an act or omission which occurs independently of the exercise of his [or her] will'. The defence of mental impairment is set out in s 27 of the Code:

> A person is not criminally responsible for an act or omission if at the time of doing the act he [or she] is in such a state of mental disease or natural mental infirmity as to deprive him [or her] of capacity to understand what he [or she] is doing, or of capacity to control his [or her] actions, or of capacity to know that he [or she] ought not to do the act or make the omission.

All seven members of the High Court were of the opinion that s 27 of the Code encompasses involuntary action where the automatism resulted from a mental disease, natural mental infirmity or disorder of mind: *R v Falconer* (1990) 171 CLR 30. If, however, it is shown that the automatism arose from a mental condition that could *not* be classified as a result of a mental disease, natural mental infirmity or disorder of the mind and the act occurred involuntarily because of this mental condition, the accused would be entitled to a complete acquittal.

After the High Court decision, Mary Falconer's case was set down for a re-trial so that the issue of automatism could be put to the jury. However, Mary Falconer decided at that stage to plead guilty to manslaughter. This plea infers that the act of shooting was voluntary, but that Mary Falconer did not discharge the gun with the intention of killing her husband.

The plea was heard on 19 March 1991 and Nicholson J delivered the sentence on 27 March 1991. He sentenced her on the basis that the crime merited a sentence of six years' imprisonment. He allowed credit against that for the period of 14 months she had spent in custody, which he scaled up to two years. He also allowed a further reduction of one year because of the guilty plea and other mitigating factors.

In relation to the remaining period of three years, Nicholson J considered that a suspended sentence was an appropriate disposition and finally, after three hearings and some two and a half years since the shooting of her husband, Mary Falconer walked free.

The distinction between automatism as relating to involuntariness and automatism as subsumed within the defence of mental impairment is well ingrained in the common law. Section 4.2(3) of the *Criminal Code* (Cth) also makes the traditional distinction between involuntary conduct arising from impaired consciousness and conduct that is willed but committed while mentally impaired.

In the recent Canadian Supreme Court decision in *R v Stone* [1999] 2 SCR 290, Bastarache J outlined how the law had developed two tests to establish whether or not the condition of automatism was a mental disorder: the 'internal cause theory' set out by Martin JA in *R v Rabey* (1977) 37 CCC (2d) 461 and the 'continuing danger theory' referred to by La Forest J in *R v Parks* [1992] 2 SCR 871. Bastarache J found that *both* approaches are relevant factors in determining in which category a condition falls, and other policy factors may also be taken into account to provide an 'holistic' approach: [1999] 2 SCR 290 at 396–8.

The High Court in *Falconer*'s case also developed a further theory to take into account evidence of dissociation. This can be referred to as the sound/unsound mind theory. These theories will be analysed in turn.

The internal cause theory of insane automatism

The internal cause theory distinguishing between sane and insane automatism was developed by Martin JA of the Ontario Court of Appeal in *R v Rabey* (1977) 37 CCC

(2d) 461 in which he stated (at 477): 'In general, the distinction to be drawn is between a malfunctioning of the mind arising from some cause that is primarily internal to the accused, having its source in his [or her] psychological or emotional make-up, or in some organic pathology, as opposed to a malfunctioning of mind which is the transient effect produced by some specific external factor such as, for example, concussion.' This distinction is aimed at placing mental states such as those caused by physical blows, hypnotic influences or drugs firmly in the camp of automatism as it relates to voluntary conduct. The rationale appears to be that an internal weakness may be more likely to lead to recurrent violence than automatism brought about by some intervening and usually external cause. Therefore automatism caused by some internal factor should be subsumed within a defence of mental impairment in order that the accused may be detained rather than completely acquitted.

The continuing danger theory

In *R v Kemp* [1957] 1 QB 399 (at 407) it was stated that a mental disorder for the purposes of the common law defence of insanity may be permanent or temporary, curable or incurable. In *Bratty v Attorney General for Northern Ireland* [1963] AC 386 (at 412) Lord Denning attempted to put a rider on this by stating that 'any mental disorder which has manifested itself in violence and is prone to recur is a disease of the mind. At any rate it is the sort of disease for which a person should be detained in hospital rather than be given an unqualified acquittal'.

This continuing danger theory found favour with Sholl J in *R v Carter* [1959] VR 105 and *R v Meddings* [1966] VR 306. In the latter case, Sholl J stated (at 309) that the 'potentiality of recurrence...might be regarded as a discrimen between cases of irrational behaviour due to some transient cause affecting the mind, other than disease of the mind, and cases of irrational behaviour due to defective reason from disease of the mind'.

La Forest J in *R v Parks* [1992] 2 SCR 871 at 906–7 stated that the purpose of a separate defence of mental disorder (as it is called in Canada) has always been the protection of the public against recurrent danger. The possibility of recurrence, although not determinative, may be looked upon as a factor at the policy stage of the enquiry on the issue of insanity. The question of what to do with those considered not criminally responsible because of mental impairment can be seen here as overtly influencing the content of the defence of mental impairment. If the irrational behaviour is in danger of recurring, then its cause will be seen as falling within the defence of mental impairment. Thus, the effect of the condition influences the definition of its cause.

The sound/unsound mind theory

The sound/unsound mind theory is a more sophisticated version of the internal cause theory aimed specifically at dissociation. Dissociation may arise from external stress factors or as a result of some forms of neurological or other general medical conditions.

In *R v Radford* (1985) 42 SASR 266, King CJ set out the test for determining whether dissociative states should fall within automatism as it relates to voluntary conduct or automatism subsumed within the defence of mental impairment. In that case, Radford shot and killed a woman whom he believed to have been the lover of his ex-wife. Radford had served in Vietnam and at the time of the shooting he claimed that he thought he was shooting a soldier dressed in army gear. He stated that he had become very detached from the situation as though he 'had gone into a sort of cocoon' (at 268). Psychiatric evidence was called by the defence to the effect that the accused had been in a 'state of derealization' that was closely akin to dissociation and this had been brought about by the emotional stress of the accused's marriage break-up. The psychiatrist was also of the opinion that this state was not caused by any disease, chronic disorder or disturbance of the mind.

The trial judge ruled that this evidence did not raise the issue of involuntary action apart from the defence of insanity. Counsel for the defence did not wish to raise insanity and therefore confined the issue to whether or not intention had been proved. Radford was convicted of murder. On appeal, the Supreme Court of South Australia set aside the conviction and ordered a retrial on the basis that the question of automatism as it relates to voluntary conduct should have been left to the jury. In the course of his judgment, King CJ stated (at 276): 'The significant distinction is between the reaction of an unsound mind to its own delusions or to external stimuli on the one hand and the reaction of a sound mind to external stimuli, including stress producing factors, on the other hand.'

At his re-trial, Radford was convicted of murder and this was upheld by the Court of Criminal Appeal of South Australia: *R v Radford (No 2)* (1987) 11 Crim LJ 231.

In *R v Falconer* (1990) 171 CLR 30, Toohey J, Mason CJ, Brennan and McHugh JJ all approved of King CJ's test for distinguishing between dissociative states that relate to voluntary conduct and those that are subsumed within the defence of mental impairment. Gaudron J (at 85) adopted a similar test, but introduced the concept of states of mind experienced by a 'normal' person: '[T]he fundamental distinction is necessarily between those mental states which, although resulting in abnormal behaviour, are or may be experienced by normal persons (as, for example and relevant to the issue of involuntariness, a state of mind resulting from a blow to the head) and those which are never experienced by or encountered in normal persons.'

Mason CJ, Brennan and McHugh JJ also proposed an objective standard gloss to the sound/unsound mind distinction. They stated (at 55):

> [T]he law must postulate a standard of mental strength which, in the face of a given level of psychological trauma, is capable of protecting the mind from malfunction to the extent prescribed in the respective definitions of insanity. That standard must be the standard of the ordinary person: if the mind's strength is below that standard, the mind is infirm; if it is of or above that standard, the mind

is sound or sane. This is an objective standard which corresponds with the objective standard imported for the purpose of provocation.

The result of these statements appears to be that where a state of dissociation is in issue, King CJ's test will be applied and the standard will be an objective one, that of the 'ordinary' or 'normal' person.

The Canadian approach is also to posit an objective standard of the 'normal' person. Bastarache J stated in *R v Stone* [1999] 2 SCR 290 at 392–3: 'In cases involving claims of psychological blow automatism, evidence of an extremely shocking trigger will be required to establish that a normal person might have reacted to the trigger by entering an automatistic state.'

Critique

Trying to distinguish between automatism as it relates to involuntary conduct and automatism as it relates to the defence of mental impairment is exceptionally difficult and all the theories set out above can be criticised.

The internal/external theory has led to arbitrary results. Sleepwalking has been considered to be a form of sane automatism in the Canadian case of *R v Parks* [1992] 2 SCR 871, yet was classified as insane automatism in the English case of *R v Burgess* [1991] 2 QB 92. Similarly, dissociation brought on by a traumatic marriage breakdown has been considered to be a form of sane automatism in Australia in the case of *R v Mansfield* unreported, acquittal 5 May 1994, Supreme Court of Victoria, Hampel J, and insane automatism in Canada: *R v Joudrie* unreported, 9 May 1996, Court of Queen's Bench of Alberta, No 9501-1280-C6. Further, in *R v Quick* [1989] 1 WLR 287 the Court of Appeal held that hypoglycaemia, which was brought on by the accused's use of insulin, amounted to sane automatism because it was brought on by an external factor. However, in *R v Hennessy* [1973] 1 QB 910 (at 293) Lord Lane CJ suggested that hyperglycaemia caused by a failure to take insulin is an 'inherent defect', which could be subsumed within the defence of insanity.

In addition, some conditions may not lend themselves to being easily classified as arising from internal or external causes. For example, Peter Fenwick writes that because sleepwalking is known to run in families and has a marked genetic component, it can be viewed as arising from internal factors: 'Somnambulism and the Law: A Review' (1987) 5 *Behavioral Sciences and the Law* 343–57. At the same time, however, he points out that 'external trigger factors such as tiredness, drugs, alcohol, stress, also often play a part' (at 350).

The internal cause theory may therefore be of assistance in relation to distinguishing between clear-cut cases as say a blow to the head producing concussion and severe mental illnesses such as schizophrenia. However, it is of limited use in relation to complex medical conditions such as hyperglycaemia, hypoglycaemia, sleepwalking and dissociation.

The continuing danger theory has also been criticised on the basis that it may unfairly hold that conditions such as epilepsy, sleepwalking, hypoglycaemia and hyperglycaemia must of necessity fall within the defence of mental impairment because they are likely to recur. This is despite such conditions lending themselves to control through medication and good health practices: B McSherry, 'Defining What is a "Disease of the Mind"; The Untenability of Current Legal Interpretations' (1993) 1 *Journal of Law and Medicine* 76–90 at 83.

The main difficulty with the sound/unsound mind theory lies in distinguishing between the reaction of an unsound mind and that of a sound mind, given the vagaries of determining who is an 'ordinary' or 'normal' person. The distinction between the two may largely depend upon the susceptibility of the accused to emotional shock and stress. For example, if there is evidence that the accused was not normally affected by stress, then he or she may have a good defence if the psychological blow is severe. On the standard of the ordinary normal person, he or she would be displaying abnormal behaviour that an ordinary person might very well experience in the same circumstances. On the other hand, if the accused's dissociative state is triggered by an 'everyday' form of stress, then he or she is to be regarded as having an unsound mind on the basis that the reaction of a normal person would not be so severe. What is the real difference? In the latter case, the accused is simply more susceptible to stress.

There is an added difficulty in determining what amounts to 'stress producing factors' for the purposes of assessing the external stimuli that may cause a sound mind to react. In *R v Mansfield* unreported, acquittal 5 May 1994, Supreme Court of Victoria, Hampel J, the accused was acquitted on the basis that he was in a dissociative state as a result of the external stress of a marital breakdown when he stabbed his estranged wife to death. It is debatable whether or not a marital breakdown is sufficient external stimuli to cause an ordinary, normal person to cause another to act in an involuntary way. King CJ sounded this warning in *R v Radford (No 2)* (1987) 11 Crim LJ 231 at 232: 'Feelings of jealousy and resentment over the breakdown of matrimonial and other sexual relationships and hatred of a rival lover are commonplace human emotions. The law must firmly repress any tendency for people harbouring such dark emotions to give in to them by way of murderous violence.'

A further problem occurs with the concept of dissociation as giving rise to involuntary behaviour in the light of recent psychological literature. E Michael Coles and SM Armstrong state that goal-directed behaviour can occur in states of impaired consciousness where some partial awareness exists. In their view only reflex movements or well-learned 'habits' such as those explored in experimental psychology under the term 'automaticity' can truly be considered involuntary in the sense that they are not goal-directed behaviours: 'Hughlings Jackson on Automatism as Disinhibition' (1998) 6(1) *Journal of Law and Medicine* 73–82. Albert Bandura refers to 'automatisation' as not being akin to unconscious activity. He writes that '[d]ifferent activities can be performed simultaneously, if they are regulated by different subsystems': *Social Foundations of Thought and Action* (Englewood Cliffs, NJ: Prentice Hall, 1986) p 459. John Bargh and Tanya Chartrand have also recently argued that there is a complex interaction between automatic perceptual activity and conscious judgments: 'The Unbearable Automaticity of Being' (1999) 54(7) *American Psychologist* 462–79.

The idea that involuntary and intentional behaviour should be viewed as on a continuum casts doubt on the current acceptance of mental disorder as negating voluntariness as well as intention, which will be explored in the next section. If current psychological thinking is correct, behaviour can still be purposeful or goal-directed even when performed in states of altered consciousness. This point was recently in issue in the Supreme Court of Victoria decision in *R v Leonboyer* unreported, 7 September 2001, CA of the SC of Vic, [2001] VSCA 149, Phillips CJ, Charles and Callaway JJA. The defence called evidence from a psychiatrist and a psychologist that Leonboyer was in a dissociative state at the time of stabbing his girlfriend to death after she told him she had been seeing another man. In contrast, the two psychiatrists called by the Prosecution gave evidence that 'any complex, directed and purposeful action is difficult to conceive as being carried out by someone whose mind is so disorganised that they cannot will their actions' (at 18 per Phillips CJ). A forensic psychiatrist, Paul Mullen, gave evidence that the act of opening the knife, aiming, directing and striking the victim numerous times all pointed to there being purpose, direction and will behind those actions (at 18 per Phillips CJ). Leonboyer was convicted of murder and an appeal against conviction was dismissed by a majority of two judges to one.

An alternative approach is to have all forms of automatism considered as conditions giving rise to the defence of mental impairment rather than considering some forms as giving rise to involuntary conduct. The Canadian Psychiatric Association has suggested that automatism be subsumed within the existing Canadian defence of not criminally responsible on account of mental disorder: *Brief to the House of Commons Standing Committee on Justice and the Solicitor General,* Subcommittee on the Reform of the General Part of the Criminal Code, 9 November 1992. This suggestion was based on the view that automatism always involves some form of mental disorder.

There are two main benefits to this approach. The first is that if conditions such as dissociative states, epilepsy, somnambulism or hyperglycaemia can be seen as potentially affecting reasoning processes in a similar way to severe mental illnesses, the courts will no longer have to rely on unworkable and artificial tests of what are conditions stemming from internal or external causes.

The second main benefit of subsuming all forms of mental disorder within a general defence is that once a person has been found not criminally responsible, a range of dispositional options becomes available. More flexible dispositional options apart from indefinite detention are gradually being enacted in Australian jurisdictions, including the prospect of unconditional release of the acquittee. This means that those who have committed serious offences while, for example, suffering from a dissociative state can be assessed at the dispositional stage in determining whether or not they should be discharged absolutely or be subject to some form of medical treatment.

The main drawback to having a broad defence of mental impairment is the stigma that may attach to those found not guilty on this basis. Individuals whose automatism results from epilepsy, for example, may not wish to be labelled mentally disordered. It may be that a change to the name of the defence to something like 'cognitive dysfunction' may assist.

It is nevertheless worthwhile considering how a defence could be worded to cover conditions such as dissociation and sleep disorders. A defence that encompasses a range of mental disorders might be established as follows: 'A person is not criminally responsible for an offence if he or she was suffering from a mental disorder at the time of the commission of the offence such that his or her ability to reason was substantially impaired.'

With such a defence, the important first step is to establish that the accused was suffering from some form of mental disorder. This could be defined as including mental illness, a severe intellectual disability or a condition of severely impaired consciousness. The latter could be further defined as a condition in which an individual's awareness of him or herself, the environment and the relation between the two is severely affected. Dissociative states may therefore fall within this category of mental disorder. The next step would then be for a jury to consider what effect the mental disorder had on the individual's ability to reason. This requirement would narrow somewhat the range of disorders that could afford an accused a defence.

At present, the outcome of criminal proceedings where evidence of dissociation is raised will largely depend upon the vagaries of medical evidence called at the trial. Having a defence of mental impairment that encompasses dissociative states may help avoid the problems associated with medical witnesses testifying as to the ultimate issue of whether or not dissociation falls within the categories of sane or insane automatism. The focus will simply be on whether or not the accused was suffering from a dissociative state at the time of the crime.

Considering mental disorder only in terms of a separate defence may go some way towards simplifying the complex law in this area.

Mental impairment and unintentional conduct

Background

Mental impairment may on rare occasions be relevant to the fault element of a crime. Such use of evidence of mental impairment has been a relatively recent phenomenon and generally evidence of mental impairment has been raised to cast doubt on whether or not the criminal conduct was intentional. As with automatism, raising evidence of mental impairment to negate intention may lead to a complete acquittal. There does not seem to be any case law as to whether or not evidence of mental impairment may be admissible in relation to recklessness or negligence. Ian Leader-Elliott, however, has argued that mental impairment may be relevant to these fault elements as well as intention: 'Case Note: Insanity, Involuntariness and the Mental Element in Crime' (1994) 18 Crim LJ 347–57 at 355.

There have been a handful of cases in Canada and Australia dealing with this area. It has become much more of an issue in some American states that have abolished the defence of insanity.

The current law

In Australia, the leading case on this point is that of *Hawkins v The Queen* (1994) 179 CLR 500. On 27 October 1990 a 16-year-old boy, Andrew Hawkins, shot and killed his father. He stated that he had intended to commit suicide in his father's presence, but at the last moment, in a disturbed state of mind, he turned the rifle towards his father and pulled the trigger without intending to kill his father.

Andrew Hawkins was in fact tried three times for murder. At his first trial, he raised the defence of insanity, but the jury was unable to reach a verdict. At his second trial, the accused withdrew the defence of insanity and he was convicted of murder. The Tasmanian Court of Criminal Appeal, however, allowed an appeal from conviction and ordered a third trial: *Hawkins (No 2)* (1993) 68 A Crim R 1.

At the third trial, counsel for the defence sought to adduce evidence of 'mental disease' not as a basis for a separate defence of mental impairment, but as a basis for showing that the accused did not possess the requisite intention for the crime of murder. Underwood J conducted a *voir dire* to determine the relevance and admissibility of this evidence. The defence called two expert witnesses. One gave evidence that the accused was suffering from a diagnosable mental disease at the time of the shooting, which he labelled an 'adolescent identity disorder'. The other expert stated that the accused had been suffering from an 'adolescent adjustment disorder', which could be regarded in law as a 'mental disease'.

Underwood J ruled that this medical evidence was inadmissible for any purpose other than the insanity defence. The Court of Criminal Appeal of Tasmania dismissed an appeal by the accused on the ground that the ruling that the evidence was inadmissible did not cause any miscarriage of justice: *Hawkins (No 2)* (1993) 68 A Crim R 1. The accused then appealed to the High Court.

In a joint judgment, the High Court agreed that evidence of mental disease should be excluded in determining the issue of the voluntariness of the criminal act. However, the High Court went on to say that there was no reason 'for excluding evidence of mental disease in determining whether an act done by a person who is criminally responsible for the act was done with a specific intent': *Hawkins v The Queen* (1994) 179 CLR 500 at 513.

The Court said that since evidence of intoxication may be led to negate intention, 'it would be anomalous to exclude evidence of other forms of mental abnormality in determining the same issue' (at 513). The High Court remitted the matter to the Court of Criminal Appeal of Tasmania to either make an order dismissing the appeal if it considered that no substantial miscarriage of justice had actually occurred or, alternatively, to consider substituting a conviction of manslaughter instead of ordering a new trial. The Court of Criminal Appeal by a majority of two judges to one subsequently ordered that there be a fourth trial of the matter: *Hawkins v The Queen (No 3)* [1994] 4 Tas R 376. Andrew Hawkins then pleaded guilty to manslaughter and was sentenced on 11 July 1995 by Cox J to six years' imprisonment to date from 29 October 1990 when he had first been taken into custody.

In its judgment, the High Court cautioned that the use of evidence of mental disease to negate intention can arise 'only on the hypothesis that the accused's mental condition at the time when the incriminated act was done fell short of insanity': (1994) 179 CLR 500 at 517. In reaching this conclusion, the High Court relied upon a series of Canadian cases in which mental impairment falling short of 'insanity' has been held to negate the fault element.

The Canadian cases, however, deal primarily with mental impairment as it relates to what was termed 'capital murder'. Prior to 1967, s 202A(2)(a) of the Canadian *Criminal Code* defined capital murder as that which is 'planned and deliberate'. This definition was repealed in 1967 (1967–68 c 15, s 1) but revived in 1976, when the *Criminal Law Amendment Act (No 2)* 1976 divided murder into first degree and second degree murder. Section 214(2) defined first degree murder as planned and deliberate, a concept that survived revision in 1985. The distinction between first and second degree murder is now contained in s 231 of the *Criminal Code*.

In *More v The Queen* [1963] 41 DLR (2d) 380 at 382, Cartwright J pointed out that the requirement that the killing be 'planned and deliberate' for capital murder meant something more than simply intentional. The word deliberate he took to mean 'considered, not impulsive'. Most of the Canadian cases therefore deal with evidence of mental impairment in relation to whether the killing was planned and deliberate. However, the Quebec Court of Appeal has interpreted Cartwright J's words in *More*'s case as meaning that mental impairment falling short of a separate defence may be used to cast doubt on the accused's ability to form a specific intent: *R v Lechasseur* [1977] 38 CCC (2d) 319 at 320. The Ontario Court of Appeal and the Nova Scotia Supreme Court have also referred to the admissibility of evidence of mental impairment 'falling short of insanity' as being relevant to negate the specific intent for murder reducing the offence to manslaughter: *R v Baltzer* [1974] 27 CCC (2d) 118; *R v Browning* [1976] 34 CCC (2d) 200; *R v Stevenson* [1990] 58 CCC (2d) 464. There may be a link between these Canadian cases and the fact that Canada has never had a defence of diminished responsibility, unlike England, Scotland and the Australian jurisdictions of the Australian Capital Territory, the Northern Territory, New South Wales and Queensland.

It is in the USA that evidence of mental impairment has been raised the most often in order to negate intention. In 1976, Montana abolished the separate defence of insanity and evidence of mental impairment became relevant only to the question as to whether or not the accused acted with the requisite intention: *Montana Code Ann.*, Stat. 46-14-102 (1979). Idaho followed this example in 1982 (*Idaho Code*, Stat. 18-207 (1982)), Utah in 1990 (*Utah Code Ann.*, 76-2-305 (1990)) and Kansas in 1995 (*Kan. Stat. Ann.* 22-3220 (1995)). In *State v Shackford* 127 NH 695, 506 A 2d 315 (1986), the Supreme Court of New Hampshire held that the 'product' test of insanity (where the accused is not criminally responsible if the criminal act was the product of mental disease or defect) was really related to whether or not insanity negated criminal intent.

Critique

Raymond L Spring has argued that the American approach to mental impairment as negating criminal intention is a step in the right direction because eliminating a separate insanity defence 'should reduce substantially the opportunity for jury confusion': 'The Return to Mens Rea: Salvaging a Reasonable Perspective on Mental Disorder in Criminal Trials' (1998) 21(2) *International Journal of Law and Psychiatry* 187–96 at 194. However, evidence of mental impairment has not been generally accepted in relation to voluntariness in the USA. In other countries, abolishing the insanity defence and allowing evidence of mental impairment to be relevant only to voluntariness and intention may lead to further confusion.

Spring argues that focusing on mental impairment and intention returns the law to its legitimate objectives because the traditional insanity defence was not intended to be a rule to cover all cases of mental impairment. However, that approach ignores the long history of excusing those who lack the ability to reason from criminal responsibility. It is a lack of reasoning capacities that was always the focus, rather than a lack of intention.

The abolition of the insanity defence in favour of mental impairment as negating intention also fails to take into account situations where an accused *does* intend to commit a criminal act, but this intention is the result of delusions. For example, in *R v Hadfield* (1800) 27 St Tr 1281 the accused tried to kill King George III. He was motivated by the belief that through his own (Hadfield's) death, he was destined to save the world. He knew that killing was illegal and punishable by death and he therefore shot at the king in order to be hanged. He fully intended to cause the King's death. If there were no separate defence assessing Hadfield's ability to reason, he would be held criminally responsible despite evidence of delusions.

It is interesting to note that the English Court of Appeal has recently rejected the argument that intention is relevant where both prosecution and defence agreed that the accused was suffering from a psychosis at the time he broke into a house: *Attorney-General's Reference (No 3 of 1998)* [1999] 2 Cr App R 214. This Court of Appeal reference followed a decision by a judge of the Crown Court to acquit the accused on the basis that the prosecution had not proved that the accused had intended to commit the crime charged. The judge found that if there is a lack of intention because of psychosis the accused is entitled to a complete acquittal. The reference in this case was limited to the question as to what needs to be proved in determining whether or not the accused did the act. The Court of Appeal held that the Crown must prove that the accused caused a certain event, but once insanity was in issue, the accused's state of mind ceased to be relevant.

In commenting on this case, JR Spencer points out that while the Court of Appeal's decision clearly shows that the trial judge was incorrect in acquitting the accused, nothing further can be done about 'a visibly dangerous defendant...wrongly acquitted': 'Insanity and Mens Rea', [2000] 59(1) *Cambridge Law Journal* 9–11 at 11. On a broad level, this raises the issue that if mental impairment is accepted as negating intention, a complete acquittal may result in circumstances where some form of psychiatric detention may be more appropriate.

The High Court decision in *Hawkins* and a few of the Canadian cases refer to mental impairment 'falling short of insanity'. What that means is open to debate, but more importantly, even mental impairment that is not considered serious enough to affect a person's ability to reason may need treatment. As outlined in the background section, the traditional justification for detaining those found not criminally responsible because of insanity centres upon the notion of incapacitation to prevent further harm to the public. There is, however, a more modern justification for detention and that is for treatment. Recent changes to the law in certain jurisdictions to enable a wider range of dispositional options other than preventive detention may help emphasise the treatment rationale. Acquitting those with some form of mental impairment because their conduct is 'involuntary' or 'unintentional' means that potentially recurrent disorders may go untreated. At least if conditions such as sleepwalking or dissociative states are brought within a separate defence of mental impairment, more flexible dispositional options may enable the individual to obtain treatment for their disorder.

Intoxication

Background
On 23 February 1997, a professional rugby player called Noa Nadruku was charged with assaulting two women outside a Canberra nightclub. There was evidence that he had punched both women in the face. In the lead-up to the assaults, Nadruku had consumed so much alcohol that he was barely conscious.

Magistrate Madden described Nadruku's actions as follows: 'The two young ladies were unsuspecting victims of drunken thuggery, effectively being king hit. The assaults were a disgraceful act of cowardice...The behaviour is deplorable, intolerable and unacceptable': *SC Small v Noa Kurimalawai*, unreported, 22 October 1997, Magistrates' Court of the ACT, No CC97/01904, Transcript of Proceedings, p 11.

However, Magistrate Madden (at 11) went on to acquit Nadruku on the grounds that '…the degree of intoxication is so overwhelming to the extent that the defendant, in my view, did not know what he did and did not form any intent as to what he was doing'.

Nadruku's acquittal was widely reported in the Australian media and many commentators expressed their outrage at the operation of the 'drunks' defence'. The then Federal Attorney-General, Daryl Williams, stated that he would ask the Victorian, South Australian and Australian Capital Territory Attorneys-General to adopt the approach of the *Criminal Code* (Cth): 'States Urged to Dump Drunk's Defence', *Media Release*, 29 October 1997. In early December 1997, the then Federal Minister for Justice, Senator Amanda Vanstone, stated that the defence would be removed from Commonwealth criminal law and that 'the use of the drunks' defence has sent a disturbing message to those who get intoxicated and engage in violent behaviour': 'Government to Ensure Early Removal of Drunks' Defence', *Media Release*, 2 December 1997.

The South Australian and Victorian Parliaments subsequently conducted inquiries into the law relating to intoxication: Attorney-General's Office (SA), *Intoxication and Criminal Responsibility*, Discussion Paper (July 1998); Law Reform Committee, Parliament of Victoria, *Criminal Liability for Self-Induced Intoxication*, Report (Melbourne: VGPS, May 1999). In 2000, the Australian Capital Territory introduced the most restrictive provision in Australia such that self-induced intoxication is no longer relevant to assessing intention or voluntary behaviour: *Crimes Act* 1900 (ACT) s 339. However, it would seem that this has been superseded by s 31 of the *Criminal Code* (ACT), which states that intoxication is irrelevant to offences involving basic intent.

Despite the common use of the term 'drunks' defence', intoxication has never been a 'defence' to criminal conduct. It instead developed as a factor that could be taken into account in assessing whether the accused's conduct was voluntary or, more commonly, intentional.

Most of the case law deals with drunkenness and intoxication in the context of imbibing too much alcohol. However, an accused may have taken other drugs on their own or in combination with alcohol. The law does not distinguish between the causes of intoxication, but an article by Shantha Rajaratnam, Jennifer Redman and Michael Lenné suggests that it should: 'Intoxication and Criminal Responsibility' (2000) 7(1) *Psychiatry, Psychology and Law* 59–69.

Alcohol use has been associated with violence and risk taking. There is also an association between central nervous system stimulants such as cocaine and amphetamines and hallucinogens such as phencyclidine (PCP) and violent behaviour. In addition, there is a well-established association between the use of anabolic steroids and violence. In comparison, drugs such as cannabis and opiates such as heroin have not been associated with violent behaviour. Rajaratnam, Redman and Lenné stress that the degree of intoxication from taking alcohol and/or other drugs varies from individual to individual and each case needs to be considered on its merits.

In England, prior to the early nineteenth century, a person who voluntarily consumed alcohol before committing a criminal act was in no better position, and sometimes in a worse position than a sober criminal. In the sixteenth century, the rule was set out in *Reniger v Feogossa* (1551) 75 ER 1 at 31: 'If a person that is drunk kills another, this shall be felony, and he shall be hanged for it, and yet he did it through ignorance, for when he was drunk he had no understanding nor memory; but inasmuch as that ignorance was occasioned by his own act and folly, and he might have avoided it, he shall not be privileged thereby.'

The first reported case that suggested intoxication could be taken into account in certain circumstances was that of the 1819 case of *R v Grindley* (referred to in *R v Carroll* (1835) 7 C & P 145; 173 ER 64). In that case, Holroyd J held that evidence of intoxication could be taken into account in considering whether or not an act of murder was premeditated or committed in the heat of the moment.

Subsequent nineteenth-century cases showed inconsistencies as to how intoxication could be taken into account: Law Reform Committee, Parliament of Victoria, *Criminal Liability for Self-Induced Intoxication*, Report (Melbourne: VGPS, May 1999) pp 18–20. In *DPP v Beard* [1920] AC 479, the House of Lords referred to drunkenness being a factor that could be relevant in assessing a specific intent as an element of an offence. Subsequently, the House of Lords in *DPP v Majewski* [1977] AC 443 divided crimes into 'offences of specific intent' and 'offences of basic intent' and allowed intoxication as a factor to be taken into account in relation to the former, but not the latter.

The current law

Australian jurisdictions differ in the approach taken towards evidence of intoxication. In relation to the fault element, Queensland, Tasmania, Western Australia and New South Wales follow the *Majewski* approach. South Australia, Victoria, and the Northern Territory follow the Australian common law approach that holds that intoxication may be relevant to intention in general without dividing it up into basic or specific. Section 15(5) of the *Criminal Code* (ACT) states that self-induced intoxication cannot be considered in assessing whether an act or omission was intended or voluntary.

At common law, evidence of intoxication in extreme cases may support the claim that the accused's actions were involuntary: *R v O'Connor* (1980) 146 CLR 64. None of the *Criminal Codes* refer to the relevance of self-induced intoxication to the question of voluntary conduct. The case law appears to hold that where an offence charged does not require proof of an intention to cause a specific result, evidence of self-induced intoxication cannot provide a foundation for a plea of involuntariness: *Snow v The Queen* [1962] Tas SR; *R v Palmer* [1985] Tas R 138; *Bennett* (1989) 45 A Crim R 45; *R v Kusu* [1981] Qd R 136; 4 A Crim R 72; *R v Miers* [1985] 2 Qd R 138; *Cameron* (1990) 47 A Crim R 397 at 410; *R v Battle* (1993) 8 WAR 449; *Haggie v Meredith* (1993) 9 WAR 206. In New South Wales, s 428G of the *Crimes Act* 1900 (NSW) now makes it clear that self-induced intoxication cannot be taken into account in determining whether the relevant conduct was voluntary.

Evidence of intoxication has been used most commonly in order to negate the fault element of a crime rather than as grounds for involuntary conduct. This is perhaps partly because of the difficulty in getting a jury to accept that the accused could carry out complex actions, yet claim that this conduct was unwilled due to intoxication. Indeed, the idea that the movements of the body can be divorced from the will has been the subject of debate in philosophical literature: HLA Hart, *Punishment and Responsibility* (Oxford: Oxford University Press, 1968) pp 90–112; EM Coles and D Jang, 'A Psychological Perspective on the Legal Concepts of "Volition" and "Intent"' (1996) 4(1) *Journal of Law and Medicine* 60–71.

Because evidence of intoxication is usually raised in relation to intention, it is worthwhile considering this in some detail.

The main decision at common law dealing with intoxication is that of *R v O'Connor* (1980) 146 CLR 64. In that case, the accused was caught rifling through a car owned by a police officer. When the officer found the accused, the latter had removed a map and a knife from the car. The accused went to run away, but the officer caught him and arrested him. During the arrest, the accused opened the blade of the knife and stabbed the officer. The accused was charged with theft and with wounding with intent to resist arrest.

At his trial, O'Connor gave evidence that he had taken fourteen Avil travel-sickness tablets and also drunk three to four glasses of Galliano liqueur and three bottles of beer during the day of the events. The trial judge directed the jury that the offences were crimes of specific intent and intoxication could be taken into account when considering these charges but that it was irrelevant to an alternative charge of unlawful wounding. The jury accordingly found the accused not guilty of theft and wounding with intent to resist arrest, but guilty of unlawful wounding.

The accused appealed to the Supreme Court of Victoria. It allowed the appeal and entered a verdict of acquittal on the alternative charge of unlawful wounding. The Solicitor-General of Victoria applied for special leave to appeal to the High Court. Special leave was granted and a majority of the Court consisting of Barwick CJ, Stephen, Murphy and Aickin JJ all delivered separate judgments dismissing the Solicitor-General's appeal. The majority was of the opinion that evidence of intoxication may be tendered to assist in raising a doubt as to the voluntary character of the criminal conduct and that such evidence may be tendered even where the offence is one of strict liability. They also held that evidence of intoxication could be relevant to cast doubt as to whether or not the accused possessed the requisite fault element in relation to the unlawful act.

The minority, consisting of Wilson, Gibbs and Mason JJ preferred to follow the English approach to evidence of intoxication set out in *Director of Public Prosecutions v Majewski* [1977] AC 443 in holding that evidence of intoxication was only relevant to crimes of specific intent. The minority was concerned with public policy in reaching their decisions. Mason J stated (at 110):

> [T]here are two strands of thought whose thrust is to deny that drunkenness is an excuse for the commission of crime. One is essentially a moral judgment—that it is wrong that a person should escape responsibility for his [or her] actions merely because he [or she] is so intoxicated by drink or drugs that his [or her] act is not willed when by his [or her] own voluntary choice he [or she] embarked on the course which led to his [or her] intoxication. The other is a social judgment—that society legitimately expects for its protection that the law will not allow to go unpunished an act which would be adjudged to be a serious criminal offence but for the fact that the perpetrator is grossly intoxicated.

The majority of the High Court refused to follow *Majewski* on the basis, first, that the distinction between crimes of specific and basic intent lacks logic and, secondly, because the social policy arguments in favour of holding an accused liable for depriving him or herself of the capacity to act voluntarily or intentionally would provide an unjustifiable exception to fundamental common law principles.

The common law approach to intoxication still holds sway in Victoria and South Australia. The *Criminal Law Consolidation (Intoxication) Amendment Act* 1999 (SA) retained the *O'Connor* approach, but made some procedural changes in relation to evidence of intoxication.

Section 31 of the *Criminal Code* (NT) states that a person is 'excused from criminal responsibility for an act, omission or event unless it was intended or foreseen by him [or her] as a possible consequence of his [or her] conduct'. Section 7(1) states:

> In all cases where intoxication may be regarded for the purposes of determining whether a person is guilty or not guilty of an offence—
> (a) it shall be presumed that, until the contrary is proved, the intoxication was voluntary; and
> (b) unless the intoxication was involuntary, it shall be presumed evidentially that the accused person foresaw the natural and probable consequences of his [or her] conduct.

The presumption in s 7(1)(b) is an evidentiary rather than a legal one that requires an accused to raise sufficient evidence of intoxication. It is still up to the prosecution to prove beyond reasonable doubt that the accused's conduct was intended or foreseen. The common law approach to intoxication and intention therefore applies in the Northern Territory: *Attorney-General's Reference No 1 of 1996* [1998] 7 Tas R 293 at 318 per Wright J; 305 per Cox CJ; 313 per Underwood J.

The *Beard/Majewski* approach is reflected in the Code jurisdictions of Queensland, Tasmania and Western Australia. In Queensland and Western Australia, intoxication may be considered in relation to crimes that have 'an intention to cause a specific result' as an element of the offence: *Criminal Code* (Qld) s 28; *Criminal Code* (WA) s 28.

Section 17(2) of the Tasmanian *Criminal Code* sets out the requirement that evidence of intoxication goes to whether or not the accused was 'incapable of forming the specific intent essential to constitute the offence'. Such evidence therefore goes to the question of capacity rather than the fact of intention. In *Attorney-General's Reference (No 1 of 1996)* [1998] 7 Tas R 293, the Supreme Court of Tasmania seems to imply that intoxication may be relevant to negate other fault elements such as knowledge: R Bradfield, 'Case and Comment' (1999) 23 Crim LJ 41–7.

In New South Wales, the *Majewski* approach was taken up in the *Crimes Legislation Amendment Act* 1996 (NSW), which inserted ss 428A–428I into the *Crimes Act* 1900 (NSW). Self-induced intoxication may now only be taken into account in relation to whether the accused 'had the intention to cause the specific result necessary for an offence of specific intent': *Crimes Act* 1900 (NSW) s 428C. This also appears to be the situation in the Australian Capital Territory: *Criminal Code* (ACT) s 31. Section 10 of the *Criminal Code* (ACT) states that the provisions dealing with intoxication have immediate application.

Where evidence of intoxication is raised by the defence to negate the requisite fault element, the prosecution may attempt to counteract this by claiming that the evidence showed that the accused became intoxicated in order to commit the crime, alcohol being known as a disinhibitor: *Attorney-General (Northern Ireland) v Gallagher* [1963] AC 349 at 382 per Denning LJ.

Critique

There have been numerous law reform proposals that have looked at how intoxication should be taken into account in assessing criminal responsibility. The Law Reform Commission of Victoria (*Mental Malfunction and Criminal Responsibility*, Report No 34 (Melbourne: LRCV, 1990) paras 218–19), the Law Reform Committee (Parliament of Victoria, *Criminal Liability for Self-Induced Intoxication*, Report (Melbourne: VGPS, May 1999), the South Australian Mitchell Committee (South Australian Criminal Law and Penal Methods Reform Committee, Fourth Report, *The Substantive Criminal Law* (1977) p 48), the New Zealand Criminal Law Reform Committee (*Report on Intoxication as a Defence to a Criminal Charge* (1984) para 45) and the Criminal Law Officers Committee (CLOC) (*Chapters 1 and 2, General Principles of Criminal Responsibility*, Final Report, (December 1992) p 51) have all recommended that the *O'Connor* approach to evidence of intoxication conforms best to general principles of criminal law. Ashworth refers to this approach as the 'simplest' one: *Principles of Criminal Law* (3rd edn, Oxford: Oxford University Press, 1999) p 225.

The main argument against the *O'Connor* approach is that it may lead to what are seen as undeserved acquittals. This argument was particularly apparent in relation to the acquittal of Noa Nadruku. In 1995, the Law Commission noted in *Legislating the Criminal Code: Intoxication and Criminal Liability*, Report No 229 (London: HMSO, 1995) pp 45–6, paras 5.20, 5.22:

> We think it significant that on consultation many respondents concerned with the practical operation of the *Majewski* rule—namely the Bar and a significant minority of the Queen's Bench Division judges—expressed support for...the abolition of the *Majewski* principle without replacement...We were, however, impressed by the practical considerations urged upon us by, in particular, the majority of judges of the Queen's Bench Division. They expressed concern about the effect of:
>
>> even one high profile case where there was an acquittal because the alleged offender was too drunk to form the required intent. The majority believe that such an acquittal would be viewed by the public as another example of the law, and inevitably the judges who apply that law, being out of touch with public opinion and public perception of fault.

While the majority of the High Court's approach to evidence of intoxication in *O'Connor*'s case caused much controversy, there is no evidence that it has given rise to an increase in acquittals on the ground of intoxication: see, for example, Law Reform Commission of Victoria, *Criminal Responsibility: Intention and Gross Intoxication*, Report No 6 (Melbourne: LRCV, 1986) p 19. In fact, it is still a rare occurrence for an accused to be acquitted on this basis.

If the majority approach in *O'Connor* is to be rejected, it doesn't necessarily follow that the best way to take evidence of intoxication into account is to divide crimes up into those of specific and basic intent. Lord Simon in *DPP v Morgan* [1976] AC 182 stated at 216:

> By 'crimes of basic intent', I mean those crimes whose definition expresses (or, more often, implies) a mens rea which does not go beyond the actus reus. The actus reus generally consists of an act and some consequence. The consequence may be very closely connected with the act, or more remotely connected with it: but with a crime of basic intent the mens rea does not extend beyond the act and its consequence, however remote, defined in the actus reus.

This quotation appears to refer to the division between the physical element as conduct and the physical element as the results or consequences of conduct. It is relatively simple on that division to see that murder is a crime of specific intent. What is prohibited in the crime of murder is the death of the victim rather than the conduct that caused the death. It is irrelevant what conduct was undertaken that caused the death; providing the conduct of the accused *results* in the death of the victim, the physical element of murder will be established.

However, Stephen J pointed out in *R v O'Connor* (1980) 146 CLR 64 at 105 that while murder is generally characterised as a crime of specific intent, other serious crimes such as manslaughter and assault are characterised as crimes of basic intent. He stated that such a distinction is 'neither clearly defined nor easily recognisable [and]…does not reflect or give effect to any coherent attitude either as the relative wrongfulness of particular conduct or the degree of social mischief which that conduct is thought to involve'.

It is also very difficult to find any rationale for holding that intoxication is relevant to certain offences and not to others. For example, why should intoxication be taken into account in relation to an attempt to commit an offence of basic intent and yet not in relation to the latter? The division is often arbitrary and lacking any guiding principles.

Further, Barwick CJ stated in *R v O'Connor* (1980) 146 CLR 64 at 87 that the blameworthiness that may be attached to the accused's behaviour in becoming intoxicated in the first place should not be superimposed over the criminal conduct so as to presume that the accused acted voluntarily or with the requisite state of mind.

There are alternatives to the *Majewski* approach. There is a natural urge to want to punish a person for getting so drunk in the first place that he or she causes harm. But if that is the case, why not simply create an offence of committing a dangerous act while under the influence of intoxication? Section 154 of the *Criminal Code* (NT) provides an example of such an offence. This states:

> (1) Any person who does or makes any act or omission that causes serious danger, actual or potential, to the lives, health or safety of the public or to any person (whether or not a member of the public) in circumstances where an ordinary person similarly circumstanced would have clearly foreseen such danger and not have done or made that act or omission is guilty of a crime and is liable to imprisonment for 5 years.
>
> …
>
> (4) If at the time of doing or making such act or omission he [or she] is under the influence of an intoxicating substance he [or she] is liable to further imprisonment for 4 years.
>
> (5) Voluntary intoxication may not be regarded for the purposes of determining whether a person is not guilty of the crime defined by this section.

The Victorian Law Committee rejected calls for the enactment of a similar provision in Victoria: *Criminal Liability for Self-Induced Intoxication*, Report (May 1999) pp 96–102. The reasons for rejecting such an offence included the possibility that it would encourage plea bargaining and that it might increase the number of compromise jury verdicts. That is, a jury might find it easier to convict an accused of the special offence if they could not agree on whether he or she was guilty of the principal offence. The Committee was also of the opinion that such an offence undermines the general principle that an accused should only be convicted where the offence was committed voluntarily and intentionally. The Committee (at para 6.62, p 100) quoted Robert Richter QC, who stated: 'It seems to me that looking at a new offence is saying, "Look, you are not guilty of the crime, but we will punish you for the crime anyway under a different guise and a different name".'

Another alternative is to consider intoxication a form of mental impairment for the purposes of the defence of mental impairment. Where there is a range of dispositional options in place, a supervision order that releases a person on certain conditions may be suitable in the case of someone who is mentally impaired due to intoxication. The benefit of this approach is that an accused can be found not criminally responsible and this accords with established principles, but a range of dispositional options could become available. This could assuage community concerns that there is a 'drunks' defence' that allows complete acquittals.

The Victorian Law Reform Committee agreed that this proposal offered real advantages, but ultimately decided that no change to the law was necessary: para 6.68, p 103. However, if a broader perspective were taken to evidence of mental impairment in general, then a practical alternative would be to subsume evidence of intoxication and other conditions such as dissociation within a defence of mental impairment. The Northern Territory Parliament has included 'involuntary intoxication' within the definition of mental impairment for the purposes of its reformulated defence of mental impairment: *Criminal Code* (NT) s 43A. It did not, however, take the next step of including voluntary intoxication within the ambit of the defence.

Whatever approach is taken, it is clear that there are no easy answers as to how best to take into account evidence of intoxication. Law reform committees tend to favour the *O'Connor* approach because it accords with general principles of criminal responsibility. Why should a person who does not will or intend his or her actions be punished? Governments, on the other hand, tend to look towards special rules to govern those who commit crimes while intoxicated. Matthew Goode writes in Attorney-General's Office, *Intoxication and Criminal Responsibility*, Discussion Paper (July 1998) p 42, para 6.2:

> Parliaments tend to the opinion that letting defendants such as Mr Nadruku escape the criminal sanction is scandalous and should not be allowed to happen. In this they may well be representing the views of the public as a general proposition—certainly a vocal section of the general public. The courts and law reform bodies

tend to say that letting the occasional defendant such as Mr Nadruku escape the criminal net is a small price to pay for keeping away any alternative which will be complex, confusing and unjust to others. If both views may be conceded to have some justice, taken from their particular perspective, what then?

In assessing these different approaches, it is worthwhile remembering that in practice, acquittals on the basis of intoxication are rare. There is also some reason to believe that those accused who raise evidence of intoxication will show some awareness of intention sufficient to warrant conviction: R Shines, 'Intoxication and Responsibility' (1990) 13 *International Journal of Law and Psychiatry* 9–35; C Mitchell, 'The Intoxicated Offender—Refuting the Legal and Medical Myths' (1988) 11 *International Journal of Law and Psychiatry* 77–103.

The defence of mental impairment

Background

In the case of Andre Chayna outlined at the beginning of this chapter, the seven psychiatrists who gave evidence at her trial agreed that she was in a psychotic state after the killings. The evidence, however, differed as to whether or not she was mentally impaired at the time of the killings.

The nature of the mental impairment suffered by Chayna is essential to proving the first part of the defence of mental impairment, that she suffered a condition that can be classified as stemming from an internal cause. Modern conceptions of the defence of mental impairment serve to exculpate an accused from criminal responsibility because of the accused's inability to know the nature and quality of the conduct or that the conduct was wrong. In the Code jurisdictions and South Australia, there is an added component of the mental impairment causing an inability to control the accused's conduct. Most jurisdictions follow along the lines of the traditional *M'Naghten Rules*, which arose out of the controversy surrounding the nineteenth-century case of Daniel M'Naghten.

M'Naghten was tried for the murder of Edward Drummond, the private secretary of the Prime Minister of England, Sir Robert Peel. Evidence was led to show that M'Naghten suffered from the delusion that he was being persecuted by 'the Tories' and that in order to end this persecution, he shot and killed Drummond whom he supposedly mistook for Peel. Lord Tindall CJ instructed the jury that they could return a verdict of not guilty on the ground of insanity if they were of the opinion that the accused did not have the use of his understanding so as not to know that he was doing a wrong or wicked act.

M'Naghten was accordingly found not guilty on the ground of insanity by the jury. This led to a detailed debate that took place in the House of Lords concerning the question of whether or not the rules of law governing the defence of insanity were satisfactory. In June 1843, certain questions were placed before the common law judges on the existing law of insanity, with particular reference to the subject of delusions.

With one dissent, the judges agreed on the answers and these have become known as the *M'Naghten Rules* (1843) 8 ER 718. The most well-known rule (at 722) set out by Tindall CJ on behalf of all the judges, save Maule J, states:

> [T]o establish a defence on the ground of insanity, it must be clearly proved that, at the time of the committing of the act, the party accused was labouring under such defect of reason, from disease of the mind, as not to know the nature and quality of the act he [or she] was doing; or, if he [or she] did know it, that he [or she] did not know he [or she] was doing what was wrong.

The current law

All nine Australian criminal law jurisdictions employ insanity defences largely based upon the *M'Naghten Rules*. These rules still apply at common law in New South Wales, and the statutory provision in Victoria echoes the language used in them: *Crimes (Mental Impairment and Unfitness to be Tried) Act* 1997 (Vic) s 20. The Australian Capital Territory, the Northern Territory, Queensland, South Australia, Tasmania, Western Australia and s 7.3 of the *Criminal Code* (Cth) include a further 'volitional' arm concerning whether or not the accused lacked the capacity to control his or her conduct: *Crimes Act* 1900 (ACT) s 428N; *Criminal Code* (ACT) s 28; *Criminal Code* (NT) s 43C; *Criminal Code* (Qld) s 27; *Criminal Law Consolidation Act* 1935 (SA) s 269C; *Criminal Code* (Tas) s 16; *Criminal Code* (WA) s 27. The provisions dealing with mental impairment in the *Criminal Code* (ACT) do not apply to offences until 1 January 2006 or other prescribed date under regulation: *Criminal Code* (ACT) s 9. Section 428N of the *Crimes Act* 1900 (ACT) would thus seem to apply until such date.

Modern conceptions of the defence involve two questions:

1 Was the accused suffering from some form of mental impairment that can be classified as 'internal'? The words used to describe such an impairment differ between the jurisdictions.
2 Did the mental impairment affect the accused's understanding of his or her actions or (in the six jurisdictions outlined above) capacity to control his or her conduct?

The 'defect of reason' part of the *M'Naghten Rules* has become somewhat lost as the focus has shifted to classifying the mental impairment and its effect.

Internal causes of mental impairment

Just what conditions will constitute mental impairment for the purposes of this defence varies from jurisdiction to jurisdiction. One of the initial difficulties with this criterion is that a clear definition of mental impairment, or even mental illness, has eluded members of the medical as well as the legal professions. Sylvia Bell has pointed out the failure of international attempts at a universal definition and the problematic experiences of legislators in New Zealand when attempting to create a generic definition of mental disorder: 'Defining Mental Disorder' in W Brookbanks (ed), *Psychiatry and the Law: Clinical and Legal Issues* (Wellington: Brooker's Ltd, 1996) pp 71–92 at 71. Bell attributes this failure to the inexact nature of psychiatric diagnosis and the constantly changing diagnostic criteria as our knowledge of psychiatric disorders is refined and syndromes are viewed in different ways.

M Gelder, D Gath, R Mayou and P Cowen (eds), in *The Oxford Textbook of Psychiatry* (3rd edn, Oxford: Oxford University Press, 1996), state at 57 that:

> [M]ost psychiatrists begin by separating mental handicap and personality disorder from mental illness...they diagnose mental illness if there are delusions, hallucinations, severe alterations of mood, or other major disturbances of psychological functions. In practice, most psychiatrists allocate psychiatric disorders to diagnostic categories such as schizophrenia, affective disorders, organic mental states, and others; by convention they agree to group these diagnostic categories together under the rubric of mental illness.

On this basis, Finbarr McAuley has suggested a definition of mental illness as 'a pervasive inability to engage reality: as a failure of "reality testing" to use the term of art favoured by psychiatrists': *Insanity, Psychiatry and Criminal Responsibility* (Dublin: The Round Hall Press, 1993) p 35.

Five terms have been used in attempting to legally define mental impairment and each will be discussed in turn.

'Disease of the mind'/'mental disease'

The *M'Naghten Rules* still apply in New South Wales and therefore the concept of 'disease of the mind' is still in use in that state. The Code jurisdictions of Queensland and Tasmania refer to a 'mental disease'. This has been held to be the same as 'disease of the mind': *R v Falconer* (1990) 171 CLR 30.

We have already discussed the internal cause theory that has been used to distinguish between sane and insane automatism. A 'disease of the mind' is legally defined as being caused by an internal condition. King CJ in *R v Radford* (1985) 42 SASR 266 at 247 referred to the concept of a disease of the mind as a condition arising from an 'underlying pathological infirmity of the mind'. This idea of a disease of the mind as arising from something internal rather than external has been adopted by the High Court in *R v Falconer* (1990) 171 CLR 30. Because epilepsy, somnambulism, hyperglycaemia and cerebral arteriosclerosis have been viewed as having internal rather than external causes, they have been viewed as diseases of the mind.

The main problem with the term 'disease of the mind' is that it has no meaning in the psychiatric context. More modern conceptions of the defence of insanity have therefore avoided using this term.

'Mental impairment'

Some of the newer versions of the insanity defence refer very broadly to mental impairment. The Victorian defence uses this term without defining it. Section 1 of the *Criminal Code* (WA) defines mental impairment to include 'intellectual disability, mental illness, brain damage and senility'. Similarly, s 269A(1) of the *Criminal Law Consolidation Act* 1935 (SA) defines mental impairment as 'mental illness, intellectual disability or a disability or impairment of the mind resulting from senility'. Section 43A of the *Criminal Code* (NT) refers to the term including 'senility, intellectual disability, mental illness, brain damage and involuntary intoxication'.

Section 7.3(8) of the *Criminal Code* (Cth) and s 27 of the *Criminal Code* (ACT) also use the term 'mental impairment', but go further than the other definitions by including the term 'severe personality disorder'.

As a term, 'mental impairment' in itself means little in psychiatric parlance, but it is broad enough to encompass a range of disorders that may affect a person's ability to reason.

'Mental illness'

Legislative references to the defence of mental impairment existing in the Australian Capital Territory, New South Wales, the Northern Territory, South Australia, Western Australia and at the federal level all refer to the term 'mental illness': *Criminal Code* (ACT) s 27; *Mental Health (Criminal Procedure) Act* 1990 (NSW) s 22(1)(b); *Criminal Code* (NT) s 43A; *Criminal Law Consolidation Act* 1935 (SA) s 269A(1); *Criminal Code* (WA) s 1; *Criminal Code* (Cth) s 7.3(9).

At common law, King CJ in *R v Radford* (1985) 42 SASR 266 at 247 referred to the *M'Naghten Rules*' concept of 'disease of the mind' as simply meaning 'mental illness'. It is obviously a key term, but do the legal definitions correspond with expert medical opinion?

It has already been pointed out that Finbarr McAuley's definition of mental illness involves a 'pervasive inability to engage reality'. The legal definition of mental illness suggested by King CJ in *R v Radford* (1985) 42 SASR 266 at 247 does not, however, correspond with this approach. King CJ defined mental illness as an 'underlying pathological infirmity of mind'. This definition was adopted by the High Court in *R v Falconer* (1990) 171 CLR 30 and was incorporated into s 7.3(9) of the *Criminal Code* (Cth). That section defines 'mental illness' in the context of mental impairment as:

> [A]n underlying pathological infirmity of the mind, whether of long or short duration and whether permanent or temporary, but does not include the reaction of a healthy mind to extraordinary external stimuli.

Section 43A of the *Criminal Code* (NT) follows the *Criminal Code* (Cth) definition of mental illness. The *Criminal Law Consolidation Act* 1935 (SA) also uses the phrase 'pathological infirmity of mind' and takes the unusual step of making express reference in a footnote to the definition to the High Court judgment in *R v Falconer*.

The phrase 'underlying pathological infirmity of mind' has not been given a definitive meaning in the criminal law. The best indication of the meaning of the expression is provided by the High Court in *R v Falconer* (1990) 171 CLR 30. As previously discussed, four members of the Court referred to a presumption that an accused person has a degree of mental strength possessed of a 'normal' (at 85 per Gaudron J) or 'ordinary' (at 55 per Mason CJ, Brennan and McHugh JJ) person. If there is evidence that the accused experienced a state of mind that is not usually experienced by a normal or ordinary person, the defence of mental impairment may be raised. If there is evidence that the accused experienced a state of mind that a normal or ordinary person could have experienced in relation to external stress, then 'sane automatism' may be raised.

As previously discussed, this approach is problematic because it begs the question: who is the ordinary or normal person?

'Mental dysfunction'

Legislative reforms in the Australian Capital Territory previously led to a new term being introduced into Australian law. Section 428N of the *Crimes Act* 1900 (ACT) refers to 'mental dysfunction'. This is defined in s 428B as:

> [A] disturbance or defect, to a substantially disabling degree, of perceptual interpretation, comprehension, reasoning, learning, judgment, memory, motivation or emotion.

Although there is no reported judicial consideration of the definition in the criminal context, there has been a brief mention of the same definition that is used in the *Mental Health (Treatment and Care) Act* 1930 (ACT). In *Burnett v Mental Health Tribunal* unreported, 21 November 1997, SC of ACT, [1997] ATSC 94, p 5, Crispin J pointed out that this broad definition focuses not on the causes of the mental dysfunction, but upon their effects. It seems, however, that the provisions dealing with mental dysfunction in the Australian Capital Territory will be superseded by the defence of mental impairment set out in s 28 of the *Criminal Code* (ACT) when this comes into force on 1 January 2006 or earlier date prescribed under regulation. This provision follows that of the *Criminal Code* (Cth).

The *Oxford Textbook of Psychiatry* identifies mental illnesses by reference to the symptoms of psychiatric illnesses or syndromes: M Gelder, D Gath, R Mayou and P Cowen (eds) (3rd edn, Oxford: Oxford University Press, 1996) p 57. These symptoms are referred to as 'delusions, hallucinations, severe alterations of mood, or other major disturbances of psychological functions'. The legal definition of 'mental dysfunction' that existed in the Australian Capital Territory corresponds with this medical definition. Further, by not specifying the particular conditions required to establish the defence, the definition of mental dysfunction is perhaps the most capable of all the terms used of adapting to changing medical definitions of mental illness and diagnostic criteria as research in psychiatry progresses.

The effect of the mental impairment on understanding

To establish the defence of mental impairment, it must be proved not only that the accused suffered from some form of mental impairment at the time of the offence, but also that the mental impairment had the effect that the accused did not know or, in the Code jurisdictions, understand the nature and quality of the conduct or that the conduct was wrong.

There are two ways in which the word 'know' may be interpreted. It may mean to know in a 'verbalistic' sense: that is, in a sense akin to learning a mathematical formula by rote. The second interpretation of 'know' connotes some deeper form of understanding as in the appreciation of the effect of conduct upon other people. The actual use of the term 'understanding' rather than 'know' in the Code jurisdictions reflects this idea of a deeper form of appreciation.

In *Willgoss v The Queen* (1960) 105 CLR 295, however, the High Court held that a mere intellectual apprehension of the wrongness of the act amounts to knowledge under the *M'Naghten Rules*. The Court rejected an argument to the effect that 'knowledge' requires a moral appreciation of the effect of conduct. The High Court's decision in *Willgoss* therefore follows the narrow interpretation of the verb 'to know'.

Part of the rationale behind this decision may lie in the fact that the Court did not wish to excuse a person with an antisocial personality disorder from criminal responsibility. If knowledge is said to require a moral appreciation of the effect of an act on others, a person with an antisocial personality disorder could be viewed as not having this requisite degree of knowledge, resulting in him or her being found not guilty because of mental impairment.

There therefore appears to be some discrepancy between the Code and other jurisdictions in relation to the scope of the effect of the mental impairment on the accused's cognitive capacities.

The first alternative for the establishment of the defence of mental impairment in the Australian Capital Territory, New South Wales, the Northern Territory, South Australia, Victoria and at a federal level is to show that the accused's mental impairment had the effect that he or she did not know the nature and quality of the conduct. This is based on the first limb of the *M'Naghten Rules*, which has rarely been used.

There is some ambiguity in the case law as to the meaning of the words 'nature and quality'. The English Court of Criminal Appeal in *Codere* (1916) 12 Cr App R 21 held that 'nature and quality' refers only to the physical character of the conduct.

However, other cases suggest that 'nature and quality' not only refers to the physical character of the conduct, but also to the *significance* of the conduct itself. For example, the High Court in *Willgoss v The Queen* (1960) 105 CLR 295 at 300 stated that the nature and quality of the conduct 'refers to the physical character of the act, in this case, a capacity to know or understand the significance of the act of killing'. Similarly, in the Canadian case of *Cooper v The Queen* (1979) 51 CCC (2d) 129 Dickson J stated (at 145) that the test for appreciating the nature and quality of the conduct involved the 'estimation and understanding of the consequences of the act'.

It would seem that if the first, narrower interpretation of the words 'nature and quality' hold sway, a smaller group of people will be afforded the defence of mental impairment. This proposition is exemplified by the English case of *R v Dickie* [1984] 3 All ER 173 in which the accused was charged with arson. The accused had set fire to a wastepaper basket and sat watching a blank television screen while the fire burned the carpet and smoke filled the room. There was evidence that he was in the manic phase of manic-depressive psychosis and that he was not aware of the dangerousness of his conduct. The Court found that the accused did know the nature and quality of his actions because he knew he was setting fire to a wastepaper basket; the fact that his psychosis prevented him from appreciating the dangerousness of his conduct was deemed irrelevant.

The Queensland and Western Australian Criminal Codes avoid using the words 'nature and quality' and instead refer to the capacity to understand what the accused is doing. This appears to follow the broader approach to the question set out in *Willgoss*. Section 16(1)(a)(i) of the Tasmanian *Criminal Code* refers to the capacity to understand the 'physical character of the act or omission'. This may reflect the narrower approach set out in *Codere*.

In practice, this branch of the defence is rarely used, rendering this discussion largely semantic.

The second alternative for the establishment of the defence of mental impairment is to show that the accused did not know that the conduct was wrong or, in Queensland, Tasmania and Western Australia, that he or she ought not do the act or omission. Again, this is based upon the *M'Naghten Rules* and, in particular, Dixon J's interpretation of the term 'wrong' in *R v Porter* (1933) 55 CLR 182 at 190: 'What is meant by wrong is wrong having regard to the everyday standards of reasonable people…[T]he main question…is whether…[the accused] was disabled from knowing that it was a wrong act to commit in the sense that ordinary reasonable men understand right and wrong and that he [or she] was disabled from considering with some degree of composure and reason what he [or she] was doing and its wrongness.'

In the Victorian legislation, the *Criminal Code* (Cth), and the *Criminal Code* (NT), these words have now been summarised to read 'he or she could not reason with a moderate degree of sense and composure about whether the conduct, as perceived by reasonable people, was wrong': *Criminal Code* (Cth) s 7.3(1)(b); *Criminal Code* (NT) s 43C(b); *Crimes (Mental Impairment and Unfitness to be Tried) Act* 1997 (Vic) s 20(1)(b).

This interpretation of 'wrong' makes it clear that there is more than simply a legal component to the term. It is significant in fact situations such as that of *R v Hadfield* (1800) 27 St Tr 1281. As previously mentioned, in that case, the accused attempted to kill King George III. He was motivated by the belief that he was destined, by dying, to save the world. He knew that killing was contrary to law and he therefore shot at the king in order to be hanged. Knowledge of the illegality of the act was his very reason for doing it. Under Dixon J's interpretation of the word 'wrong', a person in Hadfield's position would be found not criminally responsible, whereas if it only means contrary to law, a person in Hadfield's position would not be afforded a defence of mental impairment.

The effect of the mental impairment on volition

The Code jurisdictions, South Australia, and, in the future, the Australian Capital Territory, include a third alternative to the establishment of the defence of mental impairment. These jurisdictions refer to the capacity or ability to control the accused's conduct or actions. Section 16(1)(b) of the Tasmanian *Criminal Code* is a little different in referring to whether or not the act or omission was done or made 'under an impulse which [the accused] was in substance deprived of any power to resist'. Section 7.3(1)(c) of the *Criminal Code* (Cth) also includes a 'volitional' component.

There have been two ways in which the capacity to control one's conduct can be interpreted. One way is to see it as broadening the defence considerably so that it covers those who know that they ought not do the act but are unable to resist an impulse to act. This was referred to by McMillan J in *R v Moore* (1908) 10 WALR 64 (at 66) as follows:

> This section deals with the defence of insanity, and it shows in what cases persons who would otherwise be responsible for their acts are free from responsibility because they are insane. It treats as insane certain persons who under the old law would not have been treated as insane. It accepts the medical theory of uncontrollable impulse, and treats people who are insane to the extent that they have not the capacity to control their actions, whether from mental disease or natural mental infirmity, as being persons who are irresponsible.

This notion of 'uncontrollable impulse' is reflected in the wording of the Tasmanian provision and is also reflected in *Wray v The King* (1930) 33 WALR 67 at 68–9.

In Victoria and New South Wales and, currently, in the Australian Capital Territory, the incapacity to control conduct can be taken into account in assessing whether or not the accused knew that the conduct was wrong. As Dixon J explained in *Sodeman v The Queen* (1952) 86 CLR 358 (at 215): '[I]t is important to bear steadily in mind that if through disorder of the faculties a prisoner is incapable of controlling his [or her] relevant acts, this may afford the strongest reason for supposing that he [or she] is incapable of forming a judgment that they are wrong, and in some cases even of understanding their nature.'

In practice, the volitional arm of the defence of mental impairment has been used very rarely in the Australian jurisdictions in which it exists. The rarity of the use of the volitional component may be explained in part because the accused's lack of capacity to control his or her actions must be a result of a 'mental disease' or the like which has not in the past been interpreted to include personality disorders or impulse-control disorders. Where the issue has been raised, its lack of success may be due to the fact that 'it might be perceived as an "easy out" for persons who are seeking an excuse for yielding to temptation': EA Tollefson and B Starkman, *Mental Disorder in Criminal Proceedings* (Toronto: Carswell, 1993) p 41.

Critique

There is currently some confusion as to the types of mental impairment that will form the basis for the defence of mental impairment. The evidence of the psychiatrists given in *Chayna*'s case shows how diagnoses can differ substantially. Current legal definitions of 'disease of the mind' or 'mental illness' seem to be too far away from psychiatric conceptions of mental illness as a 'failure of reality testing'.

There therefore needs to be adequate guidance as to what constitutes mental impairment for the purpose of the defence in order to avoid leaving the matter entirely open to psychiatric and psychological evidence as to which conditions will fall within the defence. It would not seem to be impossible to develop a statutory definition of mental impairment that reflects modern psychiatric thinking to give guidance to a jury determining whether or not mental impairment existed at the time of the killing. The broad definition set out in s 428B of the *Crimes Act* 1900 (ACT) appears to be an adequate starting point in this regard. While such a definition may encompass a wider range of forms of mental impairment than is currently the case, it must be kept in mind that there is another step in the process of proving the defence. The mental impairment must have affected the person's understanding of his or her actions or capacity to control his or her conduct.

This then leads to the main point of contention concerning the defence of mental impairment. How broad should it be? The focus purely on reasoning or cognitive processes in the traditional *M'Naghten Rules* has been criticised as too narrow. The Murray Report, *The Criminal Code: A General Review*, in Western Australia (1983) and the O'Regan Reports on the *Criminal Code* in Queensland (Criminal Code Review Committee, *Report of the Criminal Code Review Committee to the Attorney-General*, Interim Report (1991) and Final Report (June 1992)) recommended retention of the additional volitional component in the defence in those states. The reasoning behind this was that limiting the defence of mental impairment to those whose reasoning processes are affected means that many people who should be afforded a defence are not. Some mental disorders may lead to an inability to control behaviour. For example, in *Wray v The King* (1930) 33 WALR 67, the accused was charged with the murder of a taxi driver. There was uncontradicted medical evidence that the accused was suffering from dementia praecox, which deprived him of the capacity to control his actions. In the *Diagnostic and Statistical Manual of Mental Disorders* (4th edn revised, Washington, DC: American Psychiatric Association, 1994) a chapter is devoted to 'impulse-control disorders'. These include kleptomania, which is characterised by the recurrent failure to resist impulses to steal objects; pyromania, which is characterised by a pattern of setting fires for pleasure, gratification, or relief of tension; and pathological gambling. Also included as a mental disorder is 'intermittent explosive disorder', which is characterised by episodes of failure to resist aggressive impulses that result in serious assaults or destruction of property. Should such disorders fall within a defence of mental impairment?

There are a number of specific criticisms that may be aimed at excusing persons from criminal responsibility on the basis of loss of control.

First, the problem with loss of control tests in general is that it is impossible to devise an objectively verifiable test to determine when an accused could not control his or her conduct and when he or she would not: AS Goldstein, *The Insanity Defense* (New Haven, CT: Yale University Press, 1967) pp 67–8. Certainly it can be argued that the question raised is really not so different from the questions of degree that arise throughout the law. It is impossible to draw absolute lines when considering other legal concepts such as 'intention' or 'knowledge' or 'negligence'.

However, there remains a further problem with loss of control tests and that is that such tests are based on an abandoned system of faculty psychology, which divided the mind into separate and unrelated compartments.

According to James Chaplin's *Dictionary of Psychology* (2nd edn, New York: Dell, 1982), 'faculty psychology' refers to 'the discredited doctrine that the mind is constituted of a number of powers or agencies, such as intellect, will, judgment and attentiveness, which produce mental activities' (p 174). While introductory psychology texts may still separate 'cognition' from 'emotion', much contemporary research is based on an holistic model that explores the interaction between feelings and thought processes. According to this holistic model, there can be no serious impairment of one mental function without some form of impairment of the others. For example, modern psychological research implies that in 'complex emotional experiences, such as pride, disappointment, jealousy, or contempt, cognitive appraisal must play a role': RL Atkinson, RC Atkinson, EE Smith and DJ Bern, *Introduction to Psychology* (10th edn, Fort Worth: Harcourt Brace Jovanovich, 1990) p 412.

The law relating to mental impairment stems from the notion that an individual must possess the ability to reason about the significance of conduct in order for the criminal law to apply. Loss of control tests assume that a person can know that what he or she is doing is wrong, yet be unable to control his or her actions. In reality, such tests assume that cognition remains completely unaffected, and this contradicts not only the holistic standpoint of modern psychology but also the view that the ability to reason plays an essential part in controlling conduct. Jerome Hall writes in 'Mental Disease and Criminal Responsibility' (1958) 33

Indiana Law Journal 212–25 at 223: 'What the proponents of "irresistible impulse" are in effect telling us is that the most distinctive and potent function on earth— human understanding in its full amplitude—can be normal but nonetheless impotent even as regards killing or raping or robbing. That is the thesis they are advancing and do not forget that. It can only mean that intelligence is unrelated to the control of human conduct.'

It appears to be more logical from a psychological viewpoint to follow the approach of Dixon J in *Sodeman*'s case and simply take into account an incapacity to control conduct as evidence that the accused did not know that what he or she was doing was wrong. If knowledge of wrongfulness is defined as the ability of a person to reason 'with a moderate degree of sense and composure', it is not necessary to prove the *complete* absence of a person's ability to reason before that person can be excused from criminal responsibility. This liberalises the strict cognitive approach of the traditional *M'Naghten Rules*, while preventing those who are able to reason about their conduct from being so excused. Such a test sits far more readily with traditional concepts of criminal responsibility than does a strict test of volition.

It was argued in the previous sections that a broad defence of mental impairment could encompass conditions such as dissociation and intoxication because they affect a person's cognitive processes. Because of the conceptual difficulties with a volitional component of a defence, it is not necessary to broaden such a defence further to include a separate volitional arm. The primary focus of a defence of mental impairment should return to the accused's ability to reason about his or her actions.

Diminished responsibility

Background

In the case of Andre Chayna set out at the beginning of the chapter, the Court of Criminal Appeal of New South Wales upheld the accused's appeal against conviction and substituted a verdict of manslaughter: (1993) 66 A Crim R 178. This was on the basis that there was sufficient evidence to make out the defence of diminished responsibility. This defence is available in the Australian Capital Territory, New South Wales, the Northern Territory and Queensland: *Crimes Act* 1900 (ACT) s 14; *Crimes Act* 1900 (NSW) s 23A ; *Criminal Code* (NT) s 37; *Criminal Code* (Qld) s 304A. There is no mention of the defence in the current version of the *Criminal Code* (ACT), but it could possibly be included in a future Chapter dealing with Homicide offences. It is unclear whether the legislature of the Australian Capital Territory has purposefully omitted this defence. For the purposes of this section we will refer to the defence currently set out in the *Crimes Act* 1900 (ACT).

As with the defence of provocation, diminished responsibility serves to reduce a charge of murder to manslaughter. However, unlike provocation, but like the defence of mental impairment, the accused bears the burden of proof in relation to the defence of diminished responsibility. The standard of proof is on the balance of probabilities.

Diminished responsibility is a more limited defence than that of mental impairment in that it only relates to reducing murder to manslaughter, whereas the defence of mental impairment is a general defence to all serious crimes. The outcome of the two defences also differs. If a person is found not guilty because of mental impairment, the accused may be released unconditionally or be subject to a custodial or non-custodial supervision order. If diminished responsibility is successful, there is the imposition of a sentence for manslaughter of, for example in New South Wales, up to 25 years' imprisonment. The benefit for someone like Andre Chayna in raising diminished responsibility is that the time for imprisonment is fixed. Raising the defence of mental impairment still brings with it the risk of an indefinite custodial supervision order.

Diminished responsibility began as a plea in mitigation in the Scottish courts in the mid-eighteenth century as a way of dealing with 'mental weakness' falling short of insanity and as a way of avoiding the death penalty. Its origins can be found in the seventeenth-century development of 'partial insanity', which operated to lessen and moderate the punishments of those whose reason was partially affected.

Diminished responsibility became a partial defence to murder in the mid-nineteenth-century case of *HM Advocate v Dingwall* (1867) 5 Irvine 446 and was later enacted in the UK under s 2 of the *Homicide Act* 1957 (UK). In 1974, diminished responsibility was introduced in New South Wales as a way of avoiding a mandatory life sentence for murder. Its rationale is therefore strongly rooted in the need for an alternative punishment and disposition to that of death, life imprisonment or indefinite detention in a psychiatric institution. This practical basis to the defence has had the consequence that there have been many criticisms made of its content. How can responsibility be diminished when the law deals in absolutes? Surely an accused is responsible or not for his or her actions. These criticisms will be explored after the current law is set out.

The current law

Despite differences in the wording of the defence in the four Australian jurisdictions, the defence of diminished responsibility consists of three elements:
- the accused must have been suffering from an 'abnormality of mind';
- the abnormality of mind must have arisen from a specified cause; and
- the abnormality of mind must have substantially impaired the accused's capacity to
  - understand his or her actions;
  - know that he or she ought not to do the act; or
  - control his or her actions.

Abnormality of mind

The term 'abnormality of mind' has no medical foundation, but has been taken to cover a broad range of impairment, far broader than currently allowed for the defence of mental impairment. Lord Parker CJ in *R v Byrne* [1960] 2 QB 396 (at 403) defined this term as follows:

> A state of mind so different from that of ordinary human beings that a reasonable [person] would term it abnormal. It appears...to be wide enough to cover the mind's activities in all its aspects, not only the perception of physical acts and matters, and the ability to form a rational judgment as to whether an act is right or wrong, but also the ability to exercise will-power to control physical acts in accordance with that rational judgment.

In consultations with the New South Wales Law Reform Commission, several psychiatrists pointed out that almost everyone who kills could be said to be suffering from an 'abnormality of mind': New South Wales Law Reform Commission, *Partial Defences to Murder: Diminished Responsibility*, Report No 82 (May 1997) p 45.

Cause of the abnormality of mind

The requirement that the abnormality arise from a specified cause attempts to limit the term to some degree. In the Australian Capital Territory, the Northern Territory and Queensland, the abnormality must arise from a condition of arrested or retarded development of mind, any inherent cause or be induced by disease or illness: *Crimes Act* 1900 (ACT) s 14(1); *Criminal Code* (NT) s 1; *Criminal Code* (Qld) s 304A. These causal factors appear designed to exclude external environmental influences or stresses.

The New South Wales Law Reform Commission considered the traditional causes were 'quite arbitrary and may generate a high level of complexity and confusion in relation to the expert evidence which is led in diminished responsibility cases': New South Wales Law Reform Commission, *Partial Defences to Murder: Diminished Responsibility*, Report No 82 (May 1997) p 49. Their proposal, which has now been enacted in s 23A of the *Crimes Act* (NSW) is that an abnormality of mind must arise from an 'underlying condition', which is defined in s 23A(8) as a pre-existing mental or physiological condition, other than a condition of a transitory kind.

The New South Wales Law Reform Commission explained the rationale for this terminology as follows (at 56):

> The term 'arising from an underlying condition' is intended to link the defence to a notion of a pre-existing impairment requiring proof by way of expert evidence, which impairment is of a more permanent nature than a simply temporary state of heightened emotions. This does not mean that the condition must be shown to be permanent. It simply requires that the condition be more than of

an ephemeral or transitory nature. So, for example, a severe depressive illness which is curable would still be considered to come within the definition of 'underlying condition', notwithstanding that it is not permanent. On the other hand, a transitory disturbance of mind brought about by heightened emotions, such as extreme anger in typical cases of 'road rage', would be excluded from the definition of 'underlying condition' and therefore could not form the basis of a plea of diminished responsibility.

Examples of cases where diminished responsibility has been raised include where the accused had severe depression, antisocial personality disorder or an intellectual disability: New South Wales Law Reform Commission, *Partial Defences to Murder: Diminished Responsibility*, Report No 82 (May 1997) para 3.9.

Effect of the abnormality of mind

The abnormality of mind must have substantially impaired the accused's capacity to understand what he or she was doing, the wrongness of the act or the ability to control his or her actions. In the old parlance, the term used was 'mental responsibility', a term still used in the Australian Capital Territory: *Crimes Act* 1900 (ACT) s 14(1); *Crimes Act* 1900 s 23A(8); *Criminal Code* (NT) s 37; *Criminal Code* (Qld) s 304A. The term 'mental responsibility' has been criticised as having no medical validity.

There has been some case law in relation to what is meant by 'substantially impaired'. In *R v Byrne* [1960] 2 QB 396 Lord Parker CJ (at 404) in delivering the judgment of the Court stated that substantial impairment was a matter of degree and that it signified more than 'some impairment'. In *R v Simcox* [1964] Crim LR 402 the Court of Criminal Appeal stated (at 403): 'It is a matter for the jury approaching the matter in a broad commonsense way and taking into consideration all the circumstances, not only the medical evidence but the man's history, conduct, and the whole circumstances of the case.'

In *R v Lloyd* [1967] 1 QB 175 the Court of Criminal Appeal stated (at 176) that the jury should be directed that substantial 'does not mean total...[but at] the other end of the scale substantial does not mean trivial or minimal'.

In the case of Andre Chayna, the Court of Criminal Appeal substituted manslaughter for the murder verdict because of there being evidence that Chayna was suffering from an abnormality of mind caused by depression. They found that the trial judge had misdirected the jury on this point. Gleeson CJ stated that if the proper direction had been given to the jury:

> the jury could not reasonably have failed to conclude that at the time of all three killings the appellant was suffering from abnormality of the mind caused by major depressive illness, and that on that account her responsibility for her acts was substantially impaired. I find this conclusion virtually irresistible in relation to the killing of the two children, but I believe it also follows in relation to the killing of the sister-in-law: (1993) 66 A Crim R 178 at 189.

A serious depressive illness could be said to be an 'inherent cause' of the abnormality of mind or 'underlying condition' under the new terminology in New South Wales.

Critique

In New South Wales, the Law Reform Commission considered some of the criticisms with the defence of diminished responsibility, but recommended its retention and set out recommended amendments: Report No 82, *Partial Defences to Murder: Diminished Responsibility* (May 1997). These were largely echoed in the *Crimes Amendment (Diminished Responsibility) Act* 1997 (NSW). In comparison, the Law Reform Commission of Victoria considered and rejected the possibility of enacting the defence in Victoria in 1991: *Mental Malfunction and Criminal Responsibility,* Report No 34 (Melbourne: LRVC, 1990) p 53 and more recently, the MCCOC has recommended its abolition: *Chapter 5, Fatal Offences Against the Person,* Discussion Paper (June 1998) p 129.

A number of arguments have been presented in favour of retaining such a defence. The first is that diminished responsibility reflects a valid distinction between being fully and partially culpable for the death of another. The gap between full culpability and the defence of mental impairment is too extreme. Diminished responsibility enables a midway point on the spectrum of culpability. It enables the jury to recognise a mixture of some blameworthiness and some ground for excuse.

It also provides a way for avoiding the defence of mental impairment that brings with it the possibility of indefinite detention in a psychiatric institution. The defence of diminished responsibility developed partly to compensate for the narrow cognitive focus of the defence of mental impairment as well as to enable an accused to be given a defined sentence for manslaughter. It may also afford a defence to women who kill their abusive partners where the woman is suffering depression or battered woman syndrome.

The arguments in favour of the abolition of this defence are, however, persuasive. There are serious conceptual difficulties with this defence. Diminished responsibility is in essence an artificial concept aimed at lessening the severity of punishment, without going so far as to completely acquit the accused. There are profound difficulties with the concept of being partially but not wholly criminally responsible, but apart from that, when the concept is explored more fully, it appears that the defence is not about responsibility at all.

There are two questions that arise in the course of a criminal trial. First, was the accused responsible for his or her actions? Secondly, what form should the disposition order take? The defence of diminished responsibility blurs these two questions. In fact, the primary emphasis seems to be on the question of disposition rather than on a finding of responsibility. In reality, the defence exists *only* where the essential elements of murder are present. In truth, it is the sentence that is being *diminished* rather than the accused's responsibility.

In relation to the elements of the defence, because of the vagueness of the concept of 'abnormality of mind' there is a difficulty in clearly defining the scope and operation of diminished responsibility. This has led to 'a dichotomy of approaches' in attempting to distinguish this defence from that of the defence of mental impairment: MCCOC, *Chapter 5, Fatal Offences Against the Person*, Discussion Paper (June 1998) p 123. The definition of abnormality of mind means that those with personality disorders or an inability to control their conduct can be afforded a defence. It wrongly allows people to avoid murder convictions where they know what they are doing and intend to kill.

There are also practical problems associated with expert testimony relating to diminished responsibility. These include the problems with conflicting evidence and the possibility of experts for hire as well as the tendency of experts to answer the ultimate issue as to the effect of the abnormality of mind, which is really a matter for the jury to decide: B McSherry, 'Expert Testimony and the Effects of Mental Impairment: Reviving the Ultimate Issue Rule?' (2001) 24 *International Journal of Law and Psychiatry* 13–21. In the case of Andre Chayna (1993) 66 A Crim R 178 at 189 Gleeson CJ made the following comment about the defence then operating in New South Wales: 'The variety of psychiatric opinion with which the jury was confronted strongly suggests that the operation of s 23A of the *Crimes Act* 1900 (NSW) depends upon concepts which medical experts find at least ambiguous and, perhaps, unscientific.'

Psychiatrists and psychologists must of necessity rely on what the accused says. If the term abnormality of mind is given a broad definition as has occurred in the past, there is a danger that conditions may be fabricated, much more so than in the case of the defence of mental impairment.

The New South Wales Law Reform Commission made recommendations about reformulating the defence, most of which are now incorporated into s 23A of the *Crimes Act* 1900 (NSW). This now reads as follows:

> (1) A person who would otherwise be guilty of murder is not to be convicted of murder if:
> (a) at the time of the acts or omissions causing the death concerned, the person's capacity to understand events, or to judge whether the person's actions were right or wrong, or to control himself or herself, was substantially impaired by an abnormality of mind arising from an underlying condition, and
> (b) the impairment was so substantial as to warrant liability for murder being reduced to manslaughter.
>
> ....
>
> (8) In this section:
> *Underlying condition* means a pre-existing mental or physiological condition, other than a condition of a transitory kind.

The New South Wales Law Reform Commission recommended that the defence refer to an 'abnormality of mental functioning arising from an underlying condition': New South Wales Law Reform Commission, Report No 82, *Partial Defences to Murder: Diminished Responsibility* (May 1997) p 51. This element was proposed with the assistance of mental health professionals who wanted to overcome confusion about what is meant by 'mind'. The New South Wales legislature, however, decided to retain the term 'abnormality of mind' presumably because, despite not being a medical term, it has worked relatively well in practice: S Yeo, 'Reformulating Diminished Responsibility: Learning from the New South Wales Experience' (1999) 20 *Singapore Law Review* 159–76 at 169.

The term 'underlying condition' was added because the New South Wales Law Reform Commission noted that expert witnesses often experienced difficulty in nominating a cause of the abnormality of mind and it was difficult to develop workable distinctions between the three causes: p 48, para 3.39. By replacing the three causes with the expression 'underlying condition', the Commission sought to simplify the aetiology of the abnormality of mind.

The reformulated defence requires that not only must there be an abnormality of mind in existence, that abnormality must have affected the person's capacity to understand events, judge whether the person's actions were right or wrong or control him or herself. This puts into statutory form what Lord Parker CJ stated in *R v Byrne* [1960] 2 QB 396 at 403 concerning the effect of an abnormality of mind. The addition of a volitional component—the inability to control conduct—can be criticised in the same manner as the volitional component in the defence of mental impairment. As explored above, it is impossible to know when a person is incapable of controlling conduct and when he or she chooses not to.

Finally, the New South Wales Law Reform Commission recommended abandoning the term 'mental responsibility' in favour of assessing whether the person's capacity was so substantially impaired as to warrant reducing murder to manslaughter. This was altered slightly by the legislature to an assessment of impairment of capacity *and* whether the impairment was so substantial as to warrant reducing murder to manslaughter. This requirement is designed to focus the jury's attention on the 'essentially moral choice which they are required to make': p 51, para 3.42.

The reformulated defence may be more workable than its predecessor. However, the basic conceptual difficulties with the defence still remain. The better approach may be to concentrate on reformulating the defence of mental impairment and enacting more flexible dispositional options rather than continuing with such a flawed defence.

Infanticide

Background

Maryanne Cooper's childhood was marked by abuse and physical violence. At the age of 12, she was made a state ward and lived for some time in state-run institutions or in foster homes. From about the age of 15, she started experiencing auditory hallucinations and was subsequently diagnosed with severe depression. When she was 19, she gave birth to Samantha and when she was 20, to Chloe. The father of the two girls physically abused Maryanne and at one point she fled to a women's refuge, then stayed with members of the Salvation Army before moving to a Housing Commission flat.

Within three months of Chloe's birth, Maryanne began to experience more intense auditory hallucinations with the voices telling her that she was not a good mother and that Chloe did not love her. When Chloe was six months old, Maryanne put her hand over the baby's mouth and nose and held it there until the baby stopped breathing. Maryanne pleaded guilty to infanticide and was put on a good behaviour bond for four years: *R v Maryanne Jane Cooper* unreported, 31 August 2001, SC of NSW, Simpson J, [2001] NSWSC 769.

Maryanne Cooper may have raised the defence of mental impairment, but instead chose to plead guilty to infanticide. Infanticide is unique in that it operates in Victoria and New South Wales as both an offence as well as a partial defence. This means that a woman can be either charged with or plead guilty to the offence of infanticide or, if she is charged with murder, she may raise evidence to reduce murder to the lesser offence of infanticide: *Crimes Act* 1958 (Vic) s 6(1); *Crimes Act* 1900 (NSW) s 22A. If successful as a partial defence, the woman will be sentenced as if she had been found guilty of manslaughter. Infanticide also operates in Tasmania and Western Australia, but only as an offence: *Criminal Code* (Tas) s 165A; *Criminal Code* (WA) s 287A. There is no mention of infanticide in the current version of the *Criminal Code* (ACT).

The practice of infanticide has had a long and controversial history. In the time of Plato and Aristotle, the exposure of weak and deformed infants was generally accepted and occasionally encouraged: M Tooley, *Abortion and Infanticide* (Oxford: Clarendon Press, 1983) p 316; Laila Williamson, 'Infanticide: An Anthropological Analysis' in Marvin Kohl (ed), *Infanticide and the Value of Life* (New York: Prometheus Books, 1978) pp 61–75 at 61. The general acceptance of infanticide in many different cultures appears to be related to the unavailability or ineffectiveness of contraception, and some anthropologists have viewed it as a widely used method of population control: Susan Scrimshaw, 'Infanticide in Human Populations: Societal and Individual Concerns' in Glenn Hausfater and Sarah Blaffer Hardy (eds), *Infanticide: Comparative and Evolutionary Perspectives* (New York: Aldue Publishing Co, 1984) p 440. It was not until the seventeenth century that an Act was passed in England making it an offence to conceal the death of an illegitimate child: *An Act to Prevent the Destroying and Murthering of Bastard Children* 21 James 1 c 27 (1624). This was repealed in 1803 (*Lord Ellenborough's Act* 42 Geo 3 c 58) and infanticide was put on the same footing as homicide in that the prosecution had to prove that the child had been born alive and that someone, usually the mother, had killed it. Concealment of birth was subsequently made a separate offence: *Offences Against the Person Act 1828* (UK) s XIV. It was not until 1922 that the *Infanticide Act* (UK) was passed, enabling the reduction of murder to manslaughter.

During the twentieth century, a medical rationale developed as the basis for infanticide. Infanticide was seen as less than murder because the mother's mental state was disturbed due to the effects of childbirth or lactation. In 1922, the defence of infanticide was only available to a woman who had caused the death of her 'newly born' child. The *Infanticide Act* 1938 (UK) superseded the 1922 Act. It changed the words 'newly born' to 'under the age of 12 months'. The Australian provisions that were enacted in the twentieth century followed the English model quite closely.

It is unclear whether or not the burden of proof is on the accused to prove the elements of the defence on the balance of probabilities or on the prosecution to disprove any of the elements beyond reasonable doubt. The Law Reform Commission of Victoria has recommended that the burden of disproving the defence of infanticide should rest on the prosecution: Law Reform Commission of Victoria, *Mental Malfunction and Criminal Responsibility*, Report No 34 (Melbourne: LRCV, 1990) Recommendation 28.

The current law

As explored in Chapter 3, infanticide may operate as an offence as well as a defence in Victoria and New South Wales. For infanticide to be successful as a partial defence, it must be shown that:
- The accused was the natural mother of the victim. Adoptive mothers, fathers and other carers are excluded: *Crimes Act* 1900 (NSW) s 22A(1), (2); *Criminal Code* (Tas) s 165A; *Crimes Act* 1958 (Vic) s 6(1), (2); *Criminal Code* (WA) s 281A(1); and
- The victim must be less than 12 months old: *Crimes Act* 1900 (NSW) s 22A(1), (2); *Criminal Code* (Tas) s 165A; *Crimes Act* 1958 (Vic) s 6(1), (2); *Criminal Code* (WA) s 281A(2).

At the time of the killing, the accused's state of mind must also have been disturbed by reason of childbirth or, in the relevant jurisdictions apart from Tasmania, the effect of lactation: *Crimes Act* 1900 (NSW) s 22A(1), (2); *Criminal Code* (Tas) s 165A; *Crimes Act* 1958 (Vic) s 6(1), (2); *Criminal Code* (WA) s 281A(1).

Critique

The historical motivation for infanticide is problematic. Many argue that it was intended to provide a more lenient disposition in recognition of the perceived special needs of, and pressures on, new mothers. Others, however, suggest that it was passed in order to obtain convictions against women who were thought to be securing acquittals or lenient treatment from juries under the existing law, particularly where it carried the death penalty: M Jackson (ed), *Infanticide* (Aldershot: Ashgate, 2002); R Lansdowne, 'Infanticide: Psychiatrists in the Plea Bargaining

Process' (1990) 16 *Monash University Law Review* 41–63; K Laster, 'Infanticide: A Litmus Test for Feminist Criminological Theory' (1989) 22 *Australian and New Zealand Journal of Criminology* 151–66; B McSherry, 'The Return of the Raging Hormones Theory: Premenstrual Syndrome, Postpartum Disorders and Criminal Responsibility' (1993) 15 *Sydney Law Review* 292–316; A Wilczynski, *Child Homicide* (London: Greenwich Medical Media, 1997); C Alder and J Baker, 'Maternal Filicide: More than one story to be told' (1997) 9(2) *Women and Criminal Justice* 15–39.

If Mary-Anne Cooper had killed her older daughter, she would not have been able to plead guilty to infanticide. The defence/offence of infanticide has therefore been criticised as being arbitrary in its operation and too much based on a medical explanation of child killing. The New South Wales Law Reform Commission recommended in 1997 that infanticide be abolished: New South Wales Law Reform Commission, *Partial Defences to Murder: Provocation and Infanticide*, Report No 83 (October 1997) p 103, para 3.7. The MCCOC has also recommended that there be no partial defence or special offence of infanticide: *Chapter 5, Fatal Offences Against the Person*, Discussion Paper (June 1998) p 139. However, the Law Reform Commission of Victoria has previously recommended its retention: Law Reform Commission of Victoria, *Mental Malfunction and Criminal Responsibility*, Report No 34 (Melbourne: LRCV, 1990) Recommendation 27.

Some of the arguments that have been advanced in favour of retaining the defence of infanticide centre around the need to recognise the particular difficulties that mothers may face following childbirth. Although the defence is couched in medical terms, it is one way of enabling the social and psychological stresses of child-rearing to be taken into account. Some studies suggest that infanticide may be pleaded where it is not technically available: R Lansdowne, 'Infanticide: Psychiatrists in the Plea Bargaining Process' (1990) 16 *Monash University Law Review* 41–63.

The unusual characteristic of having infanticide as an offence and defence in Victoria and New South Wales also carries with it certain procedural advantages. As shown by the case of Maryanne Cooper, it can operate to allow the accused to avoid a murder charge and the pressures associated with a trial for murder.

Finally, while infanticide is on the same sentencing scale as manslaughter, the New South Wales Law Reform Commission has pointed out that a conviction for infanticide 'ensures the imposition of a more lenient sentence': New South Wales Law Reform Commission, *Partial Defences to Murder: Provocation and Infanticide*, Report No 83 (October 1997) para 3.45, p 125. It can be argued that there should be such leniency available for women who kill their young children because there are usually tragic circumstances surrounding such killings.

In contrast, a number of arguments have been advanced in favour of the abolition of the defence of infanticide. First, it is based on an uncertain medical foundation that links women's biology to criminal responsibility. There is no causal link between the effect of lactation and a psychiatric disturbance of the mind. If there is severe depression or psychosis following childbirth, then an accused such as Maryanne Cooper could use the defence of mental impairment.

As currently formulated, infanticide is a medically unsound concept. There is no evidence that lactation or the giving of birth 'disturbs the balance' of a mother's mind. A small number of women do suffer severe post-natal depression, where infanticide would certainly be relevant if they killed the child, but the killings of young children more commonly occur in the context of stresses and pressures of parenthood, together with lack of support from partners and the community, exhaustion or illness: A Wilczynski, *Child Homicide* (London: Greenwich Medical Media, 1997).

Secondly, women who kill children more often do so because of the social and psychological stresses of child-raising rather than the effect of childbirth. The defence of infanticide ignores this and may force mental health professionals to distort their diagnoses in order to conform with the requirements of the legislation: R Lansdowne, 'Infanticide: Psychiatrists in the Plea Bargaining Process' (1990) 16 *Monash University Law Review* 41–63 at 54.

Thirdly, the defence of infanticide reflects an outdated and paternalistic view of women being in danger of mental instability due to childbirth: B McSherry, 'The Return of the Raging Hormones Theory: Premenstrual Syndrome, Postpartum Disorders and Criminal Responsibility' (1993) 15 *Sydney Law Review* 292–316. This suggests that women are inherently weak and not responsible for their actions and the current formulation of the defence deflects attention away from the structural problems of mothering and onto the individual woman's alleged inadequacies.

Finally, because the defence is limited to the killing of children under the age of 12 months, it may lead to arbitrary results. If Maryanne Cooper had killed her eldest child, she could not have pleaded guilty to infanticide because the child was aged over 12 months. An adoptive mother or a primary carer of a child other than the natural mother also cannot raise this defence.

As stated above, both the New South Wales Law Reform Commission and the MCCOC have recommended the abolition of infanticide as both a defence and offence. A different approach would be to consider substantially widening the offence/defence. If it is accepted that infanticide operates to provide a sympathetic way of treating women who kill their children, the question arises as to why the reduced offence should apply only to the killing of the accused woman's newborn child. The effects of isolation and depression may (and do) lead to killings of older children too. A further question might be why should the offence/defence be limited to mothers? If it is about recognising the possible pressures of parenthood or primary care where the person is left without support during a stressful and difficult time, rather than a necessarily biologically female 'condition'—though one still much more frequently experienced by women in this society—why should it not be available also to fathers and other carers? Would such an extension be acceptable? Or would it be seen as condoning the abuse of children by adults who, it could be argued, have a responsibility to control themselves in the interests of the vulnerable child entrusted to them?

On balance, the definition of the current offence/defence cannot be supported and the law may not be ready to allow a defence based on social conditions for fear that this may 'open the floodgates'. It may be better to allow women such as Maryanne Cooper to raise a reformulated defence of mental impairment with flexible disposition options than to continue with a medically unsound defence.

Conclusion

The current model of criminal responsibility views serious offences as being constituted by a physical and a fault element minus a defence. In this model there is no need to provide a rationale for defences as negating voluntary conduct or intention or other fault element because they exist in a separate realm of their own.

The complexities of the current legal situation in relation to mental impairment and criminal responsibility stem largely from the admissibility of evidence of mental impairment to negate voluntariness and intention.

There are two fundamental questions that need to be addressed in considering mental disorder and criminal responsibility. The first question is whether or not the accused should be found criminally responsible if he or she was suffering from a form of mental impairment at the time of the crime. The fundamental principle of criminal law is that individuals must only be punished if they are able to reason for criminal actions that are 'willed' in some way. Surely if the accused's ability to reason was substantially impaired because of some form of mental disorder, whatever the cause, he or she should not be found criminally responsible.

Interestingly, section 29 of the *Criminal Code* (ACT) sets out that mental impairment cannot be relied on to deny voluntariness or the existence of a fault element. When this section comes into operation, it will be interesting to see whether this clarifies the law in this area. An alternative approach to simplifying the law is to have mental impairment considered only as the basis for a separate defence such as: 'A person is not criminally responsible for an offence if he or she was suffering from a mental disorder at the time of the commission of the offence such that his or her ability to reason was substantially impaired.'

Having such a broad defence would not only avoid the difficulties associated with showing the accused's act were involuntary or unintentional, it could also justify the abolition of the flawed defences of diminished responsibility and infanticide.

There is then a separate question that arises as to what should happen to someone who has caused the death or injury of another while suffering from some form of mental disorder. If there is evidence that the individual concerned was unaware that a dissociative state, for example, would occur, then perhaps an absolute discharge would be appropriate.

It is clear that there is no easy solution to the problems posed by this difficult area of the law. However, a unifying test of criminal responsibility for those suffering from mental impairment at the time of committing a crime may be preferable to using evidence of mental impairment to negate voluntariness or intention. Providing there are flexible dispositional options including absolute discharge for those found not criminally responsible, a broad defence of mental impairment may help simplify the law and bring it into line with current psychological theories.

CHAPTER 12

Defences based on external pressures

Introduction

Mark Hinchcliffe was a member of a motorcycle gang called the Coffin Cheaters. His wife, Jacqueline, had met him when she was 17 and was 'enthralled' by his authority. Mark assaulted her a couple of weeks after they met, and for the next 16 years subjected her to sexual abuse and beatings that included picking her up in a 'death hold' that would render her unconscious. Mark demanded she have sex with other men while he watched and he forced her to have a tattoo on her back stating 'Property of Mark Hinchcliffe'. Mark's involvement with the Coffin Cheaters eventually led to him being away quite often. Jacqueline embarked on an affair with Michael Wright. Mark found out about the affair and beat Jacqueline senseless. He then tried to extort money from Michael before turning up at Michael's work and bashing him. Mark was jailed for these assaults. Jacqueline subsequently killed Michael by firing seven shots at him when he opened the front door of his house. There was evidence from a psychologist that he believed Mark had given Jacqueline an ultimatum to kill Michael or else he would kill her. Jacqueline was convicted of murder and sentenced to 15 years' jail: N Mercer, 'Kill or Be Killed', *Age*, 18 December 2001, p 11.

The physical and fault elements for murder were clearly established on the facts of this case. Jacqueline had an intention to kill and caused Michael's death. Should she, however, have been afforded some sort of defence based on the threats and pressures placed on her throughout her relationship with Mark? This chapter deals with cases in which the physical and fault elements of a crime have been made out, but in which the accused acted in response to threats from another person (duress/marital coercion) or in order to avert dire consequences (necessity).

The defence of duress, or compulsion as it is sometimes known, serves to excuse a person from criminal responsibility where he or she has committed a criminal act because of fear produced by threats of death or grievous bodily harm. At present, in all Australian jurisdictions apart from the Northern Territory, duress would not provide a defence to an accused in Jacqueline's position since duress is not available as a defence to a charge of murder. It is, however, available as a complete defence to other serious crimes. In the Northern Territory, s 41 of the *Criminal Code* allows for murder to be reduced to manslaughter if there was coercion of such a nature as to have caused a reasonable person similarly circumstanced to have acted in the same or similar way.

A gender-specific subset of duress is 'marital coercion', which is available as a defence in South Australia, Victoria and Western Australia: *Criminal Law Consolidation Act* 1935 (SA) s 328A; *Crimes Act* 1958 (Vic) s 336; *Criminal Code* (WA) s 32. This affords a defence to criminal acts apart from murder where a married woman commits the offence under threats or pressure from her husband. Thus, if Jacqueline had merely injured Michael, the defence of marital coercion may have been open to her.

A person may also claim that he or she committed a crime because it was necessary to do so in a situation of a sudden or extraordinary emergency. The cases where necessity has been taken into account generally relate to driving offences. In *Willer* (1986) 83 Cr App R 224, the accused was acquitted of a charge of reckless driving where he claimed that it was necessary to do so to avoid serious bodily harm to himself and his passengers from a gang of youths: *Willer* (1986) 83 Cr App R 224. Similarly, it was held that necessity was available when the accused broke the road traffic offence of speeding in order to get his gravely ill son to hospital: *R v White* (1987) 9 NSWLR 427.

In comparison, necessity has not been accepted where prisoners have led evidence that they escaped from prison because they feared for their life inside it: *R v Damson* [1978] VR 536; *R v Loughnan* [1981] VR 443; *Perka et al v The Queen* (1985) 14 CCC (3d) 385; *Rogers* (1996) 86 A Crim R 542. The defence also failed where the accused made threats and placed imitation bombs in schools demanding that the principals undertake to engage in anti-nuclear activities: *Dixon-Jenkins* (1985) 14 A Crim R 372.

At common law and in Tasmania, necessity is not available to a charge of murder. The statutory defence of sudden or extraordinary emergency in the Northern Territory, Queensland and Western Australia, however, is not limited in this way.

The common law has established that defences based on external pressures cannot justify the killing of an innocent person: *Abbott v The Queen* [1977] AC 755 at 764–5 per Lord Salmon. The rationale for this is the belief that an 'ordinary' person would always choose to sacrifice his or her own life rather than kill an 'innocent' person. This can be contrasted with the defences of self-defence or provocation, where the victim either attacked the accused first or provoked an attack and thus is not viewed as 'innocent'.

On occasion, the courts in England and New Zealand have referred to 'duress of circumstances' to cover external pressures other than threats from persons: *R v Conway* [1989] 1 QB 290; *Police v Kawiti* [2000] 1 NZLR 117. This does not seem to have been the case in Australia, but there is nevertheless some confusion between that which constitutes the categories of duress and necessity. Woolf LJ referred in *R v Conway* [1989] 1 QB 290 at 297 to duress of circumstances being 'an example of necessity'. On the other hand, the New Zealand Law Commission has referred to necessity as being a species of duress: *Battered Defendants: Victims of Domestic Violence Who Offend*, Preliminary Paper 41 (August 2000) p 62, para 198.

This may have been why Woolf LJ stated in *R v Conway* [1989] 1 QB that it was not clear whether a 'general defence of necessity' exists. In Australia, however, a general defence has been recognised at common law, but there has been a requirement that the danger be of such a nature as to exert immense pressure on the person concerned because of its imminence, suddenness or gravity: *R v Loughnan* [1981] VR 443.

There is a further problem with the rationale for duress and necessity as defences. Both have traditionally fallen within the category of 'justification' defences in that the focus was initially on the justifiability or not of the accused's conduct. However, like the defence of self-defence, duress and necessity have developed in such a way as to involve a focus on what the accused believed at the time of the threat or emergency. This means that both defences have taken on characteristics of what have been traditionally labelled 'excuse' defences.

As with the defences of self-defence and provocation, the accused bears the evidential burden in relation to raising duress or necessity, and the prosecution bears the legal burden of establishing that the accused did not act under duress or because of an emergency. The only exception to this is with the statutory defence of marital coercion that exists in South Australia. Section 328A of the *Criminal Law Consolidation Act* 1935 (SA) states that it is a defence 'to prove that the offence was committed in the presence, and under the coercion, of the husband'. This implies that the accused bears the legal burden rather than simply the evidential burden. In *Goddard v Osborne* (1978) 18 SASR 481 the Supreme Court of South Australia stated (at 495) that the effect of s 328A 'was to remove the onus of disproving marital coercion from the shoulders of the Crown and to transfer it to those of the accused'. Why the legal burden should be on the accused in South Australia in relation to marital coercion appears to be an inexplicable anomaly, particularly since duress is not treated in the same way in that state.

In this chapter we will critically analyse the defence of duress and marital coercion together before further considering the general defence of necessity.

Duress and marital coercion

Background

In *DPP (Northern Ireland) v Lynch* [1975] AC 653 at 686, Lord Simon described the defence of duress as denoting 'such [well-grounded] fear, produced by threats, of death or grievous bodily harm if a certain act is not done, as overbears the actor's wish not to perform the act, and is effective, at the time of the act, in constraining him [or her] to perform it'.

Previously, we have outlined how a serious offence can be viewed as consisting of a physical element plus a fault element minus a defence, as shown again in Figure 12.1.

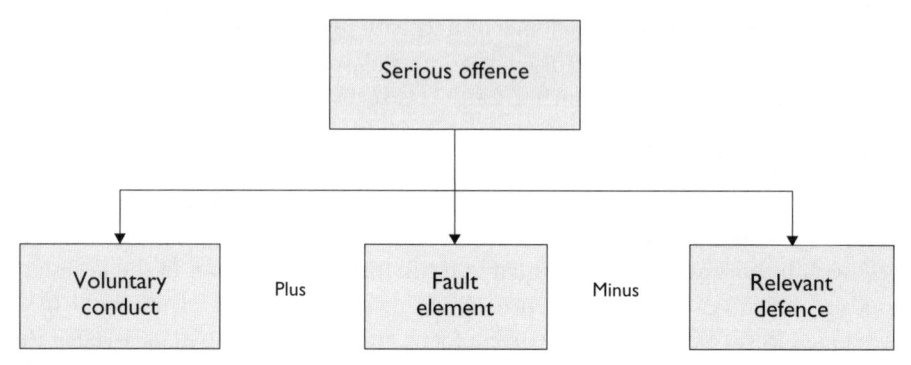

Figure 12.1 Modern division of serious offences

Evidence of duress has been considered not only as a separate defence but also as operating to negate voluntariness or the fault element of an offence, as shown in Figure 12.2.

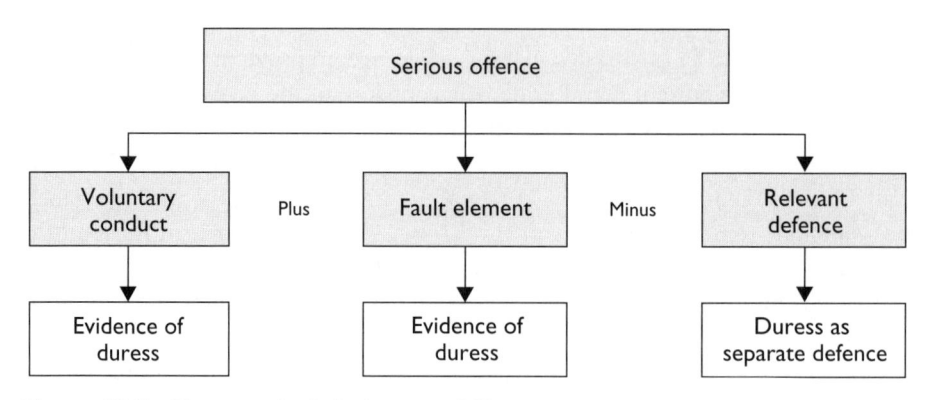

Figure 12.2 Duress and criminal responsibility

Evidence of duress has been referred to as overpowering the will of an individual. For example, in *Attorney-General v Whelan* [1934] IR 518 at 526, Munaghan J stated that 'where the excuse of duress is applicable it must…be clearly shown that the overpowering of the will was operative at the time the crime was actually committed, and, if there were reasonable opportunity for the will to reassert itself, no justification can be found in antecedent threats'. However, equating duress with a lack of will is misleading as, unlike automatic behaviour, the conduct is willed and therefore voluntary. Cox J stated in *R v Palazoff* (1986) 43 SASR 99 (at 105): '[I]n a case of duress, the *actus reus* is voluntary, or willed, and intended, but is, in a real and very relevant sense, undesired. The maxim is *coactus volui*, but the force is not compulsion, strictly so called, but persuasion created by a dilemma.'

Evidence of duress has also occasionally been used to negate a particular state of mind. For example, in *R v Steane* [1947] 1 KB 997, the accused had been charged under the Defence Regulations, during the Second World War, of broadcasting to the allies with intent to assist the enemy. He claimed that he had only done so out of fear that he or his family would be placed into a concentration camp. This evidence was used to negate the requirement that he intended to assist the enemy.

It appears that the third way of approaching duress, that is, viewing it as a separate defence, is the most accepted. It is recognised as a separate defence at common law in New South Wales, South Australia and Victoria. The statutory provisions in the Code jurisdictions of the Northern Territory, Queensland, Tasmania and Western Australia reflect the common law with some variation, as will be examined in the next section. It also exists as a statutory defence in the Australian Capital Territory and at the Commonwealth level: *Criminal Code* (ACT) s 40; *Criminal Code* (Cth) s 10.2.

Duress is a complete defence in that it leads to an acquittal. Limitations are, however, applied to when duress can be raised, the chief limitation being that it is not available to a charge of murder except in the Northern Territory where it operates to reduce murder to manslaughter.

The rationale for limiting the scope of the defence to crimes other than murder or attempted murder lies in the policy argument that human life must be preserved and the purpose of the criminal law is to set a standard of conduct with which ordinary people must comply. In *R v Howe* [1987] AC 417 (at 433) Lord Hailsham talked of the situation:

> where the choice is between the threat of death or *a fortiori* of serious injury and deliberately taking an innocent life. In such a case a reasonable man [*sic*] might reflect that one human life is at least as valuable as his own or that of his loved one. In such a case a man cannot claim that he is choosing the lesser of two evils. Instead, he is embracing the cognate but morally disreputable principle that the end justifies the means.

In *R v Gotts* [1992] 2 AC 412 at 424, Lord Jauncey of Tullichettle suggested that the scope of the defence should be further limited because of a climate of violence and rising terrorism. These remarks can be placed in the context of the Irish Republican Army's bombing campaigns on various targets in Northern Ireland and Great Britain including mortar attacks on the British Prime Minister's 10 Downing Street residence and London's Heathrow Airport in the early 1990s. Lord Jauncey of Tullichettle may also have had in mind the rise of weapons and substances capable of inflicting mass injuries that were not around when the defence of duress was originally formulated. This further limitation to the scope of the defence has been taken up in the Code jurisdictions, Tasmania being the state with the most exclusions.

In some jurisdictions, duress is not available to perpetrators of serious crimes such as homicide. In *DPP (Northern Ireland) v Lynch* [1975] AC 653 a majority of the House of Lords held that duress should be available to an accessory to murder because an accessory bears a lesser degree of guilt than the person who actually commits the murder. In *R v Darrington and McGauley* [1980] VR 353, the Full Court of the Supreme Court followed this decision and held that the defence of duress was only denied to a principal in the first degree. The decision in *Lynch*'s case was overturned by the House of Lords in *R v Howe* [1987] AC 417 on the basis that the law should 'stand firm recognising that its highest duty is to protect the freedom and lives of those under it. The sanctity of human life lies at the root of this ideal': at 443–4 per Lord Griffiths. Prior to the decision in *R v Darrington and McGauley*, other Australian cases did not allow for the defence of duress to be used by an accessory to murder and although the situation remains to be decided in Australia, it may be that *Howe*'s case will be followed.

In the Northern Territory, Queensland and Western Australia, duress is not available as a defence to accessories to murder: *Criminal Code* (NT) s 12; *Criminal Code* (Qld) s 7; *Criminal Code* (WA) s 7. In contrast to this strict approach, in Tasmania, duress is available to accessories to serious offences including murder: *Smith v The Queen* unreported, 6 March 1979, CCA Tas, Cosgrove, Crawford and Nettleford JJ. At common law, duress may also be raised by an accessory after the fact, including to the offence of murder: *R v Williamson* [1972] 2 NSWLR 281.

It is unclear at common law as to whether the defence is open to an accessory in relation to a charge of attempted murder. The weight of opinion at present seems to be that it is unavailable: *R v Gotts* [1992] 2 AC 412; *R v Howe* [1987] AC 417 at 445.

Another limitation to the use of this defence is that at common law, it is not available to an accused who voluntarily enters a situation where duress may be predicted: *R v Hurley and Murray* [1967] VR 526 at 543 per Smith J; *Baker and Ward* (1999) 2 Cr App R 335. The situation usually envisaged here is where the accused joins a criminal association, the members of which subsequently threaten him or her in order to make him or her commit a crime. The question here will be whether or not the accused knew that at the time of joining the association, that there was a risk of duress arising. This will be a matter of fact for the jury to decide: *Shepherd* (1987) 86 Cr App R 47. In the Code jurisdictions, the defence is not available to a person who voluntarily became a party to a criminal or unlawful association: *Criminal Code* (NT) s 40(2); *Criminal Code* (Qld) s 31(2); *Criminal Code* (Tas) s 20(1); *Criminal Code* (WA) s 31(4). This is also the case under section 40(3) of the *Criminal Code* (ACT).

'Marital coercion' can be viewed as a subset of duress. Until the nineteenth century, there was a common law presumption that certain offences committed by a married woman in the presence of her husband were committed under his coercion. This presumption has been abolished in Australia: *Crimes Act* 1900 (NSW) s 407A: *Criminal Law and Procedure Ordinance* 1933 (NT) s 55(2) (now repealed); *Criminal Code* (Qld) s 32 (now repealed); *Criminal Law Consolidation Act* 1935 (SA) s 328A; *Criminal Code* (Tas) s 20(2); *Crimes Act* 1958 (Vic) s 336(1); *Criminal Code* (WA) s 32. There is no such equivalent section in the Australian Capital Territory.

There is some debate as to whether or not a common law *defence* of marital coercion still exists in New South Wales and the Australian Capital Territory: Victorian Law Reform Commissioner, *Criminal Liability of Married Persons*, Report No 3 (Melbourne: LRCV, 1975), para 13. A statutory defence of marital coercion is available in South Australia, Victoria and Western Australia. Since there appear to be no cases in recent years that have raised a common law defence of marital coercion, only the statutory provisions will be the subject of this chapter.

As with the defence of duress in all jurisdictions apart from the Northern Territory, the defence of marital coercion is not available on a charge of murder: *Criminal Law Consolidation Act* 1935 (SA) s 328A; *Crimes Act* 1958 (Vic) s 336(2); *Criminal Code* (WA) s 32. In Western Australia, the scope of the defence is even more limited in that it is not available to those offences that have the element of grievous bodily harm or an intention to cause such harm: *Criminal Code* (WA) s 32. A further limitation is that the defence is only available to a lawfully married woman: *Brennan v Bass* (1984) 35 SASR 311; *R v Court* (1912) 7 Cr App R 127 at 129; *R v Ditta* [1988] Crim LR 42; *Criminal Law Consolidation Act* 1935 (SA) s 328A; *Crimes Act* 1958 (Vic) s 336; *Criminal Code* (WA) s 32. It is unavailable to a woman in a de facto marriage, a polygamous marriage or where the woman mistakenly believed she was legally married: *Brennan v Bass* (1984) 35 SASR 311; *R v Ditta* [1988] Crim LR 42.

There is a great deal of overlap between the defences of duress and marital coercion in that a woman who commits a crime because of threats from her husband would be able to use either defence.

The current law

The Victorian Supreme Court analysed the requirements for the defence of duress to be made out at common law in *R v Hurley and Murray* [1967] VR 526. Smith J stated (at 537) that a defence of duress would be relevant if eight factors existed:
- there was a threat that death or grievous bodily harm would be inflicted unlawfully upon a human being if the accused failed to do the act;
- the circumstances were such that a person of ordinary firmness of mind would have been likely to yield to the threat in the way the accused did;
- the threat was present, continuing, imminent and impending;
- the accused reasonably apprehended that the threat would be carried out;
- the accused was induced to commit the crime because of the threat;

- the crime was not murder, 'nor any other crime so heinous so as to be excepted from the doctrine';
- the accused did not expose him or herself to the threat; and
- the accused had no means of preventing the execution of the threat.

In *Emery* (1985) 18 A Crim R 49 at 56 the Victorian Court of Criminal Appeal approved of this comprehensive analysis. However, the Court warned that the jury should not be directed in such terms as this would involve a danger that they would think that the burden of proof rested on the accused to establish the defence. In *R v Abusafiah* (1991) 24 NSWLR 531 at 544–5, Hunt J set out a model direction for use by New South Wales courts in relation to the burden of proof. According to Hunt J, the jury should be directed that the legal burden is on the prosecution to eliminate any reasonable possibility that the accused acted under duress. In order to do this, the prosecution must establish either:

- when the accused performed the criminal conduct, there was no reasonable possibility that he or she did so by reason of a threat that death or grievous bodily harm would be inflicted; *or*
- there was no reasonable possibility that a person of ordinary firmness of mind would have yielded to the threat in the way in which the accused did.

In *Lanciana* (1996) 84 A Crim R 268 the Victorian Court of Criminal Appeal generally approved of this direction, but the judges were of the opinion that the words 'could' or 'might' should be substituted for the word 'would' in the latter direction: at 272 per Callaway JA with whom Phillips CJ and Southwell AJA concurred. In *Zaharias* (2001) 122 A Crim R 586, Winneke P, Vincent JA and O'Bryan AJA agreed that 'would' have yielded was acceptable and the differences between the words 'would' and 'could' were more apparent than real in the context of jury directions.

The essential element of the defence is therefore the existence of threats that induced the accused to commit a crime. In all jurisdictions other than Queensland, Tasmania and Western Australia, the accused's behaviour is measured against an objective standard. The defence of marital coercion is somewhat broader than that of duress because the latter in most jurisdictions is confined to threats of death or grievous bodily harm whereas coercion is defined more broadly. In Western Australia and South Australia, there is no objective component to marital coercion, but this component remains in Victoria.

Threats of the infliction of death or grievous bodily harm

The defence of duress is usually based upon threats of death or grievous bodily harm. The latter has been held at common law to mean really serious injury: *R v Perks* (1986) 41 SASR 335 at 346–7 per White J; *DPP v Smith* [1961] AC 290; *Pemble v The Queen* (1971) 124 CLR 107. In the Code jurisdictions, the threats must relate to bodily injury that endangers life or causes permanent injury to health or that is likely to do so: *Criminal Code* (NT) s 1; *Criminal Code* (Qld) s 1. The definition also encompasses serious disfigurement or the loss of a distinct part or an organ of the body: *Criminal Code* (Tas) s 1; *Criminal Code* (WA) s 1. Section 40 of the *Criminal Code* (NT) does not specify the type of threat, but contains the limitation that a reasonable person similarly circumstanced would have acted in the same or a similar way.

The common thread for identifying which threats will be accepted as forming the basis for the defence of duress appears to be that they are capable of overbearing the mind of a person of ordinary firmness of character: *R v Abusafiah* (1991) 24 NSWLR 531 at 545.

The threat at common law need not be directed at the accused but can be indirect in the sense that it is aimed at a third person, whether a member of the accused's family or not. In *R v Hurley and Murray* [1967] VR 526 Smith J stated (at 542): '[O]nce one goes beyond threats to the accused himself [or herself] I can see no justification, either in logic or convenience, for the laying down of a list of relationships of attachments which will define the limits of the doctrine...I consider that the true view is that a threat made known to the accused to kill or do grievous bodily harm to any human being can be sufficient to found a defence of duress.'

The Northern Territory and Tasmanian provisions are silent as to this point: *Criminal Code* (NT) s 40; *Criminal Code* (Tas) s 20(1). However, the Queensland provision was amended in 1997 to include threats to another: *Criminal Code* (Qld) s 31(1)(d). Section 31(4) of the *Criminal Code* (WA) is the only provision that expressly limits the threats to those directed at the accused.

The threats made to the accused must be continuing in the sense that they are effective in acting upon the accused's mind at the time the criminal conduct occurred. At common law and in Queensland and the Northern Territory, the threatener need not be physically present when the criminal conduct was carried out: *R v Hurley and Murray* [1967] VR 526 at 543 per Smith J; *R v Brown* (1986) 43 SASR 33; *Emery* (1978) 18 A Crim R 49 at 57; *Goddard v Osborne* (1978) 18 SASR 481 at 490; *R v Williamson* [1972] 2 NSWLR 281; *R v Valderrama-Vega* [1985] Crim LR 220; *Criminal Code* (Qld) s 31(1)(d); *Criminal Code* (NT) s 40. However, in Western Australia and Tasmania, the threatener must be actually present at the time the offence is committed: *Criminal Code* (WA) s 31(4); *Criminal Code* (Tas) s 20; *R v Pickard* [1959] Qd R 475 at 477 per Stanley J; *Clark* (1980) 2 A Crim R 90; *Rice v McDonald* (2000) 113 A Crim R 75, Slicer J.

In Victoria, in its statutory defence of marital coercion, there is no requirement in the legislation that the husband be present at the time in which the accused commits the offence. In Western Australia, the act must be done in the presence of the husband: *Criminal Code* (WA) s 32. In South Australia, the husband's presence is also required, but this has been interpreted as the husband being close enough to influence the accused into doing what he wanted done: *Goddard v Osborne* (1978) 18 SASR 481 at 493 (SC SA).

In relation to duress, at common law the threat of grievous bodily harm or death must generally be of an imminent nature in the sense that it will be carried out there and then or within a short time thereafter: *R v Hudson and Taylor* [1971]

2 QB 202; *R v Williamson* [1972] 2 NSWLR 281; *R v Damson* [1978] VR 536; *R v Brown* (1986) 43 SASR 33. This also appears to be the situation by implication in the Northern Territory: *Criminal Code* (NT) s 40. The other Code jurisdictions use the term 'immediate' rather than 'imminent': *Criminal Code* (Qld) s 31(1)(d); *Criminal Code* (Tas) s 20(1); *Criminal Code* (WA) s 31(4). This requirement of immediacy was referred to by Stanley J in *R v Pickard* [1959] Qd R 475 at 476: 'In my opinion the word "immediate" qualifies the words "death" or "grievous bodily harm". In my opinion the word "immediate" obviously cannot mean some wholly indefinite future time and place. It must be related to some very short time after the doing or the omission of the act.'

The main question here in all jurisdictions is really whether or not the threatened harm is too remote from the commission of the criminal conduct. In *R v Hudson and Taylor* [1971] 2 QB 202 at 206–7 the Court of Criminal Appeal explained this as follows:

> It is essential to the defence...that the threat shall be effective at the moment when the crime is committed. The threat must be a 'present' threat in the sense that it is effective to neutralise the will of the accused at that time...a threat of future violence may be so remote as to be insufficient to overpower the will at the moment when the offence was committed...
>
> When, however, there is no opportunity for delaying tactics, and the person threatened must make up his [or her] mind whether he [or she] is to commit the criminal act or not, the existence at that moment of threats sufficient to destroy his [or her] will ought to provide him [or her] with a defence even though the threatened injury may not follow instantly, but after an interval.

Threats may often be factually demonstrable, but occasionally the matter will depend upon a belief by the accused. In such a case, the common law requires that the accused believed on reasonable grounds that the threat would be carried out. Lord Lane CJ in *R v Graham* [1982] 1 WLR 294 at 300 put the question to be asked as follows: 'Was the defendant, or may he [or she] have been, impelled to act as he [or she] did because as a result of what he [or she] reasonably believed [the threatener] had said or done, he [or she] had good cause to fear that if he [or she] did not so act [the threatener] would kill him [or her]?'

In the Northern Territory and Tasmania, the accused's belief that the threat would be carried out is tested subjectively in that it need not be based on reasonable grounds: *Criminal Code* (NT) s 40(1)(b); *Criminal Code* (Tas) s 20. In Queensland and Western Australia, there is no reference to a belief that the threat would be carried out. Rather, the belief pertains to being unable otherwise to escape the carrying out of the threats: *Criminal Code* (Qld) s 31(1)(d); *Criminal Code* (WA) s 31(4).

The threat must have compelled the accused to commit the criminal conduct: *R v Hurley and Murray* [1967] VR 526 at 543 per Smith J; *R v Abusafiah* (1991) 24

NSWLR 531 at 535 at 428 per Hunt J; *R v Brown* (1986) 43 SASR 33 at 57; *Criminal Code* (NT) s 40; *Criminal Code* (Qld) s 31(1)(d); *Criminal Code* (Tas) s 20; *Criminal Code* (WA) s 31(4). The defence will not be made out in the situation where the accused independently decided to commit the offence.

The defence of marital coercion is broader in its scope in that the term 'coercion' is not confined to threats. For example, s 336(3) of the *Crimes Act* 1958 (Vic) defines 'coercion' as follows:

> For the purposes of this section, *coercion* means pressure, whether in the form of threats or in any other form, sufficient to cause a woman of ordinary good character and normal firmness of mind, placed in the circumstances in which the woman was placed, to conduct herself in the manner charged.

The term 'pressure' is a broader term than 'threats' alone. It may, for example, encompass economic or moral pressure: *R v Richman* [1982] Crim LR 507. This could, for example, include claims that the husband would leave the accused and force her to bring up her children on her own or that he will cut off her access to income. The South Australian and Western Australian provisions do not specify the types of coercion that will form the basis for the defence, but it would seem that this term encompasses more than simply threats.

In relation to the defence of duress, in all jurisdictions there is a legal duty on the accused to escape from the person making threats should a reasonable opportunity to do so present itself: *R v Baker and Ward* (1999) 2 Cr App R 335; *R v Abusafiah* (1991) 24 NSWLR 531; *Criminal Code* (ACT) s 40(2)(b); *Criminal Code* (NT) s 40(1)(b); *Criminal Code* (Qld) s 31(1)(d); *Criminal Code* (Tas) s 20(1); *Criminal Code* (WA) s 31(4).

At common law and in the Northern Territory, there is also an expectation that the accused report the threat to a police officer. However, the defence may be made out where the accused could have sought police protection but failed to do so because he or she thought that it would not be effective: *R v Brown* (1986) 43 SASR 33 at 40 per King CJ; *R v Damson* [1978] VR 536 at 539; *Goddard v Osborne* (1978) 18 SASR 481 at 491; *R v Hudson and Taylor* [1971] 2 QB 202 at 207; [1971] 2 WLR 1047; [1971] 2 All ER 244; *Criminal Code* (NT) s 40(1)(d). Evidence of battered woman syndrome has been accepted to explain why an accused did not escape the situation by seeking police protection: *R v Runjanjic and Kontinnen* (1991) 56 SASR 114 at 120 per King CJ.

In relation to the defence of marital coercion, there is no legislative requirement in any of the jurisdictions that police protection be sought. In *Goddard v Osborne* (1978) 19 SASR 481, the Supreme Court of South Australia held that a woman's failure to report her husband's threats to the police would not preclude reliance on the defence of marital coercion.

The objective element

At common law, in relation to the defence of duress, the circumstances must have been such that a person of ordinary firmness of mind would have been likely to yield to the threat in the way in which the accused did: *R v Hurley and Murray* [1967] VR 526 at 543 per Smith J; *R v Palazoff* (1986) 43 SASR 99 at 108 per Cox J; *R v Valderrama-Vega* [1985] Crim LR 220. Under s 40(1)(c) of the *Criminal Code* (NT) there is the requirement that 'a reasonable person similarly circumstanced would have acted in the same or a similar way'. Section 40(2)(c) of the *Criminal Code* (ACT) refers to the conduct being a reasonable response to the threat.

In Queensland, Tasmania and Western Australia, there is no such requirement. All that matters is that the accused believed that he or she was unable otherwise to escape the carrying of the threats into execution: *Criminal Code* (Qld) s 31(1)(d); *Criminal Code* (Tas) s 20; *Criminal Code* (WA) s 31(4).

In *R v Palazoff* (1986) 43 SASR 99 at 109 Cox J described the person of ordinary firmness of mind as having 'the same age and sex and background and other personal characteristics (except perhaps strength of mind) as the [accused]': see also *R v Abusafiah* (1991) 24 NSWLR 531.

In *R v Runjanjic and Kontinnen* (1991) 56 SASR 114 the Supreme Court of South Australia held that evidence of battered woman syndrome (discussed in Chapter 10) may be relevant first to the question of whether or not a woman of ordinary firmness of mind would have been likely to yield to the threat in the way the accused did and, secondly, to the question as to why such a woman would not escape the situation rather than participate in criminal activity.

In relation to marital coercion, only the Victorian legislation has an objective component. As pointed out above, s 336(3) of the *Crimes Act* 1958 (Vic) defines 'coercion' as pressure that is sufficient to cause 'a woman of ordinary good character and normal firmness of mind' to carry out the criminal act. This requirement is not relevant in South Australia or Western Australia.

The other aspect of this objective element in Victoria is that the 'woman of ordinary good character' must be placed in the position in which the accused was placed. Section 336(4) of the *Crimes Act* 1958 (Vic) is relevant here:

> Without limiting the generality of the expression "the circumstances in which the woman was placed" in sub-section (3), such circumstances shall include the degree of dependence, whether economic or otherwise, of the woman on her husband.

Taking into account the circumstances in which the accused was placed attempts to provide a balance between having a purely objective component and a purely subjective one.

Critique

The main criticisms that have been made concerning duress revolve around the wording of the elements of the defence and its unavailability to a charge of murder. The defence of marital coercion has been questioned as irrelevant given the existence of the defence of duress and as sexist in its assumptions. These criticisms will be considered in turn.

Elements of the defence
Threats or coercion

The defence of duress centres around threats of death or grievous bodily harm—a 'do this or else' scenario. 'Coercion' in the defence of marital coercion is defined more broadly to include economic or moral pressure. Deciding upon what sorts of external pressures should establish duress depends upon whether a broad or narrow approach is taken to the use of the defence.

The Model Criminal Code Officers Committee (MCCOC) approach in proposing uniform legislation encompasses a threat rather than pressure or coercion. Section 10.2 of the *Criminal Code* (Cth) sets out the model defence of duress as follows:

> (1) A person is not criminally responsible for an offence if he or she carries out the conduct constituting the offence under duress.
> (2) A person carries out conduct under duress if and only if he or she reasonably believes that:
>   (a) a threat has been made that will be carried out unless an offence is committed; and
>   (b) there is no reasonable way that the threat can be rendered ineffective; and
>   (c) the conduct is a reasonable response to the threat.
> (3) This section does not apply if the threat is made by or on behalf of a person with whom the person under duress is voluntarily associating for the purpose of carrying out conduct of the kind actually carried out.

Section 40 of the *Criminal Code* (ACT) follows this model. The section does not outline what is meant by the word 'threat'. Will something other than a threat of death or grievous bodily harm suffice? There is also no mention of the threat having to be of immediate or imminent harm. The benefit of not having a strict definition of the word 'threat' is that it still opens up the defence to enable consideration of economic or moral factors. However, to broaden out the defence even further, it may be preferable to use such a word as 'pressure' instead. We will examine in the next section whether an objective component can serve to limit the defence so that it does not become too broad.

The next issue is whether or not the person making the threat needs to be present when the accused committed the offence. There is no mention of such a requirement in s 10.2 of the *Criminal Code* (Cth). The Ontario Court of Appeal in *R v Ruzic* (1998) 128 CCC (3d) 97 held that such a requirement was unreasonably stringent. The Court opted for a more flexible approach to the common law defence.

Certainly freeing up the defence to allow a jury to consider a wider variety of external pressures than simply threats of death or grievous bodily harm would mean that women such as Jacqueline Hinchcliffe could more readily avail themselves of such a defence. If the basis for such a defence is broadened in this way, should an objective component provide an adequate limitation? If so, how should it be formulated?

An objective component

We have outlined how the defence of duress in Australian jurisdictions other than Queensland, Tasmania and Western Australia requires that the circumstances must have been such that a person of ordinary firmness of mind would have yielded to the threat in the way the accused did. The person of ordinary firmness of mind may be imbued with all the characteristics of the accused.

It is unclear whether imbuing the ordinary person with the characteristics of the accused is still good law given that the High Court in *Stingel v The Queen* (1990) 171 CLR 312 held that only age is relevant in determining the standard of self-control to be expected of the ordinary person. It could be argued, however, that *Stingel* relates only to the defence of provocation and is irrelevant to the defence of duress. The requirement that the accused's acts be measured against those of the person of ordinary firmness of mind seems similar to the test relating to dissociative states in the use of automatism. In *R v Falconer* (1990) 171 CLR 30 Toohey J, Mason CJ, Brennan and McHugh JJ proposed an objective standard gloss to the sound/unsound mind distinction. They stated (at 55):

> [T]he law must postulate a standard of mental strength which, in the face of a given level of psychological trauma, is capable of protecting the mind from malfunction to the extent prescribed in the respective definitions of insanity. That standard must be the standard of the ordinary person: if the mind's strength is below that standard, the mind is infirm; if it is of or above that standard, the mind is sound or sane. This is an objective standard which corresponds with the objective standard imported for the purpose of provocation.

That last sentence, however, seems to imply that the ordinary person's standard of mental strength is not one which contains the characteristics of the accused.

We examined the difficulties associated with constructing a workable ordinary person test in Chapter 10 in the section on provocation. Given the current uncertainty about the ordinary person test in relation to duress, it is worthwhile considering whether there is some alternative to using the concept of a person of ordinary firmness of mind in this defence.

In relation to the defence of marital coercion, the addition of the requirement in Victoria that the woman be of good character appears to inject a moral component into the defence. This has been criticised on the basis that the assumption underlying it, that a woman of bad character would be less hesitant in committing crimes than one of good character, is fallacious: S Yeo, 'Coercing Wives into Crime' (1992) 6 *Australian Journal of Family Law* 214–28 at 222. For this reason, rephrasing the objective component to include a concept of 'good character' is rejected.

The intractable problems with the idea of 'ordinariness' lead to the question: Why have an objective component at all? The Law Commission for England and Wales, for example, recommended a purely subjective defence of duress in 1993: *Legislating the Criminal Code: Offences Against the Person and General Principles*, Criminal Law Bill in Report No 218 (London: HMSO, 1993) cl 25.

We pointed out in Chapter 10 how a purely subjective test is problematic because it fails to distinguish between the elements of an offence and the elements of a defence. A mental state forming part of a defence requires an objective test in an attempt to measure blameworthiness. Before a society decides to exercise compassion by exculpating an accused from criminal liability, it is entitled to demand that the accused lacked any blameworthiness in relation to the plea relied on.

As with self-defence, without some form of objective component, it would seem that an accused who may be excessively fearful or apprehensive would be able to react violently towards others with perfect impunity. While a purely subjective defence may aid abused women who commit crimes due to their partners' coercion, it may also mean that more men would be afforded a defence on the basis of unreasonable mistaken beliefs that they were being threatened.

Section 10.4(2) of the *Criminal Code* (Cth) refers to the objective component for self-defence as whether or not the conduct is a reasonable response in circumstances as the accused perceives them to be. Section 10.2 of the *Criminal Code* (Cth), as with section 40 of the *Criminal Code* (ACT), also uses the concept of reasonableness in its model defence of duress. As set out in the previous section, there is emphasis placed on a reasonable belief, that there be no reasonable way that the threat can be rendered ineffective and that the conduct is a reasonable response to the threat.

The use of reasonableness rather than the concept of a person of ordinary firmness of mind could well be suited to the defence of duress. Its emphasis on the subjective belief of the accused allows for sufficient account to be taken of an accused's personal characteristics such as sex, ethnicity, age and religion. The objective element provides for limitations on behaviour deemed appropriate by society as represented by members of the jury.

Should duress be available to a charge of murder?

The main rationale for not allowing duress to be a defence to murder is the belief that human life must be preserved and the purpose of the criminal law is to set a standard of conduct with which ordinary people must comply. Unlike in situations of self-defence, where duress or necessity are involved, the victim is innocent. In addition, there is a belief that because of a climate of violence and rising terrorism, the defence of duress must be limited to crimes other than where there is an intention to kill. This is on the basis that the law should act as a deterrent to those who may succumb too easily to terrorist threats.

In comparison, four main arguments have been posed in support of duress as a defence to murder. First, when there is a choice between dying oneself or killing another, a person should be allowed to save his or her own life. Stanley Yeo has pointed out that '[a]lthough someone who chooses to die rather than kill another deserves praise, the criminal law should not require heroism on pain of conviction for murder': 'Private Defences, Duress and Necessity' (1991) 15 Crim LJ 139–51 at 104.

Secondly, it will only be in very rare circumstances that an accused would raise a defence of duress. A jury can adequately assess an accused's claims. The possibility of fabrication is no greater than for a defence such as provocation where it is the accused who portrays the victim's actions.

Thirdly, the CLOC was of the view that there should not be any restrictions placed on when the defence of duress may be raised: Criminal Law Officers Committee, *Chapters 1 and 2, General Principles of Criminal Responsibility*, Final Report (December 1992). It suggested that the objective element of duress is enough of a limitation as to its scope and quotes with approval the following passage written by Yeo in 'Private Defences, Duress and Necessity' (1991) 15 Crim LJ 139–51 at 143: 'Once a person is under the influence of a threat, whatever he or she does depends on what the threatener demands. The crime demanded might be trivial or serious but it has no necessary connection with the type of threat confronting the accused. Policy reasons would, however, insist on a requirement that the accused's response was reasonably appropriate to the threat.'

The CLOC's approach follows that of the Law Reform Commission of Victoria, which recommended in 1990 that the defence of duress be available to a charge of murder: *Homicide*, Report No 40 (Melbourne: LRCV, 1991) p 106.

Finally, disallowing the defence of duress to a charge of murder does not act as a deterrent as the threat of immediate death constitutes a greater threat than that of future punishment.

If duress is available to a charge of murder, should it be a complete or partial defence? Three of the five Law Lords in *Howe* [1987] 1 AC 417 suggested that murder be reduced to manslaughter as a consequence of a successful defence of duress: at 436 per Lord Bridge, at 438 per Lord Brandon, at 445 per Lord Griffiths. This is currently the situation in the Northern Territory where s 41 of the *Criminal Code* (NT) allows for murder to be reduced to manslaughter where there was 'coercion of such a nature that it would have caused a reasonable person similarly circumstanced to have acted in the same or a similar way'. The rationale for reducing murder to manslaughter lies in the similarity between duress and provocation: both involve a killing by the accused while deprived of self-control or power to withstand pressure from another. Others have argued that it should serve to exculpate an accused completely in certain circumstances: D O'Connor and P Fairall, *Criminal Defences* (3rd edn, Sydney: Butterworths, 1996) p 157; Law Reform Commission of Victoria, *Duress, Necessity and Coercion*, Report No 9 (Melbourne: VLRC, 1980) para 4.19; Criminal Law and Penal Methods Reform Committee, South Australia, *The Substantive Criminal Law*, Fourth Report (1977) para 12.5.

Given the opposition that has existed towards allowing duress as a defence to murder, from a policy perspective, it may be more advantageous to have it as a partial rather than a complete defence.

Should marital coercion exist?

The existence of marital coercion as a defence has been justified on the basis that wives may be particularly vulnerable to pressure from their husbands to commit crimes. The Victorian Law Reform Commissioner has stated in *Criminal Liability of Married Persons*, Report No 3 (Melbourne: LRCV, 1975) para 16:

> Where a wife, as is still commonly the case, has to look to her husband for support and shelter, and especially when she has young children to care for, the pressure upon her of insistent demands, and of threats of abandonment, may in many cases be just as difficult for her to resist as threats of physical violence sufficient to found a defence of duress. Moreover, the duty and habit of loyalty and co-operation which arise from the special relationship of husband and wife will commonly make it more difficult for a wife to resist pressure from her husband than from a stranger.

It should be noted that this passage was written in 1975 and attitudes to the 'special relationship' of husband and wife may have changed since then. PJ Pace and Stanley Yeo, however, have argued that there is a need to recognise the particular vulnerability of married women to pressure from their husbands: PJ Pace, 'Marital Coercion—Anachronism or Modernism' [1979] Crim LR 82–9 at 85; Stanley Yeo, 'Coercing Wives into Crime' (1992) 6(3) *Australian Journal of Family Law* 214–28 at 215. This may be particularly relevant to women in the situation of Jacqueline Hinchcliffe where there has been a long history of abuse.

In comparison, the abolition of the defence of marital coercion has been called for on the basis that it is sexist because it unduly favours women over men. Secondly, its underlying premise is based on the assumption that women may be easily subjugated under the will of men: MCCOC, *Principles of Criminal Responsibility and Other Matters*, Interim Report (1990) para 12.12. Sometimes when there are calls for the defence's abolition, it is recommended that the defence of duress be broadened at the same time: Law Reform Commission of Victoria, *Duress, Necessity* and Coercion, Report No 9 (Melbourne: LRCV, 1980) para 5.03; Review of Commonwealth Criminal Law, *Principles of Criminal Responsibility and Other Matters*, Interim Report (1990) paras 12.21 and 12.38. The rarity of the use of the defence of marital coercion has also provided a rationale for calls for its abolition: JC Smith, *Smith and Hogan Criminal Law* (10th edn, London: Butterworths, 2002) pp 265–6; English Law Commission, *Defences of General Application*, Working Paper No 55 (London: HMSO, 1974) para 63. These arguments were considered by the Victorian Law Reform Commissioner in *Criminal Liability of Married Persons*, Report No 3 (Melbourne: VLRC, 1975), but abolition was rejected in favour of legislative changes to the *Crimes Act* 1958 (Vic). The Victorian sections on marital coercion were duly introduced in 1977 by the *Crimes (Married Person's Liability) Act* 1977 (Vic) and are now the most detailed in Australia.

If it is retained, then it is necessary to consider whether it should only be made available to married women. The Law Reform Commissioner of Victoria when considering the defence of marital coercion received a submission that the defence should be available for women living in de facto relationships. This was rejected on the ground that 'the State does not have the same concern to preserve the stability of "de facto" relationships as it has to preserve the stability of marriages': *Criminal Liability of Married Persons*, Report No 3 (Melbourne: VLRC, 1975) para 83. It could be argued that this reliance on the sanctity of marriage is outdated given the rise in de facto cohabitation and greater societal acceptance of the fact. Stanley Yeo argues in his article 'Coercing Wives into Crime' (1992) 6(3) *Australian Journal of Family Law* 214–28 at 224: 'It is highly contentious to confine the defence to legal marriages. Surely, a female partner of a de facto relationship would suffer just as much coercion as a legally married wife. The factors which create the possibility of coercion, namely, intimacy and gendered power imbalance, are found as much in de facto relationships as amongst legally married couples.'

Given that duress could be expanded to take into account a broader range of threats than currently exists in most jurisdictions, the weight of argument appears to be on the side of abolishing a separate defence of coercion. This was the conclusion that Stanley Yeo reached in his article 'Coercing Wives into Crime' (1992) 6(3) *Australian Journal of Family Law* 214–28 at 228: 'Ultimately, and provided a wide defence of duress is in place, the demise of marital coercion is justified on the basis that it reinforces the inequality and inferiority of women in the eyes of both the community and the law.'

Necessity

Background
On 8 August 2000, the 'conjoined' twins Jodie and Mary were born on the Maltese island of Gozo. They were joined at the pelvic bones and shared a single bladder,

anus and vagina. They had a separate brain, heart, limbs and most vital organs. The parents travelled to England to get expert advice as to what could be done, if anything, to separate the twins.

The parents were told that the twins could be separated, but the operation would kill the weaker twin, Mary, because her heart and lungs were too deficient to oxygenate and pump blood throughout her body. However, if there was no operation, both Jodie and Mary would die within three to six months because Jodie's heart would fail under the strain of having to circulate life-sustaining oxygenated blood to Mary and herself.

The parents were devout Roman Catholics and decided not to consent to the operation, but to leave the matter in God's hands. The hospital in which the twins were being cared for went to the High Court of Justice in England seeking a declaration that the operation could be performed. Johnson J granted this.

The parents then appealed to the English Court of Appeal. Separate legal representation was provided for the twins and the Court allowed the Roman Catholic Archbishop of Westminster and the Pro-Life Alliance to make written submissions. The three judges dismissed the parents' appeal and allowed the operation to proceed. Although leave to appeal to the House of Lords was granted, the parents elected to take the matter no further.

As a result of the operation, Mary quickly died and Jodie survived, her recovery amazing the surgeons.

The three judges of the Court of Appeal gave separate reasons for their decision. Lord Justice Ward held that the killing of Mary was justified as it was akin to a form of 'legitimate self-defence [by] the doctors coming to Jodie's defence and removing the threat of fatal harm to her presented by Mary's draining her lifeblood': *Re A (Children) (Conjoined Twins: Surgical Separation)* [2001] 2 WLR 480 at 536. He also referred to family law principles as dictating that the parents or judge must make the best overall decision for the two babies. Given that Mary was 'designated for death' and that the operation was likely to be successful in giving Jodie an ordinary life span, allowing the operation was the best decision overall.

Lord Justice Walker placed emphasis on the operation being in the 'best interests' of each of the twins. He held that Mary's death would not be the purpose of the operation, but that she would die because her body on its own was not and never had been viable.

Lord Justice Brooke in comparison relied on the 'doctrine of necessity'. His judgment is the most important for the purposes of our discussion here and will be referred to throughout the analysis of necessity that follows.

In general, necessity involves a claim by a person that he or she was compelled to do what he or she did by reason of some extraordinary emergency. The concepts of justification *and* excuse have been used as rationales for the defence.

The accused's behaviour in a situation of necessity is sometimes described as justified because it is recognised that the law can on occasion be broken to avoid a greater harm than would occur by obeying it. This is sometimes referred to as the 'greater good' principle. For example, *Mouse's* case (1608) 77 ER 1341 concerned an action for trespass for throwing the plaintiff's goods overboard from a barge. It was held that not only the crew but also other passengers could do this in order to lighten the barge and prevent it capsizing in a storm. The rationale for this decision was that throwing the goods overboard was a lesser harm than the potential loss of lives.

The accused's behaviour in a situation of necessity is also said to be excused because of the situation of emergency confronting him or her: *R v Loughnan* [1981] VR 443; *Moore v Hussey* (1609) Hob 93; 80 ER 243. Obedience to the law would impose an intolerable burden on the accused in such a situation. A defence of necessity provides an opportunity to take into account feelings of panic or reactions to a sudden or extraordinary emergency. The Supreme Court of Canada in *Perka v The Queen* (1985) 14 CCC (3d) 395 at 386 described the latter principle as follows: 'Necessity rests on a realistic assessment of human weakness, recognising that a liberal and humane criminal law cannot hold people to the strict obedience of laws in emergency situations where normal human instincts, whether of self-preservation or of altruism, overwhelmingly impelled disobedience. The defence must, however, be strictly controlled and scrupulously limited to situations that correspond to its underlying rationale.'

In the conjoined twins case, Brooke LJ was faced with the dilemma that the House of Lords held in *R v Dudley and Stephens* (1884) 14 QBD 273 that necessity was unavailable to a charge of homicide. The facts of that case are well known.

Dudley, Stephens, Brooks and a 17-year-old boy, Parker, were cast adrift in an open boat 1600 miles from land. On the twentieth day, after nine days without food and seven without water, Dudley and Stephens agreed to kill Parker, who was the weakest of the four, and eat his flesh. Brooks refused to take part in the killing. Dudley then killed Parker and the three men survived by eating Parker's flesh. When they were subsequently rescued, Dudley and Stephens admitted what had happened and were charged with murder. The jurors declined to give their view whether the facts amounted to murder and asked for the advice of the Court of Queen's Bench. Lord Coleridge CJ in delivering the judgment of the Court held that the accused were guilty of murder and sentenced them to death. The Executive later commuted this mandatory penalty to six months' imprisonment.

In holding that the defence of necessity was not available to a charge of murder, Lord Coleridge CJ stated (at 287–8):

> To preserve one's life is generally speaking a duty, but it may be the plainest and the highest duty to sacrifice it. War is full of instances in which it is a man's duty not to live, but to die…It is not correct, therefore, to say that there is any absolute or unqualified necessity to preserve one's life…It is not needful to point out the awful danger of the principle which has been contended for. Who is to be the judge of this sort of necessity? By what measure is the comparative value of lives to be measured? Is it to be strength, or intellect, or what? It is plain that the

principle leaves to him who is to profit by it to determine the necessity which will justify him deliberately taking another's life to save his own...it is quite plain that such a principle once admitted might be made the legal cloak for unbridled passion and atrocious crime.

In the conjoined twins case, Brooke LJ distinguished the facts of *Dudley and Stephens* from those before him. He stated that the House of Lords in *Dudley and Stephens* did not have in mind 'a situation in which a court was invited to sanction a defence (or justification) of necessity on facts comparable to those with which we are confronted in the present case': [2001] 2 WLR 480 at 558.

This case has opened up the availability of the defence of necessity to a charge of murder. This will be explored further in the Critique section.

As with the defence of duress, the defence of necessity is available where all the elements of the crime have been made out, and the accused's ability to choose is affected by the emergency situation. As with duress also, the accused's ability to will the act remains unaffected; it is the accused's choice of conduct that is affected. We will now consider the current law before examining how best to formulate a defence of necessity and whether or not it should be available to a charge of murder.

The current law

The common law governs the defence in New South Wales, South Australia and Victoria. Interestingly, the common law also appears to apply in Tasmania. The *Criminal Code* (Tas) is silent as to the defence and pursuant to s 8, it appears that the common law is applicable. The *Criminal Codes* of the Australian Capital Territory, Northern Territory, Queensland and Western Australia contain the defence of sudden or extraordinary emergency which substantially follows the common law defence: *Criminal Code* (ACT) s 41; *Criminal Code* (NT) s 33; *Criminal Code* (Qld) s 25; *Criminal Code* (WA) s 25. Section 10.3 of the *Criminal Code* (Cth) also sets out a model defence of sudden or extraordinary emergency.

In *R v Loughnan* [1981] VR 443 (at 448) Young CJ and King J summarised the elements of the defence of necessity as follows:

> [T]here are three elements involved in the defence of necessity. First, the criminal act or acts must have been done only in order to avoid certain consequences which would have inflicted irreparable evil upon the accused or upon others whom he [or she] was bound to protect.
>
> The [second] element [is] that the accused must honestly believe on reasonable grounds that he [or she] was placed in a situation of imminent peril. Thus if there is an interval of time between the threat and its expected execution it will be very rarely if ever that a defence of necessity can succeed.
>
> The [third] element of proportion simply means that the acts done to avoid the imminent peril must not be out of proportion to the peril to be avoided. Put in

another way, the test is: would a reasonable [person] in the position of the accused have considered that he [or she] had any alternative to doing what he [or she] did to avoid the peril.

The defence of sudden or extraordinary emergency in the Northern Territory, Queensland and Western Australia is similar in that there must be an emergency, the accused must have good cause to fear death or serious injury and the situation must be such that an ordinary person possessing ordinary power of self-control could not reasonably be expected to act otherwise.

The scope of the defence of necessity is also restricted at common law in that it may be denied to an accused who has created the situation of emergency him or herself: *Perka et al v The Queen* (1985) 14 CCC (3d) 385 at 403 per Dickson J. There must also be no other alternatives open to the accused: *Perka v The Queen* (1985) 14 CCC (3d) 385 at 386; *Rogers* (1996) 86 A Crim R 542 at 550–1. There are no such explicit restrictions placed on the defence in the Northern Territory, Queensland or Western Australia.

The three elements of the defence of necessity will be explored under the following categories:
- the nature of the emergency;
- the accused's belief; and
- the objective component.

The nature of the emergency

The early case law held that necessity could not arise from threats from another as this was encompassed by the defence of duress: see, for example, *DPP (Northern Ireland) v Lynch* [1975] AC 653 at 694 per Lord Simon HL. This distinction has since been abandoned, causing confusion as to where duress ends and necessity begins.

In *R v Loughnan* [1981] VR 443 (at 448) Young CJ and King J stated that the range of threats forming the defence of necessity was a 'matter of debate', but referred to the threat of death as falling within the boundaries of the defence. Crockett J (at 460) focused on the concept of the balancing of harms to discover what amounted to 'irreparable evil'. In his view, any type of threatened harm could be relevant provided that the threatened harm was greater than or at least comparable to the crime committed by the accused to avoid it: see also *R v White* (1987) 9 NSWLR 427. Brooke LJ in *Re A (Children) (Conjoined Twins: Surgical Separation)* [2001] 2 WLR 480 at 573 also referred to the accused's act being required 'to avoid inevitable and irreparable evil'.

The 'irreparable evil' spoken of in *Loughnan*'s case may be aimed at a person other than the accused. It appears that this other person must bear a special relationship to the accused. In *R v Loughnan* [1981] VR 443 at 448, Young CJ and King J refer to the threat being inflicted 'upon the accused or upon others whom he [or she] was bound to protect'. This does not seem to be a requirement in situations of necessary medical treatment. For example, in *R v Davidson* [1969] VR 667 the accused argued that he used an instrument to procure a miscarriage because it was necessary to preserve the woman from serious danger to her life or physical or mental health. In the Northern Territory, Queensland and Western Australia, there is no express requirement of a special relationship between the accused and the person endangered.

In the Australian Capital Territory, Northern Territory, Queensland and Western Australia, the provisions refer to a 'sudden or extraordinary emergency', which is not further explained. However, in *Larner v Dorrington* (1993) MVR 75 (at 79) the Supreme Court of Western Australia referred specifically to the fear of 'death or serious physical injury'.

At common law, there is some authority that the emergency situation must be an imminent one. As Young CJ and King J pointed out in *R v Loughnan* [1981] VR 443 (at 448): 'if there is an interval of time between the threat and its expected execution it will be very rarely if ever that a defence of necessity will succeed'.

In *Re F (Mental Patient: Sterilisation)* [1990] 2 AC 1 there was some relaxation of the imminence requirement. The defence of necessity was raised with regard to the non-consensual sterilisation of an intellectually disabled woman who was in a sexual relationship. There was medical evidence that she would not be able to cope with pregnancy and giving birth, but it is questionable that the 'peril' of getting pregnant was in fact 'imminent'. Lord Goff stated (at 75): '[T]he relevance of an emergency is that it may give rise to a necessity to act in the interests of the assisted person, without first obtaining his [or her] consent. Emergency is however, not the criterion or even a prerequisite; it is simply a frequent origin of necessity which impels intervention. The principle is one of necessity not emergency.'

Similarly, Gleeson CJ in *Rogers* (1996) 86 A Crim R 542 at 546 referred to 'urgency and immediacy' as factual considerations rather than 'technical legal conditions'.

The Code provisions do not refer to imminence but a 'sudden or extraordinary emergency'. A sudden emergency is one that is unexpected and this has been held to include a loud noise at the back of a car while it is being driven: *R v Pius Piane* [1975] PNGLR 53 and being chased at high speed by a car: *R v Warner* [1980] Qd R 207.

An extraordinary emergency, on the other hand, may not entail this notion of suddenness or unexpectedness. It may persist over a period of time such as living in a war zone: *Pagawa v Mathew* [1986] PNGLR 154 (National Court of Justice) or being cast adrift on the high seas: *R v Dudley and Stephens* (1884) 14 QBD 273.

The accused's belief

At common law, the accused must honestly believe on reasonable grounds that a situation of emergency has arisen. If the accused is ignorant of circumstances of necessity then the defence cannot be relied upon. In *Limbo v Little* (1989) 45 A Crim R 61 (at 88), Martin J, with whom Kearney and Rice JJ concurred, stated: '[I]t is [not] relevant or permissible [in seeking to establish the defence of necessity] to attempt to prove facts which were not evident to the offender at the time of the offence.'

The situation of emergency may not in fact exist. It will be enough if the accused honestly and reasonably (but mistakenly) believed that the situation existed: *R v Loughnan* [1981] VR 443 at 448 per Young CJ and King J; *Limbo v Little* (1989) 45 A Crim R 61 at 88 per Martin J; *R v Conway* [1988] 3 WLR 1238 at 1244.

The Criminal Codes of the Northern Territory, Queensland and Western Australia all have provisions relating to a mistake of fact: *Criminal Code* (NT) s 32; *Criminal Code* (Qld) s 24; *Criminal Code* (WA) s 24. Reading these provisions with that of the defence of sudden or extraordinary emergency, it would seem that the latter may still be relied upon even where an emergency does not exist. For example, in *R v Pius Piane* [1975] PNGLR 52 the accused was charged with dangerous driving causing death. He claimed that a loud noise at the back of the truck that he was driving caused a momentary lack of attention. The Supreme Court of Papua New Guinea (at 56 per Lalor J) allowed the defence of emergency on that basis that 'whether there was in fact a state of emergency or not, the situation was such that the driver could quite honestly and reasonably believe that there was an emergency in the back of the truck'.

The objective component

All of the jurisdictions impose an objective standard in relation to necessity, but this is phrased in different ways.

In *R v Martin* [1989] 1 All ER 652 (at 653–4), Simon Brown J, in delivering the judgment of the Court of Appeal, expressed the test as whether or not 'a sober person of reasonable firmness, sharing the characteristics of the accused, [would] have responded to that situation by acting as the accused acted'. In *R v Loughnan* [1981] VR 443 at 448, the test was stated as: 'would a reasonable man in the position of the accused have considered that he had any alternative to doing what he did to avoid the peril?'

The Queensland and Western Australian provisions refer to whether an ordinary person, possessing ordinary power of self-control, could not reasonably be expected to act otherwise. Section 33 of the *Criminal Code* (NT) expressly refers to 'an ordinary person similarly circumstanced'. In *Larner v Dorrington* (1993) MVR 75 (at 79) the Supreme Court of Western Australia referred to the ordinary person as having the 'characteristics of the accused person'.

While the majority of formulations refer to the ordinary person, it is unclear just what characteristics of the accused will be taken into account in relation to the test. The Supreme Court of Victoria left this open in *R v Loughnan* [1981] VR 443 and other cases have not clarified the issue.

In some of the cases, a test of proportionality has been used in applying the ordinary person test. In *R v Davidson* [1969] VR 667 (at 671) Menhennit J stated that an important element of the objective test was that the accused's act was 'not out of proportion to the danger to be averted'. Similarly Brooke LJ in *Re A (Children) (Conjoined Twins: Surgical Separation)* [2001] 2 WLR 480 at 573 refers to a requirement that 'the evil inflicted must not be disproportionate to the evil avoided.' In this regard, Desmond O'Connor and Paul Fairall in *Criminal Defences*

(Sydney: Butterworths, 1996) p 113 write that: 'By parallel reasoning with self-defence and provocation, it is submitted that proportionality is but an element to be considered in determining whether the accused acted out of necessity.'

In *Rogers* (1996) 86 A Crim R 542 at 545 at 546, Gleeson CJ referred to the 'proportionality or reasonableness' of the response without mentioning the ordinary or reasonable person. It is therefore unclear at common law what the objective component of the defence contains.

Critique

As with the critique of duress, we will examine the elements of the defence and then look at whether necessity should be available as a defence to murder. Because of the conceptual confusion surrounding the defence of necessity, it is worthwhile considering what limits should be placed on its scope. This will be a theme in the following sections.

The elements of the defence
The nature of the emergency

As set out above, there is some uncertainty as to what constitutes an emergency for the defence of necessity. If the defence of duress is to exist, it may be best to confine the circumstances where this may be raised to evidence of threats or pressure from one person to the accused while necessity arises from emergency situations.

Section 10.3(1) of the *Criminal Code* (Cth) sets out a model defence as follows:

> A person is not criminally responsible for an offence if he or she carries out the conduct constituting the offence in response to circumstances of sudden or extraordinary emergency.

Section 41 of the *Criminal Code* (ACT) is similar. These provisions depart from the common law, where there has been some freeing up of the requirements of urgency and immediacy: *Rogers* (1996) 86 A Crim R 542 at 546 per Gleeson CJ.

The references by Crockett J in *R v Loughnan* [1981] VR 443 at 460 and Brooke LJ in *Re A (Children) (Conjoined Twins: Surgical Separation)* [2001] 2 WLR 480 at 573 to the accused's act being required 'to avoid inevitable and irreparable evil' seem singularly unhelpful in formulating a defence of necessity because the concept of evil is such a nebulous one: Deidre Greig, 'Criminal Responsibility and the Concept of Evil' (1996) 3(2) *Psychiatry, Psychology and Law* 163–78.

Limiting necessity to situations of a sudden *or* extraordinary emergency is one way of circumscribing the scope of the defence. However, Brooke LJ in *Re A (Children) (Conjoined Twins: Surgical Separation)* [2001] 2 WLR 480 at 572 stated that: 'There are sound reasons for holding that the existence of an emergency in the normal sense of the word is not an essential prerequisite for the application of the doctrine of necessity. The principle is one of necessity, not emergency.'

Brooke LJ was following what Lord Goff had said in *Re F (Mental Patient: Sterilisation)* [1990] 2 AC 1 at 75 that an emergency was not the criterion or even a prerequisite for necessity to be raised. However, the rare situations where necessity has arisen in the criminal law have occurred in what can be classified as extraordinary emergencies: drifting in a life boat on the high seas, escaping in a car from physical danger, living in a war zone or operating to save one baby's life at the expense of her twin's.

Limiting necessity to sudden or extraordinary emergencies fails to solve the use of necessity to justify medical procedures such as abortion, sterilisation of those incapable of consenting to medical treatment, or operations on unconscious patients. Jonathan Rogers suggests the test is somewhat different in these cases, depending more on the 'best interests' of the patient rather than necessity in a utilitarian sense: 'Necessity, Private Defence and the Killing of Mary' [2001] Crim LR 515–26.

It may be more appropriate to consider specific statutory provisions to cover such circumstances. For example, ss 282 and 259 of the *Criminal Codes* of Queensland and Western Australia respectively have codified a form of necessity in relation to surgical treatment as follows: 'A person is not criminally responsible for performing in good faith and with reasonable care and skill a surgical operation upon any person for his [or her] benefit, or upon an unborn child for the preservation of the mother's life, if the performance of the operation is reasonable, having regard to the patient's state at the time and to all circumstances of the case.'

Having such a provision in conjunction with a defence of sudden or extraordinary emergency may be one way of clarifying the doctrine of necessity in different circumstances. We will return to this point when discussing whether or not necessity should be a defence to murder.

The objective element

As explored above, the objective element at common law is unclear. Section 10.3 of the *Criminal Code* (Cth) sets out a model as to what the accused must believe:

> (2) This section applies if and only if the person carrying out the conduct reasonably believes that:
> circumstances of sudden or extraordinary emergency exist; and
> committing the offence is the only reasonable way to deal with the emergency; and
> the conduct is a reasonable response to the emergency.

Section 41(2) of the *Criminal Code* (ACT) is the same. The objective component is thus couched in terms of reasonableness. Most jurisdictions already have a requirement that the accused's belief be reasonable. Couching the conduct in terms of a reasonable *response* bypasses the problems associated with the 'ordinary' or 'reasonable' person. As previously explored in the context of duress, having an objective component couched in terms of reasonableness provides for limitations on behaviour deemed appropriate by society as represented by members of the jury.

Should necessity be available to a charge of murder?

One of the intractable debates concerning the area of external pressures being placed on an accused concerns whether necessity—and duress—should be available as defences to murder. As previously noted, in *Dudley and Stephens* at 277–88, Lord Coleridge referred to circumstances of emergency where the highest duty may be to sacrifice one's life rather than take another's. This rationale for rejecting necessity as a defence for murder also underlies the House of Lords decision in *R v Howe* [1987] AC 417, which rejected duress as a defence to murder either by a principal offender or an accessory.

Some of the reasons for allowing an accused to raise defences based on external pressures to a charge of murder were explored in the Critique section on duress. There is a body of philosophical literature solely exploring killing in emergency situations and this will be discussed in this section.

One of the reasons for so much confusion about the scope of necessity is that writers often do not differentiate between whether or not they are referring to it as a justification or an excuse. As previously explored in Chapter 2, defences 'justifying' a crime focus on the accused's act whereas those 'excusing' a person from criminal responsibility are generally viewed as concentrating on the accused's personal characteristics: P Alldridge, 'The Coherence of Defences' [1983] Crim LR 665–72; S Yeo, 'Proportionality in Criminal Defences' (1988) 12 Crim LJ 211–27 at 212–13.

In *Re A*, Brooke LJ in referring to necessity as involving a choice between two 'evils' is approaching necessity as a justification for a wrongful act. Jonathan Rogers refers to this as a 'utilitarian' doctrine of necessity: 'Necessity, Private Defence and the Killing of Mary' [2001] Crim LR 515–26 at 521. A utilitarian or consequentialist rationale for behaviour aims to identify conduct that will result in the greatest 'good' for the greatest number in society. Necessity in this sense can be used to justify the killing of one person to save two or more persons. Consider, for example, the following scenario.

JC Smith refers to an emergency situation that was revealed in an inquest into the sinking of the ferry *Herald of Free Enterprise*: *Justification and Excuse in the Criminal Law* (London: Sweet & Maxwell, 1989) pp 73–9. As the ferry was sinking, several passengers were trying to get onto the deck by ascending a rope ladder. One young man was on the ladder and, suffering from shock, was unable to go up or down. The other passengers were shouting at him to no avail. Finally, he was pushed off the ladder and he fell into the water and was not seen again. Several other passengers then escaped up the ladder to safety.

There may be a strong public interest in preserving the greater number of lives in such a situation. It could be argued that pushing one passenger to his or her death can be justified in order to save more lives.

Compare, however, the scenario posed by Judith Thomson in her book *Rights, Restitution and Risk: Essays in Moral Theory* (Cambridge, MA: Harvard University Press, 1986) p 95. A surgeon is faced with five patients dying unless they immediately get organ transplants—two need one lung each, two need a kidney each and a fifth needs a heart. Their time is almost up when a young man appears for his yearly check-up. He has the right blood type and is in excellent health. Is the surgeon justified in killing the young man in order to save five others? A utilitarian approach to necessity would say yes, but, as Judith Thomson points out, everyone to whom this scenario is told is of the view that the surgeon should not proceed. This scenario shows that 'not just anything is permissible on the ground that it would yield a net saving of lives': JJ Thomson, 'Self-Defense' (1990) 20 *Philosophy and Public Affairs* 283–310 at 309.

If necessity is seen as an *excuse* then the focus shifts from a balancing act between two 'evils' to the plight of the actor. In the first scenario, the passengers can be 'excused' because we can imagine their feelings of panic in the situation of emergency confronting them. It is more difficult to excuse a surgeon who chooses to kill a healthy young man even where the motive is to save the lives of others. The situation in the second scenario does not give rise to the same feelings of empathy towards the surgeon as to those in extraordinary emergencies.

Jeremy Horder argues that certain killings may be permissible in a 'one-off emergency': 'Self-Defence, Necessity and Duress' (1998) 11(1) *Canadian Journal of Law and Jurisprudence* 143–65. He writes at 156: 'The moral monstrosities threatened by unbounded consequentialism can, however, be avoided by confining the occasions on which such overridings (of the right to life of an innocent person) may take place to one-off emergencies, so that there can be no argument by analogy that would force such overridings on to a wider moral and political agenda.'

The CLOC has also taken this 'one-off' approach and followed the Code jurisdictions rather than the common law in formulating a defence of sudden or extraordinary emergency that is available in relation to all offences: Criminal Law Officers Committee, *Chapters 1 and 2, General Principles of Criminal Responsibility*, Final Report (December 1992) p 67; *Criminal Code* (Cth), s 10.3. As outlined above, the defence is available where circumstances of sudden or extraordinary emergency exist. In the first scenario, one could certainly argue this is the case. In the second, patients waiting for transplants could be viewed as an 'ordinary' rather than an 'extraordinary' occurrence.

By focusing on what the accused reasonably believed in relation to the circumstances, this provision is approaching necessity as an excuse rather than a justification.

In the case of *Re A* the situation of the conjoined twins could be described as one of 'extraordinary' emergency. If there were no operation, both Jodie and Mary would die. If the operation went ahead, one would die, but one could be (and was) saved. Having a test of reasonableness as proposed by the MCCOC would help limit the defence in such extraordinary situations.

But where does that leave necessity in relation to more 'ordinary' situations where medical treatment may arise? For example, a surgeon who operates on an unconscious patient is technically committing an assault because there is no consent, but his or her actions are justified on the grounds of 'necessity'. In such circumstances, surgeons are able to operate without fear of prosecution. Menhennit J referred to the necessity of preserving a woman from serious danger to her life or her physical or mental health in relation to a doctor 'procuring a miscarriage': *R v Davidson* [1969] VR 667 at 672. Necessity has also been used to justify forms of medical treatment upon those considered incompetent to consent to such treatment: *Re F (Mental Patient: Sterilisation)* [1990] 2 AC 1; *R v Bournewood Community and Mental Health NHS Trust, ex parte L* [1998] 3 WLR 107.

As mentioned above, it may be better to consider these cases of medical treatment as examples of a 'best interests' of the patient test rather than of the doctrine of necessity in action. Lord Goff stated in *Re F (Mental Patient: Sterilisation)* [1990] 2 AC 1 (at 75) in relation to operating on a person incompetent to consent to medical treatment: '[N]ot only (1) must there be a necessity to act when it is not practicable to communicate with the assisted person, but also (2) the action taken must be such as a reasonable person would in all the circumstances take, acting in the best interests of the assisted person.'

Lord Goff distinguished between emergency cases and those in which the disability is permanent. In relation to the former, he stated (at 77) that the treatment should be confined to that which is necessary in the short term in the patient's interests. These restrictions, however, would not apply in the case of a patient with a permanent disability such as an intellectual disability as the patient is incompetent to consent. In that situation, the health professional must act in the patient's best interests.

While it is uncertain whether this precise test applies in Australia, Lord Goff's focus on the patient's interests seems to be moving necessity beyond situations of sudden or extraordinary emergency. Legislative provisions dealing with such medical situations could be drafted such as ss 282 and 259 of the *Criminal Codes* of Queensland and Western Australia respectively, which are set out above. This would be one way of legislatively distinguishing between more 'ordinary' cases of medical treatment and situations of sudden or extraordinary emergency.

In an interesting twist of fate, the Supreme Court of Queensland was also recently asked to decide as to whether conjoined twins should be separated. Justice Chesterman, in *State of Queensland v Alyssa Nolan (an infant)* unreported, 31 May 2001, SC of Qld, [2001] QSC 174, referred to the defence of sudden and extraordinary emergency in s 25 of the *Criminal Code* (Qld) as well as s 282 as justifying the separation of conjoined twins. He found that the doctrine of necessity relied on in

Re A was a 'creature of the common law' that found only a very limited role in the Code (at para 17). He went on to state (at para 24): '[Section] 282 abnegates criminal responsibility for a surgeon who performs an operation in good faith and with reasonable care if it is for the patient's benefit and if the operation is reasonable having regard to all the circumstances of the case. The language is wide enough to encompass the relevant facts here.'

Justice Chesterman found that the stronger twin, Alyssa, was to be regarded as the patient for the purposes of s 282 as Bethany had developed severe pulmonary oedema and her death was an immediate prospect. Without an operation to separate the two, Alyssa would also die within hours of Bethany. While Chesterman J did not distinguish between 'ordinary' and 'extraordinary' cases of medical treatment, his decision points to the importance of the existence of such a provision when difficult cases arise.

If necessity is to be available to a charge of murder, it is worthwhile making it a partial rather than a complete defence in order to assuage the fear that it might become a 'legal cloak for unbridled passion and atrocious crime' in the words of Lord Coleridge CJ in *R v Dudley and Stephens* (1884) 14 QBD 273 at 288.

Conclusion

It has been argued that the defence of duress should be broadened to allow a jury to consider a wider variety of external pressures than simply threats of death or grievous bodily harm. This would mean that women like Jacqueline Hinchcliffe could more readily avail themselves of such a defence and there would be no need for a separate defence of marital coercion. Necessity, in contrast, should be restricted to situations of sudden or extraordinary emergency.

Both duress and necessity should be limited by the use of an objective component based on the concept of reasonableness rather than the ordinary person. Section 10.2 of the *Criminal Code* (Cth) in its model defence of duress emphasises reasonable belief: that there be no reasonable way that the threat can be rendered ineffective and that the conduct is a reasonable response to the threat. Section 10.3(2) of the *Criminal Code* (Cth) in its model defence of sudden or extraordinary emergency also emphasises reasonable belief, reasonable response and committing the offence being the only reasonable way to deal with the emergency. These provisions seem much more workable than those dealing with amorphous concepts of the ordinary or reasonable person.

It has also been suggested that both duress and necessity be available to a charge of murder, but that they be partial rather than complete defences. If the emphasis is placed more on excusing the accused's belief rather than justifying the conduct, reducing murder to manslaughter is a useful halfway point between letting the accused avoid any criminal responsibility and holding him or her guilty of murder.

Bibliography

Advisory Committee on the Australian Judicial System (David Jackson, Chairman), Report (Canberra: Constitutional Commission, 1987).

Akindemowo O, *Information Technology Law in Australia* (Sydney: LBC Information Services, 1999).

Alder C and Baker J, 'Maternal Filicide: More than One Story to be Told' (1997) 9(2) *Women and Criminal Justice* 15–39.

Alexander R, *Domestic Violence in Australia: The Legal Response* (3rd edn, Sydney: The Federation Press, 2002).

Alldridge P, 'The Coherence of Defences' [1983] *The Criminal Law Review* 665–72.

Alldridge P, 'The Doctrine of Innocent Agency' (1990) 2(1) *Criminal Law Forum* 45–83.

Alldridge P, *Relocating Criminal Law* (Aldershot: Ashgate Dartmouth, 2000).

Allen CK, *Legal Duties and Other Essays in Jurisprudence* (Oxford: Oxford University Press, 1931).

Allen J, 'Octavius Beale Re-considered: Infanticide, Babyfarming and Abortion in NSW 1880–1939' in Sydney Labour History Group, *What Rough Beast? The State and Social Order in Australian History* (Sydney: Allen & Unwin, 1982) pp 111–29.

Amarasekara K and Bagaric M, *Euthanasia, Morality, and the Law* (New York: P Lang, 2003).

American Psychiatric Association, *Diagnostic and Statistical Manual of Mental Disorders* (4th edn Text Revision, Washington, DC: APA, 2000).

Andrews L and Nelkin D, 'Whose Body is it Anyway? Disputes Over Body Tissue in a Biotechnology Age' (1998) 351 *The Lancet* 53–7.

Anonymous, 'Developments in the Law—Criminal Conspiracy' (1959) 72 *Harvard Law Review* 920–1008.

Anonymous, 'Forcible and Statutory Rape', Note, (1952) 62 *Yale Law Journal* 55–83.

Applegath LJ, 'Sexual Intercourse with a Feeble-minded Female Person: Problems of Proof' (1964–65) 7 *Criminal Law Quarterly* 480–4.

Aristotle, *The Nichomachean Ethics*, Irwin T (trans) (Indianapolis: Hackett Publishing Co, 1985).

Asai A, 'Should a Patient in a Persistent Vegetative State Live?' (1999) 18(2) *Monash Bioethics Review* 25–39.

Ashby M, 'Hard Cases, Causation and Care of the Dying' (1995) 3(2) *Journal of Law and Medicine* 152–60.

Ashby M and Mendelson D, 'Natural Death in 2003: Are We Slipping Backwards?' (2003) 3 *Journal of Law and Medicine* 260–4.

Ashworth A, *Principles of Criminal Law* (3rd edn, Oxford: Oxford University Press, 1999).

Ashworth A, 'Is the Criminal Law a Lost Cause?' (2000) 116 *The Law Quarterly Review* 225–56.

Ashworth A and Blake M, 'Presumption of Innocence in English Criminal Law' [1996] *The Criminal Law Review* 306–17.

Atkinson J, 'Violence against Aboriginal Women: Reconstitution of Community Law: The Way Forward' (1990) 46 (2) *Aboriginal Law Bulletin* 6–9.

Atkinson J, 'A Nation is not Conquered' (1996) 3(80) *Law Bulletin* 4–9.

Atkinson J, 'Voices in the Wilderness—Restoring Justice to Traumatised Peoples' (2002) 25(1) *University of New South Wales Law Journal* 223–41.

Atkinson RL, Atkinson RC, Smith EE and Bern DJ, *Introduction to Psychology* (10th edn, Fort Worth: Harcourt Brace Jovanovich, 1990).

Attorney-General's Department (NSW), *Review of the 'Homosexual Panic Defence'*, Discussion Paper No 18 (1996).

Attorney-General's Office (SA), *Intoxication and Criminal Responsibility*, Discussion Paper (July 1998).

Austin J, *Lectures on Jurisprudence* (5th edn, London: John Murray, 1885).

Australian Bureau of Statistics, *Crime and Safety Survey* (Canberra: ABS, 1999).

Australian Bureau of Statistics, *Crime and Safety Australia* (April 2002), <http://www.abs.gov.au/websitedbs/D3310114.NSF/home/statistics>, accessed October 2003.

Australian Bureau of Statistics, *Crimes Recorded by Police 2003*, <http://www.abs.gov.au/ausstats/abs@.nsf/Lookup/E93FA3CC3D9BC5C6CA256CAE001052A3>, accessed October 2003.

Australian Bureau of Statistics, *Drug-induced Deaths 1997-2001* (Canberra: ABS, 2002).

Australian Bureau of Statistics, *Women's Safety Australia 1996*, Cat No 4128.0 (Canberra: Office of the Status of Women,1996).

Australian Institute of Criminology and PricewaterhouseCoopers, *Serious Fraud in Australia and New Zealand* (Canberra: AIC and PricewaterhouseCoopers, 2003).

Australian Institute of Criminology, *Australian Crime: Facts and Figures 2002* (Canberra: AIC, 2002), <http://www.aic.gov.au/publications/facts/2002/index.html>, accessed November 2003.

Australian Institute of Criminology, *Drug Use Monitoring Australia* (Canberra: AIC, 2002).

Australian Law Reform Commission, *Aboriginal Customary Law—Recognition*, Discussion Paper No 17 (Sydney: ALRC, 1980).
Australian Law Reform Commission, *Recognition of Aboriginal Customary Laws*, Report No 31 (Sydney: ALRC, 1986).
Australian Law Reform Commission, *Multiculturalism: Criminal Law*, Discussion Paper No 48 (Sydney: ALRC, 1991).
Australian Law Reform Commission, *Multiculturalism and the Law*, Report No 57 (Sydney: ALRC, 1992).
Australian Medical Association, *Female Genital Mutilation*, Position Statement (Canberra: AMA, November 2002), <http://www.ama.com.au/web.nsf/doc/SHED-5FLUNB>, accessed November 2003.
Australian Medical Association, *Care of Severely and Terminally Ill Patients*, Position Statement (Canberra: AMA, November 2002), <http://www.ama.com.au/web.nsf/doc/SHED-5FK3DB> , accessed November 2003.
Ayres I and Braithwaite J, *Responsive Regulation: Transcending the Deregulation Debate* (New York: Oxford University Press, 1992).
Bagaric M, 'Active and Passive Euthanasia: Is There a Moral Distinction and Should There Be a Legal Difference?' (1997) 5(2) *Journal of Law and Medicine* 143–54.
Bagaric M, *Punishment and Sentencing: A Rational Approach* (London: Cavendish Publishing Limited, 2001).
Bagshaw D, Chung D, Couch M, Lilburn S and Wadham B, *Reshaping Responses to Domestic Violence: Final Report* (Adelaide: University of South Australia, 2000).
Baker BM, 'Consent, Assault and Sexual Assault' in Anne Bayefsky (ed), *Legal Theory Meets Legal Practice* (Edmonton: Academic Printing and Publishing, 1988) pp 223–38.
Bandura A, *Social Foundations of Thought and Action* (Englewood Cliffs, NJ: Prentice Hall, 1986).
Bandura A, 'Human Agency in Social Cognitive Theory' (1989) 44(9) *American Psychologist* 1175–84.
Bargh J and Chartrand T, 'The Unbearable Automaticity of Being' (1999) 54(7) *American Psychologist* 462–79.
Baume P and O'Malley E, 'Euthanasia: Attitudes and Practices of Medical Practitioners' (1994) 161(2) *Medical Journal of Australia* 137–44.
Bavin-Mizzi J, 'Understandings of Justice: Australian Rape and Carnal Knowledge Cases 1876–1924' in Kirkby D (ed), *Sex, Power and Justice: Historical Perspectives on Law in Australia* (Melbourne: Oxford University Press, 1995) pp 19–32.
Beauchamp TL, 'A Reply to Rachels on Active and Passive Euthanasia' in Beauchamp TL and Walters L (eds), *Contemporary Issues in Bioethics* (4th edn, Belmont, CA: Wadsworth Publishing Company, 1994) pp 442–9.
Beauchamp TL and Childress JF, *Principles of Biomedical Ethics* (4th edn, Oxford: Oxford University Press, 1994).

Beccaria C, *On Crimes and Punishment*, Paolucci H (trans) (Indianapolis: Bobbs-Merrill Educational, 1963, first English edn 1767).

Becker H, *The Outsiders* (New York: The Free Press, 1963).

Becket M, 'Change of Heart on Corporate Killing: Legislation Will Target Companies Rather than Individuals', *Daily Telegraph*, 26 May 2003.

Behrendt L, 'Meeting at the Crossroads: Intersectionality, Affirmative Action and the Legacies of the Aborigines Protection Board' (1997) 4(1) *Australian Journal of Human Rights* 98–119.

Behrendt L, 'Women's Work: The Inclusion of the Voice of Aboriginal Women' (1995) 6(2) *Legal Education Review* 169–74.

Bell S, 'Defining Mental Disorder' in W Brookbanks (ed), *Psychiatry and the Law: Clinical and Legal Issues* (Wellington: Brooker's Ltd, 1996) pp 71–92.

Bennett B, *Law and Medicine* (Sydney: LBC Information Services, 1997).

Biggs H, 'Euthanasia and Death with Dignity: Still Poised on the Fulcrum of Homicide' [1996] *The Criminal Law Review* 878–88.

Birsch D and Fielder JH (eds), *The Ford Pinto Case: A Study in Applied Ethics, Business and Technology* (Albany, NY: State University of New York Press, 1994).

Blackwood J and Warner K, *Tasmanian Criminal Law: Text and Cases* (Hobart: University of Tasmania Law Press, 1997).

Blagg H, Morgan N and Yavu Kama Harathunian C, 'Aboriginal Customary Law in Western Australia' (2002) 80 *Reform* 11–14.

Borowski A and O'Connor I (eds), *Juvenile Crime, Justice and Corrections* (Melbourne: Addison Wesley Longman, 1997).

Bowring J (ed), *The Works of Jeremy Bentham* (New York: Russell and Russell, 1962).

Bradfield R, 'Case and Comment: *Attorney-General's Reference No 1 of 1996 Re Weiderman*' (1999) 23 *Criminal Law Journal* 41–7.

Bradford JW and Smith SM, 'Amnesia and Homicide: The Padola Case and a Study of 30 Cases' (1979) 7 *Bulletin of the American Academy of Psychiatry and Law* 219–31.

Braithwaite J, 'On Speaking Softly and Carrying Big Sticks: Neglected Dimensions of a Republican Separation of Powers' (1997) 47 *University of Toronto Law Journal* 305–61.

Braithwaite J and Drahos P, *Global Business Regulation* (Melbourne: Cambridge University Press, 2002).

Braithwaite J and Fisse B, *The Impact of Publicity on Corporate Offenders* (Albany: State University of New York Press, 1983).

Breines I, Connell R and Eide I (eds), *Male Roles, Masculinities and Violence* (Paris: UNESCO Publishing, 2000).

Brett P, 'The Physiology of Provocation' [1970] *The Criminal Law Review* 634–40.

Bronitt S, 'Defending Giorgianni—Part Two: New Solutions for Old Problems in Complicity' (1993) 17 *Criminal Law Journal* 305–18.

Bronitt S, 'The Direction of Rape Law in Australia: Toward a Positive Consent Standard' (1994) 18(5) *Criminal Law Journal* 249–53.

Bronitt S and Amirthalingam K, 'Cultural Blindness and the Criminal Law' (1996) 20(2) *Alternative Law Journal* 58–64.
Bronitt S and McSherry B, *Principles of Criminal Law* (Sydney: LBC Information Services, 2001).
Brooks P and Gewirtz P (eds), *Law's Stories: Narrative and Rhetoric in the Law* (New Haven: Yale University Press, 1996).
Brown BJ, 'The Demise of Chance Medley and the Recognition of Provocation as a Defence to Murder in English Law' (1963) 7 *American Journal of Legal History* 310–18.
Brown D, Farrier D, Egger S and McNamara L, *Criminal Laws: Materials and Commentary on Criminal Law and Process of New South Wales* (3rd edn, Sydney: The Federation Press, 2001).
Brown H, 'Provocation as a Defence to Murder: To Abolish or to Reform' (1999) 12 *Australian Feminist Law Journal* 137–41.
Brownmiller S, *Against Our Will: Men, Women and Rape* (New York: Simon and Schuster, 1975).
Bryan JW, *The Development of the English Law of Conspiracy* (New York: Da Capo Press, 1970).
Burgess-Jackson K, *Rape: A Philosophical Investigation* (Dartmouth: Aldershot Publishing Company, 1996).
Burke RH, *An Introduction to Criminological Theory* (Cullompton, Devon: Willan Publishing, 2001).
Burnside JP, 'The Sexual Offences (Amendment) Act 2000: The Head of a "Kiddy-Libber" and the Torso of a "Child-Saver"' [2001] *The Criminal Law Review* 425–34.
Buxton R, 'Complicity in the Criminal Code' (1969) 85 *The Law Quarterly Review* 252–74.
Canadian Criminal Lawyers' Association, *Submission on Bill C-49* (1992).
Canadian Psychiatric Association, *Brief to the House of Commons Standing Committee on Justice and the Solicitor General*, Subcommittee on the Reform of the General Part of the Criminal Code, 9 November 1992.
Carcach C and Mukherjee S, 'Women's Fear of Violence in the Community', *Trends and Issues* No 135 (Canberra: AIC, 1999).
Carmody M, *Sexual Assault of People with an Intellectual Disability:* Final Report (Sydney: NSW Women's Coordination Unit, 1990).
Cashmore J and de Haas N, Commonwealth Department of Human Services and Health, *Legal and Social Aspects of the Physical Punishment of Children*, Discussion Paper (ACT: Commonwealth of Australia, May 1995).
Chamallas M, 'Consent, Equality and the Legal Control of Sexual Conduct' (1988) 61 *Southern California Law Review* 777–862.
Chaplin J, *Dictionary of Psychology* (2nd edn, New York: Dell, 1982).
Charlesworth M, *Bioethics in a Liberal Society* (Cambridge: Cambridge University Press, 1993).

Chilvers M, 'What Lies Behind the Growth in Fraud?', NSW Bureau of Crime Statistics and Research (July 2002).

Churchland P, *A Neurocomputational Perspective: The Nature of Mind and the Structure of Science* (Cambridge, MA : MIT Press, 1989).

Churchland P, *The Engine of Reason, The Seat of the Soul: A Philosophical Journey into the Brain* (Cambridge, MA: MIT Press, 1995).

Churchland P and Churchland P, *On the Contrary: Critical Essays, 1987–1997* (Cambridge, MA: MIT Press, 1998).

Cica N, 'Abortion Law in Australia', Parliamentary Research Paper 1 (1998).

Clarkson CMV, 'Complicity. Powell and Manslaughter' [1998] *The Criminal Law Review* 556–61.

Clough J and Mulhern C, *Butterworths Tutorial Series: Criminal Law* (Sydney: Butterworths, 1999).

Clough J and Mulhern C, *The Prosecution of Corporations* (Melbourne: Oxford University Press, 2002).

Cohen M, 'Inciting the Impossible' [1979] *The Criminal Law Review* 239–44.

Coke E, *Institutes of the Laws of England: Third Part* (London, 1680).

Coleman P, 'Incest: A Proper Definition Reveals the Need for a Different Legal Response' (1984) 49 *Missouri Law Review* 251–88.

Coles EM and Armstrong SM, 'Hughlings Jackson on Automatism as Disinhibition' (1998) 6(1) *Journal of Law and Medicine* 73–82.

Coles EM and Jang D, 'A Psychological Perspective on the Legal Concepts of "Volition" and "Intent"' (1996) 4(1) *Journal of Law and Medicine* 60–71.

Colvin E, Linden S and Bunney L, *Criminal Law in Queensland and Western Australia* (3rd edn, Sydney: Butterworths, 2001).

Cook D, *Rich Law Poor Law: Different Responses to Tax and Supplementary Benefit Fraud* (Milton Keynes: Open University Press, 1989).

Coomaraswamy R, *Integration of the Human Rights of Women and the Gender Perspective: Violence Against Women* E/CN.4/2002/83, 31 January 2002.

Coss G, '"God is a righteous judge, strong and patient: and God is provoked every day": A Brief History of the Doctrine of Provocation in England' (1991) 13 *Sydney Law Review* 570–604.

Cretney A and Davis G, 'Prosecuting "Domestic" Assault' [1996] *The Criminal Law Review* 162–71.

Criminal Law Officers Committee, *Chapters 1 and 2, General Principles of Criminal Responsibility*, Discussion Draft (1992).

Criminal Law Officers Committee, *Chapters 1 and 2, General Principles of Criminal Responsibility*, Final Report (December 1992).

Criminal Law and Penal Methods Reform Committee, South Australia, *The Substantive Criminal Law*, Fourth Report (1977).

Criminal Law Revision Committee, *Offences Against the Person*, Report No 14 (London: HMSO, Cmnd 7844, 1980).

Criminal Law Revision Committee, *Theft and Related Offences*, Report No 8 (London: HMSO, Cmnd 2877, 1966).

Crocker P, 'The Meaning of Equality for Battered Women Who Kill Men In Self-Defense' (1985) 8 *Harvard Women's Law Journal* 121–53.

Crofts T, *The Criminal Responsibility of Children and Young Persons: A Comparison of English and German Law* (Aldershot: Ashgate, 2002).

Cross R, 'The Reports of the Criminal Law Commissioners (1833–1849) and the Abortive Bills of 1853' in Glazebrook PR (ed), *Reshaping the Criminal Law* (London: Stevens & Sons, 1978) pp 5–20.

Cunneen C and McDonald D, *Keeping Aboriginal and Torres Strait Islander People out of Custody: An Evaluation of the Implementation of the Recommendations of the Royal Commission into Aboriginal Deaths in Custody* (Canberra: ATSIC, 1997).

Cunneen C, *Conflict, Politics and Crime* (Crows Nest, NSW: Allen & Unwin, 2001).

Daly K, 'Inequalities of Crime' in Goldsmith A, Israel M and Daly K (eds), *Crime and Justice: An Australian Textbook in Criminology* (2nd edn, Sydney: Lawbook Company, 2003) pp 105–22.

Damasio A, *Descartes' Error: Emotion, Reason and the Human Brain* (New York: GP Putnam, 1994).

Damasio A, *The Feeling of What Happens: Body and Emotion in the Making of Consciousness* (New York: Harcourt Brace, 1999).

Davies J, 'Guardian to Decide if Woman Dies', *Age*, 12 March 2003.

Davies M, *Asking the Law Question: The Dissolution of Legal Theory* (2nd edn, Sydney: Lawbook Co, 2002).

Davies M and Naffine N, *Are Persons Property? Legal Debates About Property and Personality* (Aldershot: Dartmouth Publishing Company, 2001).

de Soto H, *The Mystery of Capital* (London: Black Swan Books, 2001).

Delisle R, '*Stone*: Judicial Activism Gone Awry to Presume Guilt' (1999) 25 *Criminal Reports* (5th) 91–6.

Dennis I, 'The Rationale of Criminal Conspiracy' (1977) 93 *The Law Quarterly Review* 39–64.

Dennis I, 'The Law Commission Report on Attempt and Impossibility in Relation to Attempt, Conspiracy and Incitement: (1) The Elements of Attempt' [1980] *The Criminal Law Review* 758–79.

Dennis I, 'The Criminal Attempts Act 1981' [1982] *The Criminal Law Review* 5–16.

Dennis I, 'The Mental Element for Accessories' in Smith P (ed), *Criminal Law: Essays in Honour of JC Smith* (London: Butterworths, 1987) pp 40–67.

Dennis I, 'The Critical Condition of Criminal Law' (1997) 50 *Current Legal Problems* 213–49.

Department of Justice and Attorney-General, *Dangerous Industrial Conduct*, Discussion Paper, 2000.

Department of Justice, Statistics and Research Unit Stats Flash 112, *Trends in Shopstealing*, February 2002.

Derrida J, *Positions* (Chicago: University of Chicago Press, 1981).
Descartes R, *Treatise of Man*, Hall TS (trans), (Cambridge: Harvard University Press, 1972, first published 1637).
Devlin P, *The Enforcement of Morals* (London: Oxford University Press, 1965).
Dobash RE and Dobash R, *Violence Against Wives* (London: Open Books, 1980).
Domestic Violence Legislation Working Group, *Model Domestic Violence Laws*, Discussion Paper (Canberra: AGPS, November, 1997).
Domestic Violence Legislation Working Group, *Model Domestic Violence Laws*, Report (Canberra: AGPS, April, 1999).
Domestic Violence Legislation Working Group, *Submission in Response to the Model Domestic Violence Laws*, Discussion Paper (Canberra: Attorney-General's Department, 1998).
Donnelly H and Cumines S, 'From Murder to Manslaughter: Partial Defences in New South Wales—1990 to 1993', *Sentencing Trends No 8* (Sydney: NSW Judicial Commission, 1994) pp 1–6.
Donnelly H, Cumines S and Wilczynski A, *Sentences for Homicides in New South Wales 1990–1993: A Legal and Sociological Study* (Judicial Commission of NSW, Monograph Series No 10, 1995).
Dowie M, 'Pinto Madness' (1977), <http://www.motherjones.com/mother_jones/SO77/dowie.html>, accessed 17 February 2003, also reproduced in Birsch D and Fielder JH (eds), *The Ford Pinto Case: A Study in Applied Ethics, Business and Technology* (Albany, NY: State University of New York Press, 1994) 15–36.
Dresser R, 'Culpability and Other Minds' (1992) 2(1) *Southern California Interdisciplinary Law Journal* 41–88.
Duff RA, *Criminal Attempts* (Oxford: Oxford University Press, 1996).
Duff RA, *Intention, Agency and Criminal Liability* (Oxford: Basil Blackwell, 1990).
Dunford L and Pickford V, 'Is There a Qualitative Difference Between Physical and Psychiatric Harm in English Law?' (1999) 7 *Journal of Law and Medicine* 36–46.
Drugs and Crime Prevention Committee, Parliament of Victoria, *Inquiry into Fraud and Electronic Commerce*, Discussion Paper (Melbourne: AGPS, March 2003).
Dworkin R, *Life's Dominion. An Argument about Abortion and Euthanasia* (London: Harper Collins, 1993).
Easteal P, 'Battered Woman Syndrome: What is "Reasonable"?' (1992) 17(5) *Alternative Law Journal* 220–3.
Easteal P, 'Rape in Marriage: Has the Licence Lapsed?' in P Easteal (ed), *Balancing the Scales—Rape, Law Reform and Australian Culture* (Sydney: The Federation Press, 1994) pp 107–23.
Easteal P, *Voices of the Survivors* (Melbourne: Spinifex Press, 1994).
Easteal P, *Less than Equal* (Sydney: Butterworths Australia, 2001).
Edwards S, 'No Defence for a Sado-Masochistic Libido' (1993) 143 *New Law Journal* 406–7.

Ellard J, 'New White Elephants for Old Sacred Cows: Some Notes in Diagnosis' (1992) 26(4) *Australian and New Zealand Journal of Psychiatry* 546–9.

Elliott DW, 'Dishonesty in Theft: A Dispensable Concept' [1982] *The Criminal Law Review* 395–410.

English Law Reform Committee, *Offences Against the Person*, Fourteenth Report, Cmnd 7844 (1980).

Enker AN, 'Mens Rea and Criminal Attempt' (1977) 845(4) *American Bar Foundation Research Journal* 845–79.

Evans EP, *The Criminal Prosecution and Capital Punishment of Animals* (London: Faber and Faber, 1987, first published 1906).

Ewing C, *Battered Women Who Kill: Psychological Self-Defense as Legal Justification* (Massachusetts: Lexington Books, 1987).

Family Law Council, *Female Genital Mutilation*, Report (June 1994).

Farmer L, *Criminal Law, Tradition and Legal Order* (Cambridge: Cambridge University Press, 1997).

Farrugia PJ, 'The Consent Defence: Sports Violence, Sadomasochism, and the Criminal Law' (1997) 8(2) *Auckland University Review* 472–502.

Fattah E, *Criminology: Past, Present and Future* (Basingstoke: Macmillan Press Ltd, 1997).

Favazza AR, *Bodies Under Siege* (Baltimore: Johns Hopkins University Press, 1992).

Feinberg J, *The Moral Limits of the Criminal Law: Harm to Others* (New York: Oxford University Press, 1984).

Fels A, 'The Trade Practices Act and World's Best Practice: Proposals for Criminal Penalties for Hard-Core Collusion', *Current Issues in Regulation: Enforcement and Compliance* (Melbourne: AIC/Regnet Conference, September 2002).

Fenwick P, 'Somnambulism and the Law: A Review' (1987) 5 *Behavioral Sciences and the Law* 343–57.

Ferrante A, Morgan F, Indermaur D and Harding R, *Measuring the Extent of Domestic Violence* (Sydney: Hawkins Press, 1996).

Finn J, 'Case and Comment: *Machirus*' (1997) 21 *Criminal Law Journal* 51–3.

Finnis JM, 'Bland: Crossing the Rubicon?' (1993) 109 *The Law Quarterly Review* 329–37.

Fisse B, 'Sentencing Options Against Corporations' (1990) 1(2) *Criminal Law Forum* 211–58.

Fisse B, *Howard's Criminal Law* (5th edn, Sydney: The Law Book Company Ltd, 1990).

Fisse B, 'Corporate Criminal Responsibility' (1991) 15 *Criminal Law Journal* 166–74.

Fisse B, 'Criminal Law: The Attribution of Criminal Liability to Corporations: A Statutory Model' (1991) 13 *Sydney Law Review* 277–97.

Fisse B and Braithwaite J, *Corporations, Crime and Accountability* (Cambridge: Cambridge University Press, 1993).

Fletcher GP, 'Two Kinds of Legal Rules: a Comparative Study of Burden-of-Persuasion Practices in Criminal Cases' (1968) 77 *Yale Law Journal* 880–935.

Fletcher G, 'The Metamorphosis of Larceny' (1976) 89(3) *Harvard Law Review* 469–530.

Fletcher GP, *Rethinking Criminal Law* (Boston: Little Brown and Co, 1978) pp 40–57.

Flew A, 'The Principle of Euthanasia' in AB Downing and B Smoker (eds), *Voluntary Euthanasia: Experts Debate the Right to Die* (London: Peter Owen, 1986) pp 40–57.

Ford R, '"Lady-friends" and "Sexual Deviationists": Lesbians and Law in Australia, 1920s–1950s' in D Kirkby (ed), *Sex, Power and Justice: Historical Perspectives on Law in Australia* (Melbourne: Oxford University Press, 1995) pp 33–49.

Foucault M, *Madness and Civilisation: A History of Insanity in the Age of Reason* (London: Tavistock, 1967).

Foucault M, *The Order of Things* (New York: Vintage Books, 1973).

Foucault M, *Power/Knowledge* (Brighton: Harvester Press, 1980).

Fox R, 'The Meaning of Proportionality in Sentencing' (1994) 19 *Melbourne University Law Review* 489–511.

Fox R and Freiberg A, *Review of Statutory Maximum Penalties* (Melbourne: Victorian Government Publishing Office, 1989).

Freckelton I, 'Masochism, Self-Mutilation and the Limits of Consent' (1994) 2(1) *Journal of Law and Medicine* 48–76.

Freckelton I, 'When Plight Makes Right: The Forensic Abuse Syndrome' (1994) 18 *Criminal Law Journal* 29–49.

Freckelton I, 'Stalker Sentencing and Protection of the Public' (2001) 8(3) *Journal of Law and Medicine* 233–9.

Freiberg A, 'The Disposition of Mentally Disordered Offenders in Australia' (1994) 1(2) *Psychiatry, Psychology and Law* 97–118.

Freiberg A, 'Regulating Markets for Stolen Property' (1997) 30 *Australian and New Zealand Journal of Criminology* 237–58.

Gabriel S, 'Child Destruction: A Prosecution Anomaly Under Both the Common Law and the Criminal Codes' (1997) 21 *Criminal Law Journal* 32–9.

Gale F, Naffine N and Wundersitz J (eds), *Juvenile Justice: Debating the Issues* (St Leonards: Allen & Unwin, 1993).

Gardiner S, 'Recklessness Refined' (1993) 109 *Law Quarterly Review* 21–7.

Garland D, *Punishment and Moral Society* (Oxford: Clarendon Press, 1990).

Garnsey D, 'Rugby League Player Jailed for On-Field Assault' (1995) 5(2) *Australian and New Zealand Sports Law Association Newsletter* 7.

Gaylin W, Kass LR, Pellegrino ED and Siegler M, 'Doctors Must Not Kill' in Baird RM and Rosenbaum SE (eds), *Euthanasia: The Moral Issues* (New York: Prometheus Books, 1989) pp 25–8.

Gelder M, Gath D, Mayou R and Cowen P (eds), *Oxford Textbook of Psychiatry* (3rd edn, Oxford: Oxford University Press, 1996).

Gelsthorpe L, 'Feminism and Criminology' in Maguire M, Morgan R and Reiner R (eds), *The Oxford Handbook of Criminology* (3rd edn, Oxford: Oxford University Press, 2002) pp 112–43.

Gibbs H, Chairperson, *Review of Commonwealth Law, Principles of Criminal Responsibility and Other Matters*, Interim Report (Canberra: AGPS, 1990).

Gillespie C, *Justifiable Homicide* (Columbus, OH: Ohio State University Press, 1989).

Gillett G, 'Euthanasia, Letting Die and the Pause' (1988) 14 *Journal of Medical Ethics* 61–8.

Gilligan C, *In a Different Voice: Psychological Theory and Women's Development* (Cambridge, MA: Harvard University Press, 1982).

Glasbeek H, *Wealth by Stealth: Corporate Crime, Corporate Law and the Perversion of Democracy* (Toronto: Between the Lines, 2002).

Glazebrook PR, 'Should We Have a Law of Attempted Crime?' (1969) 85 *Law Quarterly Review* 28–49.

Goldstein AS, *The Insanity Defense* (New Haven, CT: Yale University Press, 1967).

Goodall H and Huggins J, 'Aboriginal Women are Everywhere: Contemporary Struggles' in Saunders K and Evans R (eds), *Gender Relations in Australia: Domination and Negotiation* (Sydney: Harcourt Brace Jovanovich, 1992) pp 415–21.

Goode M, *Criminal Conspiracy in Canada* (Toronto: Carswell, 1975).

Goode M, 'Stalking: Crime of the Nineties?' (1995) 19 *Criminal Law Journal* 21–31.

Goode M, 'Contemporary Comment—Two New Decisions on Criminal "Jurisdiction": The Appalling Durability of Common Law' (1996) 20 *Criminal Law Journal* 267–82.

Goode M, 'The Tortured Tale of Criminal Jurisdiction' (1997) 21 *Melbourne University Law Review* 411–59.

Goode M, Attorney-General's Office, *Intoxication and Criminal Responsibility*, Discussion Paper (July 1998).

Grabosky P and Braithwaite J, *Of Matters Gentle: Enforcement Strategies of Australian Business Regulatory Agencies* (Melbourne: Oxford University Press and Australian Institute of Criminology, 1986).

Grabosky P and Smith R, *Crime in the Digital Age: Controlling Telecommunications and Cyberspace Illegalities* (Leichardt, NSW: The Federation Press, 1998).

Grabosky P, Smith R and Dempsey G, *Electronic Theft: Unlawful Acquisition in Cyberspace* (Cambridge: Cambridge University Press, 2001).

Gray S, '"I Didn't Know, I Wasn't There": Common Purpose and the Liability of Accessories to Crime' (1999) 23 *Criminal Law Journal* 201–17.

Graycar R and Morgan J, *The Hidden Gender of Law* (2nd edn, Sydney: The Federation Press, 2002).

Greig D, 'Criminal Responsibility and the Concept of Evil' (1996) 3(2) *Psychiatry, Psychology and Law* 163–78.

Griew E, 'Dishonesty: The Objections to Feely and Ghosh' [1985] *The Criminal Law Review* 342–54.

Griffith S, 'Explanatory Letter to the Attorney-General Queensland with Draft Code' as cited in Edwards E, Harding R and Campbell I (eds), *The Criminal Codes* (4th edn, Sydney: The Law Book Company Ltd, 1992).

Griggs L, 'The Ownership of Excised Body Parts: Does an Individual Have the Right to Sell?' (1994) 4(1) *Journal of Law and Medicine* 223–8.

Grisso T, 'Society's Retributive Response to Juvenile Violence: A Developmental Perspective' (1996) 20 *Law and Human Behavior* 229–47.

Groves M, 'Commentary' (1998) 22 *Criminal Law Journal* 357–61.

Hale M, *The History of the Pleas of the Crown* (London: Professional Books Ltd, 1971, first published 1736) Vol 1.

Hall J, 'Mental Disease and Criminal Responsibility' (1958) 33 *Indiana Law Journal* 212–25.

Hall J, *General Principles of Criminal Law* (2nd edn, Indianapolis: The Bobbs-Merrill Co Inc, 1960).

Halpin A, 'The Test for Dishonesty' [1996] *The Criminal Law Review* 283–95.

Harding S, *Feminism and Methodology* (Milton Keynes: Open University Press, 1987).

Hart HLA, 'The House of Lords on Attempting the Impossible' (1981) 1 *Oxford Journal of Legal Studies* 149–66.

Hart HLA, *Law, Liberty and Morality* (London: Oxford University Press, 1963).

Hart HLA, *Punishment and Responsibility* (Oxford: Oxford University Press, 1968).

Hart HLA and Honoré A, *Causation in the Law* (Oxford: Clarendon Press, 1959).

Hay D, 'Property, Authority and the Criminal Law' in Hay D, Linebaugh P, Rule JG, Thompson EP and Winslow C (eds), *Albion's Fatal Tree: Crime and Society in Eighteenth Century England* (London: Allen Lane, 1975) pp 17–63.

Hayes SC and Craddock G, *Simply Criminal* (Sydney: The Federation Press, 1992).

Hazell R, *Conspiracy and Civil Liberties* (London: Bell, 1974).

Healey K (ed), *Euthanasia* (Sydney: The Spinney Press, 1997).

Heenan M and McKelvie H, *Rape Law Reform Evaluation Project*, Report No 2: *The Crimes (Rape) Act 1991: An Evaluation Project* (Melbourne: Department of Justice, 1997).

Henderson E, 'Of Signifiers and Sodomy: Privacy, Public Morality and Sex in the Decriminalisation Debates' (1996) 20 *Melbourne University Law Review* 1023–47.

Hepburn L, *Ova-Dose? Australian Women and the New Reproductive Technology* (Sydney: Allen & Unwin, 1992).

Higgins K, 'Exploring Motor Vehicle Theft in Australia', *Trends and Issues* No 67 (Canberra: AIC, 1997).

HIH Royal Commission, *The Failure of HIH Insurance*, Vol. 1 (Canberra: Commonwealth of Australia, 2003).

Hocking B, 'Commentary on *Dellapatrona and Duffield*' (1995) 19 *Criminal Law Journal* 164–71.

Hocking J, *Lionel Murphy: A Political Biography* (Cambridge: Cambridge University Press, 1997).

Holder R, 'Domestic and Family Violence: Criminal Justice Interventions' *Australian Domestic and Family Violence Clearinghouse*, Issues Paper 3 (2001).

Holder R, 'Playing on the Football Field: Domestic Violence, Help-Seeking and Community Development', *Domestic Violence: Current Responses, Future Directions* (Sydney: Relationships Australia, 1998).

Holdsworth W, *A History of English Law* (London: Sweet & Maxwell, 1966) Vols 3, 8.

Holland W, *The Law of Theft and Related Offences* (Scarborough, Ontario: Thomson Canada, 1998).

Holroyd J, 'A New Criminal Law of Fraud: The Recent Proposals of the Law Commission of England and Wales' (2003) *The Journal of Criminal Law* 67(1) 31–6.

Home Office, *The 1996 British Crime Survey* (London: Research and Statistics Directorate, 1996).

Home Office, *Violence: Reforming the Offences Against the Person Act 1861* (1998), <http://www.homeoffice.gov.uk/docs/vroapa.html>, accessed October 2003.

Hopkins A, *Making Safety Work: Getting Management Commitment to Occupational Health and Safety* (St Leonard's: Allen & Unwin, 1995).

Horder J, *Provocation and Responsibility* (Oxford: Clarendon Press, 1992).

Horder J, 'Self-defence, Necessity and Duress' (1998) 11(1) *Canadian Journal of Law and Jurisprudence* 143–65.

Hough M, *Anxiety About Crime: Findings from the 1994 British Crime Survey*, Home Office Research Study No 147 (London: Home Office, 1995).

House of Assembly, *Hansard*, Vol 358, 6 June 1981.

House of Lords Select Committee, *Report of the Select Committee on Murder and Life Imprisonment* (London: HMSO, 1989).

Hubble G, 'Feminism and the Battered Woman: The Limits of Self-Defence in the Context of Domestic Violence' (1997) 9(2) *Current Issues in Criminal Justice* 113–23.

Hughes G, 'Computers, Crime and the Concept of "Property"' (1990) 1 *Intellectual Property Journal* 154–63.

Hubble G, 'Rape by Innocent Agent' (1997) 21(4) *Criminal Law Journal* 204–12.

Hubble G, 'Osland v The Queen' (1999) 23 *Criminal Law Journal* 109–13.

Hulls R, Attorney-General of Victoria, Second Reading Speech, Crimes (Workplace Deaths and Serious Injuries) Bill, *Hansard*, 22 November 2001.

Hunt A and Wickham G, *Foucault and Law* (London: Pluto, 1994).

Hunter R and Stubbs J, 'Model Laws or Missed Opportunity' (1999) 24(1) *Alternative Law Journal* 12–16.

Hutchinson A and Monahan P, 'Law, Politics and the Critical Legal Scholars: The Unfolding Drama of American Legal Thought' (1984) 36 *Stanford Law Review* 199–245.

Ierodiaconou M, '"Listen to Us!" Female Genital Mutilation, Feminism and the Law in Australia' (1995) 20 *Melbourne University Law Review* 562–87.

Industry Commission, *Work, Health and Safety*, Commonwealth of Australia (1995) Vol 1.

Institutes of the Laws of England (1787) 3 Inst 47.

Jackson M (ed), *Infanticide* (Aldershot: Ashgate, 2002).

Jayasuriya L, 'Understanding Australian Racism' (2002) 45(1) *Australian Universities Review* 40–4.

Johnson K, Andrew R and Topp V, *Silent Victims: A Study of People with Intellectual Disabilities as Victims of Crime* (Melbourne: Office of the Public Advocate, 1988).

Johnson P, 'The Unnecessary Crime of Conspiracy' (1973) 61(5) *California Law Review* 1137–88.

Johnstone R, 'Economic and Sociological Approaches to Law' in Hunter R, Ingleby R and Johnstone R (eds), *Thinking About Law* (St Leonards: Allen & Unwin, 1995) pp 61–85.

Jones B (ed), *The Penalty is Death: Capital Punishment in the Twentieth Century* (Melbourne: Sun Books, 1968).

Jones TH, 'Insanity, Automatism and the Burden of Proof on the Accused' (1995) 111 *The Law Quarterly Review* 475–516.

Justinian, *Digest of Justinian*, Mommsen T (trans), Krueger P and Watson A (eds) (Pennsylvania: University of Pennsylvania Press, 1985) Book Forty-Eight.

Kadish S, 'Complicity, Cause and Blame: A Study in the Interpretation of Doctrine' (1985) 73 *California Law Review* 324–410.

Kadish S, *Blame and Punishment; Essays in the Criminal Law* (New York: Macmillan, 1987).

Kelly HA, 'Rule of Thumb and the Folklaw of the Husband's Stick' (1994) 44(3) *Journal of Legal Education* 341–65.

Kelman M, 'Interpretative Construction in the Substantive Criminal Law' (1981) 33 *Stanford Law Review* 591–673.

Kerridge I, Lowe M and McPhee J, *Ethics and Law for the Health Professions* (Katoomba, NSW: Social Science Press, 1998).

Khouri N, *Honor Lost: Love and Death in Modern Day Jordan* (New York: Atria Books, 2003).

KPMG Australia, *Fraud Survey 2002* (April 2002).

Kuhse H and Singer P, 'Active Voluntary Euthanasia, Morality and the Law' (1995) 3(2) *Journal of Law and Medicine* 129–35.

Kuhse H and Singer P, 'Voluntary Euthanasia and the Nurse: An Australian Study' (1993) 30(4) *International Journal of Nursing Studies* 311–22.

Kuhse H, Singer P, Baume P, Clarke M and Rickard M, 'End-of-Life Decisions in Australian Medical Practice' (1997) 166(4) *Medical Journal of Australia* 191–6.

Kusha HR, *The Sacred Law of Islam* (Aldershot: Ashgate, 2002).

Lacey N, *State Punishment* (London: Routledge, 1986).

Lacey N, 'A Clear Concept of Intention: Elusive or Illusory?' (1993) 56 *Modern Law Review* 621–42.

Lacey N, 'In(de)terminable Intentions' (1995) 58 *Modern Law Review* 692–5.

Lacey N, *Unspeakable Subjects* (Oxford: Hart Publishing, 1998).

Lacey N, 'Legal Constructions of Crime' in Maguire M, Morgan R and Reiner R (eds), *The Oxford Handbook of Criminology* (3rd edn, Oxford: Oxford University Press, 2002) pp 264–85.

Lacey N and Wells C, *Reconstructing Criminal Law: Critical Perspectives on Crime and the Criminal Process* (2nd edn, London: Butterworths, 1998).

Lake M, 'Between Old World "Barbarism" and Stone Age "Primitivism": The Double Difference of the White Australian Feminist' in Grieve N and Burns A (eds), *Australian Women: Contemporary Feminist Thought* (Melbourne: Oxford University Press, 1994).

Lanham D, 'Larsonneur Revisited' [1976] *The Criminal Law Review* 276–81.

Lanham D, 'Accomplices and Withdrawal' (1981) 97 *The Law Quarterly Review* 575–92.

Lanham D, 'Euthanasia, Painkilling, Murder and Manslaughter' (1994) 3 *Journal of Law and Medicine* 146–55.

Lanham D, *Cross-Border Criminal Law* (Melbourne: FT Law & Tax Asia Pacific, 1997).

Lanham D, 'Danger Down Under' [1999] *The Criminal Law Review* 960–9.

Lanham D, 'Principles of Causation in Criminal Law' in Freckelton I and Mendelson D (eds), *Causation in Law and Medicine* (Hampshire: Ashgate Publishing Ltd, 2002) pp 211–27.

Lansdowne R, 'Infanticide: Psychiatrists in the Plea Bargaining Process' (1990) 16(1) *Monash University Law Review* 41–63.

Laster K, 'Infanticide: A Litmus Test for Feminist Criminological Theory' (1989) 22 *Australian and New Zealand Journal of Criminology* 151–66.

Law Commission for England and Wales, *General Principles, Parties, Complicity and Liability for the Acts of Another*, Working Paper No 43 (London: HMSO, 1972).

Law Commission for England and Wales, *Codification of the Criminal Law, General Principles: Inchoate Offences: Conspiracy, Attempt and Incitement*, Working Paper No 50 (London: HMSO, 1973).

Law Commission for England and Wales, *Defences of General Application*, Working Paper No 55 (London: HMSO, 1974).

Law Commission for England and Wales, *Criminal Law: Report on Conspiracy and Criminal Law Reform*, Report No 76 (London: HMSO, 1976).

Law Commission for England and Wales, *Criminal Law: Attempt and Impossibility in Relation to Attempt, Conspiracy and Incitement*, Report No 102 (London: HMSO, 1980).

Law Commission for England and Wales, *Criminal Law: A Criminal Code for England and Wales*, Report No 177 (London: HMSO,1989).

Law Commission for England and Wales, *Assisting and Encouraging Crime*, Consultation Paper No 131 (London: HMSO, 1993).

Law Commission for England and Wales, *Legislating the Criminal Code: Offences Against the Person and General Principles*, Criminal Law Bill in Report No 218 (London: HMSO, 1993).

Law Commission for England and Wales, *Consent in the Criminal Law*, Consultation Paper No 139 (London: HMSO, 1995).
Law Commission for England and Wales, *Legislating the Criminal Code: Intoxication and Criminal Liability*, Report No 229 (London: HMSO, 1995).
Law Commission for England and Wales, *Legislating the Criminal Code: Unintentional Manslaughter*, Report No 237 (London: HMSO, 1996).
Law Commission for England and Wales, *Legislating the Criminal Code: Involuntary Manslaughter*, Report No 237 (London: HMSO, 1996).
Law Commission for England and Wales, *The Law of Dishonesty: Money Transfers*, Report No 243 (London: HMSO, 1996).
Law Commission for England and Wales, *Legislating the Criminal Code: Fraud and Deception*, Consultation Paper No 155 (London: HMSO, 1999).
Law Commission for England and Wales, *Fraud*, Report No 276 (London: HMSO, 2002).
Law Reform Commission of Canada, *Homicide*, Working Paper No 33 (1984).
Law Reform Commission of Canada, *Secondary Liability: Participation in Crime and Inchoate Offences*, Working Paper No 45 (1985).
Law Reform Commission of Victoria, *Criminal Responsibility: Intention and Gross Intoxication*, Report No 6 (Melbourne: LRCV, 1986).
Law Reform Commission of Victoria, *Rape and Allied Offences: Substantive Aspects*, Discussion Paper No 2 (Melbourne: LRCV, 1986).
Law Reform Commission of Victoria, *Sexual Offences Against Children*, Report No 18 (Melbourne: LRCV, 1988).
Law Reform Commission of Victoria, *Sexual Offences Against People with Impaired Mental Functioning*, Report No 15 (Melbourne: LRCV, 1988).
Law Reform Commission of Victoria, *Mental Malfunction and Criminal Responsibility*, Report No 34 (Melbourne: LRCV, 1990).
Law Reform Commission of Victoria, *Death Caused by Dangerous Driving*, Discussion Paper (Melbourne: LRCV, 1991).
Law Reform Commission of Victoria, *Homicide*, Report No 40 (Melbourne: LRCV, 1991).
Law Reform Commission of Victoria, *Homicide Prosecutions Study*, Report No 40 (Melbourne: LRCV, 1991).
Law Reform Commission of Victoria, *Rape: Reform of Law and Procedure*, Appendixes to Interim Report No 42 (Melbourne, LRCV, 1991).
Law Reform Commission of Victoria, *Rape: Reform of Law and Procedure*, Report No 43 (Melbourne: LRCV, 1991).
Law Reform Commissioner of Victoria, *Criminal Procedure: Miscellaneous Reforms* (Melbourne: LRCV, 1974).
Law Reform Commissioner of Victoria, *Criminal Liability of Married Persons*, Report No 3 (Melbourne: LRCV, 1975).

Law Reform Commissioner of Victoria, *Duress, Necessity and Coercion*, Report No 9 (Melbourne: LRCV, 1980).

Law Reform Commissioner of Victoria, *Provocation and Diminished Responsibility as Defences to Murder*, Report No 12 (Melbourne: LRCV, 1982).

Law Reform Commissioner of Victoria, *Murder: Mental Element and Punishment* (Melbourne: LRCV, 1984).

Law Reform Committee, Parliament of Victoria, *Criminal Liability for Self-induced Intoxication*, Report (Melbourne: VGPS, May 1999).

Lea J and Young J, *What is to Be Done About Law and Order? Crisis in the Nineties* (London: Pluto Press, 1993).

Leader-Elliott I, 'Battered But Not Beaten: Women Who Kill in Self-Defence' (1993) 15 *Sydney Law Review* 403–60.

Leader-Elliott I, 'Case Note: Insanity, Involuntariness and the Mental Element in Crime' (1994) 18 *Criminal Law Journal* 347–57.

Leader-Elliott I, 'Sex, Race and Provocation: In Defence of Stingel' (1996) 20 *Criminal Law Journal* 72–96.

Leader-Elliott I, 'Offences of Dishonesty: the South Australian Version', unpublished paper presented at the South Australian Law Society Conference (31 May 2003).

Leader-Elliott I and Naffine N, 'Wittgenstein, Rape Law and the Language Games of Consent' (2000) 26(1) *Monash University Law Review* 48–73.

Leaver A, *Investigating Crime* (Sydney: LBC Information Services, 1997).

Lees S, *Ruling Passions: Sexual Violence, Reputation and the Law* (Buckingham: Open University Press, 1997).

Leigh M, 'The United States and the Statute of Rome' (2001) 95(1) *American Journal of International Law* 124–31.

Levi M, *Regulating Fraud: White Collar Crime and the Criminal Process* (London: Tavistock Publications, 1987).

Lewis D, 'The Punishment That Leaves Something to Chance' (1989) 18(1) *Philosophy and Public Affairs* 53–67.

Lim YF, *Cyberspace Law* (Melbourne: Oxford University Press, 2002).

Lipton J, 'Property Offences in the Electronic Age' (1998) *Law Institute Journal* 54–8.

Lipton J, 'Property Offences into the 21st Century' (1999) 1 *Journal of Information Law and Technology*, <http://elj.warwick.ac.uk/jilt/99-1/lipton.html>, accessed November 2003.

Llewelyn K, 'Some Realism about Realism—Responding to Dean Pound' (1931) 44 *Harvard Law Review* 1222–64.

Lombroso C, *L'uomo Delinquente* (Turin: Fratelli Bosca, 1876).

Longford Royal Commission, Victoria, *The Esso Longford Gas Plant Accident: Report of the Longford Royal Commission* (1999).

Lowman J and MacLean BD (eds), *Realist Criminology: Crime Control and Policing in the 1990s* (Toronto: University of Toronto Press, 1992).

Lundstedt AV, *Legal Thinking Revisited* (Stockholm: Almqvist & Wiksell, 1956).
Luria AR, *The Working Brain* (London: The Penguin Press, 1973).
Lynch ML, Michalowski R and Byron Groves W, *The New Primer in Radical Criminology: Critical Perspectives on Crime, Power and Identity* (3rd edn, Monsey, NY: Criminal Justice Press, 2000).
MacCormick N, *Legal Right and Social Democracy* (Oxford: Oxford University Press, 1982).
Magnusson R, *Angels of Death: Exploring the Euthanasia Underground* (Melbourne: Melbourne University Press, 2002).
Maguire M, 'Crime Statistics, Patterns, and Trends: Changing Perceptions and their Implications' in Maguire M, Morgan R and Reiner R (eds), *The Oxford Handbook of Criminology* (2nd edn, Oxford: Oxford University Press, 1997) pp 135–88.
Makkai T and McGregor K, *Drug Use Monitoring Australia: 2002 Annual Report on Drug Use Among Police Detainees* (Canberra: AIC, 2003).
Markus A, *Race: John Howard and the Re-Making of Australia* (Sydney: Allen & Unwin, 2001).
Mars G, *Cheats at Work: An Anthropology of Workplace Crime* (London: Allen & Unwin, 1982).
Mason G, *The Spectacle of Violence: Homophobia, Gender and Knowledge (Writing Corporealities)* (London: Routledge, 2002).
Matthews R and Young J (eds), *Issues in Realist Criminology* (London: Sage Publications, 1992).
Mayhew P, 'Counting the Costs of Crime in Australia', *Trends and Issues* No 247 (Canberra: AIC, 2003).
McAuley F, *Insanity, Psychiatry and Criminal Responsibility* (Dublin: The Round Hall Press, 1993).
McAulay F and McCutcheon P, *Criminal Liability* (Dublin: Round Hall Sweet & Maxwell, 2000).
McConville J, 'Computer Trespass in Victoria' (2001) 25 *Criminal Law Journal* 200–7.
McConville M, Sanders A and Leng R, *The Case for the Prosecution: Police Suspects and the Construction of Criminality* (London: Routledge, 1991).
McCullough J, *Blue Army* (Melbourne: Melbourne University Press, 2001).
McCutcheon JP, 'Omissions and Criminal Liability' (1993–1995) 28–30 *Irish Jurist* (ns) 56–78.
McCutcheon P, 'Morality and the Criminal Law: Reflections on Hart–Devlin' (2002) 47 *The Criminal Law Quarterly* 15–38.
McKelvie H, 'Property in the Body' (1998) 6(1) *Journal of Law and Medicine* 16–18.
McMahon M, 'Battered Women and Bad Science: The Limited Validity and Utility of Battered Woman Syndrome' (1999) 6(1) *Psychiatry, Psychology and Law* 23–49.
McSherry B and Somerville M, 'Sexual Activity Among Institutionalized Persons in Need of Special Care' (1998) 16 *Windsor Yearbook of Access to Justice* 107–16.
McSherry B, 'Automatism in Australia Since Falconer's Case' (1996) December *International Bulletin of Law and Mental Health* 3–8.

McSherry B, 'Criminal Detention of Those with Mental Impairment' (1999) 6 *Journal of Law and Medicine* 216–21.
McSherry B, 'Defining What is a "Disease of the Mind": The Untenability of Current Legal Interpretations' (1993) 1 *Journal of Law and Medicine* 76–90.
McSherry B, 'Expert Testimony and the Effects of Mental Impairment: Reviving the Ultimate Issue Rule?' (2001) 24 *International Journal of Law and Psychiatry* 13–21.
McSherry B, 'No! (means no?)' (1993) 18(1) *Alternative Law Journal* 27–30.
McSherry B, 'The Return of the Raging Hormones Theory: Premenstrual Syndrome, Postpartum Disorders and Criminal Responsibility' (1993) 15 *Sydney Law Review* 292–316.
Meehan E, *The Law of Criminal Attempt—A Treatise* (Calgary: Carswell Legal Publications, 1984).
Mercer N, 'Kill or Be Killed', *Age*, 18 December 2001.
Michael J and Adler M, *Crime, Law and Science* (Montclaire, NJ: Paterson Smith, 1933).
Mildren D, 'Redressing the Imbalance Against Aboriginals in the Criminal Justice System' (1997) 21 *Criminal Law Journal* 7–22.
Mill JS, *On Liberty* (Harmondsworth: Penguin, 1974; first published 1859).
Mirrlees-Black C, Home Office Research Study 191, *Domestic Violence: Findings from a New British Crime Survey Self-Completion Questionnaire* (London: Home Office, 1999).
Mitchell C, 'The Intoxicated Offender—Refuting the Legal and Medical Myths' (1988) 11 *International Journal of Law and Psychiatry* 77–103.
Mitchell Committee, *Criminal Law and Penal Methods Reform Committee of South Australia* (Adelaide: Government Printer, 1973).
Model Criminal Code Officers Committee, *Chapter 3, Theft, Fraud, Bribery and Related Offences*, Report (December 1995).
Model Criminal Code Officers Committee, *Chapter 5, Non Fatal Offences Against the Person*, Discussion Paper (August 1996).
Model Criminal Code Officers Committee, *Chapter 5, Sexual Offences Against the Person*, Discussion Paper (November 1996).
Model Criminal Code Officers Committee, *Chapter 3, Conspiracy to Defraud*, Final Report (May 1997).
Model Criminal Code Officers Committee, *Chapter 5, Fatal Offences Against the Person*, Discussion Paper (June 1998).
Model Criminal Code Officers Committee, *Chapter 7, Administration of Justice Offences*, Report (July 1998).
Model Criminal Code Officers Committee, *Chapter 5, Non Fatal Offences Against the Person*, Report (September 1998).
Model Criminal Code Officers Committee, *Chapter 5, Sexual Offences Against the Person*, Report (May 1999).
Model Criminal Code Officers Committee, *Chapter 4, Damage and Computer Offences*, Discussion Paper (January, 2000).

Model Criminal Code Officers Committee, *Chapter 4, Damage and Computer Offences*, Report (January 2001).
Moloney GJ, 'Attempts' (1991) 15 *Criminal Law Journal* 175–85.
Moreton-Robinson A, 'Troubling Business: Difference and Whiteness Within Feminism' (2000) 15 *Australian Feminist Studies* 343–52.
Moreton-Robinson A, *Talkin' Up the White Woman: Indigenous Women and Feminism* (St Lucia: University of Queensland Press, 2000).
Morgan J, 'Provocation Law and Facts: Dead Women Tell No Tales, Tales are Told About Them' (1997) 21 *Melbourne University Law Review* 237–76.
Morgan J, *Who Kills Whom and Why: Looking Beyond Legal Categories*, VLRC Occasional Paper, 2002.
Morse S, 'Immaturity and Irresponsibility' (1998) 88(1) *The Journal of Criminal Law and Criminology* 15–67.
Morse S, 'Craziness and Criminal Responsibility' (1999) 17 *Behavioral Sciences and the Law* 147–64.
Mortimer J, *Rumpole and the Golden Thread* (Harmondsworth: Penguin Books Ltd, 1983).
Mouzos J, *Femicide: The Killing of Women in Australia 1989–1998* (Canberra: AIC, 1999).
Mouzos J, *Homicidal Encounters: A Study of Homicide in Australia 1989–1999* (Canberra: AIC, 2000).
Mouzos J, 'Indigenous and Non-Indigenous Homicides in Australia—A Comparative Analysis', *Trends and Issues* No 210 (Canberra: AIC, 2000).
Mouzos J and Carcach C, *Weapon Involvement in Armed Robbery*, AIC Research and Public Policy Series No 38 (Canberra: AIC, 2001).
Mouzos J and Rushforth C, 'Family Homicide in Australia', *Trends and Issues* No 255 (Canberra: AIC, 2003).
Mullen P, 'Dangerousness, Risk and the Prediction of Probability' in Geldner MG, Lopez-Ibor JJ and Andreason N (eds), *New Oxford Textbook of Psychiatry* (London: Oxford University Press, 2000) pp 2066–78.
Mullen P, 'Euthanasia: An Impoverished Construction of Life and Death' (1995) 3 *Journal of Law and Medicine* 121–8.
Mullen P, 'The Dangerousness of the Mentally Ill and the Clinical Assessment of Risk' in Brookbanks W (ed), *Psychiatry and the Law* (Wellington: Brooker's Ltd, 1996) pp 93–116.
Mullen P, Pathé M and Purcell R, *Stalkers and Their Victims* (Cambridge: Cambridge University Press, 2000).
Murray, M, *The Criminal Code: A General Review*, Report (1983).
Naffine N, *Feminism and Criminology* (St Leonards: Allen & Unwin, 1997).
National Committee on Violence, *Violence: Directions for Australia* (Canberra: Australian Institute of Criminology, 1990).
National Occupational Health and Safety Commission, *Compendium of Workers' Compensation Statistics Australia 2000–2001* (Canberra, 2002).

Naylor, B, 'The Law Reform Commission of Victoria Homicide Prosecution Study: The Importance of Context' in Strang H and Gerull S, *Homicide: Patterns, Prevention and Control* (Canberra: Australian Institute of Criminology, 1993).

Naylor B, 'Reporting Violence in the British Print Media: Gendered Stories' (2001) 40 *Howard Journal* 180–94.

Neal D, 'Corporate Manslaughter' (1996) 70 *Law Institute Journal* 39–41.

Nelson D and Perrone S, 'Understanding and Controlling Retail Theft', *Trends and Issues* No 152 (Canberra: AIC, 2000).

New South Wales Department for Women, *Heroines of Fortitude: The Experiences of Women in Court as Victims of Sexual Assault* (Woolloomooloo, November 1996).

New South Wales Law Reform Commission, *People with an Intellectual Disability and the Criminal Justice System*, Report No 80 (December 1996).

New South Wales Law Reform Commission, *Partial Defences to Murder: Diminished Responsibility*, Report No 82 (May 1997).

New South Wales Law Reform Commission, *Partial Defences to Murder: Provocation and Infanticide*, Report No 83 (October 1997).

New Zealand Criminal Law Reform Committee, *Report on Intoxication as a Defence to a Criminal Charge* (1984).

New Zealand Law Commission, *Battered Defendants: Victims of Domestic Violence Who Offend*, Preliminary Paper 41 (August 2000).

Niemann G, 'Attempts' (1991) 2(3) *Criminal Law Forum* 549–67.

Noble T, 'Hospital Welcomes Abortion Decision', *Age*, 24 January 2002.

Norrie A, 'Legal and Moral Judgment in the "General" Part' in Rush P, McVeigh S and Young A (eds), *Criminal Legal Doctrine* (Aldershot: Ashgate/Dartmouth Publishing Company Limited, 1997) pp 1–27.

Norrie A, *Crime Reason and History: A Critical Introduction to Criminal Law* (2nd edn, London: Butterworths, 2001).

Norrie A, 'Criminal Law to Legal Theory: The Mysterious Case of the Reasonable Glue Sniffer' (2002) 65(4) *Modern Law Review* 538–55.

Northern Territory Government, Department of Justice, Law Reform Committee, <http://www.nt.gov.au/justice/graphpages/lawmake/lawref.shtml>, accessed 18 June 2003.

O'Connor D and Fairall P, *Criminal Defences* (3rd edn, Sydney: Butterworths, 1996).

O'Regan, R, Criminal Code Review Committee, *Report of the Criminal Code Review Committee to the Attorney-General*, Interim Report (1991).

O'Regan, R, Criminal Code Review Committee, *Report of the Criminal Code Review Committee to the Attorney-General*, Final Report (June 1992).

O'Shane P, 'Is There Any Relevance in the Women's Movement for Aboriginal Women?' (1976) 12 *Refractory Girl* 31–4.

Odgers S, 'Criminal Cases in the High Court of Australia: McAuliffe and McAuliffe' (1996) 20 *Criminal Law Journal* 43–7.

Opie H, 'Aussie Rules Player Jailed for Behind-Play Assault' (1996) 6(2) *Australian and New Zealand Sports Law Association Newsletter* 3.

Orchard GF, 'Impossibility and Inchoate Crimes—Another Hook in a Red Herring' [1993] *New Zealand Law Journal* 426–7.

Pace PJ, 'Marital Coercion—Anachronism or Modernism' [1979] *The Criminal Law Review* 82–9.

Paciocco D, 'Death by *Stone*-ing: The Demise of the Defence of Simple Automatism' (1999) 26 *Criminal Reports* (5th) 273–85.

Packer H, *The Limits of the Criminal Sanction* (London: Oxford University Press, 1969).

Padfield N, 'Clean Water and Muddy Causation: Is Causation a Question of Law or Fact, or Just a Way of Allocating Blame?' [1995] *The Criminal Law Review* 683–94.

Palmer H, 'Dr Adams' Trial for Murder' [1957] *The Criminal Law Review* 365–77.

Perrone S, 'Workplace Fatalities and the Adequacy of Prosecutions' (1995) 13(1) *Law in Context* 81–105.

Phillips J, 'Sexual Assault, Multiple Disabilities and the Law' (1996) 7 *Australian Feminist Law Journal* 157–62.

Phillips R, 'Young Boy Acquitted of Manslaughter', 9 December 1999, World Socialist Web Site, <http://www.wsws.org/articles/1999/dec1999/tria-d09_prn.shtml>, accessed 11 June 2003.

Pickard T and Goldman P, *Dimensions of Criminal Law* (Toronto: Emond Montgomery, 1992).

Pinchbeck I and Hewitt M, *Children in English Society* (London: Routledge and Kegan Paul, 1973) Vol 1.

Pineau L, 'Date Rape: A Feminist Analysis' (1989) 9 *Law and Philosophy* 217–43.

Polk K and Ranson D, 'Patterns of Homicide in Victoria' in Chappell D, Grabosky P and Strange H (eds), *Australian Violence: Contemporary Perspectives* (Canberra: AIC, 1991) pp 53–118.

Polk K and White R, 'Economic Adversity and Criminal Behaviour: Rethinking Youth Unemployment and Crime' (1999) 32(3) *Australian and New Zealand Journal of Criminology* 284–302.

Polk K, 'Masculinity, Honour, and Confrontational Homicide' in Daly K and Maher L (eds), *Criminology at the Crossroads: Feminist Readings in Crime and Justice* (New York: Oxford University Press, 1998) pp 188–205.

Porter S, Birt AR, Yuille JC, Herve HF, 'Memory for Murder: A Psychological Perspective on Dissociative Amnesia in Legal Contexts' (2001) 24 *International Journal of Law and Psychiatry* 23–42.

Proudhon P-J in *Oxford Dictionary of Quotations* (4th edn, Oxford: Oxford University Press, 1992).

Queensland Aboriginal and Torres Strait Islander Women's Task Force on Violence (2000), <http://www.qldwoman.qld.gov.au/publications/atsiviolence.doc>, accessed October 2003.

Queensland Domestic Violence Taskforce, Report (1988).
Queensland Law Reform Commission, *Female Genital Mutilation*, Report No 47 (September, 1994).
Quinney R, *The Social Reality of Crime* (Boston: Little Brown and Co, 1970).
Quinney R, *Critique of Legal Order* (Boston: Little Brown and Co, 1974).
Quinney R, 'Class, State and Crime' in J Jacoby (ed), *Classics of Criminology* (New York: Waveland Press Inc, 1994, first published 1980) pp 106–15.
Rachels J, 'Active and Passive Euthanasia' (1975) 292(2) *New England Journal of Medicine* 78–80.
Rachels J, 'Active and Passive Euthanasia' in TL Beauchamp and L Walters (eds), *Contemporary Issues in Bioethics* (4th edn, Belmont, CA: Wadsworth Publishing Company, 1994) pp 439–42.
Rajaratnam S, Redman J and Lenné M, 'Intoxication and Criminal Responsibility' (2000) 7(1) *Psychiatry, Psychology and Law* 59–69.
Reilly A, 'Loss of Self-control in Provocation' (1997) 21 *Criminal Law Journal* 320–35.
Remick LA, 'Read Her Lips: An Argument for a Verbal Consent Standard in Rape' (1993) 141 *University of Pennsylvania Law Review* 1103–51.
Review [Committee] of Commonwealth Criminal Law, *Principles of Criminal Responsibility and Other Matters*, Interim Report (July 1990) (Canberra: AGPS, 1990).
Ribeiro RA, 'Criminal Liability for Attempting the Impossible—Lady Luck and the Villains' (1974) 4(2) *Hong Kong Law Journal* 109–32.
Richards D, 'Male Circumcision: Medical or Ritual?' (1996) 3(4) *Journal of Law and Medicine* 371–6.
Richards M, *The Hanged Man—The Life and Death of Ronald Ryan* (Melbourne: Scribe Publications, 2002).
Robbins IP, 'Double Inchoate Crimes' (1989) 26(1) *Harvard Journal on Legislation* 1–116.
Robertson G, *The Justice Game* (London: Vintage, 1999).
Rogers J, 'Necessity, Private Defence and the Killing of Mary' [2001] *The Criminal Law Review* 515–26.
Rood D, '2 Weeks After Food Stops, "BWV" Dies', *Age*, 8 July 2003.
Royal Commission into Aboriginal Deaths in Custody, *National Report—Overview and Recommendations* (Canberra: AGPS, 1991).
Royal Commission on Human Relationships, *Royal Commission on Human Relationships*, Final Report (Canberra: AGPS, 1977).
Rush P, *Criminal Law* (Sydney: Butterworths, 1997).
Rush P and Young A, 'A Crime of Consequence and a Failure of Legal Imagination: The Sexual Offences of the Model Criminal Code' (1997) 9 *The Australian Feminist Law Journal* 100–33.
Sakurai Y and Smith R, 'Gambling as a Motivation for the Commission of Financial Crime', *Trends and Issues* No 256 (Canberra: AIC, 2003).
Sallmann P and Willis J, 'Editorial: Criminal Conspiracy: Takes One to Tango?' (1982) 15 *Australian and New Zealand Journal of Criminology* 129–30.

Sayre FB, 'Criminal Conspiracy' (1922) 35 *Harvard Law Review* 393–427.
Sayre FB, 'Criminal Attempts' (1928) XLI(7) *Harvard Law Review* 821–59.
Sayre FB, 'Mens Rea' (1932) *Harvard Law Review* 974–1026.
Schacht SP and Ewing DW, *Feminism and Men: Reconstructing Gender Relations* (New York: New York University Press, 1998).
Schopp R, *Justification Defenses and Just Convictions* (Cambridge: Cambridge University Press, 1998).
Schulhofer SJ, 'Taking Sexual Autonomy Seriously: Rape Law and Beyond' (1992) 11 *Law and Philosophy* 35–94.
Scott ES, Reppucci ND and Woolard JL, 'Evaluating Adolescent Decision Making in Legal Contexts' (1995) 19 *Law and Human Behavior* 221–44.
Scrimshaw S, 'Infanticide in Human Populations: Societal and Individual Concerns' in Hausfater G and Hardy SB (eds), *Infanticide: Comparative and Evolutionary Perspectives* (New York: Aldue Publishing Co, 1984) pp 439–62.
Security Australia, 'Shoplifting up to $2m daily', (1996) 16(4) *Security Australia* 38.
Seligman MEP, *Helplessness: On Depression, Development and Death* (San Francisco: Freeman, 1975).
Seligman MEP and Maier SF, 'Failure to Escape Shock' (1967) 74 *Journal of Experimental Psychology* 1–9.
Seymour J, *Childbirth and the Law* (New York: Oxford University Press, 2000).
Seymour J, 'The Legal Status of the Fetus: An International Review' (2002) 1 *Journal of Law and Medicine* 28–40.
Shearer IA, *Starke's International Law* (Sydney: Butterworths, 1994).
Sheehy E, Stubbs J and Tolmie J, 'Defending Battered Women on Trial: The Battered Woman Syndrome and its Limitations' (1992) 16 *Criminal Law Journal* 369–94.
Sherlock RK and Sherlock RD, 'Sterilizing the Retarded: Constitutional, Statutory and Policy Alternatives' (1982) 60 *North Carolina Law Review* 943–83.
Shines R, 'Intoxication and Responsibility' (1990) 13 *International Journal of Law and Psychiatry* 9–35.
Shorter E, *A History of Psychiatry* (New York: John Wiley & Sons Inc, 1997).
Sivapragasam M, 'For Whose Benefit Anyway?' (1997) 22(4) *Alternative Law Journal* 170–2.
Skene L, *Law and Medical Practice: Rights, Duties, Claims and Defences* (Sydney: Butterworths, 1998).
Smart C, 'Feminist Approaches to Criminology or Postmodern Woman Meets Atavistic Man' in Morris A and Gelsthorpe L (eds), *Feminist Perspectives in Criminology* (Milton Keynes: Open University Press, 1990) pp 71–84.
Smart C, 'Law's Truth/Women's Experience' in Graycar R (ed), *Dissenting Opinions* (Sydney: Allen & Unwin, 1990) pp 1–20.
Smith JC, 'Case Comment: R v Meredith' [1973] *The Criminal Law Review* 253–4.
Smith JC, 'Case Comment: R v Caldwell' [1981] *The Criminal Law Review* 393–6.

Smith JC, *Herald of Free Enterprise*: *Justification and Excuse in the Criminal Law* (London: Sweet & Maxwell, 1989).
Smith JC, 'Criminal Liability of Accessories: Law and Law Reform' (1997) 113 *The Law Quarterly Review* 453–67.
Smith JC, 'Obtaining Cheques by Deception or Theft' [1997] *The Criminal Law Review* 396–405.
Smith JC, *The Law of Theft* (8th edn, London: Butterworths, 1997).
Smith JC, 'Manslaughter: R v Khan: Commentary' [1998] *The Criminal Law Review* 830–3.
Smith JC, *Smith and Hogan Criminal Law* (10th edn, London: Butterworths, 2002).
Smith KJM, 'Liability for Endangerment: English *Ad Hoc* Pragmatism and American Innovation' [1983] *The Criminal Law Review* 127–36.
Smith KJM, *A Modern Treatise on the Law of Criminal Complicity* (Oxford: Clarendon Press, 1991).
Smith KJM, 'Withdrawal in Complicity: A Restatement of Principles' [2001] *The Criminal Law Review* 769–85.
Smith R, 'Measuring the Extent of Fraud in Australia', *Trends and Issues* No 74 (Canberra: AIC, 1997).
Smith R, Wolanin N and Worthington G, 'e-Crime Solutions and Crime Displacement', *Trends and Issues* No 243 (Canberra: AIC, 2003).
Smith S, 'Shoplifting Diversion in Victoria' (1985) 10 *Legal Services Bulletin* 256–61.
Somerville M, 'Labels versus Contents: Variance Between Philosophy, Psychiatry and Law in Concepts Governing Decision-Making' (1994) 39(1) *McGill Law Journal* 179–99.
Sorell T, *Moral Theory and Capital Punishment* (Oxford: Blackwell, 1987).
South Australian Criminal Law and Penal Methods Law Reform Committee: *The Substantive Criminal Law*, Fourth Report (1977).
Spann G, 'Pure Politics' in Delgado R and Stefancic J (eds), *Critical Race Theory* (2nd edn, Philadelphia: Temple University Press, 2000) pp 21–34.
Spencer JR, 'Trying to Help Another Person Commit a Crime' in Smith PF (ed), *Criminal Law: Essays in Honour of JC Smith* (London: Butterworths, 1987) pp 148–69.
Spencer JR, 'Insanity and Mens Rea' [2000] 59(1) *Cambridge Law Journal* 9–11.
Spring RL, 'The Return to Mens Rea: Salvaging a Reasonable Perspective on Mental Disorder in Criminal Trials' (1998) 21(2) *International Journal of Law and Psychiatry* 187–96.
Springvale Legal Service, *Lawyers Practice Manual* (Melbourne: Law Book Co) 1.5.402.
Stacy HM, *Postmodernism and Law: Jurisprudence in a Fragmenting World* (Aldershot: Ashgate/Dartmouth, 2001).
Steel A, 'The Appropriate Test for Dishonesty' (2000) 24 *Criminal Law Journal* 46–59.
Steel A, 'Vaguely Going Where No-one has Gone: The Expansive New Computer Access Offences' (2002) 26 *Criminal Law Journal* 72–97.

Steinberg L and Cauffman E, 'Maturity of Judgement in Adolescence: Psychosocial Factors in Adolescent Decision Making' (1996) 20 *Law and Human Behavior* 249–72.

Steinberg M, *Handbook for the Assessment of Dissociation: A Clinical Guide* (Washington: American Psychiatric Press, 1995).

Stephen J, *A History of the Criminal Law of England* (3rd edn, London: Richard Clay & Sons, 1883) Vol 2.

Stone A, 'The Ethical Boundaries of Forensic Psychiatry: A View from the Ivory Tower' (1984) 12(3) *Bulletin of the American Academy of Psychiatry and Law* 209–19.

Stubbs J and Tolmie J, 'Feminisms, Self-Defence, and Battered Women: A Response to Hubble's "Straw Feminist"' (1998) 10(1) *Current Issues in Criminal Justice* 75–84.

Sullivan C, 'The Response of the Criminal Law in Australia to Computer Abuse' (1988) 12 *Criminal Law Journal* 228–50.

Sundby SE, 'The Reasonable Doubt Rule and the Meeting of Innocence' (1988) 40 *Hastings Law Journal* 457–510.

Sutherland EH, 'White-collar Criminality' (1940) 5 *American Sociological Review* 1–12.

Sweet R, 'Legal Issues in Reproductive Rights' (2002) 9 *Journal of Law and Medicine* 266–70.

Syrota G, 'A Radical Change in the Law of Recklessness' [1982] *The Criminal Law Review* 97–106.

Szego J, 'Wife Did Not Want to "Linger On"', *The Age*, 25 December 2002.

Taft A, Hegarty K and Flood M, 'Are Men and Women Equally Violent to Intimate Partners?' (2001) 25(8) *Australian and New Zealand Journal of Public Health* 498–500.

Taylor J, 'Rape and Women's Credibility: Problems of Recantations and False Accusations Echoed in the Case of Cathleen Crowell Webb and Gary Dotson' (1987) 10 *Harvard Women's Law Journal* 59–116.

Taylor N, 'Reporting of Crime Against Small Retail Businesses', *Trends and Issues* No 242 (Canberra: AIC 2002).

Taylor N, 'Robbery Against Service Stations and Pharmacies: Recent Trends', *Trends and Issues* No 223 (Canberra: AIC, 2002).

Temkin J, 'Impossible Attempts: Another View' (1976) 39 *Modern Law Review* 55–69.

Temkin J, *Rape and the Legal Process* (2nd edn, Oxford: Oxford University Press, 2002).

The Macquarie Dictionary (3rd edn, NSW: Macquarie University, 1997).

Thomson JJ, *Rights, Restitution and Risk: Essays in Moral Theory* (Cambridge, MA: Harvard University Press, 1986).

Thomson JJ, 'Self-Defense' (1990) 20 *Philosophy and Public Affairs* 283–310.

Tollefson EA and Starkman B, *Mental Disorder in Criminal Proceedings* (Toronto: Carswell, 1993).

Tolstoy L, *Anna Karenina* (New York: Signet, 1961, first published 1875).

Tooley M, *Abortion and Infanticide* (Oxford: Clarendon Press, 1983).

Toy M, 'Doctors Endorse Dwarf Abortion', *Sydney Morning Herald*, 4 July 2000.

Trade Practices Act Review Committee, *Review of the Competition Provisions of the Trade Practices Act* (the Dawson Review) (Canberra: Commonwealth of Australia, January 2003).

Triggs G, 'Australia's War Crimes Trials' in McCormack TLH and Simpson GJ, *The Law of War Crimes: National and International Approaches* (The Hague: Kluwer Law International, 1997) pp 123–49.

Trudel G and Desjardins G, 'Staff Reactions Toward the Sexual Behaviors of People Living in Institutional Settings' (1992) 10(3) *Sexuality and Disability* 173–88.

Turner JN, 'The James Bulger Case: A Challenge to Juvenile Justice Theories' (1994) 68(8) *Law Institute Journal* 734–7.

Tushnet M, 'Critical Legal Studies: A Political History' (1991) 100 *Yale Law Journal* 1515–44.

Urlich R, 'Physical Discipline in the Home' [1994] *Auckland University Law Review* 851–60.

Vanstone A, Federal Minister for Justice, 'Government to Ensure Early Removal of Drunks' Defence', *Media Release*, 2 December 1997.

Vaughan GM and Hogg MA, *Introduction to Social Psychology* (2nd edn, Sydney: Prentice Hall Australia Pty Ltd, 1998).

Verkaik R, 'Six Railway Managers Charged with Manslaughter', *Independent*, 10 July 2003.

Victoria Police, *Crime Statistics 2001/02*, <http://www.police.vic.gov.au/ShowContentPage.cfm?ContentPageId=4841>, accessed November 2003.

Victorian Drug and Crime Prevention Committee, *Inquiry into Fraud and Electronic Commerce*, Discussion Paper (Melbourne: VDCPC, 2003).

Victorian Law Reform Commission, *Sexual Offences: Law and Procedure*, Discussion Paper (Melbourne: VLRC, 2001).

Victorian Law Reform Commission, *Defences to Homicide*, Options Paper (Melbourne: VLRC, 2003).

Victorian Law Reform Commission, *Sexual Offences: Law and Procedure*, Interim Report (Melbourne: VLRC, 2003).

Vygotsky LS, *Selected Psychological Investigations* (Moscow: Izd Akad Pedagog Nauk RSFR, 1956).

Vygotsky LS, *Development of the Higher Mental Functions* (Moscow: Izd Akad Pedagog Nauk RSFR, 1960).

Walker J, *First Australian National Survey of Crimes Against Businesses* (Canberra: AIC 1995).

Walker LE, *The Battered Woman* (New York: Harper & Row, 1979).

Walker LE, *The Battered Woman Syndrome* (New York: Springer, 1984).

Walker LE, *Terrifying Love* (New York: Harper Perennial, 1989).

Walker LE, 'Understanding Battered Woman's Syndrome' (1995) 31(2) *Trial* 30–4.

Wallace A, *Homicide: The Social Reality* (Sydney: NSW Bureau of Crime Statistics and Research, 1986).

Waller L and Williams CR, *Criminal Law: Text and Cases* (9th edn, Sydney: Butterworths, 2001).

Ward E, 'Rape of Girl-Children by Male Family Members' 215 *Australian and New Zealand Journal of Criminology* (1982) 90–9.

Waye V, 'Rape and the Unconscionable Bargain' (1991) 16 *Criminal Law Journal* 94–105.

Weatherburn D, Lind B and Ku S, 'The Short-Run Effects of Economic Adversity on Property Crime: An Australian Case Study' (2001) 34(2) *Australian and New Zealand Journal of Criminology* 134–48.

Weiner D, 'Stalking—Does the Law Work?' (2001) 75(8) *Law Institute Journal* 67–71.

Weinert HR, 'Social Hosts and Drunken Drivers: A Duty to Intervene?' (1985) 133 *University of Pennsylvania Law Review* 867–94.

Wells C, *Corporations and Criminal Responsibility* (Oxford: Oxford University Press, 1993).

Wells C and Morgan D, 'Whose Foetus Is it?' (1991) 18 *Journal of Law and Society* 431–47.

Wheelwright K, 'Corporate Liability for Workplace Deaths and Injuries—Reflecting on Victoria's Laws in the Light of the Esso Longford Explosion' (2002) 7(1) *Deakin Law Review* 323–47.

White DV, 'Sports Violence as Criminal Assault: Development of the Doctrine by Canadian Courts' (1986) 6 *Duke Law Journal* 1030–54.

Wieviorka M, *The Arena of Racism* (London: Sage, 1995).

Wilczynski A, *Child Homicide* (London: Greenwich Medical Media, 1997).

Wilkie M, *Women Social Security Offenders: Experiences of the Criminal Justice system in Western Australia* (Nedlands, WA: Crime Research Centre University of Western Australia, 1993).

Williams CR, 'The Shifting Meaning of Dishonesty' (1999) 23 *Criminal Law Journal* 275–84.

Williams CR, *Property Offences* (3rd edn, Sydney: LBC Information Services, 1999).

Williams CR, 'Development and Change in Insanity and Related Defences' (2000) 24(3) *Melbourne University Law Review* 711–36.

Williams D, Federal Attorney-General, 'States Urged to Dump Drunk's Defence', *Media Release*, 29 October 1997.

Williams G, *Criminal Law—The General Part* (2nd edn, London: Stevens & Sons, 1961).

Williams G, 'Recklessness Redefined' (1981) 40(2) *Cambridge Law Journal* 252–83.

Williams G, 'Temporary Appropriation Should be Theft' [1981] *The Criminal Law Review* 129–41.

Williams G, 'Offences and Defences' (1982) 2 *Legal Studies* 233–56.

Williams G, *Textbook of Criminal Law* (2nd edn, London: Stevens & Sons, 1983).

Williams G, 'Criminal Omissions—the Conventional View' (1991) 107 *Law Quarterly Review* 86–98.

Williams P and Urbas G, 'Heroin Overdoses and Duty of Care', *Trends and Issues* No 188 (Canberra: AIC, 2001).

Williamson Laila, 'Infanticide: An Anthropological Analysis' in Kohl M (ed), *Infanticide and the Value of Life* (New York: Prometheus Books, 1978) pp 61–75.

Willis J, 'Manslaughter by the Intentional Infliction of Some Harm: A Category that Should be Closed' (1985) 9 *Criminal Law Journal* 109–24.

Wilson C and Brewer N, 'The Incidence of Criminal Victimisation of Individuals with an Intellectual Disability' (1992) 27(2) *Australian Psychologist* 114–17.

Wilson JQ (ed), *Crime and Public Policy* (San Francisco: ICS Press, 1983).

Wilson JQ and Herrnstein RJ, *Crime and Human Nature* (New York: Simon and Schuster, 1985).

Wolfenden Committee, *Report of the Committee on Homosexual Offences and Prostitution* (London: HMSO, 1957) Cmnd 257.

Woolard JL, Repucci ND and Redding RE, 'Theoretical and Methodological Issues in Studying Children's Capacities in Legal Contexts' (1996) 20 *Law and Human Behavior* 219–28.

Yeo S, 'Proportionality in Criminal Defences' (1988) 12 *Criminal Law Journal* 211–27.

Yeo S, *Compulsion in the Criminal Law* (Sydney: Law Book Co Ltd, 1990).

Yeo S, 'Private Defences, Duress and Necessity' (1991) 15 *Criminal Law Journal* 139–51.

Yeo S, 'Coercing Wives into Crime' (1992) 6(3) *Australian Journal of Family Law* 214–28.

Yeo S, 'Power of Self-control in Provocation and Automatism' (1992) 14 *Sydney Law Review* 3–22.

Yeo S, 'Battered Woman Syndrome in Australia' (1993) 143 *New Law Journal* 13–14.

Yeo S, 'Sex, Ethnicity, Power of Self-control and Provocation Revisited' (1996) 18 *Sydney Law Review* 304–22.

Yeo S, 'Reformulating Diminished Responsibility: Learning from the New South Wales Experience' (1999) 20 *Singapore Law Review* 159–76.

Yeo S, 'Revisiting Excessive Self-Defence' (2000) 12(1) *Current Issues in Criminal Justice* 39–57.

Young J, 'Incessant Chatter: Recent Paradigms in Criminology' in Maguire M, Morgan R and Reiner R (eds), *The Oxford Handbook of Criminology* (Oxford: Oxford University Press, 1994) pp 69–124.

Young J, 'Left Realist Criminology: Radical in its Analysis, Realist in its Policy' in Maguire M, Morgan R and Reiner R (eds), *The Oxford Handbook of Criminology* (2nd edn, Oxford: Oxford University Press, 1997) pp 473–98.

Index

abetting 438, 439, 441
abnormality of mind 542
   cause of 542–3
   effect of 543–4
abortion 113, 137, 139–40, 142, 143, 151
accessorial liability 437–53
   assisting and encouraging crime 448–50
   definitions 438–41
   fault elements 448–50
   mere presence 442–5
   omissions 442–5
   physical elements 438–41
   supplying goods and advice 442–5
   withdrawal by an accessory 445–8
accessories after the fact 450
accused's loss of self-control 488–90
acting dishonestly 288–95
acting in concert 428–33
acts in criminal law 66–9
Adler, Mortimer 5
age of consent 230–4
aggravated assault 160
aggravated burglary 329–31
aggravated robbery 316–19
aggravation, factors of 166–7
agreement
   between two or more persons 396–8
   and conspiracy 393–8
aiding 438, 439, 441
Alldridge, Peter 434, 437, 473
Allen, Judith 137, 138, 142, 143
appropriation
   and consent 275–8
   definition 273, 282
   meaning of 281–3
   and property 272–8, 281–3
Aristotle 41–2

armed robbery 316–19
Ashworth, Andrew 21–2, 49–50, 55, 69, 122, 130, 151, 170, 255, 369, 378, 387, 500
assault 155–71
   aggravated 160
   common 157, 158, 168
   and consent 188–202
   defences to 183–5, 188
   factors of aggravation 166–7
   with intention to commit another crime 160
   lawful 181–8
   on particular classes of people 160–1
   and recklessness 151, 169, 171
   and related offences 152–5
   resulting in harm 161–3
   statistics 95, 205
   by the threat of force 158–9, 164–6
   by the use of force 159–60
   use of reasonable force 182–3, 185–8
assisting and encouraging crime 448–50
Atkinson, Carlie 156
Atkinson, Judy 93, 156
attempt
   fault element 379, 385–7
   impossibility 415–6
   inchoate offences 376–88
   physical element 379, 380–3
Austin, John 70
Australian Competition and Consumer Commission (ACCC) 260, 366
Australian Law Reform Commission 163, 199, 200, 497
Australian Securities and Investments Commission (ASIC) 260, 366
automatism
   as defence 52, 54, 71, 472, 508–9, 511

internal cause theory of insane
        automatism   511–12, 532

Bagaric, Mirko   17
Baker, Brenda M   219
Ballingal, Sara   24, 28
Bandura, Albert   71
Barker, Richard   323, 328
battered woman syndrome   424–5, 475, 478,
        479–82, 495–6
Bayefsky, Anne   220
Beauchamp, Tom   68
Beccaria, Cesare   38
Becker, Howard   10
Behrendt, Larissa   13
belief in owner's consent   293–4
belief that owner cannot be found   294
Bell, Derek   15
Bell, Sylvia   531–2
belonging to another, property   268–72,
        280–1, 344
Bentham, Jeremy   38, 39
Biggs, Hazel   68
Blake, Meredith   55
blameworthiness   63, 65
Bland, Anthony   133
bodily harm   162, 168
body parts as property   267–8
body/mind and criminal responsibility   60,
        106, 108
Bonollo, Maria   299
Bracton, Henrici de   41
brain dead   99, 105
Braithwaite, John   146–7, 366
breaking and entering   325–6
Brett, Peter   498
Bronitt, Simon   215, 445
Brooks, Peter   50
Brow, Adam   298–9
Brown, Bernard   484
Browne-Wilkinson, Lord   136, 281
Brownmiller, Susan   205
Bryan, James Wallace   389
Bulger, James   42
burden of proof and defences   54–8
Burgess-Jackson, Keith   211
burglary   253, 308, 319–31
    aggravated   329–31
    breaking and entering   259, 325–6
    entry   322–3
    entry as a trespasser   323–5
    fault elements   326–7
    physical elements   322–6
    statistics   95, 252, 319

    with intent to commit another offence
        326–7
Burke, Roger Hopkins   9
Butcher, Glen   115

capitalist society   33
Cartesian dualism   60
Cashmore, Judy   186
causation
    and criminal law   81–5
    of death   99–104, 105–6
cause of the abnormality of mind   542–3
Chamallas, Martha   215
Chaplin, James   539
characteristics of the ordinary person   495–6
Charlesworth, Max   134
Chayna, Andre   502–3, 530, 540, 541, 543
Cheshire, David   101
child destruction   140–1, 142, 151
childbirth, offences relating to   137–43
children
    and reasoning   41–6
    sexual offences against   228–38
Chilvers, Marilyn   280
Churchland, Paul and Patricia   60
claim of right   290–3
Clough, Jonathan   151, 387
Coke, Edward   39, 58, 96, 97, 98
Collins, Stephen   324
complicity   411, 424–7
    accessorial liability   437–53
    acting in concert   428–34
    doctrine of common purpose   453–62
    innocent agency   434–7
    principal offenders   425–6, 428–34, 450
computer crime   31
computer fraud   279, 360–4
concurrence of physical and fault elements
        65, 79–81
conduct
    intentional   66, 71
    involuntary   508, 509
    voluntary   66, 70–1
consent
    age of consent   230–4
    and appropriation   275–8
    and assault   188–202
    definition   216–17
    and fraud   220–2
    mistaken belief in   224–5, 226, 227, 236
    and sexual assault   209–22, 224–7
    social context of   211–20
    without   209–11, 387
conspiracy   388–408

the agreement 393–9
agreement between two or more
  persons 396–8
definition 391
to defraud 388, 391–2, 404–5
fault element 403–6
impossibility 416–18
physical element 391–9
unlawful act 398–9
constructive murder 108, 115–19, 151
continuing danger theory 512
Cook, Dee 335
Cooper, Maryanne 546–7, 549, 550
corporate crime 62
corporate criminal responsibility 31–8, 62, 148
corporate homicide 144–51
corporate manslaughter 150
corporations, offences involving 364–7
counselling 438, 439, 441
Crabbe, Douglas 106–7, 111
Crafts, Anne 110
crime
  assisting and encouraging 448–50
  defining 4–5, 48
  elements of 'serious' 58–65
  fault elements 58–60, 63–5, 69–81
  measuring 22–4
  model 6–7
  physical elements 58–60, 65–9, 79–81
  statistics 22–4, 90–1, 92, 94, 95, 153, 205, 252, 256–7, 308, 319
criminal law
  acts and omissions 66–9
  aims of 17–22
  corporate responsibility 31–8, 62
  elements 58–65
  and gender 47, 90–2
  individual responsibility 31–8
  physical and intellectual disabilities 48
  and race 47
  reason and rationality 38–48
  social context 40, 51, 94–5
  structuring 49–50
  subjective versus objective fault elements 63–5, 482–4
  voluntary conduct 66, 70–1
criminal negligence manslaughter 68–9, 78–9, 121–2, 123
criminal responsibility
  corporate 31–8, 62, 148
  individual 31–8, 60
  mind/body 60
  minimum age 42–6

criminology
  critical 8–11
critical criminology 8–11
critical legal studies 8–11
critical race theory 15–16
Crocker, Phyllis 478
culpable driving causing death 123–4
cultural background and provocation 497
Cunneen, Chris 16, 93

Daly, Kathy 13
Damasio, Antonio 60
dangerous act manslaughter 127–9, 130, 151
Davies, Margaret 4, 6, 38
Davis, Corey 42
de Hass, Nicola 186
De Stefano, Frank 251–2
death
  causation of 99–104
  of a human being 98–9
deception
  obtaining a financial advantage by 349–57
  obtaining property by 338–49, 351–2
  physical elements 339–41, 351
  property offences involving 282, 333–8
defences 51–3
  to assault 183–5, 188
  automatism 52, 54, 71, 472, 508–9, 511
  burden of proof 54–8
  coercion 565
  duress 52, 553, 555–70
  duress and murder 568–9
  justification and excuse 53–4
  marital coercion 554, 564, 565, 569–70
  mental impairment 503, 530–40, 551
  mental state 502–7
  provocation 52, 91, 184–5, 188, 499–501
  self-defence 52, 53, 91, 183, 184, 188, 469–84
  and sexual offences 234–6
  threats 565–6
  see also mental state defences
defences based on external pressures 553–5
  duress and marital coercion 554, 555–70
  necessity 52, 570–82
degree of force or violence 315
Dennis, Ian 31, 384, 389, 400
Derrida, Jacques 12
Descartes, René 60
deterrence and punishment 18
Devlin, Lord Patrick 4, 20–1, 55, 200
diminished responsibility 52, 540–6
Dimozantos, Angelo 408–9

Index

'disease of the mind' 532
dishonesty 304–7, 346–9, 367–70
  acting dishonestly 288–95
  definition 303
  fault element 356–7, 405–6, 407
  High Court's approach in *Peters*'s case 300–2, 406
  meaning in other Australian jurisdictions 302–4
  meaning of 295–6
  narrow approach in Victoria 297–300
  'ordinary' or 'community standard' approach 296–7
doctrine of common purpose 453–62
Dolphin, John 277
domestic violence 91–2, 93, 153–4, 155–7, 206, 496
Duff, Antony 60, 65, 69, 170, 378, 415
duress and marital coercion 52, 553, 555–70
duress as a defence to murder 568–9
duty of care 48, 68, 124–6, 127, 130, 133
Dworkin, Ronald 134

Easom, John 286
Easteal, Patricia 335
Edmund-Davies, Lord 381
Edwards, Susan 201
effect of the abnormality of mind 543–4
effect of the mental impairment of volition 537–8
effect of the mental impairment on understanding 535–7
elements of 'serious' crimes 58–65
encouraging crime 448–50
endangering life or personal safety 176–81
Enker, Arnold 387
Enlightenment 38, 40
entry 322–3
entry as a trespasser 323–5
entry to a building or part of a building 325–6
Esau, Abel 203–4, 226
escape murder 118
Esso Australia Pty Ltd 145–6
euthanasia 67–8, 131–7
  involuntary 131, 132
  non-voluntary 131, 132, 133, 135, 137
  voluntary 131, 132, 134–7
evidential burden 55–6
excessive self-defence 475–8
excuse as defence 53–4
Ewing, Charles 481

Falconer, Mary 469–72, 473, 488, 489–90, 491–2, 494, 501, 509, 510–11
Farmer, Lindsay 40
Fattah, Ezzat 23
fault, subjective versus objective 63–5
fault elements
  accessorial liability 448–50
  assault and related offences 167–70
  attempting to commit crime 379, 385–7
  burglary 326–7
  concurrence of physical element 79–81
  conspiracy 403–6
  criminal law 58–60, 69–81
  dishonesty 356–7, 405–6, 407
  incitement 412
  intention 69–74
  knowledge 74–6
  murder 106–14, 151
  negligence 64, 77–9
  obtaining property 346–9
  property offences 283–95
  recklessness 72, 74–6, 109–10, 114
  robbery 314–15
  sexual assault 72, 74, 76, 77, 222–5
  stealing 283–95
  subjective versus objective 63–5, 69, 482–4
  theft 283–308
  wilful blindness 76–7
Feinberg, Joel 19
Fels, Allan 366
female genital mutilation 163, 196–7, 198–9
feminist empiricism 13
feminist theories 12–15
financial advantage
  meaning of 353–6
  obtaining by deception 349–57
  physical elements 352–56
financial transactions as property 264–7
Finlay-Jones, Robert Astley 509–10
Fisse, Brent 36, 37, 212, 213
Fletcher, George 261
force, use of reasonable 182–3, 184, 185–8
force/violence 310–12
Ford Pinto case 147
Foster, Michael 53
Foucault, Michel 11, 40, 41
fraud 333–8, 367
  computer 279, 360–4
  and consent 220–2
  and theft 258, 336–8, 357–60
Freckelton, Ian 188–9, 481
Freeman, Alan 15
Freiberg, Arie 253, 255, 259
fungibles 287–8

616 Index

Garland, David 18
gender and criminal law 47, 90–2
general or basic intention 70–1
Gillespie, Cynthia 475
Gillian, Carol 47
Glasbeek, Harry 35
Glazebrook, PR 384
Goldman, Phil 218
Goode, Matthew 529
Goff, Lord 581
Grabosky, Peter 366
Graycar, Regina 19, 142, 212
Green, Malcolm 493
grievous bodily harm 162, 168
   intention to cause 107, 109, 114, 170
   recklessness as to 72, 107, 109–10, 114, 151, 171
gross negligence manslaughter 121–2
Groves, Matthew 180
guilty mind 60, 63

Hall, Jerome 539
harm, prevention of 18–19
Hart, Herbert 4, 17, 20–1, 63, 64, 69, 70, 84, 200
Hawkins, Andrew 518–19
Healey, Kelly 89–90
Heenan, Melanie 214, 216, 217
Herald of Free Enterprise 144, 149
HIH Royal Commission 366, 367
Hinchcliffe, Jacqueline 553, 582
Hinks, Karen 277
Holdsworth, William 484
Holland, Winifred 331
Holroyd, Jessica 369
homicide 89–151
   corporate 144–51
   lawful 94
   statistics 119
   unlawful 94
homosexual intercourse 233
homosexuality 20
Honoré, Tony 84
Hopkins, Andrew 37
Horder, Jeremy 499, 580
horseplay, rough 188, 193–4
Hubble, Gail 482
Hunter, Rosemary 154

impossibility 413–22
   attempts 415–16
   conspiracy 416–18
   incitement 418–19
incapacitation and punishment 18

incest 236–8, 410
inchoate offences 51, 373–6, 422–3
incitement 408–13
   fault element 412
   impossibility 418–19
   physical element 409–10
indecent assault 206–27
Indigenous communities and violence 93, 156
Indigenous customary law 197–8, 199–200, 235–6, 290–1
Indigenous people and homicide 92–3
individual criminal responsibility 31–8, 60
industrial revolution 63
infanticide 141–2, 546–51
innocent agency 434–7
insane automatism, internal cause theory 511–12, 532
insanity *see* mental illness
intellectual disabilities and criminal law 48
intent to commit another offence, burglary with 326–7
intention
   to cause grievous bodily harm 107, 109, 114, 170
   and criminal law 69–74, 388
   fault element 69–74
   general or basic 70–1
   to kill 108–9, 114
   and motive 74
   oblique 72–3
   to permanently deprive 283–8, 307–8, 346, 348
   recklessness as to causing death 72, 109–10
   and sexual assault 222–4, 388
   specific 71–2
intentional conduct 66, 71
internal cause theory of insane automatism 511–12, 532
intoxication 72, 521–30
involuntary euthanasia 131, 132
involuntary manslaughter 119–120, 127

Jeffrey, Trevor 101
Johnson, Phillip 390, 400, 401
jurisdiction 24–31
   minimum age for criminal responsibility 42
   protective approach 28–9
   terminatory theory 27–8
   territorial nexus/substantial link approach 29–30
   territorial theory 24, 25–7

justification as defence 53–4

Kant, Immanuel 31
Kelly, Anthony-Noel 267
Kelman, Mark 9, 46, 66, 475
Kerridge, Ian 134, 163
knowledge as fault element 74–6
Kovacs, Stephanie 338–9, 345
Ku, Simon 254
Kusha, HR 5

Lacey, Nicola 14–15, 16, 19, 21, 40, 112, 211
Lake, Marilyn 15
Lambie, Shiralee Ann 333, 345, 351
land, theft of 264
Lanham, David 136
larceny 258, 261, 268, 274, 275, 285
law, common 39–40
Law Reform Commission of Victoria *see* Victorian Law Reform Commission
lawful assaults 181–8
Lawrence, Alan 275–6
Lea, John 6
Leader-Elliott, Ian 482, 497, 518
Lees, Sue 206
legal burden of proof 56
legal reasoning and rationality 39–40
legal studies
 critical 8–11
liability, accessorial 437–53
 assisting and encouraging crime 448–50
 definitions 438–41
 fault elements 448–50
 mere presence 442–5
 omissions 442–5
 physical elements 438–41
 supplying goods and advice 442–5
 withdrawal by an accessory 445–8
liability offences, strict and absolute 61–3
Lind, Bronwyn 254
Lipton, Jacqueline 279
Llewelyn, Karl 6
Lombroso, Cesare 3
Lowe, Michael 134, 163
Lowman, John 6
Lundstedt, Anders Vilhelm 21
Luria, Aleksandr Romanovich 71

McAuley, Finbarr 53, 59, 71, 499, 532
MacCormick, Neil 19
McCullough, Jude 185–6
McCutcheon, Paul 21, 22, 53, 59, 71, 499
McDonald, David 93
McKelvie, Helen 214, 216, 217

McKewen, Cindi 176–7
MacLean, Brian 6
McMahon, Marilyn 480
McPhee, John 134, 163
Magnusson, Roger 136
Maguire, Mike 23
Maher, Lisa 13
malice, transferred 110–12, 113
manslaughter 72, 89–95, 119–31
 causation of death 99–104, 105–6
 corporate 150
 criminal negligence 68–9, 78–9, 121–2, 123
 current law 97–104
 dangerous act 127–9, 130, 151
 death of a human being 98–9
 gross negligence 121–2
 involuntary 119, 120, 127
 negligent 68–9, 78–9, 121–2
 physical elements 95–106
 unlawful act 127–9, 130
 voluntary 119, 120
marital coercion 554, 564, 565, 569–70
marital rape 206
Mars, Gerald 253
Martin, Edwin 111
Marx, Karl 10
Matthews, Horrie 349
Matthews, Roger 6
Mayhew, Pat 319
'mental disease' 532
'mental dysfunction' 534–5
mental illness
 defence 502–7, 533–4
 and reasoning 41
 and responsibility for criminal acts 40–1
mental impairment
 defence 503, 530–40, 551
 effect on understanding 535–7
 effect on volition 537–8
 sexual offences against individuals with 238–46
 and unintentional conduct 517–21
 see also intellectual disabilities
mental impairment defence of 530–40
mental impairment and involuntary conduct 71, 507–17
 continuing danger theory 512
 internal cause theory of insane automatism 511–12, 532
 sound/unsound mind theory 512–14
mental state defences 502–7
 diminished responsibility 52, 540–6
 'disease of the mind'/'mental disease' 532

infanticide 546–51
'mental dysfunction' 534–5
'mental illness' 533–4
'mental impairment' 533
mental impairment and involuntary conduct 71, 507–17
mental impairment and unintentional conduct 517–21
'mere presence' 442–5
Michael, Jerome 5
Mill, John Stuart 8, 9, 18–19, 20, 21, 200, 378
mind/body and criminal responsibility 60, 106, 108
mistaken belief in consent 224–5
Mitchell, Ronald 110
M'Naghten, Daniel 530–1
M'Naghten Rules 531, 535, 538, 540
Model Criminal Code 30–1
Model Criminal Code Officers Committee (MCCOC) 30, 36, 105, 113–14, 118, 124, 130, 136, 143, 148, 151, 154–5, 166–7, 170, 171, 175, 176, 178, 179, 180, 187, 188, 202, 209, 219, 222, 224, 226, 233, 234, 235, 236, 238, 241, 245, 259, 260, 262, 271, 272, 278, 279, 280, 281, 282–3, 285, 305, 306, 308, 310, 315, 316, 318–19, 322, 328–9, 330, 331, 336, 338, 345, 347, 348–9, 353–4, 355, 356, 357, 359–60, 361, 363, 365, 367, 368, 369, 370, 374, 388, 403, 407, 408, 412, 436, 447, 476, 483, 486, 499, 501, 544, 545, 549, 550, 565, 568, 569, 577, 580, 581
Moore, John 268
morality, preservation of 19–21
Morgan, Derek 113
Morgan, Jenny 19, 50, 142
Morris, Lord 413
motive and intention 74
Mouzos, Jenny 90, 91, 92, 93, 95, 119, 473
Mulhern, Carmel 151, 387
Mullen, Paul 172, 175, 504
murder
  causation of death 99–104, 105–6
  constructive 108, 115–19, 151
  current law 97–104
  death of a human being 98–9
  duress as a defence 568–9
  escape 118
  fault elements 106–14, 151
  physical elements 95–106
Murphy, Lionel 373–5
Mustill, Lord 112, 113, 201

Nadruku, Noa 521–2
Naffine, Ngaire 12, 14, 211
nationality principle 26
necessity 52, 570–82
negligence
  fault element 64, 77–9
  manslaughter, gross or criminal 68–9, 78–9, 121–2, 123
negligent omissions 48, 124–6
New South Wales Law Reform Commission 240, 242–3, 545–6, 549, 550
Nitschke, Phillip 132
non-voluntary euthanasia 131, 132, 133, 135, 137
Norrie, Alan 32, 36, 40, 42, 45, 46, 63, 70, 74, 108, 136, 254, 450
Nowytarger, Morris 404

objective versus subjective fault 63–5, 69
oblique intention 72–3
obtaining a financial advantage by deception 349–57
obtaining by deception 351–2
obtaining property by deception 266, 338–49, 344–9, 351–2
O'Connor, Daniel 176–7
offences 50–1
  elements 58–65
  endangering life or personal safety 176–81
  fraud and theft 357–60
  inchoate 51, 373–6
  involving corporations 364–7
  liability, strict and absolute 61–3
  relating to childbirth 137–43
  sexual and children 236–8
omissions
  and accessorial liability 442–5
  in criminal law 66–9
  negligent 48, 124–6
ordinary person
  characteristics 495–6
  the ordinary woman 495–6
  test 490–5, 497–9
Osland, Heather 424–6, 430–2, 433, 434

Paltros, Nicholas 404
Parsons, Roumald Charles 265–6
passive personality principle 26
Pathé, Michelle 172, 175
Patrick, Andrea 173
Perera, Romel 342
Perrone, Santina 33

personal adornment 191–2
personal safety, endangering 176–81
Peters, Philip 300–1, 306, 406
physical disabilities and criminal law 48
physical elements
   accessorial liability 438–41
   acts and omissions 66–9
   assault and related offences 158–67
   attempting to commit crime 379, 380–3
   burglary 322–6
   and causation 81–5
   concurrence of fault element 79–81
   conspiracy 391–9
   criminal law 58–60, 65–9, 79–81
   deception 339–41, 351
   incitement 409–10
   indecent assault
   murder and manslaughter 95–106
   property 263–4, 343–4, 351–6
   robbery 309–14
   theft 263–83, 343–4
   voluntary conduct 66, 70–1
Pickard, Toni 218
Pineau, Lois 215–16
Polk, Kenneth 254
postmodern feminism 13–15
postmodernism 11–12, 65
Preddy, John 265
pregnancy, termination of 113, 139–40, 143
presence and accessorial liability 45
preservation of morality 19–21
presumption of innocence 54–5, 58
prevention of harm 18–19
Priestley Eleven 49–50
Priestley, Mervyn 479
principal offenders and complicity 425–6, 428–33, 450
procuring 438, 439, 441
property
   acting dishonestly 288–95
   appropriating 272–8, 281–3
   belief in owner's consent 293–4
   belief that owner cannot be found 294
   belonging to another 268–72, 280–1, 344
   body parts 267–8
   claim of right 290–3
   crimes and drug use 254–5
   fault elements 283–95
   financial transactions 264–7
   fungibles 287–8
   information 267
   intention to permanently deprive 283–8, 307–8
   meaning of dishonesty 295–6

   obtaining by deception 266, 338–49, 344–9, 351–2, 357–60
   physical elements 263–4, 343–4, 351–6
   stealing cars, boats and planes 287
   subject of theft 278–80
   taking 272–5
   willingness to pay 294–5
property offences involving deception 282, 333–8
property offences involving stealing 251–60
protective approach and jurisdiction 28–9
protective principle 26
provocation 469–72, 484–501
   accused's loss of self-control 488–90
   characteristics of the ordinary person 495–6
   cultural background 497
   as defence 52, 91, 184–5, 188, 499–501
   definition 185, 486
   ordinary person test 490–5, 497–9
   self-defence and 52, 469–72, 484–501
   by women 50
provocative conduct 486–8
punishment 17–18
Purcell, Rosemary 172, 175

Quinney, Richard 10, 33, 62, 63, 365

race and criminal law 47
race theory, critical 15–16
Rachels, James 67–8
rape
   consent 209–22, 224–7
   definition 214
   fraud and consent 220–2
   innocent agency 435–6
   intention 222–4
   marital 206
   mistaken belief in consent 224–5, 226, 227
   physical element 208, 214
   and recklessness 74, 76, 77, 222–4
   social context of consent 211–20
   statistics 95, 205–6
   and without consent 209–11, 387
rational actor 40–6
rationality
   in the criminal law 38–48
   legal 39–40
realism 6–8
reason
   and children 41–6
   in the criminal law 38–48
   and mental illness 41

reasonable force, use of   182–3, 184, 185–8
'reasonable man'   46–8, 485
reasoning, legal   39–40
Reilly, Alex   485, 495, 501
reckless driving causing death   123
reckless endangerment   177
recklessness
    and assault   151, 169, 171
    as to causing death or grievous bodily harm   72, 106, 109–10, 114, 151, 169, 171
    as fault element   72, 74–6, 109–10, 114
    and sexual assault   74, 76, 77, 222–4
Reid, Darryl and Wayne   152, 154, 188
Remick, Lani Anne   218, 220
requirement of intent to permanently deprive   307–8
retribution and punishment   17–18
robbery   308–19
    armed/aggravated   316–19
    degree of force or violence   315
    fault elements   314–15
    nature of threats   316
    physical elements   309–14
    statistics   308
    threatens violence   312, 313–14
    timing of the use of force   315–16
    uses force/violence   310–12, 313–14
Royall, Kym   89–90
Rush, Peter   214
Ryan, Morgan   373
Ryan, Ronald   118

sadomasochism   188–90, 191, 194–6, 200–2
Salem, Ismael Mahommed   152
Salmond, Lord   381, 384, 397
Saunders, John   110
Sayre, Francis   378, 379
self-control, accused's loss of   488–90
self-defence
    as defence   52, 53, 91, 183, 184, 188, 469–84
    excessive   475–8
    inadequacy of evidence to support a 'syndrome'   479–80
    limited assistance to a claim of   480–1
    medicalising a social problem   481–2
    and provocation   52, 91, 469–72, 484–501
    subjective/objective elements   482–4
    women's reactions to violence   91, 478–82
sentencing legislation   18
sexual assault   203–6
    consent   209–22, 224–7
    fraud and consent   220–2
    intention   222–4, 388

mistaken belief in consent   224–5, 226, 227, 236
and recklessness   74, 76, 77, 222–4
social context of consent   211–20
statistics   95, 205–6
without consent   209–11
sexual intercourse/indecent assault   207–9
sexual offences against children and young people   228–38
    age of consent   230–4
    defences   234–6
    incest   236–8
    Indigenous customary law   235–6
sexual offences against individuals with mental impairment   238–46
sexuality, penetrative/coercive model   212, 215, 216, 219
Sheehy, Elizabeth   495
shoplifting   256–8
Sivapragasam, Mayuran   335
Sleigman, Martin   478
Smart, Carol   14, 212
Smith, John Cyril   433
Smith, Roger   413
Smith, Thomas   101
social context
    of consent   211–20
    and criminal law   40, 51, 94–5
social welfare   21–2
Somerville, Margaret   246
Sorell, Tom   93
sound/unsound mind theory   512–14
Spann, Girardeau   15
specific intention   71–2
sports violence   193–4, 198
Spring, Raymond   520
stalking   24, 28–9, 171–6
standpoint feminism   13
stealing   258, 283–95, 309–10, 337
Steel, Alex   306, 349, 363
Steinberg, Marlene   510
Stonehouse, John   376–7
Stubbs, Julie   154, 482, 495
subjective versus objective fault   63–5, 69
subjective/objective elements of self-defence   482–4
substantial link approach and jurisdiction   29–30
supplying goods and advice accessorial liability   45
surgery and consent   192–3
Sutcliffe, Brian   24, 28
Sutherland, Edwin H   32
Sweet, Robyn   104–5

Taylor, Lord Justice   382
Taylor, Natalie   253
Temkin, Jennifer   227
terminatory theory   27–8
territorial nexus/substantial link
    approach   29–30
territorial theory   24, 25–7
theft   260–308
    and fraud   258, 336–8, 357–60
    of land   264
    physical elements   263–83, 343–4
    statistics   95, 252–3
Thompson, Judith   580
threatens violence/seeks to put person in fear
    of immediate force   312
threats
    and defence   565–6
    of the infliction of death or grievous bodily
        harm   560–3
    and stalking   171–6
Tolmie, Julia   482, 495
transferred malice   110–12, 113
trespasser, entry as a   323–5

universality principle   26
unlawful act and conspiracy   398–9
unlawful act manslaughter   127–9, 130
Urlich, Rochelle   186

victimisation
    female   153
    property offences   253
    surveys   23
Victorian Law Reform Commission   48, 52,
    57, 71, 91, 113, 123, 129, 204, 212, 214,
    222, 224, 226, 237, 238, 242, 245, 477,
    482, 499, 500, 501, 544, 548, 549, 568,
    570
violence
    domestic   91–2, 93, 153–4, 155–7, 206, 496

    and force, use of   206, 310–1
    and Indigenous communities
    and robbery   310–12, 313–14
    women's reactions to   91, 153,
voluntary conduct   66, 70–1
voluntary euthanasia   131, 132, 1.
voluntary manslaughter   119, 120
Vose, Paul   171–3
Vygotsky, Lev   71

Walden, Herbert   290–1
Walker, John   320
Walker, Lenore   478, 479–80, 481
Walsh, John   388
Weathburn, Don   254
Wells, Celia   19, 33, 112, 113
Welzel, Hans   70
White, Rob   254
wilful blindness   76–7
Williams, Anthony   408
Williams, Glanville   5, 17, 56, 70, 307,
    444
willingness to pay   294–5
Wilson, James Q   7
withdrawal by an accessory   445–8
without consent   209–11
woman
    and homicide   90–2
    the ordinary   495–6
    pregnant   112–13
    and provocation   50
women's reactions to violence   91, 153,
    478–82
work-related deaths   33

Yeo, Stanley   476, 477, 479, 497
Young, Alison   214
Young, Jock   6, 7
young people, sexual offences
    against   228–38

93, 156

478-82

-7